Microeconomics

Essays in Theory and Applications

This book, the fourth volume of Franklin M. Fisher's collected articles, contains work in microeconomics spanning four decades. Principal sections include essays on stability and disequilibrium, welfare economics and consumer theory, and applications of microeconomics. Topics include the decision whether or not to use statistical methods to adjust the census, the economics of water in the Middle East, as well as the effect of computer reservations systems on airlines and the economics of United Fund drives. An autobiographical essay serves as an epilogue.

Franklin M. Fisher is Professor of Economics at the Massachusetts Institute of Technology. He is the author of well over one hundred papers and fourteen other books, including, most recently, *Economic Analysis of Production Price Indexes* (with Karl Shell; Cambridge University Press, 1997). For the past several years he has been Chair of the Harvard Middle East Water project, an international study of the economics of water in the Middle East that has attracted considerable attention. Professor Fisher received the John Bates Clark Award of the American Economic Association in 1973. He is a Fellow of the Econometric Society, served as its president in 1979, and for many years was editor of its journal, *Econometrica*.

Microeconomics

Essays in Theory and Applications

FRANKLIN M. FISHER

edited by Maarten-Pieter Schinkel

CAMBRIDGE
UNIVERSITY PRESS

CAMBRIDGE UNIVERSITY PRESS
Cambridge, New York, Melbourne, Madrid, Cape Town, Singapore, São Paulo

Cambridge University Press
The Edinburgh Building, Cambridge CB2 2RU, UK

Published in the United States of America by Cambridge University Press, New York

www.cambridge.org
Information on this title: www.cambridge.org/9780521624237

First published 1999
This digitally printed first paperback version 2005

A catalogue record for this publication is available from the British Library

Library of Congress Cataloguing in Publication data
Fisher, Franklin M.
  Microeconomics: essays in theory and applications edited by Maarten-Pieter Schinkel
    p.   cm.
  Includes index.
  ISBN 0-521-62423-1 (hardcover)
    1. Microeconomics.   2. Equilibrium (Economics).   3. Welfare economics.
  4. Economics.   I. Title.
  HB172.F498   1999
  338.5 – dc21

                                                    98-24905
                                                       CIP

ISBN-13 978-0-521-62423-7 hardback
ISBN-10 0-521-62423-1 hardback

ISBN-13 978-0-521-02329-0 paperback
ISBN-10 0-521-02329-7 paperback

to Carl Kaysen
teacher, mentor, colleague, and friend

Contents

Part III: Applications of Microeconomic Theory

Part IV: Industrial Organization, Economics, and the Law

A. INDUSTRIAL ORGANIZATION AND ANTITRUST: ADDITIONAL REFLECTIONS

B. QUANTITATIVE METHODS AND THE LAW: RECENT WORK

Part V: Public Policy Applications

Introduction

The papers in this volume extend from my first published paper (Chapter 12) to very recent work. Generally, they are papers in theoretical and applied microeconomics. As in previous volumes (Fisher, 1991, 1992a, 1992b), I have not reprinted papers that have been superseded by my other books.

The chapters of Part I ("Disequilibrium and Stability"), particularly those of Part IA ("Models of Disequilibrium Behavior"), reflect my principal theoretical interest of the 1970s and early 1980s other than as discussed in my book on the subject (Fisher, 1983). In approximately 1970, I became convinced that the single most important lacuna in economic theory is our inability to explain whether or how competitive economies not in general equilibrium succeed in getting there. In part under the (usually) benign influence of Frank Hahn, who visited MIT in 1971, I explored that interest for well over a decade.

I remain convinced that the problem of disequilibrium and stability is one of central importance. Briefly, the elegant nature of the economics of equilibrium, beginning with the analysis of the plans of optimizing agents, has caused economists to concentrate on situations in which those plans are mutually compatible. But the work of the Invisible Hand cannot be understood by looking only at situations in which that work has been completed. Further, the central tenets of Western capitalism as to the desirability of free markets – the relations between competitive equilibrium and Pareto efficiency – become empty propositions if positions of competitive equilibrium cannot be achieved or can be achieved only slowly. These propositions are further discussed in Chapter 1, which also summarizes both the literature and my work as of the mid-1980s. It will be seen that the state of the art remains unsatisfactory. This may be both a consequence and a cause of the phenomenon that the profession largely continues to ignore such issues or, at least, to behave as though they had long been satisfactorily resolved.

1

This is not only a matter of high-powered general equilibrium theory.[1] We do not even have a really satisfactory analysis of how competitive firms set prices in a single market, since each firm is supposed to take prices as given. I therefore began my study of these issues by examining the problem of price change in an oversimplified setting. That resulted in Chapter 2, which deserves its subtitle of "A Preliminary Paper." In that paper, I tried to formulate a model in which more or less competitive firms set prices by hunting for the "correct" competitive price. To do this, I had to require that not all information was perfect and instantaneous, and the obvious choice was to allow customers to search among firms in an attempt to find the firm with the lowest price. Each firm was then assumed to adjust prices according to whether it sold more or less than its planned supply. It was not very hard to find assumptions under which this process converged to (partial) competitive equilibrium.

Chapter 2 was written in the early days of what was to become the extensive literature on search processes. Indeed, it was written at about the same time as the well-known article by my colleague, Peter Diamond (1971), which, in a somewhat similar model, showed how a search process could end up at a monopoly price. The difference in conclusion stemmed from a difference in purpose. Diamond quite reasonably set up a search model and found out where it led. I, on the other hand, was beginning a research program to discover whether relatively plausible disequilibrium stories could have a competitive ending. If not, then the underpinnings of microeconomics would be shaky indeed. I therefore built a model designed to have such an ending.

Unfortunately, that construction could not be regarded as fully satisfactory. As Michael Rothschild (1973) pointed out in his review of the early search literature, the firms described in Chapter 2 do not behave very sensibly. They take their demands to be independent of price even though they can readily observe that their sales are higher at lower prices than at higher ones. Chapter 3 was an attempt to remedy this failing by building a model in which the market power that disequilibrium conferred on firms asymptotically disappeared. This proved remarkably difficult to do in any very convincing way, and the question of how (or even if) one gets to equilibrium in a partial setting remains without a rigorous theoretical answer.

The fact that disequilibrium leads to perceived market power and that

---

[1] Indeed, it is not a matter of theory only. The habits of equilibrium analysis and the failure to think about adjustment processes infect the way in which economists analyze real-life phenomena and the policy recommendations that they give. This extends from macroeconomics and rational expectations to the analysis of antitrust cases (see Fisher et al., 1983).

this influences the path and possibly the equilibrium of the system was to reemerge, this time in a general disequilibrium context. As discussed in Chapter 1 in my book on disequilibrium (Fisher, 1983), I showed that one could model price offers based on perceived market power. Further, the question of whether the economy reaches a Walrasian equilibrium or remains transaction-constrained depends directly on what happens to such perceptions. Indeed, the question of whether agents are constrained by the need for money also depends on such matters. In a sense, the two revolutions in economic theory of the 1930s – the Keynesian possibility of the liquidity trap and non-Walrasian equilibrium on the one hand and the introduction of imperfect competition on the other – turn out to be related.

Before Chapter 3 was written, I had turned my attention directly to the problems of disequilibrium and stability in a general competitive setting. The first fruit here was Chapter 4.

As described in Chapter 1, stability theory began with tâtonnement, where a fictitious auctioneer adjusts prices in the direction of excess demand while nothing else happens. After a promising beginning, however, the hope that this (in any case hopelessly unrealistic) model would generally lead to stability was dashed in 1960 by the discovery of a class of counterexamples (Scarf, 1960). At about the same time, new models were being developed. These new "non-tâtonnement" or "trading processes" did not do away with the auctioneer but permitted trade as well as price change to take place in disequilibrium. (Despite the powerful results that were obtained, for many years much of the profession continued to believe that stability theory concerned only tâtonnement.)

Two basic models of trading processes were developed. One of these was the Edgeworth Process in which trades were assumed to take place if and only if a group of agents could improve themselves by trading at constant prices.[2] The second was the Hahn Process, whose driving assumption was that markets are organized so well that, after trade, unsatisfied buyers and unsatisfied sellers of the same commodity cannot both remain.

For reasons discussed in Chapter 1, I regarded (and still regard) the Hahn process as the one likely to lead to really satisfactory models, and, in the early 1970s, I began to write a series of papers designed to explore and extend it. In large part, this led to my 1983 book, in which the analyses of the relevant papers are given and improved; however, Chapters 4 and 5 were not entirely subsumed in that volume.

[2] For a more detailed discussion and bibliography see Chapter 1 of this volume or Fisher (1983).

Chapter 4 is the more important of these two pieces. It represents an attempt to do away with the fictitious auctioneer.[3] I observed that if one regards goods sold by different sellers ("dealers") as different goods, then the Hahn Process assumption becomes truly compelling. Of course, such a treatment permits dealers to make price offers, and here I used the unsatisfactory device of Chapter 2 in which each dealer simply adjusts his or her price according to whether sales are greater or less than planned. One must also do something to ensure that, in equilibrium, the prices charged by dealers in the same good come together. This approach still seems to me to be a useful one, but it was only very partially continued in my later work.

As noted, that work mainly resulted in my earlier book (Fisher, 1983). There I tried to analyze what is really the main problem: Does an economy in which agents recognize and act on the arbitrage opportunities created by disequilibrium tend to converge? The answer turns out to be difficult, and one might reasonably say that the major interest of the book lay in the study of disequilibrium itself rather than in the stability theorem proved. Chapter 1 summarizes the results reached.

Chapters 5 and 6 represent two alternate attempts to model the results of disequilibrium awareness. In Chapter 5 (written before the work leading directly to my earlier book), agents are assumed to discover constraints on their trading and to optimize taking those constraints into account.[4] Queues form, and some agents do not get served. It is shown that so long as (after trade) agents with an unsatisfied excess demand have that demand of the same sign as their unconstrained ("target") demand, then certain stability properties follow. Indeed, under fairly plausible assumptions, the only rest points of the model will be Walrasian, even though one begins with constraints on trade. The assumptions, however, make sense only in the neighborhood of Walrasian equilibrium.

The model of Chapter 5, like the work in my 1983 book, is based on the Hahn Process. Chapters 6 and 7, by contrast, deal with the Edgeworth Process. I cannot say that my 1983 book aroused very widespread interest – the profession continuing its practice of overlooking such issues – but some people were very interested indeed (among them, Maarten-Pieter Schinkel, the editor of the present volume). One of these was Dale Stahl II, who visited MIT in the mid-1980s. He and I combined our work

---

[3] Incidentally, the remark in Chapter 3 that this is like trying "to play *Hamlet* without the Prince of Norway" is not a slip. The role of Fortinbras in *Hamlet* is that of one who is extraneous to the action but cleans everything up.

[4] In neither Chapter 5 nor Chapter 6, however, do agents understand that prices will change.

and wrote Chapter 6. That paper presents an alternate model in which agents are aware of disequilibrium. In it, unsatisfied demand is rationed by a system of queues. The result is a stability theorem based on the Edgeworth Process.

Despite this foray, I continue to believe that the Edgeworth Process is not an attractive model for out-of-equilibrium trading. Indeed, the simple assumption on which it is based is not nearly as appealing as it first appears. One of the reasons for this is explored in Chapter 7. (Other reasons are given in Chapter 1.) Chapter 7 has a mildly interesting history. In 1975, I was invited to give the F. W. Paish Lecture at the meeting of the Association of University Teachers of Economics in Sheffield, England. I thought it was time to reflect on the state of the stability literature and presented an address that was later published as Fisher (1976) and (somewhat revised) as Chapter 2 of my (1983) book on disequilibrium. In doing so, I commented that one of the problems with the Edgeworth Process assumption is that it might require very large numbers of agents to find each other in order to produce a mutually improving trade at given prices. Reflecting on this, Paul Madden produced a paper (1978) in which he showed that, provided every agent always held a positive amount of every commodity, the trades involved could always be bilateral. At about the same time, David Schmeidler (privately) pointed out to me that the number of agents required for an Edgeworth Process trade need never exceed the number of commodities.

I felt that neither of these results, while interesting, really provided a satisfactory answer to my objection. Particularly if one dates commodities, the number of commodities is likely to exceed by far the number of agents, so Schmeidler's bound does not seem very helpful. Moreover, the assumption that every agent always holds a positive amount of every good is far too strong to be sensible, particularly in a model of disequilibrium. But it was not until the late 1980s that I tried to explore the consequences of relaxing that assumption.

The result was the present Chapter 7, in which I show that the number of agents that might have to be involved in an Edgeworth Process trade is substantial. Further, some of the required trades could be quite complicated indeed, involving circumstances in which certain agents were induced to make trades that they did not want in order to induce others to make trades that the original agents found desirable. Some years later, one of my undergraduate students, A. D. Tsai, proved (in an as-yet unpublished paper) that the problem of finding such trades is NP-hard, so that the assumption that trade takes place whenever a group of agents can improve themselves by it is by no means a weak one.

It is evident that what is involved here is a basic question about the way in which markets come into being and are organized. It is worth remarking that this was so far from the interests then popular in economic theory that for more than a year I was unable to obtain a time in which to speak on the subject of Chapter 7 in MIT's own theory workshop.[5] When Tsai, with some difficulty, finally got to speak at a theory lunch, the students found the topic quite an eye-opener.

The papers reprinted in Part IB ("Associated Models of Stability Analysis") are generally earlier than those in Part IA and hark back to a simpler set of considerations in stability theory. In part because of the prominence of the gross substitutes property in the early days of tâtonnement and in part because of their role in Leontief systems, the properties of nonnegative square matrices were of considerable interest when I was a student some forty years ago. I was self-taught in linear algebra but went on to teach that subject to economists for a long time. Nonnegative square matrices provided an interesting and relevant exercise.

The theorem on such matrices that I found most natural and appealing was one that my colleague, Robert Solow, had published some years before I came to MIT (Solow, 1952). It showed that the largest (Frobenius) eigenvalue of such matrices lay between the greatest and the least of the column sums thereof (and strictly between if the matrix was indecomposable[6]). When Albert Ando and I wrote a paper for the *American Political Science Review* (Fisher and Ando, 1962), we needed to find a way to describe Solow's Theorem to political scientists (who, in those days, at least, could not be expected to know about eigenvalues and Frobenius' theorems). The result was Chapter 8, which shows that the Frobenius root is actually a weighted average of the column sums.

Solow's Theorem seemed so appealing that I wondered whether having all the column sums less than unity might not be necessary as well as sufficient for the Frobenius root to be less than one. Of course, since the column sums are not independent of the units in which the underlying variables are measured, this could not be directly true, but some thought produced Chapter 9, in which I show that it is necessary that there exist some choice of units for the underlying variables in which the

---

[5] Harvard was more flexible.
[6] There was a confusion of language. What many economists tended to call "decomposable" was what mathematicians tended to call "reducible" – the property that identical renumbering of rows and columns would make the matrix block triangular. What mathematicians tended to call "decomposable," the same economists tended to call "completely decomposable" – the property that identical renumbering of rows and columns would make the matrix block diagonal. I use the economists' terminology.

condition on the column sums is satisfied. Chapters 8 and 9 were written in the early 1960s, before I became really interested in stability analysis.

Chapters 10 and 11 were written in 1971 immediately after my decision to enter the subject. They were written during, and as a direct result of, Frank Hahn's visit to MIT in 1971. Hahn gave a graduate course on general equilibrium, part of which concerned stability. (Arrow and Hahn, 1971, was just being published.) Both Daniel McFadden (then also visiting MIT) and I attended the course. In one session, Hahn asked McFadden to present the paper he had written for the *Festschrift* for Sir John Hicks (McFadden, 1968). That paper showed how Hicks' remarks on stability in the appendix to *Value and Capital* (Hicks, 1939) could be justified by a model in which different markets had widely different speeds of adjustment. While McFadden's *tour de force* proved global results, its local version, at least, was based on a theorem related to those on non-negative square matrices.[7] McFadden stated that this theorem (the Fisher–Fuller Theorem[8]) was quite difficult to prove. Since it seemed to me to be of the same class of theorems as those I regularly dealt with in my class, I incautiously and immodestly suggested that it couldn't be very difficult. Fortunately, I was able to sketch the fairly simple proof, given in Chapter 10, by the end of McFadden's lecture, showing (perhaps) that I was immodest but not foolhardy.

Chapter 11 had a similar origin. Hahn happened to mention in class that he knew of no examples other than the Cobb–Douglas of a utility function generating demands that had the gross substitute property. He added that perhaps that was the only one. As someone who lectured on consumer theory and used the linear expenditure system produced by a generalized Cobb–Douglas utility function as an example, I observed that this was almost certainly not true. I then set to work to characterize the set of utility functions with the appropriate property. Because at that point I was becoming convinced by McFadden, W. M. Gorman, and others that consumer theory is best done by means of the expenditure function rather than directly by use of the utility function, I produced Chapter 11 (but not by the end of Hahn's lecture).

The chapters in Part II ("Welfare Economics and Consumer Theory") and those in Part III ("Applications of Microeconomic Theory") reflect topics in pure and applied microeconomics that have caught my attention at various times. The first of these chapters, Chapter 12, was my first published paper. It was written when I was a junior at Harvard College

---

[7] So-called Hicksian matrices can be written in the form A–sI, where A is a non-negative matrix, s is a scalar, and I is the unit matrix.

[8] M. E. Fisher is not related to me. See Fisher and Fuller (1958).

and being given a quite unusual education in economics by my tutor, Carl Kaysen.[9] He posed the question of what to make of the Kaldor–Hicks–Scitovsky welfare criterion if the gainers from a change did not actually compensate the losers. This prompted me to think about value judgments on income distribution; while the paper I wrote did not answer Kaysen's question, it seemed interesting in its own right.

At the time the paper was written, in the mid-1950s, welfare economics was a subject whose principal results were all negative. The discipline had emerged from a long history in which it had seemed possible to prove positive results about a normative subject, and economists had finally come largely to understand the difference between natural assumptions about behavior and value judgments. But writers were so careful not to confuse these two things, they often refused to make value judgments at all where those judgments would be likely to command less than nearly universal agreement. In particular, whenever a proposed economic measure would bring about a change in income distribution, the usual conclusion was that since one would have to make a value judgment as to whether the distributional change was good or bad, one could say no more about the problem.

In Chapter 12, I attempted to move beyond this, not by imposing my own (no doubt entirely persuasive) views as to income distribution, but by axiomatizing the properties that value judgments were likely to have. (For example, if one moves from a worse distribution to a better one, it may be natural to assume that the distributions passed through on the way are an improvement on the starting point.) Proceeding in this manner, I found it possible to reach at least some conclusions.

While I retain a fondness for Chapter 12, it certainly bore (and bears) a number of earmarks of having been an undergraduate paper written by an inexperienced author.[10] In particular, so new was I to the subject that it never occurred to me that the fact that indifference curves could not cross meant anything other than that they were parallel along rays – a very special case, indeed (that of homotheticity). For the most part, this did not matter, since the body of the paper dealt with a single-

[9] For a description of this, see the Epilogue.
[10] Aside from substance and style, it turned out to have a very high number of typographical errors, largely because it represented my first experience at proofreading. I proofread the paper with the assistance of my father, who was very helpful but persuaded me to allow him to read the galleys while I read the original manuscript. Particularly because my father was totally unfamiliar with mathematical notation, this was not a good arrangement, and I have been careful to avoid it ever since (even with mathematically sophisticated assistants).

commodity world, but it did matter for the generalization given in the Appendix.[11] This fact was picked up by Peter Kenen (then a Harvard graduate student), who wrote a critical comment. Edward Chamberlin, the editor of the *Quarterly Journal of Economics* (in which the original paper had been published), suggested that Kenen and I write jointly on the issue, and the result was Chapter 13, which showed that the slip was not of much consequence.

While I was embarrassed by the slip, I was, of course, quite excited by the adventure of publishing a professional paper.[12] Indeed, I expected the world to sit up and take notice. This did not happen – the paper did not become widely noticed and cited – but, in retrospect, I hardly feel disappointed. The paper brought me to the attention of Robert Solow (who read it before it was published) and hence indirectly to the MIT faculty. Further, the one person who did claim to be influenced by it – and who has repeatedly (and overgenerously) continued to cite it ever since in his own work axiomatizing value judgments – was Amartya Sen. (See, in particular, Sen, 1997.) If my paper was to influence only one person, that was surely the right person to influence.

My interest in the axiomatization of value judgments concerning income distribution did not end with Chapters 12 and 13. While I was at the University of Chicago in 1959–60, Jerome Rothenberg and I discussed a paper written by Robert Strotz (Strotz, 1958), with whom both of us were friendly. In a paper subtitled "A Paradox in Distributive Ethics," Strotz had adapted a set of axioms on decisions under uncertainty due to Herman Chernoff (1954) and turned them into axioms about income distribution value judgments. Strotz showed that while those axioms appeared sweetly reasonable, they had the surprising implication that all that could matter in comparing two situations was the total amount of income. Distributional considerations would cease to matter altogether.

Rothenberg and I thought this deserved a serious answer, and the result was Chapter 14, in which we argued that the apparent sweet reasonableness of the Strotz axioms was not real. Strotz replied (Strotz,

---

[11] That generalization was the source of some amusement in my family, all of whom were proud that I had published such a paper but none of whom were technically equipped to understand it. My aunt, Ethel Fisher Korn, was particularly amused by the last sentence of the Appendix, which, after giving the matrix generalizations of some of the theorems expressed in scalars in the text, stated, "which was to be expected." "Ah, yes," said Aunt Ethel, "I certainly expected exactly that."

[12] I was only partially gently deflated by my roommate, Richard Friedberg, who, when I proudly showed him the galley proofs, remarked, "Frank, it looks just like one of the real ones."

1961), and we added a rejoinder (Fisher and Rothenberg, 1962), neither of which is reprinted here.[13]

Chapter 14 marked my last foray into welfare economics for a considerable time. The late John McGowan and I dipped into the subject briefly when we wrote Chapter 15. That chapter deals with the question of how to decide whether advertising is excessive when it changes consumer tastes. This, in turn, involves the question of whether the consumer obtains increased utility from the consumption of advertised products.

Modeling changes in consumer taste had already been a serious concern of mine. In the late 1960s, Karl Shell and I began an investigation into the economic theory of price indices that eventually resulted in two books on the subject (Fisher and Shell, 1972, 1998). In the paper that eventually became the first essay in our 1972 book (Fisher and Shell, 1968), we considered the effect of taste changes on the cost-of-living index. We showed there that the theory of the cost-of-living index could be reformulated to accommodate such changes. In so doing, we pointed out that there is no basis in consumer theory for asserting that if someone has unchanging tastes and happens to be on the same indifference curve in two periods, then he or she is equally well off in both periods. This is because the utility levels associated with the indifference curves are arbitrary and cannot be assumed to be the same in different periods. Such an assumption has no meaning.

In the course of that discussion, Shell and I also mentioned that there was certainly no justification for the proposition that if two *different* people happen to have the same tastes and are on the same indifference curve, then they are equally happy. Yet, in effect, the notion that such a statement is "natural" persists.[14] In the mid-1980s, a series of papers by Dale Jorgenson and Daniel Slesnick followed up on a suggestion by John Muellbauer to use the model of household equivalence scales (introduced by Anton Barten as a positive descriptive device[15]) as a tool with which to make welfare comparisons. In effect, this means assuming that consumers differ in their tastes only because of parameters such as family size, age, education, and so forth, so that their utility functions can all be represented as the same function, provided one includes such para-

---

[13] Rothenberg, who has a legendary fondness for puns, somehow managed to persuade Strotz (against his better judgment) to give his paper the subtitle, "Paradox Regained," to go with our subtitle of "Paradox Lost." We then subtitled our rejoinder "Paradox Enow," which certainly made Strotz regret going along with us. (As the title of Chapter 7 exemplifies, I have not given up this sort of thing.)

[14] See Sen, 1997, p. 208n.

[15] See Chapter 16 for references.

meters as arguments. The Muellbauer–Jorgenson–Sleznick procedure then assumed that if two consumers have equal values of the resulting generalized utility function, then they are equally well off. But this is simply a generalized version of the error pointed out above. Whatever the positive merits of household equivalence scales, such welfare comparisons do not follow. Chapter 16 explores this matter in detail.

The fact that I had been away from consumer theory and welfare economics for some time showed when I wrote Chapter 16, however. In one of my examples, I, too, implicitly fell into the trap of supposing that there is something special about a situation in which two consumers are on the same indifference curve. Moreover, in doing so, I forgot a theorem that Shell and I had proved twenty years earlier. The fact that there was a problem with the example being pointed out by Daniel Leonard (1990) led me to write Chapter 17 as a reply. That paper is reprinted here because I believe that it contains instructive material.

Chapters 16 and 17 deal with consumer theory as well as with welfare economics. Chapter 18 deals with consumer theory alone (as does Chapter 19, which could have been included in Part II). It has a slightly amusing history. In 1987, A. Leroux (1987) posed the question of what conditions on the utility function are necessary and sufficient for goods to be normal (have their consumption increasing in income). He gave a sufficient condition that is difficult to interpret. As this question seemed similar in form (but not in substance) to the question of what conditions on the utility function would be necessary and sufficient for all goods to be gross substitutes – the question I had answered in Chapter 11 – I thought I might try my hand at it. At this point, my wife induced me to spend time at a health spa in Florida. While there, I was introduced to several new activities, one of which was an "herbal wrap" in which I was wrapped in a sweet-smelling and warmly damp grass mat and told to relax in a darkened room. Not being particularly sleepy at first, I thought about the normal goods problem. Without a paper and pencil at hand, I found it too difficult to think about the problem in terms of the utility function but quickly realized (what I should have known anyway) that it was far easier to deal with the expenditure function. The result was the theorem presented in Chapter 18, which came to me as I was drifting off.

The chapters in Part III ("Applications of Microeconomic Theory") are more applied than are the chapters so far discussed, although this is true more in the sense that the chapters are focused on particular problems than in the sense that they are heavily empirical. In particular, Chapter 19, as already remarked, could have been included with the papers reprinted in Part II. Its genesis was as follows.

In the early 1970s, I became active in Jewish philanthropy. (That activity has continued to this day. I am presently the president of the New Israel Fund – a fund that supports civil rights, women's rights, Arab–Jewish cooperation, and similar causes in Israel.) At the time, it was not common practice for professors to ask each other for money for charity. I did, and, because percentage increases in donations got a great deal of credit, I soon became chairman of the Faculty Advisory Cabinet of the United Jewish Appeal – an office that sounds far, far grander than it really was. On the principle that a skilled vampire can find blood in anything, I began to think about the economics of United Fund drives, and the result was Chapter 19. Joking aside, there is a real thrill in using one's professional skills to illuminate or assist a worthwhile cause. Chapter 19 gave me a small hint of this, but it was not until the work reported in Part V that I came fully to realize the satisfaction that can be had in this way.

Chapter 20, I suppose, can be regarded as a very early attempt in this direction. It was also very naïve. When I wrote it, in the early 1960s, American agricultural policy had resulted in the accumulation of a government stockpile of grains. Congress provided for this to be distributed to developing countries. Unfortunately, this raised the problem that such distribution would depress prices and hence reduce the supply of local agricultural products – a perverse result. Chapter 20 outlined a possible scheme to get around this. I sent the paper to George McGovern, then the head of the distribution program. It produced a polite one-sentence thank you and no further response.

Chapter 21 was a follow-up to Chapter 20. It was written when my late colleague, Paul Rosenstein-Rodan, arranged an invitation to a meeting in Rome on "Collective Economy" whose theme that year (1963) was world hunger. Compared to the rhetoric of the other papers, Chapter 21 seemed very dry. On the other hand, it had some analytic content. I pointed out that the effect of food disposal on local food prices (and hence on local food supply) depended not only on the elasticity of demand but also on the elasticity of local supply. This might serve to moderate the problem.

Chapters 22 and 23 grew out of work that I did in the mid-1960s for the Institute for Naval Studies (INS), a Cambridge offshoot of a U.S. Navy–sponsored think tank.[16] The Navy was experiencing difficulties retaining enlisted men beyond their first term of service. This problem was considered particularly acute as regarded electronic technicians, in whom the Navy invested considerable training. Sociolo-

---

[16] That work was jointly written with Anton Morton.

gists at INS conducted a survey to discover the likelihood of reenlistment in response to various incentives (college scholarships, housing, and the like), and they needed a way to evaluate the relative costs and benefits of the proposed incentive programs. They asked me to assist in doing this.

The task was not a simple one (particularly given the state of the computational art at the time). One had to specify the degree to which inexperienced or partly experienced personnel could substitute for experienced ones. (This was accomplished by another survey, with the results being modeled in terms of a Cobb–Douglas production function for simplicity.) The real complication came because of the fact that experienced men could be obtained only by inducting inexperienced men some years earlier and training them. This meant that the optimal use of a reenlistment incentive program involved solving a dynamic programming problem. At the time, this was far from simple. Both computer hardware and available software were not nearly as capable as they are today.[17] I wrote an algorithm that could be shown to converge, but it did not seem to do so in finite time without a good deal of human intervention. (This was particularly so because the Navy wanted to test very extreme cases which tended to produce overflows or starting points in which the entire population of the world had to be inducted in year 1.) But we finally got the job done and could analyze the results.

The results were not what the Navy wanted to hear. We consistently found that, no matter what the reenlistment incentive offered, the efficient thing to do was *not* to encourage reenlistment aggressively, but to put up with low reenlistment rates. So narrowly focused were I and my colleagues on evaluating incentives that we had written two papers before I realized what was producing this apparently anomalous result. The study was done during the years of the military draft. While the draft was not directly used to secure sailors, many first-term enlisted men joined the Navy rather than be drafted into the Army.[18] As a result, the Navy found that it could attract first-termers without having to pay wages that competed with those that could be earned in civilian occupations. After the first term was up, however, sailors were no longer subject to the draft, so that naval wages were forced to be more competitive. This made experienced men relatively much more expensive than first-term enlistees, which accounted for our result.

---

[17] When, many years later, I worked on a far, far more complicated non-linear problem (see Chapter 30), I was pleasantly astonished to discover how far the state of the art had progressed.

[18] Incidentally, the study antedated the Vietnam War.

While the United States Navy was not very interested in hearing this, our study did arouse some interest in the British Admiralty (where there was no conscription effect). I lived in London (visiting the London School of Economics and Oxford University) in the fall of 1966 and was invited to the Admiralty for discussion (and hospitality). In the summer of 1967, I was invited to return to a conference and to present a paper on "Aspects of Cost-Benefit Analysis in Defence Manpower Planning" (Chapter 23), which gave a general methodological reflection on the subject.

That conference was attended by military personnel from several countries. To my great pleasure, I was invited two years later (this time by J. N. Wolfe of the University of Edinburgh) to a British conference on the Armed Services and Society, attended by extremely capable officers from all three of Her Majesty's Services.[19] I presented Chapter 22, which I consider the best summary of the INS study.

The chapters in Part IV ("Industrial Organization, Economics, and the Law") come from a much later time. For the most part, they represent my work in industrial organization done after the publication of the identically named first volume of my collected works (Fisher, 1991). (The exception is Chapter 26, which probably should have been included in that volume.) The chapters in Part IVA ("Industrial Organization and Antitrust: Additional Reflections") give some general thoughts on the field; those in Part IVB ("Quantitative Methods and the Law: Recent Work") are more specific.

In 1989, I published my paper "Games Economists Play: A Noncooperative View" (Chapter 12 of Fisher, 1991). In that paper I was critical of game theory as a way of studying oligopoly – a view I continue to hold. Largely because of this, I was asked by the organizers of the annual Brookings Conference on Microeconomics to write a review article on the relevant sections of the recently published *Handbook of Industrial Organization* (Schmalensee and Willig, eds., 1989).[20] I'm sure that the organizers did this in the expectation that my views would be controversial, and the result (Chapter 24) did not disappoint them. (My poetry quotations also provoked replies in kind from the two discussants, Timothy Bresnahan and Joseph Farrell.) I continue to hold to the views expressed in my two articles on the subject. I do not believe that our understanding of real-life oligopolies is much enhanced by the use of

---

[19] 1969 was a time of student unrest, and (so it was said) there were contingency plans for the conference to meet in Edinburgh Castle, which could be easily defended in an emergency. Of course, this never happened, but we did have a delightful reception in the castle as guests of the Regiment.

[20] Alvin Klevorick reviewed the remainder of the *Handbook*.

game-theoretic language to describe possible outcomes, but I am resigned to being in a distinct minority.

Chapter 25 is more general. It was written on the occasion of a visit to Spain in 1993, during which I spoke at the Centrode Estudios Monetarius Y Financierus (CEMFI) in Madrid. The chapter gives a brief and updated overview of my thoughts on competition policy and draws on some of the cases in which I have been involved.

As mentioned, Chapter 26 is a bit older. It is also more theoretical. Richard Posner had claimed (Posner, 1975) that the social cost of monopoly includes not only the usual dead-weight loss but also most or all monopoly rents, since these represent the value of the resources used to attain or maintain the monopoly in question. He argued that this must be true because there is free entry into the business of obtaining monopolies so that rent-seeking behavior will dissipate all the gains. I thought this argument quite wrong. Posner (whom I admire as an academic and a judge) had fallen into the kind of trap that awaits those who try to generalize relatively easy economic arguments to situations where they do not apply. As spelled out in the chapter, the fact that someone would spend up to the anticipated monopoly rent in order to obtain a given monopoly does not mean that he or she has to do so. There may be no barriers to entry into the business of obtaining a monopoly generally, but that does not mean that there are no barriers to entry into competition with a particular monopoly once that monopoly has been obtained.

The chapters in Part IVB are more specific than those in Part IVA; they are drawn from my participation in two matters of litigation. The first of these, Chapter 27 (written with Peter Fox-Penner, Joen Greenwood, William Moss, and Almarin Phillips), concerned the bankruptcy of the Washington Public Power Supply System. That system, which had the acronym WPPSS (perhaps aptly pronounced "Whoops!") was a collection of public power authorities in the state of Washington. WPPSS had begun to build nuclear power plants, relying on forecasts done by or for its members as to future needs for electricity. Unfortunately, as too often happens,[21] the forecasters thought in terms of quantities only and forgot that demand depends on price. Since the cost of the nuclear plants would add substantially to the rates charged customers, the forecasted demand could not materialize, and the system went bankrupt. This left the system's bondholders high and dry, and the litigation was the result. It was my task to testify as to how prudent economics would surely have uncovered the error. As my second book, written in association with Carl Kaysen (Fisher and Kaysen, 1962), had been one of the first economet-

---

[21] Compare attitudes toward water. See Chapter 30.

ric studies of electricity demand, this was a natural thing for me to do. (It was also natural to dedicate the paper to Kaysen on the occasion of his seventieth birthday.) The case settled during trial in a manner pretty favorable to the bondholders.[22]

Chapter 28 (written with Kevin Neels) also involves litigation that settled during trial, but that litigation was very different from the WPPSS case. In the late 1970s, the advancing computer technology made it possible for airlines to provide travel agents with computer reservation systems (CRSs). These systems permitted agents not only to acquire information very quickly but also to make reservations directly with the airline computers, issue boarding passes, and perform other services. The two largest domestic airlines, American and United, were also the airlines with the most advanced internal reservation systems. They refused to participate in a joint industry development and put out their own CRSs.

Both American and United made use of the fact that busy travel agents, faced with several choices as to what flight to suggest, will naturally tend first to suggest the flight that is first on the computer screen and then work down. In particular, travel agents will seldom search further screens if there is a relatively satisfactory flight available on the first screen presented. Particularly where a trip involves connections, it is not obvious how the flights should be ordered best to suit consumer preferences, so some algorithm is required.

American and United each chose an algorithm that gave its own flights preference. Further, each of them permitted other airlines to purchase status as "co-hosts"; this effectively meant that the co-host would not be discriminated against as strongly as would non-co-hosts.

After a while, the government intervened and imposed regulations intended to halt this practice. When that occurred, American and United greatly raised the fee that they charged other airlines for bookings made on the CRSs. Meanwhile, a large number of other airlines sued American and United under the antitrust laws, claiming major injury in the form of diverted business.

The first of the cases to come to trial involved a large number of plaintiff airlines, and the lawyers involved chose not to focus on the display bias issue very directly. Perhaps as a result, the defendants prevailed.

The situation was different in the case in which I was involved. Here the plaintiffs (Continental Airlines and others associated with the Texas Air group) did rather better. American settled before trial, and United

---

[22] I had testified extensively at deposition, but the case settled before I was called at trial.

did so while the jury was out, both settlements being quite satisfactory to the plaintiffs.

The problems associated with CRSs did not end with the cases or with the regulations, however. Indeed, it is my belief that they cannot be satisfactorily resolved without major structural change in the ways in which CRSs are owned and receive revenue. Chapter 28 also discusses these matters of public policy.

The two chapters in Part V ("Public Policy Applications") are purely about public rather than private issues, and in both the matters discussed, I received no fee. The first of these, Chapter 29 (written with Brian Palmer), concerns what I consider to be a long-standing injustice in the American electoral system, an injustice, moreover, that has been continued and exploited for political ends. (This is not to say, however, that there are no sincere advocates on both sides of the matter.) It has long been recognized that the decennial census of population undercounts certain elements of the population both absolutely and in relative terms.[23] The people involved tend to be minority members (primarily African Americans and Hispanics) and to be poor. Such persons tend to wish not to cooperate with government inquiries and may live in neighborhoods in which census takers do not enjoy working. Since census results are used for the apportionment of seats in Congress and in state legislatures, as well as for the distribution of certain federal funds, such differential undercounting implies an inequity in political power and representation.

Many years ago, it began to be suggested that statistical sampling methods might rectify that problem, and that suggestion has become increasingly prominent over the years. In the 1980s, a number of cities and states sued to compel such adjustment, and I testified as to the general way in which such methods work. That suit was opposed by the Bureau of the Census, largely because the post-census sampling taken in 1980 was felt to have been inadequate for adjustment, and that view prevailed. The bureau then began plans for such adjustment in advance of the 1990 census, but such planning was interrupted by the ruling of the secretary of commerce that no adjustment would take place. A series of lawsuits then ensued, after which the secretary (then Robert Mosbacher) promised to consider the question in an unbiased manner.

Secretary Mosbacher again ruled against adjustment, this time overriding the views of the Census Bureau. Moreover, he did so, as Chapter 29 describes, in a decision that can most charitably be described as a

---

[23] For references, see Chapter 29. The recognition that there is an undercount goes back to Thomas Jefferson, and the recognition that the percentage undercount is different for some groups than for others goes back to at least 1890.

cascade of errors, totally misusing and misinterpreting the results and methods on which he supposedly relied. I testified in the resulting litigation, and Chapter 29 is based on that testimony.

The secretary's decision was upheld by the District Court as not so arbitrary as to constitute an abuse of discretion, even though the district judge said that, had he himself to make the decision, he would probably have decided in favor of adjustment. That ruling was reversed by the Court of Appeals and then reinstated by the Supreme Court. The matter did not end there, however. The question as to whether to use statistical methods to adjust the 2000 census is currently a matter of considerable controversy with Republicans attempting to prejudge the issue against adjustment through congressional action.

Such an attempt is hardly accidental. Poor people and minorities tend to live in urban areas that traditionally vote for the Democratic Party. It is very hard to escape the suspicion that Secretary Mosbacher's decision was not merely a colossal perversion of statistical methods but also politically driven.

The project discussed in Chapter 30 has also given me the opportunity to use my professional skills in the public arena. Since 1982, I have been the chair of the Harvard Middle East Water Project, a joint effort of Israelis, Palestinians, Jordanians, and a central team in Cambridge. The project is being performed under the auspices of the Institute for Social and Economic Policy in the Middle East of Harvard University's John F. Kennedy School of Government. It seeks to promote rational economic thinking about water, both as a tool to management and policy and, more importantly, to assist in the settling of water disputes. Frankly, it is our hope to remove water as a cause of friction in the Middle East peace process.

Because of the sensitive nature of that process and the subject of water, I am currently limited as to what I can say or publish concerning this topic (although I expect that limitation to end eventually). I can therefore make only a few observations: First, Chapter 30 was a relatively early paper in the project. It does not tell the full story by any means. Second, while the mode of thinking that the project involves appears to be fairly revolutionary among those involved in the analysis of water problems, it is (or should not be) so among economists. When I spoke about the project in the MIT economics department, my chair, Paul Joskow, remarked, "What an interesting application." He was entirely correct.

In any event, the opportunity to make this application at this time has been most exciting. It has involved political and diplomatic issues as well as a fascinating piece of economic analysis. Moreover, the project still holds the prospect of making a serious contribution to the resolution of water disputes, to better water management, and to peace. At the suggestion of my colleague Peter Temin, I have been dictating my memoirs of the project since it really took off in October 1993. If all goes well, I shall one day tell the full story.

The Epilogue presents memoirs of a somewhat different kind. A few years ago I was invited to write an autobiography for a series of books entitled *Makers of Modern Economics*. I suppose that there are many able to resist such an invitation, but I am too vain to be one of them. The resulting essay makes an appropriate epilogue to the present volume.

This book was edited by Maarten-Pieter Schinkel (with some assistance from Charles Morcom). He has done a very large amount of work and has become more familiar with my work than I am myself. That cannot be its own reward, and I am very grateful to him.

As always, I thank Theresa Benevento for secretarial and administrative assistance. Without her help, my professional life would be impossible.

Anyone who gets as far as the Epilogue will realize the immense debt that I feel to Carl Kaysen, who plucked me out of an elementary economics class in 1953, taught me economic theory, and has advised and befriended me ever since. This book contains the paper I wrote as his undergraduate student (Chapter 12) and a paper written for his seventieth birthday (Chapter 27). Moreover, some of the issues in the Harvard Middle East Water Project (Chapter 30) go back to lectures on petroleum conservation that I first gave as Carl's teaching assistant in 1957. It is a pleasure to dedicate this book to him.

REFERENCES

Arrow, K. J. and F. H. Hahn (1971). *General Competitive Analysis*. San Francisco: Holden-Day; New York: Oliver & Boyd.

Chernoff, H. (1954). "The Rational Selection of Decision Functions." *Econometrica*, **22**, 422–43.

Diamond, P. A. (1971). "A Model of Price Adjustment." *Journal of Economic Theory*, **3**, 156–68.

Fisher, F. M. (1976). "The Stability of General Equilibrium: Results and Problems." In M. J. Artis and A. R. Nobay (eds.), *Essays in Economic Analysis (The Proceedings of the Association of University Teachers of Economics, Sheffield 1975)*, Cambridge, UK: Cambridge University Press.

(1983). *Disequilibrium Foundations of Equilibrium Economics*. Cambridge, UK: Cambridge University Press.

(1991). *Industrial Organization, Economics, and the Law*. London: Harvester-Wheatsheaf; Cambridge, MA: MIT Press.

(1992a). *Aggregation: Aggregate Production Functions and Related Topics.* London: Harvester-Wheatsheaf; Cambridge, MA: MIT Press.

(1992b). *Econometrics.* London: Harvester-Wheatsheaf; Cambridge, MA: MIT Press.

Fisher, F. M. and A. Ando (1962). "Two Theorems on *Ceteris Paribus* in the Analysis of Dynamic Systems." *American Political Science Review,* **56,** 110–13. Reprinted in A. Ando, F. M. Fisher, and H. A. Simon, *Essays on the Structure of Social Science Models.* Cambridge, MA: MIT Press, 1963.

Fisher, F. M. in association with C. Kaysen (1962). *A Study in Econometrics: The Demand for Electricity in the United States.* Amsterdam: North-Holland.

Fisher, F. M., J. J. McGowan, and J. E. Greenwood (1983). *Folded, Spindled, and Mutilated: Economic Analysis and U.S. v. IBM.* Cambridge, MA: MIT Press.

Fisher, F. M. and J. Rothenberg (1962). "How Income Ought to Be Distributed: Paradox Enow." *Journal of Political Economy,* **70,** 88–93.

Fisher, F. M. and Karl Shell (1968). "Taste and Quality Change in the Pure Theory of the True Cost-of-Living Index." In J. N. Wolfe (ed.), *Value, Capital, and Growth, Papers in Honour of Sir John Hicks.* Edinburgh: Edinburgh University Press.

(1972). *The Economic Theory of Price Indices: Two Essays on the Effects of Taste, Quality, and Technological Change.* New York: Academic Press.

(1998). *Economic Analysis of Production Price Indexes.* Cambridge: Cambridge University Press.

Fisher, M. E. and A. T. Fuller (1958). "On the Stabilization of Matrices and the Convergence of Linear Iterative Processes." *Proceedings of the Cambridge Philosophical Society,* **54,** 417–25.

Hicks, J. R. (1939). *Value and Capital.* New York: Oxford University Press (Clarendon Press).

Leonard, D. (1990). "Household Equivalence Scales: Comment." *Review of Economic Studies,* **57,** 325–7.

Leroux, A. (1987). "Preferences and Normal Goods: A Sufficient Condition." *Journal of Economic Theory,* **43,** 192–9.

Madden, P. (1978). "Why the Edgeworth Process Assumption Isn't That Bad." *Review of Economic Studies,* **42,** 581–96.

McFadden, D. (1968). "On Hicksian Stability." In J. N. Wolfe (ed.), *Value, Capital, and Growth, Papers in Honour of Sir John Hicks.* Edinburgh: Edinburgh University Press.

Posner, R. A. (1975). "The Social Costs of Monopoly and Regulation." *Journal of Political Economy,* **83,** 807–27.

Rothschild, M. (1973). "Models of Market Organization with Imperfect Information." *Journal of Political Economy,* **81,** 1283–1308.

Scarf, H. (1960). "Some Examples of Global Instability of the Competitive Equilibrium." *International Economic Review,* **1,** 157–72.

Schmalensee, R. and R. D. Willing, eds. (1989). *Handbook of Industrial Organization.* 2 vols. Amsterdam and New York: North-Holland.

Sen, A. (1997). *On Economic Inequality.* (Expanded Edition with a Substantial Annexe by J. E. Foster and A. Sen.) Oxford: Clarendon Press.

Solow, R. M. (1952). "On the Structure of Linear Models." *Econometrica*, **20**, 29–46.

Strotz, R. (1958). "How Income Ought to Be Distributed: A Paradox in Distributive Ethics." *Journal of Political Economy*, **66**, 189–205.

Strotz, R. (1961). "How Income Ought to Be Distributed: Paradox Enow." *Journal of Political Economy*, **69**, 271–8.

PART I

Disequilibrium and Stability

The Formation
of Economic Magnitudes:
Disequilibrium and Stability (1990)

1.   Introduction

The title of this Conference is "The Formation of Economic Magnitudes." Yet, if the papers prepared for it are true to the course of modern economic theory, most of them will, in a very real sense, not concern that subject at all. Modern economic theory is overwhelmingly a theory of equilibrium. It analyzes positions from which there is no incentive to depart, positions at which the plans and expectations of economic agents are mutually compatible. It is almost silent on the question of how such positions get reached, on how economic magnitudes get formed if they do not happen already to be in equilibrium.

Equilibrium analysis is an elegant and powerful tool, providing considerable illumination of the way in which real economies operate. But the total concentration on equilibrium now characteristic of formal economic models runs the serious risk of misunderstanding the basic insights of economics itself. Thus, the proposition that competitive industries earn no profits in long-run equilibrium is an important (if elementary) theorem. To take this to mean that competitive industries *never* earn profits is not only wrong, it is to lose sight of the fundamental role that profits and losses play in the allocation of resources when demand or technology changes. The proposition that competitive equilibria and Pareto-optima are closely related is a basic insight. The policy prescription that (under the conditions of the two Welfare Theorems) government interference with a competitive system is bound to be inefficient requires more than this, however; it requires the assurance that competitive economies are close to equilibrium most of the time. That assurance cannot be provided by only examining the properties of equilibria.

Nor are such issues restricted to microeconomics. To take a leading modern example, the statement that agents will eventually learn

This chapter was prepared for a conference on "The Formation of Economic Magnitudes," held in Paris, 1987, and published in French in Cartelier (1990).

about and act on systematic profit opportunities is an appealing assumption. The proposition of the rational expectations literature that agents always instantaneously understand the opportunities thrown up by an immensely complex and changing economy is breathtakingly stronger. That proposition begs the question of how agents learn and of the role that arbitrage plays in the formation of economic magnitudes. To take an older example, the proposition that, under some circumstances, there can exist underemployment equilibria was the major contribution of the Keynesian literature. To show that the economy can tend toward such equilibria is a much harder proposition, requiring analysis of dynamic, disequilibrium behavior.

Indeed, such dynamic, disequilibrium analysis is always required if we are to understand the formation of economic magnitudes. Certainly, if the economy does not spend most of its time near equilibrium, disequilibrium analysis is the only useful kind. Even if equilibrium is the usual case, however, disequilibrium analysis is indispensable. For one thing, only such analysis can provide the assurance that our equilibrium theories are consistent; if equilibrium is the usual case, we need to know why. Further, only analysis of the dynamic path that a stable system follows in disequilibrium can tell us to which of several possible equilibria that system will go. This is a matter of considerable importance, not only because multiplicity of equilibria is the rule rather than the exception, but also because, as we shall see, analysis of disequilibrium shows that the dynamic behavior involved often changes the equilibrium that is eventually reached.

There are two fairly common mistakes that must be avoided in considering such matters. First, one must not confuse the tautology that the economy will move away from positions that are not equilibria with the much deeper and unproven proposition that the economy always converges to equilibrium (let alone the proposition that it spends most of its time near equilibrium). In more specific terms, the fact that agents will seize on profitable arbitrage opportunities means that any situation in which such opportunities appear is subject to change. It does not follow that profitable arbitrage opportunities disappear or that new opportunities do not continually arise in the process of absorbing old ones.

The second mistake is the belief that such problems can be avoided by redefinition of terms so that there is no such thing as disequilibrium. For example, the non-clearing of markets by prices is sometimes said not to be an example of disequilibrium because agents form queues with the length of the queue determined by the shadow price of time as well as by money prices. This may be a valuable way to think about what happens when markets fail to clear, but it reformulates rather than solves that question. (What happens to money prices? How do the queues themselves disappear over time?) Certainly, there is a sense in which the disequilibrium behavior of any given system can be represented as the equilibrium behavior of a larger system in which the original one is embedded. To say this, however, is only to say that there is some definite outcome out of equilibrium in the smaller system. To insist that therefore there is no such thing as disequilibrium is to rob the term "equilibrium" and all equilibrium analysis of meaning. For if "equilibrium" is to be a useful concept in analyzing a particular system, then one must contemplate the possibility of points that are not equilibria of that system. The fact that such points can be represented as equilibria in some larger system does not change this.

If equilibrium analysis is to be justified, the crucial question that must first be answered is one of stability. That question in its most interesting and general form is as follows. Suppose an economy is made up of agents who understand that they are in disequilibrium and perceive and act on profit opportunities. Does the action of those agents lead the economy to converge to equilibrium, and, if so, to what sort of equilibrium? I shall refer to this as the "key question" of stability analysis.

It is important to note, however, that, while stability of competitive general equilibrium is perhaps the only disequilibrium question addressed in a long literature, that literature has seldom addressed the key question directly. Rather, as we shall see, writings on the stability of general equilibrium have only recently endowed agents with much perception. Instead, agents have been supposed to make their plans as though disequilibrium did not exist, and the interaction of those plans has been modelled only as an afterthought at best.

Why should this be? The answer may be related to the phenomenon of concentration on equilibrium and to the distaste or at least disinterest with which many theorists regard the stability literature. Economic analysis is extremely powerful when considering the optimizing behavior of the individual agent. It is comfortable with positions in which the plans of those agents are mutually compatible. It must break untrodden ground to describe what happens when this is not so. This means modelling both the way in which trade takes place when agents' plans cannot be completely fulfilled and how agents react to frustration. Neither aspect can be properly done by considering equilibrium behavior.

2.   Tâtonnement and Its Failure

As already indicated, however, the study of stability has historically been marked by failure to model out-of-equilibrium behavior as more than an afterthought. That was particularly true of the development that characterized the first twenty years or so of the subject – the study of tâtonnement.

It was P. A. Samuelson (1941) who took the first crucial step in the study of stability. Reacting to a suggestion of J. R. Hicks (1939) that "perfect stability" might be defined in terms of demand curves that slope down after various prices are allowed to adjust, Samuelson pointed out that there could be no study of stability without an explicit dynamic model. He assumed that price-adjustment takes place out of equilibrium by prices moving in the direction indicated by the corresponding excess demands,[1] an assumption that can be written in its general form as:

$$\dot{p}_i = H^i(Z_i(p)) \qquad (i = 1, \ldots, c), \tag{1}$$

where there are c commodities, subscripted by i, p is the vector of prices, $Z_i(p)$ the excess demand for commodity i when prices are p, and the $H_i(.)$ are continuous and sign-preserving functions. (A dot over a variable denotes differentiation with respect to time.) Samuelson proposed the study of (1) as the *only* out-of-equilibrium adjustment mechanism.

Models of this type are known as "tâtonnement" models. They suffer from the obvious lack of reality of the assumption that only prices adjust out of equilibrium, with agents constantly recontracting rather than trading (let alone consuming and producing). Yet that assumption (which goes nicely with the fictitious Arrow-Debreu world in which all markets open and close at the dawn of time) may not be the most troublesome one for purposes of understanding disequilibrium behavior. Since price adjustment equations such as (1) are also characteristic of the later, non-tâtonnement literature, it is worth discussing this in detail.

Whose behavior does equation (1) represent? It cannot reflect directly the behavior of the individual agents whose demands are to be equilibrated. Indeed, we now see a central conundrum: In a perfectly competitive economy, all agents take prices as given and outside of their control. Then who changes prices? How do sellers know when demand or costs rise that they can safely raise prices without losing all their customers? At a formal level such questions are deep ones.

[1] If price is zero and excess demand negative, price is assumed to remain zero. I generally ignore this complication in what follows.

It only begs the price-adjustment question to say (as is often done) that (1) reflects the behavior of an "auctioneer" whose job it is to adjust prices in such a way.[2] Most real markets do not have such specialists. Those markets that do have them are such that the specialist is rewarded for his or her endeavors. To understand where and how such price-setting takes place requires analysis of how markets equilibrate. That cannot be done by adding (1) as an afterthought, nor is it likely to be done satisfactorily in the tâtonnement world where only prices adjust and there are no consequences to remaining in disequilibrium.

The fact that there are no such consequences provides some justification for the way in which the behavior of the agents themselves is treated in tâtonnement models. Disequilibrium never enters the dreams of those agents; they construct their excess demands as though prices are fixed and unchanging and as though their desired transactions will in fact take place. Since nothing happens until prices have adjusted to equilibrium (assuming that ever occurs), agents may have nothing to gain by being more sophisticated about what is really happening.

Tâtonnement models, then, do little about the two basic facets of disequilibrium behavior. They model the out-of-equilibrium interaction of agents in terms of price adjustment only, without any basis for such adjustment mechanism. Further, since such an unsatisfactory adjustment mechanism does not permit agents to find their plans frustrated in any meaningful sense, there is no analysis of the way in which agents react to such frustration.

Despite these defects, the analysis of tâtonnement was the exclusive subject of the first twenty years or so of the stability literature (roughly 1940–60). This is understandable when one recalls that the subject was then in its infancy. Perhaps because the adjustment process in (1) seems the simplest case and perhaps because, even so, until the late 1950s major results seemed very hard to come by, no serious attention seems to have been paid in this period to the underlying defects of the model. What is more surprising is the casual view still sometimes encountered that stability analysis necessarily means the study of tâtonnement. Perhaps partly because of the obvious defects of the tâtonnement model and

---

[2] The auctioneer may have been invented by J. Schumpeter in lectures at Harvard and was probably introduced into the literature by Samuelson. Despite the fact that the construct is often referred to as the "Walrasian auctioneer," it does not appear in the work of L. Walras (who did, however, suppose that prices adjust in the direction indicated by excess demands). Interestingly, F. Y. Edgeworth wrote (1881, p. 30): "You might suppose each dealer to write down his *demand*, how much of an article he would take at each price, without attempting to conceal his requirements; and these data having been furnished to a sort of market-machine, the *price* to be passionlessly evaluated." I am indebted to P. Newman for this reference.

partly because of the total collapse of the tâtonnement effort in 1960, that casual view tends to be accompanied by a disdain for the entire subject of stability.

As just indicated, however, the late 1950s seemed a time of considerable promise for tâtonnement results. This was largely because of the introduction of Lyapounov's Second Method into the economics literature, rather than because of the attractive nature of the tâtonnement model itself.

Following Samuelson's introduction of equation (1), the literature (which was not voluminous) concentrated on the question of whether (1) was locally stable. Essentially, this is the question of whether (1) tends to converge to a rest point (a point at which $\dot{p} = 0$, here identical with a Walrasian equilibrium) if it begins close enough to that rest point. Such concentration on local properties seemed natural, for it allowed linear approximation, and the properties of autonomous linear differential equations are completely known.

Less understandable save in historical terms was the early concentration on the relations between local stability of (1) and the conditions for Hicksian "perfect stability" – an attribute that, as already mentioned, has nothing directly to do with stability at all. Those conditions – the alternation in sign of the principal minors of the Jacobian of the excess demand functions – were shown by Samuelson (1941, 1947) and L. Metzler (1945) to be equivalent to the local stability of (1) on the very strong assumption that all goods are gross substitutes (excess demand for any good goes up when the price of any other good increases).[3]

Since the alternation of the principal minors is not a particularly interpretable property, the Samuelson-Metzler results are properly to be regarded as a lemma rather than a theorem, but it was a long while before any further progress was made. That was done independently by F. H. Hahn (1958) and T. Negishi (1958). Each of these authors realized that the economic structure of the problem could be further exploited and each showed – Hahn using Walras' Law and Negishi the homogeneity of degree zero of the excess demand functions – that the gross substitutes assumption itself implied the Hicks conditions on the principal minors and hence the local stability of (1).

This quite neat contribution was eclipsed, however, by the really big development of the late 1950s, the introduction of Lyapounov's Second

---

[3] Years later, D. McFadden (1968), writing in the Hicks *Festschrift*, showed that the Hicks conditions imply global stability of (1) on very strong assumptions about relative speeds of adjustment in different markets.

Method.[4] This was done in a pair of papers by K. J. Arrow and L. Hurwicz (1958) and Arrow, H. D. Block, and Hurwicz (1959).

Lyapounov's Second Method works as follows. Continuing with (1) as an example of a differential equation, suppose that there exists a function, $V(p)$, which is continuous, bounded below, and decreasing through time except at a rest point of (1). The existence of such a function, called a "Lyapounov function," implies that (1) is *quasi-stable*, that is, that every limit point of the time-path of p is a rest point. If that path can be shown to remain in a compact set, then p approaches the set of rest points. If, in addition, rest points are locally isolated or unique given the initial conditions, then (1) is a *globally stable* process; it converges to some rest point no matter where it starts. (Recall that the rest points of (1) are Walrasian equilibria.)[5]

This powerful tool was used by Arrow, Hurwicz, and Block to demonstrate the global stability of tâtonnement under apparently different strong restrictions on the excess demand functions. The first such restriction was that of gross substitutes, thus completing the early literature. Unfortunately, as we now realize, both this and nearly every other restriction considered was a special case of the assumption that the Weak Axiom of Revealed Preference applies to *market* demand functions – a very strong restriction indeed. As a result, Arrow *et al.*'s conjecture, that tâtonnement is *always* stable given only those restrictions (such as Walras' Law) that stem from the basic assumptions of microeconomic theory, was a bold one indeed.

In fact, that conjecture is wrong. H. Scarf (1960) quickly provided a counter-example of an exchange economy with non-pathological consumers in which (1) is not stable. As we now know from the work of H. Sonnenschein and others, that example implies the existence of an open set of economies for which a similar result holds.[6] Indeed, so far as anything useful is known, it appears to be that stability rather than instability of tâtonnement is a special case.

---

[4] A. Lyapounov (1907). Lyapounov's "First Method" for proving stability is the explicit solution of the differential equations involved, an alternative never available at the level of generality of the stability literature.

[5] The limit point, however, generally depends on the initial conditions. For a more extended discussion as well as exact statements and proofs, see F. M. Fisher (1983). Note that G. Debreu (1970) has shown that local isolation of equilibria is true almost everywhere in the appropriate space of economies given certain differentiability assumptions.

[6] Sonnenschein (1972, 1973), Debreu (1974), and R. Mantel (1976) show that the basic assumptions of economic theory do not restrict the excess demand functions except by continuity, homogeneity of degree zero, and Walras' Law. Since Scarf's example shows that such restrictions do not imply stability of (1) and since properties such as the signs of the real parts of the eigenvalues of the Jacobian matrix of (1) are continuous, instability must hold on an open set.

Scarf's counter-example was thus of major historical importance. Its true analytical importance today, however, is not often realized. Scarf did not show that stability analysis was guaranteed to be unfruitful. (Indeed, as we shall see, a very fruitful development immediately began in the early 1960s.) Rather Scarf showed that *tâtonnement* would not generally lead to stability. This means that the facile proposition that disequilibrium is cured by fast-enough price adjustment is not generally true (although, of course, it may be true in special circumstances).

If price adjustment alone is not sufficient to guarantee stability, however, then equilibrium economics must rest on the assumption that quantities also adjust. While, as we shall see, such an assumption does indeed lead to more satisfactory stability results, it has a major consequence. When trade takes place out of equilibrium (and even more when disequilibrium production and consumption occur), the very adjustment process alters the equilibrium set.

This is easily seen even within the simplest model of pure exchange. In such a model, the equilibrium prices and allocations depend on the endowments. If trade takes place out of equilibrium, those endowments change. Hence, even if the trading process is globally stable, the equilibrium reached will generally not be one of those corresponding to the initial endowments in the static sense of the Walras correspondence. Rather the equilibrium reached will be path-dependent, dependent on the dynamics of the process taking place in disequilibrium.

If such effects are large, then the popular enterprise (ironically led by Scarf himself (1973)) of computing points of general equilibrium from the underlying data of the economy is quite misleading. The points computed by such algorithms are the equilibria corresponding statically to the initial endowments of the economy. They are not the equilibria to which the economy actually tends given those endowments. Hence such algorithms make dangerous predictive (or prescriptive) tools.

More important than this, the principal tool of equilibrium analysis – comparative statics – is called into question. Displacement of equilibrium will not be followed by convergence to the new equilibrium indicated by comparative statics. Rather it will be followed by a dynamic adjustment process that, if stable, generally converges to a different equilibrium. While general comparative-statics results are not plentiful in general equilibrium analysis, the foundation for such results, even in a partial equilibrium setting, has become shaky.

Out-of-equilibrium effects may, of course, be small. But we have no reason to believe that they are. The failure of tâtonnement means that we cannot escape by assuming that quantity-adjustment effects are negligible relative to price effects. The doubtful project of tacking anonymous price adjustment onto an equilibrium model is known to be a failure. Further progress requires more serious attention to what happens out of equilibrium, and we see that what happens out of equilibrium can have a serious effect on equilibrium itself.

3. Trading Processes: The Edgeworth Process

The failure of tâtonnement, however, does not imply the failure of stability analysis, and the early 1960s saw the beginning of a more fruitful development. Not surprisingly perhaps, that development involved a closer look at out-of-equilibrium behavior.[7] In particular, while (1) remained the equation supposedly explaining price adjustment, trade was now allowed to take place out of equilibrium, and some thought was given to the specification of trading rules. The resulting models were called "non-tâtonnement" processes, but as that name is not particularly descriptive, I prefer to call them "trading processes."

Trading processes made only a modest concession to realism in allowing trade to take place out of equilibrium. Households (the original models concerned only pure exchange) were permitted to trade endowments out of equilibrium, but no consumption could take place until equilibrium was reached. Indeed, the pre- and post-equilibrium situations were unnaturally separated, for equilibrium involved an exhaustion of trading opportunities with previously planned consumption then allowed but trade already over. This was perhaps an inevitable development, given the dominance of the Arrow-Debreu model of general equilibrium in which markets for all present and future goods clear at the beginning of time, but can be considered only a first step in the analysis of the disequilibrium behavior of actual economies.

As already observed, the price-adjustment equation (1) was retained in trading processes. The task then was to specify the adjustment equations describing changes in endowments. Here there quickly developed one restriction common to all models (in one form or another). That was the assumption that trade at constant prices cannot increase an agent's wealth, since goods of equal value must be exchanged. I shall refer to this as the "No Swindling" assumption.

That progress might be made by considering trading processes becomes apparent when one realizes that the No Swindling assumption alone implies that any Lyapounov function that works in tâtonnement

[7] The first paper to suggest (by example) that there might be considerable pay-off in a closer look at the adjustment process appears to have been Hahn (1961a) which considered specialization of (1) instead of restrictions on excess demands as a way of making progress in tâtonnement. (See also A. Kagawa and K. Kuga, 1980.)

also works for trading processes in pure exchange. Essentially this is because, with prices constant, trade in endowments cannot change any household's ordinary demand for any commodity, since wealth will be unaffected. While such trade can certainly change a particular household's *excess* demand for the commodity traded by changing its actual stock, such effects must cancel out in pure exchange when summing over households. Hence trade in endowments does not change aggregate excess demands, and those demands only move with prices. It follows that if such movement is consistent with a Lyapounov function when only prices move, then it is still consistent when trade in endowments is permitted.

This is an interesting result, incorporating both some consideration about out-of-equilibrium behavior and the properties of the underlying theory of the consumer. Surprisingly, it shows that stability proofs will generally be no harder for trading processes (in pure exchange) than for tâtonnement. Unfortunately, this does not get us very far, since we know that such proofs are usually not available for tâtonnement. Further specification of trading processes beyond the No Swindling assumption is required if real progress is to be made.

Such specification took the form of two alternative assumptions about the way trade takes place. The first of these, the "Edgeworth process," was introduced by H. Uzawa (1962) (see also Hahn, 1961b); the second, the "Hahn process" (named by Negishi, 1962), made its first published appearance in a paper by Hahn and Negishi (1962). Each of the two processes involves what turns out to be a deceptively simple and appealing assumption about out-of-equilibrium trade.

The basic assumption of the Edgeworth process is that trade takes place if and only if there exists a set of agents whose members can all increase their utilities by trading among themselves at the then ruling prices. With some complications stemming from the possibility that initial prices may not permit any such trade, it is easy to see that at least quasi-stability must follow. This is because, for each agent, the utility that would be achieved were trade to stop and the endowment then held to be consumed must be non-decreasing and strictly increasing if that agent engages in trade. Hence the sum (or any other monotonic function) of such utilities must be non-decreasing and strictly increasing out of equilibrium. The negative of the sum can then be used as a Lyapounov function.

This is very neat, but problems emerge when one begins to think hard about the basic assumption involved. In the first place, it is easy to construct examples in which the only Pareto-improving trades that are possible involve large numbers of agents. Indeed, the only upper bound on such constructions (other than the number of agents) is the number of commodities itself. Since we wish to deal with models in which all present and future goods are involved, that upper bound cannot be an effective one. Hence the assumption that trade must take place if such a Pareto-improving possibility exists places a massive requirement on the information flow among agents.[8]

A somewhat deeper problem lies in the other part of the Edgeworth-process assumption. Since trade is voluntary, it seems very natural to assume that trade takes place only when the agents engaging in it are all made better off. Once one considers the possibility of moving from trading processes in the direction of what I have referred to above as the "key question," however, the usefulness of this assumption in the form employed in the Edgeworth process becomes very doubtful.

The "key question" is that of whether the economy is driven to equilibrium by the behavior of arbitraging agents taking advantage of the opportunities thrown up by disequilibrium. But speculating agents can certainly engage in trade not because they believe that their utility will be directly increased by each trade but because of the sequence of trades they expect to complete. An agent who trades apples for bananas in the hope that he or she can then make an advantageous trade of bananas for carrots may not care for bananas at all. More realistically, agents sell goods for money, not because they expect happily to consume the money they receive but because they expect to use the money to buy something else. The basic assumption of the Edgeworth process, however, is that every individual transaction is utility increasing – that agents would gain from each leg of a transaction even if trade were to stop so that later legs could not be completed. Whether the fact that individuals engage in trade because they *expect* to gain can be used to extend the Edgeworth process to cover multi-part transactions is not known and seems doubtful.

One cannot avoid this problem if one wishes to examine the serious out-of-equilibrium behavior of agents who have non-naïve expectations.

---

[8] Let there be n agents and $c \geq n$ commodities. With the exception of agent n, let agent i hold only commodity i and desire only commodity $i + 1$. Let agent n hold only commodity n and desire only commodity 1. Then the only Pareto-improving trade involves all n agents. The problem is quite similar to that involved in coalition formation in the theory of the core, and D. Schmeidler has shown (privately) that, if $c \leq n$, the existence of some Pareto-improving trade implies the existence of such a trade for no more than c agents. P. Madden (1978) proves that the existence of a Pareto-improving trade implies the existence of a Pareto-improving bilateral trade, provided that every agent always has a positive amount of every commodity, but such a condition cannot be reasonably expected to hold. (Whether a weaker condition on agents' holdings might produce a weaker but still interesting result is an open question. The construction of the example above suggests such a possibility. See, for an extensive treatment of this, Fisher (1989).)

The fact that the economy is not in equilibrium means that some expected trades may not materialize. In turn this means that agents who expected to gain from such trades will be disappointed. As a result, they may very well regret having taken past actions – actions they would not have taken had they realized what was to occur.

This phenomenon is not restricted to speculative actions. If one considers the extension of the analysis of trading processes to permit out-of-equilibrium production and consumption, one encounters a similar difficulty with the extension of the Edgeworth process. Both consumption and production involve technically irreversible acts – the consumption of goods or the transformation of inputs into outputs. If those acts are taken on mistaken expectations about later occurrences – either later prices or the ability to complete later transactions – then they will sometimes be regretted. This is hard to accommodate in a model whose Lyapounov function depends on agents always having non-decreasing utilities.

4.   The Hahn Process

The second of the two important trading processes, the Hahn process, places a much less severe informational requirement on trades than does the Edgeworth process. In the Hahn process it is supposed that goods are traded in an organized way on "markets." (How such markets get organized is a question for a different level of analysis.) It is assumed that prospective buyers and sellers of a given good can find each other and trade if they desire to do so – indeed, in some versions (Fisher 1972), this is taken to define what is to be meant by a "market."

Naturally, out of equilibrium, it can and often will happen that prospective buyers and sellers of a given good cannot all complete their planned transactions in that good. There may thus be unsatisfied sellers or unsatisfied buyers. The principal assumption of the Hahn process is that markets are "orderly," in the sense that, *after trade*, there are not both unsatisfied buyers and unsatisfied sellers of the same commodity. Only on one side of a given market are agents unable to complete their planned transactions.

This assumption can easily be seen to lead in the direction of a stability proof. Trade is supposed to take place instantaneously or outside of time relative to the rest of the process, and we look only at post-trade situations. Since markets are orderly, after trade, any agent with unsatisfied excess demand for apples, say, finds that there is aggregate excess demand for apples. Since (1) is retained as the price adjustment equation, the price of apples must be rising. Similarly, any agent with unsatisfied excess supply for bananas finds that there is aggregate excess supply for bananas. Then the price of bananas must be falling, unless that price is already zero. Since anything an agent wants to buy and cannot buy is becoming more expensive, and any non-free good that an agent wants to sell and cannot sell is becoming cheaper, any agent with either unsatisfied excess demand or unsatisfied excess supply of non-free goods is becoming worse off. In slightly more formal terms, the agent's *target* utility – defined as the utility that the agent would get if he or she completed all planned transactions – is non-increasing and strictly decreasing if the agent's plans are frustrated.[9] It follows that the sum of such utilities over agents (or any monotonic function of the utilities of individual agents) will serve as a Lyapounov function, decreasing except in equilibrium when all agents can complete their planned transactions.

This shows the quasi-stability of the Hahn process. If one either assumes or proves boundedness of the prices, it is possible to show global stability, since expenditure minimization and the strict quasi-concavity of indifference curves implies that all limit points must be the same.

It is important to understand the difference between the Lyapounov functions of the Edgeworth and Hahn processes. In the Edgeworth process, the utilities that increase out of equilibrium are the actual utilities that agents would obtain if trade ceased and they had to consume their endowments. In the Hahn process, the utilities that decrease out of equilibrium are the target utilities that agents expect to get by completing their transactions at current prices. In effect, out of equilibrium, those expectations are not compatible; agents jointly expect more than can be delivered. As the Hahn process goes on, agents revise their expectations downward until they do become mutually compatible and equilibrium is reached.

Of course, since the two processes are quite different, it will sometimes happen in the Hahn process that trade leads to a decrease in the utility that an agent would get if that were his or her last trade. This is not a defect, however. Indeed, as can be seen from our earlier discussion of the Edgeworth process, such a property is desirable, since we want to focus on ultimate plans, not myopic desires as the reason for trade.

Moreover, continuing to look ahead toward the "key question" and more realistic models, the Hahn process has another desirable feature that the Edgeworth process lacks. Since the Lyapounov function of the Hahn process involves declining target utilities, it should be fairly easy

---

[9] With the exception of disposing of free goods. It is tiresome to have to constantly repeat this, and I shall not always do so hereafter.

to accommodate the decline in utility that occurs when an irreversible consumption or production action is taken and later regretted. This turns out to be the case (Fisher 1976a, 1977).

Before we can properly get to such matters, however, we must deal with an underlying problem. The basic assumption of the Hahn process, that markets are "orderly" in the sense described, cannot be reasonably maintained without deeper consideration. The problem at issue can be seen by considering the following example.

Suppose that there are at least three commodities: apples, bananas, and croissants. Suppose that, at non-zero current prices, before trade, apples and bananas are in excess supply and croissants in excess demand. Suppose further that some agent, A, owns only apples and wishes to trade for bananas. Suppose that another agent, B, wishes to sell bananas and buy croissants, but does not wish to sell bananas for apples. Then even though A and B can meet each other, no trade between them will take place at current prices. This means that, post-trade, there can perfectly well be agents with an unsatisfied excess demand for apples and also agents with an unsatisfied excess supply of apples. The apple market in this example is not "orderly," and such situations cannot be ruled out merely by supposing that agents can find each other readily.

This problem appears first to have been recognized in the modern literature by R. Clower (1965), who pointed out (in a different context) the need to sell before one can purchase. But a homely example comes readily to hand.[10] A familiar English nursery rhyme states:

> Simple Simon met a pieman going to the fair.
> Said Simple Simon to the pieman, "Let me taste your ware."
> Said the pieman to Simple Simon, "Show me first your penny."
> Said Simple Simon to the pieman, "Indeed, I haven't any."

This is a clear example of a Hahn process economy in crisis. Markets are sufficiently well organized that willing buyers and willing sellers can meet. Indeed, in the rhyme, the prospective buyer and seller of pies meet on their way to the marketplace (the "fair"). Nevertheless, no trade takes place because the buyer has nothing to offer the seller that the seller is willing to accept.

The case of Simple Simon, however, points up one possible way to think about this problem. It does so by introducing an element so far conspicuously lacking from stability analysis. The pieman does not ask

[10] I apologize for using again the same light-hearted example that I have already employed on two previous occasions (Fisher, 1976b, p. 14, 1983, p. 33). It is so apt as to be irresistible.

Simple Simon for apples or bananas or croissants; instead he asks for money, and the time has plainly come to consider the introduction of money into stability analysis.

Indeed, that introduction cannot be long delayed in any case. Aside from the Simple Simon problem under discussion and the use of money in the intermediate stages of arbitrage transactions, one cannot get beyond pure exchange without introducing it. This is for a reason that, interestingly, does not apply in equilibrium.

Firms, unlike households, are usually assumed to maximize profits. Suppose that some firm produces a large excess supply of some commodity, say toothpaste. Out of equilibrium, even with toothpaste in aggregate excess supply, the price of toothpaste can be positive. If that price is high enough, and if there is no standard medium of exchange in which profits are measured, the toothpaste producing firm may regard itself as making a positive profit, *even though it sells no toothpaste*. This means that the firm's inventory of toothpaste need not be offered for sale, so that the excess supply of toothpaste will have no effect on the price.[11] Only by insisting that profits be measured in a common medium of exchange (and a common unit of account) can we ensure that firms producing commodities other than the exchange medium have an incentive to sell those commodities. This makes money indispensable.

The introduction of money into Hahn process models was begun by Arrow and Hahn (1971). They assumed that one of the commodities, "money," plays a special role in that all transactions must involve it. They then assumed that agents first formulate "target excess demands" – excess demands constructed by maximizing utility functions subject to budget constraints in the usual way – but that these must be distinguished from "active excess demands," constructed as follows. If an agent has a negative target excess demand for a given commodity, then that agent wishes to sell it. Since commodities can be offered for sale whether or not the supplier has any money, active excess demand in such a case is assumed to equal target excess demand. On the other hand, positive target excess demands cannot generate offers to buy unless they are backed up by money, so Arrow and Hahn assumed that the agent allocates his or her available money stock over the goods for which he or she has a positive excess demand. This leads to the assumption that any good for which the agent has a positive target excess demand is also one for which that agent has a positive active excess demand, with

[11] The device of assuming that the firm distributes toothpaste dividends to its stockholders hardly seems satisfactory.

the active excess demand never exceeding the target one (agents do not offer to buy more than they really want and always make a positive offer for anything they want). It is active, rather than target demands that are assumed to obey the orderly markets assumption and unsatisfied aggregate excess active demand that is assumed to affect prices according to (1).

With this in hand, Arrow and Hahn were able to isolate the Simple Simon problem by assuming that no agent ever runs out of money. If this assumption holds, then it is easy to see that the Hahn process stability proof goes through in much the same way as before. Prices change in the direction indicated by unsatisfied aggregate active demands; unsatisfied individual active demands have the same signs (post-trade) as the corresponding aggregate demands; finally, unsatisfied individual target demands have the same signs as the corresponding unsatisfied individual active demands. Hence target utilities are still decreasing out of equilibrium.

As already indicated, the introduction of money permits the introduction of firms, and this was done in Fisher (1974).[12] Firms are assumed to be subject to the orderly markets assumption, but to maximize profits which they ultimately distribute to their shareholders. Shareholders expect to spend those profits. Because of the orderly markets assumption, any firm that cannot complete its planned transactions must revise its forecast of profits downward. Households then find their target utilities decreasing both because of the direct influence of the orderly market phenomenon on their own transactions and because of the declining fortunes of the firms they own. The sum of household utilities can thus again be used as a Lyapounov function. While boundedness is now a more complex matter, a global stability proof follows nicely from it, employing both profit maximization on the part of firms and expenditure minimization on the part of households to show that all limit points are the same. Money and the target-active excess demand distinction are handled as before.

This is a pretty story, and one that can even be extended to permit out-of-equilibrium production and consumption, as indicated above (Fisher, 1976a, 1977). But the difficulties are all too apparent.

The role of money in this model is very much an afterthought. Agents plan their target excess demands as though they were in equilibrium. In so doing, they take no account of the cash constraint imposed by the institutional structure. Instead, they allocate their money stocks to their

---

[12] A parallel introduction of firms into the Edgeworth process was accomplished by F. M. C. B. Saldanha (1982).

positive excess demands as though any cash difficulty will necessarily be only temporary, so that ultimately target transactions will be completed.

That naïveté is also reflected in the assumption that agents make a positive offer for every good for which they have a positive target excess demand. So long as we remain in an Arrow-Debreu world where all markets open and close at the dawn of time, this may not matter. Once we begin to be serious about disequilibrium, however, and to permit consumption and production to take place before equilibrium is reached, it matters a lot. It is not reasonable to suppose that agents facing a liquidity crisis always allocate funds to all demanded commodities. Some of those commodities may not be needed for years, while others may be required for near-term consumption.

And of course the afterthought method of allocating cash is related to the most obvious difficulty. The Simple Simon problem has not been solved, but merely well defined. It is still necessary to assume that agents never run out of money. This may be hard to swallow in any case; it is particularly unpalatable when agents make their money-allocation plans as though their planned sales would always materialize.

In the same connection, the time has come to remember how awkward the price-adjustment assumptions are in all these models. We are not dealing with a case in which agents, faced with impending cash shortage when planned sales do not occur, can lower their prices. Rather, we are still in a world in which price is set anonymously, and sellers who might benefit from lower prices are just out of luck.[13]

In other respects as well the model is less than satisfactory. Money is assumed to be a commodity entering the utility function. This is required in order to ensure that agents wish to hold money in equilibrium, avoiding the "Patinkin problem" (D. Patinkin, 1949, 1950, 1965). But that problem arises because equilibrium in this Arrow-Debreu world means a cessation of trading opportunities. If equilibrium had the more natural property of involving the carrying out of previously planned transactions at previously foreseen prices, then the transactions motive for holding money would not disappear. Yet such a version of equilibrium requires agents to care about the timing of their transactions.

In several ways, then, the defects of the more sophisticated Hahn process models point the way toward possible progress. In one way or

[13] Some progress can be made here. Fisher (1972) provides a model in which goods are identified by the dealers who sell them. In such a model, the orderly markets assumption is essentially trivial, since there is only one agent on the supply side of any "market." Since prices are set by suppliers (with buyers searching for low prices), they can be adjusted when planned sales do not occur and cash is low. But there are plenty of other difficulties with such a model. See M. Rothschild (1973).

another, those defects are all related to the fact that the agents in such models (as in all the models considered so far) pay very little attention to the fact that the economy is in disequilibrium. They go on believing that prices will not change and that transactions will be completed. Disequilibrium behavior and phenomena are modelled at best as an afterthought. Plainly, the difficulties encountered cannot be solved in such a context. A full disequilibrium model is required and must be built if we are to address the "key question" of whether arbitraging actions drive the economy to equilibrium.

5.   Towards a Full Disequilibrium Model

So far as I know, the only attempt to examine the stability question in the context of a full disequilibrium model in which consumption and production take place out of equilibrium and agents consciously act on arbitrage opportunities is that of my recent book (Fisher 1983; see also Stahl and Fisher 1988). As will be seen, that attempt to answer the "key question" cannot be considered truly successful, but there is, I think, much to be learned from it and from its inadequacies.

I begin by considering a problem of only moderate importance which nevertheless exemplifies the need for dropping equilibrium habits of thought when thinking about disequilibrium problems. This problem arises when one allows consumption and production to take place out of equilibrium.

It is common, correct, and necessary to regard commodities consumed or produced at different dates as different commodities even if they are physically indistinguishable. In the Arrow-Debreu world where nothing ever happens until equilibrium is reached, this does not matter; a commodity with a different date is just a different commodity traded on a different market and with its own price. If consumption or production takes place out of equilibrium, however, then commodity dates take on a new significance. Only currently dated commodities can be consumed or produced; future commodities can only be traded. Hence, allowing disequilibrium consumption or production means allowing some commodity dates to be passed before equilibrium is reached. Since there can only be trading in current or future commodities, but no trading in "pasts," this means that trading in some commodities becomes impossible as the adjustment process unfolds.

To see why this creates a difficulty, consider the following example. For simplicity, assume that commodities are dated by year. At midnight on December 31, 1987, trade in 1987 toothpaste ceases. Since we are out of equilibrium, this can mean that there are agents who cannot buy as much

1987 toothpaste as they had planned. Since they must now make do with a different amount than planned, this can cause a discontinuity in their behavior.

An obvious solution to this difficulty presents itself, however. Assume that toothpaste is a durable good (a somewhat different analysis applies to pure perishable commodities). Then, at midnight on December 31, 1987, 1987 and 1988 toothpastes are perfect substitutes. Our agent may not be able to buy the 1987 toothpaste he or she planned, but this will not create any discontinuity, since 1988 toothpaste can be purchased instead.

The problem cannot be made to go away so easily, however. Since 1987 toothpaste is a different commodity from 1988 toothpaste, the two commodities have different prices. If those prices do not coincide at midnight on December 31, 1987, then discontinuity is still a real possibility.

It is very tempting to reply to this that the two prices *must* coincide at that time, because the two commodities are then perfect substitutes. *That temptation must be resisted.* The proposition that the prices of perfect substitutes must coincide is an *equilibrium* proposition. It rests on the argument that arbitrage will erase any difference between the prices. But that working of arbitrage is what a full stability model is supposed to be about. We cannot, in a disequilibrium framework, simply assume that arbitrage will be successful by the time the crucial hour arrives.

There is an important sense, however, in which this difficulty is more apparent than real. That difficulty stems from the treatment of the markets for 1987 and 1988 toothpaste as wholly distinct, with prices set anonymously according to some rule such as (1). In fact, this is unlikely to be the case. Instead, the same firms that sell 1987 toothpaste are also likely to sell 1988 toothpaste and to quote prices for both. Similarly, dealers specializing in wheat futures are unlikely to deal in futures for only one date. But if the same seller (or, more generally, the same dealer) quotes prices for both 1987 and 1988 commodities, then he or she will have an active interest in making sure that those prices come together at midnight on December 31, 1987, since otherwise arbitrage at the dealer's expense will be possible.

There are three lessons to be learned from all this. First, one cannot think about disequilibrium problems using only equilibrium habits of thought. Certain issues that seem not to matter in equilibrium can matter quite a lot out of it. Second, the farther one gets into serious disequilibrium analysis, the less satisfactory is the assumption of anonymous price adjustment. Third, disequilibrium considerations have something to do with the institutional structure of transactions and the way in which markets are organized – subjects on which no work has been attempted in the disequilibrium context, but which are crucial if we are ever to gain a satisfactory understanding of the formation of economic magnitudes.[14]

Such subjects, however, are truly difficult, for they involve analysis of what happens when agents interact and their plans do not mesh. It is far easier to consider how those plans get formulated, and the analysis of Fisher (1983) does this at some length, producing a number of results on the way in which agents plan to take advantage of the arbitrage opportunities they see thrown up by changing prices. In the course of so doing, the positive cash assumption of Arrow and Hahn becomes far less arbitrary, since agents now optimize their planned transactions, paying attention to their money stock. Interestingly, it emerges that one reason for trading in the shares of firms is because anticipated dividend streams permit liquidity transfers from one period to another, and, out of equilibrium, such transfers may be needed.

Such arbitraging actions come principally from allowing agents to expect prices to change. But allowing agents to be conscious of disequilibrium means more than this; it also means allowing them to realize that their transactions may be limited in extent. So long as we retain anonymous price adjustment, we must suppose that such constraints are regarded as absolute. This has led to a literature on the analysis of equilibria under such circumstances – so called "fixed price equilibria."[15]

More interesting for the study of true disequilibrium is what happens when we allow agents to believe that they can alter the constraints they face by making price offers. Consider, for example, the case of a seller who believes that the amount that can be sold at a given price is limited. If the seller also believes that a lower price will bring more sales, then the constraint expresses expected sales as a function of price and becomes an ordinary, downward-sloping demand curve. In this case, the seller will only refrain from offering a lower price for the usual reason in the analysis of monopoly: a lower price must be given on all units to be sold, and marginal revenue will fall short of marginal cost.

This leads to a number of interesting problems. First, there is the distinct possibility in such cases that equilibrium will be non-Walrasian. Specifically, the economy can be stuck in a position where agents believe

---

[14] For work on transaction arrangements in general equilibrium, see D. Foley (1970) and Hahn (1971).

[15] While such circumstances are sometimes referred to as "disequilibrium," they are not properly so-called, since what is involved is non-Walrasian equilibrium, rather than dynamic adjustment. See A. Drazen (1980) for a survey of the literature.

they face binding transaction constraints and do not attempt to get round them with price offers because they believe that it would be unprofitable to do so. In macroeconomics, this can be regarded as a version of the original Keynesian question as to underemployment equilibrium. Hahn (1978) shows that it can happen with the beliefs of the agents rational in some sense.

Second, the crucial question of whether an equilibrium is Walrasian or non-Walrasian becomes the question of whether perceived monopoly power vanishes in equilibrium. This is not a question that can be answered by only analyzing equilibria; it pretty clearly depends on the experiences agents encounter on the way to equilibrium (assuming that some equilibrium is reached). In this regard, it is interesting that, as Fisher (1983) shows, there is a relation between the nature of the equilibrium and the question of whether or not liquidity constraints are actually binding therein. Only where perceptions of monopoly power remain (and change over time in certain ways after equilibrium is reached) will the equilibrium be non-Walrasian and cash remain a problem.

Whether or not a given equilibrium is Walrasian, however, some clarification of the role of money is achieved. We saw above that the equilibria of trading processes (or of tâtonnement models, for that matter) were merely exhaustions of trading opportunities. In a full model, such as the one under discussion, transactions do not cease in equilibrium; rather, equilibrium involves the carrying out of previously made optimal plans involving planned transactions at correctly foreseen prices. This means that the transactions demand for money does not disappear in equilibrium. While money in this model is an interest-bearing asset (so that there is no explanation for equilibrium holding of non-interest-bearing money), this explains why agents hold that asset rather than others bearing the same rate of interest in equilibrium, even though money itself enters neither utility nor production functions.

6.   Dynamics and Stability in a Full Model

All this is very interesting, but it says little about what happens when agents interact out of equilibrium and plans are frustrated. What can be said about such interactions and about the "key question" of whether they lead to stability? Alas, it is here, as already indicated, that the analysis under discussion produces less than satisfactory answers.

We have already seen that one cannot retain the old anonymous price-adjustment equation (1) left over from tâtonnement days. Individual price adjustment is essential. But how does such price adjustment take place? The answer suggested above is that prices are set optimally depending on perceived monopoly (or monopsony) power. That is all well and good, but it does not take us very far. How do such perceptions get formed and change? How do institutions arise determining which agents make price offers and which choose among offers? Out of equilibrium, where offers and acceptances will not match, how does partial matching take place?

On these crucial questions, Fisher (1983) offers relatively little guidance. Rather, price movements, like all other movements in the model, are assumed to be restricted by a vague but strong restriction called "No Favorable Surprise" (NFS). To understand that restriction, and the motivation for it, requires us to step back for a moment and consider the purpose of stability analysis.

Real economies are subject to a succession of exogenous shocks. The discovery of new products, new processes, new sources of raw materials, new demands, and new ways of organizing production are, as emphasized by J. Schumpeter (1911), the driving forces of economic development and growth. It is unreasonable to suppose that such Schumpeterian shocks are all foreseen and can be incorporated as part of equilibrium. Rather, equilibrium analysis, if it is useful at all, is so because the economy rapidly adjusts to such shocks, approaching a new equilibrium long before the next shock occurs.

The role of stability analysis, then, is to analyze the question of whether such adjustment in fact takes place. This means analyzing the part of the Schumpeterian model occurring after the initial innovation, when imitators enter and act on the profit opportunities they see. What I have called the "key question" can be interpreted as the question of whether such action does in fact lead the system to absorb a given Schumpeterian shock. Evidently, then, the first task of stability analysis is to answer this question on the assumption that further Schumpeterian shocks do not occur.

There is more to it than this, however. In a full model, where agents form their own expectations, there is the possibility that agents will perceive Schumpeterian opportunities that do not exist. If such agents have the resources with which to back their perceptions, equilibrium will at least be postponed. The entrepreneur who believes that he or she can profitably build a better mousetrap and who has the money to invest will affect the economy even if the world does not in fact beat a path to the door. Stability implies that such occasions disappear, at least asymptotically, and no stability proof in a complete model can succeed without either proving or assuming that this happens.

The basic first step in an adequate analysis of stability as a full attack on the "key question," therefore, is the weak one of showing that arbitrage leads to equilibrium if no new unforeseen opportunities arise. This is the assumption of "No Favorable Surprise." More precisely, NFS assumes that agents are never surprised by the unforeseen appearance of new, favorable opportunities causing them to deviate from previously formed optimal plans if those plans are still feasible. In other words, any plan now optimal is assumed to have been feasible a short time ago. Useful new opportunities (technological change, for example) must be foreseen at least a short time before agents actually change plans so as to act on them.

It is not hard to see that, as in the Hahn process which is a special case, NFS implies that agents' target utilities are declining out of equilibrium. While agents can be doing quite well in a foreseen way (including taking advantage of foreseen technological progress), any abrupt departures from what was expected must mean declines in utility (if they matter at all). With this in hand, a global stability proof can be made to follow, although the details are technically complex and require a number of non-primitive assumptions on the dynamics involved.

The problem with this is that NFS itself is not a primitive assumption, either. It is all very well to argue as above that one must exclude further exogenous Schumpeterian shocks in examining stability. It is far stronger to rule out the favorable opportunities that may suddenly arise in the course of adjustment to an existing shock.

Evidently, this difficulty arises precisely because we have no good model of how agents interact in reacting to disequilibrium. This causes us to be unable to describe exactly how endogenous surprises do or do not arise and makes NFS a somewhat unsatisfactory assumption.[16]

Like earlier models, then, the analysis of Fisher (1983) is only partially successful. It is strongest when dealing with the plans of individual agents or with equilibrium. It is weak when considering how those plans interact when they cannot all be fulfilled and how agents then change their expectations. While it succeeds in doing away with anonymous price adjustment, it tells us very little about how prices are in fact set. We still have much to learn about the formation of economic magnitudes.

To learn how economic magnitudes are formed requires serious modelling of disequilibrium. If we are ever to understand how resources are allocated, how consumption and production are organized, how prices come to be what they are and the role that they play, we must

---

[16] There is at least one other problem with NFS. The agents in the model being described have point expectations and no subjective uncertainty. (They are all economists – often wrong but never uncertain.) It is an open question as to whether there exists a version of NFS that is both palatable and strong enough to produce a similar stability result when subjective uncertainty is permitted.

examine disequilibrium behavior. Among other things, this means examining the ways in which agents change their expectations when their plans are frustrated. Obviously, such questions cannot be begged by using equilibrium tools. (In particular, the assumption of rational expectations can tell us nothing at all about how disequilibrium works.) We cannot simply examine positions in which economic magnitudes happen to be such that there is no tendency to change. To understand the workings of the "Invisible Hand" it is not enough to understand what the world looks like when the "Invisible Hand" has nothing to do.

REFERENCES

Arrow, K. J., H. D. Block, and L. Hurwicz (1959). "On the Stability of the Competitive Equilibrium II," *Econometrica* 27, 82–109.
Arrow, K. J. and F. H. Hahn (1971). *General Competitive Analysis*. San Francisco: Holden-Day/New York: Oliver & Boyd.
Arrow, K. J. and L. Hurwicz (1958). "On the Stability of the Competitive Equilibrium I," *Econometrica* 26, 522–52.
Cartelier, J. (ed.) (1990). "A Formation Des Grandeurs Economiques," *Nouvelle Encyclopedia Diderot*. Paris: Press Universitaires de France.
Clower, R. W. (1965). "The Keynesian Counterrevolution: A Theoretical Appraisal," in F. H. Hahn and F. P. R. Brechling (eds.), *The Theory of Interest Rates*. London: Macmillan/New York: St. Martin's Press.
Debreu, G. (1970). "Economies with a Finite Set of Equilibria," *Econometrica* 38, 387–92.
    (1974). "Excess Demand Functions," *Journal of Mathematical Economics* 1, 15–21.
Drazen, A. (1980). "Recent Developments in Macroeconomic Disequilibrium Theory," *Econometrica* 48, 283–306.
Edgeworth, F. Y. (1881). *Mathematical Psychics*. Reprinted New York: Augustus M. Kelley, 1967.
Fisher, F. M. (1972). "On Price Adjustment without an Auctioneer," *Review of Economic Studies* 39, 1–15. Reprinted as Chapter 4 in this volume.
    (1974). "The Hahn Process with Firms but No Production," *Econometrica* 42, 471–86.
    (1976a). "A Non-Tâtonnement Model with Production and Consumption," *Econometrica* 44, 907–38.
    (1976b). "The Stability of General Equilibrium: Results and Problems," in M. J. Artis and A. R. Nobay (eds.), *Essays in Economic Analysis (The Proceedings of the Association of University Teachers of Economics, Sheffield 1975)*. Cambridge: Cambridge University Press.
    (1977). "Continuously Dated Commodities and Non-Tâtonnement with Production and Consumption," in A. S. Blinder and P. Friedman (eds.), *Natural Resources, Uncertainty, and General Equilibrium Systems: Essays in Memory of Rafael Lusky*. New York: Academic Press.

(1983). *Disequilibrium Foundations of Equilibrium Economics*. Cambridge: Cambridge University Press.

(1989). "It Takes t^* to Tango: Trading Coalitions in the Edgeworth Process," *Review of Economic Studies* 56, 391–404. Reprinted as Chapter 7 in this volume.

Foley, D. K. (1970). "Economic Equilibrium with Costly Marketing," *Journal of Economic Theory* 2, 276–91.

Hahn, F. H. (1958). "Gross Substitutes and the Dynamic Stability of General Equilibrium," *Econometrica* 26, 169–70.

(1961a). "A Stable Adjustment Process for a Competitive Economy," *Review of Economic Studies* 29, 62–5.

(1961b). "On the Stability of Pure Exchange Equilibrium," *International Economic Review* 3, 206–13.

(1971). "Equilibrium with Transaction Costs," *Econometrica* 39, 417–40.

(1978). "On Non-Walrasian Equilibria," *Review of Economic Studies* 45, 1–18.

Hahn, F. H. and T. Negishi (1962). "A Theorem on Non-Tâtonnement Stability," *Econometrica* 30, 463–9.

Hicks, J. R. (1939). *Value and Capital*. New York: Oxford University Press (Clarendon Press).

Kagawa, A. and K. Kuga (1980). "On Professor Hahn's Tâtonnement Stability Theorem: Comment and Example," *Review of Economic Studies* 47, 813–16.

Lyapounov, A. (1907). "Problème Général de la Stabilité du Mouvement," *Annales de la Faculté des Sciences de l'Université de Toulouse* 9, 203–474.

McFadden, D. (1968). "On Hicksian Stability," in J. N. Wolfe (ed.), *Value, Capital, and Growth. Papers in Honour of Sir John Hicks*. Edinburgh: Edinburgh University Press.

Madden, P. (1978). "Why the Edgeworth Process Assumption Isn't That Bad," *Review of Economic Studies* 45, 279–84.

Mantel, R. (1976). "Homothetic Preferences and Community Excess Demand Functions," *Journal of Economic Theory* 12, 197–201.

Metzler, L. (1945). "The Stability of Multiple Markets: The Hicks Conditions," *Econometrica* 13, 277–92.

Negishi, T. (1958). "A Note on the Stability of an Economy Where All Goods Are Gross Substitutes," *Econometrica* 26, 445–7.

(1962). "The Stability of a Competitive Economy: A Survey Article," *Econometrica* 30, 635–69.

Patinkin, D. (1949). "The Indeterminacy of Absolute Prices in Classical Economic Theory," *Econometrica* 17, 1–27.

(1950). "A Reconsideration of the General Equilibrium Theory of Money," *Review of Economic Studies* 18, 42–61.

(1965). *Money, Interest and Prices* (second edition). New York: Harper & Row.

Rothschild, M. (1973). "Models of Market Organization with Imperfect Information: A Survey," *Journal of Political Economy* 81, 1283–1308.

Saldanha, F. M. C. B. (1982). *Essays on Non-Tâtonnement Stability*. Unpublished Doctoral Dissertation, Massachusetts Institute of Technology.

Samuelson, P. A. (1941). "The Stability of Equilibrium," *Econometrica* 9, 97–120.
   (1947). *Foundations of Economic Analysis*. Cambridge, Mass.: Harvard
   University Press.
Scarf, H. (1960). "Some Examples of Global Instability of the Competitive
   Equilibrium," *International Economic Review* 1, 157–72.
   (1973). *The Computation of Economic Equilibria* (in collaboration with
   T. Hansen). New Haven: Yale University Press.
Schumpeter, J. (1911). *The Theory of Economic Development*. Fourth printing of
   English translation, Cambridge Mass.: Harvard University Press, 1951.
Sonnenschein, H. (1972). "Market Excess Demand Functions," *Econometrica* 40,
   549–63.
   (1973). "Do Walras' Identity and Continuity Characterize the Class of
   Community Excess Demand Functions?" *Journal of Economic Theory* 6,
   345–54.
Stahl, D. and F. M. Fisher (1988). "On Stability Analysis with Disequilibrium
   Awareness," *Journal of Economic Theory* 46, 309–21. Reprinted as Chapter
   6 in this volume.
Uzawa, H. (1962). "On the Stability of Edgeworth's Barter Process," *International
   Economic Review* 3, 218–32.

CHAPTER 2

Quasi-Competitive Price Adjustment by Individual Firms: A Preliminary Paper (1970)

1. Introduction

One of the principal unfilled holes in microeconomic theory is of deep importance. We have a satisfactory theory of equilibrium in perfect competition; despite great and admirable labor by many leading theorists, we have no similarly satisfactory theory of how equilibrium is reached.[1] Such adjustment models as have been proposed and studied generally are less than satisfactory, for they rest on assumptions (often plausible ones) about the way in which prices behave in different markets taken as a whole, rather than on a model of individual behavior. Thus, as is well known, the tâtonnement process involves the assumption that the rate of change of price is proportional to excess demand, and even the non-tâtonnement processes that have been studied incorporate a similar price adjustment mechanism while allowing trade to take place out of equilibrium. Yet, as Koopmans has pointed out,[2] it is far from clear whose behavior is described by that price adjustment process in markets where there is in fact no auctioneer to conduct it.

The problem can be described in a related but different way. In a perfectly competitive market, all participants take price as given and believe that they cannot affect it; yet when that market is in disequilibrium, the price is supposed to move. The Invisible Hand is a little too invisible in this, the center of its activities.

And indeed, the problem of an adequate theory of price adjustment is of obvious importance. For one thing, we now know that even if such a theory leads to a single-market-price process, the exact form of the process and the way in which it is or is not accompanied by quantity

I am indebted to the members of the MIT-Harvard Mathematical Economics Seminar for helpful comments.

This research was sponsored by the National Bureau of Economic Research and forms part of an ongoing project that the Bureau hopes to publish when complete, pending approval of its board of directors.

[1] See Negishi (1962) for an excellent survey of the literature.

[2] Koopmans (1957), p. 179.

adjustments will matter for stability. For another thing, the classic ambiguity in econometric models as to whether demand (or supply) curves are to be normalized for price or for quantity[3] reflects our lack of a theory of how prices are changed.

I wish I could claim to have satisfactorily resolved this problem and provided a satisfactory general model of price adjustment. This is not the case. The present paper makes a tentative start in this direction by considering a very simplified model of a single market with perfectly competitive features, but in which firms themselves change prices. To focus on the price-adjustment question, I have stripped the model of all but the features bearing directly on such adjustment and thereby robbed it of possible realism. The reintroduction of such features and the study of more complicated and more interesting cases along the same lines will be a matter for further work.

Indeed, another way of looking at the present, preliminary study is as an attempt to provide a more formal apparatus for the one area in which individuals in a competitive market have always been described as affecting prices. This is in the standard classroom discussion of the Marshallian cross where, when price is above equilibrium, sellers are described as bidding down price and conversely when price is below equilibrium. Building a reasonable model of that process at the same level of simplicity seems to me to be a useful first step in an attack on the problem of competitive price adjustment by individuals.

2.   The Model: General Outline

In the model, there is a basic asymmetry between buyers and sellers.[4] Firms set and change their prices and decide on their production in a manner to be described in a moment. Given those prices, consumers engage in a search procedure to find a low-priced firm from which to buy. If that firm is sold out, they may attempt to buy from another firm, and so forth. Depending on the way in which quantity demanded from each firm coincides with its expectations, each firm then changes its price and the process is repeated. The model is a wholly partial one and, moreover, demands and production are in flow terms and are unchanging so that the underlying market situation is not affected by the results of the activity described. As I said, I have stripped the problem to the simplest possible case.

---

[3] See Schultz (1938), for example.
[4] I have in mind a retail market, but the asymmetry could be reversed in, say, a model of the labor market.

How do firms set prices and decide on production plans? Each firm knows that it is in a competitive market and believes that it faces a flat demand curve at a market price which it does not control or affect. Unfortunately, it does not know with certainty what that price is. Thus each firm sets what it believes to be the market price and determines its production by the corresponding point on its marginal cost curve (where marginal cost equals price). If it sells less than it expected (zero, or close to it, in general), then it lowers its price. If it has to turn away unsatisfied customers, then it raises its price. In short, each firm adjusts its own price with the rate of change a monotonic function of its own excess demand.[5] This is, of course, an adjustment process of the classical type, but it takes place at the level of the individual firm, where there is no ambiguity as to whose behavior is involved. At that level, the essential plausibility of such an adjustment process means something.

As a matter of fact, it is not necessary for the results that every firm adjust price in just this way, so long as some firm with the highest price does so if it fails to sell out, and some firm with the lowest price also does so if it has unsatisfied customers. These are firms who have made the most extreme assumptions about price and have been proven wrong. Firms not in this position may adjust prices in any continuous way.

Consumers, on the other hand, as already stated, take the prices set by firms and make the most of them. If information is instantaneous, perfect, and costless, then all consumers will attempt to buy from the lowest-price firm if they buy at all. If information does not have these properties but instead there is some cost or disutility to acquiring it, then it may be that consumers will try to buy from different firms.[6] Either of these is allowed by the model, although the second is the more general. Rather general limits are placed upon the lack of information that consumers can have. Thus, consumers distinguish stores only by price, and a low-price store always has at least as many customers as a high-priced one; this seems to be the least one can impose to preserve the competitive aspect of the model.

Not every consumer who tries to buy from a given store may be able to do so, for some stores may be sold out. Disappointed customers may go home or they may go to another store. Provided that the search procedure of the consumers takes place very quickly relative to the rate at

---

[5] Monotonicity is rather stronger than is necessary; see below.
[6] I have borrowed from Stigler's oligopoly theory to suit the present quasi-competitive case. See Stigler (1961, 1964).

which firms change prices (I have assumed it instantaneous, for simplicity), it turns out that the very general restrictions on the search procedure just mentioned lead the whole adjustment process to converge to competitive equilibrium.

While it is thus not necessary for the stability results to much restrict the search behavior of consumers, it is well to realize that some types of search behavior permitted by the formal assumptions are hardly compatible with the assumed behavior of the firms. As described above, the search behavior of consumers can be considered as having two principal aspects which might be termed "efficiency" and "indefatigability."

Efficiency of search we have already partially discussed. We assume that consumers' search is not counterproductive so that a low-priced firm has at least as many customers as a high-priced one. While this suffices for the stability results, however, the search had better be more efficient than this for the firms' behavior to be sensible. If the number of customers attempting to buy from a firm does not depend upon price (while the *amount* they attempt to buy does), every firm will in fact face a demand curve with the same elasticity as total industry demand and it is unreasonable to suppose that the sellers will not recognize this.

Similarly, we have allowed consumers turned away at one store to go and search for another. There is nothing in the formal assumptions to prevent them from going on and on until they find a store with unsold output, although if search is costly in money or utility, they may well prefer to give up. If they are indefatigable, however, then (to take but a single example) when all firms are at the equilibrium price, any single firm (if it is clever) will realize that if it raises its price slightly, it will *not* lose its entire demand or anything like it, since it will end up with the same number of customers anyway, even though they will buy less.

Thus, in both aspects, the generality which we shall allow the assumptions on the search behavior of consumers to have is in part only apparent. For the firms' behavior to be sensible, consumers must be fairly efficient at finding low-priced firms and they must not go on doggedly searching for an open store for too long.

3.   The Formal Model

We now formalize the preceding discussion. Mostly as a matter of convenience we assume that all firms are alike in most respects, that all consumers are alike in most respects, and that there is a finite but large number of each.

Each firm has a marginal cost curve of the usual type (and these are all the same). If a firm believes the market price to be p, and so sets its own price, it will plan to produce where marginal cost equals p. Denote by $S(p)$ the total amount that would be produced by all firms together if they all simultaneously took p to be the market price. $S(p)$ is thus the ordinary industry supply curve, obtained by horizontally summing the (in this case identical) firm marginal cost curves in the standard way.

In fact, however, at any moment of time, all firms may not charge the same price. We denote by $f(p)$ the fraction of firms who do charge price p. Naturally, $f(p)$ will change in the course of the adjustment process.

Define $s(p) = f(p) S(p)$. Then $s(p)$ is the total amount actually offered for sale at price p.

We now turn to the consumers. Each of them has a demand curve (and these are all the same). Denote by $D(p)$ the total amount that would be demanded by all consumers together if they all faced the same price, p. Thus $D(p)$ is the industry demand curve obtained by horizontally summing the (in this case identical) individual consumer demand curves in the usual way.

The actual demand facing the firm or firms who offer goods at a particular price p is not a simple function of $D(p)$. It depends on the search procedure of the consumers and on the prices set by the other firms. Indeed, the same consumer can contribute to the demand facing several firms, if his searching first leads to some that are sold out. When a consumer finally succeeds in finding an open firm charging price p, however, his demand is assumed to depend only on p and not on the search history.[7]

We denote by $d(p)$ the total demand actually facing the set of firms who charge price p.

We assume:

Assumption 3.1. $S(p)$ and $D(p)$ are continuous. $D(p)$ is monotonic non-increasing and $S(p)$ is monotonic non-decreasing. There is a unique equilibrium price, $p^* > 0$, at which $S(p^*) = D(p^*)$.

Assumption 3.2. Denote the price charged by the i-th firm by p_i and the excess demand facing that firm by x_i. The price adjustment process for the i-th firm is given by

$$\dot{p}_i = H^i(x_i), \tag{3.1}$$

---

[7] For simplicity, we ignore the possibility that the last consumer to find a particular store open might satisfy some but not all of his demand there.

where H^i is continuous and has the following properties:

$$H^i(x_i) \gtreqqless 0 \qquad \text{according as } x_i \gtreqqless 0; \tag{3.2}$$

$$H^i(\infty) > 0; \qquad H^i(-\infty) < 0. \tag{3.3}$$

Thus, H^i is sign-preserving and is bounded away from zero except as x_i approaches zero. The obvious assumption is to take H^i monotonic, but this is not strictly necessary.

Note that the H^i are allowed to be different for different firms. To assume them all the same would be more restrictive than necessary and would assume away an important feature since it would imply in many circumstances that if a single price is ever established, separate prices can never recur. There is no reason why the H^i cannot be allowed to depend on p_i as well as x_i (or indeed on the prices and excess demands of other firms as well), so long as the sign-preserving property is retained. All that is required is a continuous adjustment in the direction indicated by excess demand and at a rate that does not approach zero unless excess demand does.

As a matter of fact, not even this is required of all firms. It would suffice to require it to be true at any time of at least one firm charging the minimum price if that firm has positive excess demand and of at least one firm charging the maximum price if that firm has negative excess demand. The remaining firms may behave in any continuous way.

We assume that the differential equations involved have a unique solution. In view of the continuity assumptions, this is innocuous since it follows from the results below that a zero price and a negative excess demand cannot occur together.

We turn now to the search procedure followed by consumers. As indicated, we take this to be instantaneous and restrict it explicitly only by the following (admittedly strong) assumption.

Assumption 3.3.

  (A)   If $p < p'$, the number of consumers attempting to buy from a firm charging price p is at least as great as the number attempting to buy from a firm charging price p'.

  (B)   Every consumer attempts to buy from at least one firm.

  (C)   The demand facing any particular firm is a continuous, single-valued function of the prices set by all firms.[8]

Assumption 3.3(A) states that consumers are at least as good at finding a low-price firm as they would be if they chose a firm at random;

---

[8] This ignores the fact that the switch of one consumer in a finite set from one firm to another creates a small discontinuity.

search is not counterproductive. The assumption could doubtlessly be weakened (and made more plausible) by requiring only that the probability of any consumer finding a low-price firm is at least as great as the probability that he finds a high-price one; in this case, the results below would have to be restated in terms of probabilities. Further discussion of implicit restrictions on consumer search was given in the preceding section.

Assumption 3.3(B) in effect defines the set of consumers. Note that not every consumer need *succeed* in buying; he may give up after one or more attempts.

Assumption 3.3(C) reinforces Assumption 3.3(A) in that it requires that the output of the process depend only on the prices. Continuity is a natural and indispensable requirement.

Note that we do not explicitly require two firms that charge the same price to have the same number of customers and the same demand. Nonetheless, this follows as an easy consequence of Assumption 3.3(A) and (C), as we shall now prove.

4. Preliminary Results

Lemma 4.1. *If two firms charge the same price, p', they encounter the same demand.*

Proof. Let d^i and d^j be the demands facing the two firms. Let p_i and p_j be their prices. Fix the prices of the remaining firms. Fix $p_j = p'$ and take a sequence of values of p_i converging to p' from below. By Assumption 3.3(A), $d^i \geq d^j$ everywhere in this sequence and, by Assumption 3.3(C), this is also true in the limit. Hence when both prices are p', $d^i \geq d^j$. It is only a matter of notation, however, to show $d^j \geq d^i$, and the lemma is proved. (The case of $p' = 0$ is easily handled by continuity.)

This somewhat embarrassingly strong consequence of Assumption 3.3 (it is not required in the stability proof below) would be avoided if that assumption were weakened to one about probabilities. It is an inevitable consequence of assuming that firms can be distinguished only on the basis of price; when their prices are the same, they turn out to be indistinguishable.

We now consider the question of when certain of the firms will sell out or have excess supplies, thus preparing the way for a discussion of the stability properties of the model. In what follows, p_{min} and p_{max} will respectively denote the lowest and the highest prices among those charged by the set of firms at a given time.

Lemma 4.2. *If $p_{min} < p^*$, then for all firms charging p_{min}, $x^i > 0$.*

Proof. In view of Lemma 4.1, we need only prove that $d(p_{min}) >$ $s(p_{min})$. From Assumption 3.3(A) and (B), however, it follows immediately that the fraction of consumers attempting to buy from firms charging p_{min} is at least $f(p_{min})$, the fraction of firms charging that price. Naturally, at p_{min}, $D(p_{min}) > S(p_{min})$. Thus,

$$d(p_{min}) \geq f(p_{min})D(p_{min}) > f(p_{min})S(p_{min}) = s(p_{min}). \qquad (4.1)$$

Thus, if the lowest price is below equilibrium, every firm charging that price sells out. Lest it be thought that the whole business is as simple as this, it may be well to point out that the parallel statement is *not* true of firms charging the highest price when that price is above equilibrium. Indeed, the fact that consumers can attempt to buy from more than one firm can readily lead to situations in which all firms sell out despite the fact that the highest price is above equilibrium. Thus, for example, suppose that all but one of the firms charge very low prices and produce very low outputs, and that the remaining firm charges a price above p^*. All customers may first try to buy from the low-priced firms, but very few of them may be able to do so. They may then turn to the high-priced one and exhaust its capacity as well, even though had all firms charged the high price there would have been excess supply.

It is true, however, that a high-price firm cannot sell out if a lower-price firm fails to do so. This we now prove.

Lemma 4.3. *Let p and p' be among the prices charged by the set of firms. Assume p < p'. If, for firms charging p', $x^i \geq 0$, then $x^i \geq 0$ for all firms charging p.*

Proof. By Assumption 3.3, at least as many consumers attempt to buy from the firm charging p as from the firm charging p'. It follows from Assumption 3.1, however, that the demand of each consumer is no less at p than at p'. Finally, from the latter assumption, the supply offered by the firm charging p is no greater than that offered by the firm charging p'.

With this result in hand, we can now show that if *every* firm is at or above equilibrium, the firms charging the highest price cannot sell out.

Lemma 4.4. *Suppose $p_{max} \geq p_{min} \geq p^*$, with at least one of the strict inequalities holding. Then, for firms charging p_{max}, $x^i < 0$.*

Proof. Suppose not. Then by Lemma 4.3, every firm must have $x^i \geq 0$. Let $g(p_i)$ be the fraction of consumers who succeed in buying from a firm charging p_i, for $p_i < p_{max}$. Then $g(p_i) D(p_i) = f(p_i) S(p_i)$. Let $g(p_{max})$ be the fraction of consumers who *attempt* to buy from a firm charging p_{max}, so that $d(p_{max}) = g(p_{max}) D(p_{max})$. Note that $\Sigma g(p_i)$ (where the sum is over all firms and includes $g(p_{max})$) need not total to unity since some consumers may give up the search. If $d(p_{max}) \geq s(p_{max})$, and all firms sell out, then

$$\sum g(p_i)D(p_i) \geq \sum f(p_i)S(p_i). \qquad (4.2)$$

From Assumption 3.1, however,

$$\sum g(p_i)D(p_i) \leq (\sum g(p_i))D(p^*) \leq D(p^*), \qquad (4.3)$$

with the *first* inequality strict if $D(p)$ is strictly decreasing to the right of p^*. Similarly,

$$\sum f(p_i)S(p_i) \geq (\sum f(p_i))S(p^*) = S(p^*), \qquad (4.4)$$

with the inequality strict if $S(p)$ is strictly increasing to the right of p^*. Since p^* is a unique equilibrium point, however, at least one of the inequalities in (4.3) and (4.4) must be strict, which contradicts (4.2), proving the lemma.

Continuity considerations enable us to extend Lemma 4.4 to show that if p_{max} is bounded above equilibrium and p_{min} is close enough to equilibrium, then firms charging p_{max} will fail to sell out. Thus:

Lemma 4.5. *For any $\varepsilon > 0$, there exists a $\delta > 0$ such that $p_{max} > p^* + \epsilon$ and $p_{min} > p^* - \delta$ imply that, for firms charging p_{max}, $x^i < 0$.*

Proof. In view of Lemma 4.4, it suffices to consider the case in which $p_{min} < p^*$.

Suppose the lemma were false. Then (4.2) would hold as before. Since equilibrium is unique, however, and p_{max} is bounded away from p^* (and hence from p_{min}), either there exists an $\eta > 0$ such that $D(p_{max}) < D(p_{min}) - \eta$ for all $p_{min} < p^*$ and $p_{max} > p^* + \varepsilon$, or else there exists an $\eta > 0$ such that $S(p_{max}) > S(p_{min}) + \eta$ for all such p_{min} and p_{max}, or both. In any case, the argument yielding (4.3) and (4.4) now shows that there exists an $\alpha > 0$ such that

$$\sum g(p_i)D(p_i) - \sum f(p_i)S(p_i) < D(p_{min}) - S(p_{min}) - \alpha \qquad (4.5)$$

for all relevant price configurations in which $g(p_{max})$ is bounded away from zero (as it must be if $d(p_{max})$ exceeds $s(p_{max})$). By choosing δ sufficiently small, however, the right-hand side of (4.5) can obviously be made negative, contradicting (4.2).

5. The Stability Theorem

We are now in a position to prove:

Theorem 5.1. *As time goes to infinity, all prices converge to p^*.*

Proof. There are three regimes to consider: (I) $p_{min} \leq p_{max} \leq p^*$; (II) $p_{min} < p^* < p_{max}$; (III) $p^* \leq p_{min} \leq p_{max}$.

By Lemma 4.2 and Assumption 3.2, p_{min} is increasing everywhere in regime (I) except in equilibrium, and it is obvious from the specific assumptions made on the adjustment process that if the system starts in regime (I), it either converges to equilibrium or passes into regime (II).

Postponing consideration of the latter regime for a moment, consider regime (III). Here, by Lemma 4.4, p_{max} is always decreasing except in equilibrium. Moreover, since, by Lemma 4.2, p_{min} is increasing whenever it is below p^*, a system that begins in or enters regime (III) cannot leave it, but must converge to equilibrium.

There remains regime (II). By Lemma 4.2, in this regime, p_{min} is always increasing. Hence either the system passes out of regime (II) into regime (III) and then converges to p^*, or else it remains in regime (II) with p_{min} converging to p^*. We now show that, in the latter case, p_{max} cannot remain bounded away from p^*.

Suppose p_{max} remains above $p^* + 2\varepsilon$, for some $\varepsilon > 0$. By Lemma 4.5, there exists a $\delta > 0$ such that $p_{min} > p^* - \delta$ and $p_{max} > p^* + \varepsilon$ imply p_{max} decreasing. *A fortiori,* this is true for $p_{max} > p^* + 2\varepsilon$, and, indeed, it is clear from this and Assumptions 3.2 and 3.3(C) that the rate of decrease is bounded away from zero. Since the case we are now considering is one in which p_{min} converges to p^*, a time will certainly come about, for any given $\delta > 0$, after which $p_{min} > p^* - \delta$. It is now clear that p_{max} cannot remain above $p^* + 2\varepsilon$, and, since ε was arbitrary, p_{max} must converge to p^*.

6.   Discussion and Possible Extensions

Some of the assumptions of the model are fairly clearly relatively inessential. These include: the assumption that (3.1) holds for *all* firms; the assumption of a finite number of participants; the statement of Assumption 3.3 in terms of search outcomes rather than probabilities; and the differential equation framework with consumer search taking no time.

These last two points may be of interest when one tries to extend this sort of model to more interesting cases. I have not yet really attempted this, but the following thoughts occur rather naturally in contemplating what is involved.

First, if one attempts to remain in a partial equilibrium framework, but considers two or more markets, it is not easy to see what becomes of Lemmas 4.2–4.5. This is because equilibrium in a particular market depends on the prices in the other markets. Those prices are not single ones, however, as different firms in those markets may charge different prices out of full equilibrium. Different consumers will face different prices in the other markets, depending on the outcomes of their search, and this makes it unclear how the lemmas should be extended, since what constitutes equilibrium price in a particular market then depends on such search outcomes.

Second, within a partial framework, it seems clear that the most one could hope to do directly along the lines of the present theorem (but not the present model) is to prove stability for those cases in which it would be true of tâtonnement, since a special case is that in which each market only has one firm. It is true that if all of the functions, H^i, were the same, then the assumptions would imply that all the prices in a single market converged to a common (moving) price, thus justifying the classical single-price adjustment mechanism, but the assumption of equal speeds of adjustment for all firms makes this fairly trivial and uninteresting. It is easy to see that if speeds of adjustment are not the same for all firms, then reduction to the single-price adjustment model will not in fact take place.

On the other hand, to use only a partial equilibrium framework would be to fail to exploit the features of the quasi-competitive model here outlined. If we move to a general equilibrium framework, we can allow demands to change depending on purchases, and the question of which consumers buy from which sellers – the outcome of the search – will then become essential.

Obviously, the problem is not going to be easy. Aside from the major difficulties of proof, there are the equally important ones of deciding how the model should be extended. Some of these have just been mentioned; another, possibly minor one, is that the asymmetry of buyers and sellers in this paper may not be immediately appropriate in a context in which who buys and who sells depends upon price.

Indeed, it is clear that the present model is only a beginning. The strong result fairly easily obtained in Theorem 5.1 is not surprising at this stage if one considers how easy it is to prove stability in a single-price adjustment process for a single market. It is for this reason that I have called this "a preliminary paper."

REFERENCES

T. C. Koopmans, *Three Essays on the State of Economic Science* (New York: McGraw-Hill Book Company, 1957).
T. Negishi, "The Stability of a Competitive Economy: A Survey Article," *Econometrica*, **30** (1962), 635–69.

H. Schultz, *The Theory and Measurement of Demand* (Chicago: University of Chicago Press, 1938).

G. J. Stigler, "The Economics of Information," *Journal of Political Economy*, **69** (1961), 231–25.

G. J. Stigler, "A Theory of Oligopoly," *Journal of Political Economy*, **72** (1964), 44–61.

CHAPTER 3

Stability and Competitive Equilibrium in Two Models of Search and Individual Price Adjustment (1973)

1. Introduction

The question of how prices change out of equilibrium in a competitive model where all participants take them as given is an important and largely open one in economic theory. In my earlier paper (Fisher, 1970) I presented a model that approached the competitive equilibrium for a single market but in which prices were set by individual firms. That model was extended to one of general equilibrium in Fisher (1972). In both cases firms set prices and customers (with less than perfect information) searched over firms for the most advantageous prices. Firms then adjusted their prices in the direction indicated by the excess demand they encountered, since firms were assumed to believe they were unable to affect the "true" market price that they sought to find.[1]

The trouble with these models, as Rothschild (1973) has forcefully pointed out, is that the assumed behavior of firms may not make much sense. Firms in these models overlook the fact that they are uncertain as to the actual market price, and, more important, they overlook the fact that the imperfection of consumer information gives them a certain amount of market power. A firm that raises its price will not lose all its customers and it cannot escape the attention of high-priced firms that there are customers inquiring as to price who end up going elsewhere. In such a situation, it is not reasonable for firms to behave as though they faced perfectly elastic demand curves, and, while one can argue that if customer search is efficient enough, demand curves will be almost flat, this hardly seems fully satisfactory.

I am indebted to Peter Diamond for discussion of part of this paper, but remain responsible for errors.

The research was sponsored by the National Bureau of Economic Research. It is not an official National Bureau publication since the findings reported herein have not yet undergone the full critical review accorded the National Bureau's studies, including approval of the Board of Directors.

[1] Leaving aside their special focus on the stability of competitive equilibrium, both Fisher (1970) and Fisher (1972) belong to the growing literature on search models, as does the present paper. See Rothschild (1973) for a survey.

In the present paper, therefore, I deal with a model of a single market with customer search in which firms are quite conscious of what is going on and adjust their prices to maximize profits taking into account their monopoly power. (There is, however, no uncertainty on the part of firms.) As in my earlier papers, one of the objects is to tell a competitive-like story in some sense, so that I assume to begin with that each firm takes its rivals' prices as given. This leads to a model of price adjustment with close affinity to the Edgeworth–Bertrand oligopoly model or to the Chamberlinian large group case, and, indeed, the stability theorem proved in this part of the paper says in itself nothing directly about convergence to competitive equilibrium but is of more general applicability to models of search or of monopolistic competition.[2]

The Edgeworth–Bertrand oligopoly model, however, has the well known difficulty that the firms therein fail to realize that their own behavior changes the prices of their rivals even though the adjustment process ought to make this clear to them. If there are enough of them, each one might ignore the effects of his own price changes, but he can hardly ignore the fact that other prices are constantly changing. To some extent, this is taken care of by having firms move continuously toward their continuously changing profit-maximizing optima, rather than blindly jumping the whole way. Even so, this hardly seems an adequate answer to the objection that the firms are behaving rather stupidly.

Accordingly, I then go on to the examination of a similar model in which firms realize perfectly what is happening and move instantly to an equilibrium point at which each firm's price and output are profit maximizing given the prices of all the others – the equilibrium point of the earlier model. I then build in some competitive-like assumptions about the efficiency of consumer search and the learning behavior of consumers and show that the model converges to a competitive equilibrium. In this model, the initial market power of firms is asymptotically eroded away. This section, which contains what are perhaps the main results of the paper, may be considered as an attempt similar to Fisher (1970) to provide a sensible disequilibrium story with a competitive ending. Depending partly on one's predilections, however, the story may seem rather less than more sensible, and, indeed, one way of looking at the

---

[2] One way of looking at this part of the paper is as a contribution to the literature on stability of oligopoly models of price adjustment parallel to the various studies of the stability of the Cournot oligopoly model. See Bishop (1962), Fisher (1960–61), Hahn (1962), McManus and Quandt (1960–61), Ogukuchi (1964), Theocharis (1959–60). For a model of monopolistic competition in general equilibrium that contains some stability analysis, see Negishi (1960–61).

results is as showing how hard it is to tell a sensible competitive dis-equilibrium story.

Despite their similarities, the two models discussed (which I shall refer to as the "adjustment model" and the "equilibrium model," respectively) can be considered as separate and possibly of separate interest. It is easy to see, however, that with appropriate (rather strong) assumptions, they can be joined together, so that the equilibrium model describes the equilibrium path of the adjustment model, as it were. If the changes in equilibrium induced by consumer learning take place slowly relative to the speed with which firms adjust, then the two models jointly describe a process in which firms discover what is going on and the whole market ends up at competitive equilibrium. The final section of the paper is devoted to joining the two models.

2.   Notation and General Features of the Models

In the present section, I introduce the notation, the features, and the assumptions that the two models have in common.

There are n firms, each selling the same perishable commodity. The price set by the ith firm is denoted by p_i, the vector of such prices by p, and the vector of the $n - 1$ prices excluding the ith, by $p(i)$. The output of the ith firm is denoted by x_i.

The ith firm has a cost function $C_i(x_i)$, taken to be twice differentiable. Denoting differentiation by primes, we assume:

G.1 $C_i''(x_i) > 0.$

Of course, this need only apply in the relevant range. Moreover, for some (but not all) purposes, constant marginal costs will do, so long as some of the other inequalities (involving marginal revenue) are strict.[3]

The demand facing the ith firm is denoted by d_i and is given by

$$d_i = F^i(p_i, p(i)). \tag{2.1}$$

I shall begin by taking these functions also as twice differentiable, and, while this is partly a matter of convenience, it requires some explanation.

The process whereby these demand functions arise is often (but not always necessarily) going to be interpreted as one of consumer search. Given the prices set by firms, consumers search for the lowest price. Such search is costly in terms of utility or money, so that, in general, not all

---

[3] A similar remark holds for most of the other strict inequalities assumed elsewhere in the paper but I shall not bother observing it each time.

consumers succeed in finding the lowest-priced firm. Such search takes place very quickly relative to the adjustment process of firms, and we shall take it as instantaneous. Consumers attempt to buy from only one firm at a time.[4] What is involved in differentiability is the assumption that there are enough consumers and their search patterns are sufficiently distinct that the demand facing a given firm changes smoothly as a function of the prices. One can suppose, for example, that the many consumers have some knowledge of some of the parameters of the price distribution but not complete knowledge. When we come to the equilibrium model, I shall alter this assumption somewhat, as it will become very important that firms charging sufficiently low prices be able to sell as much as they want to sell.

It would not be implausible for some purposes to take all the functions F^i as the same and symmetric in the elements of $p(i)$, but there is no reason to do this. At this level of generality, some firms may then have special advantages in the search process, for example, by reason of location. Note, however, that firms do not acquire a reputation for low or high prices. The outcome of consumer search depends only on current prices, not on price histories.

I denote differentiation of F^i with respect to p_i by $F_p^i < 0$ and differentiation with respect to p_k, $k \neq i$, by F_k^i. Second derivatives are denoted in similar fashion.

The marginal revenue of the ith firm is denoted by M^i. It is given by

$$M^i = p_i + \frac{F^i}{F_p^i} = p_i\left(1 + \frac{1}{\eta_i}\right),$$ (2.2)

where η_i denotes the own-price elasticity.

We assume

G.2 $\dfrac{\partial M^i}{\partial d_i} - C_i''(d_i) < 0$

or, equivalently,

G.2' $\dfrac{\partial M^i}{\partial p_i} - C_i''(d_i)F_p^i > 0.$[5]

---

[4] This was not the case in Fisher (1970) in which customers turned away from a sold-out store could try again instantly. To introduce this explicitly into the present model would make d_i depend on the x_k, $k \neq i$, and would be a massive complication, although for some of our purposes – those of the adjustment model – this could be implicitly handled since the x_k depend on the prices given the cost curves.

[5] Actually, G.2 or G.2' need not be assumed to hold globally. Taking them to hold where required by the second-order condition for the firm's maximum problem would be enough. There seems little harm in the stronger assumption, however, and it is a little easier to work with.

Each firm, given its demand curve, its cost curve, and its assumptions about the prices set by other firms, is assumed to have a nonnegative profit-maximizing price-output combination (unique, in view of G.1 and G.2) at which marginal revenue equals marginal cost, i.e.,

$$p_i + \frac{F^i}{F_p^i} = C_i'(F^i(p_i, p(i))). \tag{2.3}$$

(We ignore corner solutions for convenience.) The value of p_i that satisfies (2.3) when $p(i)$ is the vector of *actual* prices charged by the other firms will be denoted by $\bar{p}_i$.

We assume there is a set of prices at which (2.3) is *simultaneously* satisfied for all $i = 1, \ldots, n$ (a Nash equilibrium point). The ith such price is denoted by $\tilde{p}_i$. Thus, $\bar{p}_i = \tilde{p}_i$ if $p(i) = \tilde{p}(i)$ (but possibly not only then). There is no harm in assuming $\tilde{p} > 0$. However, at this stage, $\tilde{p}$ need not be unique.

The commodity being sold is perishable, so that purchases at one time do not affect demand at another. Moreover, unsatisfied demand or excess supply in one period does not affect demand or supply decisions at any other time. This is very much a partial equilibrium model.

3.   The Adjustment Model

We now consider what happens if every firm takes the other firms' prices as given and adjusts p_i in the direction of $\bar{p}_i$. We shall prove that under some fairly strong, but perhaps not unreasonable assumptions such a process converges to $\tilde{p}$. As it happens, the assumptions involved will also imply that $\tilde{p}$ is unique. (In the ensuing discussion, $\tilde{p}$ can be taken to be any particular price vector satisfying (2.3) for all firms.)

The general strategy of the proof is to show that the firm with $p_i/\tilde{p}_i$ smallest finds, if $p_i < \tilde{p}_i$, that $\bar{p}_i > \tilde{p}_i$, so that it has an incentive to raise its price. Similarly, we shall show that the firm with the largest $p_i/\tilde{p}_i$ finds, if $p_i > \tilde{p}_i$, that $\bar{p}_i < \tilde{p}_i$, so that it has an incentive to lower its price.[6] To accomplish this, we need to consider the determinants of $\bar{p}_i$. Clearly, $\bar{p}_i$ is a function of the elements of $p(i)$ and of the parameters of the ith firm's demand and cost curves. We prove the following.

Lemma 3.1.   *Let α be any of the variables or parameters on which $\bar{p}_i$ depends. Then $\partial \bar{p}_i/\partial \alpha$ has the opposite sign to $(\partial M^i/\partial \alpha - \partial C_i'/\partial \alpha)$.*

---

[6] There is a natural parallel to proofs of uniqueness and stability in the gross substitute case of general equilibrium. This is not surprising; the natural assumption to make is that the wares of the different firms are gross substitutes in the eyes of the consumers. We shall indeed assume this in a moment.

Proof. Obvious from (2.3) and G.2′. If raising α makes marginal revenue greater than marginal cost, then the firm will wish to expand output and lower price.

Let $p_m/\tilde{p}_m = \min_k p_k/\tilde{p}_k$ and $p_M/\tilde{p}_M = \max_k p_k/\tilde{p}_k$. We now consider assumptions that will guarantee that if $p_m < \tilde{p}_m$ a movement of other firms' prices from $\tilde{p}(m)$ to $p(m)$ will lower firm m's marginal revenue below its marginal cost. The same assumptions will similarly ensure that if $p_M > \tilde{p}_M$, a movement of other firms' prices from $\tilde{p}(M)$ to $p(M)$ will raise firm M's marginal revenue above its marginal cost. By Lemma 3.1, firm m will then want to increase and firm M will want to decrease their respective prices. In what follows, we concentrate on firm m, the proof for firm M being similar.

The first two assumptions seem harmless enough (I wish the same could be said for the later ones). We begin with

A.1 $F_k^i \geq 0, \qquad k \neq i \qquad i, k = 1, \ldots, n.$

In other words, an increase in price by some other firm does not decrease the demand facing a given one.

Next define

$$\phi^i(\lambda) \equiv F^i(\lambda p_i, \lambda p(i)) \tag{3.1}$$

for fixed p. We assume:

A.2 $\phi^{i\prime}(\lambda) < 0 \qquad$ all $\qquad i.$

This is hardly empty, but seems pretty reasonable. One way of justifying it is to suppose that if all prices increase proportionally, the number of consumers attempting to buy from the ith firm does not increase. Moreover, the amount that any one of them wants to buy will certainly be less, given the attempt, since p_i has increased too. The essential feature is that while some consumers may not buy at all if all prices are high, and those who do will generally buy less, the distribution of buying consumers over firms depends on the price ratios and not on their absolute level. A.2 is weaker than this.

In fact, it is not necessary to assume that A.2 holds everywhere; it would be sufficient to assume that it holds along the ray through $\tilde{p}$.

We can now prove the following lemma.

Lemma 3.2. *Under G.1, A.1, and A.2, if $p_m < \tilde{p}_m$, then C_m' is higher at p than at $\tilde{p}$.*

Proof. Since marginal cost is increasing, one need only show that the mth firm faces higher demand at p than at $\tilde{p}$. Let $\lambda = p_m/\tilde{p}_m < 1$. Let prices move from $\tilde{p}$ to $\lambda\tilde{p}$. By A.2, F^m must rise. Now let prices move from $\lambda\tilde{p}$

to p. In view of the definition of m, $\lambda = p_m/\tilde{p}_m \leq p_k/\tilde{p}_k$ for all $k \neq m$, so such a move leaves p_m unchanged and does not decrease any other p_k. By A.1, therefore, F^m does not fall. Hence, the entire move from $\tilde{p}$ to p has increased firm m's output and the lemma follows from increasing marginal cost as remarked at the outset.

The task now clearly is to ensure that in such a move from $\tilde{p}$ to p, the mth firm's marginal revenue does *not* rise, or at least does not rise as far as its marginal cost. Since, at p, marginal revenue equals marginal cost for all firms, this will be enough to secure the desired result.

Unfortunately, it is not generally true that such behavior of marginal revenue is guaranteed by relatively general or innocuous assumptions such as A.1 or A.2, and, accordingly, the stability and uniqueness proofs here given are restricted to a reasonable but hardly universal class of demand functions, F^i.

The first way to proceed is to observe that, as $p_m < \tilde{p}_m$, there is some presumption that marginal revenue is lower at p than at $\tilde{p}$. To put it a bit more formally, in view of (2.2), we require:

$$p_m\left(1 + \frac{1}{\eta_m}\right) \leq \tilde{p}_m\left(1 + \frac{1}{\tilde{\eta}_m}\right), \tag{3.2}$$

where $\tilde{\eta}_m$ denotes the value of η_m when all prices are $\tilde{p}$. Since $p_m < \tilde{p}_m$, this will certainly be so if elasticity doesn't change too much as prices go from $\tilde{p}$ to p. Indeed, since in such a movement demand would have to get more elastic to upset (3.2), and since the reciprocal of elasticity is involved, it is clearly enough if demand is already very elastic at p. Further, since it is quite acceptable for our purposes for the mth firm's marginal revenue to rise, so long as it does not rise as far as that firm's marginal cost (which certainly does rise, by Lemma 3.2), the constraint required on the behavior of demand elasticity is not as great as indicated by (3.2).

Accordingly, we might simply assume the desired result as to the behavior of marginal revenue relative to marginal cost. However, it is probably worth first going into the matter in somewhat more detail to see in a different way what is involved.

Consider the construction used in the proof of Lemma 3.2 where we began at $\tilde{p}$ and moved first to $\lambda\tilde{p}$ and then to p, with $\lambda = p_m/\tilde{p}_m < 1$. Is it reasonable to suppose that the mth firm's marginal revenue does not increase too much in those two steps?

Taking first the move from $\tilde{p}$ to $\lambda\tilde{p}$, all prices decrease in the same proportion. That means that the good sold on the market under study is getting cheaper relative to all other goods. It is not unreasonable to suppose that, as this happens, customers become no more sensitive to price, because the financial rewards to incurring the disutility of bargain hunting have gone down. But if demand does not become more elastic and the mth firm's price falls, that firm's marginal revenue must decrease.

There is a slight difficulty with this argument, however. If price sensitivity goes down when all prices decrease in the same proportion, then low-priced firms (of which firm m may very well be one) may not keep their advantages and may find their share of customers decreased. If this occurs to a sufficient extent, A.2 may be violated. On the other hand, if customers look only at price ratios in searching over firms (which is one way of justifying A.2), then the elasticity of the number of customers buying from the mth firm with respect to p_m is the same at $\lambda \tilde{p}$ as at $\tilde{p}$. Total demand elasticity is the sum of this and the elasticity of demand from the average customer buying from the mth firm. It is not unreasonable to suppose that, given the customers who buy from it, the mth firm finds marginal revenue decreasing in p_m. In this case, marginal revenue for that firm certainly decreases as we move from $\tilde{p}$ to $\lambda \tilde{p}$.

It thus seems reasonable on either argument that, as we move from $\tilde{p}$ to $\lambda \tilde{p}$, the marginal revenue of the mth firm decreases or at least does not increase so fast as does marginal cost.

The movement from $\lambda \tilde{p}$ to p is another story, however. Here p_m is constant and other firms' prices are nondecreasing and, in general, increasing. It is very hard to say what effect this will have on the mth firm's demand elasticity, but there are certainly some cases in which it will increase (absolutely). Indeed, this will surely be a case often implied by the assumptions of the equilibrium model in the next section. It is not hard to show that the condition under which such an increase in p_k, $k \neq m$ increases marginal revenue less than marginal cost for firm m is:

$$\frac{F_p^m F_k^m - F^m F_{pk}^m}{\left(F_p^m\right)^2} < C_m'' F_k^m, \tag{3.3}$$

but it is hard to interpret this condition. It does say, of course, that the effect on the mth firm's demand elasticity of an increase in the kth firm's price should be small relative to the slope of the mth firm's marginal cost curve. If we recall that, by the previous argument, we are starting from a position $(\lambda \tilde{p})$ at which the mth firm's marginal cost exceeds its marginal revenue, we see that (3.3) can be relaxed somewhat and still let us end up at p with the mth firm in the same situation.

Accordingly, whether from such detailed considerations or by assuming that the price movements in question don't change η_m very much, we shall assume:

A.3. For any price vector, p: if $1 > p_m/\tilde{p}_m = \min_k p_k/\tilde{p}_k$, then $M^m < C'_m$. If $1 < p_M/\tilde{p}_M = \max_k p_k/\tilde{p}_k$, then $M^M > C'_M$.

This is obviously a quite restrictive assumption, although the discussion leading up to it makes it appear that its consequences are worth exploring. It is crucial in the uniqueness and stability proofs about to be given but plays no role in the equilibrium model of the next section. It may be considered that a stability or uniqueness proof that uses it is on the same (or perhaps firmer) footing than the similar proofs for general equilibrium which restrict the nature of the excess demand functions by such assumptions as that of gross substitution.[7]

We can now observe the following.

Lemma 3.3. *Under G.2' and A.3, if $1 > p_m/\tilde{p}_m$, then $\bar{p}_m > p_m$. If $1 < p_M/\tilde{p}_M$, then $\bar{p}_M < p_M$.*

Proof. Obvious from Lemma 3.1.

Theorem 3.1. *Under G.2' and A.3, $\tilde{p}$ is unique.*

Proof. Suppose not. Let $p \neq \tilde{p}$ be another Nash equilibrium point (a joint solution to (2.3)). Then, for every firm, given $p(i)$, $\bar{p}_i = p_i$. However, either $p_m/\tilde{p}_m < 1$ or $p_M/\tilde{p}_M > 1$ or both. Since the proof is essentially the same in both cases, take $p_m/\tilde{p}_m < 1$ for the sake of definiteness. Then, by Lemma 3.3, $\bar{p}_m > p_m$, which is a contradiction.

Now suppose that firms adjust their prices continuously in the direction of their desired profit-maximizing prices, according to

$$\dot{p}_i = H^i(\bar{p}_i - p_i) \qquad (i = 1, \ldots, n), \tag{3.4}$$

where the H^i are continuous and sign-preserving. We shall show that this process is globally stable and converges to $\tilde{p}$. The issue arises, however, of why firms do not move instantaneously to the $\bar{p}_i$ instead of continuously. One reason may be that adjustments in price involve adjustments in output that are costly if made too fast; another is that firms do learn from experience enough to know that other prices do not change and calculating where to go on the basis of unchanging prices merely indicates the direction in which to start moving. (Discontinuous adjustments could be handled but only for slow enough speeds of adjustments.) In a

---

[7] Negishi (1960–61) uses the gross substitution assumption in a stability analysis of monopolistic competition that contains some features similar to those of the present adjustment model.

sense, the next section handles a case in which the whole process is short-circuited.

Theorem 3.2.   *Under G.2′ and A.3, the process* (3.4) *is globally stable and converges to $\tilde{p}$.*

Proof.   It is obvious that $\tilde{p}$ is the only equilibrium point of (3.4). Define

$$V \equiv \max_k \left| \frac{p_k}{\tilde{p}_k} - 1 \right|.$$
(3.5)

Then V is obviously continuous and bounded below. Moreover,

$$V = \max\left\{ \left(\frac{p_M}{\tilde{p}_M} - 1 \right), \left(1 - \frac{p_m}{\tilde{p}_m} \right) \right\}.$$
(3.6)

It follows from Lemma 3.3 that if $p \neq \tilde{p}$, V is decreasing. This at once establishes that the time path of prices is bounded and shows that we may take V as a Lyapounov function, proving global stability in view of the uniqueness of $\tilde{p}$.

4.   The Equilibrium Model

These results are not too surprising; neither are they very competitive. In a sense they are preliminary to those of the present section in which we turn to the behavior of the equilibrium prices, $\tilde{p}$. This section can be regarded as an examination of the equilibrium path of prices in the adjustment model of the preceding section – a point to which we shall return below – or as an examination of a model in which all firms realize fully what is happening and move instantaneously to the Nash equilibrium point, $\tilde{p}$.[8] The object of this section is to build a reasonably plausible system in which such action converges to the competitive equilibrium, despite the initial presence of frictions and market imperfections entirely recognized by the participants.

To do this certainly requires some restrictive assumptions, although we can now dispense with the special assumptions of the adjustment model. In particular, we must now pay some attention to the search behavior of consumers which has so far played at most an implicit role. Clearly, if consumers are very bad at searching, firms will always have monopoly

---

[8] Uniqueness of $\tilde{p}$ is not technically required, but the hypothesized behavior of firms does not make much sense unless $\tilde{p}$ is unique or all firms somehow know which $\tilde{p}$ is the one to which to move.

power, so the assumptions that we shall employ are directed at the effectiveness of consumer search.

The first of these assumptions is that if a firm sets a price sufficiently low – "sufficiently" being defined alternatively in absolute or relative terms – it finds that its demand curve is flat over some range of outputs large enough that at the upper end of that range the firm's marginal cost exceeds the price in question. In other words, the firm can sell a range of outputs that exceeds its "capacity," defined as what it would be willing to sell if it operated entirely at that price. This means that such a firm is found by a large number of consumers and, of course, that individual firms are small relative to the market. We shall refer to this case as one in which $M^i = p_i$, but it must be borne in mind that the condition on marginal cost is involved as well.

It is interesting to note that one can get a long way toward a competitive result by assuming that a firm that lowers its price enough can sell all it wants to sell. For the most part it is not necessary to assume also that firms setting slightly higher prices lose all their customers. Indeed, to some extent, such an assumption turns out to be positively harmful.

We thus assume:

E.1. For every $i = 1, \ldots, n$, there exists a price vector, q^i, such that $M^i = p_i$ if $p_i \leq q_i^i$ and $p(i) \geq q^i(i)$.[9]

Various versions of E.1 are obtained by various choices of the q^i, as will appear below.

One possibility that is not quite covered by the formal statement of E.1, but that we mean to include, is that $M^i = p_i$ if $p_i \leq p_k$ for $k = 1, \ldots, n$ and $k \neq i$. We shall denote this case by $q_i^i = p_{\min}$ and $q^i(i) = \hat{p}_{\min}(i)$. More generally, we sometimes allow $q(i)$ to depend on p_i.

Since we shall be dealing exclusively with the behavior of $\bar{p}$ in this section, it would suffice to take the various versions of E.1 to hold only if $p = \bar{p}$. In that case, we might regard E.1 as something that holds asymptotically for the adjustment model, but such a treatment has some difficulties for combining the two models and, in the interests of simplicity, we shall not pursue it further.

We shall also assume:

E.2. For every $i = 1, \ldots, n$ if $p(i) \geq q^i(i)$ and $p_i > q_i^i$, then $M^i > q_i^i$.

This is weaker than assuming that marginal revenue is a decreasing function of price (although I shall refer to it that way for mnemonic

---

[9] I follow the usual conventions for vector inequalities. $x > y$ means $x_i > y_i$, all i; $x \geq y$ means $x_i \geq y_i$, all i; $x \geqq y$ means $x \geq y$ but $x \neq y$.

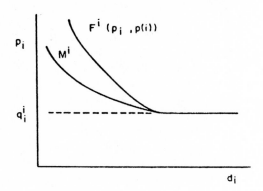

FIGURE 3.1

convenience). It means (since marginal revenue cannot exceed price), that the ith firm's demand curve flattens out smoothly as q_i^i is approached from above, as in Fig. 3.1.

We now define the ith firm's competitive supply as

$$s^i(p_i) \text{ is that value of } x_i \text{ at which } C_i'(x_i) = p_i \qquad (4.1)$$

(recall that x_i is the output of the ith firm).

We define $p_{\min} = \text{Min}_i\, p_i$, and $p_{\max} = \text{Max}_i\, p_i$.

If all elements of p happen to be the same, then if their common value is r, we denote the n-component vector whose components are all equal to r, by $\hat{r}$. As before, $\hat{r}(i)$ denotes a similar $n - 1$ component vector. Thus, for example, $\hat{p}_{\max}$ denotes an n-component vector each of whose elements are equal to $p_{\max}$.

Total demand is denoted by $D(p)$ and is given by

$$D(p) \equiv \sum_{i=1}^{n} F^i(p_i, p(i)). \qquad (4.2)$$

It is understood that if $M^i = p_i$, so that the ith firm faces a demand curve that is flat over some intervals, then $F^i(p_i, p(i))$ in the above sum is the maximum demand facing the ith firm. It is obviously innocuous to assume:

E.3. (Weak negative monotonicity of demand) $D(\hat{p}_{\max}) \leq D(p) \leq D(\hat{p}_{\min})$; $D(\lambda\hat{p})$ is nonincreasing in λ for $\lambda > 0$.

We denote by X the total output produced by the n firms, so that

$$X \equiv \sum_{i=1}^{n} x_i. \qquad (4.3)$$

Similarly, we denote by $S(p)$ the sum of the $s_i(p_i)$.

We assume:

E.4. If $D(p) > X$, then, for at least one $i = 1, \ldots, n, \bar{p}_i > p_i$.

In other words, if total demand exceeds total output, at least one firm would find it profitable to raise its price, given the prices of the other firms. Clearly, this implies $p \neq \bar{p}$. This assumption is, in a way, also an assumption about the search behavior of consumers. It says that in a situation of unsatisfied *total* demand, consumers are not so sensitive to individual prices that an attempt by any firm to raise its price even a little would lead to a very large loss of business as consumers instantly rush to other firms who are unable or unwilling to supply them. If consumers realize that low prices are unrealistic in such a situation then they may not be so ready to react to small price rises.

Note that E.4 does not imply that firms never find it profitable to turn away customers. Moreover, it is much weaker than assuming that firms with excess demand always raise prices. Nevertheless, it is uncomfortable to have to assume it directly rather than deducing it from other considerations.

I shall refer to E.4 as stating that "total excess demand is not optimal for everyone."

We now assume that there exists a unique competitive price, p^*, with the property that total demand equals total competitive supply at that price. Thus:

E.5. There exists a unique (scalar) price, p^*, such that $D(\hat{p}^*) = S(\hat{p}^*)$.

The uniqueness of p^* is not very restrictive, given increasing marginal costs and weak negative monotonicity of demand.

We can now prove the following lemma.

Lemma 4.1. *Under G.1 (increasing marginal costs) and E.3–E.5, $p^* \geq \tilde{p}_{max} \geq \tilde{p}_{min}$ is impossible, unless $p^* = \tilde{p}_{max} = \tilde{p}_{min}$.*

Proof. Suppose not. Since marginal revenue cannot exceed price, it follows that when prices are $\tilde{p}$ the ith firm has $M^i \leq \tilde{p}_i \leq p^*$ and $M^i < p^*$ for at least one i. Profit maximization then implies $C_i'(x_i) \leq p^*$, with the strict inequality holding for at least one i. Since marginal cost is an increasing function of output, this implies $x_i \leq s_i(p^*)$ and $X < S(\hat{p}^*)$. By E.3 (weak negative monotonicity of demand), however, $D(\tilde{p}) \geq D(\hat{\tilde{p}}_{max})$ $\geq D(\hat{p}^*) = S(\hat{p}^*)$ by E.5. The desired result now follows from E.4 (total excess demand not optimal for everyone).

Note that E.1 (flat demand curves) and E.2 (decreasing marginal revenue) play no role in Lemma 4.1. They are crucial, however, in the parallel case of Lemma 4.2.

Lemma 4.2. *Under* G.1, E.1–E.3, *and* E.5, $\tilde{p}_{max} \geq \tilde{p}_{min} \geq p^*$ *is impossible unless* $\tilde{p}_{max} = \tilde{p}_{min} = p^*$, *provided that for all* $i = 1, \ldots, n$, q_i^i *in* E.1 *obeys any of the following*:

- (a) $q_i^i = p_{min}$;
- (b) $q_i^i \geq \tilde{p}_{min}$;
- (c) $q_i^i \geq \tilde{p}_i$;
- (d) $q_i^i \geq p^*$,

and $q^i(i)$ *obeys any of the following*:

- (e) $q^i(i) = \hat{p}_{min}(i)$;
- (f) $q^i(i) \leq \hat{\hat{p}}_{min}(i)$;
- (g) $q^i(i) \leq \tilde{p}(i)$;
- (h) $q^i(i) \leq \hat{p}^*(i)$.

(Any of (a)–(d) *can be combined with any of* (e)–(h))[10]

Proof. Suppose not. Then, by E.1 (flat demand curves), in any of the cases listed, when prices are $\tilde{p}$, every firm, were it to charge p^* with other firms' prices fixed, would find $M^i = p^*$. By E.2 (declining marginal revenue), therefore, $M^i \geq p^*$ for all i, and $M^i > p^*$ for some i. Profit maximization then implies $C_i'(x_i) \geq p^*$ for all i, with the strict inequality holding for at least one i. Since marginal cost is increasing, by G.1, this implies $x_i \geq s_i(p^*)$ and $X > S(\hat{p}^*)$. By E.3 (weak negative monotonicity of demand), however, $D(\tilde{p}) \leq D(\hat{p}_{min}) \leq D(\hat{p}^*)$. Since firms that do not have $M^i = p_i$ have $x_i = F^i(p_i, p(i))$, and the remaining firms certainly have no excess supply, it must be true that $X \leq D(\tilde{p}) \leq D(\hat{p}^*) = S(\hat{p}^*)$, by the definition of p^*, which is a contradiction.

The conditions on q^i in the statement of Lemma 4.2 obviously require some discussion. In general, E.1 asserts that if the ith firm charges a low enough price and the prices charged by other firms are sufficiently high, then the ith firm faces a flat demand curve in the relevant range of outputs in the sense that it finds marginal revenue equal to price. The conditions of Lemma 4.2 are different possibilities for defining "low enough" and "sufficiently high." While generality is achieved by allowing all 16 combinations of the conditions, their meaning can be seen by discussing the four obvious pairwise ones.

The first possibility, (a) and (e), is that the lowest-priced firm always faces a flat demand curve. This is a strong assumption about the efficiency of consumer search.

---

[10] In fact, (a)–(d) (and, indeed, E.1 itself) need only hold for $p_i \geq p^*$, but this does not seem very interesting. There are other cases as well.

The second possibility, (b) and (f), can be regarded as follows. In some real sense (possibly because of the stability theorem proved in the preceding section), the price vector, $\bar{p}$, is the vector of "normal" prices that will be charged. Since these prices will persist, consumers will tend to know about their range and will flock to any firm that lowers its price to or below the lower end-point of that range, particularly if other firms do not.

The third possibility, (c) and (g), can be looked at in much the same way. $\bar{p}_i$ is the "normal" price for firm i which may differ from the "normal" price for other firms because of locational or other differences. Consumers will rush to any firm charging at or below its own normal price, provided that other firms are not also charging below their own normal prices.

Finally, the combination of (d) and (h) puts an absolute price into the picture. In this version, demand is large enough below the competitive price that firms charging at or below it can sell all they want, provided that other firms are charging at least that price. This is consistent with the usual notion that competitive firms are small relative to demand and with the fact that total demand certainly exceeds total supply below the competitive price.

I have discussed all these cases as though the conditions of Lemma 4.2 were all equalities. Allowing inequalities in these cases merely says that what matters is that the ith firm should face a flat demand curve if it charges a low enough price and other firms' prices are sufficiently high. It really does not matter for these results if it would also have a flat demand curve with a higher price or with other firms' prices somewhat lower. An upper (not a lower) bound is thus needed for q_i^i and lower (not upper) bounds for the elements of $q^i(i)$. It is more natural to think in terms of equalities, however.

We can now obviously combine these results to obtain the following.

Theorem 4.1. *Assume G.1 and E.1–E.5. Further, let q^i satisfy any of the conditions in Lemma 4.2, for all $i = 1, \ldots, n$. Then $\bar{p}_{max} \geq p^* \geq \bar{p}_{min}$ and $\bar{p}_{max} > p^* > \bar{p}_{min}$ unless $\bar{p}_{max} = p^* = \bar{p}_{min}$.*

Proof. This is an immediate consequence of Lemmas 4.1 and 4.2.

This seems a somewhat interesting result, showing that the competitive price must be bracketed by the Nash equilibrium prices, so that the model in the preceding section converges to a set of prices bracketing the competitive one.[11] It clearly implies the following.

---

[11] We must ensure, however, that the assumptions of Theorem 4.1 do not contradict the assumptions or method of proof of Theorem 3.2. This is the task of the next section.

Corollary 4.1.   *Under the assumptions of Theorem* 4.1, *if all elements of* $\tilde{p}$ *are the same, their common value is* p^*.

This symmetric case is very special, however. It is more realistic to allow firms to differ and to have different advantages. Clearly, such an asymmetric situation will typically not lead to convergence to a single competitive price unless those advantages disappear over time. We now consider a way in which this can happen, observing that to do so would seem to require penalizing firms with persistently high prices. It is interesting to note that, in the symmetric case, such a stick is not needed; the carrot of high sales at low prices is enough.[12]

Thus, we proceed by introducing an assumption as to consumer learning over time that will lead the elements of $\tilde{p}$ all to converge to p^*. We do this by supposing that consumer information about the distribution of prices charged by the firms can improve through time if some aspects of that distribution are sufficiently stable, so that the monopoly power of firms can last only in a situation of fluctuating prices. We denote time by t and assume:

E.6   Suppose that there exists a (scalar) price, p^0, and a time, t_0, such that for all $t > t_0, p_{\min} \leq p^0$.[13] Then, for any scalar $\delta > 0$, there exists a time t_1, such that, for all $t > t_1$, if $p_h = p_{\max} > p^0 + \delta$, then $\bar{p}_h < p_h$.

In other words, if the minimum price charged by the firms remains below some level long enough, then the maximum-priced firm will not find it ever profitable to have its price too far above that same level. This seems to be a reasonably weak assumption regarding the ability of consumers to find out about continued low prices. Note, however, that the identity of the firms charging $p_{\min}$ and $p_{\max}$ need not be invariant over time. Note also that it is not assumed that the variance of prices must decrease, merely that if the lowest price is *always* below some value, p^0, then other prices cannot remain bounded above that p^0 as consumers come to rely on being able to purchase at prices at or below p^0.

Clearly, if consumers are learning about the price distribution, the demand facing any given firm will change over time. It is not unreasonable to suppose, however, that total demand is not too affected by this so that $D(\hat{p}^*)$ does not change. In any case, this is required in what follows, and we assume it as:

E.7. p^* is invariant over time.

---

[12] I am indebted to a referee for emphasizing this point.
[13] It would be possible to weaken this to a strong inequality by assuming in Theorem 4.2 below that if $\tilde{p}$ is ever $\hat{p}^*$, then it is always $\hat{p}^*$, but this seems arbitrary.

We are now almost ready to show that all prices converge to p^* and all outputs to $s_i(p^*)$ in the equilibrium model, but in order to do so, we must first prove a stronger version of Lemma 4.1.

Lemma 4.3. *Under* G.1 (*increasing marginal costs*) *and* E.3–E.5, *for any scalar* $\varepsilon > 0$, *there exists another scalar* $\delta > 0$, *such that* $p^* + \delta > \tilde{p}_{max}$ *implies* $\tilde{p}_{min} > p^* - \varepsilon$.

Proof. Suppose that it is the hth firm that charges $\tilde{p}_{min}$ and suppose that $p_h < p^* - \varepsilon$. Then an argument identical to that of the proof of Lemma 4.3 shows

$$x_h < s_h(p^* - \varepsilon) < s_h(p^*). \tag{4.4}$$

Now, for any $\delta > 0$, if the firms charge $\tilde{p}$ and $\tilde{p}_{max} < p^* + \delta$, then the same argument shows that

$$x_i < s_i(p^* + \delta) \qquad i = 1, \ldots, n. \tag{4.5}$$

It follows that

$$X < \sum_{\substack{i=1 \\ i \neq h}}^{n} s_i(p^* + \delta) + s_h(p^* - \varepsilon). \tag{4.6}$$

Since the s_i are clearly continuous, we can choose δ small enough that $X < S(\hat{p}^*)$. On the other hand, by continuity of the demand functions,[14] by lowering δ towards zero, it is clear that $D(\tilde{p})$ cannot remain bounded below $D(\hat{p}^*)$ in view of E.3 (weak negative monotonicity of demand). Since, by the definition of p^*, $S(\hat{p}^*) = D(\hat{p}^*)$, a choice of δ sufficiently small establishes that $D(\tilde{p}) > X$, which contradicts E.4 (total excess demand not optimal for everyone).

We can now prove the following.

Theorem 4.2. *Assume* G.1 (*increasing marginal costs*) *and* E.1–E.7. *Further, let* q^i *satisfy any of the conditions in Lemma* 4.2, *for all* $i = 1, \ldots, n$. *Then, if firms always charge* $\tilde{p}$, $\mathrm{Lim}_{t\to\infty} p_i = p^*$ *and* $\mathrm{Lim}_{t\to\infty} x_i = s_i(p^*) = \mathrm{Lim}\, F^i(p_i, p(i))$, *for all* $i = 1, \ldots, n$.

Proof. By Theorem 4.1, $\tilde{p}_{min} \leq p^*$, which is assumed constant by E.7. By E.6 (consumers learn about persistently low prices), therefore, for any $\delta > 0$ there exists a time t_1 such that $\tilde{p}_{max} > p^* + \delta$ is impossible for $t > t_1$. Since, by Theorem 4.1, $\tilde{p}_{max} \geq p^*$, it is clear that $\tilde{p}_{max}$ must approach p^*.

---

[14] The case in which $M^i = p_i$ is one of upper semicontinuity rather than continuity. It is easy to see, however, that it presents no problem under our assumptions, since we are lowering prices and increasing demand, something that certainly happens if we encounter such a situation. (It is also true that the prices being lowered remain bounded above the minimum price, but this is not enough to rule out all such cases.)

It now follows from Lemma 4.3 that, for any $\varepsilon > 0$, there exists a time t_2 such that $\tilde{p}_{\min} < p^* - \varepsilon$ is impossible for $t > t_2$. Since we know that $\tilde{p}_{\min} \leq p^*$, it follows that $\tilde{p}_{\min}$ approaches p^*. Hence all prices converge to p^*.

Further, under the conditions of Lemma 4.2, with all $\tilde{p}_i = p^*$, every firm finds $M^i = p^*$. It follows readily that all x_i converge to the corresponding $s_i(p^*)$. Finally, since $S(\hat{p}^*) = D(\hat{p}^*)$, there can be no firm with unsatisfied customers, since otherwise there would be at least one firm with excess supply who would certainly not be in equilibrium. The last statement of the theorem now follows, although I have not troubled to be precise about taking limits for the case of $M^i = p_i$ where F^i is defined only as an interval rather than a point.

It is an interesting question as to how the world looks to firms in such an equilibrium. It is clear that the argument just given implies that firms are selling at the upper limit, in some sense, of the flat section of their demand curve. However, were any of them to lower price even a little, that section would greatly expand. This is, of course, part of the standard competitive picture, but it does reveal the problem that in equilibrium, even though demand curves are flat, each firm must encounter a definite demand at the competitive price so that specific customers can satisfy their demands by purchasing from specific firms. I cannot pretend fully to have understood this seeming paradox which is certainly not special to the present paper.

Before moving on, we may remark that the convergence of the elements of $\tilde{p}$ to p^* is consistent with the heuristic discussion already given as to the plausibility of the various conditions of Lemma 4.2, in particular as to the special role played by the $\tilde{p}_i$ or by $\tilde{p}_{\min}$. Such convergence takes place as consumers learn more and more about what is going on. Such knowledge makes it increasingly difficult for high-price firms to hold onto their customers for a given spread between high and low prices. As the $\tilde{p}_i$ converge to p^*, this is reflected in the fact that the "normal" spread of prices diminishes.

5.   Combining the Two Models

While the adjustment model and the equilibrium model each seem of independent interest, it is clearly worthwhile discussing the circumstances under which they can be combined into a single model. In such a model, firms choosing profit-maximizing positions in the belief that other firms' prices will remain unchanged will be led to a set of prices and outputs that bracket the competitive position and that approach that position asymptotically as consumers learn about low prices.

In order to do this, however, two issues must be discussed. The first (and perhaps the more obvious) of these is readily handled. It is clear that combining the two models requires that firms react much faster than consumers – a reasonably sensible assumption, since this is the main business of firms. If the speeds of adjustment in the firms' dynamic process (3.4) are very high relative to those in the consumer learning process as reflected in E.6, then the firms of the adjustment model will spend most of their time very close to the equilibrium path of $\bar{p}$. If we now modify E.6 slightly so that its conclusion holds if the minimum price is almost always (rather than invariably) below some stated level and never much above it, then the whole process can clearly be treated as a single one and the results of the preceding two sections combined to show convergence to the competitive equilibrium.[15]

The second issue is both deeper and more difficult. It is the question of whether the assumptions embodied in the various versions of E.1 (flat demand curves at low enough prices) may not prevent the results of the adjustment model from holding.

The problem is easy to state. The proofs of uniqueness and stability in the adjustment model rested on showing that if $1 < p_M/\bar{p}_M = \max_k p_k/\bar{p}_k$, then $\bar{p}_M < p_M$ and similarly, that if $1 > p_m/\bar{p}_m = \min_k p_k/\bar{p}_k$, then $\bar{p}_m > p_m$. There is nothing to prevent the possibility, however, given E.1, that the firm charging p_M has a flat demand curve (it might be the lowest-priced firm even though it is the highest-priced one relative to the Nash equilibrium prices) and therefore has no incentive to lower its price, because it can already sell all it wants to sell. Similarly, there is nothing to prevent the firm charging p_m from facing a flat demand curve and having no incentive to raise its price because it will lose a great many customers.

The formal difficulty comes in assumptions G.2' and A.3. Once in a region in which marginal revenue equals price, it will not be true that if marginal revenue and marginal cost are equal at some price they will become unequal at a different price in that region. In a region where a firm can take marginal revenue equal to price, changing price just means moving up or down the marginal cost curve while keeping marginal cost equal to price. Naturally, in such a region, the profit-maximizing price will be the highest such price, and we shall make use of this below. The

---

[15] E.6 has to be slightly modified because when $\bar{p}$ changes as the result of consumer learning, there is no guarantee that the identity of the firm that has the lowest equilibrium price, $\bar{p}_{min}$, will be unchanged or that, if it is, convergence in the adjustment model to the new $\bar{p}_{min}$ will be monotonic. Hence, prices might all be very briefly above p^* without further assumptions. It is true, however, that for any $\varepsilon > 0$, there exist speeds of adjustment in the adjustment model fast enough that p_{min} eventually remains below $p^* + \varepsilon$.

fact remains, however, that adjustments to disequilibrium in such a region can be *output* adjustments only and our proofs in Section 3 depended on there being *price* adjustments. The remainder of this section is devoted to an exploration of the ways in which this problem can be overcome.

It is clear that the problem in question arises if demand curves are flat in the wrong places, so to speak. It is an embarrassment much like that involved in E.4 (total excess demand not optimal for everyone) to have to assume that this does not happen so that the adjustment process does not get trapped by the market being too perfect, as it were. To have to do so once more points up the difficulty of telling a full price adjustment story with a competitive ending.

Nevertheless, we alter E.1 (flat demand curves) to the much stronger

E.1' For every $i = 1, \ldots, n$, there exists a price vector, q^i, such that $M^i = p_i$ *if and only if* $p_i \leq q_i^i$ and $p(i) \geq q^i(i)$.

Even this strengthening of E.1 is not enough to handle the present problem, for not all the (modified) versions of E.1 used in the previous section will be free of the difficulty, even with some further assumptions. Thus, in the symmetric case where all $\tilde{p}_i$ are the same, the case in which the lowest-price firm always finds marginal revenue equal to price cannot be handled, since if all firms charge the same price higher or lower than the common value of $\tilde{p}_i$, it may be the case without further strong assumptions that none of them has an incentive to move. A similar statement holds for the case in which a firm charging a price less than or equal to p^* has a flat demand curve if all other firms charge at least p^*.[16]

There are, however, ways in which this can be handled without sacrificing the results of the equilibrium section. These ways at first sight seem to involve weakening certain versions of E.1 since they involve assuming flat demand curves only in a restricted set of cases. This is not the case, however, because here the "only if" part of E.1' becomes crucial and rather restrictive.

We begin with the case of p_M, which turns out to be the easier one to handle. We assume throughout the remainder of this section that G.2' and A.3 hold wherever flat demand curves are not involved, and that E.1–E.5 hold.[17]

---

[16] The difficulty cannot be evaded in either case by having flat demand curves occur only if other firms charge strictly more than the given one. This would impose a discontinuity in marginal revenue which would contradict E.2.

[17] Of course, in what follows, $\tilde{p}_i$ is taken to be the profit-maximizing price if there is more than one solution to (2.3) given $p(i)$.

Theorem 5.1. *If q_i^i in E.1′ is either $\tilde{p}_i$ or $\tilde{p}_{\min}$, then if $p_M/\tilde{p}_M > 1$, firms charging p_M do not face a flat demand curve.*

Proof. $p_M > \tilde{p}_M \geq \tilde{p}_{\min}$ in this case.

The case of p_m is somewhat more difficult and there are alternative ways to proceed. The first of these is parallel to one of those in the preceding theorem.

Theorem 5.2. *If q_i^i in E.1′ is $\tilde{p}_i$, then, if $p_m/\tilde{p}_m < 1, \overline{p}_m > p_m$.*

Proof. If firms charging p_m do not face flat demand curves (because some element of $p(m)$ is less than the corresponding element of $q^m(m)$), then the problem under discussion does not arise. If such a firm does face flat demand curves, then, as already observed, its profit-maximizing price will certainly be at least as great as the highest price at which the demand curve is flat. This is $\tilde{p}_m > p_m$, however.

Note that these results do not restrict $q^i(i)$. One way of letting $\tilde{p}_{\min}$ rather than $\tilde{p}_i$ play a crucial role in considering p_m, as it can for p_M as shown by Theorem 4.1, involves such restrictions.[18]

Theorem 5.3. *Let q_i^i in E.1′ be min $(p^*, \tilde{p}_{\min})$ and let every element of $q^i(i)$ be max $(p^*, \tilde{p}_{\min})$. Then the results of Theorems 3.1, 3.2, and 4.1 all hold.*

Proof. It is clear in considering the proof of Lemma 4.2 that the crucial features are maintained, since the present case satisfies either (b) and (f) or (d) and (h) of that lemma. There is thus no difficulty about Theorem 4.1.

Turn now to the question of the uniqueness of $\tilde{p}$ (Theorem 3.1). Let $p \neq \tilde{p}$ be another Nash equilibrium point. Then, if $p_M/\tilde{p}_M > 1$, certainly (as in the proof of Theorem 3.1), $\overline{p}_M < p_M$, which is a contradiction. On the

---

[18] There is another way to deal with the flat demand curve problem as regards p_m without restricting either q_i^i or $q^i(i)$. Suppose that there is only one firm for which $p_i/\tilde{p}_i = p_m/\tilde{p}_m$. Clearly, such a firm will have its profit-maximizing price at least as great as q_i^i. We may as well assume, therefore, that $p_m = q_m^m$. This means that if the mth firm were to raise its price a little, its demand curve would no longer be flat. At such a slightly higher price, however, we would certainly have G.2′ and A.3 applying and $\overline{p}_m > p_m$ by Lemma 3.3. The trouble with this argument is that it rests on supposing that the firm charging p_m could raise its price slightly above q_m^m without losing the property that $p_m/\tilde{p}_m = \min_k p_k/\tilde{p}_k$. To handle the case of ties in this way would require strengthening the assumptions and arguments leading to A.3 (or E.2) so that any subset of firms each of which can be taken to be the mth has the property that jointly raising all the prices of firms in the subset does not decrease the difference between marginal revenue and marginal cost for at least one of them. While it is plausible that the total demand facing the set of firms should go down in such circumstance, and hence that some firm's marginal cost should decrease, I cannot see any very plausible reason to suppose that marginal revenue will not also decrease, since the crucial movement above the region where demand curves are flat will certainly decrease elasticity. I have thus not pursued this line of development, although some such treatment could probably be worked out.

other hand, if $p_M/\tilde{p}_M \leq 1$, then $p_m/\tilde{p}_m < 1$. Then either firm m does not face a flat demand curve, in which case the proof of Theorem 3.1 is unchanged, or else it does. In the latter case, its profit-maximizing price is at least as great as $\tilde{p}_{min}$. If $\tilde{p}_m = \tilde{p}_{min}$, then $\bar{p}_m > p_m$, which is a contradiction.

We are left with the case in which $\tilde{p}_m > \tilde{p}_{min}$. If firm m faces a flat demand curve, however, every other firm must be charging at least p^*. Since Theorem 4.1 assures us that unless all $\tilde{p}_i = p^*$, which we know cannot be the present case, $\tilde{p}_{min} < p^*$, it must be true that the firm for which $\tilde{p}_i = \tilde{p}_{min}$ has its price above $\tilde{p}_i$. In that case, however, $p_M/\tilde{p}_M > 1$, contrary to assumption.

The proof of stability (Theorem 3.2) is similar. The function V of (3.5) is certainly not increasing, since $p_M/\tilde{p}_M > 1$ implies $\bar{p}_M < p_M$ and, if $p_m/\tilde{p}_m < 1$, then either $\bar{p}_m > p_m$, or else (in the case of a flat demand curve) $\bar{p}_m = p_m = \tilde{p}_{min}$. Hence the time path of prices is bounded. Now define:

$$V^* \equiv \max\{(p_M/\tilde{p}_M - 1), 0\} + \max\{(1 - p_m/\tilde{p}_m), 0\}. \tag{5.1}$$

Then both terms in V^* are nonincreasing, and the argument given in the proof of uniqueness shows that, for $p \neq p^*$, the first term must be decreasing if the second term is stationary. Since V^* is continuous and bounded below, it is a Lyapounov function and global stability is proved, since $\tilde{p}$ is unique.

It is clearly also true that:

Theorem 5.4.   *Let q_i^i in E.1$'$ be* min $(p^*, \tilde{p}_i)$ *and let the element of $q^i(i)$ corresponding to the kth price be* max $(p^*, \tilde{p}_k)$, *for all $k \neq i$. Then the results of Theorems* 3.1, 3.2, *and* 4.1 *all hold.*

Proof.   The proof is similar to that of Theorem 5.3, save that the case of the mth firm facing a flat demand curve is simpler, since then its profit-maximizing price is at least $\bar{p}_m$.

Clearly, it is also possible to combine the two cases, using q_i^i from one and $q^i(i)$ from the other.

The trouble with all this, however, is that the argument leading to a special role in E.1$'$ for the elements of $\tilde{p}$ becomes somewhat circular. We argued that those elements were the "normal" prices that consumers would come to expect. Such a view, however, rested in part on the stability result of Theorem 3.2. If that result requires that $\tilde{p}$ play such a role, then the story, while certainly consistent, is perhaps not fully convincing.[19]

---

[19]   Clearly, assigning a special role to p^* does not raise the same difficulties, although it is still quite restrictive.

There are two ways around this problem. The first is to suppose that $\bar{p}$, which is the configuration from which price movements do not take place, has somehow become established for some time and we are considering the effects of sudden displacements from it. The second is to show that there are versions of E.1' that, together with the other assumptions, lead to all prices becoming at least $\bar{p}_{\min}$.

Since Theorem 5.3 makes only $\bar{p}_{\min}$ play a special role, we may suppose that, after such convergence takes place, the processes previously described take over. We show that this will be the case if flat demand curves occur only for the lowest-price firm if and only if that firm charges at most p^* while other firms charge at least p^*. Indeed, it suffices that this be true only where the lowest price is at most $\bar{p}_{\min}$, so that the process here described joins up naturally with that of Theorem 5.3.

Theorem 5.5. *Let q_i^i in E.1 be min $(p^*, p_{\min})$ or min $(p^*, p_{\min}, \bar{p}_{\min})$. Let every element of $q^i(i)$ be max $(p^*, p_{\min})$. Then $\bar{p}_{\min}$ is unique and all prices in the adjustment model must eventually remain greater than $\bar{p}_{\min} - \delta$, for any scalar $\delta > 0$.*

Proof. Suppose $p_{\min} < \bar{p}_{\min}$. Then certainly $p_m/\bar{p}_m < 1$. If $p_m \neq p_{\min}$, then p_m is increasing and will continue to do so until the firm charging $p_{\min}$ also becomes the firm whose price is lowest relative to the corresponding element of $\bar{p}$. So we may as well take $p_m = p_{\min}$.

Now, if the mth firm does not face a flat demand curve, then p_m is increasing. If it does face a flat demand curve, then all other firms must be charging at least p^*. It is clear, however, that the results of Theorem 4.1 hold in this case, so that $\bar{p}_{\min} \leq p^*$. Hence, the mth firm will still face a flat demand curve at $\bar{p}_{\min} > p_m$, so p_m will certainly increase.

Note that the assumptions of Theorem 5.5 do not imply that $\bar{p}$ is unique (or even that all Nash equilibrium points have the same $\bar{p}_{\min}$). Such uniqueness follows only when the process described in Theorem 5.3 takes over.

We may also observe the following.

Theorem 5.6. *If all $\bar{p}_i$ are the same, then the assumptions of Theorem 5.5 imply convergence of all prices in the adjustment model to the common value of $\bar{p}_i = p^*$.*

Proof. Theorem 4.1 certainly holds in this case, whence all $\bar{p}_i = p^*$. If $p_M/\bar{p}_M > 1$, therefore, it must be true that $p_M > p^*$ and the Mth firm does not face a flat demand curve. Hence p_M decreases. The proof of Theorem 5.5, however, shows that $p_m/\bar{p}_m < 1$ certainly implies that p_m increases, and the desired result is now evident.

We may remark that in this symmetric case, all the problems of this section become much less difficult. Taking both q_i^i and all elements of $q^i(i)$ equal to p^*, for example, produces the same result as that just obtained.

Theorem 5.7.   *If q_i^i in E.1′ and all elements of $q^i(i)$ are equal to p^* and if all $\tilde{p}_i$ are equal, then prices in the adjustment model converge to the common value of $\tilde{p}_i = p^*$.*

Proof.   Theorem 4.1 certainly implies that all $\tilde{p}_i = p^*$ in this case. The desired result now follows from Theorems 5.1 and 5.2, and the proof of Theorem 3.2. Note that, as with Corollary 4.1, neither Theorem 5.6 nor 5.7 requires the assumptions about consumer learning involved in E.6 and E.7. The assumption of symmetry is enough without this. It is pretty strong, however.

REFERENCES

R. L. Bishop, The stability of the Cournot oligopoly solution: Further comment, *Rev. Econ. Stud.* **29** (1962), 332–336.

F. M. Fisher, The stability of the Cournot oligopoly solution: The effects of speeds of adjustment and increasing marginal cost, *Rev. Econ. Stud.* **28** (1960–61), 125–135. Reprinted as Chapter 14 in Fisher, *Industrial Organization, Economics, and the Law*. London: Harvester-Wheatsheaf; Cambridge, MA: MIT Press. 1991.

Quasi-competitive price adjustment by individual firms: A preliminary paper, *J. Econ. Theory* **2** (1970), 195–206. Reprinted as Chapter 2 in this volume.

On price adjustment without an auctioneer, *Rev. Econ. Stud.* **39** (1972), 1–15. Reprinted as Chapter 4 in this volume.

F. H. Hahn, The stability of the Cournot oligopoly solution, *Rev. Econ. Stud.* **29** (1962), 329–331.

M. McManus and R. E. Quandt, Comments on the stability of the Cournot oligopoly model, *Rev. Econ. Stud.* **28** (1960–61), 136–139.

T. Negishi, Monopolistic competition and general equilibrium, *Rev. Econ. Stud.* **28** (1960–61), 196–201.

K. Ogukuchi, The stability of the Cournot oligopoly solution: A further generalization, *Rev. Econ. Stud.* **31** (1964), 143–146.

M. Rothschild, Models of market organization with imperfect information: A survey, *Journal of Political Economy*, **81** (1973), 1283–1308.

R. O. Theocharis, On the stability of the Cournot solution of the oligopoly problem, *Rev. Econ. Stud.* **27** (1959–60), 133–134.

CHAPTER 4

On Price Adjustment without an Auctioneer (1972)

1. Introduction

As is well known, a major defect with existing models of competitive disequilibrium is the assumption that prices move as monotonic functions of excess demands as though adjusted by a fictitious auctioneer. Such a model of price adjustment, common to both tâtonnement and non-tâtonnement processes,[1] describes nobody's actual behaviour in most markets. Yet it is clearly a relatively easy way out of the dilemma of deciding how prices move when every firm takes them as given.[2]

In my earlier paper (Fisher, 1970), I considered a highly simplified model of a single market in which firms quoted individual prices and consumers searched for low quotations, with search not being costless. In that model, firms were assumed to believe themselves in competition, in the sense that the demand curves that they faced were flat or almost flat at a true (but unknown) market price that they attempted to charge. Individual prices were adjusted by the individual firms as functions of the excess demands that they themselves encountered. I was able to show that under rather general restrictions on the search procedures used by consumers, the market always converged to the competitive partial equilibrium.

The present paper extends that analysis (with some alterations) to the case of general equilibrium in an exchange economy. A stability theorem is proved with prices still under the control of real rather than invisible participants. Interest centres not on the details of proof (indeed, I have

Research on this article was financed by the National Bureau of Economic Research, which is not, however, responsible for any of the statements made or views expressed herein. It forms part of an ongoing project that the Bureau hopes to publish when complete, pending the approval of its board of directors.

[1] See Negishi (1962) for a summary.

[2] The problem has been pointed out by Koopmans, among others. See Koopmans (1957, p. 179). Models of resource allocation in which some prices are under the control of individual custodians who follow rules related to those of the present paper have been studied by Koopmans (1951, pp. 93–95) and Arrow and Hurwicz (1960). I am indebted to Leo Hurwicz for these references.

borrowed much of the apparatus from Arrow and Hahn[3]) but on the construction of a model without an auctioneer. While that model is still pretty unrealistic and involves some strong assumptions, I believe it to be the case that some of the assumptions common to the present model and to the analysis of what Negishi has termed the "Hahn process"[4] are more natural in the present context than in the original. Despite the additional assumptions that I have been forced to make, therefore, I hope this paper will be regarded as an attempt at playing *Hamlet* without the Prince of Norway.

2.   The Model: General Description

The model has two main nonstandard features. The first of these is taken over bodily from Arrow and Hahn [1971, Chapter XIII]. Since assuming a barter economy out of equilibrium means assuming that individuals who can make mutually advantageous trades can find each other (even though such trades need not be merely bilateral), it is obviously sensible to introduce money in its role as a medium of exchange. That is essentially its only role here; no more than a rudimentary monetary theory is intended, and it is convenient if we think of money as a *numéraire* that also is desired for its consumption properties but that has, by convention, come to be used as the exclusive medium of exchange. Following Arrow and Hahn, the only excess demands that are allowed to affect prices are the "active" excess demands that have money to back them up.

The other convention that we suppose society to have adopted before we come upon the picture is that of recognizing certain individuals as "dealers" in each commodity (other than money). These dealers operate by each setting his own price for his commodity and waiting for others to come and transact business with him, up to the extent of his own demand or supply for that commodity. There are many dealers in each commodity; some of them may be sellers, some buyers. Some may be either sellers or buyers depending on their view of the price at which they can transact and the prices in other markets. Some may cease to act as dealers depending on prices. I shall discuss these matters in detail below.

In the description that follows, it will often facilitate discussion to take

---

[3] Arrow and Hahn (1971), Chapter XIII. I am grateful to the authors for allowing me access to the unpublished manuscript.

[4] Negishi (1962, pp. 663–65). The original paper is Hahn and Negishi (1962). As stated, I have followed the rather more satisfactory version in Arrow and Hahn (1971).

all dealers as sellers and all customers as buyers, but this is usually merely a convenience.

In addition to the recognized dealers in each market, there are the customers, consisting, in the general case, of all individuals who are not dealers in the given commodity. (Of course, some or all of these will be dealers in some other commodity; that is how they make their money.) Each customer searches among the dealers in a particular commodity (in a way described in a moment) in an attempt to find that dealer whose price is most advantageous (low if the customer is a buyer, high if he is a seller). He offers to buy from (or sell to) that dealer an amount gotten from maximizing his utility function given the prices known to him and the constraint that only money can be used as a medium of exchange.[5]

Every dealer believes that he faces a flat or almost flat demand curve and names that price which he believes to be the market price. If, after the search procedure just described, he finds a non-zero excess demand for his own wares, then he adjusts his price in the direction indicated by that excess demand.

Clearly, this assumption that dealers adjust prices in this way, while more attractive than at the level of a fictitious auctioneer, is still not so appealing as one would wish. (Note, however, that a dealer only has to manage his own excess demand on one side of his market; he does not have to balance the excess demands of others on both sides.) It would clearly be preferable to have dealers recognize that they are in disequilibrium and to adjust their prices in a way explicitly consistent with utility maximization. I have been unable to do this, however.

In order for the assumed dealer behaviour both to make sense and to generate an interesting model, certain restrictions must be put on the search behaviour of customers. If every customer surveyed only a single dealer before buying, dealers would quickly learn that they did not face flat demand curves. This would tend to be true (without further assumptions) even if customers surveyed more than one dealer, if they surveyed only a few. We must therefore suppose that customers survey the prices of many dealers (or at least that most customers do). On the other hand, if all customers had perfect information as to all prices, they would all attempt to buy from the lowest-price dealer. While such behaviour is not explicitly ruled out of the model, it does create some awkward problems for some of the later assumptions, and it leads to a model that is at best uninterestingly special. So we shall assume that information is less than perfect or, what amounts to much the same thing, that searching is costly

[5] In one version of the model customers may attempt to buy from several dealers simultaneously. This is discussed below.

in terms of utility. (Alternatively, we can assume perfect information combined with different locational or other costs associated with doing business with different dealers that prevent everyone from rushing to the lowest-priced dealer even if they know who he is. This variant is briefly discussed at the end of the paper.)

This leaves us with a situation in which the typical customer knows the prices of many but not all dealers. Unfortunately, it appears necessary in the present model to assume that the set of dealers whose prices are known to a given customer does not change over time. This rules out the possibility that customers take repeated *random* samples of dealer prices (although they may begin the process with a single randomly selected sample). This appears indispensable, partly for technical reasons of continuity, but mostly because equilibrium will require not only that total excess demands be zero in each market but also that customers and dealers be exactly matched. If repeated random search procedures were permitted, there would be nothing to prevent all customers from arriving at the same dealer and upsetting equilibrium. Obviously, this sort of problem calls for a treatment in which equilibrium is established in some probabilistic sense, but such a treatment carries its own difficulties and is a fit subject for a later paper. If we assume that the whole adjustment process is of short duration, then the assumption that the set of dealers known to a given customer is unchanging may be palatable.

3.   Notation and Preliminary Assumptions

There are H individuals, denoted by $h = 1, \ldots, H$ and n commodities other than money, denoted by $i = 1, \ldots, n$. The hth individual's actual stock of the ith commodity at time t is denoted by $\bar{x}_{hi}(t)$; his desired stock is denoted by $x_{hi}(t)$. The difference between these, the hth individual's excess demand for the ith commodity, is denoted by $z_{hi}(t) \equiv x_{hi}(t) - \bar{x}_{hi}(t)$. Similarly, the hth individual's stock of money at time t is denoted $\bar{m}_h(t)$ and his desired stock of money, $m_h(t)$. Following Arrow and Hahn, we shall refer to the $z_{hi}(t)$ as *target* excess demands; they have no effect on prices (when they are positive) unless they are backed up by purchasing power as described below.

For the ith commodity, there is a set of individuals who are dealers. We denote that set by D_i. Every dealer, d, in D_i quotes a money price for the ith commodity; we denote that price at time t by $p_i^d(t)$. The amount that a dealer wishes to sell at that price is, of course, the negative of his own excess demand. A fuller description of dealer behaviour is given below.

The amount of the ith commodity that the hth customer wishes to buy from the dth dealer (purchasing power considerations aside) is denoted by $z_{hi}^d(t)$. We assume that each customer wishes to transact business only with that dealer in the set known to him who offers the most advantageous price, so that $z_{hi}^d(t) = z_{hi}(t)$ for d that particular dealer and $z_{hi}^d(t) = 0$ for d all other dealers in that commodity whether or not their prices are known to h. For the commodities in which h himself is a dealer, $z_{hi}^h(t) = z_{hi}(t)$ and all other $z_{hi}^d(t) = 0$. This last is a matter of notational convenience.

Each individual, h, has a strictly quasi-concave differentiable utility function,

$$U_h(x_{h1}, \ldots, x_{hn}, m_h),$$

where the time argument has been omitted. His target excess demands are derived by maximizing this subject to his budget constraint:

$$\sum_{i=1}^{n} \sum_{d \in D_i} p_i^d z_{hi}^d + m_h - \overline{m}_h = 0, \tag{3.1}$$

given

$$z_{hi} = \sum_{d \in D_i} z_{hi}^d \tag{3.2}$$

and the fact that x_{hi}^d is non-zero for at most one $d \in D_i$. We shall assume that the marginal utility of money is always positive.

Where there is no danger of confusion, we shall use x_h, z_h, and $\overline{x}_h$ to represent the vectors of the x_{hi}, z_{hi}, and $\overline{x}_{hi}$, respectively.

We denote the total stock of the ith commodity in the economy by $\overline{X}_i$ and the total stock of money by $\overline{M}$. Since we are dealing with a pure exchange economy, these are invariant over time. Where convenient, $\overline{X}$ will denote the vector of the $\overline{X}_i$.

We denote by p_i the vector of the p_i^d and by p the vector of the p_i.

4. Quasi-Equilibrium and Competitive Equilibrium

Definition 4.1. A quasi-equilibrium is a set of non-negative prices, p, and non-negative stocks, $\overline{x}_1, \ldots, \overline{x}_H, \overline{m}_1, \ldots, \overline{m}_H$, such that: (a) for every h and i, $z_{hi} \leqq 0$ and $m_h = \overline{m}_h$; (b) $\sum_h \overline{x}_h = \overline{X}$ and $\sum_h \overline{m}_h = \overline{M}$.[6]

---

[6] Since z_{hi}^d is non-zero for at most one $d \in D_i$, (3.2) implies that in a quasi-equilibrium $z_{hi}^d \leqq 0$ for all h, i, and d. Even in a later version of the model, all non-zero z_{hi}^d, for given h and i, will have the same sign. It is thus a matter of indifference whether we use $z_{hi}^d \leqq 0$ or $z_{hi} \leqq 0$ in the definition of quasi-equilibrium.

In view of (3.1), it is clear that $p_i^d = 0$ if $z_{hi}^d < 0$ for any h, i, and $d \in D_i$.

Definition 4.2. A competitive equilibrium is a quasi-equilibrium in which for every i, $p_i^d = p_i^r$ for all d and r in D_i.

Thus the difference between a quasi-equilibrium and a competitive equilibrium lies in whether the different prices quoted by different dealers for a given commodity are or are not the same. The principal stability result given below establishes convergence to the set of quasi-equilibria; additional assumptions are required to ensure that this is also the set of competitive equilibria and that a unique limit is attained.

There are undoubtedly different ways of accomplishing this. The simplest is to assume:

Assumption 4.1. Let d and r both be in D_i. If $p_i^d < p_i^r$, then $\sum_h z_{hi}^d > \sum_h z_{hi}^r$. We shall discuss this assumption after the following lemma.

Lemma 4.1. *Under Assumption 4.1, every quasi-equilibrium is also a competitive equilibrium.*

Proof. Suppose that we are in quasi-equilibrium but that for some i and d and r in D_i, $p_i^r > p_i^d$. Then $p_i^r > 0$ and it follows from the definition of quasi-equilibrium and the budget constraints that $\sum_h z_{hi}^r = 0$. Assumption 4.1 then implies that $\sum_h z_{hi}^d > 0$, but this means that at least one of the z_{hi}^d must be positive, which is in contradiction to the definition of quasi-equilibrium.

Assumption 4.1 is fairly strong. It is not unreasonable to assume that the *demand* facing a dealer who offers a low price is greater than that facing one who offers a high one; this is the least one might expect if the market is going to be competitive. Assumption 4.1, however, goes beyond this and speaks of the target *excess* demand facing a dealer, that is, target demand relative to his own supply. What is ruled out, given the natural assumption about demand, is the possibility that information is sufficiently imperfect that dealers who happen to want to offer relatively small amounts can get away with relatively high prices because the demand facing them just happens to be relatively low by the same amount as their supply, i.e., that the market is so imperfect as to permit a very special kind of negative correlation between dealers' prices and the supplies they want to offer. Since each dealer wants to offer more at a higher price than at a low one and his price behaviour is not tied to this, this seems only to rule out a rather exceptional case.

It would suffice, however, to take Assumption 4.1 to hold only for prices in quasi-equilibrium as it plays no direct role save in the proof of Lemma 4.1. If it fails, then only convergence to the set of quasi-equilibria is established below. If the reason for its failure is market imperfection due to locational or other advantages of some dealers, then such convergence is itself interesting, even if prices are not equalized. If there are no such advantages and information is relatively good, then, as stated, Assumption 4.1 does not seem too unreasonable.

5. Purchasing Power and Active Demands[7]

As already observed, demands have little influence in this model unless they are backed up with money. Following Arrow and Hahn, we assume that the adjustment process is fairly rapid and that individuals do not care by what sequence they achieve their target demands. Accordingly, we assume that if an individual is limited at a particular moment by the amount of money in his possession, then he rations his purchases by distributing the money so as to attempt to make some positive purchase of each good for which he has a positive excess demand. We assume that he believes these attempts will succeed and that all prices will remain at their current levels (see below).

Formally speaking, define a_{hi} as the *active* excess demand of individual h for commodity i. Define a_{hi}^d as his active excess demand from the dth dealer. Denote by a_h^+ the vector of those a_{hi}^d that are positive and by p^+ the vector of corresponding prices.

Assumption 5.1.

(a) If $z_{hi}^d \leqq 0$, $a_{hi}^d = z_{hi}^d$;

(b) If $z_{hi}^d > 0$, and $\bar{m}_h > 0$, $0 < a_{hi}^d \leqq z_{hi}^d$ and $p^{+\prime} a_h^+ \leqq \bar{m}_h$;

(c) If $z_{hi}^d > 0$ and $\bar{m}_h = 0$, $a_{hi}^d = 0$.[8]

To avoid burdening the notation, we continue to omit the time argument.

6. Dealer Behaviour and the Hahn Assumption

The crucial feature of the Hahn process is that at any moment each individual's excess demand for any commodity is either zero or of the same sign as aggregate excess demand for that commodity. In the present context, this is a relatively natural assumption, since we shall in effect consider the same commodity sold by two different dealers as two dif-

---

[7] As already indicated, this section and much of what follows is closely derived from Arrow and Hahn [1971, Chapter XIII].

[8] There are no credit institutions in this economy. The crucial feature of Assumption 5.1, however, is not this but the fact that non-zero target excess demands have the same sign as the corresponding active excess demands and are at least as great in absolute value.

ferent commodities for this purpose. Nevertheless, this requires some additional assumptions about dealer behaviour and we have some choice as to how to go about it.

So long as a dealer is only a seller (or only a buyer) and publicly known to be so, the Hahn assumption is immediate. As we have set it up, a selling dealer will be the only trader in his wares with a non-positive excess demand. All his customers have a non-negative one or they would not be his customers. It is natural to assume that he either sells all he cares to or else sells as much as he can, whichever is less. In the first case, the dealer has a zero excess demand after these transactions while all unsatisfied customers have a positive one; in the second case, only the dealer is unsatisfied with a negative excess demand. The case for a buying dealer is similar.

At low enough prices, however, a dealer who usually sells may wish to buy. If he continues to act as a dealer when he buys and it is known that he sometimes does this, then there is nothing to prevent customers who wish to sell from attempting to do business with him even when he is still selling. Since those attempts depend only on prices while his own decision to buy or sell depends on his own stock, it will not do to suppose that everyone knows at what price the changeover comes.

There is more than one way to get around this. The most obvious way is to make the dealer play the role of the traditional fictitious auctioneer in his own market so that if the demand from buyers facing him exceeds his own intended sales, he buys from all sellers and instantaneously resells to buyers until either all buyers or all sellers have been satisfied.

An alternative that seems somewhat more satisfactory than this in a model that attempts to eliminate fictitious auctioneers (other than by replacing them with real ones) is available, however. We can suppose that a given dealer acts as such only while selling (or buying). When his situation becomes such as to make him desire to buy, we can suppose that he then acts as a customer in making his purchases. To do this, we must suppose that he can be thought of as always acting both as a dealer and as a customer; when his excess demand for his own commodity is negative, then we treat him as expressing his intentions as a dealer while having a zero excess demand as a customer. When his excess demand is positive, then we treat him as expressing that demand as a customer while having a zero excess demand as a dealer. Obviously, which he does depends on which he believes will yield the higher utility. We can thus take him as only a selling dealer and always known as such, posting a selling price even when intending to sell zero and adjusting that price according to the rules given below. Having done this, the Hahn assumption is again a very natural one, since when acting as a customer the dealer is not acting on his *own* market in the relevant sense.

This is a fairly attractive way to proceed, particularly if we do not strive for the utmost generality and suppose that all dealers in a particular commodity are either sellers or buyers. This is the standard picture of firms who come on to the market at high enough prices but leave it *as firms* when prices are low, even though the individuals owning the firms may purchase the same commodity at low prices from other firms.[9]

It might also be possible, though somewhat cumbersome, to suppose that every dealer posts a selling and a buying price but typically has a non-zero offering in only one of these capacities, acting, in effect, as two dealers. In this case, it would seem reasonable to assume that his selling price is never less than his buying price, but this assumption would have to be made explicit and, in a real sense, *ad hoc*, for there is nothing in the price adjustment process given below that guarantees it, different prices not being directly tied together.

In any case, we shall assume:

Assumption 6.1 (Hahn process). At all times, if $a_{hi}^d \neq 0$, then $a_{hi}^d a_i^d > 0$, where $a_i^d = \sum_h a_{hi}^d$.

This is a natural assumption only if we assume that trading takes place instantaneously.[10] Otherwise there is nothing to prevent a customer who wishes to buy from arriving at a dealer who wishes to sell with the trade not being totally consummated for a non-zero time interval.[11] Provided we assume trading takes place fast enough that this can be ignored, the Hahn process assumption seems more natural here than in impersonal markets with fictitious auctioneers.

---

[9] In this case every customer must be considered a *potential* dealer, however.

[10] So that the Hahn process assumption holds after trade. There is no difficulty with the question of whether excess demands are pre- or post-trade, since we shall ensure continuity of prices and stocks below.

[11] In Arrow and Hahn [1971, Chapter XIII], the parallel assumption to Assumption 6.1 is taken to hold at time zero and continuous trading rules are postulated which then imply that it holds at all times thereafter. Such an alternative is not readily available in the present context because of the inherent discontinuity in the demands made by a given customer on a given dealer when that dealer's price becomes the minimum in the set known to the customer. Such a customer suddenly arrives at the dealer and only instantaneous trading will keep Assumption 6.1 valid at such a moment. On the other hand, that Assumption is highly palatable in the present context and we can take instantaneous trading to be an approximation, the whole continuous adjustment process taking place much slower than such trades.

The other difficulties raised by this inherent discontinuity are discussed in the next section.

7.   Trading Rules, Price Adjustment, and Continuity

We now discuss the rules according to which trade takes place and prices adjust. For the most part, these have already been indicated.

The first rule is that of pure exchange:

$$\sum_h \bar{x}_h = \bar{X}; \sum_h \bar{m}_h = \bar{M}. \tag{7.1}$$

Next, we impose the condition that an individual cannot change his wealth by exchange. This is a little complicated to state formally because an individual's stock of a given commodity is composed of former purchases from different dealers. At any moment of time, however, the price at which he values a given commodity is the price offered by that dealer with whom he finds it most advantageous to do business. Let $\tilde{p}_h$ be the vector of such prices (one for each commodity), and $\tilde{p}'_h$ its transpose. Then:

$$\tilde{p}'_h \dot{x}_h + \dot{m}_h = 0 \tag{7.2}$$

where the derivatives exist.

Unfortunately, such derivatives need not always exist. Obviously, there will be moments at which the identity of the most advantageous dealer in commodity i changes. If the new most advantageous dealer has a larger excess supply than the old, then h may find himself suddenly able to increase his stock of commodity i. Since we have assumed such trades instantaneous, $\dot{x}_{hi}$ fails to exist at such a moment. Noting, however, that at the moment of changeover the prices of the old and the new most advantageous dealer must be the same (since prices will move continuously), we can alter (7.2) as follows, letting $\hat{t}$ be the moment in question:

$$\lim_{t \to \hat{t}^+} \{\tilde{p}_h(\hat{t})' \bar{x}_h(t) + \bar{m}_h(t)\} = \lim_{t \to \hat{t}^-} \{\tilde{p}_h(\hat{t})' \bar{x}_h(t) + \bar{m}_h(t)\}. \tag{7.3}$$

In fact, only (7.2) is *directly* needed in the proof below.

The assumption that wealth cannot increase through exchange is not so innocuous here as in the more traditional context, however. At any moment in time, there can be several prices for the same commodity. We are therefore ruling out *instantaneous* arbitrage. We have, in effect, already done this by allowing a given customer only to trade with a single dealer in a given commodity *at a time*. If all dealers in a given commodity are sellers (or all buyers), then this is no problem. If not, then we must assume the problem away, allowing a given individual to act *only* as a seller or *only* as a buyer at a given moment in time with a given set of prices. We have, in fact, already assumed that there are no transactions with arbitrage as their object since demands are derived from utility maximization. Customers and dealers are assumed to act so as directly to secure stocks for consumption, not for resale, although resales may of course take place if prices change, as may capital gains. Relaxation of this assumption is an obvious place for further work. If it seems too strong in the general context, then the reader is free to suppose that markets are organized so that the dealers in any given commodity are all sellers and the customers all buyers, or the reverse.[12]

The remaining trading rules were essentially specified in the preceding section. Trade takes place instantaneously until either the dealer or all his customers have a zero excess demand for his wares. Changes are rationed over unsatisfied customers, if any.

The basic price adjustment mechanism that we shall employ has also been indicated. Each dealer takes a non-zero active excess demand facing him as an indication that he has misjudged the market price. He thus adjusts price as a sign-preserving continuous function of the active excess demand for his own goods. Thus:

Assumption 7.1.

    (a)   If $p_i^d > 0$, or $p_i^d = 0$ and $a_i^d \geqq 0$, then $\dot{p}_i^d = F_i^d(a_i^d)$, where F_i^d is continuous and sign-preserving, and bounded away from zero save as a_i^d goes to zero.

    (b)   If $p_i^d = 0$ and $a_i^d < 0$, then $\dot{p}_i^d = 0$.

We shall later comment on some modifications of this assumption that make a later assumption more plausible and in which F_i^d also depends on $\bar{m}_d$ or on a_{di}^d.

The price of money, of course, is assumed to be constant.

Now there are some continuity problems connected with the process we have described. One of these is common to most studies of the stability of general equilibrium; the others are special to the present paper. Such problems are important because we wish to assume that the crucial variables have a uniquely determined path as a solution of the differential equations and Lipschitz Conditions may be violated.

The common problem is that raised by the non-negativity of prices. The change-over in regimes represented by the difference between (a) and (b) of Assumption 7.1 is not always a continuous one. Such suggestions as have been made in the literature to get around this seem rather arbitrary.[13] As is common, we shall assume that this does not create a problem for the existence and continuity of solution paths.

Similarly, we shall assume that the other continuity problems are negligible, but these require considerably more discussion.

---

[12] Again, in this case, every customer must be considered a potential dealer when he changes from buying to selling.
[13] See Arrow and Hahn [1971, Chapter XI] and Nikaidô and Uzawa [1960].

The source of such problems has already been made clear. It is the switching of customers from one dealer to another when prices change. This makes it evident that the demand of a given customer for the goods of a given dealer cannot be taken to be a continuous function of prices. Moreover, as we have seen, even the stocks possessed by a given individual are not continuous in prices because we have allowed trading to take place instantaneously.

This latter fact is really the heart of the difficulty. If the only problem were the discontinuity in the demands made on dealers, we could get around it by assuming that there are sufficiently many customers with sufficiently varied awareness of dealers that the total active excess demand for a given dealer's wares, a_i^d, can be taken as a continuous function of all the prices. This is unfortunately not sufficient, since the basic variables in the differential equations are not merely the prices but also the individual stocks. As observed in the preceding section, there is nothing so far to prevent a dealer who at a given moment becomes the most advantageous one for a given customer from having an excess supply (or relatively smaller excess demand) so that the customer suddenly finds himself able to carry out his purchasing plans.

There are at least two ways around this, each with its own difficulties. The first of these is to take Assumption 4.1 as applying to *active* rather than *target* excess demands. (It is easy to see that this together with Assumption 5.1 would still imply the result of Lemma 4.1.) This seems strong, but taken alone, perhaps not overly so. If one then adds the assumption indicated in the previous paragraph, that the total active excess demand facing a dealer is continuous in the prices, then one obtains the far stronger result that dealers charging the same price encounter identical active excess demands.[14] If we are prepared to accept this, then the discontinuities in individual stocks can be made to disappear by assuming that dealers all use the same continuous rules to ration their sales among their active customers, and that these rules are such as to make the $\bar{x}_h$ continuous in the prices.

This is the simplest way out of the continuity problem, but it obviously involves a pretty strong assumption about the similarity of dealers. An alternative that does not involve that assumption is available at the price of a mild complication of the model that may not be altogether a natural one.

Suppose that we drop the assumption that a customer always expects his transactions to be successfully completed. We might then assume that

---

[14] *Proof.* Let p_i^r approach $p_i^d > 0$ from above. For $p_i^r > p_i^d$, $a_i^r < a_i^d$ and for $p_i^r < p_i^d$, $a_i^r > a_i^d$. Continuity then yields the desired result. The case of both prices zero is readily handled by continuity, given this.

a customer realizing that the lowest-priced dealer will be sold out does not place his full active demand with that dealer but instead places some of his orders with the next lowest-priced one or even the next few lowest-priced ones.[15] (Orders are assumed to be non-cancellable.) Naturally, the total of his orders so placed will generally be less than if he placed them solely with the lowest-priced dealer. If we assume that the orders placed with any dealer are continuous functions of the prices, the discontinuity problem is avoided entirely.

The price paid for this alternative is that we have gone further away from a relatively simple utility-maximization model. We have, however, already gone one step in this direction in Assumption 5.1 in providing no utility-maximization rationale for the way in which a customer distributes his active excess demands when constrained by the availability of money, so perhaps we may accept this further step. If we do, then Assumption 5.1 itself must be altered somewhat, since we now allow some non-zero a_{hi}^d to correspond to zero z_{hi}^d. *Provided that we still require non-zero z_{hi}^d to correspond to non-zero a_{hi}^d of the same sign* (whenever there is money to back up positive excess demands), then no essential differences arise in the proofs below. We do, of course, require this, since we assume that *some* non-zero order is still placed with the lowest-priced dealer.

We shall refer to this case as the multi-order (as opposed to the single-order) case. It will seldom require distinguishing in what follows.

In any event, we shall assume that the trading rules are such as to make the rates of change of prices and of individual stocks continuous in the levels of the same variables; indeed, that they satisfy Lipschitz Conditions. Alternatively, we shall assume that any discontinuities can safely be ignored. We thus assume that the time path of prices and individual stocks is continuous in the initial conditions and uniquely determined given the initial conditions and the elapsed time.

8. Boundedness of Variables

It is obvious that the assumption of pure exchange, eq. (7.1), implies that individual stocks remain bounded. Boundedness of prices, however, requires additional assumptions.

Such boundedness can be ensured in several ways. One such way begins by assuming:

---

[15] In the case of customers who are sellers and dealers who are buyers, the customer offers part of his supply to dealers below the highest-priced one if the latter will not take it all.

Assumption 8.1. Drop for a moment the assumption that the price of money is unity and denote it by p_m. If $p \neq 0$ and $p_m = 0$, then $\sum_h m_h < \overline{M}$.

This is the requirement that money can serve as a *numéraire*, since it prevents the price of money from being zero. Now resume the convention that $p_m = 1$.

Assumption 8.1 does not by itself suffice to establish the boundedness of prices unless we also strengthen Assumption 7.1.[16] One way that will readily suffice is to restrict the functions F_i^d by:

Assumption 7.1'. For every i and d, there exists a scalar $K_i^d > 0$ such that for all a_i^d,

$$F_i^d(a_i^d) \leqq K_i^d a_i^d.$$

Lemma 8.1. *Under Assumptions 8.1 and 7.1', the time path of prices is bounded.*

Proof. Let

$$V \equiv \sum_{i=1}^n \sum_{d \in D_i} \frac{(p_i^d)^2}{K_i^d} \tag{8.1}$$

Then Assumption 7.1' implies:

$$\dot{V} = 2\sum_{i=1}^n \sum_{d \in D_i} \frac{p_i^d \dot{p}_i^d}{K_i^d} = 2\sum_{i=1}^n \sum_{d \in D_i} \frac{p_i^d F_i^d(a_i^d)}{K_i^d}$$

$$\leqq 2\sum_{i=1}^n \sum_{d \in D_i} p_i^d a_i^d \leqq 2\sum_{i=1}^n \sum_{d \in D_i} p_i^d z_i^d$$

$$= \overline{M} - \sum_h m_h \tag{8.2}^{17}$$

where

$$z_i^d \equiv \sum_h z_{hi}^d \tag{8.3}$$

and the final equality in (8.2) follows from Walras' Law. Assumption 8.1 and homogeneity of degree zero now show that for large enough prices $\dot{V} < 0$ from which boundedness can easily be inferred.

---

[16] I am indebted to Kenneth Arrow for pointing out an error in an earlier proof and to Frank Hahn for discussion of this point.

[17] The final inequality in (8.2) is true even in the multi-order case on the innocuous assumption that households' multiple orders are still constrained by their inability to spend more money than they have, so that the budget constraints (3.1) hold as weak inequalities when the z_{hi}^d are replaced by the corresponding a_{hi}^d.

An alternative way to proceed is not to restrict the F_i^d but instead to strengthen Assumption 8.1 to:

Assumption 8.1'. For every subset of commodities, J (not including money), and every collection of subsets of dealers in these commodities, $R_j, j \in J$, such that J and at least one R_j are not empty, there exists a commodity $j^* \in J$, a dealer $r^* \in R_j^*$, and a scalar $K > 0$ such that if

(a) $\dfrac{p_j^r}{p_i^d} > K$ for all $j \in J, r \in R_j$ and all $i \notin J$ and all $i \in J, d \notin R_j$

(b) $p_j^r > K$ for all $j \in J, r \in R_j$

then

(c) $z_{j^*}^{r^*} \leq 0$.

Aside from the cumbersome notation, what Assumption 8.1' says is that if the prices of any set of dealers become indefinitely large relative to all other prices and to the price of money, then at least one dealer in the set will face a persistently non-positive target excess demand.[18] This is not terribly unreasonable and it clearly leads to:

Lemma 8.2. *Under Assumption* 8.1', *the time path of prices is bounded.*

Proof. Suppose not. Then there is a set of dealers, say R, such that all their prices become indefinitely large relative to all other prices. One such dealer in R must then find that he faces a target excess demand (and therefore, by Assumption 5.1, an active excess demand) that remains non-positive whence it is clear (from Assumption 7.1) that his price cannot continue to increase, contradicting the fact that he is in R.

We shall henceforth assume boundedness of prices; the assumptions of this section are not required in what follows.

9. Behaviour of Individual Target Utilities

In this section, we show that individual *target* utilities are non-increasing over time.

Let $\mathscr{D}$ denote the Cartesian product of the D_i $(i = 1, \ldots, n)$. At any moment in time, an individual has non-zero target excess demands for the wares of at most one dealer in each commodity. We can denote any such set of dealers for the hth individual by $s_h \in \mathscr{D}$. Then we can think

---

[18] As pointed out by Kenneth Arrow, this does not follow from Assumption 8.1 and Walras' Law, which only allows one to establish that at least one dealer in the set has a negative excess demand, not that it is the *same* dealer for all prices in the set high enough.

of his target utility as a function of s_h, that is, as a function of the set of dealers with which he chooses to do business. Naturally, given his information as to prices, he chooses that s_h which maximizes his target utility. We denote the chosen s_h by s_h^*. As before, we denote by $\tilde{p}_h$ the vector of prices quoted by the dealers with whom h wishes to trade, the dealers represented by s_h^*.

Lemma 9.1. *For any t at which s_h^* does not change, $\dot{U}_h \leq 0$, provided that $\bar{m}_h(t) > 0$.*[19]

Proof. Differentiating the budget constraint, (3.1), and observing that only the dealers corresponding to s_h^* matter, we obtain:

$$\dot{\tilde{p}}_h' z_h + \tilde{p}_h' \dot{x}_h + \dot{m}_h - \{\tilde{p}_h' \dot{\tilde{x}}_h + \dot{\bar{m}}_h\} = 0. \tag{9.1}$$

Since $\bar{m}_h > 0$, Assumption 5.1 assures us that $z_{hi} \neq 0$ implies $z_{hi}a_{hi} > 0$. Further, for any dealer d with whom h wishes to trade, the Hahn process assumption (Assumption 6.1) states that $a_{hi}a_i^d > 0$. By Assumption 7.1, therefore, the first term in (9.1) is non-negative. The term in brackets in (9.1) is zero by (7.2). Hence:

$$\tilde{p}_h' \dot{x}_h + \dot{m}_h \leq 0. \tag{9.2}$$

Differentiating the target utility function, however, we observe that:

$$\dot{U}_h = \sum_i U_{hi} \dot{x}_{hi} + U_{hm} \dot{m}_h \tag{9.3}$$

where the additional subscript on U_h denotes differentiation. Since U_h is maximized subject to the budget constraint, then for all i except those for which both $x_{hi} = 0$ and $\dot{x}_{hi} = 0$ (that is, except for corner solutions which we may disregard),

$$U_{hi} = \lambda_h \tilde{p}_{hi}; \; U_{hm} = \lambda_h. \tag{9.4}$$

Thus, substituting in (9.3),

$$\dot{U}_h = \lambda_h (\tilde{p}_h' \dot{x}_h + \dot{m}_h) \leq 0 \tag{9.5}$$

by (9.2) and the fact that the marginal utility of income is non-negative. We now show that constancy of s_h^* is inessential.

Lemma 9.2. *For any t at which $\bar{m}_h(t) > 0$, U_h is continuous and non-increasing.*

Proof. This is guaranteed by Lemma 9.1 for all t for which s_h^* is unchanging. At a t at which s_h^* does change, however, $\dot{U}_h$ may be undefined.

---

[19] This is essentially Lemma 1 of Arrow and Hahn [1971, Chapter XIII]. Note that it is *target*, not actual utility, that decreases as individuals find earlier plans unachievable.

Denote by $U_h(s_h)$ the value of U_h that would obtain were s_h the set of dealers chosen by h. Let S_h be the set of dealers known to h (one for each commodity). ($S_h \subseteq \mathscr{D}$.) Then

$$U_h = U_h(s_h^*) = \max_{\{s_h \in s_h\}} U_h(s_h). \tag{9.6}$$

Moreover, since the prices move continuously through time, a change in s_h^* takes place only when the maximum occurs simultaneously for more than one s_h. This ensures continuity of U_h at such points and, together with Lemma 9.1, readily implies that U_h is non-increasing.

Lemma 9.3. *For any t for which for all h, $\bar{m}_h > 0$ and for which $a_i^d \neq 0$ for some i and $d \in D_i$, U_h is non-increasing for all h and, for some h, U_h is strictly decreasing, unless all such non-zero a_i^d are negative and correspond to zero p_i^d.*[20]

Proof. At such a moment, there is at least one $a_{hi} \neq 0$, and for that h the first term in (9.1) is now strictly positive, implying the strong inequality in (9.2) and (9.5). If for that h, s_h^* is not changing at that moment, then this proves the lemma.

Now suppose that s_h^* is changing at the moment in question. Since trade takes place instantaneously, $a_{hi} \neq 0$ when the new set of dealers has been chosen, whence it is clear that U_h must be decreasing to the right of t.

Consider now the points to the left of t. Suppose that the change in s_h^* occurs in the identity of the dealer in that commodity for which $a_{hi} \neq 0$. Since consideration of the trading assumptions makes it clear that shifting to a new dealer as his price passes that of an old one can satisfy a non-zero excess demand but cannot create one, $a_{hi} \neq 0$ just to the left of t. On the other hand, suppose that the shift in dealers occurs in some other commodity. Since, for that i for which $a_{hi} \neq 0$, $\bar{x}_{hi}$ does not jump at such a moment, since demands, x_{hi}, are continuous in the prices and wealth, and since wealth does not change merely through trading, $z_{hi}(= x_{hi} - \bar{x}_{hi})$ must be non-zero to the left of t, since it clearly is at t. If $\bar{m}_h$ was also non-zero just to the left of t, so was a_{hi}. The only way in which $\bar{m}_h$ could suddenly become non-zero at t while being zero just to the left of t, however, is if the change of dealers suddenly allows h to sell something at a non-zero price which he wished to sell before but could not. In that case, $a_{hj} \neq 0$ just to the left of t for some j whose price was non-zero.

In any of these cases, U_h must have been decreasing just to the left of t, and, since it is also decreasing just to the right of t, it must

---

[20] This trivial exception is overlooked by Arrow and Hahn [1971, Chapter XIII].

be decreasing at t, by the considerations given in the proof of Lemma 9.2.

10.   Assuming Money Stocks Positive

It is now clear where we can go. Still following Arrow and Hahn, we can make the sum of utilities a Lyapounov function, provided that we can assume:

Assumption 10.1.   For all h and all $t \geqq 0, \overline{m}_h(t) > 0.$

This is a very strong assumption, yet it may be more reasonable in the present context than in that of the traditional auctioneer where Arrow and Hahn found it difficult to ensure with simple conditions.

Since money is required as a medium of exchange and since it has a positive marginal utility, it seems reasonable to assume that individuals never plan to have their money stock be zero at any time. Rather, money stocks can be zero if individuals are badly mistaken about the amounts that they will be able to sell, the limiting case being when they can sell nothing at all.

Now consider a selling dealer. He controls the price at which he attempts to sell. We have already assumed that if he quotes a positive price and fails to sell as much as he expected at it, then he will take this as an indication that he has quoted a higher-than-market price and will lower his price. We have made the rate of that price change dependent on the amount of excess supply. It takes little more to suppose that the speed of adjustment can also be a function of the fraction of his supply that goes unsold, or, even simpler, of his own money stock. In other words, our model will allow us to assume that a selling dealer who is badly wrong and sees his money stock declining to zero takes quick action to reverse the situation by rapidly lowering his price. So long as the rate of price change is a sign-preserving continuous function of the excess demand facing the dealer, there is no reason why it cannot also depend on his money stock or similar factors.

This kind of consideration is not available, of course, in a model with a fictitious auctioneer; it crucially depends on the control over price possessed by an individual dealer in the present model.

While important, however, such considerations do not immediately remove all the problems associated with Assumption 10.1. For one thing, the case of a buying dealer is not symmetric with that of a selling dealer. A buying dealer, seeing his money stock vanishing, might reduce his buying price, but as the unexpected vanishing of the money stock would have to come from an inability to sell (since he will never buy more than he intended), such behaviour is inconsistent with the assumption that prices are adjusted only when a dealer faces a non-zero excess demand. Moreover, the case of a selling dealer facing a zero demand (as opposed to excess demand) at all positive prices because nobody wants his commodity cannot be handled in this way.

Nevertheless, the ability of selling dealers to adjust prices downward is of some aid in the acceptance of Assumption 10.1, particularly if we think of institutional arrangements where sellers are typically dealers and buyers typically customers. In such circumstances, we can assume that the haphazard workings of the market do not shut individuals out completely, because they can adjust their own prices. Only the case in which an individual has nothing to sell of any value remains a problem.[21]

We now adopt Assumption 10.1.

11.   Stability of Equilibrium

We can now use the proof of Arrow and Hahn essentially unchanged to show:

Theorem 11.1. *Every limit point of the path of prices and individual endowments is a quasi-equilibrium.*

Proof. Clearly, $U_h(x_h, m_h) \geqq U_h(\bar{x}_h, \bar{m}_h)$ and we may take U_h as bounded from below.

Let $L \equiv \sum_h U_h$. Then, by Lemma 9.3 and Assumption 10.1, L is decreasing at any t for which some $a_i^d \neq 0$ unless that $a_i^d < 0$ and $p_i^d = 0$. A point at which $a_i^d = 0$, however, is, by the Hahn process assumption, a point at which all the corresponding $a_{hi}^d = 0$ and, by Assumption 5.1 and Assumption 10.1, all the corresponding z_{hi}^d must be zero as well. Moreover, for those i and $d \in D_i$ for which $a_i^d \leqq 0$, the corresponding $z_{hi}^d \leqq 0$. In view of the budget constraints, therefore, the only points at which L is not decreasing (and is therefore stationary by Lemma 9.2) must also have $m_h = \bar{m}_h$. It clearly follows that all such points are quasi-equilibria.

Thus we may take L as a Lyapounov function and it follows that every limit point of the path of prices and individual stocks is a quasi-equilibrium.

[21] The special role of money in the Arrow-Hahn model (and the present one) emphasizes the rather unnatural character of the assumption that utility maximization accounts for demands while everyone believes that his transactions will be completed. If individuals realized what was happening, they would have liquidity preference, but such preference occurs only *ad hoc* as in the present section rather than as a result of utility maximization. Still it is better to have it appear *ad hoc* than not at all. I am indebted to Christopher Bliss for raising this point.

It is probably worth emphasizing that this result holds in both the single-order and the multi-order case, as do all our principal results.

It does not seem possible to establish more than this, the quasi-stability of quasi-equilibrium,[22] so long as quasi-equilibria are not necessarily full competitive equilibria. We can prove, however:

Theorem 11.2. *If Assumption* 4.1 *holds, then the economy is globally stable; that is, from any initial position, it converges to a competitive equilibrium.*[23]

Proof. By Lemma 4.1, all quasi-equilibria are also competitive equilibria and, hence, by Theorem 11.1, all limit points are competitive equilibria. Now, in view of Lemma 9.2, for every h, U_h converges to a limit, say U_h^*. If we write $x_h = x_h(p, \bar{x}_h, \bar{m}_h)$ and $m_h = m_h(p, \bar{x}_h, \bar{m}_h)$ as the demand functions, then:

$$U_h^* = \lim_{t \to \infty} U_h = U_h\{x_h(p^*, \bar{x}_h^*, \bar{m}_h^*), m_h(p^*, \bar{x}_h^*, \bar{m}_h^*)\}, \qquad (11.1)$$

where p^*, $\bar{x}_h^*$, and $\bar{m}_h^*$ are limit points of the path of prices and individual stocks. Let x_h^* and m_h^* be the values of x_h and m_h, respectively, at that point. Obviously, for all those commodities for which $\tilde{p}_{hi}^* \neq 0$ (where, as before, $\tilde{p}_h^*$ is the subvector of p^* that is relevant to h) $x_{hi}^* = \bar{x}_{hi}^*$, while for all other commodities, $x_{hi}^* \leqq \bar{x}_{hi}^*$; moreover, $m_h^* = \bar{m}_h^*$. Otherwise, the limit point would not be a quasi-equilibrium.

Now, suppose that $(p^{**}, x_h^{**}, \bar{m}_h^{**})$ were another limit point with corresponding limiting target demands x_h^{**} and m_h^{**}. Then such a point has similar properties.

However,

$$U_h(x_h^{**}, m_h^{**}) = U_h(x_h^*, m_h^*) = U_h^* \qquad (11.2)$$

and, since U_h is strictly quasi-concave:

$$\tilde{p}_h^{*\prime}(x_h^* - x_h^{**}) + m_h^* - m_h^{**} < 0, \qquad (11.3)$$

unless $m_h^* = m_h^{**}$ and $x_{hi}^* = x_{hi}^{**}$ for all commodities with non-zero prices in $\tilde{p}^*$.

Since all quasi-equilibria are also competitive equilibria, at such points, all dealers in a given commodity quote the same price. Hence $\tilde{p}_h^*$ is the

---

[22] See Negishi [1962, pp. 648–649].
[23] Actually, Assumption 4.1 is not needed directly. It would obviously suffice to assume that all of the limit points that, by Theorem 11.1, are all quasi-equilibria are also competitive equilibria. Indeed, many of the results can be obtained if only one such limit point has all prices strictly positive. This can be seen by taking that point to be the one defined by a single star in the proof below.

same for all h, and we may drop the subscript. Now sum (11.3) over all individuals, obtaining:

$$\tilde{p}^{*\prime}\left(\sum_h x_h^* - \sum_h x_h^{**}\right) + \sum_h m_h^* - \sum_h m_h^{**} < 0. \tag{11.4}$$

This is impossible, however, since (by the definition of quasi-equilibrium):

$$\sum_h m_h^* = \sum_h \overline{m}_h^* = \overline{M} = \sum_h \overline{m}_h^{**} = \sum_h m_h^{**}, \tag{11.5}$$

while for all commodities for which $\tilde{p}^*$ has a non-zero component,

$$\sum_h x_{hi}^* = \sum_h \overline{x}_{hi}^* = \overline{X}_i = \sum_h \overline{x}_{hi}^{**} \geqq \sum_h x_{hi}^{**}. \tag{11.6}$$

Thus there is a unique set of limiting target demands for all commodities with non-zero prices at any limit point (and, indeed, for all commodities). Hence there is also a unique set of limiting target endowments for all such commodities and for money; moreover, p^* can be seen to involve a unique set of limiting prices for such commodities.[24] It follows that the set of commodities for which the prices in any limit point are zero is the same in all limit points, hence these prices also converge.

There remains the question of the individual stocks of those commodities that have zero price in the limit. Since the wealth of any individual is not affected by his holdings of these commodities, his target demand for each of them obviously approaches a definite limit that, of course, must be no bigger than his stock. If we assume free disposal, then we can take these limiting demands to also be limiting stocks; otherwise, the limiting excess individual stocks of free goods are apparently undetermined, a fact that we shall not consider an exception to the theorem.[25]

---

[24] This follows because we have already assumed the utility functions differentiable with the first-order conditions for a maximum (9.4) holding for commodities demanded in non-zero amounts. It follows that if any individual h has $x_{hi}^* > 0$ and $x_{hj}^* > 0$, the ratio, p_i^*/p_j^* is uniquely determined. Indeed, if the first-order condition on money given in the second part of (9.4) holds for some h, then p_i^* is determined for any i for which $x_{hi}^* > 0$ for that h. Since $m_h^* = \overline{m}_h^*$, it follows from Assumption 10.1 that the second part of (9.4) does hold for *every* h even in the limit. Since $\tilde{p}_i^* > 0$ implies $x_{hi}^* > 0$ for some h, all positive prices are uniquely determined.

Indeed, even if Assumption 10.1 did not imply the second part of (9.4), prices would fail to be determined only if the set of commodities (including money) and the set of individuals just happened to be partitionable into two (or more) disjoint subsets with each subset of individuals holding a particular proper subset of the commodities at equilibrium.

[25] As already indicated, Arrow and Hahn fail to recognize this rather unimportant problem of how much of the bag each individual gets caught holding when the music stops.

12.   Extensions

It is pretty clear that much the same apparatus can be used to handle the case in which there are different costs in terms of utility associated with buying from different dealers (for example because of locational differences). The limiting case of this occurs when every individual knows every price but does not necessarily seek to buy from the lowest-priced dealer because of such cost considerations. In such a case, it is easy to see that the proof of Theorem 11.2 can be used to establish convergence to a quasi-equilibrium without assuming that some limit point is also a full competitive equilibrium. This is so because the crucial question is that of whether all prices are known to all individuals, so that the subscript can be dropped before the sum is taken in (11.4).

In general, however, we would not expect cases with different locational advantages to different dealers also to be cases in which dealer prices in a given commodity were all the same in equilibrium. This is hardly a defect; it suggests that a similar convergence process can be used to establish the stability of equilibria involving such rents.

Other suggestions for further work have already been given. Once we abandon the fictitious auctioneer, the problem becomes richer. In some ways, that richness leads to greater difficulty; in some, as I hope this paper has shown, it facilitates analysis by making various assumptions relatively more reasonable. In the present paper, that seemed true of the Hahn process assumption (Assumption 6.1) and the assumption of non-zero money stocks (Assumption 10.1) as well as of the nature of the adjustment process itself. Yet the model of the present paper is only one way of eliminating the auctioneer, and much additional work remains to be done both in terms of easing the assumptions of the present analysis and in terms of altogether different approaches.

REFERENCES

Arrow, K. J., and Hahn, F. H. *General Competitive Analysis* (San Francisco, Holden Day, 1971).

Arrow, K. J., and Hurwicz, L. "Decentralization and Computation in Resource Allocation", pp. 34–104 in R. W. Pfouts, ed., *Essays in Economics and Econometrics, A Volume in Honor of Harold Hotelling* (Chapel Hill, University of North Carolina Press, 1960).

Fisher, F. M. "Quasi-Competitive Price Adjustment by Individual Firms: A Preliminary Paper", *Journal of Economic Theory*, **2** (1970), 195–206. Reprinted as Chapter 2 in this volume.

Hahn, F. H., and Negishi, T. "A Theorem on Non-Tâtonnement Stability", *Econometrica*, **30** (1962), 463–469.

Koopmans, T. C. "Analysis of Production as an Efficient Combination of Activities", Chapter III in T. C. Koopmans, ed., *Activity Analysis of Production and Allocation* (Cowles Commission Monograph 13) (New York, John Wiley & Sons, 1951).

Three Essays on the State of Economic Science (New York, McGraw-Hill Book Company, 1957).

Negishi, T. "The Stability of a Competitive Economy: A Survey Article", *Econometrica*, **30** (1962), 635–669.

Nikaidô, H., and Uzawa, H. "Stability and Non-negativity in a Walrasian Tâtonnement Process", *International Economic Review*, Vol. **1** (1960), 50–59.

CHAPTER 5

Quantity Constraints, Spillovers, and the Hahn Process (1978)

1. Introduction

In recent years there has been considerable interest in general equilibrium (or disequilibrium) models in which agents perceive that they cannot complete their desired transactions and hence choose their demands by optimizing subject to quantity constraints on their trading activity. [Examples are Clower (1965), Patinkin (1965), Leijonhufvud (1968, 1973), Barro and Grossman (1971), Benassy (1975, 1976, multilith, forthcoming), Frevert (1970), Hayashi (multilith), Varian (April 1975, April 1977), and Veendorp (1975).] Such constraints affect not only the markets in which they occur, but they also "spill over" in their effects on other markets because they can alter demands for all goods. The leading case, of course, is that in which the realization of unemployment affects demands by consumers, and, indeed, much of the literature has concentrated on such phenomena as an explanation for the existence of Keynesian underemployment equilibria. However, the phenomenon involved can be much more general, and one should expect that it leads to equilibria that are not Walrasian (competitive) in a general model as quantity-constrained demands all get satisfied. [Probably the most satisfactory proofs of existence are those of Benassy (1975, 1976, multilith, forthcoming).]

Despite the fact that the subject is one of disequilibrium behaviour, however, most of the work has concentrated on showing the existence of such non-Walrasian equilibria and relatively little is known about the dynamic stability of adjustment processes in such models. Such analyses as are available [e.g. Frevert (1970), Hayashi (multilith), Varian (April 1975, April 1977), and Veendorp (1975)] typically involve relatively simple models or very strong restrictions of the gross substitute type. One principal purpose of the present paper, therefore,

Research for this chapter was supported by the National Science Foundation, Grant 43185. I am indebted to Hal Varian for helpful conversations and to the editors and referees of the *Review of Economic Studies* for criticism but retain responsibility for errors.

110

is to consider a relatively general model of stability under quantity constraints.

If satisfactory discussions of stability are largely lacking from the quantity constraint literature, however, that literature does provide an important feature the lack of which makes more traditional discussions of stability most unsatisfactory indeed – the consciousness on the part of the agents that they are in disequilibrium. The stability literature typically proceeds by assuming that agents expect their transactions to be completed and that they formulate their demands accordingly, taking prices as given and (usually) unchanging. [See Fisher (1976) for a recent survey and discussion; earlier surveys are given in Negishi (1962) and Arrow and Hahn (1971).] I shall not here be concerned with the assumptions as to prices but shall concentrate on the completion-of-transactions aspect which is clearly unsatisfactory in itself in models that have long since passed beyond the tâtonnement stage to allow disequilibrium trading to occur. [For some work on price adjustment by individual agents, see Fisher (1970, 1971, 1973, 1977).] Thus the second principal purpose of this paper is to consider how existing stability models can be modified to accommodate the kind of consciousness of disequilibrium that is expressed in the use of quantity constraints.

As it happens, it turns out to be quite easy to go some distance in this direction as regards the class of stability models using what I consider to be the most satisfactory non-tâtonnement adjustment process so far developed, the Hahn Process.[1] Indeed, to a certain extent this has already been done by Arrow and Hahn (1971, Ch. XIII). They at least localize the problem that one must offer something of value before one can buy by developing a model in which all purchases must be made for a particular commodity, "money", and demands not backed up with money are not effective ("active") demands but only planned ("target") demands. Even in that model, however, agents act as though they expect their transactions to be completed and formulate active demands taking into account only their cash constraint and without regard for the fact that their transactions on other markets may be limited. The present paper shows one way in which such quantity restrictions can be somewhat accommodated along the lines of Arrow and Hahn (1971, Ch. XIII). It remains necessary, however, as in that analysis, to assume that agents never run out of money out of equilibrium – an assumption that is pretty

---

[1] So named by Negishi (1962). The original paper is Hahn and Negishi (1962). Arrow and Hahn (1971, Ch. XIII) develop the model for a monetary economy with cash constraints on effective demand; Fisher (1972) puts in individual price adjustment; firms are introduced in (1974), and disequilibrium production and consumption (as opposed to merely disequilibrium trading) in (1976) and (1977).

strong in contexts such as the present one and to which I shall return below.[2]

In order to concentrate on the problem at hand, the incorporation of quantity constraints and spillovers into the Hahn Process, I shall deal with a version of that process in which the monetary matters introduced by Arrow and Hahn are only implicit rather than giving them explicit notational treatment. Further, although consideration of quantity constraints obviously makes most sense when consumption and production are going on out of equilibrium, the complications involved in allowing such activities are large and not particularly germane to the issues here discussed. [See Fisher (September 1976, 1977).] Hence I shall deal with the case in which the only disequilibrium activity is the trading of commodities or, in the case of firms, of commitments to buy inputs and sell outputs, production and consumption being deferred until equilibrium is reached. Moreover, since most of the issues involved can be discussed in the context of pure exchange, I give explicit treatment only to that case, briefly discussing the differences involved in the incorporation of firms after the technical results. The exchange model to be discussed is closest to that of Arrow and Hahn (1971, Ch. XIII). The model with firms is closest to that of Fisher (1974). In both cases the present paper suppresses the explicit treatment of money.

The results obtained are fairly strong. We find that one possible specification of how quantity constraints are perceived and how they affect behaviour leads immediately to the quasi-stability of the equilibrium set (which includes non-Walrasian equilibria). Moreover, extension of that specification in what seems a reasonable way to allow experimentation with constraints when markets continue to clear generates a far stronger result, namely, that the adjustment process involved is stable in that from any set of initial conditions it converges to some *Walrasian* equilibrium.

Clearly, the question of the plausibility of the assumptions that lead to such results becomes one of importance. As will be seen, those assumptions seem more likely to be plausible close to Walrasian equilibrium than away from it, so that the results should be taken as providing reasons for believing that the adjustment process is locally stable and converges locally to Walrasian equilibrium even when there are quantity constraints. In other words, even though, for technical convenience, the results are stated globally, such "global" results are really only applicable so long as the system stays close enough to equilibrium for the assumptions to hold.

---

[2] That assumption has somewhat more plausibility when prices are set by individuals conscious of disequilibrium than it does in other contexts. See Fisher (1972).

2. Pure Exchange and Quasi-Stability

There are $n + 1$ commodities, numbered $0, 1, \ldots, n$, with commodity 0 being money whose price is always unity. The price of commodity i is denoted by p_i and the $n + 1$ component vector of the p_i (first element unity) by p.

Households are subscripted h. The hth household has a strictly quasi-concave, differentiable utility function, $U^h(x_h)$, where x_h denotes a vector of demands. The household's actual possessions are denoted by $\bar{x}_h$. Both x_h and $\bar{x}_h$ are functions of time, t, as are prices, but we generally suppress the time argument.

The household's Walrasian demands are obtained by maximizing its utility function subject only to its budget constraint:

$$p'(x_h - \bar{x}_h) = 0 \tag{2.1}$$

where the prime denotes transposition. We denote its Walrasian *excess* demands by $z_h(= x_h - \bar{x}_h)$. I shall refer to the components of z_h as *target* excess demands.

Now, denote the vector of the *active* excess demands (the demands the household attempts to exercise in the marketplace) by a_h. It goes without saying that if $z_{hi} \leq 0$ for all i so that [in view of (2.1)] the household is able to fulfil its unconstrained plans, with the possible exception of disposing of free goods, then $a_{hi} = z_{hi} = 0$ for all goods with positive prices and $a_{hi} \leq 0$ for all free goods. However, in general, it will not be the case that the household's target excess demands and active excess demands coincide. There are at least two reasons for this.

In the first place, it is natural to assume [following Arrow and Hahn (1971, Ch. XIII)] that purchases must be made for money. Hence, since the household may not always have enough money to effect its desired purchases, it may have to limit its positive excess demands to amounts that can be backed up with money. I shall assume that the household does this in some appropriately continuous way and that it never runs out of money. [For more extended discussion of these issues, see Arrow and Hahn (1971), and Fisher (1972, 1976)]. I return to No Bankruptcy later. The two assumptions are implicitly involved in the explicit ones below.

The second reason that active and target excess demands can differ is the one with which we are concerned in this paper. If the household realizes that it may not be able to complete all its transactions it may adjust its demands to take account of the fact that its trading on particular markets is limited. One way of modelling such behaviour is to assume that there are certain quantity constraints perceived by the household and that it chooses its active excess demands by remaximizing its utility function once it perceives those constraints.

For purposes of the present paper it is convenient to think of this process as involving two stages. In the first stage the household attempts to exercise its target excess demands (restricting its offers to buy to be consistent with its cash constraint). Queues then form and the household realizes that it may not complete its transactions and readjusts its demands by remaximizing utility accordingly. I shall be more explicit about the story in a moment, but for the present it is useful to make two remarks.

First, such a story is really a compromise. It only goes part way towards allowing households to understand what is going on, by allowing them to see the constraints only after they attempt to exercise their unconstrained demands. Particularly since the process keeps being repeated, this is not fully satisfactory.

Second, the story makes sense at best in positions close to Walrasian equilibrium. Only there is it sensible for the household to take its target excess demands as a point of departure and to believe (in the first stage of the process) that they may be satisfied.

I shall return to these matters below. Now let me give the crucial assumption that the two-step story is supposed to produce and then proceed to elaborate on that story. (Note, however, that the crucial thing is the assumption itself. The two-step story is one way in which that assumption can hold, but there is no strong reason for believing that it is the only way.)

Let A_i denote the sum of the a_{hi} over h, the total active excess demand for commodity i. The crucial assumption is:

Assumption 2.1 (Modified Hahn Process).   For every h and every $i = 1, \ldots, n$, it is always the case *post-trade* that $z_{hi}A_i \geqq 0$.

In other words, the only reason *post-trade* that a household has an unsatisfied *target* demand for some commodity is that it is on the wrong side of the market, the side with unsatisfied active demand.

To understand what this involves it is useful to tell the two-stage story already referred to. For reasons of technical convenience, it is useful to think of trade as happening instantaneously or outside of time, even though prices and endowments will be assumed to change continuously. Hence I shall tell the story as though it took place in discrete time with prices announced at the beginning of a trading "day" and not changed until after trade. [Assumption 2.1 makes sense (as does the usual Hahn Process Assumption) only *post-trade*. Before trade, when prices change, there come moments when suppliers and demanders look at each other with the wild surmise that trade can be consummated. Only after trade can unsatisfied demand appear on only one side of the market. This makes the continuous time story a little awkward (and the story leading to Assumption 2.1 harder to swallow than if it could hold *pre-trade*). See Arrow and Hahn (1971, p. 342).

After prices are announced, each household goes out and attempts to exercise its target excess demands. In doing so, it initially takes account of disequilibrium only to the extent that it reduces its positive target demands to initial positive active demands so as not to spend more money than it has on hand. [See Arrow and Hahn (1971, Ch. XIII).] The market for each commodity then develops a long and a short side (demand being the long side if demand exceeds supply so that the good is "in short supply"). Households on the short side of the market are told that their initial offers are accepted. Households on the long side are given tickets that entitle them to a place in the queue for that commodity and told that the extent to which their (positive or negative) excess demands will be satisfied will be decided in the second stage.

For convenience of language, I shall occasionally speak as though demand rather than supply is the long side.

Households now reconsider their positions *and remaximize* utility, believing correctly that, while it will be possible to move to the short side of a market and be served regardless of one's initial position in that market, it will not be possible to move to the long side. In other words, households believe correctly that they are constrained as to completing their transactions by the fact that nobody not holding a ticket for a particular queue will be served if he joins that queue. Moreover, no ticket-holder will be able to obtain more than he initially asked for. Hence households may leave queues or reduce their demands for commodities in short supply but they never join queues or increase demands for such commodities when remaximizing utility subject to the new transaction constraints.

In order for the constraints perceived by the households to be true ones, it is necessary that the queue-leaving process be such that the second-stage readjustments do not reverse the identity of the long and short side of any market. In other words, while the queue-leaving process and the movement of households to the short side of the market can result in a situation in which all those still in the queue are served and satisfy their active demands, it never results in a situation in which so many people have joined the short side and so many left the queue that the active demands of those on the original short side cannot now be satisfied.

Trade now takes place with the total short active supply rationed over the total long active demand. So long as this is done so as to satisfy appropriate Lipschitz Conditions as discussed below, the exact rationing rules do not matter. Prices now adjust in the direction indicated by total unsatisfied active excess demands and the process begins again.

Clearly, this story generates Assumption 2.1. In order to do so, however, I have had to allow households to wake up to quantity constraints only after the tickets are given out in the first stage. It is instructive to see just how strong this is by considering a particular kind of behaviour that it rules out.

Suppose that a particular household wishes (in the target sense) to sell coffee and buy tea. Suppose further that both coffee and tea are in short supply. Then the household may wish to sell less coffee than it would if tea transactions were unconstrained. In the process just described, it cannot do this by holding back from the coffee market some of the coffee it would otherwise have sold. (To allow it to do so could lead to a situation in which it has a zero post-trade active demand for coffee and a *negative* post-trade target demand with total active demand for coffee still positive.) Rather it must first supply its target amount of coffee and then realize that it is worse off in buying coffee than in buying tea since it has no ticket for the coffee queue. What is worse is that it must go on behaving like this the next day. (The problem arises because of the requirement that Assumption 2.1 holds *post-trade*.)

This makes sense only (if at all) if we suppose that queues are short enough that most or all customers are usually served. If the whole story takes place close to a Walrasian equilibrium, then households can take target demands as a first approximation in such a two-stage process since in fact they may be able to come close to satisfying those demands in the second stage. In such a situation we can suppose that the household in the example just given is unable to tell that its tea requirements will be severely restricted until it sees the size of the queue and therefore does not initially reduce its coffee supply. Nevertheless, this is very strong.

It should be clearly recognized, however, that restricting household behaviour in this way does not eliminate spillovers; it merely restricts some of the ways in which they can occur. Thus, the household in the above example, perceiving the constraints on its transactions, may very well remaximize its utility subject to those constraints and decide to sell *more* coffee. It can also decide to sell rather than buy tea or it can move to the long side of any other market, altering its demands from its Walrasian ones to take account of the transaction constraints. All such actions are spillover effects.

I have named Assumption 2.1 as I have because it is closely related to the usual Hahn Process assumption that willing buyers and sellers can readily find each other so that, after trade, there are not unsatisfied agents on both sides of the market. [I argued in Fisher (1972) that such an assumption is almost compelled in models in which individuals adjust their own prices.] Indeed, as in the story just told, one way of thinking of Assumption 2.1 is to assume that individual post-trade active and target excess demands are (weakly) of the same sign and then to add the usual Hahn Process assumption. (Note, however, that such an assumption would be entirely inappropriate as applied to pre-trade demands as it would prevent households from joining the short side of a market.)

Let me be a little more explicit about this. In all Hahn Process models without spillovers, the assumption (one way or another) is that a non-zero target excess demand for some commodity produces a non-zero active excess demand for that commodity, provided the household does not run out of money, which is assumed not to happen. Since all assumptions are in terms of post-trade demands, this means that a household that, *pre-trade*, wishes to buy a commodity in overall excess supply will do so and will increase its active pre-trade demand for that commodity, acquiring it until either its post-trade active and target demands are both zero or the commodity has switched to being in overall excess demand. All of this happens instantaneously, with time suspended, and before prices are influenced by post-trade excess demands. [This tends to make it easier but not essential to think of such models as applying after an initial period in which markets develop a long and short side. Only continuous adjustments occur thereafter. See Hahn and Negishi (1962) and Arrow and Hahn (1971, Ch. XIII).] In the present model, the same thing is true. Thus, a household that begins with a pre-trade Walrasian excess demand for some commodity of opposite sign to overall active excess demand for that commodity will be able to satisfy it and will do so as long as that overall active excess demand does not change sign. Hence, *post-trade*, it must be the case that $z_{hi}A_i \geqq 0$, which is Assumption 2.1.

Of course, this explanation requires that a pre-trade target excess demand generate a pre-trade active excess demand of the same sign. This is restrictive and will not generally be true unless households can more or less expect their target demands to be approximately satisfied. Hence, as already remarked, this sort of story makes sense only in the neighbourhood of a Walrasian equilibrium.

I now pay more explicit attention to the dynamics and mathematics of the model. I assume that the results of the above process or, more generally, of the way in which active demands are determined is such as to make:

$$a_{hi} = D^{hi}(p, \overline{X}),\tag{2.2}$$

where $\overline{X}$ denotes the vector (not the sum) of the endowments of all households. Further,

$$\dot{p}_i = G^i(A_i) \text{ unless } p_i = 0 \quad \text{and} \quad A_i < 0,$$
$$\text{in which case } \dot{p}_i = 0 \ (i = 1, \ldots, n),\tag{2.3}$$

where $G^i(.)$ is a continuous and sign-preserving function that does not approach zero except as A_i does. Finally,

$$\dot{\overline{x}}_{hi} = F^{hi}(p, \overline{X}).\tag{2.4}$$

I assume that the functions F^{hi} satisfy Lipschitz Conditions as do the result of expressing the $\dot{p}_i$ directly as functions of p and $\overline{X}$ (except for the requirement that prices stay non-negative). I further assume that trade takes place only if active demands are non-zero[3] and that the F^{hi} satisfy two further conditions, namely:

$$\sum_h \dot{\overline{x}}_h = 0 \tag{2.5}$$

and

$$p'\dot{\overline{x}}_h = 0, \quad \text{all } h. \tag{2.6}$$

The first of these rules (2.5) is an immediate consequence of the fact that we are in pure exchange, so that the total amount of each commodity is fixed. The second (2.6) is a No-Swindling Assumption which states that a household cannot alter its wealth through trading at constant prices.[4]

The adjustment process described determines prices and stocks (and implicitly all other variables) as single-valued and continuous functions of time t and initial conditions in the usual way. [The violation of Lipschitz Conditions in (2.3) is not a problem here. See Henry (January 1973, March 1973) and Champsaur, Drèze, and Henry (1977).]

The system is in equilibrium wherever all active demands are non-positive with active demands zero for all positively priced goods. It is

---

[3] Recall that things change continuously. The only interesting (if unlikely) possibility that is eliminated by this is that at a non-Walrasian equilibrium quantity constraints get adjusted in such a way that trade takes the economy to a Walrasian equilibrium with prices unchanged and post-trade active demands zero. Handling of this sort of thing is not difficult but explicitly allowing for it unduly complicates the exposition. This note should be borne in mind when considering Assumption 3.1 below.

[4] Arrow and Hahn (1971, Ch. XIII) give one example of such rules.

in *Walrasian* equilibrium wherever the same thing applies to *target* demands.

It is now easy to prove:

Theorem 2.1. *Under Assumption 2.1, the adjustment process is quasi-stable. That is, every limit point of the path of prices and stocks is a (possibly non-Walrasian) equilibrium.*

Proof. The proof is essentially the same as for the standard Hahn Process models [see Arrow and Hahn (1971, Ch. XIII) or Fisher (1974), for example], but is so short that it may as well be given here.

The Lagrangian for the household's target maximization problem can be written:

$$L_h = U^h(x_h) - \lambda_h p'(x_h - \bar{x}_h), \tag{2.7}$$

where λ_h is a Lagrange multiplier equal to the marginal utility of wealth. By the Envelope Theorem, we can evaluate $\dot{U}^h$ by differentiating (2.7) with respect to the things not wholly under the household's control, namely, prices and stocks. Doing so, we obtain:

$$\dot{U}^h = -\lambda_h \dot{p}' z_h + \lambda_h p' \dot{\bar{x}}_h. \tag{2.8}$$

However, the second term on the right-hand side of (2.8) is zero by (2.5). Moreover, λ_h is positive, and every term in the inner product in the first term on the right-hand side is non-negative, since individual target excess demands have (weakly) the same sign as total active excess demands, by Assumption 2.1, and so do price changes, by (2.3). Since utility can be taken as bounded below by the utility that would be obtained by consuming initial stocks, it is evident that the sum of target utilities over households is a Lyapounov Function.

3. Convergence to Walrasian Equilibrium

To get further than quasi-stability and obtain stability of the adjustment process requires two more steps. The first is a proof of boundedness and the second a proof either that equilibria are locally isolated or that all limit points starting from given initial conditions are the same.

Boundedness presents no problems as regards stocks, in view of (2.5). The issue as regards prices is somewhat trickier. There are two known ways to obtain boundedness of prices in Hahn Process models (other than by assuming it directly). [Details may be found in Fisher (1974).] The first of these is to assume that if relative prices become too high, the highest priced good is in non-positive excess demand. Such a method seems as applicable to active as to target excess demands. The other method for obtaining boundedness is to assume that the adjustment functions, $G^i(\cdot)$, are bounded above by rays through the origin and that money is in positive excess demand if its relative price is sufficiently low. The applicability of this method to the present case, however, would require assuming that *active* excess demand for money is positive when the relative price is sufficiently low. This is certainly a possibility but will not follow from the somewhat more natural assumption about target excess demands without rather more assumptions. [For example, there is no reason to assume (as do Arrow and Hahn, 1971, Ch. XIII) that active excess demands are always less than or equal to target excess demands.] In any case, I shall henceforward assume boundedness of relative prices.

The remainder of a global stability proof – a demonstration that equilibria are locally isolated or that all limit points are the same – is clearly not available in the present analysis without more explicit treatment of the way in which active demands are generated. Indeed, in view of Varian (1977), it is clear that local isolation is not an inevitable result. Hence one cannot proceed further down this line in a model as general as the present one, although specific analyses may be able to do so.

In any case, it seems to me to be more interesting to examine the implications of some further assumptions to which one might be led by consideration of the sort of argument leading to Assumption 2.1. As it turns out, such further assumptions do lead to stability of the adjustment process (given boundedness); moreover, they lead to convergence to a *Walrasian* equilibrium. Thus consideration of them is interesting if only to examine the differences that keep the system from getting stuck in a non-Walrasian place – or allow it to do so.

The first such assumption would be the considerable strengthening of Assumption 2.1 to:

Assumption 2.1' (Strong Modified Hahn Process).   For every h and every $i = 1, \ldots, n$, it is always the case post-trade that $z_{hi}A_i \geqq 0$ and $z_{hi}A_i > 0$ unless $z_{hi} = 0$.

This is much too strong. What it says that is not contained in the weaker Assumption 2.1 is that any non-zero target excess demand post-trade must result in a non-zero active demand of the same sign.[5] This means that quantity constraints can alter demands but not by so much

---

[5] It is probably worth remarking that the requirement that target excess demands result in non-zero action goes very deep in stability models. It is assumed without comment in Arrow and Hahn (1971, Ch. XIII) but plays a major role in what I have termed the "Present Action Postulate" which comes to the fore when disequilibrium production and consumption are introduced. See Fisher (September 1976), (1976), and (1977).

that any constrained demand balances while the corresponding unconstrained one is still unsatisfied. In terms of the two-stage story told above,
such an assumption rules out the possibility in any market at any time
that enough ticketholders leave the queue and enough households come
to the short side of the market as to allow all remaining ticketholders
to satisfy their active demands. This is not particularly plausible and it is
not surprising that it rules out non-Walrasian equilibria as limit points
to the adjustment process as it clearly does. (It also implies stability as
will be seen below.) It may be instructive, however, to compare Assumption 2.1′ (or Assumption 2.1″ below) to Assumption 2.1 above and to
Assumption 3.1 below as an aid to assessing the plausibility of the latter
two assumptions.

Now, not only is Assumption 2.1′ implausibly strong, but it is also
stronger than necessary to produce the results of interest. If we seek for
an assumption that will keep the adjustment process from getting stuck
at a non-Walrasian equilibrium, it is not necessary to have total active
and individual target demands strongly of the same sign for *all* households, *all* commodities, and *all* moments of time.

In the first place, if one is going to rule out non-Walrasian equilibria
as directly as this, one may as well do so directly in a substantially weaker
form by retaining Assumption 2.1 and adding:

Assumption 2.1″ (No Non-Walrasian Equilibria). Except at Walrasian
equilibria, there exists an $i = 1, \ldots, n$, such that $A_i \Sigma_h z_{hi} > 0$ and not both
$p_i = 0$ and $A_i < 0$.[6]

This rather weaker assumption states that, outside of Walrasian equilibrium, there is at least one commodity and one household whose unsatisfied target demand for that commodity corresponds to an unsatisfied
active demand. This is clearly weaker than Assumption 2.1′ but is still
unnecessarily strong.

To see this, let us return to the two-stage story told above. A non-
Walrasian equilibrium corresponds to the case in which, for every
market, enough ticketholders leave the queue or otherwise reduce their
demands and enough households come to the short side of the market
so that all those remaining in the queue get served. Since the reason for
moderating one's demands is the expectation that one will not be fully
served (either in that market or in some other) and since the reason for
joining the short side of the market is the spillover effect of the belief
that one will not be fully served in some other market, it seems natural
to assume that if everyone keeps getting served for a long enough time,

---

[6] I am indebted to Joseph Greenberg for this form of the assumption.

then households will readjust their views as to the constraints and will begin to experiment by remaining in some queue or ceasing to moderate their demands.

Formally, we retain Assumption 2.1 and add to it the following:

Assumption 3.1 (Eventual Experimentation).   There exists a finite time interval, $\Delta t \geqq 0$, such that, for any t^*, if for all t in the interval $[t^*, t^* + \Delta t)$, $A_i \leqq 0$ for all i and $\Sigma_{i=0}^{i=n} P_i A_i = 0$,[7] but for some h and i, $z_{hi} > 0$, then there exists a commodity j ($j = 1, \ldots, n$) such that at time $t^* + \Delta t, \Sigma_h z_{hj} A_j > 0$ and not both $p_j = 0$ and $A_j < 0$.

This apparently elaborate assumption simply makes the statement about eventual experimentation already given, the last clause merely ensuring that the experiment is not only that of trying to dispose of free goods. Some further comments are in order.

First, this is weaker than requiring experimentation on a given market whenever *that* market has had a zero active and a non-zero target excess demand for a long enough time.

Second, we could have stated the assumption directly in terms of having at time $t^* + \Delta t$ a non-zero A_j that is not just an active attempt to dispose of a free good. While this is the direct implication of Assumption 3.1, to state it that way would not capture the flavour of experimentation by at least one household on some market.

Finally, there is an important technical point. We assumed above that the resulting adjustment process can be represented by a system of ordinary differential equations with the variables being the prices and the endowments. We also assumed Lipschitz Conditions so that the solution of those equations was uniquely and continuously determined by the initial conditions. Assumption 3.1, however, makes active demands and therefore price and endowment changes dependent not only on where the system is but also on where it has recently been. This means that in the original space of prices and endowments we no longer have a system of ordinary differential equations. This is easy to fix by taking as our fundamental variables not only current prices and endowments but also the history of prices and endowments over the period $[t - \Delta t, t)$. In this expanded space, we can assume that the system is uniquely and continuously determined by its initial conditions as before. *Note, however, that this means that Assumption 3.1 has implications not just at non-Walrasian equilibria, but also at points close to non-Walrasian equilibria.* Thus, for example, if the system stays close to a non-Walrasian equilibrium for a

---

[7] Active demand for money, A_0, is the negative of the amount of money that households wish to spend after revising their demands to take account of the transaction constraints.

period $[t, t + \Delta t)$, actions taken at time $t + \Delta t$ must be similar to those that would have been taken had the system actually been at that non-Walrasian equilibrium for that time interval. This means that we are implicitly assuming that if almost everyone in all queues is getting served to the extent of his active demands, and this goes on long enough, then not all households will continue to moderate their demands until everyone can keep on being served, unless the system approaches Walrasian equilibrium. Roughly, if queues are very short for a long time, someone will realize that it pays to stay in some queue.[8]

As is fairly evident, Assumptions 2.1 and 3.1 together ensure that the limit points of the system are all Walrasian equilibria, thus strengthening the result of Theorem 2.1. However, in order to proceed to global stability, rather than quasi-stability, one more assumption is needed that has nothing to do with the issues we have been discussing. It is:

Assumption 3.2 (Indecomposability of Walrasian Equilibrium). At any Walrasian equilibrium, let S be the set of commodities (including money) that have strictly positive prices. For any proper subset of S, say S', there exists a pair of commodities, $i \in S'$ and $j \in (S - S')$, such that for some household the marginal rate of substitution between i and j is not at a corner and is equal to the ratio of their prices, p_i/p_j.

This assumption prevents the possibility that the economy breaks into two parts at a Walrasian equilibrium with one group of agents holding one set of commodities and having corner solutions with respect to a second set and the remaining agents holding the second set of commodities and having corner solutions with respect to the first set. It is required in the proof below to establish the global stability of prices but not of stocks. Note that it would make no sense to require such indecomposability out of Walrasian equilibrium.

We can now prove:

Theorem 3.1. *Under Assumptions 2.1, 3.1, and 3.2, the adjustment process is stable. That is, from any initial conditions, prices and stocks converge to some Walrasian equilibrium (with the possible exception that holdings of free goods may not converge).*[9]

Proof. The proof is very similar to that for standard Hahn Process models. [See Arrow and Hahn (1971, Ch. XIII) or Fisher (1974).]

---

[8] I am indebted to Kenneth Arrow and Jerry Green for pointing out to me some of the problems involved here and thus enabling me to correct an error in an earlier proof. Of course such complications would not occur if we took $\Delta t = 0$, which would essentially take us back to Assumption 2.1″.

[9] Note that since Assumption 2.1′ or 2.1″ implies Assumption 3.1, either of them would yield the same result.

In the expanded space in which we are working, it is evident that the sum of target utilities is still a Lyapounov Function. Moreover, as opposed to the case of Theorem 2.1, all the limit-points must be Walrasian equilibria, since Assumption 3.1 prevents the system (and target utilities) from slowing down as one approaches a non-Walrasian equilibrium in the expanded space.

Another way to say this is that Lyapounov's second method does not require that the Lyapounov Function always decline out of equilibrium, but only that it be everywhere non-increasing and *ultimately* declining out of equilibrium. Finite flat stretches can be readily accommodated, provided we expand the space in the way described.

Since we have already assumed boundedness, it remains to show that all limit points are the same. Suppose that there are two limit points, denoted by * and **. Since U^h is non-increasing and bounded below it approaches a limit that must be the same at both limit points. Hence $U^h(x_h^*) = U^h(x_h^{**})$. Because * is a *Walrasian* equilibrium, however, the strict quasi-concavity of U^h implies that:

$$p^{*\prime}x_h^* \leqq p^{*\prime}x_h^{**} \tag{3.1}$$

with the strict inequality holding unless x_h^* and x_h^{**} coincide for all commodities with a positive price at *. (Note that this statement would not hold for non-Walrasian equilibria; this is the principal place at which an attempt to prove global stability simply from Theorem 2.1 would break down, another being Assumption 3.2.)

Now, since * and ** are equilibria, the left-hand side of (3.1) is the value of actual holdings at *, while the right-hand side cannot exceed the value of actual holdings at **, valued in the prices of *. Hence,

$$p^{*\prime}\overline{x}_h^* \leqq p^{*\prime}\overline{x}_h^{**}, \tag{3.2}$$

with the strict inequality holding under the same conditions as before. Since we are in pure exchange, however, the sum of actual stocks over households is the same at both equilibrium points; hence, summing (3.2) over households will yield a contradiction unless both x_h and $\overline{x}_h$ are the same at * and ** for every household as regards all goods with positive prices at *. It is but a matter of interchanging the notation to show that the same must be true for all goods that have positive prices at **.

It remains to show that p^* and p^{**} are the same. To do this, observe that if money is the only non-free good at both * and **, then there is nothing to prove. We may thus suppose that there is some other good with a positive price at one of the equilibria, say*. By Assumption 3.2, there exists a commodity j, other than money, that has a positive price at *, such that the marginal rate of substitution between j and money for some household is not at a corner and is equal to the price ratio. Since x_h^* and x_h^{**} coincide in *all* non-free goods, that marginal rate of substitution must be the same at ** as at *, whence the price of j must be the same also. If there is another commodity with a positive price at * or **, then there is a commodity, i, with a positive price such that, for some household, the marginal rate of substitution between i and j or between i and money is not at a corner and is equal to the price ratio. Since marginal rates of substitution are the same at the two equilibria, so is the price of i. Proceeding in this way we can reach every positive price and the theorem is proved.

4.   Introducting Firms

I now briefly indicate how the above results can be adapted to models involving firms. The formalities involved are really no different from what has gone before as regards the problems at issue here and so I shall not give a formal model. [The interested reader can consult Fisher (1974) for the simplest model adaptable for the present discussion.] There is some point in discussing firms, however, not merely to indicate how to adapt the analysis, but because such discussion points up some issues regarding the plausibility of the assumptions leading to our rather strong results.

There seems no reason why Assumptions 2.1 and 3.1 should not apply to profit-maximizing firms as well as to utility-maximizing households. If Assumption 2.1 applies to firms, then, essentially as in the proof of Theorem 2.1, firms will find that their target profits (the profits they would make if they could complete all their transactions) are declining out of equilibrium. This is because the things they would like to sell but cannot sell are getting cheaper, while the things that they would like to buy but cannot buy are getting more expensive.

Given that target profits of firms are declining out of equilibrium, target utilities of households will decline also. For households there are now two reinforcing effects. First, there is the direct Hahn Process effect as for firms, essentially that involved in Theorem 2.1, which means that prices move so as to reduce the household's target utility. Second, the household's resources will decline because of the decline in its share of target profits. Thus the sum of household utilities can again be taken as a Lyapounov function and quasi-stability established.

Finally, if Assumption 3.1 is adapted to include firms, convergence to Walrasian equilibrium can be obtained by adapting the proof in Fisher

(1974). The principal addition to the proof of Theorem 3.1 is the use of profit-maximization for firms together with expenditure minimization for households to force the kind of contradiction involved in summing (3.2) above.

Thus our results can be extended to firms, although it should be observed that, for reasons unrelated to the present paper, constant returns cannot be accommodated. [See Fisher (1974).]

5.   Target Profits, No Bankruptcy, and the Modified Hahn Process

Consideration of firms, however, points up once more a central issue involved in our assumptions. In deciding on their target excess demands, consumers in the model just discussed take the *target* profits of firms as part of their resources. Assumptions 2.1 and 3.1 assume that the target excess demands so generated are related to active excess demands in particular ways. In an economy in which agents recognize that they are in disequilibrium, is this plausible?

In fact, the issue involved here is not greatly different from that involved under pure exchange where the wealth involved in computing a household's target excess demands is that which it would receive if it could sell all its resources including its labour. In both cases, the central question is how restrictions on spendable wealth are to be taken into account.

This brings us back to an assumption implicitly made throughout, namely, that no agent runs out of money in the course of the adjustment process. Without that assumption, positive target excess demands cannot be exercised at all and there is no reason that prices cannot move so as to increase target utilities. It is generally very hard, moreover, to ensure that the No Bankruptcy condition holds, although it is easier when individuals adjust prices. [See Arrow and Hahn (1971) and Fisher (1972).] When agents are conscious of disequilibrium, however, such an assumption becomes somewhat more plausible. If I know that I will have difficulty finding employment, for example, I am likely to be rather careful about spending all my money while looking for work. Certainly, I will be less likely to spend it all deliberately than I would in a world in which I erroneously thought I could find work whenever I wanted and could thus plan to live off current earnings rather than dipping into capital.

If we accept the No Bankruptcy assumption, however, there remains the question of whether Assumptions 2.1 and 3.1 are very plausible. I have already pointed out that the plausibility of the two-stage story turns, in a way, on how far from Walrasian equilibrium the system is perceived to be. The same is true for a more general reason. If the system is far from Walrasian equilibrium, the agents may feel that the target demands that they would like to exercise if they had the resources that generate them have little to do with the real world in which they live. Assumption 2.1 makes sense only if agents take their target excess demands as a reasonable starting point in constructing their active ones. If they regard quantity constraints as so severe that target excess demands are wholly unrealistic, then our analysis will not go through. This may be particularly likely where target excess demands involve spending the undistributed and unachieved profits of firms that are themselves far from being able to complete their transactions, but it can occur in pure exchange as well.

On the other hand, if target excess demands are a good starting point, then Assumptions 2.1 and 3.1 seem at least a possible story. In that case, the system is at least quasi-stable and, if the sort of experimentation involved in Assumption 3.1 is engaged in, will even converge to Walrasian equilibrium. Since target excess demands may be good starting points if the system is close to Walrasian equilibrium, this may be a reason for supposing that the process is locally, if not globally, stable and converges locally to Walrasian equilibrium. (Such an argument is only suggestive, however. A full proof of local stability would require showing that if the process starts in a region where Assumptions 2.1 and 3.1 are plausible, then it always remains in such a region.)

REFERENCES

Arrow, K. J. and Hahn, F. H. *General Competitive Analysis* (San Francisco: Holden-Day; and Edinburgh: Oliver & Boyd, 1971).

Barro, R. J. and Grossman, H. I. "A General Disequilibrium Model of Income and Employment", *American Economic Review*, **61** (March 1971), 82–93.

Benassy, J.-P. "NeoKeynesian Disequilibrium Theory in a Monetary Economy", *Review of Economic Studies*, **42** (October 1975), 503–524.

Benassy, J.-P. "The Disequilibrium Approach to Monopolistic Price Setting and General Monopolistic Equilibrium", *Review of Economic Studies*, **43** (February 1976), 69–82.

Benassy, J.-P. "Regulation of the Wage-Profits Conflict and the Unemployment-Inflation Dilemma in a 'Keyneso-Marxian' Dynamic Disequilibrium Model" (multilith).

Benassy, J.-P. "Theorie du Desequilibre et Fondements Microeconomiques de La Macroeconomie", *La Revue Economique* (forthcoming).

Champsaur, P., Drèze, J., and Henry, C. "Stability Theorems with Economic Applications", *Econometrica*, **45** (March 1977), 273–294.

Clower, R. W. "The Keynesian Counter-Revolution: A Theoretical Appraisal", in Hahn, F. H. and Brechling, F. P. R. (eds.), *The Theory of Interest Rates* (London: Macmillan, 1965).

Fisher, F. M. "Quasi-Competitive Price Adjustment by Individual Firms: A Preliminary Paper", *Journal of Economic Theory*, **2** (June 1970), 195–206. Reprinted as Chapter 2 in this volume.

Fisher, F. M. "On Price Adjustment without an Auctioneer", *Review of Economic Studies*, **39** (January 1972), 1–16. Reprinted as Chapter 4 in this volume.

Fisher, F. M. "Stability and Competitive Equilibrium in Two Models of Search and Individual Price Adjustment", *Journal of Economic Theory*, **6** (October 1973), 446–470. Reprinted as Chapter 3 in this volume.

Fisher, F. M. "The Hahn Process with Firms but No Production", *Econometrica*, **42** (May 1974), 471–486.

Fisher, F. M. "A Non-Tâtonnement Model with Production and Consumption", *Econometrica*, **44** (September 1976), 907–938.

Fisher, F. M. "The Stability of General Equilibrium: Results and Problems", in Artis and Nobay (eds.), *Essays in Economic Analysis (Proceedings of the Association of University Teachers of Economics, Annual Conference, Sheffield 1975)* (London and New York: Cambridge University Press, 1976). 3–29.

Fisher, F. M. "Continuously Dated Commodities and Nontâtonnement with Production and Consumption", in Blinder and Friedman (eds.), *Natural Resources, Uncertainty, and Dynamics: Essays in Honor of Rafael Lusky*. (New York: Academic Press, 1977).

Frevert, P. "On the Stability of Full Employment Equilibrium", *Review of Economic Studies*, **37** (April 1970), 239–251.

Hahn, F. H. and Negishi, T. "A Theorem on Non-Tâtonnement Stability", *Econometrica*, **30** (July 1962), 463–469.

Hayashi, F. "A Quantity Adjustment Process in a Pure Exchange Economy" (multilith).

Henry, C. "An Existence Theorem for a Class of Differential Equations with Multivalued Right-Hand Side", *Journal of Mathematical Analysis and Applications*, **41** (January 1973), 179–186.

Henry, C. "Problèmes, d'Existence et de Stabilité pour des Processus Dynamique Considerés en Economie Mathematique" (Laboratoire d'Econometrie de l'Ecole Polytechnique, March 1973).

Leijonhufvud, A. *On Keynesian Economics and the Economics of Keynes* (New York: Oxford University Press, 1968).

Leijonhufvud, A. "Effective Demand Failures", *Swedish Journal of Economics*, **75** (1973), 27–48.

Negishi, T. "The Stability of a Competitive Economy: A Survey Article", *Econometrica*, **30** (October 1962), 635–669.

Patinkin, D. *Money, Interest and Prices* (New York: Harper & Row, 1965).

Varian, H. "On Persistent Disequilibrium", *Journal of Economic Theory*, **10** (April 1975), 218–228.

Varian, H. "Non-Walrasian Equilibria", *Econometrica*, **45** (April 1977), 573–590.

Veendorp, E. C. H. "Stable Spillovers among Substitutes", *The Review of Economic Studies*, **42** (July 1975), 445–456.

CHAPTER 6

On Stability Analysis
with Disequilibrium Awareness (1988)

written jointly with Dale O. Stahl II

1. Introduction

Most of the existing literature on the stability of general equilibrium suffers from a common problem – the assumption that individual agents are unaware of the fact of disequilibrium.[1] Under tâtonnement, agents take current prices as given and report their demands as though the economy were in Walrasian equilibrium. In "non-tâtonnement," no-recontracting models (such as the Edgeworth process and the Hahn process), agents formulate demands again taking prices as given and paying no attention to the fact that they will often not be able to complete their planned transactions. In both types of models, the agents act as though they were in Walrasian equilibrium and simply fail to notice either that prices are not Walrasian and may change or that transactions may not be completed.[2]

Plainly, it is desirable to allow agents to have some idea of what is happening in disequilibrium and this paper attempts to do so in one particular way,[3] by allowing them to recognize that notional demands may not always be satisfied.[4] Indeed, in one sense, we go to the other extreme, permitting agents fully to understand the mechanism through which expressed demands are translated into actual trades.

We consider a wide class of deterministic mechanisms for a pure-

---

[1] For surveys, see Arrow and Hahn (1971), Fisher (1983), and Hahn (1982).

[2] There are two ways to interpret goods in non-tâtonnement models. One is that the goods are perfectly durable commodities, but nobody eats before the process terminates so what matters is the total accumulated stock. The other interpretation is that the goods are "commodity consols" that promise delivery of a constant flow of perishable commodities or services. In both interpretations trade is in "stocks."

[3] Fisher (1981, and especially 1983) gives a more ambitious, but not wholly satisfactory attempt to deal with the problem of disequilibrium awareness, permitting agents to expect price change as well as transaction restrictions.

[4] "Notional demand" is the traditional price-taking demand with *no* disequilibrium awareness. In contrast, "expressed demand" is the demand actually expressed (and acted upon) by the agent given his awareness of what happens in disequilibrium (such as rationing). The agent may expect to get something different from the demand he expresses; this expectation is referred to as "expected trade" or "target trade." Following the expression of demands, we get "actual trades."

exchange economy. Each such mechanism takes the demands expressed by agents and produces actual trades that clear all markets. We assume the trading mechanism is common knowledge. Hence, agents take the mechanism into account when formulating their expressed demands. Indeed, agents do more than that, for we assume that they understand not only how the trading mechanism generally works but also what its outcome will be in each instance. Therefore, given the prices, the expressed demands of all agents when transformed by the trading mechanism clear all markets, and agents get what they expect. Considering each trading moment as a game in which agents choose expressed demands as strategies and the market fine-tunes the trading mechanism as its strategy, agents and the market reach a Nash equilibrium at each moment of time. Nevertheless, there is "disequilibrium" in the sense that the trading mechanism distorts the opportunity sets from the usual price-taking budget sets, and agents end up with trades different from their notional demands.

The agents are required to have a large amount of information. In effect, they have momentary rational expectations of trade outcomes in this deterministic model. Note, however, that while we allow the agents to have full information about current transaction difficulties, we leave them naive about the future. Specifically, agents think nothing will change in the future, so the current period may as well (from their viewpoint) be the last. Agents do not expect prices to change and hence do not speculate in this model [unlike that of Fisher, (1983)].

Prices do change, nonetheless, reacting to signals given by the trading mechanism (the length of queues, for example). Hence, even though agents complete the transactions they expect, the economy does not stop moving until the trading mechanism ceases to produce disequilibrium signals, and notional demands, expressed demands, and actual trades all coincide. This feature of our model rules out non-Walrasian rest points.

Our principal result is that such a model is an Edgeworth process and hence globally stable. Naturally, given the way we have set it up, the equilibrium to which the model converges is Walrasian.[5]

2. The Deterministic Disequilibrium Awareness Model

The central feature of our model is the specification of a wide class of deterministic trading mechanisms. We assume pure exchange. Let z^i denote the vector of expressed demands (net of current stock) by the ith

---

[5] Whether that result would continue to hold if agents were permitted to expect price changes is at best doubtful. The Edgeworth process is not directly suited to situations of speculation and arbitrage; see Fisher (1983), pp. 30–1.

agent ($i = 1, \ldots, N$). Then a *trading mechanism* is a pair of functions (h, c). The function $h: \mathbb{R}^n \times \mathbb{R}^n \to \mathbb{R}^n$ is the *final trade function*, which for an arbitrary parameter vector $\tau \in \mathbb{R}^n$ (discussed later) takes expressed demand z^i and assigns final trade $y^i = h(\tau, z^i)$. Given a price vector p, the function $c: \mathbb{R}^n \times \mathbb{R}^n \to \mathbb{R}_+$ gives the additional *deadweight cost* imposed by the trading mechanism, so the total net costs of final trade y^i are

$$C(\tau, y^i; p) \equiv p \cdot y^i + c(\tau, y^i; p). \tag{1}$$

Typically, purchases will have a "marginal cost" $\partial C / \partial y_j \geq p_j$, while sales will have a "marginal revenue" $\partial C / \partial y_j \leq p_j$, where by "marginal revenue" is meant the marginal reduction in net costs. We require the functions $h(\cdot)$ and $c(\cdot)$ to be Lipschitzian continuous (hence differentiable almost everywhere). We also assume that $c(\cdot, 0; \cdot) = 0$, i.e., that no-trade ($y^i = 0$) is always feasible. When applicable, we assume the deadweight costs are paid in a numéraire commodity (say n).

An example of such a deterministic trading mechanism is queue-rationing (Stahl, 1988). To transform the queue-rationing model into this framework, interpret the expressed demand for time (z_n) to be the demand for time excluding the requirements of the queues. Then the only expressed demands that are altered by the trading mechanism are those for time; final trade in time is $z_n - Q(\tau, y)$. A coupon-rationing mechanism (e.g., Hahn, 1978) with tradeable coupons of intrinsic value [such as cigarettes in World War II POW camps (Radford, 1945)] is formally equivalent to queue-rationing. A third example is the quantity-rationing mechanism (e.g., Drèze, 1975) for which $c(\tau, y^i; p) = 0$. The quantity limit on purchases can be defined as $B_j \equiv L - \max\{0, \tau_j\}$, and for purchases $S_j \equiv L - \max\{0, -\tau_j\}$, for some appropriately large positive constant L.

Returning to general assumptions, the preferences of each agent are assumed to be represented by a twice-differentiable, strictly increasing, and strictly quasi-concave utility function $u^i: \mathbb{R}_+^n \to \mathbb{R}$. To avoid boundary cases, we assume that the indifference surfaces of u^i do not intersect the boundary of $\mathbb{R}_+^n$.[6] Without loss of generality, we choose an ordinal utility function that is bounded above.

Given a price vector p and an assumed strictly positive initial stock ω^i, each agent is assumed to choose an expressed demand z^i that maximizes $u^i(\omega^i + y^i)$, subject to two constraints: (1) $C(\tau, y^i; p) \leq 0$ and (2) $y^i = h(\tau, z^i) \geq -\omega^i$. The Lagrangian for this problem is

$$\mathcal{L} = u^i(\omega^i + y^i) - \lambda^i \{ p \cdot y^i + c(\tau, y^i; p) + \eta^i \cdot [y^i - h(\tau, z^i)] \}. \tag{2}$$

---

[6] Strictly increasing utility and the boundary condition are commonly assumed (e.g., Arrow and Hahn, 1971; Uzawa, 1960). We suspect a weaker assumption would suffice but not without tedious technical complications.

Note that given an interior endowment, since indifference curves do not intersect the boundary of $\mathbb{R}_+^n$, the non-negativity constraint ($y^i \geq -\omega^i$) can be safely ignored.

We define the "virtual price" as the derivative of the expression in braces $\{\cdot\}$ with respect to y^i. Since $c(\cdot)$ and $h(\cdot)$ are assumed to be Lipschitzian, left- and right-hand derivatives always exist. Let $\beta_j^i(\tau, p, y^i)$ denote the virtual price of commodity j obtained by approaching y_j^i from the positive direction, and let $\gamma_j^i(\tau, p, y^i)$ denote the virtual price of commodity j obtained by approaching y_j^i from the negative direction. The Kuhn–Tucker conditions require $\lambda^i \gamma_j^i(\tau, p, y^i) \leq \partial u^i / \partial \omega_j^i \leq \lambda^i \beta_j^i(\tau, p, y^i)$.

We shall assume *orderly markets*: that at most one side of any given market is "rationed." A buyer is rationed in commodity j if $y_j^i > 0$ and $\beta_j^i > p_j$. A seller is rationed in commodity j if $y_j^i < 0$ and $\gamma_j^i < p_j$. If some buyer (seller) is rationed in some commodity, then no sellers (buyers) are rationed in that commodity.

This brings us to the role of the parameter vector τ. We adopt the convention that $\tau_j > (<) 0$ whenever buyers (sellers) of commodity j are rationed. Then $\tau_j > 0$ implies: (a) if $y_j^i \geq 0$ then $\beta_j^i > p_j$; (b) if $y_j^i \leq 0$ then $\gamma_j^i = p_j$. Similarly, $\tau_j < 0$ implies: (a) if $y_j^i \geq 0$ then $\beta_j^i = p_j$; (b) if $y_j^i \leq 0$ then $\gamma_j^i < p_j$. Obviously then, $\tau_j = 0$ implies that neither buyers nor sellers are rationed in j.

Let $B(\tau, p)$ denote the *opportunity set*: the set of feasible trades (y^i) for agent i that satisfy the budget and quantity constraints imposed by the trading mechanism. We assume that $B(\cdot, \cdot)$ is non-empty, compact-valued, convex-valued, and continuous for all $p \gg 0$.[7]

Under these conditions, by standard proof, there is a unique continuous "target trade" function $\phi^i(\tau, p)$ that gives the trade y^i that maximizes $u^i(\omega^i + y^i)$ subject to the constraints embodied in $B(\tau, p)$. Moreover, any expressed demand z^i such that $h(\tau, z^i) = \phi^i(\tau, p)$ is optimal. Let $\zeta^i(\tau, p) \equiv \{z^i \mid h(\tau, z^i) = \phi^i(\tau, p)\}$ denote the "expressed demand correspondence." When $\tau = 0$, the opportunity set is just the usual price-taking budget set, so $\phi^i(0, p) = \zeta^i(0, p)$ is the notional demand.

We now aggregate trade behavior. Define

$$\phi(\tau, p) \equiv \sum_{i=1}^N \phi^i(\tau, p) \qquad (3)$$

and

---

[7] This is an implicit restriction on the trading mechanisms. The examples mentioned above have this property.

$$\zeta(\tau, p) \equiv \sum_{i=1}^{N} \zeta^i(\tau, p).$$

Note that when $\tau = 0$, we have $\phi(0, p) = \zeta(0, p)$, the aggregate notional demand. If, in addition, for some p^*, $0 = \phi(0, p^*) = \zeta(0, p^*)$, then p^* is by definition a Walrasian equilibrium price. Let W denote the set of *Walrasian prices*.

For those trading mechanisms that impose actual payment of dead-weight costs c when $\tau \neq 0$ (in contrast to simply utility losses), there will be a positive aggregate deadweight cost:

$$c(\tau, p) \equiv \sum_{i=1}^{N} c[\tau, \phi^i(\tau, p); p]. \tag{4}$$

In such a case, it is too much to ask that final trades $\phi(\tau, p) = 0$, since this condition is incompatible with Walras' law and the payment of the deadweight costs: $p \cdot \phi(\tau, p) + c(\tau, p) = 0$. The most we can require is that $\phi_j(\tau, p) = 0$ for all $j \neq n$ (where n is the numéraire in which dead-weight costs are paid), implying via Walras' law that $p_n \cdot \phi_n(\tau, p) + c(\tau, p) = 0$. That is, $\phi(\tau, p) = (0^{n-1}, -c(\tau, p)/p_n)$, where 0^{n-1} is the zero vector in $\mathbb{R}^{n-1}$. Of course, if the trading mechanism imposes no actual payment of deadweight costs (i.e., $c = 0$ as in the Drèze mechanism), then $\phi(\tau, p) = 0$ and all markets clear in the normal sense.

We thus say that (h, c) *is an effective trading mechanism* if for every price $p \gg 0$ there exists a unique $\tau^*(p)$ such that $\phi[\tau^*(p), p] + (0^{n-1}, -c[\tau^*(p), p]/p_n) = 0$. In other words, for any arbitrary positive price there exists a unique τ^* such that final trades "clear" (subject to deadweight costs).

Effective trading mechanisms are really the only interesting ones. If final trades do not clear, the trading mechanism is incompletely defined. Should expressed demand exceed supply in some commodity, what is the final outcome? The resolution of such discrepancies by definition yields a deterministic vector y^i for each agent such that the aggregate final trades "clear"; hence, the total process would be an effective trading mechanism. Further, suppose that $\tau^*(p)$ is not unique. If there are multiple values of τ that would work, then the mechanism remains incompletely specified until a single selection is made.

We say that (h, c) is a *regular* effective trading mechanism if (a) $\tau^*(p) = 0$ iff $p \in W$, (b) $\tau_n^* = 0$ independent of p, and (c) $\tau^*(p)$ is a piecewise Lipschitzian continuous function.[8] Recall that if $p \in W$, then $\phi(0, p) =$

---

[8] A function $f: X \to \mathbb{R}$ is "piecewise Lipschitzian continuous" if there is a partition $\{X_R\}$ of the domain such that for all k, $f(\cdot)$ restricted to the interior of X_k is Lipschitzian continuous.

0, so markets clear; in other words, $\tau^* = 0$ is a possible solution. Condition (a) requires that $\tau^* = 0$ in fact be the only outcome whenever the price is Walrasian for the given endowments. Obviously, without such a condition, we would have little hope for stability. Condition (b) says that the numéraire commodity is unrationed, which is compatible with typical rationing mechanisms in the literature. Condition (c) means that the price domain can be partitioned into a finite number of regions in the interior of which $\tau^*(\cdot)$ is C^1 almost everywhere. To see that this is a mild assumption, first note that the existence of a $\tau^*(p)$ satisfying effectiveness will follow from a familiar fixed point argument. In general, there may be multiple values of τ that would work (i.e., clear the markets). The correspondence of these "workable" τ's would be upper hemicontinuous and would admit local Lipschitzian selections. The effectiveness assumption means that one local Lipschitzian selection is made. Conditions (a) and (b) constrain this selection, and condition (c) merely assumes directly that it is piecewise Lipschitzian continuous.[9]

To summarize, agents know the trading mechanism, and take p and τ^* as fixed. [Note that we have implicitly assumed that τ^* is perfectly observable by all consumers; otherwise, the optimization problem involving $h(\tau^*, z^i)$ would be incompletely specified.] Agents choose an optimal expressed demand, $\zeta^i(\tau^*, p)$, while they expect to get $\phi^i(\tau^*, p) = h[\tau^*, \zeta^i(\tau^*, p)]$. The trading mechanism determines τ^*, hence final trades, such that all markets "clear": $\phi(\tau^*, p) = (0^{n-1}, -c(\tau^*, p)/p_n)$, so every agent gets what he or she expects. Further, $\tau^*(p) = 0$ iff p is Walrasian, in which case notional demands, expressed demands, and final trades all coincide.

It is important to recognize that whether or not actual final trades $\phi^i(\tau^*, p)$ are the same as expressed demands $\zeta^i(\tau^*, p)$, all agents correctly foresee their final trades, and hence satisfy their budget constraints and realize their anticipated utility $u^i(\omega^i + y^i)$. Consequently, "target" utility is not declining out of Walrasian equilibrium, and since this is the crucial feature of the Hahn process, we obviously cannot use that argument here. On the other hand, trade is voluntary so in a sense utility must be

---

[9] The queue-rationing and coupon-rationing trading mechanisms mentioned earlier are each regular and effective for non-critical economies. Note, however, that a coupon-rationing mechanism with marketable coupons at a fixed positive price is *not* a regular trading mechanism because if $p \in W$ and $\tau = 0$ there will be excess expressed demand since everyone will want to sell coupons and purchase more goods. On the other hand, if the coupon's market value is endogenized (as in a black market) and if τ is interpreted as the "money" value of coupon surcharges, then regularity is restored.

It is interesting to note, however, that "deterministic proportional rationing" (which gives every agent a fraction of his expressed demand) is not an effective trading mechanism because for every $p \notin W$ and τ, the mechanism can be completely undone: there is an expressed demand z^i such that $h(\tau, z^i) = \phi^i(0, p)$, the notional demand (see Bennasy, 1977).

increasing, which is a crucial step in showing that the Edgeworth process is globally stable.

3.   Dynamics

In general, price may respond to information about both the trading mechanism's signal (τ^*) and aggregate expressed demand (ζ). For convenience, we shall proceed by assuming prices respond to τ^* only. Generalization is easy provided the properties about to be assumed are preserved.

To this end, let $dp/dt = f(\tau)$, where $f(\cdot)$ is continuous and $f(\tau) = 0$ iff $\tau = 0$. Then, the set of stationary points are Walrasian equilibria. Given orderly markets and our sign convention on τ, it is natural to assume that $f(\cdot)$ is sign preserving in the sense that $f_j(\tau)$ has the same sign as τ_j, which we henceforth do. [A special case would be to have $f_j(\cdot)$ depend only on τ_j and to preserve sign.] Furthermore, we assume a minimum speed of adjustment ($\sigma > 0$) such that $|f_j(\tau)| \geq \sigma |\tau_j|$.

In the static analysis of section 2, the endowments of agents were suppressed from the notation. We must now incorporate them into the notation. Let $\underline{\omega} \equiv \{\omega^1, \ldots, \omega^N\}$ denote the distribution of stock holdings. For every $\underline{\omega}$, the static solution in more explicit notation is $\tau^*(p, \underline{\omega})$. Regularity now entails that $\tau^*(\cdot, \cdot)$ is jointly piecewise Lipschitzian.

With trade in stocks, we must consider the dynamic path of $\underline{\omega}$ as well. As we pass from a discrete time process to a continuous time process, at points of continuity $d\omega^i/dt = \lim_{T \to 0} y^i/T \equiv \hat{\phi}^i(\tau, p, \omega^i)$. Define $G(p, \underline{\omega}) \equiv (\hat{\phi}^1[\tau^*(p, \underline{\omega}), p, \omega^1], \ldots, \hat{\phi}^N[\tau^*(p, \underline{\omega}), p, \omega^N])$ to be the vector of instantaneous trades expressed as a function of $(p, \underline{\omega})$ alone.

Now because we have not assumed $\tau^*(p, \omega)$ to be globally Lipschitzian continuous, we must deal with possible discontinuities. At a point where $\tau^*(\cdot)$ is discontinuous, optimal consumer behavior will in general prescribe a discrete but finite change in stocks. To capture this behavior in our notation we define the "impulse function" $v: \mathbb{R} \to \mathbb{R}$ such that $v(t) = 0$ for all $t \neq 0$ and $\int_{-\infty}^{\infty} v(t)\, dt = 1$. Then, if stocks take a discrete jump of $\Delta\underline{\omega}$ at time t', we can express this as $d\underline{\omega}/dt = \Delta\underline{\omega}\, v(t')$. Thus, by allowing $G(p, \underline{\omega})$ to include impulse functions, the dynamic path of stocks can be expressed unambiguously as $d\underline{\omega}/dt = G(p, \underline{\omega})$.

Next define $F(p, \underline{\omega}) \equiv f[\tau^*(p, \underline{\omega})]$. Our general dynamic adjustment process is then

$$dp/dt = F(p, \underline{\omega})$$
$$d\underline{\omega}/dt = G(p, \underline{\omega}). \tag{5}$$

At points where $\tau^*(\cdot)$ is Lipschitzian continuous, $F(\cdot)$ and $G(\cdot)$ are Lipschitzian also, so that starting from such a point $(p_0, \underline{\omega}_0)$ there will exist a locally unique solution path $p(t, p_0, \underline{\omega}_0)$ and $\underline{\omega}(t, p_0, \underline{\omega}_0)$. At points where $\tau^*(\cdot)$ is discontinuous, the impulse function part of $G(\cdot)$ determines the discrete change in $\underline{\omega}(t, p_0, \underline{\omega}_0)$. At this instant, $F(\cdot)$ will take a finite jump, so dp/dt will also, but the solution path $p(t, p_0, \underline{\omega}_0)$ will remain continuous. It would be a sheer coincidence if $\tau^*(\cdot)$ had a discontinuity at the new point with the same price but discretely different stock distribution. In that rare event, a solution path may not be well defined. We assume directly that this coincidence does not occur so that (5) has a well-defined (not necessarily unique) solution path.

The central question is whether such a process is globally stable; i.e., starting at arbitrary $(p_0, \underline{\omega}_0)$ does the process always converge to some Walrasian point?

Theorem 1. *In our model of deterministic disequilibrium awareness and trade in stocks, given a regular effective trading mechanism that satisfies orderly markets, and given the preceding assumptions, the dynamic system (5) is globally stable and converges to a Walrasian equilibrium.*

Proof. At each stage, an agent is fully aware of the trading mechanism and makes a trade offer that ultimately changes his stock portfolio if and only if the correctly foreseen change will increase his utility. Therefore, u^i is always non-decreasing and is strictly increasing whenever $d\omega^i/dt \neq 0$. Thus, the temporal sequence of u^i values must converge monotonically to a limit, say $\bar{u}^i$. Moreover, given strictly increasing and strictly concave utility, the corresponding sequence of $d\omega^i/dt$ must converge to 0. (See the Appendix.)

Since the consumer is perfectly aware of the trading mechanism, he correctly foresees the deadweight costs and can avoid with certainty running out of stocks, which he will avoid since utility is strictly increasing and indifference surfaces do not intersect the boundary of $\mathbb{R}_+^n$. Thus, $\underline{\omega}(t)$ is bounded away from zero in every component for all t. Further, given twice-differentiable utility functions, along this strictly positive path of $\underline{\omega}(t)$, the first and second derivatives of $u^i(\cdot)$ are bounded.

Recall the definitions of the virtual prices β_j^i and γ_j^i. For the natural numéraire (commodity n), $\tau_n = 0$ and $\omega_n^i > 0$; hence, $\gamma_n^i(\tau, p, y^i) = \beta_n^i(\tau, p, y^i) = p_n$ for all i and all (τ, p, y^i). Thus, $\partial u^i/\partial \omega_n^i = \lambda^i p_n$. Now let $\mu_j^i \equiv (\partial u^i/\partial \omega_j^i)/(\partial u^i/\partial \omega_n^i)$ for $j \neq n$ denote the marginal rate of substitution evaluated at ω^i, and let $\hat{\gamma}_j^i \equiv \gamma_j^i/p_n$ and $\hat{\beta}_j^i \equiv \beta_j^i/p_n$. Then the Kuhn–Tucker conditions require $\hat{\gamma}_j^i \leq \mu_j^i \leq \hat{\beta}_j^i$ for all $j \neq n$ and every agent. It is convenient to let $\hat{p} \equiv p/p_n$ denote the relative prices with respect to the numéraire.

Define $\alpha \equiv \max_{i,j}\{|\mu_j^i - \hat{p}_j|\}$. Note that $\alpha \geq 0$ and equal to zero iff $\tau = 0$. To see this, (1) if $\alpha = 0$, so that $\mu_j^i = \hat{p}_j$ for all i and j, then (by strict quasi-concavity of the utility functions) the desired final trade is $y^i = 0$, which is the same as the Walrasian notional demand (i.e., the current ω^i is optimal with respect to $p \cdot y^i \leq 0$), so p is a Walrasian price. But then by regularity of the trading mechanism, $\tau = 0$. (2) If $\tau = 0$, then $\hat{\gamma}_j^i = \mu_j^i = \hat{\beta}_j^i = \hat{p}$ for all i and j, so clearly $\alpha = 0$.

We will now prove that $\alpha(t)$ converges to zero. Let $H(t) \equiv \{(i, r): \alpha(t) = |\mu_r^i - \hat{p}_r|\}$, i.e., the set of maximizers. We will consider two cases.

First, suppose t'' is a continuity point and $\alpha(t'') = \bar{\alpha} > 0$. By continuity of $|\mu_j^h - \hat{p}_j|$, $H(t)$ is upper hemi-continuous, which implies that there is an $(i, r) \in H(t'')$ and a $t' < t''$ such that, for all $t \in (t', t'')$, $(i, r) \in H(t)$ and $\alpha(t) = |\mu_r^i - \hat{p}_r| \geq \bar{\alpha}/2 > 0$. Consider two possibilities. (1) If $\alpha(t) = \mu_r^i - \hat{p}_r > 0$, then $\tau_r \geq \varepsilon > 0$, where ε depends on $\bar{\alpha}$. Hence, given the minimum speed of adjustment, $d\hat{p}/dt \geq \sigma\varepsilon > 0$. Since $u^i(\cdot)$ has bounded first and second derivatives, $d\mu_r^i/dt \to 0$ (from simple differentiation and the fact that $d\omega^i/dt \to 0$). Then, for t'' sufficiently large, $d\alpha/dt = d\mu_r^i/dt - d\hat{p}/dt < -\sigma\varepsilon/2 < 0$. (2) If $\alpha(t) = \hat{p}_r - \mu_r^i > 0$, then $\tau_r \leq -\varepsilon < 0$, so $d\hat{p}/dt < -\sigma\varepsilon$. Again, for sufficiently large t'', $d\alpha/dt < -\sigma\varepsilon/2 < 0$. Hence, for large t, $\alpha(t)$ is strictly decreasing at all continuity points. Moreover, if there were no upward discontinuities for $t > t''$, then clearly $\alpha(t)$ would monotonically decline to zero.

Second, suppose t'' is a discontinuity point. In other words, at t'', $\tau^*(\cdot)$ has a discontinuity that induces a discrete change in stocks $\underline{\omega}$, implying a discrete change in μ^i for some consumers, and hence a discrete jump in α equal to say $\Delta\alpha$. Recall that $p(\cdot)$ is continuous at all t. Let t''^+ and t''^- stand for the instant just after and just before t'', in the sense that $\Delta\alpha = \alpha(t''^+) - \alpha(t''^-)$. Let $(i, r) \in H(t''^+)$ and $(j, s) \in H(t''^-)$. By definition of α, $\alpha(t''^-) = |\mu_s^j(t''^-) - \hat{p}_s(t''^-)| > |\mu_r^i(t''^-) - \hat{p}_r(t''^-)|$. Thus,

$$\Delta\alpha = |\mu_r^i(t''^+) - \hat{p}_r(t''^+)| - |\mu_s^j(t''^-) - \hat{p}_s(t''^-)|$$
$$< |\mu_r^i(t''^+) - \hat{p}_r(t''^+)| - |\mu_r^i(t''^-) - \hat{p}_r(t''^-)|$$
$$\leq |\mu_r^i(t''^+) - \mu_r^i(t''^-)| \equiv |\Delta\mu_r^i|.$$

Since $u^i(\cdot)$ is C^2, $d\mu^i/d\omega^i$ is well defined and finite. Thus, there is a $K \in (0, \infty)$ such that $\|\Delta\mu^i\| < K \|\Delta\omega_i\|$. Then since $\|\Delta\omega^i\| \to 0$, by Lemma 2 of the Appendix, so does $\Delta\alpha$. Moreover, the cumulation of $\|\Delta\omega^i\|$ over any finite time interval $(t, t + T)$ must also converge to zero, which implies that the cumulation of jumps in α over any finite time interval must also converge to zero.

We now show that indeed $\alpha(t) \to 0$. Suppose to the contrary that the upward jumps dominate the monotone decline at continuity points for infinitely many finite time intervals $(t, t + T)$, so α is bounded above zero by say $\bar{a} > 0$. But then at continuity points $d\alpha/dt < - \sigma\varepsilon < 0$ (where ε is fixed by $\bar{a}$). Thus, the decline of the continuous component is at least $\sigma\varepsilon T$, whereas the cumulated upward jumps are vanishing, so α must eventually become negative: a contradiction, which proves the claim.

Since the μ_j^i are bounded and $\alpha(t)$ converges, prices are bounded, so prices have a well-defined limit set. Moreover, since the μ_j^i are strictly positive, and $\alpha \to 0$, the limit prices are strictly positive. Since we have a pure exchange economy with fixed finite stocks, $\underline{\omega}(t)$ is bounded and so has a well-defined limit set. Let $(p', \underline{\omega}')$ and $(p'', \underline{\omega}'')$ denote two limit points, where (p', p'') are derived from a subsequence of the respective sequences $t_\lambda \to \infty$ that generated $(\underline{\omega}', \underline{\omega}'')$.

Now we have $u^i(\omega^{i\prime}) = u^i(\omega^{i\prime\prime}) = \bar{u}^i$; i.e., the final stock allocations are on the same indifference surfaces. Moreover, since $\tau = 0$, total net costs $C(0, y^i; p') = p' \cdot y^i$. Letting $y^i = (\omega^{i\prime} - \omega^{i\prime\prime})$, then by strict quasi-concavity, $p' \cdot (\omega^{i\prime} - \omega^{i\prime\prime}) \leq 0$ with strict inequality unless $(\omega^{i\prime} - \omega^{i\prime\prime}) = 0$ (recall that prices are strictly positive). But $(\omega^{i\prime} - \omega^{i\prime\prime})$ summed over all i is identically zero (by virtue of pure exchange), so $(\omega^{i\prime} - \omega^{i\prime\prime}) = 0$ for all i. In other words, the stocks converge for each agent to (say) $\bar{\omega}^i$.

Given $\bar{\omega}^i \gg 0$ and strict quasi-concavity, the μ_j^i must also converge, which implies (since $\alpha \to 0$) that the prices must converge to a Walrasian equilibrium price. Q.E.D.

4. Conclusion

We have approached the issue of disequilibrium awareness by specifying a general deterministic trading mechanism and supposing that all agents know the trading mechanism perfectly (albeit myopically). We defined a regular effective trading mechanism such that final trades clear for every price and assumed it has the "orderly markets" property. The observable parameter of the trading mechanism (τ) was a natural signal for price adjustment.

When trade is in stocks,[10] we found that the natural sign-preserving price adjustment process is globally stable. This result followed from a regularity condition on the trading mechanism and mild conditions on agent preferences.

---

[10] Observing that a significant portion of trade in the real world is in spot flows and not stocks (or commodity consols), it would be desirable to study economies in which trading is in flows. In such economies, the income effects that plague traditional tâtonnement theory continue to be troublesome in the presence of disequilibrium awareness. While conditions for local stability (e.g., eigenvalue conditions) can be easily stated, the results are far from a satisfactory answer to stability questions.

This global stability result for trade in stocks is an improvement over the received non-tâtonnement results because agents make offers with perfect awareness of the trading mechanism, rather than blindly pursuing trade demands in complete ignorance of prices being non-Walrasian. Thus, the Edgeworth process is compatible with perfect disequilibrium awareness of this type.

On the other hand, this very result immediately implies that the Hahn process is not compatible with the kind of disequilibrium awareness studied here. This is because, with perfect awareness of the outcome of the trading mechanism, every agent gets what he or she expects. Although the system, nevertheless, keeps moving out of equilibrium,[11] there is no reason for every agent to find that prices move perversely, as in the Hahn process. Indeed, there are "favorable surprises" (see Fisher, 1981, 1983), although, of course, such surprises disappear asymptotically.

Evidently, disequilibrium dynamics are quite sensitive to the way in which agents understand what is going on. We have shown here that, in a wide class of models, allowing agents fully to understand the way in which expressed demands result in final trades leads to stability. We have not allowed agents to foresee the motion of the system, however; indeed, we have kept them from realizing that prices change, even though prices react to the very trading mechanism that agents are supposed to understand so well.

Our agents are thus unrealistically well informed and sophisticated in some respects and unrealistically ignorant and naive in others. Further work in this area is highly desirable if we are ever to understand how (or if) real economies succeed in reaching equilibrium.

Appendix

Lemma 1. *Let* $y^i = \phi^i(\tau, p)$. *Given* $0 < \varepsilon < M < \infty$, *there exists a* $\delta > 0$ *such that* $\Delta u^i \equiv u^i(\omega^i + y^i) - u^i(\omega^i) \geq \delta \, \|y^i\|$ *for all* $\varepsilon < \|y^i\| < M$. [$M$ *and* ω^i *can be chosen as large as the size of the aggregate endowment of the economy.*]

---

[11] Fisher (1983, pp. 181–184) points out that perfect foresight about the ability to transact in disequilibrium (here, perfect awareness of the trading mechanism) is likely to be uninteresting as it implies that the system never moves. That result, however, applies where the system (prices, in particular) reacts to the difference between agents' expected (target) trade and actual trade, and this difference is identically zero given perfect awareness. It is avoided here because prices react to disequilibrium signals (namely τ^*) stemming from the difference between actual trades, $\phi^i(\tau^*, p)$, and notional demands, $\phi^i(0, p)$, and this difference vanishes if and only if $\tau^* = 0$. Hence, prices keep moving even though markets "clear" (in the sense that the trading mechanism always gives agents what they expect).

Proof. Since trade is voluntary, $\Delta u^i \geq 0$ always. Hence, the only way the lemma could be false is if for some $y^i \neq 0$, $\Delta u^i = 0$. But since the feasible set is convex, $y^i/2$ is also feasible, and by strict quasi-concavity of utility, $y^i/2$ is preferred: a contradiction.   Q.E.D.

Remark 1. In a formal derivation of the continuous time model, the time path would be the limit of an appropriate sequence of discrete time paths. Between each "decision period" we can insert two artificial periods of length T, and specify that the stocks change at the constant rate y^i/T over the first artificial period, and that prices change at the constant rate of $\Delta p/T$ over the second period. By letting the length of these discrete periods shrink to zero (noting that Δp^i and hence y^i (a.e.) would also shrink to zero), we would approach the continuous time path and $\lim_{T\to\infty}(y^i/T) = d\omega^i/dt$. Thus, the continuous time corollary of Lemma 1 is that there is a $\delta > 0$ such that $du^i/dt \geq \delta \, \|d\omega^i/dt\|$ for $0 < \varepsilon < \|d\omega^i/dt\| < M < \infty$.

Lemma 2. $y^i \to 0$.

Proof. Consider a discrete time process in which y^i is the optimal change in stock for a single period. Suppose to the contrary that $\|y^i\| \geq \varepsilon > 0$ infinitely often. Then, by Lemma 1, $u^i \to \infty$: a contradiction.

                                                        Q.E.D.

Remark 2. Recalling Remark 1, the continuous time version of Lemma 2 is that $d\omega^i/dt \to 0$. Moreover, by the same argument, the cumulative stock changes $\int_{t_0}^{\infty} \|d\omega^i/dt\| \, dt < \infty$. Hence, for any $T > 0$. $\int_{t'}^{t'+T} \|d\omega^i/dt\| \, dt \to 0$ as $t' \to \infty$.

REFERENCES

K. J. Arrow and F. H. Hahn, "General Competitive Analysis," Holden-Day, San Francisco, 1971.

J. P. Bennasy, On quantity signals and the foundation of effective demand theory, *Scand. J. Econ.* **79** (1977), 147–168.

J. Drèze, Existence of an exchange equilibrium under price rigidities, *Int. Econ. Rev.* **16** (1975), 301–320.

F. M. Fisher, Disequilibrium awareness, and the perception of new opportunities, *Econometrica* **49** (1981), 279–317.

F. M. Fisher, "Disequilibrium Foundations of Equilibrium Economics," Cambridge Univ. Press, London/New York, 1983.

F. H. Hahn, On non-Walrasian equilibrium, *Rev. Econ. Stud.* **46** (1978), 1–18.

F. H. Hahn, Stability, *in* "Handbook of Mathematical Economics" (K. J. Arrow and M. D. Intriligator, Eds.), Chap. 16, North-Holland, Amsterdam, 1982.

R. A. Radford, The economic organization of a P.O.W. camp, *Economica* **12** (1945), 189–201.

D. O. Stahl, Queue-rationing and price dynamics, *Scand. J. Econ.* **24** (1988), 197–216.

H. Uzawa, On the stability of Edgeworth's barter process, *Int. Econ. Rev.* **3** (1960), 218–232.

CHAPTER 7

It Takes t^* to Tango: Trading
Coalitions with Fixed Prices (1989)

1.   Introduction

The basic assumption of the Edgeworth non-tâtonnement process is that trade takes place if and only if there exists a coalition of agents able to make a Pareto-improving trade among themselves at current, disequilibrium prices. In or out of the Edgeworth-process context, this seems an attractive assumption. There are, however, objections to it (Fisher (1976, p. 12), (1983, pp. 29–31)). One of these is that the formation of such coalitions may impose very high information requirements. In particular, a very large number of agents may have to find each other. In reply to this, David Schmeidler has observed (in a private communication) that such trading coalitions need never involve more members than the number of commodities, while Paul Madden has shown that, if all agents always have strictly positive endowments of all commodities, then such coalitions need never have more than two members. (Both results can be found in Madden (1978).)

These are not very reassuring answers to the problem at hand, however, particularly if one thinks of extending the Edgeworth-process assumption to relatively realistic settings. If consumption takes place at different times, then the same commodity at different dates will be treated as different commodities. This can easily make the number of commodities much greater than the number of agents in the economy. As for Madden's bilateral trade result, it requires strictly positive endowments of all commodities for all agents, and this is far too strong a requirement in the context of disequilibrium trade.[1]

I am indebted to a referee for comments and to Peter A. Diamond and John Moore for helpful discussion but retain responsibility for errors. I wish to dedicate this chapter to the memory of my aunt and dancing teacher, Ethel Fisher Korn, who could, if necessary, tango all by herself.

[1] Existing proofs of stability in the Edgeworth process require the positive endowment assumption anyway (Hahn (1962), Uzawa (1962), Arrow and Hahn (1971, pp. 328–337)). Thus Madden's result formally answers the criticism that large numbers of traders may be required. That answer will not be satisfactory, however, if the analysis is ever to be advanced beyond such a strong assumption.

It is therefore of some interest to see the extent to which the two existing results can be generalized. It turns out to be possible to accomplish this with very elementary methods. Unfortunately, results show that the Edgeworth-process assumption may impose very heavy information requirements on coalition formation, and that those requirements can arise in a way other than that of requiring coalitions with large numbers of agents. (Obviously, such results have some interest beyond the non-tâtonnement stability context. They directly affect what one can plausibly assume about trading at fixed prices, a subject on which there is a large literature.)

The reason for this is that, once the positive endowment assumption is relaxed, the only possible Edgeworth-process trades may take a form that I shall call "compound trade" as opposed to "simple trade". Simple trade involves a circle of transactions in which each household sells one commodity and buys another, thereby (weakly) increasing its utility. Compound trade, on the other hand, involves transactions in which some household sells one commodity and buys another even though it would prefer not to do so, because the sale involved induces another household to enter into a transaction that eventually leads to an increase in the original household's utility. I shall be precise about this below and shall show that the information on preferences required to form compound trades is considerably more detailed than that required to form simple ones. In addition, coalition size is not so easily restricted for compound trades as for simple ones.

The fact that detailed information on preferences is required for compound trades and that the number of households needed can be large suggests that the natural assumption to make in a non-cooperative, competitive setting is not that of the Edgeworth process but rather that trade will take place if and only if there exists a coalition of agents able to make a Pareto-improving *simple* trade among themselves at current prices. This makes the analysis of simple trade worth doing, and the results are easy to obtain and fairly rich. I note, however, that the possibility that compound trade may be required for Pareto improvement means that some additional trading assumption will be required to generate stability.

2.   The *t*-Wise Optimality Literature

Even for simple trades, however, the results obtained below are considerably weaker than results on the related question of when "*t*-wise optimality" – the non-existence of Pareto-improving trades involving no more than t traders for some arbitrary t – is equivalent to full Pareto optimality. (See Feldman (1973), Graham, Jennergen, Peterson, and Weintraub (1976), Madden (1975), Rader (1968), (1976), and, especially, Goldman and Starr (1982).) The reasons for that difference are very instructive and are best understood after an example.

Consider Theorem 1.1 in Goldman and Starr (1982, p. 597), a theorem originally due to Rader. It states that, provided there is a trader holding positive quantities of all goods, then the absence of any mutually-improving bilateral trade implies Pareto-optimality, so that there are no mutually-improving trades for any number of traders. Put differently, the existence of some mutually-improving trade implies the existence of a mutually-improving bilateral trade.

The proof of this theorem consists in observing that prices corresponding to the marginal utilities of the trader who holds all goods (say trader 1) must support a Pareto optimum since otherwise some mutually-improving bilateral trade would be possible. True enough. If, for trader 2, the marginal rate of substitution between some pair of goods were different from that of trader 1, then a mutually-improving bilateral trade between them would be possible at some other set of prices.

Note, however, that this leads to a contradiction only because it is assumed that no mutually-improving bilateral trade is possible at *any* prices. The equivalent assumption in the present case would be the much weaker one that no mutually-improving bilateral trade is possible at a *given* set of prices. That this does not lead to the same result can be seen by observing that, if prices happen to be equal to trader 1's marginal utilities, trader 1 will not wish to trade. Hence, the possible trade between traders 1 and 2 will not be possible at the *given* prices, and no contradiction arises. Indeed, in this situation (without further assumptions), there is nothing to prevent there being a mutually-improving trade involving several (or all) traders other than trader 1.

The general point is as follows. In showing that the existence of some mutually-improving trade implies the existence of such a trade with no more than t traders, the t-wise optimality literature effectively considers the case in which no t-wise improving trade is possible at *any* set of prices. This is a much stronger assumption than the condition that no t-wise improving trade be possible at *given* prices, and it is therefore not surprising that it leads to much stronger results.

Since trade in actual economies often takes place at given prices, however, it is interesting to know how many traders are required with prices fixed. That problem is studied here.

3.   Preliminaries: Simple Trades and Compound Trades

There are h households and n commodities. Each household has a differentiable, locally-nonsatiated, strictly quasi-concave utility function that is non-decreasing in its arguments.[2] Prices are assumed to be strictly positive. (This is mainly a convenience.[3])

Definition 1. An Edgeworth-process trade is a trade at given prices such that, with all participants in the trade on their budget constraints, no participant's utility decreases and at least one participant's utility increases.

For later purposes, observe that the strict quasi-concavity of the utility functions implies that an Edgeworth-process trade remains an Edgeworth-process trade if the amounts of each commodity traded by each participant are all mutiplied by the same scalar, λ, $0 < \lambda \leqq 1$. We can thus consider very small trades and work in terms of marginal rates of substitution.

Lemma 1.   *In an Edgeworth-process trade, it is not possible to partition the participating households into two sets, A and B, such that some household in A sells some commodity to a household in B but no household in B sells any commodity to any household in A.*

Proof.   Suppose not. Then the total wealth of households in A would be greater after the trade than before, contradicting the fact that all households must remain on their budget constraints.   ‖

Now consider an Edgeworth-process trade that involves household i selling commodity j to household i'. Household i' must sell to some other household or households, and they in turn must sell to others, and

---

[2] Strict quasi-concavity is not to be interpreted to rule out the possibility of satiation in one or more (but not all) goods, so that indifference surfaces can become parallel to one or more of the axes.

　　The assumption of differentiability can almost certainly be weakened to the requirement that indifference surfaces have unique supporting hyperplanes (Madden (1978, p. 281)), but there seems little gain in complicating the exposition to do so. Apart from the method of proof used, one needs to rule out cases such as the following. Suppose that household 1 regards apples and bananas as perfect complements while households 2 and 3 do not. In that circumstance, the three households may have a Pareto-improving trade in which 1 sells carrots to 2 for apples and to 3 for bananas. Such a trade can require three participants even though a particular household (1) participates in all transactions. This makes calculation of the minimum number of participants tedious at best, and, as the circumstance involved is quite special, it does not seem worth pursuing (although it might be possible to handle it along the lines of the treatment given to "compound" trades below). (Note that if *all* agents view a given subset of commodities as perfect complements using the same proportions, then, without loss of generality, that subset can be renamed as a composite commodity.)

[3] The principal complication avoided is that of keeping track of gifts in which one household gives a free good to another without getting anything in return.

so on. All of these households will be said to buy commodity j from household i, directly or indirectly. Denote the set of such households as $B(i, j)$.

Lemma 2. *Household i is a member of $B(i, j)$.*

Proof. Suppose not. Take A as the set of households involved in the Edgeworth-process trade that are not in $B(i, j)$. Take B as $B(i, j)$. Then Lemma 1 is contradicted. ‖

Hence every sale (or purchase) of a commodity by a household in an Edgeworth-process trade involves a circle of households and commodities, with each household in a circle buying a commodity from the preceding one and selling a commodity to the succeeding one. We can think of transactions in which a given household buys or sells more than one commodity as involving more than one circle (possibly with all the same households and almost all the same commodities).

Definition 2. An Edgeworth-process trade is called "simple" if at least one of the circles composing it is itself an Edgeworth-process trade. An Edgeworth-process trade that is not simple will be called "compound".

In other words, in a simple Edgeworth-process trade, the households participating in at least one circle would be willing to do so even if they were not also participating in other circles. Such a trade obviously can be simplified. In a compound Edgeworth-process trade, on the other hand, at least one household participating in any circle only does so because such participation is required to bring a different circle into existence.

An example will help here. Figure 7.1 shows a trade consisting of two "circles". Nodes in the diagram represent households, indicated by numbers, while arrows denote sales of commodities, indicated by letters. Thus, in the diagrammed trade, the right-hand "circle" has household 1 selling commodity a to household 2, household 2 selling commodity b to household 3, and household 3 selling commodity c to household 1. In the left-hand "circle", household 1 sells commodity d to household 4, household 4 sells commodity e to household 3, and household 3 sells commodity c to household 1.

This trade would be simple if at least one of these "circles" were (weakly) utility-improving for all its participants. But suppose that the situation is as follows. At the prices at which trade takes place, households 2 and 4 find their respective roles in the diagrammed trade to be utility increasing. Household 1, however, would not be willing to participate in the left-hand circle standing alone. That is, at the given prices, household 1 would not be willing to sell d and buy c. It would, on the

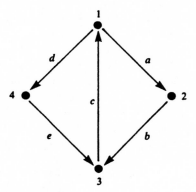

FIGURE 7.1

other hand, be happy to engage in the right-hand circle standing alone, selling *a* and buying *c*. By contrast, household 3 would be willing to participate in the left-hand circle standing alone (selling *c* and buying *e*), but would not be willing so to participate in the right-hand one (selling *c* and buying *b*). In this circumstance, neither circle, standing alone, would be an Edgeworth-process trade. Nevertheless, the entire transaction taken as a whole can be an Edgeworth-process trade, with household 1 agreeing to participate in the left-hand circle in exchange for household 3's agreement to participate in the right-hand one.

Without further assumptions, there is nothing to prevent the possibility that the only utility-improving trades possible at given prices are compound. Further, as we shall see below, without the strong assumption that all (or nearly all) households hold positive amounts of all commodities, there is nothing to prevent the possibility that the only such trades require large numbers of participants. In such cases, the assumption that those trades will nevertheless take place seems very strong and somewhat out of place in a non-cooperative, competitive setting.

To see this, consider the following. Where only utility-improving circle trades are involved, one can imagine prices being announced and each household then ranking the commodities such that, at the announced prices, it would be willing to exchange (a very small amount of) any commodity for one of higher rank. Someone (the "market") then arranges (small) circle trades accordingly.

The information required for such rankings amounts to an ordering of commodities in terms of the ratio of marginal utility to price; but the values of those ratios are not required.

By contrast, knowing whether or not a compound trade is possible requires knowledge of the ratios themselves. In a compound trade, agents are selling linear combinations of commodities in exchange for other such linear combinations. One cannot decide whether an agent will sell a particular linear combination of apples and bananas in exchange for carrots merely by knowing that he or she would sell apples for carrots and would prefer not to sell bananas for carrots. Yet knowing what linear combinations a particular agent is willing to trade is required if those combinations are to be matched up with the trading desires of other agents. Much more than a rank ordering of commodities is therefore needed.

In effect, for compound trades, one needs information on relative preference intensity. Actual marginal rates of substitution are required, not just data on which such rates exceed the corresponding price ratios. Simple trades, of course, require only the latter.

This difference in informational requirements might not seem too great if we could be sure that all compound trades involved only a few participants. As we shall see below, however, this is not the case once we leave the assumption that most households have strictly positive endowments of all commodities. When that happens, the required trades can be far more complex than that of Figure 7.1 with many more than two of the households participating in one or more circles as the *quid pro quo* for obtaining participation in another one. To find such a trade requires very detailed information on the preferences of a large number of people.

I now go on to consider what restrictions can be put on the number of required agents when the universal positive endowment assumption is relaxed.

4.   Standard t-Trades

I begin with simple trades. If an Edgeworth-process trade is simple, then at least one of the circles of which it is composed is itself an Edgeworth-process trade. Hence, in considering the maximum number of participants required for a simple Edgeworth-process trade, it suffices to assume that the trade involved is itself just a single circle.

Furthermore, if a given commodity occurs twice in such a circle, then the number of participants in the circle can be reduced while still having an Edgeworth-process trade. Consider the trade diagrammed in Figure 7.2. Here, a, b, c, and d are all different commodities. By strict quasiconcavity, we can, if necessary, reduce the size of the trade so that all participants find it strictly utility-increasing. Suppose that commodity x

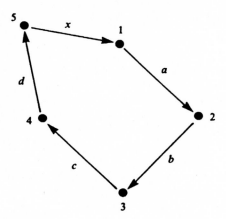

FIGURE 7.2

is the same as any one of the other four commodities. If $x = a$, then household 1 can be removed from the trade. If $x = b$, then households 1 and 2 can be removed. If $x = c$, then households 1, 2, and 3 can all be removed, making bilateral trade possible. Finally, $x = d$ implies that household 5 can be removed from the trade. There is nothing special about this example.

It follows that, in considering simple Edgeworth-process trades, it suffices to look at circles with the same number of commodities as households. It will be convenient to standardize notation as follows.

Definition 3. A standard t-trade is a circle of households, which we may as well take to be $\{1, \ldots, t\}$, and a set of commodities, which we may as well take to be also $\{1, \ldots, t\}$, such that, for $1 \leq i < t$, household i sells commodity i to household $i + 1$, while household t sells commodity t to household 1.

I shall adopt the convention that, when considering a standard t-trade, commodity 0 is taken to be commodity t, so that each household $i = 1, \ldots, t$ sells commodity i and buys commodity $i - 1$. I denote $\{i - 1, i\}$ by $S(i)$.

5.   Simple Trades: Results

The following fairly obvious fact is central to the analysis of simple trades.

Lemma 3. *Consider any household, H, and any triplet of commodities, a, b, c, with H's holdings of a and b both positive. Suppose that, at current prices, H could increase utility by selling a and buying c. Then, at the same prices, H would also find one of the following trades to be utility-increasing: (1) selling b and buying c or (2) selling a and buying b.*

Proof. Denote H's utility function by $U(\cdot)$. Let the prices of the three goods be p_a, p_b, and p_c, respectively. Then $U_a/U_c < p_a/p_c$, since H could increase utility by selling a and buying c. Evidently, either $U_b/U_c < p_b/p_c$, in which case H would find selling b and buying c to be utility increasing, or else $U_a/U_b < p_a/p_b$, in which case H would find selling a and buying b to be utility increasing.   ‖

This leads to the following lemma.

Lemma 4. *Suppose that an Edgeworth-process standard t-trade is possible with $t > 2$. Suppose further that household i $(1 \leq i \leq t)$ holds a positive amount of some commodity j $(1 \leq j \leq t)$, with j not in S(i). Then there is an Edgeworth-process trade involving no more than $t - 1$ households.*

Proof. Without loss of generality, we can take $i = 1$. Then household 1, which certainly holds commodity 1, also holds commodity j, where $1 < j < t$. By Lemma 3, either household 1 is willing to sell commodity 1 and buy commodity j or else it is willing to sell commodity j and buy commodity t.

Suppose first that household 1 is willing to sell commodity 1 and buy commodity j. Then there is a standard j-trade possible. That is, households $\{1, \ldots, j\}$ can trade with each household, g, selling commodity g to household $g + 1$ and household j selling commodity j to household 1. Since $j < t$, there are at most $t - 1$ households involved in this trade.

Now suppose that household 1 is willing to sell commodity j and buy commodity t. In this case, households $\{j + 1, \ldots, t, 1\}$ can trade with household g selling commodity g to household $g + 1$, except that household t sells commodity t to household 1, and household 1 sells commodity j to household $j + 1$. The number of households involved in this trade is $(t + 1 - j)$, and this is less than t, since $j > 1$.   ‖

It is now easy to prove the main result for simple trades:

Theorem 1. (A) *For any m, $1 < m \leq n$, let x(m) be the number of households holding at least m commodities in positive amounts. If there exists a simple Edgeworth-process trade, then there exists one with at most $t_1(m) = \text{Max}\{h - x(m), n - m + 2\}$ participants.*

(B) *For any k, $1 < k \leq h$, let $y(k)$ be the number of commodities held by at least k households in positive amounts. If there exists a simple Edgeworth-process trade, then there exists one with at most $t_2(k) = \text{Max}\{n - y(k), h - k + 2\}$ participants.*

Proof. (A) Without loss of generality, suppose that there exists an Edgeworth-process standard t-trade with $t > t_1(m)$. Since $t > h - x(m)$, at least one of the households involved in the trade must hold at least m goods. Let that household be household i. Then i holds at least $(m - 2)$ goods not in $S(i)$. Since $t > n - (m - 2)$, i must hold some good involved in the trade that is not in $S(i)$. Since $t > n - m + 2 \geq 2$, Lemma 4 now yields the desired results.

(B) Again suppose that there exists an Edgeworth-process standard t-trade with $t > t_2(k)$. Since $t > n - y(k)$, at least one of the commodities involved in the trade is held by at least k households. Let that commodity be commodity j. Then j is held by at least $(k - 2)$ households, i, with j not in $S(i)$. Since $t > h - (k - 2)$, at least one such household must be involved in the trade. Since $t > h - k + 2 \geq 2$, the desired result again follows from Lemma 4. ‖

Corollary 1. *If there exists a simple Edgeworth-process trade, then there exists one with at most*

$$t^* = \text{Min}\{\text{Min}_m t_1(m), \text{Min}_k t_2(k)\}$$

participants (where the notation is as in Theorem 1).

Proof. Obvious. ‖

Corollary 2. *If a simple Edgeworth-process trade exists, then one exists with no more than $\text{Max}\{2, \text{Min}(h - x(n), n - y(h))\}$ participants.*

Proof. Set $m = n$ and $k = h$ in Theorem 1. ‖

Corollary 2 states that, if a simple Edgeworth-process trade requires more than two participants, it need not require more than the number of households *not* holding all commodities or the number of commodities *not* held by all households.

Corollary 3 (Schmeidler). *If a simple Edgeworth-process trade exists, then one exists with no more than n participants.*

Proof. Follows from Corollary 2 and the fact that $y(h) \geq 0$. ‖

Corollary 4. *Suppose that at least $h - 2$ households hold $m \geq 2$ commodities (not necessarily the same ones). Then, if a simple Edgeworth-process trade exists, such a trade exists with no more than $n - m + 2$ participants.*

Proof. In Theorem 1(A), $x(m) \geq h - 2$. ‖

Corollary 5. *Suppose that at least $n - 2$ commodities are held by $k \geqq 2$ households (not necessarily the same ones). Then, if a simple Edgeworth-process trade exists, such a trade exists with no more than $h - k + 2$ participants.*

Proof. In Theorem 1(B), $y(k) \geqq n - 2$. ∥

These results obviously imply:

Corollary 6. *Suppose that either* (a) *at least $h - 2$ households hold all commodities in positive amounts or* (b) *at least $n - 2$ commodities are held in positive amounts by all households. If a simple Edgeworth-process trade exists, then a bilateral simple Edgeworth-process trade exists.*

This is a slightly stronger version of:

Corollary 7 (Madden). *Suppose that all households hold positive amounts of all commodities. If a simple Edgeworth-process trade exists, then a bilateral Edgeworth-process trade exists.*

6.   Simple Trades: Can Further Results Be Obtained?

The number of participants required for an Edgeworth-process trade depends on the distribution of commodity holdings and, of course, on the distribution of tastes. The results so far obtained for simple trades have made no assumptions on the distribution of tastes and have only characterized the distribution of commodity holdings by the two functions, $x(\cdot)$ and $y(\cdot)$ (respectively, the number of households holding at least a given number of commodities and the number of commodities held by at least a given number of households).

Since that information does not completely characterize the holding of commodities by households, it is easy to see that more information on the pattern of such holdings can make a considerable difference. Consider the following example:

(A) Assume $h = n > 2$, with n even. Suppose that there exists an Edgeworth-process standard n-trade with household i holding only the commodities in $S(i)$ (that is, commodities $i - 1$ and i, with commodity 0 taken to be commodity n). Then $x(2) = h$, while $x(m) = 0$ for $m > 2$. Similarly, $y(2) = n$, while $y(k) = 0$ for $k > 2$. This means that $t_1(m) \equiv n \equiv t_2(k)$ for $1 < m \leqq n$ and $1 < k \leqq h$. Evidently, $t^* = n$ in Corollary 1, and, indeed, it is obvious that the standard n-trade cannot be reduced.

(B) With the same number of goods and households as in (A), and the same standard n-trade as before, suppose that household i now holds only the commodities i and $i + 1$, instead of i and $i - 1$ (with commodity $n + 1$ taken to be commodity 1). Then the functions $x(\cdot)$ and $y(\cdot)$ are the same as in (A), so that $t^* = n$, as before. In this case, however, every household, i, owns a good involved in the standard n-trade that is not in $S(i)$, so that Lemma 4 shows the existence of an Edgeworth-process trade with fewer than n participants. In fact, it is not hard to show that there exists such a trade with $n/2$ participants, since, along the lines of the proof of Lemma 4, every odd-numbered participant in the standard n-trade can bypass participant $i + 1$.

Somewhat more surprising than this is the fact that t^* of Corollary 1 need not be the least upper bound on required trades given only the information in $x(\cdot)$ and $y(\cdot)$. To see this, consider the following example.

Suppose that there exists an $m^* \geq 3$, with $n - m^* + 2 > m^*$, such that:

$$x(m) = \begin{cases} h & \text{for } m \leq m^* \\ 0 & \text{for } m > m^*; \end{cases} \qquad y(k) = \begin{cases} n & \text{for } k \leq m^* \\ 0 & \text{for } k > m^*. \end{cases} \tag{1}$$

In other words, every household owns exactly m^* commodities, and every commodity is owned by exactly m^* households. Assume $h \geq n$. In this case,

$$t_1(m) = \begin{cases} n - m + 2 & \text{for } m \leq m^* \\ h & \text{for } m > m^*, \end{cases} \tag{2}$$

and, similarly,

$$t_2(k) = \begin{cases} h - k + 2 & \text{for } k \leq m^* \\ n & \text{for } k > m^*. \end{cases} \tag{3}$$

Then $t^* = t_1(m^*) = n - m^* + 2$. Note that, by assumption, $t^* > m^*$, so that $y(t^*) = 0$. In other words, there is no commodity owned by as many as t^* households.

Now consider any simple Edgeworth-process trade involving t^* households. Without loss of generality, we may take this to be the standard t^*-trade. There are $n - m^* + 2$ goods involved in such a trade. Each household, i, owns at least $(m^* - 2)$ goods not in $S(i)$. In order for none of these goods to be involved in the trade, those $(m^* - 2)$ goods must be the same for all t^* participants. Since we know that this is impossible, Lemma 4 tells us that there is an Edgeworth-process trade with fewer than t^* participants.

It remains to show that the functions $x(\cdot)$ and $y(\cdot)$ given in (1) can actually occur. This is easily done by having household i own commodities $\{i - 1, i, \ldots, i + m^* - 2\}$, with commodity 0 identified with commodity n and commodity $n + j$ identified with commodity j ($1 \leq j \leq m^* - 2$).

Evidently, further work along these lines can produce stronger lower bounds on the number of required participants than t^*. That further analysis would have to run in terms of the total number of commodities owned by sets of households and the total number of households that own sets of commodities.

7.   Compound Trades: Results

I now turn to the more complex case of compound trades. Here results are not so easily come by. The principal reason for this is that the result of Lemma 4 does not hold for compound trades. To see this, consider Figure 7.1 again and recall that household 1 participates in the left-hand circle only in order to participate in the right-hand one, while the opposite is true for household 3. Suppose that household 4 owns commodity c. Then, by Lemma 3, household 4 is either willing to sell c and buy d or else willing to buy c and sell e. In the latter case, bilateral trade between households 3 and 4 is possible, but suppose that the former case applies, and that household 4 has no interest in purchasing either a or b. If the left-hand circle were itself an Edgeworth-process trade, bilateral trade between households 1 and 4 would be possible, but now it is not. Household 1 is not willing merely to sell d and buy c; it is doing so only because that gives it the opportunity to sell a and buy c. If we try to replace the left-hand circle by a bilateral trade between households 1 and 4, household 3 will no longer receive e. Since household 3's participation in the right-hand circle is conditional on its getting e, household 3 will no longer participate in the right-hand circle. But, in that case, household 1 will have no reason to sell d and buy c, and the whole trade will break down.

Moreover, it is not true (as it is in the case of simple trades) that the existence of a commodity involved in the trade and held by all participants implies that the number of participants can be reduced. To see this, consider Figure 7.3. Here there are two circles, each involving the *same* three households. (Household 2 has been exhibited twice for clarity.) Suppose that household 2 gains utility from participation in the right-hand circle and loses from participation in the left-hand one, while the opposite is true for households 1 and 3. Assume that household 1 owns a and d, household 2 owns a, b, and e, and household 3 owns a and c. Thus, a is owned by all households.

For convenience, assume that all prices are equal to unity. Denoting the utility function of household i by U^i and marginal utilities by subscripts, the information given implies:

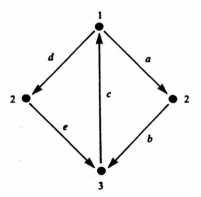

FIGURE 7.3

$$U_a^1 > U_c^1 > U_d^1, \tag{4}$$

$$U_a^2 > U_b^2; \qquad U_d^2 < U_e^2, \tag{5}$$

and

$$U_e^3 > U_c^3 > U_b^3. \tag{6}$$

Suppose that, in addition,

$$U_d^1 > U_b^1 > U_e^1, \tag{7}$$

$$U_a^2 > U_d^2; \qquad U_a^2 > U_c^2, \tag{8}$$

and

$$U_a^3 > U_e^3; \qquad U_b^3 > U_d^3. \tag{9}$$

Inequalities (4) and (7) imply that household 1 will not sell either a or d in order to purchase b or e, while (8) implies that household 2 will not sell a in order to purchase d. Hence bilateral trade between households 1 and 2 cannot take place.

Similarly, inequalities (7) and (9) imply that household 3 will not sell a to purchase b or e, while (8) implies that household 2 will not sell a in order to purchase c. Hence bilateral trade between households 2 and 3 cannot take place.

Finally, (4) implies that household 1 will not sell a in order to purchase c, while (6) and (9) imply that household 3 will not sell a in order to purchase d. Hence bilateral trade between households 1 and 3 cannot take place.

Thus, no bilateral trade is possible at the given prices,[4] and the compound trade shown in Figure 7.2 cannot be reduced even though a is owned by all participants. Basically, the reasoning that led to a different result in the case of simple trades breaks down (as before) because the trades are all interdependent. Thus, the household that owns a good that it is not trading is household 3. That household would be glad to purchase a and sell c, and, if the right-hand circle were itself an Edgeworth-process trade, this would allow household 3 to replace household 2 and deal directly with household 1. In the compound case being examined, however, households 1 and 3 have no direct interest in such a trade of a for c, and engaging in it would remove household 2's reason for participating in the left-hand circle.

This does not mean that it is impossible to obtain positive results, however. In fact, the parallelism between commodities and households breaks down in the case of compound trades, for it remains true that the presence of a household owning all goods in a multilateral trade permits a reduction in the number of participants. To see this, consider the following lemma, which gives the result parallel to (and weaker than) that of Lemma 4 for the case of compound trades.

Lemma 5. *Suppose that an Edgeworth-process trade exists with $t > 2$ participants. Suppose further that there exist two households, i and i', participating in the trade, such that the set of commodities owned in positive amounts by household i includes all commodities being traded (bought or sold) by household i'. Then there exists an Edgeworth-process trade with no more than $t - 1$ participants, one of which is household i. That trade involves no commodities or households not involved in the original trade.*

Proof. If necessary, reduce the size of the original trade so that every participant finds it strictly utility-increasing. Household i' can be thought of as buying one composite good (a linear combination of ordinary goods) and selling another. (For example, household 1 in Figure 7.1 buys c and sells a combination of a and d.) Let B denote the composite good that household i' buys, and S the composite good that it sells. Then household i owns both B and S. If household i would find it strictly utility-

---

[4] It is perhaps worth re-emphasizing the role that the assumption of given prices plays here. Nothing in the example comes close to requiring that *ratios* of marginal utilities (marginal rates of substitution) must be equal for the three participants. Indeed, from Theorem 1.2 of Goldman and Starr (1982, p. 597), a theorem originally due to Feldman, we know that the marginal rate of substitution between a and some other good must differ between two traders in such a way that bilateral trade is possible at some *different* set of prices.

increasing to sell B and buy S, then a bilateral Edgeworth-process trade between households i and i' is possible. If, on the other hand, household i would not find it strictly utility-increasing to sell B and buy S, then household i can replace household i' in the original trade, selling S and buying B.[5]   ‖

This immediately implies:

Theorem 2. *If one of the participants in an Edgeworth-process trade owns all the commodities involved in the trade, then there exists a bilateral Edgeworth-process trade.*[6]

This leads immediately to the extension of (parts of) Corollaries 2, 6, and 7, above, to the case of compound trades. (As before, h is the number of households, n the number of commodities, and $x(n)$ the number of households holding positive amounts of all commodities.)

Corollary 8. *If an Edgeworth-process trade exists, then one exists with no more than $\text{Max}\{2, h - x(n)\}$ participants.*

Corollary 9. *Suppose that at least $h - 2$ households hold all commodities in positive amounts. If an Edgeworth-process trade exists, then a bilateral Edgeworth-process trade exists.*

This is a slightly stronger version of:

Corollary 10 (Madden). *Suppose that all households hold positive amounts of all commodities. If an Edgeworth-process trade exists, then a bilateral Edgeworth-process trade exists.*[7]

Theorem 2 also implies a different generalization of Madden's result, namely:

---

[5] A similar proof generalizes Lemma 5 to:

> **Lemma 5'.** *Suppose that an Edgeworth-process trade exists with $t > 2$ participants. Suppose further that there exists a household, i, and a subset of $t' < t - 1$ households, R, participating in the trade, such that the set of commodities owned in positive amounts by household i includes all commodities that R trades (buys or sells) with households outside of R. Then there exists an Edgeworth-process trade with no more than $t' + 1 \leqq t - 1$ participants, one of which is household i. That trade involves no commodities or households not involved in the original trade.*

> I have been unable to find a use for this result that is not a consequence of the less general Lemma 5, however.

[6] I am indebted to a referee (who provided a different proof) for suggesting that this be stated explicitly.

[7] Schmeidler's result, while true, does not seem readily provable for compound trades along the lines here developed.

Corollary 11. *Suppose that an Edgeworth-process trade exists in which all the participants own the same commodities. Then a bilateral Edgeworth-process trade exists.*

This shows that diversity of ownership is essential to the need for large numbers of participants.

Unfortunately, these results do not appear to offer much hope as to the restrictions that can reasonably be put on the number of participants needed for a compound trade. Since, as already discussed, the construction of compound trades requires detailed knowledge of agents' preferences, the Edgeworth-process assumption does not appear particularly reasonable if it extends beyond simple trades. Describing how trade takes place evidently requires a more detailed story with consideration of how markets are organized.

REFERENCES

Arrow, K. J. and Hahn, F. H. (1971), *General Competitive Analysis* (San Francisco: Holden-Day and Edinburgh: Oliver & Boyd).

Feldman, A. (1973), "Bilateral Trading Processes, Pairwise Optimality, and Pareto Optimality", *Review of Economic Studies*, **40**, 463–473.

Fisher, F. M. (1976), "The Stability of General Equilibrium: Results and Problems" (F. W. Paish Lecture delivered at the A.U.T.E. meetings, Sheffield, U.K. 1975) in Artis, M. and Nobay, A. (eds.), *Essays in Economic Analysis, Proceedings of the Association of University Teachers of Economics Annual Conference, Sheffield 1975* (Cambridge: Cambridge University Press).

Fisher, F. M. (1983), *Disequilibrium Foundations of Equilibrium Economics* (Cambridge: Cambridge University Press).

Goldman, S. M. and Starr, R. M. (1982), "Pairwise, t-Wise, and Pareto Optimalities", *Econometrica*, **50**, 593–606.

Graham, D. A., Jennergen, L. P., Peterson, D. W., and Weintraub, E. R. (1976), "Trader-Commodity Parity Theorems", *Journal of Economic Theory*, **12**, 443–454.

Hahn, F. H. (1962), "On the Stability of a Pure Exchange Equilibrium", *International Economic Review*, **3**, 206–213.

Madden, P. (1975), "Efficient Sequences of Non-Monetary Exchange", *Review of Economic Studies*, **42**, 581–596.

Madden, P. (1978), "Why the Edgeworth Process Assumption Isn't That Bad", *Review of Economic Studies*, **45**, 279–283.

Rader, T. (1968), "Pairwise Optimality and Non-Competitive Behavior", in Quirk, J. P. and Zarley, A. M. (eds.), *Papers in Quantitative Economics* (Lawrence, Kansas: University Press of Kansas).

Rader, T. (1976), "Pairwise Optimality, Multilateral Optimality and

Efficiency with and without Externalities", in Lin, S. A. Y. (ed.), *Theory and Measurement of Economic Externalities* (New York: Academic Press).

Uzawa, H. (1962), "On the Stability of Edgeworth's Barter Process", *International Economic Review*, **3**, 218–232.

An Alternate Proof and
Extension of Solow's Theorem
on Nonnegative Square Matrices (1962)

Some time ago, Robert M. Solow (1952) proved a now well-known theorem, namely, that the largest characteristic root of an indecomposable nonnegative square matrix is less than unity provided that no column sum is greater than one and at least one column sum is strictly less. This note provides an alternative proof of a rather more general version of that theorem that may be useful as it exhibits the exact relation between the largest root and the column sums. As a by-product, the stronger result obtained leads to an intuitive characterization of the largest root of a submatrix of a Markov matrix.

Let $A \geq 0$ be an $n \times n$ matrix with largest characteristic root λ, which is thus real and positive. Let X be the characteristic vector associated with λ; then $X \geq 0$ with the strict inequality holding if and only if A is indecomposable. Then:

$$\sum_{j=1}^{n} A_{ij} X_j = \lambda X_i \qquad (i = 1, \ldots, n). \tag{1}$$

Summing over i:

$$\sum_{i=1}^{n}\sum_{j=1}^{n} A_{ij} X_j = \sum_{j=1}^{n}\left(X_j \sum_{i=1}^{n} A_{ij} \right) = \sum_{j=1}^{n} X_j \operatorname{Col}_j = \lambda \sum_{j=1}^{n} X_j \tag{2}$$

where Col_j is the jth column sum of A. We have immediately:

$$\lambda = \frac{\displaystyle\sum_{j=1}^{n} X_j \operatorname{Col}_j}{\displaystyle\sum_{j=1}^{n} X_j} \tag{3}$$

so that λ is a nonnegatively weighted average of the column sums of A, the weights being the X_j. This is the stronger result mentioned above. It now immediately follows that:

I am indebted to Albert Ando for helpful discussions.

$$\text{Max Col}_j \geq \lambda \geq \text{Min Col}_j \tag{4}$$

Now suppose that not all column sums are equal but that one of the equalities in (4) holds. Then all column sums not equal to λ must have zero weights in (3), that is, the corresponding X_j must be zero, hence A is decomposable.

An interesting byproduct of (3) occurs when A is a submatrix of a Markov matrix corresponding to a subset of states. Clearly, the probability of an individual in some one of those states remaining in the given subset at the next time period is a column sum of A. Moreover, as time goes on, the distribution of individuals originally in that subset at time zero, and still in that subset, approaches that given by the elements of X. It follows from (3) that the asymptotic probability of an individual who began in the subset and has stayed in the subset through time t remaining in the subset at time $t + 1$ is equal to the Frobenius root of A.

REFERENCE

Robert M. Solow: "On the Structure of Linear Models," *Econometrica*, Vol. 20, No. 1 (January, 1952), pp. 29–46.

CHAPTER 9

Choice of Units, Column Sums, and Stability in Linear Dynamic Systems with Nonnegative Square Matrices (1965)

Sufficiency conditions for the stability of a nonnegative square matrix in terms of the column or row sums thereof are, of course, well known.[1] Such conditions are not also necessary. If such a matrix is that of a dynamic system, however, the non-zero off-diagonal elements thereof are not independent of the units in which the variables are measured, and the same statement holds for the column or row sums. This paper sets out results related to the existence of a set of units in which the Solow condition on column sums holds. The basic mathematical results are already known, but it seems useful to draw them together in one place and to give them an interpretation in terms of units.

The basic theorem for first-order systems is that if the matrix is inde-composable, there exists a set of units in which all column sums are equal to the Frobenius root. This is an interpretation of a theorem of Kol-mogorov.[2] The theorem immediately implies the necessity of the existence of a set of units for which the Solow condition holds.[3] In addition, we observe that there are alternate simple ways of proving the latter result, one of which allows us to interpret a result of McKenzie (1960), as the latter author did not do.

If the original dynamic system is of an order higher than first, then the construction used in the proof of the results just described leads to the use of different units for the same variable in different time periods. This is clearly unaesthetic and we therefore show that similar results apply for a set of consistent units. A recent theorem of Bear (1963) on distributed lags is an immediate byproduct.

I am indebted to D. Belsley, A. R. Dobell, D. Levhari, P. A. Samuelson, and R. M. Solow for their comments but retain responsibility for error.

[1] See Solow (1952). An alternate proof of Solow's theorem that yields a stronger result is given in Fisher (1962).

[2] The theorem and proof (but not the interpretation in terms of units) is given in Brauer (1962), who cites Dimitriev and Dynkin (1946). I am indebted to David Levhari for this reference. An interpretation in terms of units is given in Ara (1963). I am indebted to Paul A. Samuelson for this reference.

[3] Such necessity is stated without proof in Dorfman, Samuelson, and Solow (1958, p. 256).

1.   First-Order Systems

Consider the dynamic system:

$$y(t) = Ay(t-1) \tag{1.1}$$

where $y(t)$ is an n-component column vector of variables, and A is an $n \times n$ square matrix, with $A \geq 0$. If the jth element of y is to be measured in new units, then the jth row of A must be multiplied and the jth column divided by the same appropriate conversion factor. Thus a shift of units may be described as follows. Let D be an $n \times n$ diagonal matrix with positive diagonal elements. The shift of units gives a system with a new matrix:

$$A^* = DAD^{-1}. \tag{1.2}$$

It is easy to show that if x is a latent vector of A corresponding to a latent root, λ, then (Dx) is a latent vector of A^* corresponding to the same latent root. We prove:

Theorem 1.1.   *If A is indecomposable, there exists a set of units in which all the column (row) sums of A^* equal the Frobenius root thereof.*

Proof.   Let λ be the Frobenius root of A (and therefore of any A^* derived as in (1.2)). Let x be the latent vector of A corresponding to λ. Since A is indecomposable, x is strictly positive. Now, choose:

$$D_{ii} = 1/x_i \qquad (i = 1, \ldots, n). \tag{1.3}$$

Then the vector Dx consists of all unit elements and the result for row sums follows immediately from the relation:

$$A^*(Dx) = \lambda(Dx). \tag{1.4}$$

The result for column sums follows similarly using the appropriate characteristic vector of A'.

An obvious corollary (sufficiency following from Solow (1952) or Fisher (1962)) is:

Corollary 1.1.   *Let A be indecomposable. A necessary and sufficient condition for the stability of (1.1) is that there exist a set of units in which all column (row) sums are at most unity and one such sum is less than unity. A necessary and sufficient condition for the instability of (1.1) is the existence of a set of units in which all column (row) sums are at least unity.*

We turn now to the case in which A is decomposable.[4] In this case, with suitable renumbering of variables, A can be partitioned into submatrices, A^{IJ} with A^{II} square and indecomposable and $A^{IJ} = 0$ for $J > I$

---

[4] I use the term as does Solow (1952). Bear (1963) and others use "reducible."

$(I, J = 1, \ldots, N)$. We shall take A in this canonical form. We may easily show:

Corollary 1.2. *Let A be decomposable. A necessary and sufficient condition for the stability of* (1.1) *is that there exist a set of units in which every column* (row) *sum is at most unity and at least one of the Ith set of such sums be less than unity for all $I = 1, \ldots, N$.*

Proof. (a) Sufficiency. Since A is nonnegative, the column sums of any A^{II} are at most equal to the corresponding column sums of A, and the latent roots of A are those of the A^{II}.

(b) Necessity. Since any A^{II} is indecomposable, there exists a set of units in which each of its column sums is equal to its Frobenius root which is less than unity. Suppose that the system is already in such units. Let the number of columns in A^{II} be n_I. Choose:

$$D_{ii} = k_I > 0 \qquad \left(i = \sum_{J=1}^{I-1} n_J + 1, \ldots, \sum_{J=1}^{I} n_J; \quad I = 1, \ldots, N \right). \qquad (1.5)$$

Then the A^{II} are left unaffected by the shift of units but the elements of A^{II} for $J < I$ are all multiplied by (k_I/k_J). Appropriate choice of the k_I clearly yields the desired result.

We add a few remarks. First, the necessary stability condition of Corollary 1.1 can be obtained by observing that if A is indecomposable, there exists a strictly positive vector x such that $Ax < x$.[5] The variables can then be measured as multiples of the corresponding elements of x. In a Leontief system, this amounts to measuring outputs as multiples of a producible set of positive outputs that yield a strictly positive final bill of goods, or measuring prices (using the transpose) as multiples of a set of positive prices that cover interindustry costs and leave something over for the wage-bill.[6]

---

[5] See, for example, Bear (1963, p. 520).

[6] It is also possible to give a sufficiency proof in such economic terms. Thus, suppose that every industry buys at least indirectly from every other industry. Further, suppose that there exists a set of units such that when every industry produces at unit output no industry is called on to supply more than it is producing and at least one industry has some output left over for the final bill. Cut down the output of the latter industry slightly, using part of the original deliveries to final bill to meet the interindustry input requirements. Every industry supplying the one so treated will now be able to deliver to final bill. We may treat such industries in a similar fashion and, proceeding in this way, obtain a strictly positive final bill (since every industry buys at least indirectly from every other).

Alternatively, suppose that there exists a set of units such that if all prices are equal to unity, no industry fails to cover unit costs (excluding wages) and at least one industry more than covers them. If every industry *sells* at least indirectly to every other one, then (essentially as in the output case) we can proceed by adjusting prices to obtain a price system in which every industry more than covers interindustry unit costs. As is well known, both these cases are equivalent to the condition that the Frobenius root of the input-output matrix be less than unity.

Second, the necessary and sufficient stability condition of both corollaries may be immediately obtained from a corollary of McKenzie (1960, p. 58) which states that a necessary and sufficient condition for the characteristic roots of A to be less than unity in absolute value is that $I - A$ have a dominant positive diagonal. This means (by McKenzie's extended definition of dominant diagonality) that there exist $D_{ii} > 0$ such that

$$D_{ii}(1 - A_{ii}) > \sum_{j \neq i} D_{jj} A_{ij} \qquad (i = 1, \dots, n). \tag{1.6}$$

This is clearly equivalent to:

$$1 > \sum_{j=1}^{n} (D_{jj}/D_{ii}) A_{ij} \qquad (i = 1, \dots, n), \tag{1.7}$$

which is the condition that the row sums be less than unity with an appropriate shift of units.[7]

2.   Higher-Order Systems and Distributed Lags

Suppose that, in place of (1.1), we have

$$y(t) = \sum_{\theta=1}^{T} A_\theta y(t - \theta), \qquad T > 1, A_T \neq 0, A_\theta \geqq 0, \quad (\theta = 1, \dots, T) \tag{2.1}$$

where the A_θ are each $n \times n$ matrices and $y(t)$ is, as before, an n-component vector of variables. As is well known, this can be transformed by redefinition of the variables into

$$z(t) = A z(t - 1) \tag{2.2}$$

where the first n-components of $z(t)$ are the components of $y(t)$ and the remainder are defined by (2.2) and:

$$A = \begin{bmatrix} A_1 & A_2 & \cdots & A_T \\ I & 0 & \cdot\cdot 0 & 0 \\ 0 & I & 0\cdot 0 & 0 \\ \vdots & \vdots & \vdots\vdots\vdots & \vdots \\ 0 & \cdot & \cdot 0\, I & 0 \end{bmatrix} \tag{2.3}$$

so that $z(t)$ is a Tn-component vector and A is $Tn \times Tn$. The last $(T - 1)n$ equations of (2.2) are thus definitions. We shall refer to them

[7] Indeed, dominant diagonality in McKenzie's extended sense (see 1960, p. 47) is equivalent to the existence of a set of units in which the matrix in question has a dominant diagonal in the usual sense.

as definitional equations and to the corresponding rows of A as definitional rows.

Clearly, there is no formal reason why the results of the preceding section cannot be directly applied to the analysis of (2.2). This is particularly true if we drop the units interpretation of those results and interpret them merely in terms of the existence of diagonal matrices D such that DAD^{-1} has certain properties. Nevertheless, the units interpretation is perhaps an illuminating one and it would be desirable to retain it. The difficulty with doing so here is that the constructions of the last section would generally require us to measure the same variable at different time periods in different units.

Once again, there is little formal difficulty in so doing. A man's units are his own to use as he sees fit. Indeed, the use of time-consistent units is really one of convenience and aesthetics only.[8] Nevertheless, it is interesting to observe that a good deal of our earlier results can be preserved even if we restrict ourselves to consistent units.

We now formally define consistent units as follows. A unit shift will be said to be consistent if D has the following property:

$$D_{ii} = D_{n\theta+i, n\theta+i} \qquad (\theta = 1, \ldots, T; i = 1, \ldots, n). \tag{2.4}$$

Clearly, the definitional rows of A are unchanged in any consistent units. We prove:

Theorem 2.1. *Let A be indecomposable. A necessary and sufficient condition for the stability of (2.2) is that there exist a set of consistent units in which every nondefinitional row sum is at most unity and at least one such sum is less than unity. A necessary and sufficient condition for the instability of (2.2) is that there exist a set of consistent units in which every nondefinitional row sum is at least unity.*

Proof. That the stated condition is sufficient in either case is evident since the definitional row sums are always precisely unity in any set of consistent units. It remains to prove necessity.

To accomplish this, we use a construction similar to that used in the proof of Theorem 1.1. Once more the latent vector associated with the Frobenius root is strictly positive. Further, denoting that vector by x and the vector of its first n components by $\bar{x}$, it is obvious that:

---

[8] In this respect, the situation differs only in degree from that encountered in some first-order cases. For example, it may be necessary in interpreting the results of the preceding section to measure money flows of different sectors in different monetary units. Here also, measurement in the same units is primarily a matter of convenience and aesthetics.

$$x = \begin{bmatrix} \bar{x}/\lambda \\ \bar{x}/\lambda^2 \\ \vdots \\ \bar{x}/\lambda^T \end{bmatrix} \tag{2.5}$$

where λ is the Frobenius root of A. Now, choose:

$$D_{ii} = 1/\bar{x}_i \qquad (i = 1, \ldots, n), \tag{2.6}$$

and the remaining diagonal elements of D by (2.4). As before, the latent vector of $DAD^{-1} = A^*$ corresponding to λ is Dx, and this is now a vector with its first n components unity, its next n components $1/\lambda$, and so forth. From the equation:

$$A^*(Dx) = \lambda(Dx) \tag{2.7}$$

the desired results now follow immediately.

Clearly, a similar result cannot hold for column sums if we insist on consistent units; it is easy to show by a similar construction using A' that a necessary condition for stability is the existence of a set of consistent units in which the sum of the elements of any column of A that appear in the nondefinitional rows be strictly less than unity.

As in the preceding section, if A is decomposable a similar result follows on the row sums, where at least one of the nondefinitional row sums in the Ith set is required to be strictly less than unity for every I.

As our final topic, we consider the relations between the system (2.2), which is equivalent to (2.1) and the system obtained from (2.1) by time-aggregation:

$$y(t) = By(t - 1) \tag{2.8}$$

where

$$B = \sum_{\theta=1}^{T} A_\theta. \tag{2.9}$$

D. V. T. Bear (1963) has shown that (2.8) is stable if and only if (2.1) is stable. This result is an immediate byproduct of our theorems, since it is evident that for any set of consistent units each row sum of B is equal to a nondefinitional row sum of A and conversely.

REFERENCES

Ara, K.: "A Note on Input-Output Matrices," *Hitotsubashi Journal of Economics*, Vol. 3, No. 2 (June, 1963), pp. 68–70.

Bear, D. V. T.: "The Matrix Multiplier and Distributed Lags," *Econometrica*, Vol. 31, No. 3 (July, 1963), pp. 514–29.

Brauer, A.: "On the Theorems of Perron and Frobenius on Nonnegative Matrices," Chapter 7 in *Studies in Mathematical Analysis and Related Topics: Essays in Honor of George Pólya* (G. Szegö *et al.*, eds.) Stanford, Stanford University Press, 1962.

Dimitriev, N., and E. Dynkin: "On Characteristic Roots of Stochastic Matrices," *Bulletin de l'Académie des Sciences de l'URSS*, Série Mathematique, Vol. 10 (1946), pp. 167–184.

Dorfman, R., P. A. Samuelson, and R. M. Solow: *Linear Programming and Economic Analysis*, New York, McGraw-Hill, 1958.

Fisher, F. M.: "An Alternate Proof and Extension of Solow's Theorem on Nonnegative Square Matrices," *Econometrica*, Vol. 30, No. 2 (April, 1962), pp. 349–350. Reprinted as Chapter 8 in this volume.

McKenzie, L.: "Matrices with Dominant Diagonals and Economic Theory," Chapter 4 in *Mathematical Methods in the Social Sciences, 1959* (Arrow, Karlin, and Suppes, eds.) Stanford, Stanford University Press, 1960.

Solow, R. M.: "On the Structure of Linear Models," *Econometrica*, Vol. 20, No. 1 (January, 1952), pp. 29–46.

CHAPTER 10

A Simple Proof of the Fisher–Fuller Theorem (1972)

Several years ago, Fisher and Fuller (1958) proved that if P is a real square matrix with all members of its "nested set" of principal minors non-zero, then there exists a real diagonal matrix, D, such that the characteristic roots of DP are all real, negative, and distinct. This interesting and powerful result, used by the authors to derive further results concerning convergence of linear iterative processes, has since also proved of interest to economists studying the stability of economic general equilibrium.[1]

Fisher and Fuller's original proof of their theorem, however, is quite laborious, requiring fairly detailed examination of the characteristic polynomial. As it happens, it is possible to give a much simpler proof (although not a technically more elementary one), and that is the purpose of the present note.

Fisher and Fuller consider the following condition on a real $n \times n$ matrix, P.

> (A) P has at least one sequence of non-zero principal minors, M_k of every order $k = 1, \ldots, n$, such that M_{k-1} is one of the k first principal minors of M_k.

(I shall call such a sequence of principal minors – whether its members are non-zero or not – a "nested set".) They prove:

Theorem 1.   *If P is a real $n \times n$ matrix satisfying* (A), *then there exists a real diagonal matrix, $D = $ diag (d_i) such that the characteristic roots of DP are all real, negative, and distinct.*[2]

Since the signs of the d_i may be freely chosen, there is no loss of generality (and some convenience) in replacing (A) by:

> (H) P has at least one nested set of principal minors, M_k, such that

---

[1] See especially McFadden (1968). The relevance of the Fisher–Fuller Theorem for such analyses was first noted by Newman (1959–60).

[2] This is Fisher and Fuller's Theorem 1 (1958), p. 418, together with the non-trivial part of their Corollary. The remainder of their Corollary consists of observing that the characteristic roots of DP can be scaled as desired by appropriate choice of D.

$(-1)^k M_k > 0, \quad k = 1, \ldots, n.$

(A matrix satisfying this condition will be called *Hicksian*.)

And then proving the very slightly stronger:

Theorem 1′. *If P is a real n × n Hicksian matrix, then there exists a real diagonal matrix D* = diag *(d_i) with positive diagonal elements such that the characteristic roots of DP are all real, negative, and distinct.*

This is the form of direct interest to stability theorists in economics where the d_i are the speeds of adjustment in different markets. The formal proof that Theorem 1′ implies Theorem 1 is given in the footnote.[3]

Proof. The proof is by induction on n, the theorem being obviously true for $n = 1$. We thus suppose it true for matrices of order $n - 1$. Let a bar over a matrix denote the submatrix formed by deleting the last row and column. It is clear that if P is Hicksian, so is $\bar{P}$. Hence, by the induction hypothesis it is possible to choose positive $d_1, \ldots, d_{n-1}$ so that the characteristic roots of $\overline{DP}$ are all real, negative, and distinct. Consider the characteristic roots of DP as functions of d_n. At $d_n = 0$, there is one zero characteristic root and the remaining $n - 1$ roots are those of $\overline{DP}$. It follows from the well-known fact that the characteristic roots are continuous in the elements of the matrix (and, indeed, directly from Fisher and Fuller's Lemma, 1958, p. 421) that for d_n positive and sufficiently small, all the characteristic roots of DP will still be real and distinct and $n - 1$ of them will be negative. The remaining root must then be negative also, however, since the determinant is the product of the characteristic roots and

$$(-1)^n |DP| = (-1)^n |D\|P| > 0,$$

because the d_i are positive and P is Hicksian.   Q.E.D.

As a matter of fact, it is possible to go further than this and to use similar methods to prove a somewhat stronger version (essentially implicit in the Fisher–Fuller proof, though not stated separately by them). Again we work with the Hicksian variant of the theorem, the carry-over to matrices satisfying (A) but not (H) being obvious.

---

[3] *Proof that Theorem 1′ implies Theorem 1.* Let P be a real $n × n$ matrix satisfying (A). Then there clearly exist real scalars, $c_1, \ldots, c_n$, such that $P* \equiv CP$ satisfies (H), where $C = $ diag (c_i). By Theorem 1′, there exists a real diagonal matrix, $D* = $ diag (d_i^*) with positive diagonal elements such that the characteristic roots of $D*P*$ are all real, negative, and distinct. But since $D*P* = D*CP$, this is just the conclusion of Theorem 1, with $D = D*C$.

It is, of course, obvious that Theorem 1 implies Theorem 1′ with the exception of the statement that the d_i in the latter theorem can be chosen to be all positive.

Theorem 2.   *Let P be a real $n \times n$ Hicksian matrix. Then for any α, $0 < \alpha \le 1$, there exists an $\varepsilon > 0$ and a δ, $0 < \delta < 1$, such that for all real diagonal matrices $D = \text{diag}\ (d_i)$ with positive diagonal elements satisfying $\alpha\varepsilon \le d_k/d_{k-1} \le \varepsilon$, $k = 2, \ldots, n$, the characteristic roots of DP are all real and negative. Moreover, denoting those characteristic roots by $\lambda_k(k = 1, \ldots, n)$, and numbering them in order of descending absolute value, $\lambda_k/\lambda_{k-1} < \delta$, for $k = 2, \ldots, n$.*

   Proof.   Again the proof is by induction, the theorem being obvious for $n = 1$. We thus assume the theorem true for matrices of order $n - 1$. As in the proof of Theorem 1', we use a bar over a matrix to denote the submatrix formed by deleting the last row and column, and we observe that the induction hypothesis applies to $\overline{P}$. We denote by $\overline{\varepsilon}$ and $\overline{\delta}$ the ε and δ, respectively whose existence is stated in the induction hypothesis applied to $\overline{P}$.

   It will obviously suffice to prove the theorem for D restricted to have $d_1 = 1$, since the ratios of the characteristic roots of DP are homogeneous of degree zero in the d_k. We define the set:

$$\overline{S} \equiv \{\overline{D}|d_1 = 1; \alpha\overline{\varepsilon} \le d_k/d_{k-1} \le \overline{\varepsilon}, k = 2, \ldots, n-1\}.$$

   Now, for all $\overline{D} \in \overline{S}$, the ratios, λ_k/λ_{k-1} ($k = 2, \ldots, n$) are continuous in d_n at $d_n = 0$. Since $\overline{S}$ is compact, such continuity is uniform. Denoting by $\overline{\lambda}_k(k = 1, \ldots, n - 1)$ the characteristic roots of $\overline{DP}$, it is clear that for any $\eta > 0$, there exists an $\varepsilon_n > 0$, such that if $0 < d_n < \varepsilon_n$, then for all $\overline{D} \in \overline{S}$:

$$\left| \frac{\lambda_k}{\lambda_{k-1}} - \frac{\overline{\lambda}_k}{\overline{\lambda}_{k-1}} \right| < \eta \quad (k = 2, \ldots, n-1) \tag{1}$$

and

$$\left| \frac{\lambda_n}{\lambda_{n-1}} \right| < \eta. \tag{2}$$

Clearly, (1) together with the induction hypothesis implies:

$$\frac{\lambda_k}{\lambda_{k-1}} < \frac{\overline{\lambda}_k}{\overline{\lambda}_{k-1}} + \eta < \overline{\delta} + \eta \quad (k = 2, \ldots, n-1). \tag{3}$$

Choose $\eta < 1 - \overline{\delta}$. The theorem now follows with $\delta = \overline{\delta} + \eta$ and ε chosen so that $\varepsilon < \min\ (\overline{\varepsilon}, \varepsilon_n)$, the negativity of λ_n following as in the proof of Theorem 1'.   Q.E.D.

   So far as I have been able to tell, however, McFadden's strong form of the theorem (1968, p. 348) in which the lower bound of the ratios of the d_k is dispensed with (and $\delta = 1$ is allowed so that the ratios of the roots are not bounded away from unity) cannot be simply proved by similar methods but does depend on the intimate examination of the characteristic polynomial given by Fisher and Fuller.

REFERENCES

Fisher, M. E. and Fuller, A. T. On the stabilization of matrices and the convergence of linear iterative processes. *Proc. Cambridge Philos. Soc.* **54** (1958), 417–425.

McFadden, D. On Hicksian Stability, Chapter 14 of J. N. Wolfe, ed. *Value, capital and growth: papers in honour of Sir John Hicks* (Edinburgh: Edinburgh University Press, 1968).

Newman, P. Some notes on stability conditions. *Review of Economic Studies* **27** (1959–60), 1–9.

CHAPTER 11

Gross Substitutes
and the Utility Function (1972)

As is very well known, the case in which all excess demands have the gross substitute property is one in which very strong results can be obtained concerning the uniqueness and stability of general equilibrium.[1] Considering how long this has been known,[2] it is perhaps remarkable that we apparently do not possess a convenient characterization of the class of utility functions that yield individual demand functions with the gross substitute property. The standard example of such a utility function is the Cobb–Douglas (although this is not strictly correct unless all endowments are positive; see below), but it is evident that this is not the only example, an immediate generalization being given by the Stone–Geary linear expenditure system

$$U = \prod_{i=1}^{n}(x_i - b_i)^{\gamma_i}, \qquad \sum_{i=1}^{n}\gamma_i = 1, \qquad \gamma_i > 0, \qquad i = 1, \ldots, n, \qquad (1)$$

provided that $b_i \le 0, i = 1, \ldots, n$. (Here, as later, x_i denotes the amount of the i-th good demanded).

The present note provides a characterization of the entire class of utility functions having the gross substitute property. Since the primary interest in that property is in the analysis of general equilibrium, we shall mainly concern ourselves with the demand functions that arise in a condition of exchange rather than with those that arise when income is fixed, independent of prices, the extension of the results to the latter case being given at the end of the paper. We shall also insist, therefore, that the gross

I am indebted to Frank Hahn for suggesting this problem, and to Peter Diamond, Robert M. Solow, and especially Daniel McFadden for helpful suggestions. Since the central proposition of this note turns out to be one of those that are very easy to prove once one knows what to look for, it may not be obvious to the reader what the contributions of this vast array of talent actually were. It is obvious to me, however.

[1] See, for example, Negishi (1962) or Arrow and Hahn (1971).
[2] The gross substitute assumption figured in the relations between Hicksian stability and local dynamic stability. See Metzler (1945).

substitute property be present independent of the consumer's initial endowment.[3]

We thus suppose that the consumer maximizes a utility function $U(x_1, \ldots, x_n)$ subject to the constraint

$$\sum_{i=1}^{n} p_i x_i = \sum_{i=1}^{n} p_i \bar{x}_i \equiv Y, \tag{2}$$

where $\bar{x}_i$ denotes the consumer's initial holdings of the i-th commodity, and income Y is defined by the identity in (2), but is not held constant. We assume that the solution to this maximization problem yields differentiable demand functions in the usual way. We denote by x, $\bar{x}$, and p, the vectors of the x_i, $\bar{x}_i$, and p_i, respectively.

Definition. *A utility function $U(x)$ is said to have the gross substitute property (GS) if and only if, for all semipositive endowment vectors $\bar{x}$ and strictly positive price vectors p such that $Y \equiv p'\bar{x} > 0$, the maximization of $U(x)$ subject to (2) yields demand functions with the property that*

$$\partial x_i / \partial p_j > 0, \qquad i, j = 1, \ldots, n; j \neq i. \tag{3}$$

If the strict inequality in (3) is replaced by a weak inequality, $U(x)$ will be said to have the weak gross substitute property (WGS).

Three bits of notation will be needed below. We let e_i denote the income elasticity of demand for the i-th commodity:

$$e_i \equiv (\partial x_i / \partial Y)(Y / x_i); \tag{4}$$

α_i denotes the share of expenditure devoted to the i-th commodity:

$$\alpha_i \equiv p_i x_i / Y; \tag{5}$$

and η_{ij} denotes the Allen–Uzawa elasticity of substitution between commodities i and j (a formal representation is given below).[4]

We shall show below that if all goods are normal (income elasticities nonnegative), then a necessary and sufficient condition for $U(x)$ to have GS is that, for every pair of commodities, the Allen–Uzawa elasticity of substitution exceeds the greater of the two income elasticities. To take care of the case of inferior goods, however, we prove the general

---

[3] In this regard, it may be worth pointing out that Houthakker's observation (1961, p. 720) that the assumption of universal gross substitutes implies that all demand curves are elastic with respect to own price is not correct for the form that matters in general equilibrium analysis. This is because Houthakker's argument takes total expenditure as constant and independent of prices, which it will not be if the consumer earns his income by supplying goods or factors. However, in view of *Corollary 6* below, Houthakker's observation is true of the income–constant demand curves derived from utility functions whose endowment–constant demand functions exhibit the gross substitute property even if it need not be true of the latter functions themselves.

[4] Defined for goods as though they were factors of production. See Uzawa (1962).

Theorem. *A necessary and sufficient condition for* U(x) *to have* GS *is that for every* $i, j = 1, \ldots, n, j \neq i$, *positive income Y and strictly positive price vector* p,

$$\eta_{ij} > \max\left\{e_i, e_j, e_i\left(1 - \frac{1}{\alpha_j}\right), e_j\left(1 - \frac{1}{\alpha_i}\right)\right\}. \tag{6}$$

(*A necessary and sufficient condition for* U(x) *to have* WGS *is that* (6) *hold with a weak rather than a strong inequality.*)[5]

Proof. Consider the expenditure function, giving the minimum expenditure required to obtain a given utility level:

$$Y = C(U, p). \tag{7}$$

Then denoting differentiation by subscripts in the obvious way,

$$x_i = C_i, \tag{8}$$

and

$$\eta_{ij} = CC_{ij}/C_iC_j.[6] \tag{9}$$

By Slutsky's theorem

$$\partial x_i/\partial p_j = C_{ij} - [(\partial x_i/\partial Y)(x_j - \bar{x}_j)], \tag{10}$$

whence

$$\partial x_i/\partial p_j = (C_iC_j/C)\eta_{ij} - (\partial x_i/\partial Y)(x_j - \bar{x}_j). \tag{11}$$

Hence, for this to be positive, it is necessary and sufficient that (for all i and $j \neq i$),

$$\eta_{ij} > (C/C_iC_j)(\partial x_i/\partial Y)(x_j - \bar{x}_j). \tag{12}$$

But $C = Y$, $C_i = x_i$, and $C_j = x_j$, so (12) is equivalent to

$$\eta_{ij} > e_i[1 - (\bar{x}_j/x_j)]. \tag{13}$$

For GS, it is necessary and sufficient that (13) hold for all possible choices of $\bar{x}_j$, i.e., for all $\bar{x}_j$ in the closed interval $[0, Y/p_j]$, and hence obviously necessary and sufficient that it hold for $\bar{x}_j$ at the endpoints of that interval. This yields

---

[5] η_{ij} is undefined if either x_i or x_j is zero; so, strictly speaking, the theorem only gives a condition that is necessary and sufficient at strictly positive x. Of course, GS implies that there is no open neighborhood in price space in which $x_i = 0$ identically (no real corner solutions) but WGS would allow this. It is clear from continuity, moreover, that if GS or WGS holds for all strictly positive x, then at least WGS holds when some $x_i = 0$. This problem will be ignored from now on.
[6] See Uzawa (1962).

$$\eta_{ij} > e_i, \tag{14}$$

and

$$\eta_{ij} > e_i[1 - (Y/p_j x_j)] = e_i[1 - (1/\alpha_j)]. \tag{15}$$

The theorem now follows on observing that η_{ij} is symmetric and that the proposition about WGS will hold if the strict inequality is replaced with a weak one throughout the proof.

This is an intuitive result, for it says that if indifference curves are sufficiently flat, $U(x)$ will have GS. How flat they have to be is given by the precise statement of the theorem. Another way of putting it is that the theorem shows the precise sense in which substitution effects must dominate income effects.

We can go on to state several immediate corollaries, in all of which WGS can be substituted for GS if a weak inequality is substituted for the strict one.

Corollary 1. *If all goods are normal, a necessary and sufficient condition for GS is that for every $i, j = 1, \ldots, n, j \neq i$, positive income Y, and strictly positive price vector p,*

$$\eta_{ij} > \max\{e_i, e_j\}. \tag{16}$$

Proof. If $e_i \geq 0$, then $e_i \geq e_i(1 - 1/\alpha_j)$.

As stated above, in the normal case, Allen–Uzawa substitution elasticities greater than income elasticities is necessary and sufficient for GS.

Corollary 2. *A necessary condition for GS is that for every $i, j = 1, \ldots, n, j \neq i$, positive income Y, and strictly positive price vector p,*

$$\eta_{ij} > 0. \tag{17}$$

Proof. Either $e_i \geq 0$ or else $e_i[1 - (1/\alpha_j)] \geq 0$, since $\alpha_j \leq 1$.

Hence, as we should expect, a necessary condition for all pairs of goods to be gross substitutes is that all pairs be net substitutes.

Corollary 3. *If the indifference map is homothetic, a necessary and sufficient condition for GS is that for all $i, j = 1, \ldots, n, j \neq i$, positive income Y, and strictly positive price vector p,*

$$\eta_{ij} > 1. \tag{18}$$

Proof. In the homothetic case, $e_i = 1, i = 1, \ldots, n$.

Corollary 4. *A necessary condition for GS is that for all positive income Y, and strictly positive price vector p, there exist at least one pair of commodities $i, j \neq i$, for which (18) holds.*

Proof. At least one $e_i \geq 1$.

Corollary 3 provides an easy method for generating examples of utility functions with GS. Take any constant returns production function with Allen–Uzawa elasticities of substitution bounded above unity. It also shows that the Cobb–Douglas utility function does not in fact have GS, as we have defined it, but only WGS (the same is true of the displaced Cobb–Douglas given in (1) unless all the b_i are strictly negative). This occurs (as is easy to verify by direct computation) because $\bar{x}_j$ is allowed to be zero. If the consumer does not hold any of the jth commodity and has a Cobb–Douglas utility function, its price does not affect his demand for any other commodity.

Before closing, we may ask, for completeness, about the slightly different problem in which Y is fixed in (2), so that it is the income–constant demand curves rather than the endowment–constant demand curves that are to exhibit GS. (I take the terminology to be obvious.) Obviously, it is sufficient for this that the endowment–constant demand curves exhibit GS for all semipositive endowments; what is not so clear is whether this is necessary. In fact it is necessary if all goods are normal, as is shown by the following two corollaries.

Corollary 5. *A necessary and sufficient condition for the income–constant demand curves to exhibit GS is that, for all $i, j = 1, \ldots, n, j \neq i$, positive income Y, and strictly positive price vector p,*

$$\eta_{ij} > \max\{e_i, e_j\}. \tag{19}$$

Proof. This follows from the proof of the theorem rather than from the theorem itself. In the income–constant demand curves, Slutsky's equation differs from (10) by setting $\bar{x}_j = 0$. The rest of the proof goes through as before.

Corollary 6. *A necessary condition for the endowment–constant demand curves to exhibit GS is that the income–constant demand curves do. If all goods are normal, this is also sufficient.*

Proof. The first statement (which is in any case obvious) follows from the theorem and *Corollary 5*. The second statement follows from *Corollaries* 1 and 5.

Finally, we may add two remarks. First, it follows from the proof of the theorem that if the ith good is normal, a necessary and sufficient condition for goods i and j to be gross *complements* at some price-income point, i.e., for $(\partial x_i / \partial p_j) < 0$, is that $\eta_{ij} < e_i$ at that point. This holds both for the endowment–constant and the income–constant demand curves. (In the latter case, normality is not required for this result.)

Second, the developments in the proof of the theorem can be used to obtain an alternative form of the Slutsky equation. Restricting attention, for convenience, to the income-constant version, set $\bar{x}_j = 0$ in (11), multiply through by p_j/x_i, and use the facts that $C_i = x_i$, $C_j = x_j$, and $C = Y$ to obtain

$$(\partial x_i / \partial p_j)(p_j / x_i) = a_j(\eta_{ij} - e_i), \tag{20}$$

so that the cross-elasticity of demand for good i with respect to good j is given as the fraction of income spent on good j, multiplied by the difference between the Allen–Uzawa elasticity of substitution for the two goods and the income elasticity of demand for good i.

REFERENCES

K. J. Arrow and F. H. Hahn, *General Competitive Analysis*, Holden-Day, San Francisco, 1971.

H. S. Houthakker, The present state of consumption theory, *Econometrica* **29** (1961), 704–740.

L. Metzler, Stability of multiple markets: The Hicks conditions, *Econometrica* **13** (1945), 277–292.

T. Negishi, The stability of a competitive economy: A survey article, *Econometrica* **30** (1962), 635–669.

H. Uzawa, Production functions with constant elasticities of substitution, *Rev. Econ. Studies* **29** (1962), 291–299.

PART II

Welfare Economics and Consumer Theory

CHAPTER 12

Income Distribution, Value Judgments, and Welfare (1956)

I.   Introduction

The only remaining divergence of belief (in welfare economics) seems to be on pragmatic, tactical questions: e.g., shall all changes which *could* make everyone better off but which might in fact hurt some people be made mandatory in the expectation or hope that the cumulative effects of following such a rule will be better (for all or some) than if some other rule is followed? Shall we set up a rule of unanimous consent for any new change so that compensatory bribes must be in fact paid? To answer such questions we must go beyond economics.[1]

Yes, we must go beyond economics, for it is inevitable that in discussing income distribution and its relation to welfare we must discuss value judgments, but economic analysis may enable us to see the implications of our value judgments more clearly, to discover what classes or types of value judgments lead to particular conclusions.

It is the intent of this paper to argue that the first of Samuelson's questions may be answered in the affirmative, to attempt to show that under value judgments that seem reasonably plausible, there exists a large class of situations with higher potential welfare (i.e., satisfying the Kaldor-Hicks-Scitovsky criterion)[2] than that of the present situation, but that involves widely different income distributions,[3] moves to which situations should be recommended. To reach such a conclusion, we shall have to discuss value judgments, both as to their implications and as to their acceptability. Such discussion is to be welcomed, not avoided, for it will be one of the points that this paper will attempt to demonstrate that in

The author wishes to express his appreciation to Professor Carl Kaysen, at whose suggestion this study was undertaken, to Mr. Richard Friedberg for many helpful conversations, and to Professors Robert M. Solow and John S. Chipman for their kind interest and criticism.

[1] Samuelson (1952, 37n).

[2] That an economic change is desirable if the gainers could overcompensate the losers and the losers cannot profitably bribe the gainers to oppose the change. See Little (1950, chap. VI and Appendix).

[3] A "situation" may be thought of as being completely described by the *absolute* amount of each commodity consumed by each individual in society, while a "distribution" is the *percentage* of each commodity that he consumes. We shall be more rigorous below.

183

welfare economics, as elsewhere, there can be no such thing as refusing to make value judgments.

Our problem, then, is to discover what value judgments concerning income distribution imply the existence of a large set of situations such as that just described. The difficulties involved are numerous. In essence, however, the more serious of them are formally similar. They reduce to the problem of finding some method for comparing the magnitude of two vectors where the components of one may not all be greater than or equal to those of the other. Thus we find ourselves confronted with the question of the measurement of real income in two ways: how to tell when it has increased and how to tell when a shift in its composition has increased a given person's utility. In the one case, it is possible to speak unequivocally in all situations only if prices, the weights we attach to the different components of the real income vector, are assumed unchanged; in the other, only if tastes, in some sense the weights here, are assumed constant. The central problem of welfare economics is the same. How, assuming that we have a measurable utility for each person, or more difficult, if we have an ordinal measure for each, can we assign weights to the utility of various individuals so that we may secure a scalar, ordinal (at least) measure of welfare?[4] It is with this question, in a slightly less technical form, that distribution value judgments are concerned.

It might be asked at this juncture, however, why bother discussing such a difficult problem? If we are prepared to make value judgments comparing distributions, why balk at comparing situations? The point is well taken. Perhaps the only answer is that the human mind (or at least those examples of it in the economic profession) seems to have a great desire to deny its own irrationality, to select a relative statement and behave as if it were an absolute. Thus the classical economists acted implicitly or explicitly on the value judgment that the consumer ought to get what he says he wants, and from this derived the perfectly competitive model. On a somewhat lower level, it is conceivable that a large class of value judgments that differ as regards distribution would imply the same judgment as to situations. Since we may suppose that there is even more disagreement in comparing situations than in ranking distributions, it would be helpful to have an analysis of the consequences of various distribution

---

[4] Note that we are already making the value judgment that welfare is a function of individual *utilities*. This is not inevitable; we do not, for instance, consider the utilities of non-rational beings such as the insane or even of children of much relevance for welfare. (I owe this point to Professor Robert M. Solow.)

value judgments, an analysis of the restrictions placed by such value judgments on the shape of the Bergson welfare function.[5]

It will be best, then, to begin by discussing exactly what we mean by "distribution." Of course, we are interested in the real, not the money income of the individual or of the society and this makes things somewhat more complex. Real income is not a scalar but a vector whose components are amounts of commodities. Thus, we write the real income of the jth individual in the society as:

$$\begin{bmatrix} s_{1j} \\ s_{2j} \\ \cdot \\ \cdot \\ \cdot \\ s_{nj} \end{bmatrix} = s_j$$

where s_{ij} is the amount of the ith commodity that he possesses. His money income is simply $p's_j$, where p' is the row vector of the prices obtaining at a particular moment. Similarly, for the community as a whole, real income is the vector:

$$\begin{bmatrix} C_1 \\ C_2 \\ \cdot \\ \cdot \\ \cdot \\ C_n \end{bmatrix} = C$$

where

$$C_i = \sum_{j=1}^{m} s_{ij} \qquad (i = 1, 2, \ldots, n)$$

where m is the total number of individuals in the community.

Now, it is easy to talk of the distribution of money income, for we can easily speak of the percentage that one scalar (the money income of a given individual) is of another scalar (total money income). Unfortunately, however, the case of real income is not so easy to handle, for we

[5] See Bergson (1938).

should properly mean by the distribution of real income the distribution of each component of C. Thus, whereas in the case of money income we can speak of a distribution *vector*:

$$M = (M_1, M_2, \ldots, M_m)$$

where

$$M_j = \frac{p's_j}{p'C},$$

in the case of real income we must speak of a distribution *matrix*:

$$X = [x_{ij}] \qquad (i = 1, \ldots, n)$$
$$(j = 1, \ldots, m)$$

where

$$x_{ij} = \frac{s_{ij}}{C_i},$$

the percent of the community's supply of the ith commodity that is possessed by the jth individual. If $\bar{C}$ is an $n \times n$ matrix whose diagonal elements are the elements of C and whose off-diagonal elements are zeros, then it is obvious that

$$\frac{p'\bar{C}X}{p'C} = \frac{p'S}{p'C} = M$$

S being an $n \times m$ matrix whose columns are s_j ($j = 1, 2, \ldots, m$).

Thus *for any given set of prices*[6] and real incomes, the distribution vector M, showing the percentage distribution of money income, also shows the percentage distribution of real income. Throughout the body of this paper, we shall make the assumption, for convenience only, that prices are constant (or, if it will be any more palatable, that only one commodity exists). This is done for ease of presentation only; the assumption is not necessary, and a proof of the more important theorems that does not make use of it may be found in the Appendix. In addition, we make the following assumptions:

(1) The present situation (i.e., the *terminus a quo* of a given change) is known with certainty as regards the total amount of money

---

[6] Of course, no particular significance attaches to the prices as market valuations of the commodities. Any arbitrary set of weights would do as well.

and real income and its distribution. The same is known of the effects of any change.

(2) The transition from the present situation to any other situation is made instantaneously.

(3) This transition has no effect on the availability of future alternatives. Together with assumption 2, this means that we are considering merely positions of static equilibrium without regard either for the process by which the equilibrium position is shifted or for the question of dynamic stability. Under these assumptions, in other words, we are considering a model of comparative statics. The time path of the variables involved does not concern us. These assumptions seem to be generally made in welfare economics insofar as they narrow the consideration of two situations to a comparison of their static qualities, that is, to a consideration of their relative desirabilities assuming that each could be maintained indefinitely.

However, if we agree to treat a given commodity consumed at two different times as two different commodities, then the generalization in the Appendix permits us to treat a "situation" as embracing a complete time-plan of consumption for each individual, thus removing much of the restrictiveness of the above assumption.

(4) We do *not* assume that the changes considered here have no effect on "noneconomic" components of welfare. Such considerations are presumed to be those on which (among others) the value judgments under consideration are made.

(5) Within a range large enough to include most moves from the present situation that are likely to be considered, distribution value judgments are *independent* of total income.[7]

---

[7] From now on, unless otherwise specified, we shall mean by "income" the total money income of the society, since prices are assumed constant. (In the following example, food, rather than paper money, is such a *numéraire*.)

That this assumption is somewhat restrictive may be seen from the following trivial example. Suppose a society consists of only two individuals, each of whom needs exactly three units of food per day to survive (all other needs are assumed satiated or nonexistent). Suppose further that on this desert island, under existing methods of cultivation, the food supply is only sufficient to give a total of four units per day. I think that it is clearly possible to say that it is better to give three units to one individual and one to the other than to give two units to each. In other words, it is plausible to deem the distribution vector (3/4, 1/4) better than the distribution vector (1/2, 1/2). Now suppose that through some revolution in the technology of date palm cultivation the food supply becomes sufficient, so that each of the men can live in luxury on four units a day. Then it is certainly conceivable that the same person who made the value judgment in the earlier case might now say that the distribution (1/2, 1/2) is better than (3/4, 1/4) since the unequal distribution starves one of the individuals. The point is that there are situa-

We now introduce the formal model and definitions that will be employed throughout the following two sections. Other definitions will be added as required.

Consider a society of m individuals; we set up a co-ordinate system in m-space, measuring along each axis the money income of a given individual. We denote the money income of the jth individual as y_j. Consider the set of hyperplanes:

$$Y = \sum_{j=1}^{m} y_j$$

where Y is the total money income of the community. We call these "income hyperplanes." In particular, we denote the present total income by $\bar{Y}$, and refer to the corresponding hyperplane as the "present income hyperplane."

To any point, y, in the m-space, draw the vector from the origin. The components of this vector, of course, are the incomes of the various individuals. If the income hyperplane on which the given point lies has $Y = Y^*$, then the *distribution vector* associated with that point is

$$\frac{(y_1, y_2, y_3, \ldots, y_m)}{Y^*}$$

where the numerator is, of course, the vector drawn from the origin to y. Note that a distribution vector has the property that the sum of its components is unity. Thus the several components represent the percentage shares of the corresponding individuals. Distribution vectors will be represented hereafter by the letters, R, P, Q, O, sometimes with prime marks (which no longer will denote transposes of matrices). In particular, we shall represent the present point by B, and the present point's distribution vector by P. Hence $B = P\bar{Y}$ by definition. We shall refer to distribution vectors simply as distributions where the meaning is clear.

We add the following definitions:

(a)   The symbol, b_k, denotes "is better than by value judgment k."
(b)   Similarly, g_k will denote "is at least as good as, by value judgment k." Where there are two subscripts under b or g, the respective relations hold by two value judgments.

tions, some not so trivial, in which a distribution value judgment need not be independent of total income. We shall revert to this later, merely pointing out here that we do not assume *complete* independence, but only independence within a certain range. For moves involving relatively small changes in aggregate income, this does not seem so very restrictive.

(c)   *A distribution value judgment* is a value judgment that provides
a complete ordering of distribution vectors.[8] (It may also
have other properties.) Thus, given any two distribution
vectors, R and Q, one and only one of the following relations
holds: either R b_k Q or Q b_k R or R g_k Q g_k R, where k is a
distribution value judgment. Also, O b_k Q and Q g_k R imply
O b_k R. (The g and b relations could be interchanged and
the statement would still hold. The g relation is also transitive
by itself, as is the b relation.) Note that b is not symmetric, while
g may be so and that g is reflexive while b is not. Finally,
obviously R b_k Q implies Q not b_k R, and Q not b_k R and R not
b_k Q imply R g_k Q g_k R. Also, of course, R g_k Q and Q not g_k R
imply R b_k Q. We shall use the subscripts, j and k, to denote distribution value judgments. (j may also be used to denote a particular component of a vector when there is no danger of
confusion.) b_{Ak} and g_{Ak} will mean b or g by value judgments A
and k.

(d) S_k will denote the set of points ranked at least as good as the
present one by value judgment k. As before, S_{Ak} will mean the
set of such points obtained by accepting both value judgment A
and value judgment k. We call S_k the "acceptable set" by k.

(e)   A distribution vector, Q, is *between* two others, P and R, if and
only if

$$Q_i = r_i P_i + (1 - r_i) R_i \qquad (0 \le r_i \le 1) \qquad (i = 1, \dots, m)$$

and $P \ne Q \ne R$. That is, one distribution vector is between two
others if each of its components is between the corresponding
components of the other two.[9]

(f)   A distribution value judgment, k, will be said to be *nontroughed*
from P to Q, if and only if Q g_k P implies that there exists no R
between P and Q such that P b_k R, where P, Q, and R are all

---

[8] By assumption 5, above, such orderings are independent of the level of total income.

[9] Professor John S. Chipman has pointed out privately that all theorems remain true if
"between" is defined more simply as "on the straight line between," since if Q is between
P and R in this simpler sense it is also between them in the sense defined in the text.
However, the most important use made of the concept is for the definition of "nontroughed" (definition (f)), and it does not seem reasonable to expect a distribution value
judgment to be nontroughed using the simpler sense of between and not using the more
complex sense. Moreover, if nontroughedness, using the more complex sense of between,
is a reasonable property to expect distribution value judgments to have, then *Theorem 2*
and *Corollary 1* of the next section have much more force than if the simpler notion were
employed, even though they are technically "weaker" theorems, and the same is true of
Theorems 4 and *5* and of *Corollary 5*.

distributions. (Note that $P \, g_k \, R$ is possible.) If k is nontroughed from P to *any* Q, it is said to be nontroughed at P. If it is nontroughed at *all* distributions, then it is said to be everywhere nontroughed. In other words, a distribution value judgment is nontroughed if a step in the right direction is not considered a bad step.

(g)   The symbol $\supset$ denotes "includes."

II.   The Formal Model – The Special Case

Traditionally, welfare economics has been based on an important value judgment, namely, that a situation A is better than a situation B if every individual in A is at least as well off as in B, and at least one individual is better off. So far as this goes, it is undoubtedly acceptable to most people as a tautology. But the value judgment did not stop here, but went on to say, first, that an individual's welfare increases with increasing consumption, and second, that the welfare of the individual depends *only* on what he consumes. These two statements are not at all the same thing. The first is an assumption that material wants are not satiated; the second is either a statement of fact or a statement of value or both. With the nonsatiation assumption we shall not argue. Welfare economics is not generally concerned with the problem of jaded appetites. It will be well, however, to understand exactly what is involved in the second statement.

We have just stated that the statement of the exclusive dependence of welfare on consumption is either a statement of fact or one of value or both. This is not immediately obvious. The statement has usually been made and objected to on empirical grounds. These objections have been well founded. There is no need here to belabor the point made by Veblen and Duesenberry among others that the happiness of the individual is not independent of nonconsumption factors. However, to reject the statement in question, *it is not enough to question its factual basis.* We not only must say that the welfare of the individual depends on nonconsumption factors, we must make the value judgment that such factors *ought to be considered* when discussing the welfare of the whole community. Thus the happiness of a wealthy miser might be decreased if he observed increased consumption by the poor; but this may be judged to be irrelevant, or of very little moment in considering total welfare. Of course, this is an extreme example, but the point is clear. It is possible to accept the statement that nonconsumption factors are irrelevant, not because they do not affect the happiness of the individual, but because we make a value judgment that assigns them little or no weight in the consideration of community welfare.

Thus interpreted, the traditional value judgment says that a situation A is to be considered better than a situation B, if every individual in A is able to consume at least as much as he could in B and at least one individual can consume more. We shall refer to this value judgment as *value judgment A* and shall be concerned in this section with the implications of its acceptance. In the next section we shall discuss the consequences of rejecting value judgment A and take up, so far as possible, the general case.

Thus throughout the remainder of this section it will be assumed that value judgment A is accepted, i.e., that no other value judgment discussed can contradict it. In other words, we take as an axiom that no point in S_A is in S_k^*, where S_k^* is the set of points pronounced unequivocally worse than the present one by value judgment k; similarly, no point in S_A^* is in S_k. Moreover, all points in $S_A(S_A^*)$ are in $S_{Ak}(S_{Ak}^*)$.

Let us consider the nature of the sets S_A and S_A^*. In terms of our model, S_A is the set of all points in the positive orthant drawn from B as the origin and including all points on the boundary of that orthant, while S_A^* is similarly the set of all points in the negative orthant from B, including the boundary, except for B itself. This is the case because with prices assumed constant money income is a measure of real income. Of course, the Kaldor-Hicks-Scitovsky criterion is simply the statement that a point C is better than B if, starting from C, some point in S_A, other than B itself, can be reached by a redistribution of income. This is the same as saying that C is better than B if it lies above the present income hyperplane.

We note some properties of value judgment A. First, it is not, on the face of it, a value judgment that has anything to do with distribution. We shall see shortly that this is not the case. Second, taken by itself, value judgment A does not give a complete ordering of all points in the m-space. As we shall see, taken together with certain distribution value judgments it does provide such an ordering. However, if a distribution value judgment consists *only* of an ordering of distributions, then that judgment together with value judgment A does not provide a complete ordering, generally speaking, of all points, since a point not in S_A may have a distribution vector that is judged better than P. For the present, until otherwise explicitly stated, all distribution value judgments will be assumed to provide *only* a complete ordering of distributions. The theorems stated under this assumption, however, remain valid when we add further features to the distribution value judgments involved, but such features are not needed in the proofs.

We thus have without proof:

Theorem 1. *Given any distribution value judgment, j, such that $R \, g_i \, P$ for some $R \neq P$:*

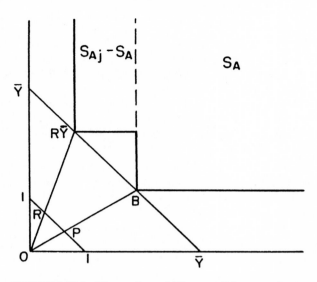

FIGURE 12.1. Illustration of *Theorem 1* for a two-man society.

(1) $S_{Aj} \supset S_A$

(2) $S_{Aj} \neq S_A$.   (See Figure 12.1)

Thus the making of a distribution value judgment widens the set of acceptable points, provided some other distribution than the present one is judged at least as good as the present one. If the value judgment made is nontroughed at P, however, we may say more than this.

Define a *direction vector*, Z, as a vector of m components (positive, negative, or zero) such that the sum of the components is zero and the sum of the squares of the components is unity. We say that the point, $W = B + \lambda°Z$, where $\lambda°$ is a nonnegative scalar, lies a distribution distance of $\lambda°$ from B in the Z direction. It is obvious that W is on the present income hyperplane and that this definition of distance is simply a special case of the usual definition. We define going from B to W as the operation of allowing λ to go from 0 to $\lambda°$ in the expression $(B + \lambda Z)$. This operation is merely a way of redistributing income, leaving total income unchanged. (Incidentally, it will be observed that the set of all direction vectors is the set of the radii of the unit hypercircle of dimension $(m - 2)$ with center at the origin and lying in the $(m - 1)$ dimension hyperplane $Y = 0$.)[10] We immediately have:

[10] This construction was suggested by Mr. Richard Friedberg.

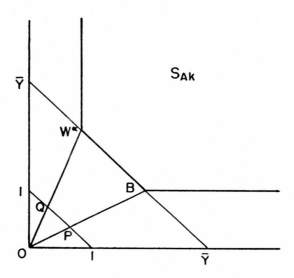

FIGURE 12.2. Illustration of *Theorem 2* for a two-man society.

Theorem 2. *Let k be a distribution value judgment nontroughed at P. From B go in any direction Z^a until a point $W^a = B + \lambda^a Z^a$ is reached such that $B\, b_k\, B + \lambda Z^a$ for $\lambda > \lambda^a$ and $W^a\, g_k\, B$. Then S_{Ak} includes all points passed through in going from B to W^a. (See Figure 12.2.)*

Proof. Let $W^a = Q\overline{Y}$. Let $C = RY$ be any point not B or W^a passed through in going from B to W^a. What we must prove is that $C\, g_k\, B$.

Since λ^a is the distribution distance from B to W^a, then:

$$Q\overline{Y} = \overline{Y} + \lambda^a Z^a.$$

Dividing by $\overline{Y}$,

$$Q = P + \frac{\lambda^a}{\overline{Y}} Z^a$$

or

$$Q_i = P_i + \frac{\lambda^a}{\overline{Y}} Z_i^{\,a} \qquad (i = 1, \ldots, m) \tag{1}$$

Similarly, if λ is the distribution distance of C from B,

$$R_i = P_i + \frac{\lambda^a}{\overline{Y}} Z_i^{\,a} \qquad (i = 1, \ldots, m) \tag{2}$$

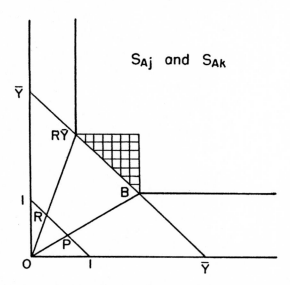

FIGURE 12.3. Illustration of *Corollary 1* for a two-man society. Hatched area is in S_{Ak} but not in S_{Aj}.

Solving (1) for $\frac{1}{\overline{Y}} Z_i^a$ and substituting in (2),

$$R_i = \left(1 - \frac{\lambda}{\lambda^a}\right) P_i + \frac{\lambda}{\lambda^a} Q_i \qquad (i = 1, \ldots, m) \tag{3}$$

But $\lambda < \lambda^a$ since C is passed through in going from B to W^a. Hence (3) shows that R is between Q and P. But by definition, W^a g_k B so that Q g_k P since both W^a and B are on the same income hyperplane. Then by the nontroughedness of k at P, R g_k P and thus C g_k B. Thus all points in or on the boundary of the positive orthant from C are in S_{Ak}, and the theorem is proved.

In other words, if starting at the present point we insist that compensation be paid by some individuals to others, and if we think any situation where only part of that compensation is paid (by and to the same individuals) is at least as good as the present one, then we must accept all points in the positive orthant from the point corresponding to that situation. The theorem has certain corollaries that we state without proof:

Corollary 1. *If j and k are two distribution value judgments such that R g_k P, R g_j P, and k is nontroughed from P to R, while j is not, then ceteris paribus $S_{Ak} \supset S_{Aj}$ and $S_{Ak} \neq S_{Aj}$. (See Figure 12.3.)*

We now take up the possibility of points below the present income hyperplane being in the acceptable set. By definition, $R \, b_k \, P$, for some distribution value judgment k, implies $R\overline{Y} \, b_k \, B$, but it is also possible that we might have $R(\overline{Y} - \varepsilon) \, g_k \, B$ for small enough positive ε. In other words, if we felt strongly enough about distribution we might feel that the situation would be improved if the distribution had improved, *even if we had to give up something in total income to do it.* That is, we might wish to achieve a better distribution even if the amount we take away from some individuals is greater than that we give to others. For example, an egalitarian who felt strongly enough about the matter might feel that an egalitarian distribution ought to be achieved even if we take more from the rich than we give to the poor. In our model, this would correspond to the feeling that movement to a better distribution compensates for going below the present income hyperplane. Note, however, that the acceptance of value judgment A puts a limit on this process. If we accept that value judgment, then the point $D = R(\overline{Y} - \varepsilon) \, g_k \, B$ cannot lie in or on the boundary of the negative orthant from B, for if it did it would be in S_k and S_{Ak}^* at the same time, contrary to assumption. Similarly, D cannot be in the negative orthant from any point $C = Q\overline{Y}$ where $P \, g_k \, Q$.

Thus we define an everywhere *compensating*[11] distribution value judgment as one for which (calling the value judgment in question k) $R \, b_k \, Q$ implies the existence of an $\varepsilon > 0$ for each fixed total income, Y^*, such that $R(Y^* - \varepsilon) \, g_k \, QY^*$ for every R and Q. Of course, value judgments may be compensating only for some R and Q, and not be everywhere compensating. Throughout what follows, it will be understood that where we speak of a compensating value judgment we mean one that is compensating for the relevant distributions. In general, the theorems and lemmas derived hold for the special limiting case of $\varepsilon = 0$, provided it is possible to fulfill their conditions in that case. We examine the properties of compensating value judgments.

Lemma 1. *Let k be a compensating distribution value judgment such that $R \, b_k \, Q \, b_k \, P$. Let $D = R(\overline{Y} - \varepsilon_1)$ and $C = Q(\overline{Y} - \varepsilon_2)$ exist such that $D \, g_k \, B \, g_k \, D$ and $C \, g_k \, B \, g_k \, C$. Then $\varepsilon_1 > \varepsilon_2$ (i.e., the better the distribution moved to, the greater the decrease in total income that will be accepted).*

Proof. Suppose $\varepsilon_1 \le \varepsilon_2$. Then consider the point $C' = Q(\overline{Y} - \varepsilon_1)$. Clearly $C' \, g_A \, C$. But $D \, b_k \, C'$. Hence $D \, b_{Ak} \, C$. But $B \, g_k \, D$ so that B

---

[11] "Compensating" because, as will be obvious later if it is not so already, such a judgment involves the notion that *compensation* in the usual sense must be paid if a move satisfying the Kaldor-Hicks-Scitovsky criterion is made and results in a distribution worse than the present one, as well as the idea that a decrease in total income may be *compensated* for by a shift to a better distribution.

b_{Ak} C contrary to assumption. Thus $\varepsilon_1 > \varepsilon_2$ and the lemma is proved.

Lemma 2. *Let k be a compensating distribution value judgment such that* $R\ b_k\ Q$. *Let* $D = R(\bar{Y} - \varepsilon_1)$, $C = Q(\bar{Y} - \varepsilon_2)$. *Then* $C\ g_{Ak}\ D$ *implies* $\varepsilon_1 > \varepsilon_2$ (*i.e., if a point with a poor distribution is ranked higher than a point with a better one, it must be because the first has a higher total income than the second*).

Proof. Suppose that $\varepsilon_2 \geq \varepsilon_1$. As in the proof of *Lemma 1* construct $C' = Q(\bar{Y} - \varepsilon_1)$. We have $D\ b_k\ C'\ g_A\ C$. Thus $D\ b_{Ak}\ C$ contrary to assumption. Hence $\varepsilon_1 > \varepsilon_2$. Q.E.D.

Now, as we remarked above, no point $D = R(\bar{Y} - \varepsilon)$ can lie within the negative orthant from B (or from any B' such that $B\ g_k\ B'$) if we are to have $D\ g_k\ B$. We may suppose, however, that some people may feel so strongly about distribution that they would be willing to accept any point with a better distribution than the present one so long as it was not in such a negative orthant, or on the boundary thereof. In other words, they would be willing to go from the present distribution to a better one, even if it meant taking away from some individuals and giving only an infinitesimal amount to others. We shall call this type of distribution value judgment *totally* compensating. As before, a distribution value judgment may be totally compensating for some distributions, partially compensating for others, and noncompensating for still others. In what follows, it will be understood that by "totally compensating," we mean totally compensating for the relevant distribution.

Let us for a moment return to *Theorem 2*. It is obvious that a special case occurs when no W^α exist save B (i.e., $\lambda^\alpha = 0$ for all α). If, in addition, k is "single-peaked" at P; that is, if for every α, $B + \lambda^2 Z^\alpha\ b_k\ B + \lambda^1 Z^\alpha$ if and only if $\lambda^1 > \lambda^2$ (i.e., distributions are ranked by their distance from the present one, the farther ones being worse) and k is also totally compensating, then S_{Ak} is identical with S_A. Of course, this is not a contradiction of *Theorem 1* whose conditions are not met. It is also quite apparent that the nontroughedness of k at P is irrelevant in this special case. Thus we have the very important corollary:

Corollary 2. *The acceptable set obtained by accepting value judgment A and refusing to make any further value judgments as to distribution is identical with that obtained by accepting value judgment A and making a totally compensating distribution value judgment that is single-peaked at P.*

In other words, the refusal to make a value judgment in this case, as in so many others, is in itself a value judgment, not only in the sense that one is saying that one *ought* to abstain from making value judgments, but also in the sense that the results obtained are those that would result from glorifying the present distribution. (Although not so strongly, since value judgment A gives us no ordering of points within the acceptable set, while a single-peaked value judgment does.)[12] One cannot abstain from making distribution value judgments; it is a "forced option," in William James' phrase, and, since we all do make value judgments, we had better make them explicit.

We examine the properties of totally compensating distribution value judgments. First, we may immediately state without proof:

Corollary 3. *If the conditions of Theorem 2 are met, and if, in addition, for every a, for any $C = B + \lambda^1 Z^a$ and $D = B + \lambda^2 Z^a$ where $B\ b_k\ C$, $B\ b_k\ D$, $C\ g_k\ D$ only if $\lambda^1 \le \lambda^2$, then that part of S_{Ak} that lies on or above the present income hyperplane is precisely the set described by Theorem 2 if and only if k is totally compensating.*

Lemma 3. *Let k be a totally compensating distribution value judgment such that $R\ b_k\ P$. Let $D = R(\overline{Y} - \varepsilon^*)$ where $\varepsilon^* > 0$ and*

(a) $B\ b_A\ R(\overline{Y} - \varepsilon)$ *for* $\varepsilon \ge \varepsilon^*$,
(b) $R(\overline{Y} - \varepsilon)\ b_k\ B$ *for* $\varepsilon < \varepsilon^*$.

Let $\theta = \max_{Q} \left(\min_{i} \left(\frac{Q_i}{R_i} \right) \right)$

where $P\ g_k\ Q$ and $i = 1, \ldots, m$.

Then:

(1) $D = \theta R \overline{Y}$
(2) $\varepsilon^* = \overline{Y}(1 - \theta)$
(3) *any point $C = Q'(\overline{Y} - \varepsilon_1)$, where $\varepsilon_1 > 0$ and $R\ b_k\ Q'$, is in S_{Ak} only if $\varepsilon_1 < \varepsilon^*$.*

Proof: (1) Since D has properties a and b, it is obvious that it must be just on the boundary of the negative orthant from some B' such that $B\ g_k\ B'$. Moreover, of all such points, D must be the closest to the present income hyperplane. (See Figure 12.4.) Hence, if $D' = \theta R \overline{Y}$ can be proven to be that point, then we shall have proved that $D = \theta R \overline{Y}$.

Without loss of generality, we may suppose that $\theta = \dfrac{Q_j}{R_j}$. Then,

---

[12] This was pointed out by Professor Solow.

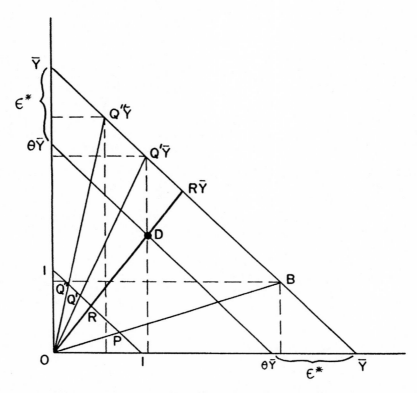

FIGURE 12.4. Illustration of location of point D of *Lemma 3* for a two-man society. $P g_k Q'$ and $P g_k Q''$.

$$D_j' = \theta R_j \overline{Y} = \frac{Q_j}{R_j} R_j \overline{Y} \qquad \text{and}$$

$$D_i' = \theta R_i \overline{Y} = \frac{Q_j}{R_j} R_i \overline{Y} \le \frac{Q_i}{R_i} R_i \overline{Y} = Q_i \overline{Y} \quad (i = 1, \ldots, j-1, j+1, \ldots, m).$$

Hence D' is on the boundary of the negative orthant from $Q\overline{Y}$, and, by assumption, $P g_k Q$ so that $B g_k Q\overline{Y}$.

Moreover, because of the way in which θ was chosen, letting $\frac{O_h}{R_h} = \min_i \left(\frac{O_i}{R_i} \right)$ for some O, different from Q, such that $P g_k O$, we have:

$$D'_h = \theta R_h \overline{Y} > \frac{O_h}{R_h} R_h \overline{Y} = O_h \overline{Y},$$

so that D' is not in the negative orthant from $O\overline{Y}$. Hence D' has properties a and b, and thus $D' = D$. Q.E.D.

(2) Since $D' = D$,

$$\sum_{i=1}^{m} \theta R_i \overline{Y} = \overline{Y} - \varepsilon^* \qquad \text{or}$$

$$\theta \overline{Y} \sum_{i=1}^{m} R_i = \overline{Y} - \varepsilon^*.$$

But R is a distribution vector; hence, by definition:

$$\sum_{i=1}^{m} R_i = 1.$$

Thus,

$$\theta \overline{Y} = \overline{Y} - \varepsilon^* \qquad \text{or}$$
$$\varepsilon^* = \overline{Y}(1 - \theta) \qquad \text{as asserted.}$$

(3) If C is in S_{Ak} then $C \, g_{Ak} \, B \, b_A \, D$ or $C \, b_{Ak} \, D$. But we know that R $b_k \, Q'$, hence, by *Lemma 2*, $\varepsilon_1 < \varepsilon^*$. Q.E.D.

We are now in a position to examine fully an important special case, namely, that of the totally compensating, strict egalitarian distribution value judgment. This states that the best distribution is $E = \left(\dfrac{1}{m}, \dfrac{1}{m}, \ldots, \dfrac{1}{m} \right)$, and that all other distributions are ranked according to their distribution distances from E, the closer ones being better. We consider the case where the judgment, in addition, is totally compensating. Note that the judgment is everywhere nontroughed. We have:

Theorem 3. *If k is the totally compensating, strict egalitarian distribution value judgment just described, then:*

(1) *S_{Ak} is the set of all points the sum of whose co-ordinates is greater than m ($\min B_i$) and which are in the interior of the space bounded by the hyperplanes*

$$y_i = \min B_j \qquad (i, j = 1, \ldots, m)$$

plus some, but not all points on those hyperplanes, the sum of whose co-ordinates is greater than m ($\min B_j$).

(2) *These hyperplanes meet at the point $D = E(\overline{Y} - \varepsilon^*)$ where E*

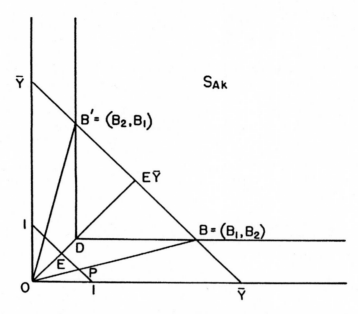

FIGURE 12.5. Illustration of *Theorem 3* for a two-man society.

is the egalitarian distribution vector and ε^* has the properties a and b of Lemma 3. (See Figure 12.5.)

(3) $\varepsilon^* = \bar{Y} - m \min B_j = \bar{Y}(1 - m \min P_j)$.

Proof. It is immediately obvious that, defining θ as in *Lemma 3*, with $R = E, \theta = m \min P_j$. Assertions 2 and 3 follow immediately from *Lemma 3*. It remains to prove assertion 1.

We first show that any point in the interior of the space described is in S_{Ak}; then that no point not in the interior or on the boundary of that space is in S_{Ak}; finally, that there exist points on the boundary that are, and points on the boundary that are not, in S_{Ak}.

Thus let C be any point in the interior of the space described. Then choose $\varepsilon = \varepsilon(C)$ greater than zero but less than ε^* such that C is in the positive orthant from the point $E(\bar{Y} - \varepsilon)$. This can always be done since $C_i > \min B_i$ for all i. Clearly, however, this latter point $b_k B$, for we have already shown that ε^* has property b. But $C\, b_A\, E(\bar{Y} - \varepsilon)$, and thus $C\, b_{Ak}$ B and is in S_{Ak}.

Now, let F be any point not in the interior or on the boundary of the space described. Then $F_i < \min B_j$ for at least one i. Construct the point $F' = (\min F_j, \min F_j, \ldots, \min F_j)$ and consider the set of points lying on higher income hyperplanes than does F' and which are in the interior of the hyperspace bounded by the hyperplanes

$$y_i = \min F_j \qquad (i = 1, \ldots, m)$$

A similar proof to that just given shows that at all these points $b_{Ak} F$. It is clear however that B is one of these points, for $B_i > \min F_j$ for all i. Hence $B\ b_{Ak}\ F$ and F cannot be a member of S_{Ak}.

As for the boundary of the set described, it suffices to show that there is at least one point on it not in S_{Ak}, and one that is in S_{Ak}. This may be done trivially by observing that D is on the boundary and is not in S_{Ak}, while B is also on the boundary and is in S_{Ak}. Lest it be thought (a mistake originally made by the author) that all points on the boundary below the present income hyperplane are not, while all points on the boundary on or above the present income hyperplane are in S_{Ak}, we consider a more general case. It is obvious, for $m > 2$, that there are points on the boundary below the present income hyperplane such that their minimum co-ordinate is $\min B_j$, but such that their other co-ordinates make their distribution vectors nearer E than is P (in terms of distribution distances) and such that at least one individual has more income than in B. The only time that this is not possible is when P is such that $\min P_j$ is the only component of P that is less than $\dfrac{1}{m}$ (even in this case the trivial example given above remains valid). Secondly, consider points on the boundary such that their distribution vectors are farther from E than is P (still in terms of distribution distances). Clearly, we cannot say that these points are in S_{Ak}, for their distribution vectors are worse than P, while they are not in the positive orthant (or on the boundary thereof) from any point B' such that $B'\ g_k\ B$.

Thus all points in the interior of the space described are in S_{Ak}; no point either in the interior of that space or on its boundary is in S_{Ak}; while there are some points on the boundary that are and some that are not in the acceptable set. Q.E.D.

Now, we are not so much interested in the *loss* in total income that would be accepted under a given distribution value judgment in going from a worse to a better distribution as we are concerned with the *increase* in total income that would be required in order to accept a shift to some worse distribution from a better one. We make the transition by stating without proof the following lemma, the proof of which is similar to that of *Lemma 3*.

Lemma 4.　*Let k be a totally compensating distribution value judgment such that $P\ b_k\ R$. Let $D = R(\bar{Y} + \delta^*)$ $(\delta^* > 0)$ such that*

(a)　$B\ b_k\ R(\bar{Y} + \delta)$ *for $\delta < \delta^*$,*
(b)　$R(\bar{Y} + \delta)\ b_A\ B$ *for $\delta \geq \delta^*$.*

For any Q such that $Q\ g_k\ P$, define $\phi^Q = \max\limits_i \left(\dfrac{Q_i}{R_i} \right)$ $(i = 1, \ldots, m)$ Let $\phi = \max\limits_Q \phi^Q$. Then:

(1)　$D = \phi R \bar{Y}$
(2)　$\delta^* = \bar{Y}(\phi - 1)$　　　(See Figure 12.6.)

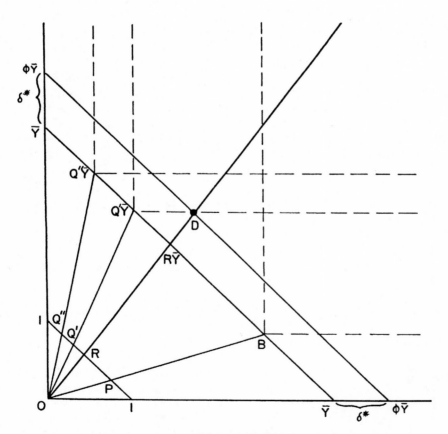

FIGURE 12.6. Illustration of location of point *D* of *Lemma 4* for a two-man society. *Q′* and *Q″* are the only distributions $g_k\ P$.

It is immediately evident that if $P = E$ (the egalitarian distribution) and if k is the strict egalitarian distribution value judgment of *Theorem 3*, then

$$\delta^* = \overline{Y}\left(\frac{1}{m \min_i R_i} - 1\right).$$

Moreover, there is a direct relation between ϕ and θ, where θ is defined as in *Lemma 3, mutatis mutandis*, as $\max_O\left(\min_i\left(\frac{O_i}{P_i}\right)\right)$ where R g_k O and $i = 1, \ldots, m$. If we choose an ε^* greater than zero, such that:

(a) $P(\overline{Y} + \delta^* - \varepsilon)$ b_k $R(\overline{Y} + \delta^*)$ for $\varepsilon < \varepsilon^*$
(b) $R(\overline{Y} + \delta^*)$ b_A $P(\overline{Y} + \delta^* - \varepsilon)$ for $\varepsilon \geq \varepsilon^*$

it is evident that to avoid contradictions we must have $\varepsilon^* = \delta^*$. Thus,

$$(\overline{Y} + \delta^*)(1 - \theta) = \overline{Y}(\phi - 1)$$
$$(\overline{Y} + \overline{Y}(\phi - 1))(1 - \theta) = \overline{Y}(\phi - 1)$$
$$\overline{Y}\phi(1 - \theta) = \overline{Y}(\phi - 1)$$
$$\phi = \frac{1}{\theta}.$$

Moreover, we have (without proof):

Theorem 4. *Let k be a totally compensating distribution value judgment such that P b_k R. Let Q be between P and R such that Q g_k P. Let $D = R(\overline{Y} + \delta^*)$, where δ^* is chosen as in Lemma 4. Define, as in Lemma 4,*

$$\phi^P = \max_i\left(\frac{P_i}{R_i}\right) \text{ and } \phi^Q = \max_i\left(\frac{Q_i}{R_i}\right) \text{ where } i = 1, \ldots, m.$$

Then:

$$\delta^* \leq \overline{Y}(\phi^Q - 1) \leq \overline{Y}(\phi^P - 1)$$

the left-hand equality holding if there exists no Q' between Q and R such that Q' g_k P, and the right-hand equality holding *only* in the special case that $P_j = Q_j$, where $\phi^P = \frac{P_j}{R_j}$ and $\phi^Q = \frac{Q_j}{R_j}$.

Furthermore, it is evident that if k is nontroughed at P, D is just on the boundary of the acceptable set described by *Theorem 2*.

The meaning of *Theorem 4* is clear. It states that if, in going from P to some distribution worse than P, we pass through some other distribution at least as good as P, then we need not require an increase in total income sufficient to bring us into S_A. In particular, if we judge one distribution to be best, then if that is passed through, the theorem applies. In the case of the strict egalitarian value judgment of *Theorem 3* this means, effectively, that if R (the distribution moved to) lies in the direction of E (the egalitarian distribution) from P and the distribution distance of R from P is greater than that of E from P (obviously, this relation is independent of total income), then we do not have to have an increase in total income sufficient to reach S_A, but only sufficient to reach S_{Ak}, as described in *Theorem 3*, to justify the move. This, of course, we already know, since we know S_{Ak} in this case. In general, however, *Theorem 4* tells us a sufficient condition that S_{Ak} be reached, for a certain distribution, at a lower total income than would suffice to reach S_A.

We now move from the consideration of totally compensating distribution value judgments to that of partially compensating or noncompensating ones. We make the following definition:

Definition.   Let k be a totally compensating distribution value judgment and j another distribution value judgment that gives the same complete ordering of distributions as k. For any two distributions, Q and R, such that $Q \, b_k \, R \, (Q \, b_j \, R)$ choose δ^K such that:

   (a) $R(\overline{Y} + \delta) \, b_A \, Q\overline{Y}$ for $\delta \geq \delta^k$
   (b) $Q\overline{Y} \, b_k \, R(\overline{Y} + \delta)$ for $\delta < \delta^k$

Similarly, choose δ^j, making the appropriate changes in superscripts and subscripts, and changing b_A in (a) to b_j. We define the *compensating coefficient of j from Q to R* as:

$$\eta^j_{QR} = \frac{\delta^j}{\delta^k}. \tag{1}$$

We assume that this ratio is independent of income at least insofar as its value at $\overline{Y}$ and $\overline{Y} - \varepsilon^k$ is concerned, where ε^k is defined analogous to ε^* in *Lemma 3*, ff., so that we might write

$$\eta^j_{QR} = \frac{\varepsilon^j}{\varepsilon^k}$$

where ε^j is defined in the obvious way. In general, however, as we shall see in the next section, compensating coefficients are *not* independent of income over the entire range of total income, or even over a substantial part of it. The above assumption, therefore, is made not for reasons of necessity (we never use it formally) but for reasons of convenience in visualizing the meanings of the relevant theorems.

Note, incidentally, that if the compensating coefficient is one for all distributions, then j and k are identical and that if it is zero, j is noncompensating for the relevant distributions. We may now state the following important theorem:

Theorem 5. *Let k be a distribution value judgment such that $P \, b_k \, Q$ and $Q \, b_k \, R$. Let $\phi = \min\limits_{O} \left(\max\limits_{i} \left(\dfrac{O_i}{Q_i} \right) \right)$ where $O \, g_k \, P$ and let this be $\dfrac{Q'_j}{Q_j}$, say.*

Similarly, let $\phi' = \min\limits_{O} \left(\max\limits_{i} \left(\dfrac{O_i}{R_i} \right) \right)$ where $O \, g_k \, P$ and call this $\dfrac{R'_h}{R_h}$, say.

$$(i = 1, \ldots, m)$$

Then:

   (1) $\eta^k_{PQ} < 1$
   (2) $R' = Q'$

and

   (3) $\max\limits_{i}\left(\dfrac{Q_i}{R_i} \right) = \dfrac{Q_j}{R_j}$

imply $\eta^k_{PR} < 1$.

Proof. Clearly, since $\dfrac{Q'_j}{Q_j} = \max\limits_{i}\left(\dfrac{Q'_i}{Q_i} \right)$, hypotheses 2 and 3 imply that:

$$\left(\frac{Q'_j}{Q_j} \right)\left(\frac{Q_j}{R_j} \right) = \frac{Q'_j}{R_j} = \max_{i}\left(\frac{Q'_i}{R_i} \right) = \frac{R'_h}{R_h}. \tag{1}$$

Now choose $\delta_1, \delta_2, \delta^*$, such that:

   (a) $Q(\bar{Y} + \delta) \, b_k \, B$ for $\delta \geq \delta_1$
   (b) $B \, b_k \, Q(\bar{Y} + \delta)$ for $\delta < \delta_1$
   (c) $R(\bar{Y} + \delta) \, b_k \, B$ for $\delta \geq \delta_2$
   (d) $B \, b_k \, R(\bar{Y} + \delta)$ for $\delta < \delta_2$
   (e) $R(\bar{Y} + \delta) \, b_A \, B$ for $\delta \geq \delta^*$
   (f) $B \, b_n \, R(\bar{Y} + \delta)$ for $\delta < \delta^*$,

where n is a totally compensating distribution value judgment giving the same complete ordering of distributions as k. By definition,

$$\eta^k_{PR} = \frac{\delta_2}{\delta^*}.$$

Now consider the points

$$C = Q(\bar{Y} + \delta_1) \text{ and } D = R(\bar{Y} + \delta_1)\frac{Q_j}{R_j}.$$

Clearly, D is on the boundary of the positive orthant from C, since $\dfrac{Q_j}{R_j} = \max_i\left(\dfrac{Q_i}{R_i}\right)$. Hence $D\ b_A\ C$. But $C\ b_k\ B$. Thus $D\ b_{Ak}\ B$.

So

$$(\bar{Y} + \delta_2) \leq (\bar{Y} + \delta_1)\frac{Q_j}{R_j}.$$

But, since $\eta_{PQ}^k < 1$ by assumption, *Lemma 4* implies

$$(\bar{Y} + \delta_1) < \bar{Y}\phi$$

so that, using (1)

$$(\bar{Y} + \delta_2) \leq (\bar{Y} + \delta_1)\frac{Q_j}{R_j} < \bar{Y}\phi\frac{Q_j}{R_j} = \bar{Y}\left(\frac{Q_j'}{Q_j}\right)\left(\frac{Q_j}{R_j}\right) = \bar{Y}\frac{R_h'}{R_h}.$$

But $\bar{Y}\dfrac{R_h'}{R_h} = \bar{Y}\phi'$ by definition, and, by *Lemma 4*,

$$\bar{Y}\phi' = (\bar{Y} + \delta^*).$$

Hence $(\bar{Y} + \delta_2) < (\bar{Y} + \delta^*)$, so that $\delta_2 < \delta^*$, and thus

$$\eta_{PR}^k < 1$$

and the theorem is proved.

In fact, a more precise expression for η_{PR}^k may be obtained. It is:

$$\eta_{PR}^k \leq \frac{\eta_{PQ}^k(Q_j' - Q_j) + (Q_j - R_j)}{Q_j' - R_j},$$

the inequality obtaining when η_{QR}^k is less than one, or when there exists some $O\ g_k\ Q$ such that $\max_i\left(\dfrac{O_i}{R_i}\right) < \dfrac{Q_j}{R_j}$. The above expression reduces when $\eta_{PQ}^k = 1$ or 0 to:

$$\eta_{PR}^k \leq 1 \qquad \text{and}$$

$$\eta_{PR}^k \leq \frac{Q_j - R_j}{Q_j' - R_j} = \frac{\bar{Y}\left(\dfrac{Q_j}{R_j} - 1\right)}{\bar{Y}\left(\dfrac{Q_j'}{R_j} - 1\right)},$$

respectively, as might be expected.

Theorem 5 seems at first glance to be rather rigid in its assumptions. In a consideration that involves the most general case, this is no doubt true. However, when we consider the value judgments that are actually likely to be made concerning distributions, we see that *Theorem 5* is somewhat more applicable than at first appears to be the case. In essence, what it states is that if we do not think a certain distribution is so much worse than the present one that we want to correct it by taking away from some and giving only an infinitesimal amount to others, then consistency demands that we hold the same view concerning any other distribution whose bad features, so to speak, are an exaggeration of those of the first. To take a specific example: if we are egalitarians but feel that at some point the gain in welfare involved in attaining an egalitarian distribution is overbalanced by the loss in welfare that would occur were we to attain that distribution simply by taking from the rich without giving more than an additional token pittance to the poor, then to be consistent, we must feel the same way about any other situation in which the rich are richer and the poor poorer. Similar remarks could be made concerning any distribution value judgment that is "single-peaked," i.e., that ranks one distribution better than all others and all others according to their distribution distance from the "peak." It does not seem unreasonable to suppose that most, if not all, of the distribution value judgments commonly made are of this type, which includes, under *Corollary 2*, the refusal to make distribution value judgments while accepting value judgment *A*.

A word or two more concerning the compensating coefficient may be in order before concluding this section of our analysis. It is, of course, evident that if we know the complete ordering of the distributions that is given by any distribution value judgment and, in addition, know its compensating coefficient for every pair of distributions, that it, taken with value judgment *A*, provides a complete ordering of all points. Moreover, it is also obvious that we have:

Theorem 6. *If k and j are two distribution value judgments yielding the same complete ordering of distributions, and for some Q such that $P\ b_k\ Q\ (P\ b_j\ Q)\ \eta_{PQ}^k < \eta_{PQ}^j$, then the increase in total income required to compensate for a move from P to Q is less under k than it is under j.*

The proof follows directly from the definition of the compensating coefficient. As a limiting case of *Theorem 6* we may note that if the compensating coefficient of a given distribution value judgment is identically zero, then *any* move that will increase total income must be considered good under that judgment, regardless of its distribution effects. Of course, this is equivalent to saying that *any* move passing the Kaldor-Hicks-Scitovsky criterion must be accepted. It is *not* the same thing as saying that distributional considerations are irrelevant, that all distributions are equally good. What we have in this case, interestingly enough, is a lexicographic ordering of points, where *any* point on a higher income plane is better than *any* point on a lower, and distributional considerations affect only the choices between two points on the same income hyperplane.

We may now sum up the results of this rather lengthy investigation of the formal consequences of accepting value judgment *A* and of making the assumptions indicated in the first section. The following factors, when operative, each tend to make points above the present income hyperplane other than those in the positive orthant from the present point judged acceptable:

(1) The present distribution is not considered the best, and distribution value judgments are actually made explicit. (*Theorems 1* and *2* and *Corollary 2*)

(2) The distribution value judgment made is nontroughed. (*Theorem 2* and *Corollary 1*)

(3) Supposing the distribution under consideration to be worse than the present one, there exists another distribution between it and the present one that is at least as good as the present one. (*Theorem 4*)

(4) The compensating coefficient between the present distribution and the one under consideration is small. (*Theorem 6*)

(5) The distribution under consideration involves an exaggeration of the bad features of some other distribution, and the compensating coefficient between that distribution and the present one is small. (This factor operates through the preceding factor.) (*Theorem 5*)

Whether or not, and under what circumstances any or all of these five factors are likely to be operative will be discussed in the final section.

III.   The Formal Model – The General Case

The time has now come for us to consider the consequences of dropping value judgment *A*. As was remarked above – and we shall revert to this later – if this is to be done, it must be done on two grounds, one of fact and one of value. Concerning the statement of fact, I think there cannot be much disagreement; it is a commonplace that people think of other things besides their own consumption. Concerning the value judgment, however, there is much to be said, both as to whether or not we should accept it and as to what accepting it entails. In this section, then, we shall attempt to develop the consequences of discarding value judgment *A* (insofar as anything can be said of them), while in the last we shall discuss the question of whether or not it ought to be discarded.

Of course, discarding value judgment A represents a break with the traditional position. Insofar as the Kaldor-Hicks-Scitovsky criterion was based on that position – on the idea that *potential* welfare has increased if a redistribution of income in the new situation would reach some point in the positive orthant from the old point – discarding value judgment A represents a break with the acceptance of that criterion also. However, in a sense we are not breaking with the classical position entirely, but discarding a part of it and strengthening another part. Insofar as we state that an individual's happiness does not depend only on his own consumption we are discarding a traditional view; but insofar as, accepting this as a fact, we assert that such feelings as arise from nonconsumption considerations are important and are worth consideration, we are following the value judgment always inherent in traditional theory, that people know what they want, and that it is best for them to receive it.

We then suppose that we are rejecting value judgment A. Now, I find it difficult indeed to conceive of anyone discarding it completely and in all situations. Surely, most proponents of such a rejection would agree that *insofar as nonconsumption factors can be ignored*, value judgment A can be accepted. In other words, *ceteris paribus*, social welfare (vague as the concept is) is probably considered by most people to be an increasing function of consumption. Of course, an ascetic might claim that greater consumption decreases social welfare by leading to greater concentration on the things of this world and disregard for those of the next; but presumably no ascetics are practicing economists, and will not have read thus far anyway. Studies of welfare economics are not typically devoted to the theory of aiding camels through needles' eyes. Hence we shall assume that value judgment A is considered valid, except insofar as nonconsumption factors are considered important enough to affect it. Increased consumption, considered in isolation, is assumed to be judged a good thing.

Furthermore, I think most people would agree that not all factors that affect an individual's subjective feeling of happiness ought to be considered as affecting social welfare. We might well agree that the feelings of a poor man who sees his friends becoming rich, while he himself can only consume as much as before, are relevant and ought to be given a good deal of weight in our thinking; but I doubt whether we would give the same weight, or even any weight whatsoever, to the injury done the sensitive feelings of a millionaire miser, who loves to have far more than anyone else, by increasing the general standard of living. The subjective feelings involved in the latter case may be quite as real and quite as acute as in the former, but in some sense we do not consider them so important. The example of the starvation economy given in the first section is another case in point. There may be times when consumption is so important that we cannot stop to consider anything else. Finally, even in the state of bliss, where everyone can consume an infinite amount if he so chooses, we may consider feelings produced by inequities of distribution to be simply silly. The point is that this type of value judgment is not independent of the level of total income. It does not seem too farfetched to argue that above a certain low level of total income, we tend to feel that a high consumption may make nonconsumption feelings less important as a welfare consideration although we may legitimately feel, as a practical matter, that in any range of income that we are likely to reach in the foreseeable future, they are still of great importance indeed.

What does all this mean in terms of the model of the last section? Roughly speaking, it means that the set of acceptable points obtained by the use of value judgment A alone, S_A, which was the positive orthant from the present point, is replaced by a new set, S_G, say, that is also a cone or combination of cones and that may or may not be included in S_A. It is evident that we cannot now even pretend to refuse to make distribution value judgments, for the rejection of value judgment A *must* be based on distributional considerations. Even if we know exactly how each distribution affects each individual's utility, it is clear that we must make a distribution value judgment in deciding which of these effects are to be taken into account and how heavily they are to be weighted. This process will tell us the location of the set S_G. Value judgment A, then, represents a limiting case where all nonconsumption considerations are given zero weight so that S_G becomes S_A, the set of all points in which there has been no decrease in the consumption of any individual.

The magnitude of the problem and the difficulty of saying anything very precise about the general case is immediately apparent, for the location of the set S_G depends on the *particular* distribution value judgments made. In particular, we must re-examine the assumption that distribution value judgments are independent of income in the relevant range. We have already seen that the weight given to nonconsumption considerations is probably not generally independent of the level of total income. Is this also true with regard to the complete ordering of distributions provided by any distribution value judgment that seems likely to be made?

In general, it seems plausible to me to continue to make the assumption that the complete ordering of distributions given by any distribution value judgment is independent of the level of total income in the relevant range. Generally speaking, attacks on value judgment A are made more or less on the basis of distribution value judgments whose orderings are independent of total income (of course, this does not say that the strength of the attack is independent of that level). As we have argued above, most people would probably accept value judgment A as a first approximation, and, provided that we restrict ourselves to relatively small changes in total income, I think we may assume that any distribution that remains constant throughout the change will not be considered significantly worse (or better) after the change than before. In other words, we continue to assume that if income distribution remains constant an increase in income is considered good. This would seem to be the least that might be granted us.

We now generalize the notion of a compensating value judgment as follows:

Definition. Let k be a distribution value judgment. Then for any two distributions, Q and R, we define δ_{QR}^k as the *compensation number* of k from Q to R if and only if:

(a) $Q\overline{Y}\, b_k\, R(\overline{Y} + \delta)$ for $\delta < \delta_{QR}^k$
(b) $R(\overline{Y} + \delta)\, b_k\, Q\overline{Y}$ for $\delta > \delta_{QR}^k$.

Note that δ_{QR}^k may be positive, negative, or zero and that the case of $\delta = \delta_{QR}^k$ has been left undefined. Obviously, we have immediately:

Theorem 7. *Let k be a distribution value judgment such that $Q\, g_k\, P$ and $P\, g_k\, R$. Then:*

(1) $\delta_{PQ}^k \leq 0$
(2) $\delta_{PR}^k \geq 0$.

Thus we have, where the subscript G denotes the presence of the general case:

Corollary 4. *Let k be a distribution value judgment and $Q\, g_k\, P$. Then S_{Gk} includes all points with distribution Q that are on or above the present income hyperplane.*

Corollary 5. *If k is a distribution value judgment such that $P\, b_k\, R$ and is nontroughed from R to P, then $\delta_{PR}^k < \infty$ implies $\delta_{PQ}^k < \infty$ for all Q between R and P.*

Moreover, it is also easy to prove on lines analogous to those of *Lemmas 1* and *2*, that if $R\, b_k\, Q$ and δ_{PQ}^k is finite, then $\delta_{PR}^k \leq \delta_{PQ}^k$ (remembering that the compensating number can be negative or zero). It is also obvious that, for consistency, we must have δ_{QR}^k at income $\overline{Y}$ equal to $(-\delta_{RQ}^k)$ at income $(\overline{Y} + \delta_{QR}^k)$.

All this is easy, if not quite trivial. It is obvious, however, that the crucial question is the value of the compensation number from P to R when P b_k R. Roughly, we may look upon this value as a sort of "trading point"; it is that increase in total income that would make us pause before rejecting any move from P to R that involved it. Defining ϕ_{PR} as $\max_i\left(\dfrac{P_i}{R_i}\right)$ $(i = 1, \ldots, m)$, it is evident by *Lemma 4* that if $\delta_{PR}^k = \overline{Y}(\phi_{PR} - 1)$ for every R worse than P, and there are no distributions as good as P or better, S_G is identical with S_A. More generally, if the above relation holds true with $\phi = \min_Q \phi_{QR}$ substituted for ϕ_{PR} (where Q g_k P)

then we are back in the special case, at least as far as that part of the acceptable set above or on the present income hyperplane is concerned, and that part of the acceptable set obtained is no different from that which would be obtained by combining value judgment A with some totally compensating value judgment giving the same complete ordering of distributions as does k. Obviously, if the compensation number is less than the above, we have what was termed in the last section a "partially compensating" distribution value judgment, and, in general, the smaller is the compensation number, the larger the acceptable set.

It is clear that the value of the compensation number depends on income for most value judgments. The question is, how does it so depend? Is there some definite relation between the two, for instance their ratio, that remains constant? The answer would seem to depend on the particular value judgment involved. In general, however, I think we may discern two opposite tendencies. For one thing, I think it is obvious that as income rises, the *absolute* increase in total income that will be required to compensate for a given shift in distribution will tend to rise. This is certainly true for a totally compensating value judgment of the last section, where the compensating number for a given shift from the present distribution to a worse one is a linear increasing function of Y. Intuitively this makes sense; we see for a shift to a given distribution different from the present one, that if as income rises it takes more and more additional income to reach S_A, then we ought to require more and more additional income to reach S_G, with rising total income, since presumably it always requires more to reach the latter set than to attain the former one. However, this is only half the story. It would apply without qualification only if we could feel sure that the weights given to distributional considerations and to nonconsumption factors by a given value judgment were independent of income. As we have seen, however, this is probably not the case. While we might advocate that a man of average means who finds his associates becoming much wealthier ought to have a substantial *percentage* increase in his income to compensate for non-consumption considerations, I doubt whether in a like situation we would require a comparable increase in the income of a millionaire. I do not think that all of this feeling is due to the difference in *relative* wealth between the two men. If the first man's absolute consumption were as high as the millionaire's, but if the rest of the society had had a comparable increase in wealth, so that his relative position was no different from before, I think we would still feel that he need not be given so large a percentage increase in wealth to compensate for a situation such as that described as that which we required when total income was lower. Put bluntly: so far as value judgments are concerned, goods may compensate for envy.

Which of these two conflicting tendencies is dominant at any given income will depend on the value judgment involved. Clearly, however, as income rises, the second tendency, insofar as it is operative, will tend to bring the compensating number closer and closer to $\overline{Y}(\phi - 1)$, the amount that a totally compensating value judgment would require under value judgment A. Perhaps, if income rises far enough, a value judgment that for low levels of total income would require high compensating numbers relative to this value may end by requiring lower ones. If this is the case, then it is an argument for adopting a policy of increasing income whenever possible, provided that one believes that, in the long run, the fact that the situation will improve compensates for the fact that the short-run situation may deteriorate. Obviously, long run and short run are relative concepts, and the speed with which the situation improves is a very relevant consideration in making such value judgments.

There does not seem to be anything more precise that we can say about the general case. Basically, this is due to the fact that the rejection of value judgment A leaves us without any general principle to go by. It does not seem possible to describe the acceptable set in the general case in any way more precise than saying that it is the set of all points $Q(\overline{Y} + \delta_{PQ}^k + a)$ where $a > 0$ and adding the observations of *Theorem 7* and *Corollaries 4* and *5*. Note, however, that by *Corollary 5*, as by *Theorem 1*, the more distributions considered better or as good as the present one, the larger the acceptable set, *ceteris paribus*. However, value judgment A is not typically discarded because the present distribution is considered very bad. I suggest that the discarding of value judgment A tends to accompany a feeling that the present distribution is really better than most others, at least insofar as a refusal to make distribution value judgments is concerned. Perhaps some make that refusal desiring the status quo for its own sake and not for the intrinsic merits of the distribution involved.[13] In any case, even the emphasis on nonconsumption factors, coupled with such a refusal, tends to have the same effect as exalting the present distribution, i.e., as opposing all changes in distribution just because they are changes.

Finally, it is self-evident that for a given ordering of distributions, $S_{Ak} \supset S_{Gk}$ and is not identical with it, provided that for any R such that $P\, g_k\, R, \delta_{PR}^k > \overline{Y}(\phi - 1)$, where ϕ is defined as before. Obviously, practically all rejections of value judgment A are made on this basis. Such action is not typically taken on the grounds that the standards set by value judgment A are too high. Hence, if we wish to argue that increases in total income are desirable under a wide variety of circumstances, we must argue both the following points: first, that value judgment A should be accepted, and second, that the compensating number should be relatively low (of course, remembering that we do not mean to exclude by the acceptance of value judgment A the existence of compensating numbers below $\overline{Y}(\phi - 1)$ for any or all distributions). These points, together with the applicability of the factors listed in the preceding section, will be discussed in the next, and final, section.

IV.   Arguments and Conclusions

We are now in a position to argue the question in point. Should changes that will increase total income be adopted if we presume that distribution effects will not be cumulative? Should, in other words, all changes that would increase *potential* welfare be recommended even though some people might suffer from them? Of course, no one will argue that *all* such changes are good. Most people, I think, would agree that there is no increase in total income large enough to compensate for the presence of a large number of zeros in the new distribution vector; some would probably hold that such is the case even if there is only one such zero. What we are arguing here is not that any conceivable income-increasing change should be made, but rather that there are good reasons to say that many such changes (perhaps all that are likely to be actually contemplated in practice) should be made because the resulting situations will be such as to be acceptable under value judgments with which many people would agree. In other words, under widely acceptable value judgments, there exists a class of situations that covers a wide range of distributions and that may be deemed desirable nonetheless.

---

[13] Of course, I do not mean by this that to refuse to make distribution value judgments in the interests of setting up and discussing general criteria is to praise intentionally the status quo, whatever it may be; I am speaking of the application of those criteria to practical situations, where to refuse to make such value judgments does have that effect.

In the two sections preceding, we listed several factors that, if operative, would tend to support such a conclusion. The time has now come to discuss whether or not they are likely to be operative. As was shown in the last section, the acceptance of value judgment A is one of these factors. Since most of the other factors involved depend to a large extent upon the acceptance of that value judgment, we shall discuss its acceptability first.

As we have already emphasized, the acceptance of value judgment A involves either a statement of fact, or one of value, or both. It is not enough simply to reject it on the grounds that the subjective happiness of the individual depends on other factors besides his own consumption; one must also add that those factors should be considered and should be given so much weight as to overcome the consumption factor in a large variety of circumstances. We must be clear as to what this means. Take, for example, the case of a community with a continually rising standard of living, that is, where most of the people are able over time to consume an increasing amount. Suppose, however, that a small group of people does not share in the general increase of wealth but sees its relative position decline although its absolute position remains the same. Granted that these people will be less happy than before, in order to reject value judgment A in this situation, we must be prepared to state that the decrease in their happiness multiplied by the importance of the group (determined by a value judgment), so to speak, is so great as to outweigh in our judgment the gain in the happiness of the rest of the community caused by the increased material benefits multiplied by the importance of the rest of the community.

I think the above example makes it plain that few would reject value judgment A in *all* circumstances. I doubt very much whether anyone would seriously claim that the decrease in happiness of a wealthy man who sees the poor faring better is sufficient to offset the increased welfare of the poor (unless one happens to be that wealthy man, of course). On the other hand, I admit that when considering individuals it is hard to accept value judgment A in all situations. The fact that a given worker, say, suddenly receives a substantial pay increase because his wife's brother-in-law's third cousin has become president of the company may cause such unrest among his peers that we deem the change harmful even though no one's absolute consumption has been decreased. However, in making such a value judgment, we must remember two things: First, that it is only the *feelings*, not the *actions*, of the other workers that can be considered, for we are considering situations of static equilibrium. Second, that we are not choosing between giving a pay increase to *all* the workers and giving it to one, but between the latter alternative and a situation where *no* pay increase is granted.

However, when all this has been said, we must admit the possibility of rejecting value judgment *A* in the above situation. The favored worker may be particularly undeserving in our eyes, or we may feel that discriminatory pay increases are bad no matter to whom they are given. Thus there are situations in which value judgment *A* may be plausibly rejected *insofar as we interpret it as relating to particular individuals*. But suppose we consider the distribution vector's components to be not the percentage share of total income of an individual, but of a *group* of individuals that we consider relatively homogeneous (another statement that may be one of fact or one of value, i.e., they *ought* to be considered as a group). In fact, of course, most distributions of total income are considered on this basis. As Little says:

Most people who consider the welfare of society do not, I am sure, think of it as a logical construction from the welfares of individuals. They think rather in terms of social or economic groups, or in terms of average, or representative men.[14]

Does this make much difference to the acceptance or rejection of value judgment *A?* I think it does. It becomes somewhat harder to construct a case in which the increased welfare accruing to one or more groups through increased consumption is offset by the *nonconsumption* reactions on the welfare of the remaining groups, again remembering that we are restricted to the comparison of two positions of static equilibrium. Value judgment *A* seems much more acceptable, to me at least, when distributions and incomes are thought of as those of groups rather than as those of individuals. Of course, the degree to which we weight the happiness of each group in considering the welfare of the entire community may still make a difference. In the limit, if we consider only the happiness of one such group to be relevant and deem that of all other groups to be of no moment whatever, then of course we must reject value judgment *A* for a large variety of situations. This is beside the point, however. It seems rather more plausible to suppose that most people in a democratic society would not be so extreme in their weighting of the relative importance of the various groups, and traditional considerations of justice may demand that groups of equal size be weighted equally. Moreover, while it may be unfortunate, it is nonetheless true that many people in our society consider material benefits (i.e., consumption) of such importance that they would give little or no weight to the nonconsumption repercussions on the happiness of other groups caused by the

[14] Little (1950), p. 49.

increase in consumption of one, remembering, again, that it is a question not of one group gaining at the *expense* of another, but of one gaining while the others do not.

However, it is not necessary that value judgment A be accepted for all conceivable situations, in order to support our argument. All that is required is that it be accepted for all points within some reasonably size-able range of the present situation (a range large enough to permit the proofs of Section II). Supposing this not to be the case, however, we may still discuss the plausibility of the compensation number, as defined in the last section, being relatively low, a situation that, as we have seen, would tend to support our argument. In the first place, be it noted, that for compensation numbers greater than that which value judgment A would require when combined with a totally compensating distribution value judgment, the same arguments that we used for accepting value judgment A apply, *pari passu*, as arguments for accepting a relatively low compensation number, for they are all arguments that tend to lessen the weight, if accepted, that is given to nonconsumption factors. Moreover, as we saw in the last section, there seems some reason to suppose that the higher is total income, the lower is the compensation number for any given shift in distribution likely to be relative to that income. I think perhaps some people would feel that, at present, the standard of living in the United States is so high as to bring this situation about. This does not mean that the condition of the working class, for example, ought not to be improved, but it does mean that we may feel that the *noncon-sumption* repercussions on the happiness of that class brought about by increases in the consumption of others are relatively unimportant at present levels of income.[15] I think it is clear that we would consider such factors less important now than during the Great Depression, but whether we consider them of very little importance is a matter of individual opinion. Value judgments, after all, are made by people, and people change. As income rises, we may find the compensation number given us by a particular person falling faster relative to income for some shifts in distributions than for others (faster for shifts that benefit shop-keepers than for those that benefit bankers, for example, although the condition of the classes whose nonconsumption feelings are under con-sideration may be the same in both cases). What this argument has been is merely an attempt to show the plausibility of supposing that in general the compensation number for a given bad shift in distribution may be

[15] Provided that we think that the noneconomic aspects of welfare are not adversely affected by the modern industrialism that has produced such high consumption levels and that external diseconomies such as smog, etc, are unimportant. (I am indebted for this point to Professor Chipman.)

lower relative to income than might be supposed from a very general consideration of the possibilities involved.

Whatever the level of the compensation number, however, and whether or not we accept value judgment A, it is clear that the first two of the factors listed at the end of Section II as supporting our argument are highly relevant. These are: first that the present distribution is not considered the best of all distributions, and that distribution value judgments are actually made; and second that, other things being equal, the distribution value judgment made is nontroughed. The applicability of the first of these factors would be self-evident were it not for the fact that to refuse to make distribution value judgments is, as was shown above, tantamount to declaring the present situation to be the best. Clearly, if pressed we all will make distribution value judgments and provided we do not rank the present distribution best this will tend to increase the acceptable set. As for whether we actually do consider the present distribution best, this is a matter of individual judgment. I think, however, that if we remember that we are abstracting from dynamic processes (i.e., from the difficulties attendant on making a change, or the availability of future alternatives before and after the change) it seems highly likely that we can find a good many people who would judge *some* other distribution better than the present one (if there are any at all, in fact, of the opposite persuasion), although how *much* better remains a matter of opinion.

As regards the second factor cited, as to the nontroughedness of distribution value judgments, I think that, if we consider the meaning of "nontroughed" as we have defined it, we will see the reasonableness of supposing that many, if not all, of the distribution value judgments that are likely to be made are of this type. Roughly speaking, what we mean by the nontroughedness of a given value judgment is that if we think a distribution where the first z individuals (groups) have more than at present and the remaining $(m - z)$ have less (we omit the consideration of elements that remain constant, for the sake of simplicity) is better than the present one, then if we attempt to reach that distribution by taking away from the latter set of individuals (groups) and giving to the former, provided no one receives more or loses more than in the better distribution, if we cut off this process at any point, the distribution involved will be no worse than the one with which we started. To take a simple example, if we have a two-man society and the present situation is one in which Tom has a good deal and Dick has only a little, and we think that a redistribution that gave them both equal amounts would be better, then nontroughedness says that if we take from Tom and give to Dick and do not pass in this way the egalitarian distribution, then any distribution that we pass through in this process will not be worse than the original one. It is at once obvious that all distribution value judgments that are "single-peaked" – that is, which consider one distribution best and rank others by their distance from it (distribution distance on the unit income hyperplane) – are nontroughed, for as we approach the "peak" we never go downhill although we may (but probably do not) encounter a plateau, so to speak. As we said above, it seems reasonable to suppose that the huge majority of the distribution value judgments that are likely to be made are of this type, and there thus seems even more reason to suppose that the huge majority of such judgments are nontroughed.

Besides, surely, even if a distribution value judgment is not single-peaked, it may well be double-peaked, with the two peaks separated by a considerable distribution distance. In such a case, the judgment is non-troughed within the neighborhood of each peak. Even if, as Samuelson says:

A policy that shifts society's utility-possibility function uniformly outward may not at the same time shift the utility-feasibility function uniformly outward, instead causing it to twist inward in some places.[16]

nonetheless the inward twists may well be at points so far away from the peak or the "slope" on which the present point lies that we care little, if anything, about them.[17]

Proceeding down the list of factors at the end of Section II, we reach those that are peculiarly applicable to the special case of value judgment A (that is, those that although they may be generally applicable do not seem capable of being proved so; their proofs all require the application of value judgment A and do not seem easily modifiable). The first of these is the condition that between the present distribution and the distribution under consideration there be some other distribution that is considered at least as good as the present one. Since this is so clearly a matter of particular circumstance we shall not pause to discuss it, merely pointing out that such may often be the case if the distribution value judgment (as seems likely) is "single-peaked."

Finally, we come to the last two factors in the special case, the conditions first that the compensating coefficient (as defined in Section II) be small, and second that the conditions of *Theorem 5* apply. As for general remarks on the factors that affect the size of the compensating coefficient, it is obvious that the observations made above as to the size of the compensation number in the general case apply here also. We note

[16] Samuelson (1950), p. 21.
[17] I owe this point to Professor Carl Kaysen.

that in the limiting case of a compensating coefficient (or compensation number) that is identically zero, any change that satisfies the Kaldor-Hicks-Scitovsky criterion is desirable whether or not compensation or bribes are actually paid.

In addition to the remarks made in the general case, the special case allows us to add a few observations concerning *Theorem 5*. Essentially, what that theorem states is that in the special case, if there is some distribution Q worse than the present one, and the compensating coefficient from P to Q is less than one, then for *all* other distributions whose bad features, so to speak, are worse exaggerations of those of Q, the compensating coefficient from P will also be less than one, always provided that with such distributions an increase in income carries us into the positive orthant from $Q\bar{Y}$ before we reach the positive orthant from some point at least as good as the present one. It does not seem at all improbable to suppose the existence of such Q as far as many distribution value judgments are concerned, and such existence implies a wider acceptable set than would otherwise be obtained. For example, we may feel, to take the case of the two-person society already given, if we are egalitarians, that a situation in which Tom has a slight bit more income than Dick is not so undesirable that we should care to correct it by taking away from Tom and giving only an infinitesimal amount to Dick. At the other extreme, provided that Dick is not starving, if Tom has tremendous wealth, we may hesitate to attain an egalitarian distribution at the sacrifice of a large part of the society's income. In either case, consistency demands (assuming value judgment A) that we do not feel that any situation in which Tom has even more than before and Dick has less should be corrected merely by taking away from Tom and giving Dick only a token amount. This simple example can easily be extended, and it does not seem unreasonable to suppose that Q's (see above) actually exist for a good many distribution value judgments that people are likely to make.

Thus, by the operation of all these factors, there seems good reason to suppose that under value judgments that are likely to be acceptable, many moves satisfying the Kaldor-Hicks-Scitovsky criterion are good moves, regardless of what happens to the distribution of income.

APPENDIX

Throughout the body of the paper the assumption has been made that prices are held constant. We now prove analogues of some of the more important theorems without making use of that assumption.[18]

---

[18] If you like, we have been assuming that only one commodity exists and are now generalizing to the multi-commodity case.

We assume that each individual has a preference field (ordinal) of the usual type and that this field is known. The symbol $u^j(x)$ will thus represent an ordinal utility function for the jth individual, one of all the monotonic transformations that could be used. For it, read "utility of x for j."

As before, assume that there are m individuals. In addition, we stipulate that there are n commodities. We also continue to assume that we are examining only situations of static equilibrium.

Thus we assume that any situation with which we are concerned can be completely represented by a *commodity matrix*

$$C = [C_{ij}] \qquad (i = 1, \ldots, n)(j = 1, \ldots, m)$$

where C_{ij} represents the amount of the ith commodity possessed by the jth individual. Note that every column of a commodity matrix is the real income vector of an individual, while each row shows how the supply of a given commodity is distributed.

In particular, we let B be the "present" commodity matrix.

Throughout, δ_{ij} will be the Kronecker delta, i.e., $\delta_{ij} = 0$ for $j \neq i$; $\delta_{ij} = 1$ for $j = i$.

Define for any commodity matrix, C, the total real income matrix, $Y(C)$, as

$$Y(C) = \left[\delta_{ij} \sum_{j=1}^{m} C_{ij} \right],$$

the indices running as before. (Hereafter we shall always assume this.)

Next, for any commodity matrix, C, define a *distribution matrix* $R(C)$ as

$$R(C) = Y(C)^{-1} C.$$

Note that each row of $R(C)$ is a *distribution vector* for the relevant commodity, identical with those used for money income in the body of the paper.

Finally, we define the relationship, C is equivalent to D, written $C \sim D$, as $C \sim D$ if and only if $u^j(C_j) = u^j(D_j)$ for all j (where C_j, of course, is the jth column of C). Of course, $C \sim C$. (The relation is also transitive and symmetric.)

We also use the following notation: $C > D$ means $C_{ij} > D_{ij}$; $C \geq D$ means $C_{ij} \geq D_{ij}$ but $C \neq D$; $C \geqq D$ means $C_{ij} \geq D_{ij}$ and includes $C = D$. This notation will be used with all matrices.

A distribution value judgment will now be supposed to give a complete ordering of distribution *matrices*, and our other notation will remain the same.

We assume that $C \sim D$ and $Y(C) \leq Y(D)$ imply $C \, g \, D$. We shall make the additional assumption that if $C \, g \, D$ and $Y(C) \leq Y(D)$ then $R(C) \, g \, R(D)$.[19]

We also assume the acceptance of value judgment A since nothing very precise could be said under our former restrictive assumptions concerning the general case, anyway, and immediately obtain a result analogous to *Theorem 1:* We define S_A as

$$S_A = \{C | C \geqq D \sim B; \text{ where } Y(D) \leq Y(B)\}.$$

Theorem A.   *Let k be a distribution value judgment such that $R(C) \, g_k$ $R(B)$ and $R(C) \nrightarrow R(B)$. Then $S_{Ak} \supset S_A$ and $S_{Ak} \neq S_A$, provided that the very special case of $C = Y(B)R(C) \sim B$ does not hold.*[20]

Analogous to *Corollary 2*, it also follows that:

Corollary A.   *$S_A = S_{Ak}$ if and only if k is such that $R(B) \, b_k \, R(C)$ for every $R(C) \nrightarrow R(B)$.*

We now proceed to generalize the notions of "betweenness" and "non-troughedness" as follows:

(a) $R(C)$ is *between* $R(B)$ and $R(D)$ if and only if for all i and j, either
 (1) $R(B)_{ij} \geq R(C)_{ij} \geq R(D)_{ij}$ or
 (2) $R(D)_{ij} \geq R(C)_{ij} \geq R(B)_{ij}$
 and $R(B) \neq R(C) \neq R(D)$.
(b)   A distribution value judgment k is *nontroughed* from $R(B)$ to $R(D)$ if and only if $R(D) \, g_k \, R(B)$ implies $R(C) \, g_k \, R(B)$ for any $R(C)$ between $R(D)$ and $R(B)$.
(c) k is *uniformly* nontroughed from $R(B)$ to $R(D)$ if and only if it is nontroughed from any $R(B^*) \sim R(B)$ to any $R(D^*) \sim R(D)$. Obviously, uniform nontroughedness implies nontroughedness.
(d) K is (uniformly) nontroughed at $R(B)$ if and only if it is (uniformly) nontroughed from $R(B)$ to *any* $R(D)$.

---

[19]   But *not* that $R(C) \, g \, R(D)$ and $Y(C) \leq Y(D)$ imply $C \, g \, D$ since this would lead to ridiculous conclusions. For example, we should be forced to conclude that if we favor the bread eaters over the wine drinkers and $R(C) \, b \, R(D)$ because relatively more bread goes to the bread eaters and relatively more wine to the wine drinkers, then C must be as good as D provided there is a bit more wine in C even if there is only one crumb of bread in C to be divided.
  What we do assume is the reasonable proposition that $R(C) \, g \, R(D)$ and $Y(C) \geqq Y(D)$ imply $C \, g \, D$, which is not at all the same thing.

[20]   Of course, any $C' > C$ is in S_{Ak}. If we assume infinitely divisible commodities, then there are an infinite number of these matrices not in S_A.

(e) k is *everywhere* (uniformly) nontroughed if and only if it is (uniformly) nontroughed at all $R(X)$. (Actually, it is obvious that if k is everywhere nontroughed, then it is everywhere uniformly nontroughed.)

(f) Z is a *direction matrix* if and only if:

(1) Z is $n \times m$

(2) $Y(Z) = 0$

(3) $|Z_i| = \sum_{j=1}^{m} (Z_{ij})^2 = 1 \qquad (i = 1, \ldots, n)$.

(g) Λ is a *distance matrix* if and only if $\Lambda = [\delta_{ij} \Lambda_{ij}] \geq 0$. Then "$D$ lies a distance Λ from B in direction Z" means $D = B + \Lambda Z$. Note that $R(B + \Lambda Z) \neq R(B)$ for $\Lambda \neq 0$ but that $Y(B + \Lambda Z) = Y(B)$.

Analogous to *Theorem 2*, we now have:

Theorem B. *Let k be a distribution value judgment that is uniformly nontroughed at $R(B)$. From any $R(B^*) \sim R(B)$ go in any direction, Z, a distance of Λ° such that $R(D) = R(B^*) + \Lambda^\circ Z \, g_k \, R(B)$ but $R(B) \, b_k \, R(B^*) + \Lambda Z$ for $\Lambda \geq \Lambda^\circ$. Then S_{Ak} includes all C such that $Y(C) \geq Y(B)$ and $R(C) = R(B^*) + \Lambda Z$ where $\Lambda \leq \Lambda^\circ$. (Of course, there will generally be a different Λ° for each B^*.)*

Proof. If $\Lambda = \Lambda^\circ$ then $R(C) = R(D)$ and the proof is trivial. If $\Lambda \leq \Lambda^\circ$ it suffices to show that $R(C)$ is between $R(B^*)$ and $R(D)$ since k is uniformly nontroughed. Suppose first that $Z_{ij} > 0$ for any given i and j. Then

$$R(D)_{ij} = R(B^*)_{ij} + \Lambda^\circ_{ii} Z_{ij} \geq R(B^*)_{ij} + \Lambda_{ii} Z_{ij}$$
$$= R(C)_{ij} \geq R(B^*)_{ij}$$

while if $Z_{ij} < 0$ the inequalities are reversed. Since $Z \neq 0$ and $\Lambda = \Lambda^\circ$ has already been discussed, one of the above expressions must have an inequality in it (of course, $\Lambda = 0$ is also trivial) and hence, $R(C)$ is between $R(B^*)$ and $R(C)$ and the theorem is proved.

Of course, modifications can easily be made for k not *uniformly* nontroughed or nontroughed from $R(B)$ to a finite number of matrices, and the like. We should note here that *Corollary 1* still applies.

As a final step in our generalization of the results of the paper, we take up compensating value judgments and their effect. Here the proofs are quite similar to those in Section II and some of them will merely be indicated. Definitions:

(a) k is said to be *compensating* from $R(B)$ to $R(C)$ if and only if $R(B)$ b_k $R(C)$ implies that for any $\Delta = [\delta_{ij}\Delta_{ij}]$ where $0 \le \Delta \le \Delta(B,C)$ (for some $\Delta(B,C) = [\delta_{ij} \Delta(B,C)_{ij}]$) $C = [Y(B) + \Delta]$ $[R(C)]$ g_k B (and the reverse, of course, for $\Delta \ge \Delta(B,C)$).

(b) k is *totally* compensating from $R(B)$ to $R(C)$ if and only if it is compensating from $R(B)$ to $R(C)$ and $\Delta(B,C)$ is such that $C = [Y(B) + \Delta]$ $[R(C)] \le B^*$ for $\Delta \le \Delta(B,C)$ where $Y(B^*) = Y(B)$ and B g_k B^*, and $C \ge B^*$ for $\Delta \ge \Delta(B,C)$.
Since B^* is arbitrary this is the same as saying that C g_A B for $\Delta \ge \Delta(B,C)$ and B b_k C for $\Delta \le \Delta(B,C)$.

(c) We shall discuss compensating and totally compensating value judgments without regard for the intervals involved. If the degree of compensation required (see below) differs depending on the interval, this will not necessitate any change in the discussion, so that we may thus speak loosely of a "compensating value judgment."

(d) Let k be any distribution value judgment and j be a totally compensating value judgment giving the same complete ordering of distribution matrices that does k. If $\Gamma(B,C)$ is the minimum compensation required for a given move by j and $\Delta(B,C)$ that required by k, define the compensating coefficient matrix of k,

$$H(B,C)=[\Delta(B,C)][\Gamma(B,C)]^{-1}.$$

Obviously, as in *Theorem 6* the smaller is H, the bigger is S_{Ak}. If $H = I$ (the unit matrix) then $k = j$. If $H = 0$ then k is non-compensating.

(e) For any $R(C)$ not g_k $R(B)$ define $\Phi(B,C)$ as

$$\Phi(B,C)= \min_{B^*}\left[\delta_{ij} \max_{j}\left(\frac{R(B^*)_{ij}}{R(C)_{ij}} \right)\right] \text{ where } i = 1,\ldots,n$$

and $R(B^*)$ g_k $R(B)$. By a proof analogous to that of *Lemma 4* it can easily be shown for k totally compensating that $Y(B) + \Delta(B,C) = \Phi(B,C)Y(B)$ and hence that $\Delta(B,C) = [Y(B)][\Phi(B,C) - I]$.

It is now easy to prove a result analogous to that of *Theorem 5*.

Theorem C.   *Let k be a distribution value judgment and $R(B)$ b_k $R(D)$. Then if there exists an $R(C)$ such that:*

(1) $Y(C) = Y(B) = Y(D)$; $R(B)$ b_k $R(C)$.

(2) *The B* in definition e above for $\Phi(B,C)$ is the same as that for $\Phi(B,D)$,*

(3) *$R(C)$ is between $R(B^*)$ and $R(D)$.*

(4) *For every i, the j in definition e for $\Phi(C,D)$ is the same as that for $\Phi(B,C)$.*

(5) *$H(B,D) \leqslant I$.*

Then $H(B,D) \leqslant I$.

Proof. This proof is exactly like that of *Theorem 5* and will hence only be sketched. It consists in showing that the point

$$D = [\Phi(C,D)][Y(B) + \Delta(B,C)][R(D)]b_A C = [Y(B) + \Delta(B,C)][R(C)]$$

and thus (since $C \, g_k \, B$ by the definition of $\Delta(B,C)$) that D is in S_{Ak}. One further shows that

$$D \leq [\Phi(C,D)][\Phi(B,C)][Y(B)][R(D)] = [\Phi(B,D)][Y(B)][R(D)]$$
$$= [Y(B) + \Delta°][R(D)],$$

where $\Delta°$ is $\Delta(B,D)$ for a totally compensating value judgment giving the same complete ordering as k. This proves the theorem.

As before, a somewhat more precise formula can be worked out, thus:

$$H(B,D) \leq [[\Phi(C,D)][I - H(B,C)]$$
$$- [H(B,C)][\Phi(B,D) - I]][\Phi(B,D) - I]^{-1}$$

(the inequality obtaining when k is not totally compensating from C to D).

As before, when $H(B,C) = I$ or 0, we have, respectively:

$$H(B,D) \leqq I \quad \text{and}$$
$$H(B,D) \leqq [\Phi(C,D) - I][\Phi(B,D) - I]^{-1}$$
$$= [\Phi(C,D) - I][Y(B)][[\Phi(B,D) - I][Y(B)]]^{-1}$$

both of which were to be expected.

REFERENCES

Bergson, A., "A Reformulation of Certain Aspects of Welfare Economics," *Quarterly Journal of Economics* 52, 1938, 310–334.

Little, I. M. D., *A Critique of Welfare Economics*, Oxford University Press, Oxford, 1950.

Samuelson, P. A., "Evaluation of Real National Income," *Oxford Economic Papers* 2, 1950.
  "Comment," in: B. F. Haley (ed.), *A Survey of Contemporary Economics, II*, Richard D. Irwin, Homewood, Ill., 1952.

CHAPTER 13

Income Distribution, Value Judgments, and Welfare: A Correction (1957)

written jointly with Peter B. Kenen

In "Income Distribution, Value Judgments, and Welfare,"[1] it was assumed that distribution value judgments are independent of the level of total income.[2] We shall show here that no such assumption can be maintained in the multi-commodity case as it either conflicts with the underlying postulate that "welfare is a function of individual utilities"[3] or else implies that all indifference maps are homothetic (indifference curves are radial blow-ups of each other). We shall then point out that the assumption in question can be dropped without changing the major results of the article in other than a formal way.

Adapting the notation of the Appendix,[4] consider a community composed of k individuals and examine a pair of distribution matrices, $R(C^m)$ and $R(C^n)$. These matrices, premultiplied by a given total real income matrix $Y(C)$, will produce two commodity matrices, C^m and C^n. Next, write $u(C^m)$ and $u(C^n)$ to denote the two $(1 \times k)$ vectors $u^j(C_j^m)$ and $u^j(C_j^n)$ of individual utilities $(j = 1, \ldots, k)$. The postulate that "welfare is a function of individual utilities" implies that:

$$R(C^m)bR(C^n) \qquad \text{if and only if} \qquad u(C^m)bu(C^n)$$

that is, one distribution of commodities is to be judged better than another, if and only if the distribution of individual utilities corresponding to the first is judged better than the distribution of individual utilities corresponding to the second. However, it is clear that individual utilities are not simply functions of commodity distributions but also depend upon the level of real income, C^m; and thus $u(C^m)$ is not uniquely determined by $R(C^m)$ but is also a function of $Y(C)$. Therefore, we cannot assume that the choice between $R(C^m)$ and $R(C^n)$, which depends upon the choice between $u(C^m)$ and $u(C^n)$, is invariant with respect to $Y(C)$.

This argument may be illustrated as follows: For a given total income, consider a point, say T, that is Pareto-optimal. If we accept value-

---

[1] Fisher (1956). The page references refer to Chapter 12 in this volume.
[2] P. 187.
[3] P. 184n.
[4] Pp. 220–25.

judgment A,[5] then clearly we must rank the distribution corresponding to T better than those corresponding to various neighboring points that are not Pareto-optimal. Now let us double real income (i.e., double all components thereof) and consider those same distributions. It is obviously quite possible that the point $2T$, which has the same distribution as T, will not be Pareto-optimal and that a point which is twice one of the neighboring points mentioned above will be so. Hence for the new level of total real income we ought to prefer some other distribution to T instead of the other way around. An examination of the ordinary box-diagram convinces one that the only case in which this effect cannot arise is where all indifference maps are homothetic, a condition much too restrictive to be assumed.

Hence the assumption that distribution value judgments are independent of the level of total real income cannot be maintained in the multicommodity case. But examination of the problem shows that the removal of this assumption does not alter any major conclusion of the article. We shall not indulge in the tedious pastime of proving the major theorems again without use of the assumption in question, but content ourselves with some general remarks on the ways in which such proofs would differ from those given in the paper.

In fact, there is no substantial difference in the statement or proof of any major theorem, for only the illustrative *Theorem 3*[6] requires the independence assumption. This is so because *Theorem 3* rests on our ability neatly to describe the set S_{Ak} in geometrical terms, while all other theorems require at most our ability so to describe the set S_A that is not dependent on the given assumption. In the Appendix, one basic change does have to be made, but that change does not invalidate the theorems of that section. There, we must now define S_A as the set described on page 222 *plus* all points that are what we may term "Pareto-preferred" to points in that set.

Finally, aside from strengthening the results of the paper in general, the removal of the independence assumption strengthens our *Corollary 2*[7] (*Corollary A* of the Appendix), which must now read as follows: The acceptable set obtained by accepting value judgment A and refusing to make any further value judgments as to distribution is identical with that obtained by accepting value judgment A and making a totally compensating distribution value judgment that is single-peaked at P and *that is independent of the level of total income with the exception of what may be termed "Pareto effects."*

---

[5] P. 191 and passim.
[6] Pp. 199–200.
[7] P. 196.

We thus conclude that the assumption of distribution value judgments as independent of the level of total income must be removed in the multi-commodity case; but also that its removal can be easily accomplished without altering either the major theorems of the paper or its general argument. They are in fact strengthened by the removal of what was perhaps the most restrictive assumption made.

REFERENCE

Fisher, F. M., "Income Distribution, Value Judgments, and Welfare," *Quarterly Journal of Economics* 70, 1956, 380–424. Reprinted as Chapter 12 in this volume.

CHAPTER 14

How Income Ought to Be
Distributed: Paradox Lost (1961)

written jointly with Jerome Rothenberg

I

A few years ago Robert Strotz propounded an apparent paradox in the ethics of income distribution and called for its resolution.[1] Briefly stated, the paradox is this: Strotz places a number of apparently ethically desirable or innocuous restrictions on the class of admissible social welfare functions in a one-commodity n-person world, yet proves that the only member of the admissible class is an apparently ethically *un*acceptable welfare function, namely, that which is maximized by maximizing total income without regard for the way in which the income is distributed among persons.[2] It must therefore be the case either that at least one of the apparently ethically acceptable conditions is in fact ethically abhorrent or that the apparently ethically abhorrent result is in fact ethically acceptable. Strotz invites the reader to decide between the alternatives and, if selecting the first, to point out the guilty condition or conditions.

This paper undertakes to do just that. In the next section we briefly summarize Strotz's paper; the following sections then discuss our objections to Strotz's assumptions; finally, we discuss the implications of these criticisms for some of the other relevant literature.

This article was written while the authors were colleagues at the University of Chicago and was partly financed by the Ford Foundation Econometrics Workshop of the Department of Economics, University of Chicago.

[1] Strotz (1958). Page references in text refer to this article.

[2] Actually, this statement of Strotz's result is a bit too strong in two minor ways. First, there is obviously a whole set of functions with the stated property, not just one; however, the same apparently ethically unacceptable maximizing rule holds for each of them. Second, Strotz's result implies that, if in an available situation, A, total income is greater than that in all other available situations, A is to be chosen, regardless of other considerations. However, if there are two or more such maximum-income situations, there is no reason why the choice *among the members of the maximal set* cannot be made on other grounds, although the final choice must be some such member. Society is allowed, in other words, to have a lexicographic ordering of situations in which total income comes first and other considerations second. This qualification hardly weakens the force of Strotz's result, however, since any positive gain in total income – no matter how small – more than compensates for any worsening of other distributional considerations – no matter how large.

II

Strotz's restrictions are ethical interpretations of Chernoff's decision-making axioms.[3] We need not discuss all of them in detail but refer the reader to the original article for the full treatment, which must be simplified here.

Strotz assumes a one-commodity world (the commodity is called "money income"). All individuals are assumed to have linear Von Neumann–Morgenstern utility functions – they have neither risk aversion nor risk preference (the utility functions may, of course, differ in intercept and slope).[4]

Points in the space whose coordinates are the individual incomes are called "distributions." The problem posed is to find a choice function that will select from the (assumed non-null) set of attainable distributions those that are ethically acceptable – that is, that satisfy the following postulates (here given informally):

> *Postulate 1* (Resolution).[5] – The choice problem is always resolved – that is, the choice function always selects at least one distribution.
>
> *Postulate 2* (Pareto optimality). – If two distributions, d_1 and d_2, are both attainable and $d_1 \geq d_2$ (in the usual sense of vector inequality),[6] then d_2 is not chosen.
>
> *Postulate 3* (Isomorphism). – The social choice is independent of the labeling of persons and of distributions – the social choice depends only on the absolute and relative size of the pieces into which the pie is cut, not on the identities of the particular individuals getting particular pieces.
>
> *Postulate 4* (Independence of Irrelevant Alternatives I). – Adding more distributions to the attainable set (and not subtracting any) can never cause a previously rejected distribution to be chosen.
>
> *Postulate 5* (Independence of Irrelevant Alternatives II). – Furthermore, if each of the new distributions is dominated by an

---

[3] Chernoff (1954). Incidentally, it will be clear from what follows that our objections to the Strotz axioms in no way apply to Chernoff's article.

[4] Subsequently, this is relaxed in favor of the assumption that all utility functions are identical up to a linear transformation – identical attitudes toward risk. The resulting theorem changes but retains much of the flavor of the one that we concentrate on here.

[5] These informal names for postulates are mostly ours and are adopted for mnemonic convenience. Strotz does use some of them.

[6] For any two vectors, x and y, $x = y$ means $x_i = y_i$ for all i; $x \leq y$ means $x_i \leq y_i$ for all i; $x \leq y$ means $x_i \leq y_i$ for all i and not $x = y$.

old distribution (as in Postulate 2), no previously chosen distribution shall be rejected.

Postulate 6 (Ends, Not Means). – If additional ways are found of bringing about distributions already available, then any distribution previously chosen shall still be chosen, and any distribution previously rejected shall still be rejected. (Of course, some of the old distributions brought about in the new ways may be accepted.)

Postulate 7 (Randomization). – If d_1 and d_2 are both ethically acceptable, then it is permissible to use any random device to choose between them.

Postulate 8 (Convexity). – Consider the distribution problem formed from a given problem by replacing the attainable set of distributions by its convex hull;[7] if d_1 and d_2 were both acceptable in the original problem, then all convex combinations of d_1 and d_2 shall be acceptable in the new problem.

Postulate 9 (Strong Independence). – Consider the set of all two-prize lottery tickets such that one prize is a distribution in the attainable set and the other is some specified distribution (which may or may not be attainable) and such that the first prize is gained with specified probability p and the second with probability $(1 - p)$, p being constant over the set of tickets. Then the lottery tickets chosen must be precisely those in which the first prize is a distribution that would be chosen in the original problem. In other words, if with probability p you will be allowed to choose from the attainable set and with probability $(1 - p)$ you will receive some specified distribution, your choice must be independent of the particular distribution specified as the second prize and of its probability.

Postulate 10 (Certainty Equivalence). – Consider the problem formed from the original problem by letting the attainable set be the set of all averages of the elements of the original set on the one hand and a specified distribution on the other, with weights p and $(1 - p)$ respectively, where p is some number such that $0 \le p \le 1$. In other words, consider the problem whose attainable set consists precisely of the certainty equivalents of the lottery tickets just described. The chosen distributions in this new problem must be precisely the certainty

---

[7] That is, by the set of all non-negatively weighted arithmetic means of the elements of the original set.

equivalents of the chosen lottery tickets in Postulate 9, that is, they must be precisely those distributions that are averages of the specified distribution and those distributions that would be chosen in the original problem.

Given these ten postulates, the theorem then follows that the only distributions chosen will be those for which total money income takes on its maximum value over the attainable set.[8]

III

I've got a little list – I've got a little list
Of society offenders who might well be underground
And who never would be missed – who never would be missed! . . .
Such as – What d'ye call him – Thing'em-bob and likewise – never-mind,
And 'St – 'st – 'st – and What's-his-name, and also You-know-who –
The task of filling up the blanks I'd rather leave to *you*.
But it really doesn't matter whom you put upon the list,
For they'd none of 'em be missed – they'd none of 'em be missed!

See how the fates their gifts allot,
For A is happy, – B is not.
Yet B is worthy, I dare say,
Of more prosperity than A!
Is B more worthy? I should say
He's worth a great deal more than A.
Yet A is happy. . . .
Ever joyous, ever gay,
Happy, undeserving A!
If I were fortune – which I'm not –
B should enjoy A's happy lot.
. . . . . .
But condemned to die is he,
Wretched meritorious B!

W. S. GILBERT, *The Mikado*

Let us begin by considering the circumstances under which value judgments about income distribution are likely to be made or to be thought relevant, in order to judge whether Strotz's theorem in fact makes us reject such judgments when we should expect them to be important – a true paradox – or whether one or more of his axioms is unacceptable because it eliminates the grounds on which such value judgments can be made without persuasive justification, thus making the theorem hardly

---

[8] Where the assumption of linear utility functions is relaxed in favor of functions all of which have the same form, the theorem is that the distribution chosen is that for which the sum of comparable individual utilities is maximized over the attainable set.

surprising or significant. In our opinion, Strotz's model is of the latter type. His postulates, together with the assumption of a one-commodity world with linear utility functions for all individuals (and subsequently, when this is relaxed, with utility functions equal for all up to a linear transformation), so critically (and unwarrantedly) constrain the possible value judgments and rarefy the world to which they are to pertain that it is no surprise to find that welfare is maximized by maximizing total income and ignoring value judgments concerning income distribution. For just this reason, his results have little bearing on real situations in which real value judgments can be made.

We turn then to the possible grounds on which value judgments concerning income distribution are likely to rest – the possible reasons for worrying about the ethics of income distribution in the first place. We can think of four principal (not mutually exclusive) categories of such grounds:

1   Interpersonal comparisons of utility are made. In other words, it is believed that different individuals have commensurably different capacities for satisfaction, and this enters into consideration. This category is recognized and discussed by Strotz (p. 205).

2   Interpersonal comparisons of utility may or may not be made, but (what is not at all the same thing) interpersonal comparisons of intrinsic *worth* or *deservingness* are. Regardless of what I think about the utility capacity of two individuals or groups (and even if I have no opinion whatsoever on that subject), I may be prepared to say that one of them, B, is "meritorious" relative to the other, A, and should be given a higher income. Such a judgment can rest on a variety of grounds, but it is the sort of judgment that all of us make at some time or another, explicitly or implicitly. Indeed, when we feel most strongly about income distribution, it is likely to be on this sort of ground that we do so. (Remember that such a judgment can take the form of a statement that all men are equally deserving or that it is morally right that each man should get what he earns, or the like.)

3   In the many-commodity real world, each distribution may result in external economies and diseconomies in consumption. Distributions may thus be judged in terms of the extent to which they take advantage of external economies and avoid external diseconomies.

4   Income distribution may be thought to have an effect on incentives to future effort and may be judged accordingly. While the

other categories might be described as "personal" reasons for normative interest in income distribution, in the sense that it is the relative consumption of particular individuals that is central, this category is "impersonal" in the sense that it is the absolute size of the (future) total distribuend that is central, and relative consumption incidental. For this reason, it is really an efficiency, rather than a strictly equity, consideration (as is also, in part, the external economy consideration).

Categories 1 and 2 are separately ruled out by Strotz's Isomorphism Postulate. This postulate asserts that individuals are to be treated anonymously; yet it is precisely the non-anonymity of individuals or of groups that is at the heart of categories 1 and 2.[9]

Further, category 3 is extravagantly limited by the fact that Strotz's world, by assumption, has only one homogeneous commodity. External consumption relations in a one-commodity world are limited to little more than altruism and jealousy, and it is highly debatable whether this particular kind of external relation is or should be included in value judgments about distribution.[10] In any case, other forms of consumption externality cannot exist in a one-commodity world.

Finally, category 4 is practically annihilated in the context of Strotz's model by a combination of Postulates 3 and 8 (Isomorphism and Convexity). Even if one is an inegalitarian in Strotz's sense – that is, one who feels "that a lopsided distribution of income is the essence of the good society" and "that it makes no difference who is rich and who is poor, provided someone is rich" (p. 196) – one may well believe that a proper system of economic incentives requires *some particular* unequal distribution of income. If we assume that the income dimension in Strotz's system is current income, then the effect of distribution on incentives means that different distributions of the same total income presage different levels of future income. We must be able to declare that some distributions of a given income are better than others. Yet we are prevented from doing so by Isomorphism and Convexity. Given some unequal distribution that is preferred, Isomorphism requires that we be indifferent between it and any distribution in the set formed by permuting the individuals and keeping the original imputations – that is, the set of distributions placed symmetrically about the 45-degree ray and including the original distribution. Thus, we must accept any equally unequal

---

[9] It makes little difference that individuals' utility functions are allowed to differ in terms of origin or unit of measurement – these differences prove ultimately irrelevant for Strotz's welfare decisions.

[10] Cf. Chapter 12, p. 190, pp. 208–10.

distribution.[11] Furthermore, Convexity requires us to accept all distributions in the convex hull of the set just described – that is, we must accept all distributions that are non-negatively weighted means of the distributions in the permutation set of the original distribution. Since the egalitarian distribution must always lie in this convex hull, this means that we cannot accept an unequal distribution without also accepting all distributions with the same or a lesser degree of inequality. No degree of inequality can ever be declared better than a lesser degree at any given level of contemporaneous income – surely a stringent requirement for someone who merely wishes to express an opinion as to incentives.[12]

Thus, all four grounds for being interested in income distribution are virtually closed off or eliminated in Strotz's system. If one accepts the system, one is not likely to expect that distributional considerations of these types will be important. The theorem should therefore occasion little surprise. However, the problem remains of deriving welfare implications from an ethical system in which distributional considerations are important. In this regard, our discussion above indicates that Postulates 3 and 8 and the one-commodity assumption merit examination.

Clearly, Postulate 3 carries the greatest weight in the system. If Isomorphism were dropped, the system would contain a wide latitude for distributional considerations. In such a context, the assumption of a one-commodity world would not much detract from the interest of the system and would be easily justified on the basis of its contribution to analytic tractability. Similarly, while the Convexity Postulate does to some extent independently restrict the applicability of distribution value judgments,

---

[11] This refers not to the attainability of any such distribution but only to its social evaluation.

[12] This interpretation assumes that the income dimension is current income. A reinterpretation of Strotz's model might make it possible to incorporate the incentive effects of distribution on future efficiency explicitly into the system in terms of the shape of the attainable set itself. Indeed, Strotz, in personal communication with one of the present authors, has indicated that such an interpretation is what he intended in his article. If the points being considered are redefined to be representative (for example, expected) values of all (or some subset of) future incomes, it is possible to reflect incentive effects by an asymmetry of the attainable set itself with respect to the 45-degree ray or a concavity of the upper boundary of the set to indicate a worsening of production possibilities as one approaches equality. This approach takes advantage of the fact that category 4 is purely an efficiency consideration and so incorporated in the production-possibility set. We do not believe this to be a fruitful interpretation for Strotz's overall intentions. In any case, however, since category 4 is so stringently circumscribed as grounds for distributional judgments (either by Postulates 3 and 8, as in the text, or definitionally, as just described), it is no surprise to discover that it can be ignored in the final result.

its strongest effects stem from the presence of Isomorphism; in the absence of the latter postulate it would be substantially unobjectionable in terms of what we have said so far (although we shall discuss it in another connection below).[13]

It is Postulate 3, therefore, that we chiefly criticize, because we believe that the kinds of concern with distribution that Isomorphism excludes (categories 1 and 2) are those that observers feel most strongly about when they want the distribution of income as well as its level taken into account. It must be admitted, however, that our view is here contrary to the basic outlook of the New Welfare Economics. (Indeed, we believe that much of the sterility of the latter stems from the exclusion of considerations of this type.) The New Welfare Economics was largely developed in an effort to see how much could be said without making interpersonal comparisons of utility. Interpersonal comparisons of worth, also, while never forbidden, are clearly contrary to the spirit of the New Welfare Economics. The Bergson Social Welfare Function need not require the anonymous and symmetrical treatment of individuals, but such treatment is widespread in the literature and is much older than the New Welfare Economics itself.[14]

If we were convinced that Strotz's treatment were within this tradition, one way of looking at his paradox would be to regard it as showing the undesirable ethical implications that can be derived from the ethics of the New Welfare Economics by a *reductio ad absurdum*. In this view, however, the paradox would be one not of distributional ethics as such but of the rather limited ethics of the New Welfare Economics.

Strotz's treatment is not, however, truly within the spirit of the New Welfare Economics, for he is willing to assume Von Neumann-Morgenstern utility functions and thus to measure intensity of preferences for his individuals, even though he does not *explicitly* compare such intensities between different individuals.[15] In this context, however, the case for comparisons of individual *worth* is even stronger than it is when intensity of preference is not measured. Where preference intensities do not "count," interpersonal comparisons of worth might seem unfair: if

---

[13] Indeed, the consequences of a somewhat different (and perhaps more broadly acceptable) version of the Convexity Postulate were investigated by one of the authors elsewhere. See Chapter 12: Definitions *e* and *f* (pp. 189–90), *Theorem 2 and Corollary 1* (pp. 193–94), and pp. 219–20.

[14] See, for example, Hildreth (1953), pp. 86–7; Harsanyi (1955), p. 320; and Samuelson (1947), p. 224.

[15] For an attempt at utilizing preference intensities with avowedly ordinal – but effectively cardinal – utility, see Goodman and Markowitz (1952), pp. 257–62; Luce and Raiffa (1957), pp. 345–48.

Citizen A counts for less than Citizen B does, one feels intuitively that this discounting ought to be outweighed in the assessment of over-all effects on social welfare when extremely intense preferences by A compete against near indifference by B, though not when both are near indifference or both have intense preferences. Such adjustments can be accomplished if preference intensities are measured – as they are in a cardinal utility function – but not when each individual has only an ordinal utility index.[16]

Furthermore, it is not the case that, when preference intensities are measured and "count," Isomorphism simply prevents interpersonal comparisons of worth from being made. Indeed, the acceptance of the Isomorphism postulate gives the same results as does the acceptance of an extremely strong assumption that makes interpersonal comparisons of preference intensity and social worth mutually independent. By choosing a unit of measurement for each individual's utility (here the constant marginal utility of one dollar) and then assigning equal total social impact to each individual in the social welfare function, Strotz is behaving as though the social worth of individuals were inversely proportional to the unit of measurement of intensity of their preferences. Isomorphism implies that the imputation (0, 100) is precisely as good as the imputation (100, 0) regardless of the actual relative intensities with which the two individuals involved prefer 100 to 0. Thus, in effect, an increase in the first individual's income by \$100 has a positive impact on welfare just equal to the negative impact of a decrease of \$100 in the second individual's income. Thus, the implicit (constant) social weights given the two individuals are inversely proportional to their (constant) marginal utilities of money. Of course, Strotz may not intend such a comparison;[17] nonetheless, Isomorphism does give the same results as a rather unacceptable, very strong set of interpersonal comparisons. Thus, Isomorphism does not really enable us to avoid making

---

[16] Strotz has communicated to one of the authors that he does not invest the Von Neumann-Morgenstern utility function with welfare significance: the preference intensities implicit in the function are not concrete psychological entities that deserve to be considered in a normative system of choice; the function is simply a "convenient" way to describe an individual's behavior under risk. Our position differs from this. We believe that preference intensities, however measured, ought to be considered in formulating normative choice systems. Whatever the merits of this dispute, however, the particular use that Strotz makes of the utility function in his normative model fashions a social choice mechanism that operates in every respect *as if* utility differences (preference intensities) mattered – and mattered a great deal. This suffices for our purposes. To avoid unnecessary philosophical argumentation, the reader may interpret most of our subsequent discussion of Strotz's model in this *as if* fashion if he wishes, since our position does not really depend on the ultimate metaphysical reality of constructs like preference intensity.

[17] In a personal communication he insists that he does not.

interpersonal comparisons (albeit implicitly). What it does is prevent us from making comparisons of capacity for satisfaction independently of comparisons of social worth. In this sense, there is no such thing as refraining from interpersonal comparisons in this area; the choice of making or not making them is a "forced option," in William James's phrase.[18]

However, if it is difficult to justify Isomorphism on the grounds that it prohibits interpersonal comparisons, it might nevertheless be argued that anonymous and symmetrical treatment of individuals is the only palatable distribution value judgment in a democratic society, as Strotz himself suggests (p. 205).[19] The widespread use of the assumptions already referred to might be taken as evidence of this, although such treatment ordinarily has stemmed from a desire for analytic convenience rather than from ethical arguments.[20] Democratic equity, however, requires only that equals be treated equally (hence, that unequals be treated unequally). It may be that this requires each person to be accorded the same social worth, but it begs the question to insist that interpersonally evaluated differences in preference intensity are not differences that "count" or that, in the light of equal worths, positing symmetric anonymous treatment of individuals in their overall welfare impacts does not imply interpersonal comparisons of utility.

Our stricture against Isomorphism, then, is as follows. Strotz's postulates entail implicit interpersonal comparisons of welfare impact in his system. The form of these comparisons is not, however, incontestably most appropriate. His implicit interpersonal comparisons represent the workings of an *im*personal decision procedure: social weights are "decided" and utility comparisons are "made" independently of any factual information about particular individuals or groups (other than information about level of money income). This seems an unfortunate restriction on normative distributional considerations in a model that has as central focus the implications of making alternative kinds of value judgments. We believe that such a model should leave open the possi-

---

[18] Cf. Chapter 12, pp. 196–97, for an analogous discussion.

[19] In this spirit it might be argued that the second quotation from *The Mikado* may be appropriate precisely because its context is W. S. Gilbert's authoritarian Japan. It would be inappropriate for the United States. On the other hand, one could retort that it is rather the liquidational anonymity, the faceless disdain, represented in the *first* quotation that reflects the authoritarian system. The respect for the dignity and uniqueness of the individual expressed in the second is more appropriate to individualistic society. But one must not push one's text too far. Some of our readers may have a little list also.

[20] Harsanyi (1955) is an exception to this; however, he states the point without presenting an argument for it.

bility of making interpersonal comparisons of worth and utility independently and on personal grounds.[21]

IV

Strotz's system allows even less scope for distributional considerations than the last section suggests. For, as a result especially of his assumption about individual utility functions, the distributions that may be chosen by the "central decision-maker," whose value judgments about income distribution give the form of the social welfare function, are not the distributions that actually obtain.[22] The former merely determine initial conditions for a subsequent redistributing procedure carried on by the population – gambling. The outcomes of the subsequent procedure are such as to make distribution value judgments very nearly superfluous.

Since everyone is assumed to have a linear Von Neumann-Morgenstern utility function (individual functions differing from one another – if at all – only in intercept and slope), everyone is just willing to accept a fair gamble (that is, everyone is indifferent between taking the gamble and not), *whatever the size of the stakes and whatever the amount of his original assets*. Each pair of individuals agrees on the odds that define a fair gamble. Consequently, whatever imputation is made by the central decision-maker, the members of the population will be just willing to employ their incomes as stakes in a series of gambles, the terms of which can be agreed upon. Since they are willing to do so, they may in fact do so (but, of course, they may just as well not do so). A no-gambling outcome is not unique. Nor is it stable. Assume that a round

---

[21] Admittedly, however, many comparisons of worth that are reflected in political decisions, such as in sumptuary taxation, depend upon the existence of many commodities, since they rest on some individuals possessing unapproved tastes. This example shows, by the way, that it may be desirable to make comparisons of worth even when comparisons of preference intensities are not made.

[22] The criticisms of this section are directed exclusively to the implications of the assumption that all individuals' utility functions are linear. As noted above, it is this assumption that enables the maximization of the welfare function to be expressed as a maximization of aggregate money income. In the more general case, which Strotz subsequently adopts of non-linear functions identical up to a linear transformation, social welfare maximization calls only for a maximization of the sum of individual ("transferable," in Von Neumann-Morgenstern terms) utilities; and this maximization cannot be given a simple translation into aggregate money income. While the more general theorem has much the same flavor as does the more restricted one and is equally subject to our criticisms in other sections, it is free from the difficulties we discuss here.

In fairness to Strotz we must point out that he has informed us that he intends the more general case to be the important one. He devotes the earlier and larger part of his paper to the linear case for expositional purposes only.

of gambling does occur. After this first round of gambles, everyone still possessed of money, but no one else, is willing to enter on another round of fair gambles (linearity ensures that this willingness is independent of income level).[23] So this is not a stable outcome either. Let us assume a second round does take place. Another group of individuals will subsequently drop out with nothing left, and third and further rounds may take place, with no stability achieved until all income has been won by one individual. This will ultimately come about because no individual becomes unwilling to take a fair gamble, no matter how much he has won or lost, so long as he has any income left. The only stable outcome of the procedure, then, is where one individual is left with the total income and everyone else has nothing, for only then can no further gambling occur.

Aside from its radical unreality, this process makes Strotz's theorem almost trivial. For, if every centrally selected distribution ends up with one individual having everything and everyone else nothing, then the original welfare choice is scarcely terribly important. The only effect it can conceivably have is to influence the relative probabilities of different individuals becoming sole winner. Value judgments have some scope here, in that an egalitarian might feel his goal approximated by equalizing these relative probabilities for all individuals, while someone who favors a small group of individuals could arrange for each of them to have a substantial chance to be sole winner. But such scope is extremely limited, since most value judgments about distribution translate very poorly into relative chances of becoming the winner who takes all.[24]

---

[23] We assume that an individual who has lost everything cannot borrow in order to continue gambling, since his expected profit is zero.

[24] This is not to insist that the problem of selecting initial relative assets for a gambling game is in itself trivial. Far from it. Indeed, most distributional treatments envisage simply distributing assets to individuals and leaving the individuals responsible for doing what they want with them. Consumption – and gambling can be considered as consumption – is the individual's business. The difficulty in the present case is that the form of "consumption" involved has an unusually radical situation for its only stable outcome, one that will invariably falsify the equity intent of the original distribution.

The situation is quite different when the assumption of linear utility is dropped in favor of one requiring merely that all individual functions be identical up to a linear transformation. For now an individual's willingness to gamble money depends upon his income level. It is no longer true that a fair gamble will always be acceptable to every pair of individuals with non-zero income. Indeed, for every pair, there will be relative incomes such that no gamble, fair or otherwise, will be acceptable to both. Given any initial allocation of stakes, there is a high probability, dependent on that imputation, that gambling will cease before one individual wins everything. This is especially true of the final imputation which maximizes the only welfare function acceptable in Strotz's system, since, by Strotz's argument (p. 201), the second-order maximization condition is

What is even more limiting is that, if we may interpret the problem of welfare choice in terms of these ultimate stable outcomes, the few value judgments that are not substantially distorted by being translated into influences on relative probabilities of winner-take-all will be rendered inoperative by Isomorphism in conjunction with nothing more objectionable than Pareto optimality (Postulate 2). Suppose distribution d_1 maximizes income. In d_1, individual 1 receives everything, everyone else nothing. Consider any other outcome d_2, with a lower total income, in which individual 2 receives everything. The permutation of d_2, d_2', in which 1, instead of 2, receives the total income of d_2, is as good as d_z (by Isomorphism). But then d_1, which makes 1 better off – since he gets a higher total income than d_2 – without making anyone else worse off (zero for everyone else), is better than d_2 (Postulate 2). Thus, no matter what value considerations might induce me to approve the initial imputation that led to d_2, they are overruled by an exceedingly small and simple subset of Strotz's postulates.

Under this interpretation, maximization of income follows almost trivially because distribution considerations have been almost completely expunged by very unrealistic assumptions concerning individual utility.

V

We now turn to a discussion of Postulate 8 (Convexity) and Postulate 10 (Certainty Equivalence). Up to now we have attempted to show that most of the grounds on which persons feel that distributional ethics are relevant to welfare choices are excluded by the combined presence of the assumption of linear utility functions, Postulate 8, and Postulate 3. It is little wonder that optimality is discovered to reside in a formula that makes distributional ethics largely irrelevant. Postulate 8 and, notably, Postulate 10 restrict the scope of distributional value judgments in a different and quite interesting manner. Even if we should accept Postulate 3, Postulate 10 especially would be unacceptable.

Consider first Postulate 8. In Strotz's system there are two postulates, 7 and 9, which deal with choices among lottery tickets and two, 8 and 10, which deal with choices among "certainty equivalents." The latter seem

that at this imputation either everyone, or everyone save at most one individual, must be unwilling to take even a fair gamble. Hence, only one individual at most is available who is willing to take a gamble biased against himself in money terms. For most reasonable utility functions, individuals will be unwilling to take a fair gamble either at high or low incomes; therefore, the maximizing imputation is highly likely to be one in which more than one individual has non-zero income.

superficially to stem from the former. Thus, if one is willing to toss a coin to select one of a pair of approved distributions, it may seem reasonable to suppose that one is responding to the mathematical expectation of the lottery and, therefore, that the certainty equivalent of the gamble – the distribution formed by a weighted mean of the pair of approved distributions, where the weights equal relative probabilities in the gamble – would be as good as the gamble. But closer inspection shows that this is not indubitable.

The crucial distinction between a lottery and a certainty equivalent is that, unless the same lottery is to be repeated a large number of times, one does not obtain the certainty-equivalent outcome either in a single instance or as an average. The alternatives in the lottery are mutually exclusive: one always obtains *either* one *or* the other, but not a combination of both. Thus, no distributions other than the acceptable pair are ever involved. It seems quite reasonable that, when one is indifferent between two acceptable outcomes, any random way of choosing between them should be acceptable. But certainty equivalents are quite different. Only figuratively is the certainty-equivalent distribution nothing more than a combination of the two approved distributions. It is, in reality, a different distribution entirely. Why *should* some third distribution be as good as two others just because it is a weighted average of the two? If, for example, both a very unequal and a perfectly equal distribution should be found (thought) conducive to incentives to high production, does this necessitate that a moderately unequal distribution be found (thought) just as conducive? We have already seen that the presence of Postulate 3 along with Postulate 8 implies that, if *any* unequal distribution should be acceptable, then *all* lesser degrees of inequality of the same total income must be acceptable as well. It must be emphasized that, so long as the nature of the social value judgments about distribution is unspecified, it is quite an arbitrary restriction on them (but, of course, not necessarily an unreasonable one) to require this modified form of monotonicity implied by Postulate 8.

The objection to Postulate 10 is of much the same type, but more serious. Whereas we have little assurance that the substance of Postulate 8 would be fulfilled for all distributional value judgments, we have strong indications that the substance of Postulate 10 would be violated by many distributional value judgments. Suppose that one is choosing among two-prize lottery tickets all of which will give the same distribution d_0 (attainable or not) if a random event E, expected with probability p, occurs, but different distributions from the attainable set if the random event *not-E*, expected with probability $1 - p$, occurs. Here, since the two prizes of each ticket are mutually exclusive, one has nothing to choose from if E

occurs. Choice among the tickets depends only on what can be won if *not-E* occurs. Thus, the choice depends only on the preference ordering of the attainable set; it is independent of the nature of d_0. This is the substance of Postulate 9 and is an entirely proper restriction on *social* value judgments about distribution.

Postulate 10 is subtly, but crucially, different. The lottery tickets chosen in the previous problem reflected only the ordering of Distributions in the attainable set (D). Suppose we have a new attainable set (D') comprising the certainty equivalents of all possible lottery tickets in the previous problem with probabilities p and $1 - p$. Postulate 10 asserts that we must choose from D' the certainty equivalents of just those lottery tickets that were chosen in the first problem. Since the latter choice was independent of d_0, depending only on the ordering of D, the former choice is also independent of d_0.

This is an extraordinarily restrictive postulate. We remember that the new attainable set of distributions (D') is very much dependent on the location of d_0. Different distributions do lead to very different conditional attainable sets. Moreover, the new problems do not at all involve choices concerning the original attainable set. They do not involve lottery tickets, where distributions in D are possible prizes. Only actual distributions in new attainable sets, D', D'', etc., are involved. Since d_0 and p $(0 < p < 1)$ can be selected unrestrictedly, new sets can be generated everywhere throughout distribution space. Furthermore, the arbitrariness of our choice of d_0 and p means that these new sets are functionally unrelated to one another in the sense of the structure of preferences about distributions. Yet we are required to make our choice from each of these spatially unrelated, widely separated sets on the basis solely of our ordering of distributions in the nowise special original set D. This is certainly a remarkable requirement.

Not only does there seem no obvious justification for imposing such a strong regularity on social preferences over the distribution space, there are persuasive grounds for believing that this regularity is unreasonable for many value judgments. We know that the location of any new "conditional set" D' relative to D depends on the location of d_0. If d_0 is especially undesirable, then D', being a weighted average of D with d_0, may approximate some of the undesirable characteristics of d_0. In such a situation we might wish to adjust our choice in D' relative to our choice in D so as partially to undo the undesirable effects of d_0. Conversely, if we consider d_0 desirable, we might wish to take advantage of its desirable properties by choosing "differently" in D' than in D (and thus differently in D' than when selecting among lottery tickets). It is true that the acceptance of Postulate 3 makes such circumstances less likely, for it prevents us from being interested in redressing the injury done by d_0 to particular *identified* individuals. Nevertheless, it is still quite plausible that, if the distribution of income in d_0 is very unequal in favor of some individual (say), in order to select acceptably in D' we might prefer a convex combination of d_0 and a distribution d, in D, which discriminated against that individual, to similar combinations of d_0 and more preferred distributions in D.[25]

This sort of situation is illustrated in Figure 14.1, which shows such a case for a two-man society. In this case the central decision-maker is a strict egalitarian (in terms of outcomes but not in terms of mathematical expectations of outcomes) who prefers d_2 to d_1 in the originally attainable set (where these are the only members of that set) and who might well be willing to choose a lottery ticket of d_2, with probability $1/2$, and d_0, with probability $1/2$, over a similar lottery ticket of d_1 and d_0 with the same probabilities; yet he would (quite plausibly) prefer $d_1' = 1/2 d_1 + 1/2 d_0$ to $d_2' = 1/2 d_2 + 1/2 d_0$ when the choice is restricted to certainty equivalents of such lottery tickets.[26] More general cases illustrating the same point could easily be constructed. Thus, if Postulate 3 prevents one from being anti-egalitarian, Postulate 10 may make it difficult to be egalitarian.

Finally, Postulate 10 is undesirable for a quite different sort of reason. It is easy to show that, if we wish to generalize the analysis to many commodities while retaining it in terms of commodity distributions, Postulate 10 may render judgments that are incompatible with Pareto optimality.[27] It will always be possible to find a d_0 such that some convex combination of it and a previously chosen (and thus Pareto-optimal) distribution is not Pareto-optimal. Although it will not always be possible

---

[25] Note that even if some d_1 was previously an acceptable distribution, Postulate 10 carries us further than do Convexity and Isomorphism. The latter imply that every attainable distribution in the convex hull of the permutation set of d_1 was also previously acceptable and that every distribution in the convex hull of the permutation set of the chosen distribution in D' is also acceptable. They do not imply that every convex combination of d_0 and an element of the convex hull of the permutation set of d_1 is acceptable – a far different matter.

[26] The fact that indulging such sentiments may require him to sacrifice some total income is, of course, no surprise.

[27] In this respect it is related to the assumption that value judgments about income distribution are independent of the total level of income. For an evaluation of the latter assumption, see Kenen and Fisher (1957), pp. 322–24; and Rothenberg (1961), chap. v. Despite the deficiencies of the latter assumption, it is considerably more palatable than Postulate 10 is, since, while the independence of total-income assumption causes no trouble on this point if all individuals have homothetic indifference maps (indifference curves that are radial blowups of one another), the more ad hoc arbitrariness of Postulate 10 irregularly violates Pareto optimality for this and any other regularization of individual indifference maps.

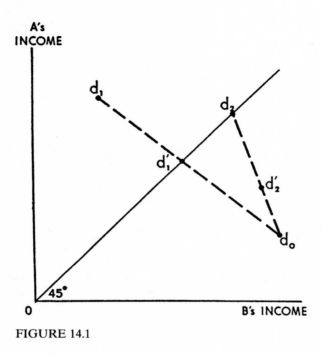

FIGURE 14.1

to find another originally attainable distribution such that the same convex combination of d_0 with it dominates the first combination in utility space, this can certainly happen. This result arises from the fact that, while in a one-commodity world radial blowups of any two initial distributions will leave preferences along rays unaffected, this is not so when there are many commodities. Because different patterns of commodity relatedness may be desirable at different levels of income, a commodity bundle that was most preferred at a low income level may be inferior at a higher level to bundles that were inferior to it at the lower level.

While Strotz's model explicitly deals with one commodity and is, therefore, formally free of this defect, it must be urged that, in a world where many commodities do in fact exist and individuals do in fact differ in tastes, choices about the distribution of a generalized purchasing power can be very nearly beside the point if the different alternatives imply substantially different sets of relative prices.[28]

---

[28] Cf. Samuelson (1947), p. 225.

VI

If Postulates 8 and, especially, 10 seem so unpromisingly arbitrary, what is offered to justify their presence in Strotz's system? Strotz accepts Postulate 8 "because of the libertarian view that, if one is willing to toss a coin to decide upon distribution d' or d'', which is in effect to distribute lottery tickets, one should be willing to distribute alternatively what each income recipient regards as the certainty equivalent of his lottery ticket – if that distribution is available" (p. 196). Since we believe that the reasoning behind this justification is basic to Postulate 10 as well, it will repay close examination.

In examining this reasoning, we must distinguish between the preferences of the central decision-maker (which include the value judgments on distribution central to the problem) and those of the individual recipients of income, whose utilities are arguments of the social welfare function. We rephrase Strotz's argument in these terms. The *social* value judgment (that of the central decision-maker) asserts that d' and d'' are equally good. A restriction on *social* preferences is that selection between alternatives may be accomplished by means of a random process: in effect, that a lottery in which they constitute the only prizes is as good as either of them. *Individual* preferences are such that, if each individual were given a lottery ticket with these prizes, he would be indifferent between it and a certainty equivalent distribution. Since all individuals by assumption possess linear utility functions,[29] they all have the same certainty equivalent for each lottery ticket – the mathematical expectation of the prizes. Thus, since all *individuals* are indifferent between each lottery ticket and a particular certainty equivalent, a form of Pareto optimality would seem to require that the *social* judgment declare the certainty equivalent equally acceptable with the lottery and, therefore, equally as acceptable as either d' or d''. Furthermore, every convex combination of d' and d'' can be envisaged as the common certainty equivalent of a similar lottery with appropriate probabilities. Thus, the same analysis declares that all convex combinations of d' and d'' are equally acceptable as is d' or d''.

It must be noted that the postulate is intended to characterize restraints on *social* preferences. Note, too, that only d' and d'' have been compared explicitly in the social preference ordering – no convex combinations of d' and d'' are mentioned. These are introduced only by examining *individual* preferences. The structure of the argument seems to be

---

[29] The same broad argument holds for Strotz's more general case of non-linear utility functions identical up to a linear transformation.

as follows: (*a*) in terms of social preferences a lottery is as good as either
d' or *d''*; (*b*) in terms of individual preferences a convex combination of
d' and *d''* is as good as a lottery; therefore, (*c*) in terms of social preferences a convex combination of *d'* and *d''* is as good as either *d'* or *d''*.
The form of individual preferences is being allowed to impose a constraint on social preferences. Is this reasonable? We believe that in the
present case it is quite unreasonable.

1   The argument is not transitive in terms of individual orderings.
     While it is all the same for social preferences whether we choose
     either *d'* or *d''* or decide by lottery, no individual for whom *d'*
     and *d''* represent different personal incomes can be indifferent
     between the two kinds of options. For the lottery is worth
     its mathematical expectation to him, and this is necessarily
     different from either *d'* or *d''*. Consequently, since each of
     these particular individuals is indifferent between the lottery
     and its certainty equivalent, not one of them can be indifferent
     between the certainty equivalent and either *d'* or *d''*. Thus,
     Strotz's "[to be] willing to toss a coin to decide upon distribu-
     tion *d'* or *d''* . . . is in effect to distribute lottery tickets," is not
     strictly true. It begs the question: Why *are* the two formulations
     equivalent? The argument, then, is quite complex: it is not on
     grounds of Pareto optimality that convexity is recommended.
     Rather, social preferences are allowed to contravene individual
     preferences (as in step 1), but the form of this contravention is
     itself regulated by individual preferences (step 3). This sort of
     procedure is not of itself necessarily unsatisfactory, since it may
     represent the perfectly reasonable situation in which social
     value judgments about income distribution are distilled from
     individual judgments about distribution. We shall indicate imme-
     diately below, however, that this is not the case in the present
     situation.

2   Convexity is being justified by suggesting that individual pref-
     erences should determine at least part of the structure of social
     preferences. The social preferences explicitly concern the evalu-
     ation of different distributions of income. The individual prefer-
     ences explicitly concern only each individual's own receipt of
     income. The former preferences are, therefore, meant explicitly
     to supplement the latter by rendering exactly the kind of deci-
     sions that the latter are unable to make. Social preferences are
     not restricted to cases where individual preferences (or indif-

ferences) are unanimous: value judgments about distribution *typically* adjudicate among alternatives in which some individuals are hurt and some benefited. Moreover, where an individual judges between two alternatives on grounds that have literally nothing to do with the desirability of the resulting relative distribution, this judgment is simply an argument of the social welfare function; it should not help to determine the form of that function. Only judgments that include considerations of distribution should influence that form. Thus, the social equivalence of either d' or d'' with the lottery is, in the general case, not concurred in by any individual (thus, by the way, under a strict application of Strotz's justification, Postulate 7 might actually be *un*acceptable). To say that the unanimous individual indifference between a lottery and its certainty equivalent does not warrant imposing social indifference between d' or d'' and that certainty equivalent is, therefore, not to violate Pareto optimality: there just is no unanimous individual judgment that these are equally acceptable.

To clarify this point somewhat, we say that, when some alternatives d_1 and d_2 are socially compared, individual preferences between d_1 and d_2 are allowed to influence the social decision – this is what it means to be arguments of the social function. For the same reason individual preferences between d_1 and d_3, and d_3 and d_2, are allowed to influence the social decision between d_1 and d_2 if there exists a *social* judgment asserting some relationship among d_1, d_2, and d_3 – that is, a social judgment that asserts that the form of the social function is such as to make d_3 relevant to the choice between d_1 and d_2. However, individual preferences between d_1 and d_3, and d_3 and d_2, are *not* allowed to influence the decision between d_1 and d_2 when it is only *individual* judgments that assert that d_3 is relevant, if these latter individual judgments are socially deemed to be irrelevant to the question of the form of the social function. In the problem at hand, since the individual preferences have nothing to do with distributional considerations, we believe that they are not relevant for determining the form of value judgments about distribution. We, therefore, believe that the unanimous individual indifference between lottery and certainty equivalents should carry very little weight in determining the social choice between socially indifferent distributions and convex combinations of them.

Nothing in the foregoing implies that there cannot be social value judgments about distribution that possess the convexity property or that these furnish inadmissible welfare functions in a normative system like Strotz's.[30] Our argument against Postulate 8 is, instead, that the restrictions on individual utility functions in Strotz's system do not provide persuasive grounds for restricting the admissible social value judgments *only* to those possessing convexity. Strotz's system is unreasonably limited thereby.

Much the same analysis applies to Postulate 10. We desire to obtain a social choice between d_1' and d_2' in D'. This choice is arrived at indirectly: There is a social decision that d_1 is preferred to d_2 in D. Given two lottery tickets, $[d_1, d_0|p(E)$ – a prize of d_1 if random event E, which has a probability of p, occurs; otherwise, a prize of $d_0]$ and $[d_2, d_0|p(E)$ – a prize of d_2 if E, which has a probability of p, occurs; otherwise a prize of $d_0]$, there is a social decision (Postulate 9) that $[d_1, d_0|p(E)]$ is preferred to $[d_2, d_0|p(E)]$. All individuals would be indifferent between lottery ticket $[d_1, d_0|p(E)]$ and its certainty equivalent $d_1' = (d_1, d_0|w = p)$ in D' (that is, the distribution in D' whose elements are a convex combination of d_1 and d_0 with weights equal to p and $1 - p$, respectively); all individuals would be indifferent between $[d_2, d_0|p(E)]$ and its comparable certainty equivalent $d_2' = (d_2, d_0|w = p)$ in D'. Therefore, the social choice between d_1' and d_2' is equivalent to the social choice between $[d_1, d_0|p(E)]$ and $[d_2, d_0|p(E)]$, which is determined by the social choice between d_1 and d_2: d_1' is socially preferred to d_2'.

We find the same distinctive mixture of social and individual preferences as in Postulate 8. A social decision determines that the social choice between distributions in D is relevant to the social choice between lottery tickets. But it is an individual decision (albeit unanimous) that asserts that the choice of lottery tickets between D and d_0 is relevant to the social choice in D'. Our same interdictions apply here as to the comparable procedure in Postulate 8. First, there can be no unanimous individual preference for d_1' over d_2', except in the trivial case of d_1 dominating d_2. The critical equivalence of lottery and certainty equivalents for individuals is no equivalence at all for society: the lottery means that either d_0 or a distribution in D will be obtained, but not a distribution in D'. Postulate 9 is, indeed, reasonable for just this reason: if not-E occurs, there is nothing to choose between the two tickets; if E occurs, only the ordering in D is relevant. This irrelevance of certainty equivalents to the social lottery is more important here than in Postulate 8

---

[30] See Fisher's treatment of a modified form of convexity in such a normative system (Fisher, 1956).

because there is a much greater likelihood that the certainty equivalent will be socially unattainable in this context than in the context of Postulate 8.[31] Strotz recognizes this factor, acknowledges that it may be a source of disagreement with Postulate 10, but does not consider its effect in allowing individual non-distributional preferences to influence the form of the social welfare function.[32]

Second, the individuals' preferences concerning lottery tickets and certainty equivalents are totally devoid of distributional content. There is little persuasive justification for allowing such preferences to influence the form of social value judgments about distribution. When we add to this how undesirable we have found the consequences of the particular restrictions at issue in Section V, it seems clear that Postulate 10 is unacceptable. The strong mapping of the distribution space that it brings about represents an undesirable and very weakly justified constraint on the whole normative model.

VII

We shall now indicate briefly the relevance of our remarks to some other recent models of the social welfare function that bear some resemblance to Strotz's. We shall consider the models of Hildreth, Goodman and Markowitz, Harsanyi, and Fisher already cited.

Hildreth's model is devised to show that acceptable social welfare functions exist that fulfil the spirit of Arrow's five conditions (value judgments) on social orderings[33] if only Arrow's Condition 3 ("The Independence of Irrelevant Alternatives") is modified to permit individuals' preference intensities to count as well as their preference orderings. To this end he postulates essentially that all individuals have Von Neumann-Morgenstern utility functions (although these are not necessarily all of

---

[31] It is surely likely that convex combinations of attainable distributions will be attainable as well, since all that seems involved is transfers of income. But exceptions occur where transfers to some distributions dissipate part of what is being transferred by adversely affecting production incentives; see our discussion in Section III, above.

[32] Strotz, p. 204. The ethical *difference* between a situation in which only lottery tickets are involved and one in which the mathematical expectation of lottery tickets – certainty equivalents – is attainable also is well brought out in Strotz's own apologue about William and Arthur (pp. 197–98). After making all too dramatic the dilemma that arises just because certainty equivalents are *not* attainable, he asserts that the keenly felt ethical difference does not in fact matter because William and Arthur are willing to gamble for all or nothing, thereby appealing to the portion of his system which, as we have seen, makes nearly all distributional considerations irrelevant. Whatever we may believe about that analysis, it does nothing to shore up the ethical persuasiveness of Postulate 10.

[33] Arrow (1951), chap. iii.

the same form). In addition, to bring about the interpersonal comparability necessary for a complete transitive social ordering, he postulates the essential equivalent of Isomorphism and a uniform restriction on all individual utility functions in terms of two particular standardized alternatives. Because he does not require an equivalent of Postulate 10, he cannot deduce that the only acceptable social welfare function is maximized where the sum of individual utilities is maximized (which is the form Strotz's theorem takes when he relaxes the linearity assumption for individual utility functions, although still requiring that they all possess the same form). What he does deduce (that acceptable social functions exist that satisfy his postulates) allows a social function that is summative in the individual utilities to be acceptable, but not uniquely acceptable.

The burden of our strictures does not apply here. Hildreth assumes Isomorphism, but in a context notably different from Strotz's. Our dissatisfaction with Isomorphism was not that it was intrinsically an unreasonable value judgment. Rather, we thought that a model designed explicitly to admit value judgments about distribution is unwarrantedly restricted by being forced to admit *only* value judgments that are isomorphic, especially where that model implies a single admissible form of welfare function. Hildreth does not make distributional considerations central; he does not attempt to derive a uniquely acceptable welfare function – in which task, of course, the acceptability of the underlying postulate system is crucial. Instead, he is only interested in showing that the spirit of Arrow's conditions involves no internal contradiction when preference intensities are admitted. Surely, postulate systems in which the distributional value judgments are isomorphic are admissible members of the set of reasonable postulate systems that are not contradictory, and, thus, dropping Hildreth's symmetry assumptions would not affect the spirit of his result.

Goodman and Markowitz also take as point of departure the modification of Arrow's conditions by the introduction of preference intensities. They, too, show that social welfare functions exist that fulfil these modified conditions; but they go much further than Hildreth does, varying a key postulate to derive alternative uniquely admissible functions or the impossibility of any. Their preferred modification results in an unweighted summation of individual rank numbers of preferences being an acceptable – and, indeed, the only acceptable – social welfare function. Since rank numbers are taken to be approximations of individual utility levels, this criterion is much the same as Strotz's. The result is obtained by postulating indicators of cardinal levels of utility for individuals, postulating further their interpersonal comparability, and by an equal weighting in the social welfare function. In contrast to Strotz and Hildreth, Goodman and Markowitz derive the individual utility indicators not from assumptions about risk-taking behavior (Von Neumann-Morgenstern utility) but rather by assuming a finite number of individual welfare-discrimination levels and postulating that rank numbers in a preference-ordering acceptably approximate these levels. Interpersonal comparability and weights are ascribed by means of two postulates, one of which is Isomorphism. The substantial formal differences between this model and Strotz's system make Postulate 10 inappropriate in the former, but Goodman and Markowitz obtain by their methods a cardinalization of social utility at least as reflective of the cardinality of individual utility as is Strotz's. One of the present authors has evaluated this system at length elsewhere and found important difficulties with this type of system.[34] For the present purpose it is enough to note that, while Isomorphism helps to bring about some of the difficulties, it does not really fall under the kind of interdiction we have made here. It is an unfortunate restriction of distributional considerations – where such considerations are deemed central to the problem of formulating social welfare functions. But Goodman and Markowitz's model does not pretend to deal with distributional value judgments. Other postulates in their system more completely bar such considerations than does Isomorphism. The proper criticism of the model from this point of view should be directed to these more exclusive postulates, but that is outside the scope of the present paper.

The third system is that of Harsanyi. This has the closest resemblance to Strotz's system. Harsanyi, too, is concerned to propose the most reasonable set of postulates he can to enable him to deduce a uniquely appropriate welfare criterion. The form of the criterion is nearly the same in both systems: maximization of the sum of individual utilities. In Strotz's system this is an unweighted sum, in Harsanyi's a weighted one. The substance is somewhat different as well. An individual's utility in Strotz's system appears to reflect only the income going to that consumer; in Harsanyi's system individual utility explicitly takes into account external relations in consumption and so is a function of the income going to everyone else as well. Indeed, Harsanyi intends to incorporate into individual utility functions some – but not all – of the substance of the kinds of value judgments about distribution for which we have argued in this paper. He does not, while we do, envisage some basic social consensus for these judgments; hence, he places them only as arguments of the social welfare function, while we have presumed

---

[34] Rothenberg (1961), chap. viii.

throughout the paper that they help determine the shape of the function itself.

Harsanyi's procedure is similar to Strotz's in postulating Von Neumann-Morgenstern utility functions for individuals. In addition he postulates that social preferences satisfy the conditions for Von Neumann-Morgenstern utility functions as well. Finally, he links individual with social utility by an apparently innocuous postulate, to wit: "If two prospects P and Q are indifferent from the standpoint of every individual, they are also indifferent from a social standpoint."[35] While this postulate would be highly acceptable in many contexts, here, in the presence of the first two assumptions, it is not so, for it enables us to deduce Strotz's Postulates 8 (and 7 and 9, for that matter) and 10, already discussed. Harsanyi's postulates are even stronger than are Strotz's, and he justifies them, respectively, as follows: the first two together are asserted to be the unique substance of rational choice – whether individual or social – under risk; the third is asserted to be the proper individualistic orientation for a democratic society.

Our criticisms of Postulates 8 and, especially, 10, thus apply, with some reservations, to Harsanyi. In Strotz's system these postulates considerably narrowed the range of admissible value judgments about income distribution. But some such valuational content is already incorporated in Harsanyi's individual utility functions. Thus, the indifference of lottery tickets and certainty equivalents in social preferences does not much affect distributional considerations. We do, however, believe that introducing external economies and diseconomies into individual utility functions does not nearly resolve the ethical issues that substantiate our conception of distributional value judgments. Secondly, we prefer to believe that the consensus necessary to enable us to incorporate such judgments into the form of the social welfare function does exist in concrete societies. This is, admittedly, a controversial point. Our conclusion, therefore, is that, while Harsanyi's postulates on the cardinality of social preferences are apparently stronger than Strotz's, it is not unlikely that Strotz's is the more restrictive of distributional considerations.

It is worth noting, finally, that it is Harsanyi's unwillingness to make the Isomorphism assumption that leaves his welfare function with a weighted sum of utilities instead of an unweighted one. This is deliberate. His weights are intended to reflect not standardized social worths (which are assumed equal to unity for everyone) but interpersonally differentiated marginal utilities. Harsanyi considers interpersonal com-

---

[35] Harsanyi (1955), p. 313.

parisons of utility to be matters of fact rather than matters of value; he is prepared to introduce such comparisons into the respective scales of his individual utility functions.[36] Harsanyi does not go as far as Strotz's special case and restrict all individuals to linear utility functions; this prevents him, as it does the other writers we have discussed, from equating maximization of summative utilities with maximization of money income.

We conclude, finally, with brief mention of a model formulated by Fisher. His purpose is explicitly to explore how one narrows down the range of indeterminacy of choice that remains after one has adopted Pareto optimization, by subsequently adopting stronger and stronger extra-individual (that is, consensual) value judgments about income distribution. The implications of imposing certain structural constraints on the value judgments (for example, a modified form of convexity) are explored. One proposition, inferable from this work, that has proved suggestive for our present critique is that the commodity space can be completely ordered by introducing value judgments that are unspecialized enough to permit considerably more latitude in the range of admissible value judgments than is evident in Strotz's or, indeed, in any of the other systems mentioned in this section. In the light of this finding it surely seems that some issues concerning income distribution have been prematurely scrapped in much of the literature, as in Strotz's work. Determinate social welfare functions can exist under far wider sets of admissible value judgments. Undue pauperizing of such a field can reduce the normative corpus to a scarecrow – "a thing of shreds and patches."[37]

---

[36] *Ibid.*, pp. 316–21.

[37] A rebuttal in Fisher and Rothenberg (1962) to Strotz's 1961 reply served mainly to sharpen and clarify the critique given in this chapter and has not been reproduced here. Its closure speaks peace after harsh dispute:

> "[L]et us end with that soft answer which proverbially turneth away wrath. Graaf aptly states: "One of the things we must continually keep in mind, therefore, is the specificity of the ethical assumptions we find ourselves making. We want to keep them as broad as possible, so that interest in our conclusions might be widespread. But we also want them to be detailed enough to yield some conclusions" (Graaf, 1957, p. 11). Too often economists, disappointed in the lack of content of the new welfare economics, have rejected the topic itself rather than go beyond Pareto optimality as the only welfare criterion. Yet hard problems are never solved by ignoring them. In being deliberately provocative by making additional and more specific value judgments, Strotz is one of the few writers in this area who has not shied away from some of the truly important issues in welfare economics. To invite and to open discussion on these issues is to do the profession a real service (Fisher and Rothenberg, 1962, pp. 92–3).

REFERENCES

Arrow, K. J., *Social Choice and Individual Values*, John Wiley & Sons, New York, 1951.
Chernoff, H., "The Rational Selection of Decision Functions," *Econometrica* 22, 1954, 422–43.
Fisher, F. M., "Income Distribution, Value Judgments, and Welfare," *Quarterly Journal of Economics* 70, 1956, 380–424. Reprinted as Chapter 12 in this volume.
Fisher, F. M., and J. Rothenberg, "How Income Ought to Be Distributed: Paradox Enow," *Journal of Political Economy* 70, 1962, 162–80.
Goodman, L. A., and H. Markowitz, "Social Welfare Functions Based on Individual Rankings," *American Journal of Sociology* 43, 1952, 257–62.
Graaf, J. de V., *Theoretical Welfare Economics*, Cambridge University Press, London, 1957.
Harsanyi, J. C., "Cardinal Welfare, Individualistic Ethics and Interpersonal Comparisons of Utility," *Journal of Political Economy* 63, 1955, 309–21.
Hildreth, C., "Alternative Conditions for Social Orderings," *Econometrica* 21, 1953, 81–94.
Kenen, P. B., and F. M. Fisher, "Income Distribution, Value Judgments, and Welfare: A Correction," *Quarterly Journal of Economics* 71, 1957, 322–324. Reprinted as Chapter 13 in this volume.
Luce, R. D., and H. Raiffa, *Games and Decisions*, John Wiley & Sons, New York, 1957.
Rothenberg, J., *The Measurement of Social Welfare*, Prentice-Hall, New York, 1961.
Samuelson, P. A., *Foundations of Economic Analysis*, Harvard University Press, Cambridge, Mass., 1947.
Strotz, R., "How Income Ought to Be Distributed: A Paradox in Distributive Ethics," *Journal of Political Economy* 66, 1958, 189–205.
   "How Income Ought to Be Distributed: Paradox Regained," *Journal of Political Economy* 69, 1961, 271–78.

CHAPTER 15

Advertising and Welfare:
Comment (1979)

written jointly with John J. McGowan

In their provocative article, Dixit and Norman (1978) apparently show that, for a variety of market structures, the equilibrium amount of advertising will be excessive. They demonstrate that this is so whether judged by preadvertising or postadvertising tastes. This is indeed a strong result.

A little reflection, however, shows that their result is in fact too strong, at least if it is to be interpreted in the obvious policy sense. According to Dixit and Norman (hereafter D–N), advertising merely serves as something that causes an outward shift of the demand curve. Their theorem can therefore be taken to apply to anything else that shifts the demand curve outward. Interpreted in these terms, for example, D–N have apparently shown that, for a variety of market structures, the equilibrium amount of research and development in product improvement is excessive. Surely something is wrong here.

The basis of D–N's approach is to evaluate the welfare effect of a change in output accompanying a change in advertising according to both preadvertising and postadvertising tastes. Thus, supposing $U(x_0)$ to be the preadvertising level of utility derived from the output x_0 and $\psi(x_i)$ to be the postadvertising level of utility from the output x_i, D–N proceed to compare $U(x_i)$ with $U(x_0)$ and $\psi(x_i)$ with $\psi(x_0)$. Using a geometric analysis for the case of a monopolist, they demonstrate that $U(x_i) < U(x_0)$ and $\psi(x_i) < \psi(x_0)$ and use this result to conclude that advertising is excessive whether judged by the tastes embodied in $U(x)$ or by those embodied in $\psi(x)$. This result is correct, as far as it goes, but it does not remove the impediment to making welfare judgments when tastes change.

In terms of the notation above, we believe the fundamental question to be: How does $\psi(x_i)$ compare with $U(x_0)$? Knowing that $U(x_i) < U(x_0)$ and $\psi(x_i) < \psi(x_0)$ does not allow one to infer that $\psi(x_i) < U(x_0)$ unless it is also known, or one is willing to assume, that $\psi(x_0) \leq U(x_0)$ or $\psi(x_i) \leq U(x_i)$. Since this latter requirement is equivalent to knowing or assuming that advertising does not increase welfare, the D–N analysis can provide no information as to whether additional advertising is beneficial or not.

The same point may be put in another way. In their analytic (as opposed to geometric) setup, D–N (p. 6) assume that demand is generated by a utility function whose arguments consist of the output of the numéraire, the output of the advertised good, *and the amount of advertising.* They then fix this last argument at two different levels (the preadvertising and the postadvertising points) and evaluate the pre- and postadvertising equilibria with the level of advertising fixed. But if the amount of advertising enters the utility function, the natural criterion for welfare evaluation is the *unrestricted* utility function so defined. Dixit and Norman's very setup assumes that utility is generated by advertising. By fixing the level of advertising in the utility function and *then* making welfare comparisons, Dixit and Norman fail to take account of this.

Should account be taken of it? Some, certainly, will argue that this should always be done. On this view, consumers, when consuming an advertised product, always get more enjoyment because of the association with advertising. This can happen either because the consumer is more informed about the properties of the product than he would be without advertising or because he takes pleasure in the association the advertised product brings. If we believe that the kind of cognac we drink reflects to us and to others our personal status, we may enjoy drinking it more. If we know that we are consuming a product that others have found reliable or otherwise of good quality, then the product may be more enjoyable to us than it would be were it not advertised, because we believe the risks associated with its consumption to be less.

It is a delicate and difficult question whether some or all of such increased enjoyment phenomena should be included in welfare comparisons. To put it another way, to the extent that advertising enters into the utility function (as it does in Dixit and Norman), the welfare question is one of how to count that entry. Dixit and Norman implicitly decide not to count it at all and thus beg the really important issue.

REFERENCE

Dixit, A. and Norman, V. "Advertising and Welfare." *The Bell Journal of Economics*, Vol. 9, No. 1 (Spring 1978), pp. 1–17.

CHAPTER 16

Household Equivalence Scales
and Interpersonal Comparisons (1987)

The measurement of inequality is an important and difficult enterprise, made harder by the fact that one wants to measure inequality of welfare rather than merely of money income. If that end is to be achieved, some way of making interpersonal comparisons must be found.

A very appealing way of making such judgments was suggested by Muellbauer (1974a, b, c). He suggested the use of household equivalence scales (Barten (1964)), useful in positive work on demand, to make households comparable for normative purposes. That use has taken its most powerful and elegant form in a recent paper by Jorgenson and Slesnick (1984a), who skillfully combine consumer-theoretic and social choice considerations to develop a measure of welfare inequality. (See also Jorgenson and Slesnick (1983), (1984b).) It is therefore convenient to use their paper as a point of departure in commenting on the entire enterprise.

As Jorgenson and Slesnick (and Muellbauer) recognise, such strong results naturally require value judgments concerning interpersonal comparisons. I believe that one such value judgment – so basic and natural-seeming that Jorgenson and Slesnick do not even discuss it – is open to very serious question.

Jorgenson and Slesnick (1984a, pp. 372–373) assume that household preferences can be represented "by means of a utility function that is the same for all consuming units", with the kth household's utility function given by:

$$U_k = U\left[\frac{x_{1k}}{m_1(A_k)}, \frac{x_{2k}}{m_2(A_k)}, \ldots, \frac{x_{Nk}}{m_N(A_k)}\right]. \tag{1}$$

Here x_{nk} denotes k's consumption of the nth commodity, and the $m_n(\cdot)$ are functions whose arguments, the A_k, are vectors of household attributes. In Jorgenson and Slesnick's paper, those attributes are family size,

I am indebted to Dale W. Jorgenson, Kevin Roberts, and two referees for extremely helpful discussion and references and to Ellen P. Fisher for emphasizing that taste differences can stem from past experiences that are income or opportunity related.

age of head, region of residence, race, and type of residence (urban vs. rural). The utility function, $U(\cdot, \ldots, \cdot)$, is common to all households that differ only in the commodity-specific household equivalence scales, $\{m_n(A_k)\}$.

For purposes of this note, I shall take this representation of preferences to be empirically correct. It implies that the indirect utility function of the kth household can be written as:

$$V_k = V\left[\frac{p_1 m_1(A_k)}{M_k}, \frac{p_2 m_2(A_k)}{M_k}, \ldots, \frac{p_N m_N(A_k)}{M_k}\right]. \tag{2}$$

Here, p_n is the price of the nth commodity, and M_k is the total expenditure of the kth household. The function $V(\cdot, \ldots, \cdot)$ is again common to all households. Jorgenson and Slesnick use it to construct measures of welfare inequality.

As already indicated, the difficulty I shall discuss does not concern the empirical validity of the assumption that differences in the tastes of households can be summarized in the form (1) or (2). Rather it lies in the issue of whether, taking that assumption as correct, one *ought* to treat households with equal values of U (or V) as being equally well off. The assumption that this is appropriate is only implicit but underlies the rest of Jorgenson and Slesnick's analysis. This is not surprising, for some such assumption is required if one is to proceed at all. (Indeed, I have no alternative to suggest.) Nevertheless, it is well to realise what is involved in so proceeding.

As a preliminary matter, it is important to realise the following. Even if two consumers have *identical* utility functions, the statement that they are equally well off if they are on the same indifference curve is a normative, not a positive statement. We cannot know that the "true" utility value associated with a given indifference curve is not much higher for one consumer than for another. Indeed, there is no operational meaning to the proposition that it is higher. But then there is no operational meaning to the proposition that the two numbers are the same. If one is going to treat two such consumers on the same indifference curve as equally well off, it must be because one has decided that they *ought* to be so treated as a matter of distributive ethics. Despite the fact that this has been well recognised in the literature (see, for example, Fisher and Shell (1968) and Sen (1979), (1984)), this point is easily overlooked.

The reason for this is that such a value judgment seems natural and appealing. Given the symmetry involved in such a case, it is hard to see how one could do anything else but treat the two consumers equally. Any other treatment would require more information – perhaps about the relative moral worths of the two people involved (Fisher and Rothenberg (1961, pp. 164–165)), perhaps about what Sen cells their relative "capabilities" or freedom to live decent lives (Sen (1984), (1985b)). These are matters that are difficult to bring "into relation with the measuring rod of money", and hence are tempting to ignore as not part of "economic welfare" (Pigou (1952, p. 11)). But if welfare comparisons are to form a basis for policy, it is dangerous to suppose that such issues do not matter merely because they are difficult ones for economists.

Once we leave the pure symmetric case, the difficulties involved in making such value judgments come to the fore. This is true even when symmetry can be restored through the use of household equivalence scales.

Suppose, for example, that there are three commodities, milk, whisky, and all other consumption. Dropping the household subscript, denote consumption of these by $x_1, x_2,$ and x_3, respectively. One of the household attributes used by Jorgenson and Slesnick (and a natural one for such use) is family size. Suppose that households of less than three members like whisky a lot and do not care for milk, while households of three of more members like milk but not whisky. To put this in terms of (1) and (2), denote households of less than three members by $A_k = S$ and larger households by $A_k = L$ (ignoring any other attributes). Normalise on households of sizes less than three, so that $m_n(S) = 1 (n = 1, 2, 3)$. Assume that, for larger households, $m_1(L) > 1$, so that larger households require more milk, other things equal, to get on the same indifference curve as small ones. If the demand for milk is price inelastic, this also means that large households consume more milk than do similarly placed small ones (see, e.g. Gorman (1976, p. 216)). Suppose, further, that $m_2(L) < 1$, so that small households require more whisky than do large ones to reach the same indifference curve, *ceteris paribus*. To make the example particularly sharp, assume that the demand for whisky is also price inelastic, so that small households consume more whisky than do similarly placed large ones. Further, assume that the value of $m_1(L)$ is very large and that of $m_2(L)$ very small. I shall assume $m_3(L) = 1$.

In these circumstances, the value judgment required for the use of household equivalence scales requires the following. Suppose that there are two households, one large and one small, with the same total expenditure, M. Suppose that the small household faces prices p_1, p_2, p_3, while the large one faces prices p_1^*, p_2^*, p_3^* which happen to be such that $p_n^* = p_n m_n(L) (n = 1, 2, 3)$. Then the value judgment in question requires us to call the two families equally well off, despite the fact that the large family faces a very high price for milk and a low one for whisky. In effect, we are required to say that a large family in such a situation is just as well (badly) off as a small family facing a high price for whisky and a low price for milk because *if the large family did not have children it would like whisky more and milk less.*

I emphasise again that the difficulty involved here has nothing to do with the empirical validity of the assumption that the effect on tastes of family size can be represented in this way. The difficulty lies in the implicit ethical statement which here requires one to treat symmetrically the ability of larger families to buy milk for their children and of smaller ones to afford more potent beverages.

This kind of problem is not restricted to the use of family size which, at least at first glance, would seem to be an ethically harmless attribute to employ. Consider, for example, the use of race as a household attribute. The tastes of an individual or a household are partly formed from experience. Hence a systematic difference between the tastes of blacks on the one hand and whites on the other may partly reflect differences in education and past differences in income. Suppose that rich whites like caviar and poor blacks like pork and beans but that differences in preferences can be expressed in terms of household equivalence scales as before. Then, similar to the milk–whisky example, the implicit ethical judgment under consideration will require us to give symmetric treatment to rich whites faced with a high price of caviar and poor blacks faced with a high price of pork and beans. While poor blacks will usually be counted as having less income than rich whites, we will not be able to treat pork and beans for poor blacks as more important than caviar for rich whites. Indeed, if rich whites face a high enough price of caviar, we can be forced to treat them as being worse off than poor blacks facing a high price for pork and beans. This sort of treatment is required by the proposition that poor blacks would like caviar if only they were rich and white. Marie Antoinette would have approved, but I suspect she would be in the minority.

Similar, although probably less dramatic examples can be constructed for the other household attributes used by Jorgenson and Slesnick (region of residence, age of household head, and urban vs. rural residence). Indeed, similar examples can be constructed for any household attribute. The two cases already examined point to certain conclusions.

To begin, even if one puts aside the question of whether differences in taste have developed for ethically neutral reasons, there are ethical questions involved in deciding how to treat such differences. The family size example shows that one may have to choose how to weigh the needs and preferences of children and adults. Where age is used as an attribute, there is an ethical statement to be made concerning how old and young should be treated. It may be an appropriate value judgment that they should be treated equally, but it is not a value judgment that should be made without consideration.[1]

What can be said in defence of such a value judgment (beyond begging the question by *defining* welfare to be equal if everyone is on the same equivalent-scale indifference curve)? Mirrlees (1982) takes the position that such a value judgment is appropriate. He argues that, if individual tastes differ only as described in (1), then each individual in the society can think of the others as possible "alternative selves". This being so, Mirrlees claims that there is no reason to prefer one such alternative self to another and hence they should be treated symmetrically.[2] Basically, the position taken is as follows. Since I can imagine what it would be like to be any other person, I ought to judge the relative welfare of any other person in terms of how I would feel were I in their shoes. But, since my utility function differs from that of any other person in a well defined, parameterizable way, that judgment just depends on the values that my utility function would have in alternative situations. (This argument extends to more general situations than those in which households differ only to the extent permitted by (1).)

I do not find this argument persuasive as a defence of the household-equivalence-scale position. Assuming that individual tastes differ as described by (1), there is nothing to prevent "true" utility from being described by:

$$U_k^* = F(U_k, A_k). \tag{3}$$

This generates the same set of indifference maps as does (1) and is empirically indistinguishable from it if all we have are demand functions.[3] In such a case, however, my view of what it would be like to be you would not be measured by the value that the function, U, would take on if I had your attributes, but rather by the corresponding value of the function U^*.

[1] Sen (1985*b*, p. 42) and Deaton and Muellbauer (1986, pp. 741–742) make the somewhat different point that taking households as the fundamental unit for comparison implicitly ignores the relative levels of welfare of the individuals within the household.

[2] Mirrlees takes this to imply that the sum of utilities should be maximised. I do not understand how his argument leads to the sum in preference to any other symmetric function.

[3] Writing (3) suggests quite explicitly that some of the A_k may be themselves matters of choice. For example, the number of children to have is often an endogenous decision in which parents change their own consumption patterns in order to be able to afford more offspring. Pollak and Wales (1979) cogently point out that this means that welfare comparisons made conditional on attributes such as the number of children are likely to be misleading. (See also Deaton and Muellbauer (1986, pp. 724–725).) This is related to but not identical with the point being made in the text which is that such conditional comparisons may be misleading whether or not household attributes are themselves objects of choice.

In terms of the first example given above, considering a large or small family as two of my "alternative selves" does not prevent me from deciding that I would be more unhappy were I the parent of a large family faced with a high price of milk than were I a single adult faced with a high price of whisky. Even if one agrees with Mirrlees that, when utility is defined over a broad enough set of goods and lifestyles, one should evaluate relative welfare in terms of the values of the then common utility function, this does not seem to get one very far so long as non-chosen attributes enter the common utility function. In any event, it does not provide a justification for proceeding by taking the values of U as the basis for comparison.

The fact that rejection of U can stem from acceptance of U^* also provides an answer to one possible objection to the stand taken in this note. As Jorgenson has pointed out to me, my examples suggest that I believe that Society should favour certain kinds of consumption over others. Is this not a rejection of the principle of consumer sovereignty?

One possible answer to this question is in the negative. The milk–whisky example does not rest on a value judgment that small families ought to like milk rather than whisky or that any particular household's consumption pattern ought to change. Rather it rests on a value judgment that the value of U obtained by a large household when children drink milk ought to be given more weight by society than the value of U obtained by a small household when its members drink whisky.

Moreover, as we have just seen, the value judgment involved can be justified in terms of the function U^* rather than U. This involves accepting households' own utility functions as given, but observing that the function, U, fails to capture the direct effect on utility of attributes such as family size. This retains consumer sovereignty in the sense of accepting what households would choose if they could choose their own attributes as well as their consumption vectors.

To say this, however, may not be to face up to the question. Some household attributes are not the objects of choice (*Jeremiah* 13:23), and hence there will always be attributes that may enter the second argument of U^* without having observable effects. To say that taking account of such effects would restore consumer sovereignty may merely be a rather empty way of avoiding a contradiction. In terms of observable choices of actual commodities, I am rejecting consumer sovereignty as the sole basis for judgment. Without a redefinition of the domain of individual utility functions, the social welfare function that embodies such value judgments as I have been suggesting cannot depend only on the utility indices of households. That function must depend as well on household consumption vectors directly. Less formally, it is hard to see how one can make the milk–whisky value judgment as described without also being willing to say that a family with children ought to be encouraged to buy milk rather than whisky. In terms of observables, the position here taken does involve a rejection of consumer sovereignty.

There are circumstances where such a rejection is justified. As the example of race illustrates, where a particular household attribute is correlated with past income or past social status, the taste differences accompanying differences in that attribute may not be ethically neutral. To treat them as if they were may simply be to build in the results of past inequities as though they no longer matter (cf. Sen (1985a, pp. 191, 196–197) and (1985b, pp. 21–22)).

A well-known Yiddish story by I. L. Peretz (1974) tells of a poor man so beaten down by poverty and mistreatment that when, after death, the heavenly judge tells him that all of Paradise is his and that he can have anything he wishes, his highest desire is for a daily hot roll and butter. It is not an accident that the hero of the story is named "Bontsha Schweig" – "Bontsha the Silent" – and no accident that a silence "more terrible than Bontsha's has ever been" descends as "the judge and the angels bend their heads in shame at this unending meekness they have created on earth" (Peretz (1974, p. 77)). The moral of the story is surely not that one should count Bontsha as at a bliss point if he gets his roll, even if, with different experiences he would have more sophisticated tastes. "*De gustibus non disputandum*" is not always an attractive ethical standard. It can lead to what Sen (1985b, p. 23) calls "an alienated, commodity-fetishist view".

REFERENCES

Barten, A. P. (1964), "Family Composition, Prices and Expenditure Patterns", in Hart, P. E., Mills, G. and Whitaker, J. K. (eds.) *Econometric Analysis for National Economic Planning* (London: Butterworths).

Deaton, A. S. and Muellbauer J. (1986), "On Measuring Child Costs: With Applications to Poor Countries", *Journal of Political Economy*, **94**, 720–744.

Fisher, F. M. and Shell, K. (1968), "Taste and Quality Change in the Pure Theory of the True Cost of Living Index", in Wolfe, J. N. (ed.) *Value, Capital and Growth: Papers in Honour of Sir John Hicks* (Edinburgh: Edinburgh University Press).

Fisher, F. M. and Rothenberg, J. (1961), "How Income Ought to Be Distrbuted: Paradox Lost", *Journal of Political Economy*, **61**, 162–180. Reprinted as Chapter 14 in this volume.

Gorman, W. M. (1976), "Tricks with Utility Functions", in Artis, M. J. and Nobay, A. R. (eds.) *Essays in Economic Analysis: Proceedings of the 1975 AUTE Conference, Sheffield* (Cambridge, U.K.: Cambridge University Press).

Jorgenson, D. W. and Slesnick, D. T. (1983), "Individual and Social Cost-of-Living Indexes", in Diewert, W. E. and Montmarquette, C. (eds.) *Price Level Measurement* (Ottawa: Statistics Canada).

Jorgenson, D. W. and Slesnick, D. T. (1984a), "Aggregate Consumer Behaviour and the Measurement of Inequality", *Review of Economic Studies*, **61**, 369–392.

Jorgenson, D. W. and Slesnick, D. T. (1984b), "Inequality in the Distribution of Individual Welfare", in Basmann, R. and Rhodes G. (eds.) *Advances in Econometrics*, **3** (Greenwich: JAI Press).

Mirrlees, J. A. (1982), "The Economic Uses of Utilitarianism", in Sen, A. K. and Williams, B. (eds.) *Utilitarianism and Beyond* (New York: Cambridge University Press).

Muellbauer, J. (1974a), "Prices and Inequality: the United Kingdom Experience", *Economic Journal*, **84**, 32–55.

Muellbauer, J. (1974b), "Household Composition, Engel Curves and Welfare Comparisons between Households", *European Economic Review*, **5**, 103–122.

Muellbauer, J. (1974c), "Inequality Measures, Prices and Household Composition", *Review of Economic Studies*, **61**, 493–504.

Peretz, I. L. (1974), "Bontsha the Silent" (H. Abel, trans.), in Howe, I. and Greenberg, E. (eds.) *Selected Stories of I. L. Peretz* (New York: Schocken Books).

Pigou, A. C. (1952), *The Economics of Welfare*, Fourth edition (London: Macmillan).

Pollak, R. A. and Wales, T. J. (1979), "Welfare Comparisons and Equivalence Scales", *American Economic Review* **69**, 216–21.

Sen, A. K. (1979), "The Welfare Basis of Real Income Comparisons: A Survey", *Journal of Economic Literature*, **17**, 1–45.

Sen, A. K. (1984), "The Living Standard", *Oxford Economic Papers*, **N.S. 36** (supplement), 74–90.

Sen, A. K. (1985a), "Wellbeing, Agency and Freedom: the Dewey Lectures 1984", *Journal of Philosophy*, **82**, 169–221.

Sen, A. K. (1985b) *Commodities and Capabilities* (Amsterdam: North-Holland).

CHAPTER 17

Household Equivalence Scales: Reply (1990)

Daniel Leonard (1990) is quite right in pointing out that I made an error in my milk-whisky example, but that is as far as it goes. It is quite easy to rearrange the example to prove the original point, and the issues involved in thinking about it are instructive.

Reverse one of the assumptions of the example so that

$$0 < m_1(L) < 1 < m_2(L) \tag{1}$$

(with $m_3(L) = m_i(S) = 1, i = 1, 2, 3$, as before). Suppose that the prices faced by the two families are such that

$$p_n^* = p_n / m_n(L) \qquad (n = 1, 2, 3) \tag{2}$$

where the starred prices are faced by the large family and the unstarred ones by the small one. Then the use of household equivalence scales to make value judgments requires that we consider both families equally well off despite the fact that the large family faces a very high price of milk and a low one for whisky.

Leonard raises objections to this amendment, however. He states that it "makes the large family an 'efficient user of milk' which is able to derive the same 'milk enjoyment' by sharing a cup of milk among parents and children as does the small family by drinking a pint per person. I find this premise unrealistic in the way it models the effect of size on a family's taste for milk."

Let's first dispose of an item of lesser importance. There is no warrant whatever for the picture of parents sharing a cup of milk with their children. The large family can perfectly well give all the milk it has to its children. What is involved appears to be that so doing gives the household more additional utility than the same amount of milk gives the small household with no children.

This may make the example seem intuitively reasonable, but there are pitfalls here, for the notion that one can actually compare the utility levels (or gains) of the two households has no non-normative basis. This was the point of my original article (and Leonard does not disagree). Hence deciding on whether examples such as the present one are realistic cannot rest on comparing what the two families do at the "same" utility level.

It is easy to fall into this trap. I did so in my original article when I set up the example. Leonard does so in the passage quoted above. Indeed, one can fall deeper. As pointed out by Leonard in correspondence with me, one can show that (1) and (2) together imply that, with equal utilities for the two families, the small family will consume more milk and less whisky than the large one – an outcome that it is tempting to label as "unappealing."

But *why* is it unappealing? Points at which the two utilities happen to be equal have no non-normative significance. The result is certainly *ethically* unappealing: It comes about because the large family faces high milk prices and low whisky prices. But that is the point of the example. Only if one insists on calling the two families equally well off in that situation does their behaviour appear unrealistic. But realism or unrealism cannot depend on our value judgments; rather, if the example is realistic, the value judgment involved is unappealing.

I suggest that the only positive test of whether assumptions on preferences are realistic must lie in consideration of what they imply about demand functions, about choices in differing price and income situations. In the present case, that means asking what (1) implies about the two families' relative consumption of milk and whisky when they face the same budget set – *not* in examining those relative consumptions at differing prices but with utility levels arbitrarily set equal.

Since this is only an example, we are free to add features consistent with (1). Assume that the demand for each beverage is elastic with respect to its own price and that the two beverages are gross substitutes. Then it is easy to show that, *at the same income and prices*, the large family *always* consumes more milk and less whisky than does the small one.[1] I don't see how intuition extends beyond this property.[2]

---

[1] The demonstration is essentially given in Fisher and Shell (1972, p. 20). Define

$$\hat{x}_i = x_i/m_i; \qquad \hat{p}_i = p_i m_i \qquad (i = 1, 2, 3). \tag{3}$$

Without subscripts, x and p denote vectors in the obvious way. px will be the inner product of p and x, and similarly for $\hat{p}\hat{x}$. Let M denote total income.

Choosing x to maximize $U(\hat{x})$ subject to $px = M$ is equivalent to choosing $\hat{x}$ to maximize $U(\hat{x})$ subject to $\hat{p}\hat{x} = M$, so we can think of the consumer as solving the latter problem.

For $i \neq k$,

$$\partial x_i/\partial m_k = (\partial \hat{x}_i/\partial m_k)m_i = (\partial \hat{x}_i/\partial \hat{p}_k)p_k m_i$$
$$= (\partial x_i/\partial p_k)(p_k/m_k). \tag{4}$$

As this discussion illustrates, the notion that there is something special about equating the utility levels of different households is dangerously seductive. As Leonard and I agree, that seduction ought to be resisted, and normative statements not confused with positive propositions.

REFERENCES

Fisher, F. M. and Shell, K. (1972), *The Economic Theory of Price Indices* (New York and London: Academic Press).
Leonard, D. (1990), "Household Equivalence Scales: Comment," *Review of Economics Studies* 57, 325–27.

$$\partial x_i / \partial m_i = (\partial \hat{x}_i / \partial m_i) m_i + \hat{x}_i = (\partial \hat{x}_i / \partial \hat{p}_i) p_i m_i + \hat{x}_i$$
$$= \hat{x}_i \{1 + (\hat{p}_i / \hat{x}_i)(\partial \hat{x}_i / \partial \hat{p}_i)\}$$
$$= \hat{x}_i \{1 + (p_i / x_i)(\partial x_i / \partial p_i)\}. \tag{5}$$

Let milk be good i. If milk demand is elastic with respect to its own price, then the final expression in (5) is negative. If milk and whisky are gross substitutes, then (4) is positive. Then a decrease in m_1 and an increase in m_2 increase milk consumption. A similar demonstration shows that the large family consumes less whisky than does the small one.

[2] Leonard shows that a modified LES system does not have the property that the large family always consumes more milk than the small one at the same prices and income. This shows that (1) is not itself sufficient for that intuitive property to hold. That fact does not matter, however, so long as (1) is consistent with examples that do possess that intuitive property.

CHAPTER 18

Normal Goods and
the Expenditure Function (1990)

1.   Introduction

A normal good is one the demand for which increases with income. Despite the simplicity of that definition and the general presumption that most goods are normal, it is surprisingly difficult to relate normality to properties of the utility function. This question was recently studied by Leroux (1987), who gave a sufficient condition for all goods to be normal. Unfortunately, that condition is not easy to interpret.

As with many propositions of consumer theory, however, it turns out that the characterization of normality is very easy to do in terms of the expenditure function. I do so in this paper, giving a necessary and sufficient condition for any particular good to be normal.[1]

Whether this provides a satisfactory solution to the problem posed by Leroux (that of characterizing normality in terms of the utility function), however, is a matter on which reasonable economists can differ. On the one hand, one can argue that the expenditure function codes all the information in the utility function so that characterizing normality in terms of the expenditure function also characterizes it in terms of the utility function. On the other hand, the demand functions themselves also code all the information in the utility function, and one would scarcely take as a solution the answer that one should calculate the demand functions and see whether they increase with income.

In any event, the characterization of normality in terms of the expenditure function has its own independent interest. This is especially so because the proof is very simple and the result quite intuitive.

2.   Results

The household has a twice continuously differentiable, locally non-satiated, strictly quasi-concave utility function, $u(x)$, where x is an n-

---

[1] After the original publication of this chapter, Eugene Silberberg brought his very closely related work to my attention. In Silverberg and Walker (1984), the corollary derived below is given as equation (7) on page 691. The present theorem, on the other hand, is closely related to but somewhat different from their results.

vector of commodities consumed. It maximizes utility subject to the budget constraint $p'x = y$, where p is the price vector, y is income, and the prime denotes transposition. In the standard way, this generates the indirect utility function, $v(p, y)$, and the expenditure function, $E(p, u)$. The demand function for good i is denoted by $D^i(p, y)$. All these functions are assumed continuously differentiable – the expenditure function twice so – and the marginal utility of income is assumed to be positive.

There are n commodities. x^i denotes the ith element of x and p^i the ith element of p. Differentiation with respect to p^i is denoted by the use of i as a subscript. Differentiation with respect to u or y is denoted by the use of the corresponding symbol as a subscript.

Since we shall be interested only in the demand for goods that are actually consumed and have positive prices, it is harmless to take $p > 0$ and confine attention to x in a neighborhood of an interior point of R^n.

Definition.   Good i is a *normal good* if and only if $D_y^i(p, y) > 0$.

Theorem. $D_y^i(p, y)$ *has the same sign as* $E_{iu}(p, u)$. *Hence the ith good is normal if and only if* $E_{iu}(p, u) > 0$.

Proof.   As is well known,

$$x^i = E_i(p, u) = E_i(p, v(p, y)),\tag{1}$$

where the second equality follows from the definition of the indirect utility function. (Note that, as the middle term indicates, the derivative is taken only with respect to the first appearance of p^i in the expression on the far right of (1).) Hence,

$$D_y^i(p, y) = E_{iu}(p, u)v_y(p, y).\tag{2}$$

But $v_y(p, y)$ is the marginal utility of income and positive, so the theorem is proved.

The intuition that illuminates this result comes from considering the following. For any fixed level of utility, u, and expenditure minimization, the income required to achieve that utility is determined as $E(p, u)$. If the consumer is given that income and allowed to maximize utility, the marginal utility of income is also determined. In symbols,

$$v_y(p, y) = v_y(p, E(p, u)) \equiv G(p, u),\tag{3}$$

say. We have the following Corollary:

Corollary.   *Good i is normal if and only if* $G_i(p, u) < 0$.

Proof.   Follows immediately from the theorem and the fact that the marginal utility of income is the reciprocal of $E_u(p, u)$.

Essentially this says that good i is normal if and only if, *with utility held constant*, an increase in the price of good i would decrease the marginal utility of income.

This is very natural. If an increase in income would lead the household to buy more of good i, then an increase in the price of good i would make a small increase in income less valuable in terms of obtaining higher utility (less bang for the buck). On the other hand, if the demand for good i is decreasing with respect to income, then an increase in the price of good i would make the saving from buying less more valuable.

Having said this, I confess that I can give no intuitive explanation for the fact that the Corollary speaks in terms of the effects of price changes on the marginal utility of income with *utility* rather than *income* held constant.[2]

REFERENCES

A. Leroux, Preferences and normal goods: A sufficient condition. *J. Econ. Theory* **43** (1987), 192–199.
E. Silberberg and D. A. Walker, "A Modern Analysis of Giffen's Paradox," *International Economic Review* **25** (1984), 687–694.

[2] Observe, however, that the sign of the derivative of the marginal utility of income with respect to p^i with income held constant is not invariant to monotonic transformation of the utility function (whereas the results obtained show that the similar derivative with utility held constant is so invariant). To see this, suppose that $u(x)$ is replaced by $u^*(x) = F(u(x))$, with $F'(\cdot) > 0$. Then $v(p, y)$ will be replaced by $v^*(p, y) = F(v(p, y))$. Differentiating:

$$v^*_{yi}(p, y) = F'(v(p, y))v_{yi}(p, y) + F''(v(p, y))v_y(p, y)v_i(p, y).$$

Appropriate choice of $F(\cdot)$ can give the second term any sign and magnitude and alter the sign of the whole expression.

PART III

Applications of Microeconomic Theory

CHAPTER 19

On Donor Sovereignty
and United Charities (1977)

There are eight degrees in alms-giving, one lower than the other. . . . [The second degree] is giving alms in such a way that the giver and recipient are unknown to each other. . . . [One way to accomplish this is by] the donation of money to the charity fund of the Community, to which no contribution should be made unless there is confidence that the administration is honest, prudent, and efficient.

Below this degree is the instance where the donor is aware to whom he is giving the alms, but the recipient is unaware from whom he received them. The great Sages, for example, used to go about secretly throwing money through the doors of the poor. This is quite a proper course to adopt and a great virtue where the administrators of a charity fund are not acting fairly.

Maimonides

I.   The Problem

It is common practice for individual charitable organizations to merge their fund raising activities. The United Fund or Community Chest, the United Jewish Appeal, and Federation of Jewish Philanthropies are well-known examples. There are obvious reasons for such mergers. By having a common fund drive, the combined organizations save considerable expenditure of resources that would otherwise be largely duplicative; moreover, prospective donors are saved the annoyance of having more than one solicitor call. For both reasons, the net receipts of the combined charities may well go up.

On the other hand, such charitable combinations impose a hidden cost on their donors. Whereas before the merger a donor could control the separate amounts that he gave to each charity, after the merger he can generally control only the total amount of his gift. The allocation of that total will generally be decided by the merged organizations. If the donor cares about that allocation, he may be less well off than before.

This phenomenon is plainest where the managements of the combined charities set the allocation explicitly; it is likely to be present, however, even where there is some effort made to accommodate donor prefer-ences. Some merged fund drives, for example, allow each donor to specify how his gift is to be allocated. Clearly, if every donor did so, there would be no utility lost from the inability to control such allocations. In practice, however, large numbers of donors do not avail themselves of this opportunity. The result of this is that a large sum of otherwise unallocated money is distributed by bargaining among the managements of the component charities. One very important element of that bargaining inevitably becomes the financial needs of each organization after taking into account the earmarked funds. Hence, if one charity gets a high proportion of the earmarked funds, it is likely to do relatively less well in the later bargaining for the undifferentiated funds than a charity receiving smaller earmarked donations.[1] If donors perceive this to be the case, then they will also perceive that their earmarking does not affect the ultimate disposition of their gifts. (Indeed, this may be one reason for the failure to earmark, although certainly not the only one.)

Moreover, if the combined fund drive accounts for a large share of the funds raised by the component charities, the same phenomenon can arise even if those charities have supplemental individual fund raising activities. A donor giving to a particular charity may be directly contributing to it but may be weakening that charity's bargaining position in the distribution of the combined charity's receipts. In this case, as in the case of earmarking, if a dollar of direct contribution results in a dollar less of allocation from the combined fund, then donor activities have no effect on ultimate allocation. If the relation is other than one-for-one, then donors can affect the ultimate allocation, but not as efficiently as if the charities were wholly separate. In either case, a utility loss is imposed on the donor.[2]

Do donors care about the allocation of their own funds or only about the existence of the charities involved? It seems plain to me that donors do care about such allocations. Certainly it would be a very strong assumption to suppose that they do not. Unless donors care, it is hard to understand why individuals give more – sometimes considerably more – to some charities than to others. While it is true that charities partake of some aspects of public goods (in the technical sense), it seems clear that donors derive satisfaction not merely from the knowledge that the charities exist but also from the sense of themselves participating in a worthy

---

[1] This does not have to be the case, of course. The management of the combined charity, for example, could take earmarking as an expression of donor preferences and divide the undifferentiated funds in the same proportion as the earmarked funds. Such a solution is unlikely to be very stable in practice, however, unless every individual charity gets as much as it would expect to get on its own. In general, bargaining over fair shares is likely to be a complicated business.

[2] If donors believe erroneously that they can completely control the allocation of their gifts, is there a *real* utility loss? For my purposes it seems unnecessary to explore this question.

cause. Unless they think all causes equally worthy, they are likely to care where their money goes.

Note that this means that utility losses can be present even if the management of the combined charities sets the postmerger allocation of funds so that each individual charity's share is the same as it was before the merger. (This may, of course, be a sensible thing to do.) Even though such an allocation is the average, in some appropriately weighted sense, of the allocations that donors would choose, there may be no donor for whom it is the preferred allocation of his own money. A donor who cares about the allocation of his own contribution and not just about the total funds going to each component charity will then be made worse off by being forced to contribute in the average proportion.

Hence, while combined fund drives provide obvious resource savings and may also involve utility gains to donors in the form of decreased annoyance,[3] they are also likely to impose utility losses on donors because of lessened or lost control over fund allocations. Two questions then arise.

First, if donors are unhappy about the way in which their money is to be allocated, are they not likely to express that unhappiness by changing the amounts they give? Since the management of the charities is likely to be sensitive to the total receipts, doesn't this mean that donors, by voting with their dollars so to speak, will influence the allocation in the way they would like it to go? At the least, one would expect this to be true if there is no problem of aggregating over donors with widely different preferences.

Second, if after the merger, receipts net of administrative and fund raising expenses go up, can that not be taken as an indication that the utility costs imposed on donors are more than offset by the resource savings? Certainly, if *gross* receipts go up, one would expect this to be an indication that donors are happier with the merger than they would be without it. Hence one might expect to judge whether the merger was worth having by looking at gross or net receipts.[4]

---

[3] As exemplified by the time and trouble of the "great Sages" described in the opening quotation. Perhaps it is worth remarking, however, that in modern times the merging of charities does not provide the donor with the satisfaction of rising one step up the Ladder of Charity of Maimonides. The feature that distinguishes the second from the third degree is the question of the anonymity of the individual ultimate recipients, and this is generally equally preserved whether or not the charities are merged.

[4] I am well aware that all of this is from the point of view of the donors only. Clearly the merger will be worth having from the point of view of the ultimate recipients if net receipts go up and each component charity gets at least as much with the merger as it would without it. It is not at all clear how one should weigh the interests of the recipients against the interests of the donors. Presumably the donors consider the interests of the recipients in making their donations (formally, the utilities or consumptions of the

The present paper shows that both of these suppositions are erroneous as general propositions. I provide a counterexample with a single donor in which the total amount given to the merged charities goes up as the postmerger allocation moves *away* from that which the donor would choose in the absence of the merger. Indeed, for a particular special case, total charitable donations are actually *minimized* at the preferred allocation (at least locally). Hence management paying attention to total receipts will generally be led away from the allocation preferred by the donor. It follows immediately that one cannot conclude the merger was worth having because gross or net receipts go up.[5] Generalization to many donors is immediate.

While the example used is, of course, special, it is in no sense pathological.[6] Indeed, as the later discussion suggests, the results will certainly hold for a wide class of utility functions. Hence, while there may be occasions on which gross (or net) receipts provide an appropriate guide to donor preferences and to the desirability of mergers from the donors' point of view, they do not do so in general.

I now proceed to the mathematics, postponing heuristic discussion until the examples have been given.

II.   The Counterexample

Assume a single donor who allocates his income y among donations to two charities, denoted x_1 and x_2, and expenditure on a single ordinary commodity, denoted x_3. We choose the units of x_3 so as to make its price unity. The donor then (with no merger) faces the budget constraint

$$x_1 + x_2 + x_3 = y \tag{1}$$

The donor maximizes a strictly quasi-concave utility function

---

recipients enter the utility functions of the donors). Is one justified in taking further account of recipient utilities than this and imposing on donors some outside sense of what their charitable obligations should be? This is not a simple question and I do not consider it further in this paper.

[5] Of course donors will probably be pleased if all charities get more than before. The issue is whether they will be sufficiently pleased to offset their annoyance at having their allocations restricted and (possibly) paying more than they would like. This depends on the relative importance in the donor's utility function of the donor's own gifts and the total moneys received by the charities.

[6] As would be, for instance, a case in which the donor insisted that the net amount received from his personal donation by a particular individual charity be at least some minimum. In such an example, the donor would obviously regard the imposition of an outside allocation following the merger just as he would an additional administrative expense and feel compelled to give more to achieve the same net result. While instructive, such an example seems too extreme to be persuasive.

$$U(x) = V(x_1) + W(x_2) + Q(x_3) \qquad (2)$$

where

$$V(x_1) = \beta_1 log(x_1 - \gamma_1)$$
$$W(x_2) = \beta_2 log(x_2 - \gamma_2) \qquad (3)$$

with the $\beta_i > 0$, $i = 1, 2$.[7] There is no need to restrict $Q(x_3)$ further than required for strict quasi-concavity. We assume until further notice that

$$\beta_1 \gamma_2 \neq \gamma_2 \beta_1 \qquad (4)$$

Counterexamples are permitted to be special, of course; it may be felt, however, that this one is objectionable in a particular way. I have made the donor's utility function depend solely on his own consumption and his own contributions – that is, on his own feeling of contributing to worthy causes. Donors can obviously also be interested in the existence and level of charities independent of their own contributions (the public good aspect of charities referred to above), and the donor whose behavior is being modelled apparently is not interested in such considerations.

Such a defect in the example is apparent rather than real, however. Let Z_1 and Z_2, respectively, denote the level of donations by all *other* individuals to the two charities. We could replace (2) by taking the donor's utility function to be

$$U^*(x, Z) = F(U(x), Z_1, Z_2) \qquad (5)$$

where $U(x)$ is given by (2). Since the Z_i are outside the control of the particular donor, however, we may as well take them as parameters and, given the weak separability of (5), treat the donor as though his utility function were simply (2). While such separability is also special, continuity will show that our results continue to hold when such separability is absent but departures from it sufficiently small. Since the purpose of a counterexample is to place the burden of proof on those believing in the propositions being negated, this is sufficient generality for our purposes.

Denoting differentiation by subscripts, the first-order conditions for the premerger optimum are:

$$V_1 = W_2 = Q_3 = -\lambda; x_1 + x_2 + x_3 = y \qquad (6)$$

where λ is a Lagrange multiplier.

Now suppose that the two charities merge and allocate their funds so

---

[7] It is necessary to assume that $x_1 > \gamma_1, x_2 > \gamma_2$ is feasible, which will certainly be true if the $\gamma_i < 0$, but can hold even if the $\gamma_i > 0$ provided income is large enough.

that the ratio of the first charity's funds to those of the second are given by k, a fixed positive constant announced to all donors. Hence $x_1 = kx_2$, and the donor now faces the problem of choosing x_2 and x_3 to maximize

$$U(kx_2, x_2, x_3) = V(kx_2) + W(x_2) + Q(x_3) \tag{7}$$

subject to

$$(k + 1)x_2 + x_3 = y \tag{8}$$

(Note that the merger changes the relative prices of x_1 and x_2, although that is not the only thing it does.)

Define $c = x_1 + x_2$, the donor's total contributions to charity. If the conjectures we are examining are correct, then such total contributions will be greatest if the merged charity sets k at the ratio which the donor would prefer, the ratio he would himself choose in the absence of the merger. I shall show that this is not the case in the present example by showing that $\partial c/\partial k \neq 0$ at the premerger optimum. It follows that the donor's contributions will *rise* rather than fall as the merged charity's managers move away from his preferred allocation in a particular direction.

The first-order conditions for the postmerger optimum are

$$kV_1 + W_2 + (k + 1)\lambda = 0; \quad Q_3 + \lambda = 0; \quad (k + 1)x_2 + x_3 = y \tag{9}$$

which involve the intuitive condition that the marginal utility of a dollar consumed equals a weighted average of the marginal utilities of dollars donated to each charity. Differentiating totally with respect to k:

$$\begin{bmatrix} k^2 V_{11} + W_{22} & 0 & k + 1 \\ 0 & Q_{33} & 1 \\ k + 1 & 1 & 0 \end{bmatrix} \begin{bmatrix} \partial x_2/\partial k \\ \partial x_3/\partial k \\ \partial \lambda/\partial k \end{bmatrix} = - \begin{bmatrix} V_1 + kx_2 V_{11} + \lambda \\ 0 \\ x_2 \end{bmatrix} \tag{10}$$

Observe that, since income is fixed, $\partial c/\partial k = -\partial x_3/\partial k$. Let D be the determinant of the matrix on the left of (10) and observe that $D > 0$ by the second-order conditions. Inverting that matrix by the adjoint method, we obtain:

$$\begin{aligned} \partial c/\partial k &= -\partial x_3/\partial k \\ &= (1/D)\{(k + 1)(V_1 + kx_2 V_{11} + \lambda) - x_2(k^2 V_{11} + W_{22})\} \\ &= (1/D)\{(k + 1)(V_1 - Q_3) + x_1 V_{11} - x_2 W_{22}\} \tag{11} \end{aligned}$$

using (9) and the fact that $x_1 = kx_2$.

Now consider setting k at the allocation the donor would himself choose, so that the first-order conditions for the premerger optimum (6) are satisfied. At such a point, $V_1 = Q_3$. Further, because of the particular character of V and W given in (3), the condition that $V_1 = W_2$ becomes

$$\frac{\beta_1}{x_1 - \gamma_1} = \frac{\beta_2}{x_2 - \gamma_2} \tag{12}$$

Hence, at such a point (evaluating V_{11} and W_{22}), (11) becomes

$$
\begin{aligned}
\partial c/\partial k &= (1/D)\left\{\frac{\beta_2 x_2}{(x_2 - \gamma_2)^2} - \frac{\beta_1 x_1}{(x_1 - \gamma_1)^2}\right\} \\
&= (1/D)\left(\frac{\beta_1}{x_1 - \gamma_1}\right)\cdot\left(\frac{x_2}{x_2 - \gamma_2} - \frac{x_1}{x_1 - \gamma_1}\right)
\end{aligned} \tag{13}
$$

However, from (12)

$$\frac{x_2}{x_2 - \gamma_2} = \frac{\beta_2 x_1 + (\beta_1\gamma_2 - \beta_2\gamma_1)}{\beta_2(x_1 - \gamma_1)} \tag{14}$$

Hence the sign of $\partial c/\partial k$ at the premerger optimum is the same as that of $(\beta_1\gamma_2 - \beta_2\gamma_1)$ and (4) states that the latter magnitude is not zero, yielding the desired result.

I now consider the special case in which the inequality in (4) does not hold and show that there exist subcases in which total donations are actually at a local minimum at the premerger optimum.[8] In order to do this most easily, observe the following properties that hold at the premerger optimum if (4) is violated and the γ_i are not zero.

First, since $\partial c/\partial k = 0$ in such a case, it follows that

$$\partial x_1/\partial k = -\partial x_2/\partial k = x_2/(k + 1); \quad \partial x_3/\partial k = 0 \tag{15}$$

Next, from (14), in this case, it must be true that

$$k = x_1/x_2 = \gamma_1/\gamma_2 \tag{16}$$

Denote by N the term in brackets on the far right-hand side of (11) and note that $N = 0$ at the premerger optimum in this case as does $(V_1 - Q_3)$.

At the premerger optimum in this case, therefore,

$$
\begin{aligned}
\partial^2 c/\partial k^2 &= (1/D)\partial N/\partial k \\
&= (1/D)\{(k + 1)V_{11} + V_{11} + x_1 V_{111} + W_{22} + x_2 W_{222}\}\left(\frac{x_2}{k + 1}\right)
\end{aligned} \tag{17}
$$

---

[8] I suspect that in some (or all) of these the minimum is global, but this is harder to show.

where use has been made of (15). From the definition of V, however,

$$V_{11} + x_1 V_{111} = \frac{\beta_1}{(x_1 - \gamma_1)^2}\left(\frac{2x_1}{x_1 - \gamma_1} - 1\right) = \frac{\beta_1}{(x_1 - \gamma_1)^2}\left(\frac{x_1 + \gamma_1}{x_1 - \gamma_1}\right) \tag{18}$$

and similarly for W. Using (12), (16), and (18), we obtain from (17):

$$\partial^2 c/\partial k^2 = \left(\frac{1}{D}\right)\left(\frac{x_2}{k+1}\right)\left(\frac{\beta_1}{(x_1 - \gamma_1)^2}\right)\cdot(k+1)\left(\frac{x_1 + \gamma_1}{x_1 - \gamma_1} - 1\right)$$

$$= \gamma_1\left(\frac{2x_2\beta_1}{D(x_1 - \gamma_1)^3}\right) \tag{19}$$

which has the sign of γ_1.

Thus, while in the very special case we are examining, total donations are maximized (at least locally) at the preferred allocation if the γ_i are negative, they are actually at a relative minimum in the equally plausible case in which the γ_i are positive.[9] As for the case in which both γ_i are zero (thus still violating (4)), as one might expect, this turns out to be very much a watershed. Indeed, in this case, total donations turn out to be wholly independent of the allocation set by the merged charity. To see this, observe that in this case the postmerger first-order conditions (9) imply

$$c = (k+1)x_2 = \frac{\beta_1 + \beta_2}{Q_3} \tag{20}$$

so that x_3 must satisfy

$$x_3 + \frac{\beta_1 + \beta_2}{Q_3} = y \tag{21}$$

an equation that is independent of k. In view of the budget constraint (1), this means that c is also independent of k.

III.   Heuristics

What can be said by way of intuitive discussion of these perhaps surprising results?[10] One way of looking at the matter is to think of the merged charities as a monopolist engaging in a tie-in sale. Without the merger, the monopolist has no control over the prices of the goods he

---

[9] Curiously, this turns out to be the case even though, in view of (12) and (16), the pre-merger allocation is independent of income so that the donor seems especially attached to it in some sense.

[10] For treatment of a somewhat analogous problem, see Edmond Phelps and Robert Pollak (1968).

sells, but after the merger he does have some aspects of control over their *relative* prices (see (8)). There is no reason to suppose that it will be optimal in the postmerger situation for the monopolist to set the relative prices as though he had no such control.

While there is a good deal in this, such an explanation ignores the fact that the "monopolist" does not simply set relative prices but instead makes a much more complicated offer. Moreover, this explanation tells us little about the behavior of the donor himself and thus begs the question somewhat.

Turning to donor behavior, it is easy to see (as remarked in an earlier footnote) that certain extreme kinds of utility functions will generate the result obtained. But the utility functions used above are not particularly extreme. What then is going on?

One way of seeing that the result is likely to be true is to generalize the extreme case just referred to as follows. Suppose the donor cares only for Charity A and is indifferent as to Charity B. Before the merger, we can think of him as purchasing "Charity A certificates" at a dollar apiece, where each certificate represents the receipt of one dollar by Charity A. After the merger, the merged charities allocate some fraction of the jointly collected funds, say 10 percent, to Charity B. From the point of view of this particular donor, this amounts to roughly a 10 percent increase in the price of Charity A certificates. We should naturally expect his demand for those certificates to fall. There is no reason, however, why it must fall by as much as 10 percent. If his demand is inelastic, the total dollar donation he makes will rise even though he would prefer an allocation with 100 percent rather than 90 percent going to Charity A.

The important point in considering this still special example is to realize that the thing bought (dollars delivered) and the amount paid (dollars donated) are not the same. With this in mind, one can now go a bit deeper and consider the underlying utility maximizing behavior involved in more general cases. Thus, consider the following argument (which, incidentally, suggests that the result is not at all restricted to the particular utility functions used in the counterexamples mathematically explored above). Consider a donor at the postmerger optimum whose preferred allocation of funds is different from that set by the charity. Clearly, given his consumption and the *total* amount donated to charity, his charitable funds are not being allocated efficiently. Now, with consumption fixed, remove the allocation constraint and permit him to allocate the same total charitable funds in an efficient way. He will do this by reallocating funds from the charity with the lower marginal utility to the charity with the higher marginal utility (see (9)), stopping when the two marginal utilities are equal. At this point, however, the marginal rate of substitution between consumption and charitable donation will have been altered. While it is possible that the marginal utility of consumption is now lower than that of donation (recall that the prices are all unity), there is no reason why this must be so. If it is not, he will wish to transfer funds from donation to consumption, thus giving less to charity at the premerger optimum than at the postmerger one.

Yet another way of looking at the matter is as follows. With consumption fixed at its postmerger value, consider the minimum expenditure on charity required to reach the postmerger utility level if allocations are not restricted. Since the allocation restriction prevents the donor from achieving his postmerger utility level efficiently, the removal of that restriction will enable him to do just as well with some money left over. Now, it may be optimal for him to spend all the money so saved on charity and even optimal for him to do so and then transfer funds from consumption to charity, but it is not inevitable that he should do so. Looked at in this way, there seems no reason to suppose that he will not wish to spend some of the money saved on consumption, in which case he will give less to charity at the premerger than at the postmerger optimum.

As these arguments suggest, removing the allocation restriction allows the donor to substitute donations to one charity for donations to the other so as to efficiently allocate his charitable funds. In doing so, however, there are effects on the marginal rate of substitution between either charity and ordinary consumption that can go more than one way.

This is the best that I have been able to do in seeking to explain the results. The astute reader will notice that I have not attempted a heuristic explanation of the results for the special cases in which (4) fails to hold and the premerger allocation turns out to be either a local minimum or a local maximum. This is left as an exercise.

IV.   Conclusions

Even before aggregation problems, therefore, it turns out that donor sovereignty over charitable allocations is unlikely to occur. Even if the managers of the merged charity pay strict attention to donors and seek to maximize gross receipts, they will not generally be led to the allocation that donors prefer. Indeed, there exist cases in which any move *away* from the donor-preferred allocation increases gross receipts.

A fortiori, it is not the case that one can conclude that such a merger is desirable from the point of view of donors by seeing whether it increases net or gross receipts. Such receipts can go up rather than down just because donors are forced to give in proportions that they do not freely choose.

Indeed, this may be the case even if the managers of the charity set the postmerger allocation equal to that which obtained before the merger (a natural thing to do, but one that will be harder to justify the farther in the past is the merger). Receipts may then go up not because donors are pleased at being saved one or more solicitations, but because they are forced to give in the average proportions even though every one of them feels worse off as a result.[11]

The interesting questions of when such mergers are desirable and how the allocations should be set must therefore be examined according to other criteria.

REFERENCE

E. S. Phelps and R. A. Pollak, "On Second-Best National Saving and Game-Equilibrium Growth," *Rev. Econ. Stud.*, Apr. 1968, *35*, 185–200.

[11] To see that such an example is possible, suppose that donors fall into two classes. Let every donor in the first class have a utility function of the partial Cobb-Douglas type discussed at the end of the preceding section, that is, with both $\gamma_i = 0$. Let the other class all have utility functions of the type described in the more general counterexample. It is easy to see that if the first group has a higher than average preferred value of k and the second group a lower, then total receipts can increase when everyone is forced to the average allocation. This will occur because the donations of the first group will remain unchanged while those of the second group will increase (for appropriate choice of the parameters).

CHAPTER 20

A Proposal for the Distribution Abroad of the United States' Food Surplus (1962)

One of the more embarrassing by-products of the United States' farm problem has been the accumulation in recent years of stocks of surplus crops. These surpluses enable others to picture the United States as hoarding food while millions in other lands go hungry. For some time it has been evident that it would be highly desirable to use the United States' farm surplus as economic aid to populous countries, especially those with severe food problems; indeed, some steps have already been taken to do this under the Food for Peace program, and more have been suggested. However, the United States government has properly hesitated to make really full-scale efforts in this direction, at least partly because of the probable effect that such efforts would have on the food export markets of such close allies as Canada and Australia, as well as of such rice producers as Burma.

This paper proposes, in broad outline, a possible method of expanding the Food for Peace program in such a way that the food export markets of friendly nations are not damaged. We are concerned, however, only with the problems raised by the undesirability of dumping our surplus on such export markets. There are certainly likely to be other problems involved in an expanded surplus disposal program, but these we do not discuss. It is hoped that despite the unrealism involved, this paper will stimulate useful discussions.

Let us begin by listing the features that a plan for disposal of the surplus should have:

1. The plan should provide for disposal of the surplus with a minimum of disturbance to the export markets of friendly nations. Also, it should be added that it would be desirable for the plan not to aggravate or induce balance of payments or foreign exchange problems in participating countries.[1]

The basic idea for this proposal was worked out in discussions with my wife, Ellen P. Fisher. I am also indebted to Harry G. Johnson, Paul A. Samuelson, and Robert M. Solow for comments and criticism.

[1] We have not concerned ourselves with the possibility of using the surplus to alleviate the

2.   Benefits under the plan should accrue primarily to those nations at which the program is primarily aimed. It seems poor strategy to adopt a plan such that the Communists can claim (falsely but plausibly) that we are really benefiting only ourselves and our rich capitalist allies at the expense of the poorer nations of the world. Moreover, while there is no objection as such to other food importers (the United Kingdom, for example) benefiting from the program, this clearly should not be allowed to happen at the expense of the underdeveloped countries at whom the program is primarily aimed. (We shall henceforth refer to the latter nations as "beneficiary" countries.)

3.   It should be clear to all that it is not possible for any country or group of countries to increase its benefits under the plan at the expense of the United States or of other exporting or beneficiary nations by deliberately falsifying its needs. Preferably, the plan should be self-policing in this respect – that is, such clarity should not be achieved by sanctions external to the workings of the program.

4.   Consistent with the other points, the program should cost the United States as little as possible. Of course, it is perfectly reasonable to *subtract* from the costs of the program the costs of storing the surplus that would be saved by the disposal thereof.

I.   The Proposal – the One-commodity Case

The demand for food by the world as a whole is probably price-inelastic; however, this is considerably less likely to be the case, at least at present prices, with the demand for food by the beneficiary nations themselves – the populous nations with serious food problems.[2] Indeed, it seems to Western eyes to be almost a contradiction in terms to speak of a country with a serious food or diet problem as having a price-inelastic demand curve for food (although the relative pressure of such problems may seem greater to those who have never experienced them than to those who have lived with them for years). The demand in such countries seems highly likely to be price-elastic, or at least not far from unitary elasticity, save for the effects of the need to make payment in foreign exchange. Moreover, if the effective constraint on purchasing relatively more at lower prices is the limited quantity of foreign exchange, then we

United States' own gold difficulties. The assumption is that dumping has been rejected as a means of surplus disposal.

[2] Cf. Malenbaum (1953), pp. 72–3, for a similar but somewhat weaker statement about the demand for wheat taken separately.

should certainly expect to see at least as much, if not more, foreign exchange spent on food imports at lower prices than at higher ones. This is somewhat more than is required for the perfect working of the plan about to be proposed, a plan that allows us to test the elasticity proposition before it is put into practice.[3]

To study the proposal, consider that an agency is set up, which we will refer to as the Food Surplus Disposal Agency (FSDA),[4] and assume that it is concerned with the distribution of surpluses of one crop only, an assumption that will later be removed. At the start of the program, and periodically thereafter until the surplus has been disposed of, each beneficiary nation will submit to the FSDA a schedule showing the total amount of food it is prepared to import at different prices. Furthermore, each such nation will agree to import from the FSDA the amount of food shown on its schedule, once the price has been determined,[5] to import the same food from no other source so long as the FSDA is prepared to sell below world market prices, and to prohibit export of the foodstuffs involved. (This last provision is to avoid arbitrage at the expense of the FSDA and to keep the market segregated.)

The FSDA will then engage in buying operations on the world market in such a way as to simulate as closely as possible the purchases that would have been made by the beneficiary nations in the absence of the plan. This can be done in a number of ways.

First, since the FSDA will undoubtedly be too big a buyer to leave world prices unaffected by its purchases, it cannot act as a price-taker in any very simple sense. Perhaps the simplest thing for it to do is to exercise the aggregate beneficiary nation demand schedule by entering into a series of contracts at successively higher prices, the first contract being at a price low enough so that suppliers are unwilling to sell the full amount that beneficiary nations are willing to buy. If such a price is sufficiently close to the market clearing price, the effect of price dis-

---

[3] The elasticities here involved are *price* elasticities on which no empirical work seems available. This is not the case with income elasticities.

[4] It would probably be desirable to make the agency an international one, at least in part, with representatives from countries participating in the program. Perhaps the whole thing could best be handled under the auspices of the United Nations Food and Agriculture Organization, as indicated by the recent United Nations resolution introduced by the United States government. There is also no reason why other countries with surpluses should not participate in the plan together with the United States.

[5] This sort of commitment differs from that involved in the International Wheat Agreement insofar as the program described makes the benefits depend directly on the amount actually purchased by beneficiary nations as well as on the amount for which they contract. However, it is clearly crucial that the agreements described in the text be binding ones. (This is somewhat different from the problem, considered below, of whether or not – given binding agreements – it would be advantageous to the beneficiary nations to submit demand schedules that did not represent their real preferences.)

crimination by the FSDA will be small. On the other hand, the ability of the FSDA to act as a discriminating monopsonist as just described is objectionable since it largely stems from the aggregation of the demands of the several beneficiary nations and thus is a market condition that would not be present in the absence of the plan. Other exporters might thus complain, with some justification, that the buying operations of the FSDA resulted in lower net yields than they would otherwise have obtained because the FSDA wielded a market power not originally present.

An alternative that the FSDA might therefore adopt is to engage in an Edgeworth recontracting procedure to locate a single market-clearing price at which all its purchases can be made. If this proves administratively difficult, an equivalent procedure would be to ask the exporting countries to file binding supply schedules with the FSDA and to choose the purchase price as that price which equates the aggregate supply thus obtained and the aggregate demand of the beneficiary nations. (It would clearly be in the interest of other exporters to file accurate schedules since they would, in fact, have to supply what they said they would supply.) It is evident that this procedure would do away with the FSDA's market power and leave the world market unaffected, on the assumption that no individual beneficiary country would be large enough to affect price in the first place. On the other hand, if the assumption is not valid, then the present procedure would destroy not only the FSDA's aggregate market power but also the individual market power of each beneficiary nation and would therefore result in *higher* net yields to exporters than they would obtain in the absence of the plan. If this effect is not large, it might be well to adopt this procedure anyway in order to secure certainty in forecasting the results of buying operations.

Finally, if the problem just raised turns out to be a serious one (or if it is not known how serious it is) the FSDA might adopt a procedure intermediate between the first two discussed. In this case, it would assign the demand curve of each beneficiary country to a separate purchasing agent. These purchasing agents would then *without collusion* exercise the demand curve given to them and try to purchase for the lowest possible price. The FSDA would thus be attempting to reproduce, by the actions of its agents, the actions that the beneficiary countries would have taken in the absence of the plan, and would thus leave the world market unaffected. The accounts of the purchasing agents would then be aggregated, as for purposes of dealing with the beneficiary nations, the FSDA will act as a single selling unit.

Whichever of these actions is taken, it will be convenient to refer to the average purchasing price paid by the FSDA as the average world market price. It will presumably be close to, if not identical with, the average price that would have obtained on the world market in the absence of surplus disposal.

The FSDA will also engage in selling operations. It will sell food to the beneficiary nations at the lowest price that will enable it to carry out its functions without financial loss, using the revenue from the sale of the food surplus it obtained for free to make up for the loss generated by the price difference. (Once it sets the selling price, it can count on selling the corresponding amount shown on the aggregate demand schedule.) If the aggregate demand schedule is at least of unitary price-elasticity, such a price will always be lower than the world market price and the effect will be that of selling to beneficiary nations below the average world price and compensating other exporters for the consequent loss of markets out of the proceeds of the sale. When we recall that some saving on storage costs will be achieved, we see that demand does not even have to be as elastic as this to be successful.

Note further that the plan need not aggravate the foreign exchange problems of beneficiary countries, for there is no reason for the FSDA not to accept payment in the currencies of major exporting nations up to the amount that it needs for its purchases. Since this is the same amount that beneficiary nations would spend in those currencies for the same purpose in the absence of the program, they can supply at least this much without aggravating their exchange problems. As already noted, even if they choose to spend only this much, demand will still be of unitary elasticity. Our plan thus meets this aspect of the first criterion listed above.

Moreover, the working of the program, as described, does not depend on the ability to determine what average world price would have been in the absence of the program. Indeed, it would be easy to carry out the buying and selling operations simultaneously, since the plan can be made quite flexible with respect to error in forecasting world price. Thus, if the FSDA finds itself about to earn extra income, because it anticipated a too high average world market price, it can lower its sales price, rebating on amounts already sold, and step up its purchases. If, on the other hand, a deficit is in prospect, the FSDA can raise its sales price (and receive extra payment for sales already made) and stop its purchases sooner than expected. Participating beneficiary countries ought to be willing to agree to such a procedure, since, if forecasts are unbiased, they would presumably receive rebates just as often as they would have to pay them. However, it might be best always to begin the year by erring on the high side in setting selling price so that rebates will tend to be paid by, rather than to, the FSDA. Of course, it should be possible to make forecasts accurate enough so that this is not a serious problem,[6] but the point remains that the proposal does not turn on the forecasting ability of the agency.

The only serious possible error in the plan, then, is that the demand schedules supplied by the beneficiary nations are misleading as to their actual requirements, thus causing the plan to fail to meet the third criterion listed above. This possibility requires some discussion. On the one hand, note that it is in the self-interest of beneficiary nations to provide a demand schedule that is accurate in the neighborhood of the FSDA selling price, for whatever amount they agree to take at that price, they will actually have to take, and this will determine their benefits. Since the FSDA selling price cannot be known in advance, this means that it is in the self-interest of each beneficiary nation to provide an accurate demand schedule over a fairly large range of prices.

On the other hand, it is also in the self-interest of the beneficiary nations as a whole to understate their requirements in the neighborhood of the average world market price. If the beneficiary nations were to understate their demand at average world market prices, the FSDA would not have to engage in buying operations at a loss to the extent required by the true demand curve. It could thus afford a lower selling price.

This is a somewhat serious point; however, it is not so serious as it at first appears, for there are a number of considerations tending to reduce the incentive to understate demand in this way. In the first place, some limit is placed on the amount by which demand at world market price can be understated by the necessity of maintaining some degree of historical plausibility. While it must be admitted that this is not a very strong restriction since the economies of the beneficiary nations are rapidly changing, nevertheless it is of some effect.[7]

Secondly, a somewhat stronger restriction is placed on understatement of demand by the need to preserve internal consistency. Thus, if demand is to be understated at average world market price, it must also be understated at prices in the neighborhood of that price in order to produce a smooth and plausible looking demand curve. However, the beneficiary nations cannot know the world market price in advance; they can only estimate it, and this cannot be easy without knowledge of the supply

---

[6] If the second buying policy, described above, is adopted, the world market price will be known in advance to the FSDA, but not to others.

[7] Robert M. Solow has pointed out that it might be possible to strengthen this restriction by an explicit requirement that aggregate demand be at least some percentage of some historical figure at world price. Such a requirement, however, would tend to destroy the simplicity of the plan which is one of its important features.

schedules of exporters. Should it happen that they underestimate average world price, for example, because of an unforeseen crop failure, then to the extent that the FSDA selling price falls near the world price they forecast, understatement of demand near that forecast will lead to lower benefits under the program than would be the case with no such understatement. There is, therefore, some risk attached to deliberate understatement of demand at forecasted average world prices, and this risk is greater in the multi-commodity case discussed below.

Finally, in view of this, it is not wholly in the interest of any beneficiary nation to grossly understate demand at forecasted prices. This is particularly true, moreover, if it believes other beneficiary nations to be so understating, since in this case additional benefits can be secured while others take the risk.

However, despite these compensating factors, it must be admitted that the problem of deliberate understatement of beneficiary nation demand in the neighborhood of average world price is a defect of the present proposal. It may be that some non-self-policing measure is called for to ensure that the plan meets the third, and thus completely satisfies the first of our criteria.

Note, however, that the remaining criteria are fully met. Clearly, the benefits under the proposal go exclusively to the beneficiary countries and are as large as is consistent with the first and the last criteria. Moreover, it will be apparent that the program is designed to benefit the beneficiary nations and that the United States, through the FSDA, is providing cheap food by subsidizing their food purchases. Indeed, the direction of benefit flow is so apparent that it would be very difficult for even the Communists to distort the interpretation of the plan's effects.

Finally, as to the last criterion, costs, we have already remarked that the costs of acquiring the surplus are costs of the farm program itself and not of the way in which the surplus is distributed. With this in mind, it is questionable whether the implementation of this program will cost anything at all.

Moreover, it is possible to find out at very little cost whether the program will work as described – that is, whether the aggregate demand curve is inelastic. Since demand schedules must be filed with the agency in advance, this can be discovered before the agency begins operations. Further, even if the schedules are inelastic for some commodities (see below), the program might well be workable for others. If necessary, we could adopt a modified version of the plan (either purchasing less than indicated by the aggregate demand schedules and selling more from the surplus, or adopting the first buying method listed above) that would largely leave export markets unaffected, thus compromising between the two evils of hoarding the surplus and simply dumping it.

Alternatively, even if the original demand schedule is so inelastic that despite the saving on storage costs the program would lose money, a more elastic schedule might be produced by agreement with the beneficiary nations. That is, by pointing out that benefits under the program depend on an aggregate demand schedule of sufficient elasticity, the FSDA might persuade beneficiary nations that it was in their interest to make their demand schedules a bit more elastic rather than forego the program entirely. Of course, if this were done, it should be the original rather than the adjusted schedules that guide the FSDA in its buying operations, and such persuasion should not be tied to the original schedules in such a way as to provide an incentive to distort them.

Finally, if the demand schedule is somewhat inelastic, and the suggested alternatives are rejected, the United States might still decide to operate the program at a moderate loss so as to obtain the consequent increase in international good will.

II.   The Proposal – the Multi-commodity Case

This completes our discussion of the proposal, save for the problem of removing the restriction introduced by considering only one surplus commodity. This would be no problem at all were it not for the fact that the surplus contains commodities that have close substitutes in consumption, making it impossible to implement a program for each commodity separately.

The problem is two-fold. First, it is unreasonable to expect beneficiary nations to provide demand schedules for some commodity without some convention as to the prices of that commodity's substitutes. Second, it is not enough to take care of repercussions of the program on the world market for a single commodity, without allowing for the effects on the markets of substitutes. This complicates the FSDA's operations.

To solve this, two policies must be followed. First, whenever the FSDA acts in the market for any commodity, it must also act in the markets for all substitutes for that commodity even though this may mean the temporary acquisition of stocks of commodities not originally in the surplus. Second, the FSDA must not set selling prices for any commodity independent of the selling prices it sets for the substitutes thereof; rather, the relative selling prices of such goods should be set simultaneously and thereafter operations should be conducted as though a single commodity were involved.

Before this can go into effect, however, several different sets of ratios

between the prices of all pairs, or sets, of substitute commodities will be
determined by the FSDA. Fortunately, the existence of more than one
close substitute is rare, so that the process need not be overly laborious.
Given these sets of ratios, the beneficiary countries will provide demand
schedules as previously described. This will be done for several different
sets of ratios; in particular, it will be done for ratios close to the most
recent average ratios prevailing on the world markets, or to some historic average or other forecast thereof, and, given these demand schedules, for ratios that appear eligible as selling price ratios in view of
the buying operations that will have to be conducted. Not all possible
ratios need be considered; rather it will be possible to restrict attention
to the demand schedules corresponding to relatively few ratios.

The FSDA will then conduct buying operations on the world markets
for the commodities in question in one of the ways described in the last
section – that is, it will exercise the demand functions of the beneficiary
nations for them, demand now being a function of the prices of more
than one commodity. It will set its relative selling prices (with the aid
of the various demand schedules) so that, given the ratios involved,
the highest price level at which its supply of some commodity is just
exhausted (including the supply from buying operations) is such that the
agency just breaks even in its operations in all the commodities in question taken together.[8]

Thus, for example, if buying and selling operations are carried on
simultaneously, suppose that the FSDA starts operations with a stock of
commodity A and none of commodity B – the only close substitute. It
will estimate the buying prices and thus estimate how much it will have
to buy of each commodity. It will then choose a ratio of selling prices
and observe, given that ratio, what level of prices would have to be set
in order to just exhaust the stock of B that it will have to purchase. If, at
that level, it sees that it will still make a profit, it will lower the relative
price of A and recompute, continuing this until no profit results. The set
of prices at which this occurs is the set that should obtain. The rest of the
program will work as in the single-commodity case. As before, if average
world prices are different from those forecast, the FSDA will alter buying
plans accordingly and reset selling prices – both relative and absolute –
adjusting the financial arrangements by rebates back and forth.

As before, world commodity markets will be left undisturbed, as the

---

[8] The fact that this rule need not in principle lead to a unique set of prices is academic, as
it will generally be quite clear which commodity is the limiting one. Thus, a good procedure to follow is to choose that set of prices satisfying the conditions in the text such that
the stock of no commodity is increased. Typically, stocks in the surplus are not evenly
divided among close substitutes.

FSDA will conduct the same buying operations that the beneficiary nations would have conducted in the absence of the program. The beneficiary nations will receive food at the lowest price level consistent with this, and the relative selling prices set by the FSDA will reflect, as they should, the relative size of the surpluses and the relative strength of beneficiary nations' demands for each commodity. (Note that it is perfectly proper that beneficiary nations with relatively strong demands for commodities in long supply should benefit more than beneficiary nations with relatively strong demands for non-surplus commodities.)

Finally, the other merits of the one-commodity proposal remain the same. Indeed, the principal defect of that proposal – the possibility of deliberate understatement of demand at average world price – is alleviated here, since the calculation of optimum plausible understatement becomes very complicated indeed and the risk of losing benefits correspondingly greater.

We must add an important *caveat*, however. Perhaps the greatest danger involved in this proposal is not that it will not work, but that it will work too well. It would indeed be unfortunate if a successful surplus disposal program, by removing perhaps the largest single visible symptom of our farm problem, led us to think that we had solved the farm problem itself. To the extent that the existence of the surplus stands as a constant reminder of the effects of our farm policy, it would be undesirable to remove it. Given this warning, however, the proposal just discussed does seem to point towards a practical means of disposing of the surplus so as to benefit the needy of the world.

REFERENCE

Malenbaum, W., *The World Wheat Economy*, 1885–1939, Cambridge, 1953.

CHAPTER 21

A Theoretical Analysis
of the Impact of Food Surplus Disposal
on Agricultural Production
in Recipient Countries (1963)

Introduction

This paper presents a theoretical analysis of the problems raised for the domestic agriculture of underdeveloped countries by the use of foreign food surpluses. The issues analyzed are twofold: (1) How large and serious a discouragement to domestic agriculture is the importation of foreign food surpluses? (2) Given the type of expenditures for economic development to which the receipts from surplus sales are devoted, by how much do such expenditures offset any negative effect of the surplus by (directly or indirectly) encouraging development of domestic agriculture? In particular, how does the expenditure in such programs required to just offset such effects compare with the receipts from the sale of the surplus? It is hoped that a rigorous theoretical statement of what is involved in these questions will prove useful in empirical work, although it is clearly not a substitute for detailed investigation.

The results obtained suggest the need for econometric analysis of price effects on both supply and demand of agricultural commodities in underdeveloped countries. It is shown that such price effects can be of considerable importance in policy evaluation. Thus, such quantitative investigation seems clearly called for, if only to establish that such effects are quantitatively small.

This paper was written while I was a National Science Foundation Postdoctoral Fellow at the Econometric Institute of The Netherlands School of Economics. An earlier version, issued as Report 6307 of the Econometric Institute, was read at the 6th Congress of Collective Economy, Rome, April 1963 and published in *The Annals of Collective Economy*. I am indebted to Marc Nerlove for helpful discussions but take sole responsibility for any errors.

The Size of the Effect

Theoretical Analysis – Open Sale

In his well-known paper on the value of United States farm surpluses to underdeveloped countries, T. W. Schultz gives an example of the possible effects on farm prices of the receipt of surplus commodities.[1] Briefly, the example is implicitly based on the proposition that the effect of a 1 percent increase in food supplies on price is measured by the reciprocal of the price elasticity of demand. It is of some importance to realize, however, that in the present context this will overstate the price effect unless the supply curve of domestic production is perfectly inelastic (a case denied by Schultz and to the discussion of which we shall return). To see this, one need only observe that if a given amount of surplus food is imported and sold on the open domestic market and prices fall, the corresponding cutback in domestic production (if it exists) will reduce *total* supplies available for consumption below the level of the total of presurplus supplies and the amount of the imported surplus. Price will not therefore fall so far as suggested by Schultz's example.

This may be illustrated diagrammatically. In Figure 21.1, DD' is the demand and SS' the domestic supply curve (plus fixed other imports, if any). Before the importation of surpluses, quantity is OQ_1 and price is OP_1. The effect of the importation of a certain amount, say I, of surplus which is then thrown on the market is the shifting of SS' to the right by an amount equal to I. Clearly, total quantity is then OQ_2 and price OP_2, with domestic production falling to OS_2. Schultz's example, however, implies that quantity will be OQ_3 and price OP_3, which overstates the price effect unless SS' is vertical.

To derive the precise magnitude of the price effect involved, let P denote price, $D = F(P)$ denote quantity demanded, $S = G(P)$ denote quantity of domestic supply,[2] and I denote the amount of imported surplus. The market clearing equation is then:

$$G(P) + I = F(P). \tag{1}$$

Let us agree to measure I as a fraction of total existing supplies, S, and consider percentage changes in price. Let E denote the absolute value of the percentage change in price induced by the importation of surpluses amounting to 1 percent of existing supplies. By differentiating equation (1) with respect to I, it is easy to show that:

[1] Schultz (1960), p. 1028.
[2] As before, a given amount of preexisting imports can be included in this; as in Schultz's example, we are assuming that other things remain equal.

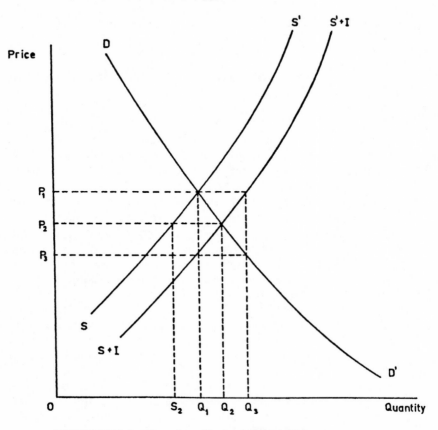

FIGURE 21.1. The price effects of the surplus.

$$E = |(dP/dI)|(S/P) = \frac{1}{\eta_S + \lambda\eta_D}, \tag{2}$$

where η_S and η_D are the price elasticities of supply and demand, respectively (measuring the demand elasticity as positive), and

$$\lambda = (S + I)/S$$

is the ratio of total demand to domestic supply, and is thus equal to unity at the point of no imported surplus. It follows that the magnitude of the price effect in question when the surplus is first imported is given to a first approximation by 1 over the *sum* of domestic demand and supply elasticities and not merely as 1 over the reciprocal of the price elasticity of demand alone as in Schultz's example.

It follows immediately, letting K be the absolute value of the percentage change in domestic supply induced by an increase in the surplus equal to 1 percent of preexisting supplies, that:

$$K = \frac{\eta_S}{\eta_S + \lambda\eta_D}. \tag{3}$$

Thus the percentage effect on domestic supply is approximately given by the price elasticity of the domestic supply curve divided by the sum of domestic supply and demand price elasticities. (Schultz's example would imply that the result is the ratio of supply to demand elasticities – clearly greater than the true figure unless supply elasticity is zero.)

The point of this analysis is not to criticize Schultz on a point not particularly important to his powerful argument. It is rather to provide a correct statement of the theoretical expression for the magnitudes of the effects of surplus on price and on domestic supply, so that such expression may serve as a basis for assessing the seriousness of such effects and the costs of overcoming them, both in *a priori* discussion and in quantitative investigation.

Theoretical Analysis – Gratis Distribution

Before turning to the consequences of the preceding analysis, it should be observed that the derived expression (3) may overstate the effects of the imported surplus, depending on the policy of the recipient government. All of the foregoing implicitly assumed that the imported surplus was sold in competition with domestic and other preexisting supplies; however, it is possible that recipient governments may choose to distribute the imported surplus gratis to the poorer segments of their populations. Surprising as it may sound, it is in fact the case that such a policy will generally be *less* harmful to domestic agriculture than the policy of sale so far considered, provided that arbitrage by the recipients can be prevented.

To see this, let P^0 be the price that results when the surplus is sold – the price at which (1) is satisfied. The total demand at that price is $F(P^0)$. Now, suppose that the surplus is distributed gratis and consider what happens when domestic supplies are offered for sale. Clearly, at P^0, no individual will now buy less than the difference between what he would have bought previously and his share of the surplus, for each individual's *total* demand will not be decreased by lowering the price on some units to zero. Further, in general, some individuals will be willing to buy more than this. It follows, summing over all individuals, that total demand in the new situation will be greater than $F(P^0) - I$, but since P^0 was the original market-clearing price, this will be greater than $G(P^0)$, so that the new market-clearing price will lie above P^0. It follows that the negative effect on domestic agriculture will be smaller than if the surplus is simply sold.

Note that since the same proposition holds on the international level, we have just shown that if arbitrage is prevented (which may be by no means as difficult an accomplishment on this level as on the domestic level), free gifts of surplus food or sales at specially low prices to under-developed countries are less damaging to normal export markets than simple dumping of the surpluses on the world market would be. This is the case whether or not such surplus transfers are accompanied by agreements concerning the maintenance of normal food imports.

Returning to the domestic problem, it is, of course, the case that a policy of gratis distribution has its drawbacks. If the surplus is not sold, the receipts from its sale are not available as funds for economic development. On the other hand, such a policy, if carefully handled, can result in cheaper food than does the policy of open sale, for just those elements of the population that require it most. At the same time it reduces the negative effect on domestic agriculture. Since the relief of hunger must certainly be an important objective, gratis distribution (or, at least, restricted sale at specially low prices) may be desirable, although the difficulty of preventing arbitrage may make such policies impractical at the domestic level.

Having pointed out this possibility, we shall now cease to consider it for the remainder of the paper since the prevention of arbitrage at the domestic level may be far harder than in international trade. We shall thus return to the assumption that imported surpluses are sold on the open domestic market, bearing in mind that the effect measured by (3) may, in fact, be larger than the effect under such alternative policies as we have just discussed.

Some Consequences

Obviously, the price elasticities of both supply and demand crucially determine the size of the effects measured by (2) and (3). I shall argue below that it is of obvious importance to attempt to measure such elasticities quantitatively rather than rest content with *a priori* argument or qualitative empirical observations. In the absence of such measurements, however, some further *a priori* discussion may not be out of place.

Most of the discussion of these matters to date seems to have centered on the likely size of the price elasticity of domestic supply – on the question of whether farmers in underdeveloped areas are at all sensitive to price incentives or disincentives. Thus Schultz[3] argues that it has become all too convenient to assume away such effects and that price elasticity of supply is likely to be greater than zero, while Olson and Khatkhate[4] take the opposite view, arguing that in underdeveloped countries there may be few alternative uses for the land and labor resources employed in agricultural production and that the supply curve may even be downward sloping because of effects on small farmers' own consumption. Dantwala, on the other hand, argues that the question is not of great importance, stating:[5]

What makes Prof. Schultz' contention irrelevant is not the insensitivity of the farmer in recipient country [sic] to price changes, but the prevalent situation – in India, for example – of inflationary pressure on agricultural – particularly food – prices resulting from deficit financing and economic development, in need of a countervailing force of additional imported supplies to keep the prices at a reasonable level.

Let us discuss this last argument first. It suggests that the principal contribution of imported surpluses is the provision of food at reasonable prices in the face of an otherwise highly inflationary situation. This may indeed be so. However, while there may be no pronounced negative effect on domestic agriculture (because of the existing upward pressure on farm prices), if farmers are at all sensitive to prices, then agriculture will not expand to the extent that it would have done in the absence of the imported surplus. The signal from the price mechanism that *more* resources are needed in domestic agriculture will not get through because of the effects of the surplus. If it is more than a pious hope that the existing surplus situation is temporary, one is forced to consider the time when surplus disposal ends. At that time, food prices in such countries may well become substantially higher than would have been the case had prices in the short run not been held down by imported surpluses. Low food prices now may be gained at the expense of high prices later on, and, while this may not be undesirable, it should surely not be undertaken incautiously.

Moreover, the extent to which food prices will be held down even in the short run by imported surpluses is not independent of the price responses of farmers. It is clear from the previous analysis that the effect of surpluses on price may be partly offset – see (2) – by such responses. If domestic supply is not perfectly price inelastic, then there will be such offsetting effects, and the effect of surpluses on price will clearly be

---

[3] Schultz (1960), pp. 1028–29.
[4] Olson (1960), pp. 1043–44, and Khatkhate (1962), pp. 187–92, respectively.
[5] Dantwala (1963), p. 87.

smaller the greater is the price elasticity of the domestic supply curve. It follows that even if one is prepared to disregard the effects of surpluses on domestic agriculture as such and is primarily concerned with prices – even if that concern is only for prices in the near future – the issue of the sensitivity of farmers to price incentives is an important one.

Is the price elasticity of domestic supply likely to be nonnegligible then? This is clearly a question which can be answered only by quantitative investigation, and there is room here for a great deal of econometric work. I have little to add to the argument of what that work would show if it were done. I should like to point out, however, that whatever weight is given to the Olson argument that resources employed in agriculture are likely not to have alternative uses, that weight must clearly become less and less over time as the countries in question develop and the demand for labor in other areas expands. Similarly, the Khatkhate argument as to the consumption of small farmers also becomes less relevant as countries develop. There does not seem to me to be sufficient evidence to conclude that price effects on supply will be of no importance or negative in the foreseeable future during the surplus disposal period. Furthermore, the argument concerning the difficulty of shifting resources out of agriculture loses much of its relevance when one considers the necessary *expansion* of domestic agriculture discussed above.[6] In balance, I must agree with Schultz that the issue of the price sensitivity of farmers is an important one that merits a good deal more careful (and quantitative) study than it appears to have received.

Whatever one thinks about the price elasticity of supply, however, the preceding theoretical analysis clearly points out the importance of the price elasticity of demand – a rather neglected parameter in these discussions. The price elasticity of demand figures importantly in the expressions for both the effect of the surplus on price (2) and the effect on domestic supply (3). Moreover, the analysis of the cost of neutralizing the effect of the surplus on domestic agriculture, to be given later, also points up the importance of the price elasticity of demand. There has been relatively little quantitative work on the estimation of the effects of price on demand, however, although there are several studies of income effects taken alone. We are thus once again reduced to *a priori* argument.

I find it hard to believe that the demand for food in food-deficit countries can be very price inelastic, especially when one considers the large income effect that is likely to occur when food prices fall. The existence of a large demand for food that is not satisfied because prices are high

---

[6] See also the evidence discussed by Dantwala (1963), p. 87.

seems to me to be a likely characteristic of food-deficit countries. If this is so, then the effects of the surplus on price and on domestic supply will be less serious than would otherwise be the case.

The Expenditure Necessary to Offset the Effect

The Comparison to Be Made

A country receiving aid in the form of food surplus from abroad can utilize the funds received from the sale of the surplus to the consuming public in various ways. On the one hand, such funds may be used for economic development in general; on the other, such funds may plausibly be used directly to offset the effects on domestic agriculture discussed in the preceding section. In either case, the use of the funds will in turn affect domestic agriculture, since even if general nonagricultural development projects are undertaken, there will be an income effect on the demand for food.[7] It is thus clearly of interest to derive a general expression for the effects (direct or indirect) of development expenditure programs on domestic agriculture and to ask how large such expenditures must be to overcome the effects of the surplus already discussed. It is natural to ask whether, given the way in which the receipts from surplus sale are spent for economic development, the effects of the surplus on domestic agriculture can be offset without the use of more funds than those generated by the sale of the surplus itself.

Theoretical Analysis

Let the amount of expenditure on a particular development program be given by X.[8] If the program in question is directly related to domestic agriculture, such expenditure will affect the domestic supply curve; we thus write:

$$S = H(P, X); \qquad H(P, 0) = G(P), \qquad (4)$$

it being understood that if there are no direct effects of the development program on domestic supply, $H_2(P, X)$ (the partial derivative of $H(P, X)$ with respect to X) is identically zero.

Whether or not the program is directed at agriculture, however, the expenditure of the surplus receipts will generally have effects on income

---

[7] I am indebted to Paul N. Rosenstein-Rodan for pointing out the necessity of altering an earlier analysis to include such demand effects.

[8] Of course, X represents the expenditure *additional* to that which would be undertaken in the absence of surplus receipts.

and hence indirectly on the demand for food. We thus rewrite the demand curve as:

$$D = \phi(P, X); \qquad \phi(P, 0) = F(P). \tag{5}$$

It is important to note that (4) cannot be taken as giving the full effects of the program on domestic supply; it gives only the direct effects. The full effects include those by way of demand and the indirect effects on price that result from (4) and (5). Accordingly, we rewrite the market-clearing equation (1) as:

$$H(P, X) + I = \phi(P, X). \tag{6}$$

Our results will be easier to interpret if written in terms of elasticities. For this purpose, let us agree to consider X as a fraction of existing income. Denoting such income by Y, the income elasticity of demand, say e_D will be given by $\phi_2(P, X)(Y/D)$. We may define a corresponding "expenditure elasticity of supply" (the percentage change in supply induced by an expenditure in the given program of 1 percent of existing income) as $e_S = H_2(P, X)(Y/S)$. By differentiating (6) totally with respect to X, the percentage change in price induced by a program expenditure of 1 percent of existing income can be shown to be:

$$(\partial P/\partial X)(Y/P) = \frac{\lambda e_D - e_S}{\eta_S + \lambda \eta_D}. \tag{7}$$

Similarly, the percentage increase in domestic supply induced by a program expenditure of 1 percent of income is given by:

$$(\partial S/\partial X)(Y/S) = \left\{ H_1(P, X)\left(\frac{\partial P}{\partial X}\right) + H_2(P, X) \right\}(Y/S)$$

$$= \frac{\eta_S e_D + \eta_D e_S}{\eta_S + \lambda \eta_D}. \tag{8}$$

To a first approximation, the full effects of a given amount of expenditure in the given program on price and domestic supply may be found by multiplying (7) and (8) by (X/Y).[9]

Finally, agree as in the preceding section to consider the surplus as a percentage of preexisting domestic supply. Combining (3) and (8), the percentage of income that will have to be expended in the given program

---

[9] The use of such approximation involves the assumption that the expenditure under discussion only negligibly affects the four elasticities involved. If the programs are large, this may not be a good assumption and would have to be abandoned in actual policy evaluation except as a first approximation.

in order to just offset an increase in imported surplus of 1 percent of pre-existing domestic supply is given by:

$$(dX/dI)(S/Y) = \frac{\eta_S}{e_D\eta_S + \eta_D e_S}. \tag{9}$$

Note that if there are no direct effects of the given program on domestic supply, then $e_S = 0$, and all the above expressions reduce to rather simpler ones; in particular, (9) becomes essentially the reciprocal of the income elasticity of demand.

We may use (9) to derive the total expenditure in the given program required to just offset the full effects of the surplus. To do this, let S^0 be presurplus domestic supply; then multiplying the right-hand side of (9) by (I/S^0) gives the required expenditure as a fraction of income; multiplication by Y then gives the desired result. Let C be the required expenditure; to a first approximation, we have:

$$C = (I/S^0)(Y)\left(\frac{\eta_S}{e_D\eta_S + \eta_D e_S}\right). \tag{10}$$

As already remarked, it seems natural to compare this with receipts from the surplus to determine whether the effects of the surplus can be offset with no additional expenditure from other sources, given the development program. Denote those receipts by $R = PI$; then:

$$C/R = (Y/PS^0)\left(\frac{\eta_S}{e_D\eta_S + \eta_D e_S}\right). \tag{11}$$

Note that the first factor is the reciprocal of the fraction of income accounted for by sales of domestic agricultural products after the effects of both the surplus and the program.[10]

Having obtained expressions for the effects in question, it will be of interest to observe that in general there always exists a policy of surplus receipt expenditure for which the ratio of C to R is highly likely to be less than unity. This will also serve as an illustrative example in our analysis. The policy in question is that of direct subsidy to domestic producers in payments per unit of output. It is reasonable to suppose that the effect of the subsidy per unit of output will be no different from the effects of price.[11] Thus, in this case:

---

[10] It is possible to use (2) and (7) to derive an equivalent expression in terms of presurplus and preprogram magnitudes, but the result is rather awkward.

[11] There is a minor issue here as to whether this will be the case if the subsidy is paid per unit of production rather than per unit brought to market. I am assuming that farmers value their own consumption at market prices and that farmers' own consumption can

$$H(P, X) = G(P + X/S) \tag{12}$$

so that

$$\frac{H_1(P, X)}{S} = H_2(P, X) \tag{13}$$

and

$$e_S = \eta_S(Y/PS). \tag{14}$$

Noting that if the effects of the surplus are to be just offset, the subsidy will have to be paid on an output of S^0 and observing that the income elasticity of demand, e_D, will generally be positive, we have:

$$C/R = (Y/PS^0)\left(\frac{1}{e_D + \eta_D(Y/PS^0)}\right) < 1/\eta_D. \tag{15}$$

It follows that for this policy, the surplus can be offset with no external funds if demand is elastic or (since income elasticity of demand is likely to be substantial) even if demand is somewhat inelastic. As argued above, this is a quite reasonable circumstance to expect to encounter, although there is practically no quantitative work thereon.[12]

Concluding Remarks

Relation to the International Problem

While this analysis has been concerned with the problem raised for domestic agriculture within underdeveloped countries by the surplus disposal program, a short digression may be in order on two ways in which our discussion relates to the similar problem of the effects on normal export markets of international surplus transfers.

The first of these has already been discussed but perhaps bears reiteration. We have shown that the effects on such export markets of free gifts of surplus food to underdeveloped countries will be less (if arbi-

---

and should be treated as an addition to demand rather than as a subtraction from supply. Alternative cases can, of course, also be analyzed.

An equivalent policy to the one under discussion is that in which the government estimates supply and demand curves and acts as monopsonist and monopolist of foodstuffs, buying from farmers at the presurplus market-clearing price and selling to consumers at the resulting postsurplus market-clearing price. A policy along these general lines is evidently followed by Japan (see UN and FAO (1958)) and I have proposed it in an international context with a rather more complicated institutional framework (see Fisher (1962)).

[12] I am indebted to Thomas J. Rothenberg for discussion of the above proof.

trage is prohibited) than the effects of open sale of the surplus on world markets. This is the case even if no agreement is involved as to the maintenance of normal imports of food. Surplus disposal by free gift (or sale on special concessionary terms) may indeed have the effects of a form of dumping; those effects are less, however, than actually dumping the same quantity of foodstuffs on the world market.[13]

Second, the example discussed in the preceding section is somewhat similar to that which led to my rather unrealistic international proposal in Fisher (1962). In both cases, receipts from the sale of the surplus to recipient countries were to be used in some way to compensate other suppliers for the consequent fall in price, and in both cases, a crucial question was whether the price elasticity of demand for food in underdeveloped countries was greater than unity (approximately). It may thus appear that I am suggesting that the receipts of the surplus be used twice – once at the international level and once at the domestic one. This is not the case, however, since the analysis of this paper has lumped normal imports into the supply function. Clearly, if demand is anywhere near price elastic, enough funds will be generated by the sale of the surplus to compensate all normal suppliers of whatever nationality for the consequent fall in price, although such a policy is clearly easier to implement at the domestic level, where more efficient policies may also be available to stimulate agriculture.

The Need for Econometric Studies

This paper has suggested two measures of the effects of the surplus program on the domestic agriculture of underdeveloped countries. The first of these (3) is a measure of the size of the effect itself; the second (11) is a comparison of the expenditure required to offset those effects by some given policy of development expenditure and the receipts from the sale of the surplus. The measure of the size of the effects involves both the price elasticity of supply and that of demand, while the measure of required offsetting expenditure involves both price and income elasticities as well as the share of domestic agriculture in total income. We have shown, however, that there exists a policy under which a nontrivial upper limit to the required expenditure involves the reciprocal of the price elasticity of demand, which parameter also enters crucially at the international level of the problem, as just discussed.

It thus seems to be of some importance to have quantitative estimates

---

[13] Receipts are then not available (or less available) for use in development programs, however.

of price elasticities of both supply and demand as well as of income effects. As mentioned above, there has been a good deal of qualitative discussion of the likely magnitude of the price elasticity of domestic supply and practically none of the price elasticity of demand. I think such qualitative discussions are useful, but it also seems to me that they have taken us about as far as they can and that the time has clearly come to apply the techniques of modern econometric analysis to the measurement of these crucial parameters. The question of the sign and size of the price response of farmers is a quantitative one and ought to be treated as such, although I realize that such treatment will not be easy in view of data limitations. Even if that response turns out to be negligible or negative, it will be something gained to have settled the question. Further, even if domestic supply is not positively price responsive, estimates of the price elasticity of demand ought to be undertaken because of the importance of that parameter for treatment of the international problem. *A fortiori*, if supply responses turn out to be nonnegligible, estimates of the price elasticity of food demand can play a crucial role in policy determination at the domestic level as well by revealing whether offsetting policies are likely to require funds generated from outside the surplus program itself.[14]

REFERENCES

Dantwala, M. L., "International Planning to Combat the Scourge of Hunger Throughout the World," *Annals of Collective Economy*, Vol. 34, 1963, pp. 71–95.

Falcon, W. P., *Farmer Response to Price in an Underdeveloped Area – A Case Study of West Pakistan*, unpublished Ph.D. Thesis, Harvard University, 1962. "Real Effects of Foreign Surplus Disposal in Underdeveloped Economies: Further Comment," *Quar. J. Econ.* Vol. 77, 1963, 323–326.

Fisher, F. M., "A Proposal for the Distribution Abroad of the United States' Food Surplus," *Review Econ. and Stat.*, Vol. 44, 1962, pp. 52–57. Reprinted as Chapter 20 in this volume.

Khatkhate, D. R., "Some Notes on the Real Effects of Foreign Surplus Disposal in Underdeveloped Economies," *Quar. J. Econ.*, Vol. 76, 1962, pp. 186–196.

National Council of Applied Economic Research, *Long Term Projections of Demand for and Supply of Selected Agricultural Commodities 1960–61 to 1975–76*, Bombay, 1962.

---

[14] Since this was written, two quantitative studies have come to my attention, both of which show positive price-responses of supply in particular contexts. They are: National Council of Applied Economic Research (1962); and W. P. Falcon (1962). See also W. P. Falcon (1963).

Olson, R. O., "Impact and Implications of Foreign Surplus Disposal on Under-developed Economies," *J. Farm Econ.*, Vol. 42, 1960, pp. 1042–1051.

Schultz, T. W., "Value of U.S. Farm Surpluses to Underdeveloped Countries," *J. Farm Econ.*, Vol. 42, 1960, pp. 1019–1030.

United Nations, Food and Agriculture Organization, "A Note on the Utilization of Agricultural Surpluses for Economic Development in Japan," UN, FAO Doc. E/CN.11/L.60, Bangkok, 1958.

CHAPTER 22

US Experience:
The Recent INS Study (1970)

This paper summarizes a cost-benefit analysis of re-enlistment incentives in the United States Navy performed some time ago at the Institute of Naval Studies (INS) (Morton et al. (1966)) and considers some of the lessons to be learned from it. See also Fisher and Morton (1967) and Fisher (1967). Since the study was undertaken before the Vietnam build-up, its direct applicability is to what one hopes will be the normal situation of a peacetime Navy.

The Perceived Problem: Re-enlistment Incentives in the US Navy

Men enlisting for the first time in the United States Navy do so for a four-year term. A very large fraction of such men leave after four years; most of the remainder become career men and continue in the Navy until retirement. At the time of the INS study the Navy perceived its first-term re-enlistment rate (the one after four years) as undesirably low. A first-term enlisted man typically spends six to twelve months largely in training and, of course, improves the skills so acquired through on-the-job experience. If he leaves at the end of the first term, the human capital that the Navy has built up through its investment in such training and experience becomes dissipated so far as the Navy is concerned. This problem was naturally felt to be particularly acute in occupations requiring extensive technical training, principally that of electronics maintenance and repair.

In this situation, thought was given to offering different incentive packages to affect favourably the crucial decision – that of first-term re-enlistment. Such packages ranged from pay increases through rapid promotion and a variety of fringe benefits. Since the offering of an incentive to re-enlist is not generally without costs, the INS study was undertaken to determine which, if any, of various proposed incentive programmes was worth undertaking and which of them was the most efficient in a cost-benefit sense.

There are two kinds of costs associated with inducing a higher proportion of first-termers to re-enlist in the Navy. The first of these are the direct costs of the incentive programme itself – the costs of the pay increases or fringe benefits used as an incentive. At least as important, however, are the indirect costs that occur when the re-enlistment rate goes up, regardless of the incentive package used. Even an exogenous rise in the re-enlistment rate (that is, one not produced by changing the incentive programme) would involve additional costs simply because pay and fringe benefits rise sharply after the first term so that an experienced man costs more than a first-termer to have in the Navy. On the other hand, while costs *per man* must therefore rise, total costs may not, since the Navy will presumably be able to operate at a given level of effectiveness with a smaller number of enlisted men when those men are relatively well trained than when they are relatively inexperienced. Deciding on the net effects of these forces is the essence of the problem.

The matter (somewhat simplified) can be looked at in the following way: At a given level of effectiveness, the Navy can operate with a smaller relatively experienced group of enlisted men or with a larger relatively inexperienced one. We can think of an indifference surface showing the various mixes of experienced and inexperienced men that give the same level of effective operation. Even with the present incentive package, operation at different points on the surface involves different costs, both because the total size of the enlisted force is different and because experienced men cost more than inexperienced ones. Moreover, to move from the present point on that surface in the direction of a more experienced and smaller Navy requires additional expenditure since such a movement requires the offering of incentives to raise the re-enlistment rate.

When we recall that the Navy must plan not just for one year but for many and that the movement to a more experienced Navy cannot generally be accomplished by hiring more experienced men from outside the military but only by using and training an appropriate number of inexperienced men in an earlier year, the complexity of the problem soon becomes apparent.

Estimating a Utility Function for the Navy: Substitution versus Official Personnel Requirements

An essential ingredient of the analysis is the construction of a "utility" function for the Navy, more precisely, the construction of the indifference surface mentioned above showing the rate at which relatively inexperienced and relatively experienced men can be substituted for each other at a given level of effectiveness. I shall now discuss that construction, restricting my attention to operational effectiveness within a given year; the intertemporal part of the problem will be considered later.

The way in which official personnel requirements are often stated implies, if taken literally, that substitution of men of one experience class for men of another is impossible. If we really believe it to be an absolute requirement that the Navy have a certain stated number of men in each experience category, then the clear implication is that the Navy operates only with fixed proportions in its labour inputs and that substitution is never desirable.

This is clearly not likely to be the case in practice, and, while our study made heavy use of officially stated personnel requirements, we did not take them merely at face value in this way. The Navy obviously can and does operate with force structures differing in some measure from officially stated *desiderata*. Indeed, the very perception of the re-enlistment problem suggests that the Navy recognizes the possibility of substituting a smaller number of experienced men for a larger number of inexperienced ones. If substitution is possible in this direction, however, it is certainly possible in the other over some range of the variables; further, if such substitution would increase effectiveness at given cost, then it can also be used to reduce costs at a given level of effectiveness (Fisher, 1967a).

The contrary view – that substitution between experience categories is impossible – may well be based on the erroneous notion that such substitution must be on a man-for-man basis with an inexperienced man expected to do the work of an experienced one at no loss of effectiveness. This is a special form of the opposite extreme from the case of no substitution, being substitution at a constant rate.

That neither extreme is particularly reasonable may be seen by considering a situation in which an experienced man leaves the Navy and it is desired to compensate for this by adding inexperienced ones. It is wrong to think that such a substitution must necessarily be a direct one with, say, two raw recruits taking over the tasks of one experienced man. In general, such direct substitution will not be possible if the effectiveness of the establishment is to remain unchanged.

Effectiveness, however, is a matter of what the personnel of an establishment can do, rather than of who they are, and substitution takes place by reorganizing the tasks performed by the personnel so that the whole establishment runs most effectively. This may result in rather indirect substitution.

Consider first the loss of an experienced man in a relatively small part of the military establishment, a given ship or a given installation, for example. Suppose, first, that the installation is not so small that the man lost is the only man of his experience working on it. What happens if such a man is removed is, naturally, not the reassignment of his tasks to raw recruits. Rather the entire operating force of the installation is to a greater or lesser extent reorganized. If the experienced man was acting in a supervisory capacity, other supervisors are worked a bit harder, stretched a bit thinner to cover for his loss. This results in a loss of effectiveness as supervision becomes less close and less efficient and as personnel with slightly less experience take over the less demanding tasks of experienced personnel. There is a similar adjustment all the way down the line, with a slight upgrading of the personnel assigned to the simpler tasks ordinarily assigned to those of more experience. Finally, raw recruits are required to take over or help with tasks ordinarily reserved for men with a very small amount of training. The loss of efficiency resulting from the loss of an experienced man is transmitted by redefining tasks and by less good supervision into a loss of efficiency in working parties. This is then compensated for by increasing the number of men available in such working parties.

To put it another way: If we agree that some number (perhaps more than one) of men with slightly less experience can compensate for the loss of a fully experienced man, then the loss of an experienced man can be translated into the loss of such a number of almost experienced men. If this can be done in general, then we can ultimately translate the loss of an experienced man into a loss of some number (perhaps quite large) of raw recruits and compensate for that loss directly. Direct substitution of raw recruits for experienced personnel need not be involved.

Further, substitution between personnel types can be accomplished in ways even more indirect than those just exemplified. We restricted ourselves above to the discussion of personnel substitution in a relatively small unit. Substitution in the entire military establishment being analysed is likely to take place in a wider variety of ways than in a small installation. For one thing, there is a wider latitude in the reassignment of personnel. When an experienced man is lost from one installation, he can be replaced by an experienced man from another; the other being chosen as one where experienced men are relatively more plentiful in order to minimize the effects of the loss. In addition, a slight loss in efficiency in a given unit can often be compensated for by a slight redefining of the missions of other units to cover the loss and an increase in personnel somewhere else in the naval establishment.

Naturally, however, the numbers of men involved in the trade-offs described are likely to depend on the situation. If experienced personnel are very scarce, it may be impossible to compensate for the loss of even one by adding a reasonable number of relatively inexperienced men. If experienced men are relatively plentiful, then they may already be performing tasks that could just as well be performed by men with less experience, and substitution may be very easy.

The whole process that I have described is quite like that of substitution of factors of production in a more conventional production function. It is not generally presumed that one factor takes the place of another by doing that other factor's job. Rather substitution is accomplished by reorganizing the production process to use the new factor combination in the most efficient way possible. Such reorganization occurs to a larger and larger degree as the passage of time allows the change in factor combination to be integrated more and more into the running of the organization.

Accordingly, our study attempted to model the substitution possibilities in a way similar to that used in the analysis of production and incorporated the essential features of those possibilities as described above.

Discussion with naval officers indicated that enlisted men could be grouped into four experience classes, with substitution within a class assumed on a man-for-man basis. The lowest experience class (the first) consisted of all first-year men.

The Navy's utility function was then defined with the sizes of the four classes as arguments. A four-factor Cobb-Douglas function (used ordinally only) was chosen for analytic convenience.[1] Thus, denoting the number of men in the ith experience class in calendar year t by Y_{it}, the Navy's utility function in year t was taken to be:

$$U_t = Y_{1t}^{\beta_1} Y_{2t}^{\beta_2} Y_{3t}^{\beta_3} Y_{4t}^{\beta_4}; \quad \sum_{i=1}^{4} \beta_i = 1. \tag{1}$$

To estimate the β_i, over 100 interviews were conducted with experienced supervisors scattered over nine ship types and six occupational groups, asking how many men of a given experience class would just compensate for the loss (or gain) of one man in another class; i.e., return them to the existing level of operational effectiveness. Given the men on-board, the implied β_i could then be determined for each interviewee from the marginal rates of substitution so described assuming his utility function to be of the form (1).

These results then had to be aggregated to obtain estimates for the overall Navy. This is not a simple matter. Experienced men in widely different trades are not perfectly interchangeable; investment in human capital becomes embodied. There are two ways around this problem.

---

[1] Our dynamic programming problem (discussed below) made such reasons a bit more compelling than usual. While only for this reason, a Cobb-Douglas was used, its parameters were varied considerably.

Table 22.1. *Cobb-Douglas exponents (βs)*

	All-Navy assumption set			Electronics assumption set	
Experience class	1	2	3	1	2
1. Basic	0.268	0.239	0.255	0.104	0.086
2. Apprentice	0.386	0.402	0.393	0.432	0.444
3. Journeyman	0.268	0.279	0.273	0.337	0.341
4. Chief	0.078	0.081	0.079	0.126	0.129

The columns headed by '1' give the parameters as estimated from interview data. While the standard errors of the estimated β_i were very small (because of the large number of observations), the fit of utility functions using the estimated β_i to the original interview data was very poor. This was largely due to a non-negligible number of observations corresponding to man-to-man trade-offs scattered over the entire range of the observations. If these are ignored, as due to insufficiently thoughtful interview responses, the fit is much improved. If trade-offs really were man-for-man, our results below would be substantially strengthened.

First, because of the Navy's special interest in electronics personnel, we performed separate analyses for them and for the Navy as a whole. Second, we showed that various assumptions about assignment of men to jobs justify using (1) as an average overall relationship, estimating the β_i as weighted geometric averages of the interview-derived parameters, the weights being the number of men in each ship-occupational category. (Details may be found in Morton et al. (1966). The human capital aggregation problem is related to the physical capital aggregation problem discussed in Fisher (1965) and (1969)). The analysis was performed both with the β_i so derived and with variations from them as given in Table 22.1, so as to ensure insofar as possible that our results were insensitive to the particular values of the parameters used.

Efficiency over Time: A Dynamic Programming Problem

It is clear, however, as already remarked, that it is not enough to define a utility function for the Navy for a given year. The Navy is an ongoing organization; the induction of men now commits expenditures to be undertaken later on; and, perhaps most important of all, experienced men at a later date can be produced only by the induction of inexperienced men at an earlier one. Accordingly, the relevant question is not what incentive package will most cheaply achieve a given standard of effectiveness in a particular year but rather what package will be most efficient taking account of the future as well as the present operation of the Navy.

Yet, while comparison of costs incurred at different points of time is a relatively straightforward matter involving discounting at some appropriately chosen discount rate, the comparison of effectiveness at different points of time is considerably more complicated. (I do not mean to imply that the choice of a discount rate is an easy matter where the public interest is involved. See Fisher (1967a) for a summary of some of the issues. In the INS study, we used 5 percent, experience with a prototype model indicating that the qualitative results were rather insensitive to the precise rate chosen). Ideally, one would want to have a utility function for the Navy stretching over many future years and showing the trade-offs that the Navy is (or is not) willing to make between effectiveness in one year and effectiveness in another or, alternatively, between men in a particular experience class in one year and men in that class in some other year. This is obviously not a feasible way to approach the problem, however; it was hard enough obtaining sensible answers at the working level as to trade-offs in particular narrowly-defined situations. To obtain meaningful answers to the very complicated questions of essentially high-level policy that would be required for the construction of such an intertemporal utility function would clearly have been out of the question. The construction of such a function would thus have rested almost entirely on unsupported assumptions on our part; in particular, it is not hard to see that this would have been true had we discounted effectiveness (measured by the utility function for a single year) in the same way as we discounted costs.

Accordingly, we had to find some way around such a construction. This we did by the attractive and not too unreasonable device of insisting that any Navy that was to result from the institution of some incentive package had to attain at least the same level of effectiveness (as measured by (1)) in every year considered as would a Navy in which officially stated personnel requirements were exactly met. In other words, we took as our standard a Navy meeting official requirements and considered possible Navies that differed therefrom by having in each year an on-board complement of men that our work on substitution told us would be at least as effective as that of our standard Navy.

Our task now became that of finding among all such admissible Navies the one that cost the least in terms of the discounted value of future expenditures. This was not merely a matter of looking at the costs of each incentive package; for each such package, there are an infinite number of ways in which an admissible Navy can be obtained depending on the pattern of recruitment. It is always possible to obtain an admissible Navy by inducting great numbers of men, but it is not generally efficient to do so. Accordingly, for each incentive package, we had to find that pattern of inductions that produced an admissible Navy at minimum cost. Such minimum costs were then compared across incentive packages to find the most efficient one.

Thus we were led to the following nonlinear programming problem for each incentive package in which the variables to be chosen were the induction rates for raw recruits over the next thirty years (which we took as long enough into the future that costs incurred thereafter would be sufficiently discounted as not materially to affect the results).

Let I_t be the number of men inducted in year t under the given incentive package. Then:

$$Y_{1t} = I_t$$
$$Y_{it} = \sum_{\theta=1}^{t-1} \lambda_{it-\theta} I_\theta + B_{it} \quad (i = 2, \ldots, 4) \tag{2}$$

Here the $\lambda_{it-\theta}$ are the fraction of the inductees of year θ in experience class i in year t, while the B_{it} are the number of men in that experience class in that year who were already in the Navy at the start of the programme (in year 0). These parameters are all derived from survival rates and the distribution of men in each longevity year over experience classes. (The first-year re-enlistment rate that would obtain if the given incentive package were instituted was estimated from interview data and a study relating re-enlistment incentives to actions. Survival rates not directly affected by incentives were held constant at historical levels. See Morton, Fisher, and Nitzberg (1966) and Morton (1965) for details. Men in training or providing instruction were treated as providing direct services only for that fraction of their time in which they were not so engaged and the Y_{it} adjusted accordingly.)

Let C be the present value of all programme costs. Then C can be written as:

$$C = a \sum_{t=1}^{30} \frac{I_t}{(1 + r)^t} + S \tag{3}$$

where: r is the discount rate; a is the expected present value of all per-man costs that will be associated with a man inducted at time 0 (costs in each future longevity year being weighted by the probability of survival into that year); and S is the similar expected present value of programme costs assignable to men already in the Navy at the start of the programme.[2]

For each incentive, we have the following nonlinear dynamic programming problem: Choose $I_1, \ldots, I_{30}$ so as to minimize (3) subject to (2) and

$$U_t \geq \overline{U}_t \quad (t = 1, \ldots, 30) \tag{4}$$

where U_t is defined by (1) and $\overline{U}_t$ is the value of (1) in year t for a Navy just meeting stated personnel requirements in that year.

It is important to note that it need *not* be efficient to operate by inducting men as needed to just meet the target level of effectiveness in each year. Such a myopic policy may be very expensive since it can clearly sometimes pay to induct more inexperienced men than needed in an early year in order to have more experienced ones on board in a later one. Indeed, this is the essence of the problem. Accordingly, the nonlinear programming problem described had to be solved. We did this for each incentive package for varying values of the parameters, and we did it once for the Navy as a whole and once for electronics personnel. (See Morton et al. (1966) and Fisher and Morton (1967).)

The Results: I. Myopic versus Farsighted Planning

The principal results were of two sorts, one largely methodological and one substantive. In the present section I discuss the methodological results, deferring the more important substantive implications to the following one.

As just stated, it need not be optimal to follow the myopic policy of each year inducting just enough men to meet current effectiveness requirements; rather, it may pay to induct extra men so as to have more experienced ones later on. As it happens, in the case of the Navy as a whole, the myopic policy does turn out to be the optimal one. The results of our investigation of substitution possibilities showed that first-year men are sufficiently substitutable for more experienced ones when all occupations are considered, that it pays to go on from year to year adjusting for any shortage or excess in the number of experienced men on board by inducting a greater or less number of new men. Within the range of the data used, this is cheaper than a more complicated policy of planning ahead.

For electronics personnel, on the other hand, this is emphatically not

---

[2] Men inducted in year thirty, for example, are assigned the discounted value of all costs committed to them while they remain in the Navy. This avoids large end effects.

the case. As might be expected, raw recruits who spend much of their time in training are not worth nearly so much in terms of effectiveness as even partially trained electronics technicians, although they are not entirely worthless. This immediately suggests that it may be very expensive to try to compensate for any shortage in experienced personnel solely by the induction of such recruits.

This is indeed the case. The Navy as of 1964 inducted about 10,000 men a year in electronics. As it happens, with the current incentive package, and the experience distribution of electronics personnel currently in the Navy, somewhat fewer men than this would have to be inducted in the first year of the programme (with the current incentive programme) to just meet the first year's target. If this is done, then the number of men in experience class 2 falls short in the second year. This can be made up for only by inducting a good many more than 10,000 men in the second year. In the third year, the Navy is then long on men in experience class 2, and, to just meet the third year's target, *very* few men need be inducted in that year. The result in the fourth year is the induction of an enormous number of men, and so forth. The process is so explosive that well before the thirtieth year several million men must be inducted into the electronics Navy in some years and less than one man in others, and the total cost of the electronics programme is well above that found for the Navy as a whole.

On the other hand, the costs and induction levels involved in the optimal solution to the dynamic programming problem are quite reasonable and are of the same order of magnitude as those actually experienced. This suggests that the Navy not only should not be, but in fact is not myopic about its electronics programme, inducting men with an eye to the future.

This also suggests that the estimated parameters from our substitutability study may not be too unreasonable. Indeed, we found that if we altered those parameters in the direction of making first-year men in electronics much less substitutable for more experienced men (beyond the point indicated in column 2 of the electronics section of Table 22.1), then the specified target levels of effectiveness could not be reached at all with electronics induction rates ranging from three to four times the actual rates. If first-year men are worse substitutes for more experienced ones than we found them to be, then the Navy's problem in electronics has no feasible solution at reasonable expenditure levels. This finding makes one pause before concluding that the substantive results about to be discussed come about because first-year men have been assumed unduly good substitutes for more experienced ones.

The Results: II. Should Re-enlistments Be Encouraged?

To those substantive results I now turn, and I may remark at the outset that they do not primarily consist of a list of which incentives turned out to be most efficient, although, naturally, such a list was produced and was almost invariant to the various changes in assumptions that were made.

Rather, the principal and, at first, surprising result was as follows for *every* choice of assumptions and parameters used. For every incentive programme, for both the Navy as a whole and for electronics, an increase in the first-term re-enlistment rate results in an increase in costs for a given effectiveness pattern. (Of course, substantially lowering the first-term re-enlistment rate may be inadvisable, because even with a draft, the Navy probably could not induct the required number of volunteers to fill the resulting annual gaps.) The Navy would do better to exercise selectivity in offering re-enlistment incentives than to try to raise the general re-enlistment rate.

This result also shows up in the relative rankings of the incentives. The present incentive system ranks better than every other incentive except one, in electronics. This incentive is an option to retire after ten rather than twenty years of Naval service, and, of course, involves the assumption of a considerable reduction in the survival rate after ten years as well as an increase in the first-term re-enlistment rate.[3]

Why should raising the re-enlistment rate at no direct costs result in a more expensive Navy? We saw above that a rise in the re-enlistment rate means a substitution of fewer but more costly relatively-experienced men for a greater number of cheaper inexperienced men. Such substitution, in the range of data and parameters studied, is cost increasing.

To illuminate the matter, suppose that inductions are in an optimal pattern and consider the induction of an additional 100 men at time t. This can be regarded as a production process that takes four years and results at time $t + 4$ in some number (<100) career men. Denote costs involved in the production process by C_1.[4] There are also savings associated with the process, for the 100 men perform useful services in their first four years and thus enable the Navy to meet requirements in those years by inducting fewer men during those years. Call those savings S_1.

---

[3] Considering only electronics personnel, two incentives offering rapid promotion to warrant officer status may be a bit less expensive than the present incentive system (the caution is due to errors of approximation in the solution). Note that these too are incentives that keep men in the enlisted Navy after four years but encourage them to leave earlier than at present.

[4] Costs and savings in this discussion may be taken as discounted to time 0.

The net cost of production of the career men involved is then $(C_1 - S_1)$, which may be positive or negative.

There are also costs and savings associated with the use of the elements of human capital so produced from $t + 4$ on. As before, they are the direct costs associated with the career men and the savings that these career men exert on later inductions to meet later targets. Call those costs C_2 and the savings S_2; the net return from using the human capital is $(S_2 - C_2)$, which again may be positive or negative.

The total net return from the induction of the 100 men, therefore, is $(S_1 - C_1) + (S_2 - C_2)$. It is easy to see, however, that, if inductions are already optimal, this sum can never be positive, for, if it were, costs would be reduced by inducting the men. Indeed, the sum will be zero for years in which current requirements are more than fulfilled and will actually be negative for those years (of which there are quite a few, including year thirty) in which current requirements are a binding constraint. It thus cannot be true that $(S_1 - C_1)$ and $(S_2 - C_2)$ are both positive, and negativity tends to dominate.

Now consider a small increase in the re-enlistment rate, other things equal. This produces in every year extra career men after a production process that takes four years but that costs nothing (for the production of the extra men). Thus, the net returns from doing this involve only $(S_2 - C_2)$. We know that these returns would fail to justify the production of the human capital at a cost of $(C_1 - S_1)$ which may be positive or negative; our result as to the effect of raising the re-enlistment rate says that such production is not justified at zero cost either.[5]

Thus, with existing later survival rates and pay scales, the Navy can accomplish a given mission more cheaply with a somewhat larger turnover of relatively inexperienced men than it can by encouraging those men to stay for an additional sixteen years. The fact that an early retirement incentive does reduce costs slightly in electronics suggests that the difficulty lies in a rate of pay and other benefits that rise with seniority in a manner not matched by rises in marginal products, so long as nearly all men staying after four years become career men who stay through twenty.

---

[5] It may be thought that choosing an optimal induction pattern for each incentive (on which choice this argument and, in part, the results depend) is an unrealistic process; it should be pointed out that these optimal patterns are not radically different from historical induction rates. This suggests that even in electronics (where, as opposed to the Navy as a whole, cost minimization is not merely a matter of myopic decision-making), the Navy does make some attempt to optimize. Even aside from this, it is reasonable to require a rational policy choice to involve optimization of this sort. If the Navy is far from an optimal induction pattern, changing that is likely to have more effect on costs than raising the re-enlistment rate.

Reflections on the Results

Of course, the reason behind this phenomenon is easy to find, and, on reflection, the results turn out not to be surprising at all. As is no longer the case in the United Kingdom, the American military forces rely on conscription to supply new recruits. Even though the Navy in the period studied did not draft men directly, enlistments in the Navy were certainly encouraged by the existence of the draft for the Army; men joined the Navy in order to avoid the Army draft and exercise choice as to their military service. One result of this system is the fact that the Armed Forces, including the Navy, are able to obtain large numbers of recruits despite the fact that the rate of pay for first-term men is far below what those same men could earn in civilian life. Indeed, it is fair to say that the conscription system imposes a large involuntary tax on enlisted men in their first term of service – this is a compelling argument against it. (See chapters by Pauly and Lillett in Miller (1968)).

On the other hand, no such compulsion is involved in the retention of career men and, accordingly, even with the existing incentive package, the Navy is forced to pay such men something approximating what they could earn in civilian occupations. Thus the ratio of the wage of a career man to that of a recruit is high, far higher than the ratio of their civilian wages and hence far higher than the ratio of their contributions to the economy in civilian life. Since the skills required by the military are not totally different from those required by the civilian economy, it is thus not surprising to discover that the same wage ratio is likewise higher than the ratio of the two men's marginal products in the Navy and, accordingly, that *given those wages* it is relatively efficient to operate by moving in the direction of a greater use of less experienced men. Where a recruit can be forced to work for practically nothing and an experienced man must be hired on the market, it is not surprising that it pays to make do with the forced labour. Were both men valued at their civilian wages, this would doubtless not be the case.[6]

Moreover, this fact has serious implications for the relations between the military and society and for the continuance of the conscription system. From society's point of view, the cost of having a man in the Navy is an opportunity cost; it is the loss of his civilian product, and this is measured by his civilian wage. The INS study therefore gives the wrong results when considered from a point of view less parochial than that of the Navy. Given the wage structure in the Navy – a wage structure maintained through conscription – the observed budgetary costs make it

---

[6] At least, it would not be so to such an extent.

optimal to maintain a relatively larger and less experienced Navy than would be the case were the true economic costs taken into account.[7] Economic decision-making can be delegated to managers (in this case the military) without loss only if the prices with which they must operate are those that reflect the true costs of the resources that they use. By the use of conscription, the United States has not only imposed an inequitable tax on certain of its young men, but it has also distorted manpower decisions. It has provided a false price structure in which the cost of first-term enlistees is held artificially low and the true cost hidden because much of it does not appear as a budgetary item.

Further, since the present false price structure distorts naval and other military manpower decisions by providing a powerful incentive toward operation with a large and inexperienced force, rational debate on the ending of the draft tends to be hampered. This is so for two reasons.

First, it is not generally recognized that because the present force structure is suboptimal when true costs are taken into account, the true costs of a volunteer military force of equal effectiveness *must* be lower than those of the present arrangement, since in a volunteer force each man must be induced to leave his civilian occupation where he earns his marginal product.

Second, leaving true hidden costs aside, the budgetary costs of a volunteer military force tend to be overestimated by all but the very thoughtful. (For a thoughtful estimate, see Oi (1967) and Chapter 5 of Miller (1968).) The natural tendency is to believe that such costs would exceed the present ones by the amount necessary to bring every first-term enlisted man in the present Service up to his civilian wage. The natural inclination to disregard substitution opportunities now works in reverse. It is not recognized in such a calculation that in a volunteer army the number of first-term men would be far less than at present for it would then be efficient to operate with the Services reduced in size and manned by experienced personnel to a greater extent than the present conscription-distorted price structure will permit.

REFERENCES

F. M. Fisher, Embodied Technical Change and the Existence of an Aggregate Capital Stock. *Review of Economic Studies*, vol. xxxii (1965), pp. 263–88. Reprinted as Chapter 2 in Fisher (1992–93).

[7] Similarly, note that the benefit to society from the receipt of a trained man from the Navy is also measured by his wage and the benefits to the civilian economy of naval training by the difference in the wages a man can command before and after such training.

F. M. Fisher, Aspects of Cost-Benefit Analysis in Defense Manpower Planning. In the *Proceedings of the Nato Conference on Manpower Research in the Defence Context*, London, 14–18 August 1967a. Reprinted as Chapter 23 in this volume.

F. M. Fisher, Reenlistments in the US Navy: A Cost-Effectiveness Study. *American Economic Review: Papers and Proceedings*, vol. LVII (1967b), pp. 32–38.

F. M. Fisher, The Existence of Aggregate Production Functions. *Econometrica* 37 (1969), pp. 553–77. Reprinted as Chapter 1 in Fisher (1992–93).

F. M. Fisher, *Aggregation: Aggregate Production Functions and Related Topics*. London: Harvester–Wheatsheaf; Cambridge, MA: MIT Press, 1992–93.

F. M. Fisher & A. S. Morton, The Costs and Effectiveness of Reenlistment Incentives in the Navy. *Operations Research*, vol. 15 (1967), pp. 373–87.

J. C. Miller (ed.), *Why the Draft? The Case for a Volunteer Army*. Baltimore: Penguin Books, 1968.

A. S. Morton, Predicting the Impact of Policy Changes from Surveys. Paper read at the American Meeting of the Institute for Management Sciences, San Francisco, February 1965.

A. S. Morton, F. M. Fisher & D. M. Nitzberg, *Cost/Effectiveness of Reenlistment Incentives* (Institute of Naval Studies, Cambridge Mass., 1966, for official use only).

W. Y. Oi, The Economic Cost of the Draft. *American Economic Review: Papers and Proceedings*, vol. LVII (1967), pp 39–62.

CHAPTER 23

Aspects of Cost-Benefit Analysis in Defence Manpower Planning (1969)

1.   Introduction

Cost-benefit (or cost-effectiveness) analysis has become in recent years a rapidly developing and highly fashionable tool in defence and other governmental operations.[1] This is as it should be. Such analysis can be an invaluable aid to systematic and rational decision making in complex situations. Yet the proper application of cost-benefit analysis requires more than just the use of the appropriate words. Complicated questions are likely to require sophisticated analysis, and proper use of the techniques of cost-benefit analysis requires detailed attention to the very hard problems that arise in particular cases. It may be all too easy to pass over such problems with a relatively perfunctory treatment, believing that one cost-benefit analysis is much the same as another.[2]

In the present paper, I shall discuss some of the hard problems that arise in cost-benefit analysis, particularly in defence manpower planning. Some of these problems have no easy solution in practice, and the analyst may have to get along with approximate or makeshift solutions. All these problems, however, must be faced as matters for conscious decision if a proper analysis with valid and useful answers is to be performed. While it may turn out in particular cases that some problems can be set aside, this cannot be assumed *ab initio* and careful attention rather than unconscious choice must be exercised.

The problems that I shall discuss do not form an exhaustive list of those that arise, nor can I give entirely satisfactory solutions to all of

This paper was begun during my tenure of a Ford Foundation Faculty Research Fellowship in Economics, while visiting the Hebrew University, Jerusalem. I am indebted to Anton S. Morton for discussion of an earlier draft.

[1] For a recent survey of the field, see Prest and Turvey (1965).

[2] While engaged in the computer runs of the quite difficult nonlinear programming problem involved in Morton, Fisher, and Nitzberg (1966), our programmer, C. R. Berndtson, encountered another programmer from a defence establishment organization. On being told that Berndtson was running a cost-effectiveness analysis program, the second programmer said that he was too and suggested that it was probably the same program. Cost-benefit analysis is not and probably never will be at that stage of development.

them. Indeed, in some cases I can do little more than call attention to the need for further analysis.

Many of the matters here discussed were suggested to me by my work as a consultant on a cost-effectiveness study of re-enlistment incentives in the United States Navy performed at the Institute of Naval Studies (INS) of the Center for Naval Analyses. This study is reported elsewhere[3] and is discussed in other papers presented to the present conference. I shall occasionally draw upon it for good and also bad examples of treatment of the problems discussed.

2.   Cost-Benefit Analysis: An Overview

In this section and the next, we begin with a general outline of a cost-benefit analysis that will provide a background for the more specific discussion to follow. Several alternative policies involving the recruitment, training, and assignment of personnel are to be considered. Each of these policies involves expenditures on different items, typically spread out over several different time periods. Also, over several different time periods, each of these policies results in a pattern of effects, frequently quite complex, affecting several different dimensions of defence capability.

For example, different patterns of recruitment and training over time involve different patterns of expenditure on pay, training expenditures, fringe benefits, and capital equipment. They will result in different time patterns of size of forces, length of service distributions, amount of training in and assignment to various tasks, and so forth.

The problem of cost-benefit analysis is to decide on a function that will reduce these variegated effects to a single criterion and then to choose the policy that is best according to that criterion. In principle, this is accomplished in the following way.

First, certain of the results of any program may relate to variables whose values are in some way constrained, in the sense that no program, however desirable on other criteria, will be considered at all if it does not satisfy such constraints. Thus programs requiring the sudden induction of abnormally large numbers of men may be simply ruled out. In a somewhat more complex circumstance, it may be required that the number of men on sea duty not exceed the number of berths and that the skill distribution of men on such duty be such as to allow the assignment of men with an appropriate mix of skills to each ship. Indeed, it

---

[3] The full study is given in Morton, Fisher, and Nitzberg (1966). The model and methodological results are given in Fisher and Morton (1967b) and substantive findings presented in Fisher and Morton (1967a). See also Chapter 22.

may be specified what the number of men in each skill category is to be in a particular year and the program sought that most efficiently achieves this goal.

It is evident that the choice of such constraints can intimately affect the result of the whole analysis. Further, the nature of such choices is not generally so obvious as may appear. For example, is it really the number of men in each skill category that one wants to fix, or is it not rather what those men can achieve in terms of their work? Questions like these are not nearly so innocent as they may seem, and I shall have a good deal to say about this later on.

For the present, however, assume that the constraints have been chosen, wisely or not. The analysis now conventionally proceeds by combining the expenditure effects of any program into a single measure called "costs" and the non-expenditure effects into a single measure called "benefits."

In principle, the problem of how to combine different expenditure items into a single one has a more-or-less well-defined and well-known solution. Expenditure items are all in money terms and can apparently be combined in the obvious way. Indeed, the only difficulty typically arising stems from the fact that expenditures at different points in time are *not* in fact in the same money terms. An expenditure now and an expenditure equal in nominal amount ten years hence are not the same thing. This difficulty is overcome by the use of discounted present value of expenditures as the cost measure. Clearly, this raises the question of what discount rate should be used for discounting; this is by no means a trivial matter, although it is fairly clear what range of alternatives is involved.

The problem of the choice of a discount rate, moreover, may not be the only one above an accounting level involved in cost calculation. Just as expenditures at different times are not immediately comparable, so expenditures at different places are not. To take the simplest example, a program that involves a given expenditure abroad may be in fact more costly than one that involves the same expenditure at home if one's country has balance-of-payments difficulties and foreign exchange is in short supply. Of course, this sort of problem can be handled by constraining the amount of foreign exchange that may be used; alternatively, effects on the balance of payments may be treated as just another benefit (positive or negative), but the latter device renames rather than solves the problem of comparing foreign and domestic expenditures.

If the problem of combining expenditures into a single cost measure has its difficult aspects, however, the problem of combining non-monetary effects of policies into a single measure of benefits is the

central and most difficult problem of cost-benefit analysis. I shall return
to this problem below.

Now, it must be recognized that the division of policy effects into monetary effects (costs) and non-monetary effects (benefits) is an arbitrary
one. Why should a deleterious non-monetary effect be counted as a
negative benefit rather than as a positive cost? Similarly, if a program by
expenditure in one time period reduces expenditure later on, there is no
reason why that later saving should not be counted as an increase in
benefits rather than as a decrease in costs. Since the decision as to what
is a cost and what a benefit is thus an arbitrary one, we may immediately
state the following conclusion:

Whatever decision procedure is used in combining benefits and costs
into a single criterion to be optimized, the resulting criterion must not
be affected by the arbitrary division of items into costs and benefits. That
division may be a useful matter of convenience in analyzing the problem;
it must not be allowed to affect the results. Another way of saying this
is that the problem of combining non-monetary effects into a single
benefit measure is but a part of the problem of combining all effects,
monetary and non-monetary, into a single measure. The larger problem
cannot be ducked.

This simple but important point has strong implications if we now
assume that the problem of combining non-monetary effects into
benefits has been solved and go on to the question of what decision
criterion should be used. There are several possibilities.

3.   What Should Be Maximized?[4]

The first possibility is to take the total costs of the program as fixed, by
higher governmental authority, for example, and, given that fixed cost
level, to maximize the benefit measure so as to buy the most benefit for
the given expenditure. If total cost really is fixed, this is an entirely appropriate thing to do, but are costs really fixed? To decide whether they are,
we have to ask what increase in benefit would be obtained by a slight
relaxation of the cost constraint. This can be discovered fairly readily by
analysis; it is technically known as the *shadow price* of the cost constraint
when benefits are maximized as described.[5] If this shadow price turns
out to be high, as it may, then one must ask whether it is reasonable that

---

[4] For an alternative discussion in the wider defence context of the problems treated in this
section, see Hitch and McKean (1960).

[5] In general, the *shadow price* of a constraint measures the amount by which the objective
to be maximized would increase if the constraint were made a little weaker. It is the price
paid in terms of the objective for having the constraint as strong as it is.

costs will really remain fixed if whoever fixes them is presented with the fact that a slight increase in costs will result in a large increase in benefits. Here is one of many places in which the policy-maker and the analyst can usefully interact. How much benefit can be bought for an increase in costs can be found by the analyst. Whether the extra benefit makes the extra cost worth incurring is a problem for the policy-maker. It is, of course, part of the same problem just mentioned, namely, the decision as to how monetary and non-monetary effects are to be combined. By breaking up the larger problem as described, the cost-benefit analyst can lay out the alternatives that are open here, even if such a laying-out does not itself determine what alternative to take. Provided that the analyst does not forget to consider the question of the extra benefits resulting from a change in the cost constraint, the method of maximizing benefit for given cost can be a very useful one.

Similar remarks apply even more forcefully to the second possible decision criterion that stands the first one on its head. This is the fixing of the benefit measure at a pre-assigned level and the minimization of costs, so as to purchase the given benefit level most cheaply.[6] The difficulty here is that whereas it is reasonable to suppose that total costs can be given outside the problem, it is most unlikely that the level of a sophisticated benefit measure will be so given. We shall see that there are good ways of solving this, however, and this alternative is the one that we shall recommend in a somewhat more complex version. In any case, here again it is a matter of considerable importance to consider the shadow price of the constraint – here the cost saving that would be obtained if the constrained level of benefits were changed. We shall have more to say about this below.

If neither of these first two alternatives is adopted, however, then the problem of combining costs and benefits into a single measure must be faced head on rather than usefully broken up. What form should such a measure take?

I shall consider two such forms. The first of these is often used but has absolutely nothing to recommend it. This is the use of the ratio of benefit to cost as the criterion to be maximized.

There are two crucial things wrong with this. In the first place, we saw in the preceding section that the division of effects into costs and benefits must not be allowed to affect the results. It is obvious, however, that max-

---

[6] It is perhaps worth reminding the reader that these two approaches lead to the same result in the following sense. Suppose that costs are first fixed and benefits maximized. Take the maximized level of benefits and fix it and then minimize costs. The optimal policy in both cases will be the same, and the minimized level of costs will be the same as the level that was fixed in the first place.

imizing a benefit-cost ratio does not meet this fundamental criterion. A policy that maximizes that ratio on a given division of effects into benefits and costs will in general not maximize it if some costs are treated as negative benefits and items moved from the denominator to the numerator and vice versa.[7]

This would be enough by itself to completely eliminate the benefit-cost ratio as a sensible decision criterion, but there are other, perhaps more subtle, reasons as well.

Even if one succeeds in combining all the dimensions of benefits into a single measure, that measure is almost certain to have only ordinal rather than cardinal properties. In other words, while meaning can be attached to the statement that in one situation benefit is higher than in another, no meaning can be given to statements as to how much higher. There is no natural unit for measuring increases in benefits. Two equivalent ways of expressing this are as follows: first, the most that can be done in combining different benefits into a single measure is to determine the marginal trade-offs between different benefits, that is, the amount by which a particular item would have to increase to just offset a small deterioration in another item. Second, any benefit measure that accurately reflects those trade-offs is as good as any other; it follows that if we have any measure of benefit that is adequate in this regard, any other measure derived from the given one by a monotonic transformation will do as well. Thus, all the information in a particular benefit measure will be preserved if we replace that measure by its square, or its logarithm, and so forth. This is just another way of saying that we can determine when benefits go up but not by how much they rise.

If the choice of a particular benefit measure is arbitrary to this degree, as in the case of the division between benefits and costs, we must be careful not to have a decision criterion that is affected by the arbitrary choice. In the present instance, this means that whether or not a particular decision is optimal must not depend on the particular choice of a benefit measure that we happen to use. Rather, such optimality must be preserved if that benefit measure is replaced by any monotonic transformation of itself, i.e., by any other benefit measure that also correctly reflects trade-offs among different benefit items.

Since if we maximize a given benefit measure, we also maximize its logarithm, its square, and so forth, it is easy to see that the invariance property just set forth is present if we choose to set costs and maximize

[7] There can be an exception to this if costs, treated as negative benefits, are combined with other benefits in the numerator in a nonlinear way; in this case, however, the crucial combination of costs and benefits is the one in the numerator and the numerator might as well be defined to include all costs and then maximized, eliminating the ratio form.

benefits. Similarly, since if we fix the level of a benefit measure, we also fix the level of its logarithm, its square, and so forth, it is easy to see that the invariance property is present if we fix benefits and minimize costs. However, a policy that maximizes a benefit-cost ratio with a given choice of benefit measure will not in general maximize such a ratio if the given benefit measure in the numerator is replaced by its square, its logarithm, and so forth. Thus the benefit-cost ratio criterion fails on this point also.

Finally, even aside from the points just made, the use of a benefit-cost ratio ignores problems of scale. There is no guarantee that the policy that maximizes such a ratio does not do so at an unreasonably small or unreasonably large level of benefits and costs, requiring, for example, the induction of very small or very large numbers of men. While this can be guarded against in the constraints, the point remains that there is really no particular reason why one should want to maximize a benefit-cost ratio except in those cases in which such maximization happens to coincide with maximizing benefit at given cost or minimizing cost at given benefit. Thus, even aside from the crucial difficulties already raised, the basic rationale for maximizing a benefit-cost ratio is extremely weak.[8]

One final alternative remains to be considered. This is the maximization of the difference between benefits and costs. If all benefits were monetary or if they could be reduced to monetary equivalents by consideration of monetary versus non-monetary trade-offs, this difference would clearly be the natural thing to maximize.[9] In the present context, however, this is not a particularly useful conclusion. The comparison of monetary and non-monetary effects of a program is precisely the problem with which we are concerned. If one can already solve that problem, then costs can and should enter as a subtraction from benefits, but this is no help in solving the central problem of comparison itself.

We conclude then that reliance on simple formulae will not lead to appropriate results, this being true in particular of benefit-cost ratios. The problem of comparing monetary and non-monetary effects of programs must be faced in a reasonably explicit form. As outlined above, this can

[8] Some of the problems in this paragraph can be avoided by the use of a *per man* (or per man-year) benefit-cost ratio. Doing this, however, requires the assumption (untrue in general) that the ratio is invariant to the number of men involved (constant returns to scale, even though items such as capital equipment are constant). In any case, there remains the question even on the per man level, as to why one should *want* to maximize the ratio of benefits to costs.

[9] The difference between benefits and cost is invariant to the treatment of costs as such or as negative benefits. It is not invariant to monotonic transformations of the benefit measure, but such monotonic transformations also destroy the reduction of non-monetary benefits to a monetary equivalent, hence are ruled out by the phrasing in the text.

be usefully done by fixing costs and maximizing benefits or by fixing benefits and minimizing costs. We shall see below that the latter method, in a rather more general form, is quite flexible and can be used to advantage to help solve the problem of benefit measure itself.

This completes our general outline of cost-benefit analysis; we now turn to a more detailed discussion of the problems involved therein.

4.   Constraints: Real or Imaginary?

We saw above that cost-benefit analysis generally takes the form of a constrained optimization problem. The constraints involved can be relatively simple or quite complicated.

4.1.   Environmental Constraints

Some of these constraints are not really matters of policy choice at all; rather, they reflect the environment within which policy making must operate. Thus, for example, a real constraint in the INS study was the number of men estimated to reenlist for a given set of incentives. This is a parameter, different in value for each incentive package, and reflects underlying social and economic motivations of enlisted personnel. Policy can change the reenlistment rate by changing the incentives offered, but, at least within the range of policies considered in the study, policy cannot change the percentage of men who will reenlist for a given set of incentives.

This sort of constraint, of course, is frequently not stated formally as a constraint but, as in the example, enters by determining the parameters and forms of the functions involved in the problem. Clearly, the estimation of such parameter values is an essential and often difficult task in the course of a cost-benefit analysis. I shall not here dwell on the great importance of securing good reliable data and of the use of modern methods of statistical inference in the performance of that task.

4.2.   Official Personnel Requirements: What Price?

There is another sort of constraint that is quite different and is a matter for policy choice. Indeed, such constraints are self-imposed by the policymaker or the analyst and require far more conscious consideration than they sometimes get.

Official personnel requirements are frequently stated in terms of the number of men with particular skills or experience that it is required to have at particular moments in time. On the simplest level, this may be just the total number of men required; more generally it is a list of numbers of men in each of several classifications. Cost-benefit analysis is then required to find the policy that achieves such goals most efficiently, i.e., that minimizes the cost of achieving them.

There is nothing wrong with this if such personnel requirements can be taken at face value as immutable, but can this really be done? This question can be approached in two ways.

The first such way is to consider directly the consequences of imposing such a constraint. In principle, such imposition means that no amount of savings in costs, no matter how large, will compensate for the slightest deviation from the stated personnel requirements, no matter how small. The personnel requirements, in the precise form stated, become a *sine qua non* of policy making; they must be satisfied at any cost. This is a position that can, of course, be consistently held; it is not a very plausible position, however. Nevertheless, it is directly implied by the imposition of personnel requirements in their usual form as constraints on the analysis.

On the other hand, it may be objected that principle is all very well, but practice is likely to prove different. It is one thing to say that the imposition of rigid constraints involves being willing to pay any finite price rather than weaken such constraints at all; it is quite another to say that the price *actually* paid will in fact be indefinitely large. This is quite true. As in the case of fixing benefits and minimizing costs already briefly discussed in the preceding section, it is quite easy for the analyst to find the actual price involved. As in that case, the price involved is technically known as the shadow price of the constraint,[10] and is a useful thing to find. Naturally, that shadow price may turn out to be low. Indeed, if the constraint is not a binding one (i.e., if it is automatically satisfied when the optimization is carried out without it), the shadow price associated with it is zero, indicating that nothing is to be gained by weakening the constraint a little. More often, however, rigid personnel requirements are likely to have a very high shadow price. Whether that price is worth paying is a matter for conscious decision.

To put this slightly differently, the shadow price of a personnel constraint gives the actual trade-off between the personnel effects of the optimal program and the monetary effects. It gives the cost saving that will be achieved if the personnel requirements are relaxed just a little. The trade-off between these two effects from the viewpoint of the policy

[10] See Hitch and McKean (1960). If constraints have more than one dimension (e.g., personnel requirements in different categories specified), there will, of course, be more than one shadow price. This makes no essential difference to the exposition in the text.

maker is another matter, however. This is the penalty (in monetary terms) that will be incurred, from his point of view, for falling short of the stated personnel requirements by just a little bit. Examination of the shadow price can aid in determining this penalty but is not of course a substitute for it. Imposing a rigid personnel constraint implies that the penalty is infinite.

Moreover, such an imposition implies that the overfulfillment of a personnel requirement is worth nothing in itself, that the over-achieving of a minimum goal is not worth any additional expenditure, no matter how small. This is a more plausible position than the infinite penalty exacted for falling short of such a goal, but it too may often be unrealistic. Again, the policy maker must decide what the trade-offs between costs and personnel effects are for him. It is wrong to suppose that the simple statement of personnel requirements in rigid form avoids making a decision as to such trade-offs. Such a procedure merely makes that decision in a particularly extreme and implausible manner.

4.3. *Substitution Possibilities*

A second way of approaching the problem is to consider trade-offs among different personnel requirements and among personnel and non-personnel effects of a program instead of simply between personnel and costs. Typically, personnel requirements are not unidimensional; rather, requirements are stated in terms of the number of men required in each of several categories. Such categorization may be in terms of skill specialization or experience or other variables.

It is not hard to see that imposing such multi-dimensional personnel requirements as constraints that must be satisfied by any program not only imposes a drastic assumption as to the trade-off between personnel and costs but also imposes such an assumption as to the possibility of substitution among men in different categories. If such requirements *must* be met (and thus, quite literally, met at all costs), then no addition of extra men in one category, however large, can compensate for falling short of the stated requirements in another category by even one man. Insistence on meeting such requirements imposes the assumption that there is no substitution possible among different categories of labour. Further, even in the unidimensional case, it also imposes the assumption that there is no substitution possible between labour of any category and capital equipment.

Are such assumptions valid? The answer is clearly no. Turn first to the simplest case, that of substitution between men and capital. Here it is easy to multiply examples of such substitution. Many, if not all, tasks that can be performed by a military establishment with a large personnel complement can also be performed by an establishment with fewer personnel and more machines. The substitution of machines for men naturally has its limits and it may not be worth performing, but this is a matter for the analysis to determine. It is simply not true that such substitution possibilities are generally absent as a matter of principle.

On the other hand, rightly or wrongly, the analyst may decide that the available capital equipment must be taken as given and the analysis performed within that constraint. This may come about either because the constraint is a real one or, more likely, because there is a limit to the size of problem that can be handled at one time. In this case, the analyst will ignore labour-capital substitution and hope that the consequences are not too severe.

Even when this is so, however, the analyst cannot afford to ignore substitution possibilities among different types of labour. This is all too easy to do, for such substitution many be more subtle than is generally realized.

In the first place, to assert that substitution among labour types is possible is not to assert that it must be on a man-for-man basis. What is at issue here is whether the loss of one man in a given category can be compensated for by the addition of *any* number of men in another category, not whether it can be so compensated by the addition of one such man. Indeed, if such substitution is possible, it is likely not even to be at a constant rate, with a fixed number of men of one type being worth a fixed number of men of another type, regardless of the total number of men of those and other types already employed. One-for-one substitution would be even more special than this. Rather the substitution possibilities are likely to depend on the number of men in each category to begin with and on the ways in which tasks can be reorganized to use men in different categories most efficiently.

Thus, let us consider what is involved in substituting raw recruits for experienced personnel. It is wrong to think that this must necessarily be a direct substitution with, say, two raw recruits taking over the tasks of one experienced man. In general, such direct substitution will not be possible if the effectiveness of the establishment is to remain unchanged. If such direct substitution were the only way in which substitution among labour categories could take place, then stating personnel requirements as constraints would be unobjectionable.

Effectiveness, however, is a matter of what the personnel of an establishment can do, rather than of who they are, and substitution takes place by reorganizing the tasks performed by the personnel so that the whole establishment runs most effectively. This may result in rather indirect substitution.

Consider first the loss of an experienced man in a relatively small part of the military establishment, a given ship or a given installation, for example. Suppose, first, that the installation is not so small that the man lost is the only man of his experience working on it. What happens if such a man is removed is, naturally, not the reassignment of his tasks to raw recruits. Rather the entire operating force of the installation is to a greater or lesser extent reorganized. If the experienced man was acting in a supervisory capacity, other supervisors are worked a bit harder, stretched a bit thinner to cover for his loss. This results in a loss of effectiveness as supervision becomes less close and less efficient, and as personnel with slightly less experience take over the less demanding tasks of experienced personnel. There is a similar adjustment all the way down the line, with a slight upgrading of the personnel assigned to the simpler tasks ordinarily assigned to those of more experience. Finally, raw recruits are required to take over or help with tasks ordinarily reserved for men with a very small amount of training. The loss of efficiency resulting from the loss of an experienced man is transmitted by redefining tasks and by less good supervision into a loss of efficiency in working parties. This is then compensated for by increasing the number of men available in such working parties.

To put it another way, if we agree that some number (perhaps more than one) of men with slightly less experience can compensate for the loss of a fully experienced man, then the loss of an experienced man can be translated into the loss of such a number of almost experienced men. If this can be done in general, then we can ultimately translate the loss of an experienced man into a loss of some number (perhaps quite large) of raw recruits and compensate for that loss directly. Direct substitution of raw recruits for experienced personnel need not be involved.

Note, further, that the numbers of men involved in the trade-offs described are likely to depend on the situation. If experienced personnel are very scarce, it may be impossible to compensate for the loss of even one by adding a reasonable number of relatively inexperienced men. If experienced men are relatively plentiful, then they may already be performing tasks that could just as well be performed by men with less experience, and substitution may be very easy. In any case, it is wrong to impose the assumption in advance that substitution is impossible. Even if experienced men are believed to be relatively scarce, a proper cost-benefit analysis will often involve recruitment and training programs changing such scarcities and thus changing the substitution possibilities. Such possibilities must not be implicitly assumed absent to begin with, particularly since scarcity of one or more types of personnel can be a subtler and more relative matter than may at first appear.[11]

Further, substitution between personnel types can be accomplished in ways even more indirect than those just exemplified. We restricted ourselves above to the discussion of personnel substitution in a relatively small unit. Substitution in the entire military establishment being analyzed is likely to take place in a wider variety of ways than in a small installation. For one thing, there is a wider latitude in the reassignment of personnel. When an experienced man is lost from one installation, he can be replaced by an experienced man from another; the other being chosen as one where experienced men are relatively more plentiful in order to minimize the effects of the loss. Further, a slight loss in efficiency in a given unit can often be compensated for by a slight redefining of the missions of other units to cover the loss and an increase in personnel somewhere else in the establishment. These effects may be difficult to quantify, but they must not be assumed to be absent. Again, the imposition of official personnel requirements as constraints that must be satisfied rules out any substitution possibilities whatsoever.

4.4. Effectiveness Constraints

How should such substitution possibilities be handled then? How should official personnel requirements, which, after all, must reflect something of importance in terms of needs, be incorporated into a cost-benefit analysis in manpower planning?

The answers lie in a consideration of what official personnel requirements are presumably designed to represent, and here we enter the area of benefit measurement. Those requirements give the number of men in each category that, in the judgment of those producing the requirements, will be just sufficient to enable the military establishment to fulfill its mission. On the other hand, we have just seen that there are likely to be substitution possibilities among different personnel categories. It follows that the configuration of personnel given in official requirements is not the only one that will just enable the establishment to fulfill its mission (although, for various reasons, it may be the configuration that most naturally occurs to those producing the requirements). Surely, however, what is required is that the establishment be able to perform its mission, not that it be able to perform it in a particular way. The constraint that

---

[11] The results of the INS study show this very strongly. What appeared before analysis to be a shortage turned out to be an oversupply. See Morton, Fisher, and Nitzberg (1966), Fisher and Morton (1967a), and Chapter 22.

must be imposed on the cost-benefit analysis, therefore, is that of mission performance – of a given level of effectiveness – rather than that of satisfying official personnel requirements.

To impose such a general effectiveness constraint, however, seems at first glance to be practically impossible. Effectiveness has many dimensions, some readily quantifiable and some more elusive, and direct measurement of effectiveness is at best extraordinarily difficult. Fortunately, there is no need to measure effectiveness directly or even to decide in principle how it should be measured.

We have just seen that official personnel requirements provide one personnel configuration at which the requisite effectiveness level is achieved. To impose that level as a minimum constraint on our analysis, we need not worry about what that level is or how to measure it; we need only concern ourselves with the alternative ways in which it can be achieved. In other words, we only need to know the set of personnel configurations that will result in the same effectiveness as will the meeting of official personnel requirements (in technical parlance, the indifference surface passing through the point given by such requirements). This is, of course, not a particularly easy thing to find directly, but we can gain much information about it by starting with official requirements and considering substitution possibilities in a more than superficial fashion.

In other words, beginning with the personnel configuration given in official requirements, consider what trade-offs can be made among personnel in different categories while leaving effectiveness unchanged. Note that it is not necessary to say what the level of effectiveness objectively *is* in order to do this, merely to say if it goes up or down. Such effectiveness-preserving trade-offs obviously lead to alternative configurations just as good as official personnel requirements in terms of effectiveness.

4.5.   Finding the Trade-offs

How can such trade-offs be found? There are ways, but there is no disguising that much more work needs to be done here.

In principle, the trade-offs required ought to be supplied by the policy maker for whom the cost-benefit analysis is being performed. It is his notions of effectiveness that must be satisfied. Unfortunately, one suspects that high-level decision makers are inclined to be a bit vague in replying to direct questions as to their marginal rates of substitution among various personnel categories. Nevertheless, it is seriously to be hoped that those who rely on personnel requirements, or at least those who produce them, will give increasing thought to specifying what alternative personnel configurations will be equally satisfactory. The present situation implies that they believe effectiveness cannot be maintained in the presence of any deviation, no matter how small, from such requirements, and that such deviations must be avoided at any price. This is simply unrealistic.

If it is unlikely that the requisite trade-offs can be specified at a high policy-making level, the analyst must investigate such trade-offs much closer to the operational level itself. In the INS study, this was done by extensive interviewing of experienced officers in charge of relatively narrowly defined small units. These officers were asked directly for the number of men in one category that would just substitute for the loss of a single man in another category, leaving effectiveness unchanged (or for the number of men in one category they would just be willing to give up to get an additional man in another category). They were encouraged to think through the sort of task rearrangement required for efficient substitution. The responses were then adjusted in various ways (involving the size of the on-board complements with which the respondents worked) to estimate the indifference surface required for the analysis.

It cannot be claimed that this is an entirely satisfactory way to proceed. This is so for at least three reasons.

First, it is relatively clear from the experience of the INS interviews that it is not easy to get officers in such situations to give thoughtful responses really reflecting the substitution possibilities open to them. Possibly, this difficulty could be at least partially overcome by refined interviewing techniques.

Second, what one wants to elicit from such interviews frequently is the marginal trade-off involved – the rate at which substitution can take place if changes are relatively very small. This is so both for technical reasons involved in the estimation of the indifference surface from the responses and, more importantly, because small changes are more likely to be easy for the respondent to consider in an accurate manner. Yet at the organizational level at which the interviews had to be conducted, the loss of a single man in a particular category sometimes meant a loss of one hundred percent and not at all a marginal loss. This can be overcome, in principle, by considering the loss of a small fraction of a man's time, but this may be hard for the respondent to do in practice.

Finally, as already discussed, substitution possibilities in a small installation are likely to be rather more restricted than in the entire military establishment for which the analysis is to be performed. Even if respondents in small installations give entirely accurate pictures of the substitution possibilities from their point of view, those pictures need not reflect the substitution possibilities in which we are basically interested.[12] This problem is one aspect of the general difficulty of performing necessarily aggregative analyses, to which we shall return in a later section. It is, of course, an excellent reason to call for more serious interplay between the analyst and the relatively high-level manpower decision makers who wish to use the results of the analysis.

Such interplay can be facilitated by the analyst, as can the examination of marginal trade-offs in general, no matter whose the trade-offs to be examined, by once more considering the shadow prices of constraints. If costs are minimized subject to official personnel requirements in their original form, then, as we have seen, one can obtain as a byproduct the cost saving that would occur if those requirements were slightly relaxed, or, alternatively, the cost increase that would have to be paid if those requirements were slightly tightened. Such a shadow price can in fact be obtained for each category of personnel in the requirements, so that we know the price in terms of costs of gaining or losing a man in each such category. It is then easy to see that the ratios of such prices net out the monetary effect and give the price of a man in category A in terms of men in category B. That is, such ratios give the number of men in category B that could be added to the official requirements for that category at no increase in costs, provided that requirements in category A are reduced by one man. This is the marginal trade-off between the two categories in terms of keeping cost constant. It serves as a useful benchmark from which to examine marginal trade-offs that keep *effectiveness* constant; one should ask whether such trades would aid or harm effectiveness. As with direct trade-offs between men and costs, judicious use of such information can aid in eliciting the true preferences of policymakers.[13] As with the direct cost-personnel relationship, it must not simply be assumed that trade-offs are impossible. The space I have devoted to this issue perhaps underrates its importance, considering the present state of the art.

4.6.   The Price of Effectiveness Constraints

Having successfully transformed official personnel requirements into an effectiveness indifference surface, an appropriate way to proceed is to insist that any policy have at least the effectiveness represented by that surface (and by official requirements). This substitutes for strictly stated

---

[12] This difficulty can be overcome if certain assumptions are satisfied concerning the way in which men are assigned to installations, but the assumptions involved can be pretty strong. This is discussed in Section 6 below.

[13] On the general use of shadow prices in this way, see Dorfman (1965).

and detailed personnel constraints a more reasonable effectiveness constraint. Subject to such an effectiveness constraint, cost is to be minimized.

There are, however, some problems involved in doing this. These problems turn out to be the same on a new level as those that led us to reject the imposition of detailed personnel requirements as constraints in the first place. Fortunately, they are not nearly so serious in the new context.

The principal such problem is that which arises with the imposition of any constraint. If an effectiveness constraint is imposed, the implied position is that no cost saving, however great, can compensate for any reduction in effectiveness below the constrained level, however small that reduction may be. Similarly, no credit is given for achieving an effectiveness level above that specified in the constraint. It may thus be more reasonable to specify the trade-off between effectiveness and cost, rather than specifying an effectiveness level.

There are three reasons for believing that this is not nearly so serious a problem as is the parallel one in the case of the imposition of a personnel requirements constraint.

In the first place, it may very well be that an effectiveness constraint correctly reflects the situation facing the military establishment. A certain state of readiness or effectiveness is to be achieved; this cannot be lowered without grave risk to national security, and there is no gain (or at least not much) from improving on it. In the strictest form, this is perhaps only approximately realistic, but it is far more realistic if such minimum goals are stated *in terms of what the establishment must be capable of doing* rather than in terms of the sorts of men it must employ.

Second, while, in principle, the imposition of any constraint implies that no cost saving will be worth any weakening of that constraint, the cost saving that will in fact be achieved by a slight weakening of a generally formulated effectiveness constraint, with substitution possibilities properly included, may not be at all great. Certainly, it is not hard to show that the cost saving involved in weakening an effectiveness constraint derived, as described, from personnel requirements is lower than the cost saving involved in a parallel weakening of those requirements themselves when they are directly imposed as constraints. Much of the cost savings involved are already taken up in the substitution possibilities. Nevertheless, the cost savings that would occur may be worth having, and this question ought not to be ignored.

Finally, and perhaps most importantly, the solution to the optimization problem of the cost-benefit analysis is far less likely to be affected by small adjustments in the level of the constraint if constraints are stated in the relatively free way involved in taking account of substitution possibilities rather than in the very rigid way involved in the imposition of official personnel requirements as direct constraints. In other words, the nature of the optimal policy is relatively more likely to be insensitive to the precise level of an effectiveness constraint than to the precise level of official personnel requirements stated directly as constraints.

The second problem involved in the use of effectiveness constraints is essentially that of substitution possibilities in a new form. It may not be possible to impose only a single effectiveness constraint, attractive though such imposition may be. The fact that a military establishment is made up of many different parts may mean that it is natural to impose constraints ensuring the achievement of minimum effectiveness levels *in each part*. If this is done, we are assuming no substitution among different parts of the establishment; that is, we assume that a reduction in the effectiveness of one part of the establishment cannot be compensated by an increase in the effectiveness of another part. This is quite possibly a valid assumption; it is far more likely to be valid than the similar assumption of no substitution among personnel of different types. Nevertheless, it deserves examination and this may not be easy.

A similar problem arises concerning effectiveness at different points in time. We shall show below that manpower planning is inevitably dynamic, that effectiveness cannot be considered at only a single time point, but that planning must take place for several years at once. As we shall see, the natural thing to do, therefore, is to insist on a minimum effectiveness level in each of those years.[14] To do this, however, is to assume that no substitution between years is possible, that no reduction in effectiveness in one year, however small, can be compensated for by an increase in effectiveness in a different year, however large. Again, this may be an entirely appropriate assumption, but it should be examined.

5.   Costs and Benefits over Time

5.1.   Why Time Effects Are Important

We have just observed that defence manpower planning is an essentially dynamic process. The costs incurred in and the benefits resulting from a particular program do not take place at a single point in time; rather they are spread out over perhaps fairly long intervals.

---

[14] This was done in the INS study. See Morton, Fisher, and Nitzberg (1966), Fisher and Morton (1967b), and Chapter 22.

There are several reasons for this. In the first place, men inducted into the military typically undergo a period of training during which they acquire the skills that they need in the service. Such training continues on the job, even after the men begin to perform useful functions. This has two effects, however. First, there are direct costs of training – instructor salaries, provision of school and other training facilities, support of the trainees during the training period, and so forth. If training takes more than a negligible period, these costs are spread out over time and their level need not be constant. Second, a man in training is not the equivalent of a fully-trained man in terms of the benefits to be derived from his service. The extent to which his services approach those of a fully-trained man affects benefits at more than one point in time. Thus the existence of a non-negligible training period leads to consideration of costs and benefits at more than a single instant.

There is, however, a much more important reason than this for considering a whole time pattern of benefits and costs. Consider an effectiveness target stated for a particular year, say 1972. As we have seen, that target is probably best stated in terms not simply those of official personnel requirements, but this does not matter for the present argument. The burden of the preceding paragraph can be taken to be as follows. Since achievement of such a target depends, in part, on the skills possessed by the personnel in the service in 1972, and since those skills must be acquired through training, costs and also benefits associated with the achievement of the 1972 goal must begin before 1972.

A stronger point, however, is the following one. Since some, at least, of the men involved in meeting the 1972 target will remain in the service after that year, and since skills acquired in the course of training do not become obsolete overnight, the funds expended on training men to meet the 1972 target will result in benefits in later years as well. Another way of saying this is that the ease with which targets later than 1972 can be met is in part dependent on the carry-over of skilled personnel from 1972. Training provides an investment in human capital, the return on which, like that on any investment, is typically received over the lifetime of the equipment involved rather than in a single year. Naturally, if no skills, training, or experience were involved, then men already in the service would have no advantage over raw recruits. If that were the case, there would be no real need to consider costs and benefits over more than a single year. One of the things that makes defence manpower planning interesting and difficult, however, is precisely that such effects cannot be ignored.

Of course, it may just turn out that planning for a single year at a time leads to an optimal course of action. Unfortunately, this cannot be assumed in advance. Perhaps an example simplified from one of the results of the INS study will make this clear.

In that study, there is some substitution between relatively experienced and relatively inexperienced men. A given effectiveness goal can be achieved with a relatively large, relatively inexperienced Navy or a relatively small, relatively experienced one. If one considers meeting just the next year's goal, the only way in which this can be done (for purposes of this example) is by varying the level of inductions, since the number of experienced personnel is a legacy from past decisions. Deciding on the level of induction for next year, however, influences or (given other factors) determines the number of experienced men who will be available to the Navy in the year after next. It thus affects the number of men who will have to be inducted in that following year in order to meet that year's goals. Obviously, it may sometimes be cheaper to induct more men next year than are needed for next year's goals in order to produce trained men for later years.

As it turns out in the INS study, this is false as regards the analysis of the Navy as a whole. Considering the entire enlisted Navy, it just so happens that there is enough substitution between relatively experienced and relatively inexperienced men and enough loss of experienced men through failure to reenlist that just meeting each year's goal as it occurs is in fact the optimal policy.

On the other hand, this result is clearly not one that can be assumed beforehand. To drive this home, consider one result of the INS analysis of electronics maintenance and repair personnel. Here relatively untrained men are very bad substitutes for relatively trained ones. The result is that a myopic policy of inducting men as needed leads to a situation where goals in later years are very difficult to meet and expenditures on electronics personnel exceed the budget for the entire Navy in those years. When one takes proper account of the carry-over between years, however, one finds that by slightly overachieving goals in some years, the costs of goal achievement in later years are dramatically reduced, and, indeed, the inductions and costs of the true optimal, nonmyopic program are perfectly reasonable.

Clearly, results like these are not accidental. They reflect the fact, as stated, that manpower policies involve investment in human capital and that the costs and benefits of any investment program take place over time and not simply at a single instant. Pretending that planning is but for a single year can, and frequently will, lead to results that are wrong and even ridiculous when considered from a longer-run point of view.

5.2. *Discounting of Costs*

Thus, cost-benefit analysis of manpower planning necessarily involves the combining of costs and benefits occurring at different moments of time. In the case of costs, such combination is relatively straightforward; what is involved is the calculation of the present discounted value of an expenditure stream.

Such discounting of future expenditures, so that future money is considered less valuable than present money, is based on a number of considerations. Important among these, for a private firm, is the fact that in a perfect capital market, maximization of present discounted value can be shown to generate an income stream that in every period provides at least as much income as does any other policy. This occurs because the firm can lend a given amount of money now and receive a larger amount later. Alternatively, the firm can invest the money in its own operations now and reap a larger reward later. In a competitive capital market, the interest rates involved in these two transactions will be equalized at the margin, after allowance for risk.

It is important to realize that the same sort of principle applies to governmental operations. If policies are financed by present taxation, then resources are being taken from the private sector. Those resources, if put to use in that sector, would result in higher output later on; hence, just as for a private firm, the worth to society of a given value of resources now is greater than the worth of the same monetary value of resources later on.

This argument suggests that the appropriate interest rate to use in discounting is the rate of growth of the entire economy. However, this is only one of several possibilities.

Consider, for example, a different reason for discounting. For various reasons, individual consumers have time preference; they do discount future consumption. In deciding how to weight tax dollars now against tax dollars later, society ought to consider that a tax dollar saved now is worth more to individuals than a tax dollar saved later on, because of individuals' own preference for current over future consumption. Thus future money should be discounted relative to present money. What rate should be used in such discounting? A clear possibility is the rate at which individuals discount the future, as represented by the rate at which they are just willing to make risk-free loans. This latter rate, however, is the rate at which the government can borrow funds.

The government borrowing rate is also an attractive rate to use, of course, if one takes a purely accounting point of view and considers the government as an entity separate from the people and one whose operations must take into account the cost of capital to it.

Indeed, this discussion does not nearly exhaust what can be said on the subject of the appropriate discount rate. For example, both the above arguments have considered society's preferences as merely reflecting the preferences and opportunities of its members as expressed in the marketplace. Perhaps society's discounting of the future ought rather to reflect the collective preferences of its members as politically expressed; these two sets of preferences need not be the same, for individuals may well desire that society as a whole give heavier weight to the future of unborn generations than they themselves are willing to do in their individual capacities. If so, market rates of interest are higher than the rates that society should use in discounting expenditures on public projects.

There are many other facets to the problem of appropriate choice of interest rate. Indeed, there is a simply enormous literature on this subject,[15] and I shall not attempt to extend the relatively superficial remarks already given, as I wish to move on to a consideration of other topics. In practice, it seems clear that alternative discount rates should be tried in a sensitivity analysis; if one is not too unlucky, all rates within a plausible range (which may be fairly narrow) may lead to roughly the same results. If not, close attention must be paid to this problem.

5.3.   Comparison of Benefits at Different Points of Time

We come then to what is in some ways a similar and in others a very different problem, the comparison of benefits occurring at different points of time.

At first glance, there seems no reason to consider this a separate problem. Do not the arguments given for the discounting of costs equally apply to benefits? Moreover, is it not sensible to discount both costs and benefits at the same rate? It is easy to see that this would indeed be the case if benefits were strictly monetary or could be reduced to monetary equivalents by consideration of monetary–non-monetary trade-offs. Where this is not feasible, however, the solution is not so easy, and this is almost inevitably the case in problems of defence manpower planning.

Suppose that for each time period, we have constructed a benefit measure; we now wish to combine those measures into a single one cov-

---

[15] Prest and Turvey [(1965), pp. 697–700] give a rather more complete survey than that given here (although still an abbreviated one), as well as references.

ering all time periods. Alternatively (and this is not really any different), suppose that, as described in an earlier section, we have formulated effectiveness goals for each time period; we now wish to combine those goals into a single one by considering possible substitution between the goals of different time periods.

The difficulty in doing this arises for a reason already briefly discussed. Unlike costs, benefits have no natural unit of measurement. A benefit measure or an effectiveness target at a moment in time is constructed by somehow making comparable the different non-monetary effects of a program. This requires only information, potentially available, on trade-offs between different effects. Having formed such a measure, however, there is nothing specially privileged about it, in the sense that any other measure reflecting the same trade-offs will do as well.

Thus, for example, suppose that we require that effectiveness, measured in a particular way, reach the level implied by official personnel requirements. We can impose precisely the same substantive constraint by deciding to square the effectiveness measure used and requiring that any program achieve the squared effectiveness level that would be achieved by official personnel requirements. Once we have done this, however, there is no way to tell which is the "true" effectiveness measure. We could have begun with the second one and claimed that the first was derived as the square root of the second. Both measures code all the observable information on trade-offs; both are entirely equivalent. Moreover, it is obvious that the square is only an example. The log, the cube, and indeed any increasing monotonic transformation will also serve. Which of these equivalent effectiveness or benefit measures one uses is purely a matter of convenience; the choice among them is a wholly arbitrary one.

The implication of this is clear, however. If the choice among equivalent representations of a benefit measure is arbitrary, the problem must not be formulated in such a way that the results depend on which measure is chosen. We have already had occasion to consider this in dealing with the benefit-cost ratio as a criterion of optimality.

Now, unfortunately, it is easy to show that if one adopts a particular measure of benefits for each time period and maximizes the present discounted value of such benefits at given costs (or maximizes the present discounted value of benefits less costs), the result will *not* be the same if the benefit measure used is replaced by its square, its log, and so forth. Similarly, if we attempt to compare effectiveness goals in different years by requiring that effectiveness rise by, say, five percent per year, we will not be making a comparison that is independent of the particular choice of one of a whole family of equivalent effectiveness measures. If an effectiveness measure rises by five percent a year, its square will rise by 10.25 percent, its square root by a bit less than 2.5 percent, and its log by no constant percentage at all. Thus the discounting of a particular benefit or effectiveness measure imposes a wholly arbitrary condition on the results of a cost-benefit analysis. Hence such discounting is inadmissible in the kind of problem we are discussing.

How then ought effectiveness in different years to be compared? There are two possibilities, and, I think, only the second is likely to be practical.

The alternative that is in principle preferable but in practice likely to be infeasible is to consider seriously the question of substitution between effectiveness levels in different years. This need not be done directly. One need not ask the meaningless question: "How much additional effectiveness in year A is required to just compensate for the loss of a unit of effectiveness in year B?" It should be apparent that such a question depends crucially on the definition of effectiveness units and is hence inadmissible if that definition is arbitrary. Rather, the question that must be asked concerns the trade-off that might be made between personnel of some type in year A and personnel of the same or different type in year B, leaving effectiveness in both years unchanged. Since what is wanted is a summary measure of effectiveness that reflects the contribution of different men in different years, only such trade-offs need be considered.

Unfortunately, however, while such questions of trade-off between different personnel types in different years can perfectly well be asked in principle, it seems clear that to ask them in practice puts an unreasonable strain on what can legitimately be expected of those answering such questions. Obtaining accurate answers to trade-off questions is, as we have seen, a tricky matter even when the trade-offs involved are fairly directly within the experience of the officers responding; questions of the present sort are likely to be unanswerable in practice.

Fortunately, on the other hand, the answer to interyear comparisons of effectiveness may be very simple in the defence manpower context. As opposed to substitution among personnel categories or between labour and capital, it is entirely plausible to suppose that substitution possibilities between years are extremely limited or altogether nil. Thus, within reasonable limits, the requirement that a country's forces always be at some minimum level of effectiveness implies that no decline from that level in one year can be compensated for by an increase in a different year. Since it is small consolation to a nation overwhelmed by enemy attack that its forces were more than prepared in another year, the assumption of no substitution among years seems a realistic one. If it is realistic, then the problem of obtaining answers to trade-off questions such as those just posed does not have to be solved; still, like all other points of this sort, the matter needs to be given more than cursory attention in performing cost-benefit analyses.

Suppose, then, that we accept the position that substitution between years is impossible. This immediately implies that there exists *no* single benefit or effectiveness measure subsuming all years. Instead, the analysis should proceed by imposing for each year considered an effectiveness constraint derived as already described and minimizing the present discounted value of costs while requiring that any program achieve in every year at least the level of effectiveness prescribed for that year by the constraints. This is the natural extension to many years of the fixing effectiveness – minimizing costs procedure outlined above. It is a flexible and powerful technique and it is far superior to an incautious attempt to summarize benefits through discounting.

5.4. End Effects

Before closing this section on effects over time, it seems appropriate to add a few words concerning so-called end effects. As we have seen, it is necessary to consider costs and benefits over several time periods rather than only for a single moment in time. How does one know where to stop? Put differently, one wants to be careful to avoid terminating the consideration of future periods in such a way as to substantially influence the results.

Fortunately, this is not hard to do in the present context. In a more general context, such end effects arise for two reasons. First, if the problem is set up to maximize a single criterion function (for example, the present discounted value of benefits less costs), end effects tend to arise unless proper provision is made for the way in which the program is to terminate. Thus, for example, in considering investment problems, one cannot forget that the world (and the problem) will not really terminate at the end of the period considered and thus one must make some provision for the amount of capital that will be left over for the next planning period. If this is not done, one can obtain foolish results involving the eating up of capital toward the end of the planning period with no provision for the future.

In the present context, this problem is readily avoided if one adopts the approach outlined above and imposes effectiveness constraints for all periods of the program. By imposing such a constraint for the last period considered, one can easily ensure that the human capital acquired during the life of the program is not simply dissipated for no reason. An effectiveness constraint for the last year of the program here plays precisely the same role as a constraint on the terminal stock of capital in a more conventional context.

Now, the imposition of an effectiveness constraint for the terminal year of the planning period ensures that the manner in which consideration of future years is terminated will not affect the program in an outrageous way. This alone is not enough to avoid end effects, however, for we must also be sure that the very choice of which year is to be the last considered does not substantially affect the results.

This is where discounting of costs comes in again. We do not consider as costs expenditures that arise after the end of the period for which we are planning.[16] Provided that we plan for a fairly long period, however, it will usually turn out that the exact date at which we end is immaterial, because costs for years toward the end of that period are already discounted by so large a factor as to make their contribution to the present discounted value of all costs negligible.[17]

Moreover, such discounting is also likely to make the results relatively insensitive to the exact levels of the effectiveness constraints for periods in the relatively distant future. This is fortunate, since inability to predict the international situation and the effects of technical change on labour-capital and inter-personnel category substitution is likely to make the formulation of constraints for such years a relatively uncertain business.[18]

6.   Aggregate vs. Disaggregate Analysis

I turn now to another topic to which I already have had occasion to refer – the level of aggregation of the analysis. The difficulty here is as follows. On the one hand, the need to have a computationally feasible and analytically reasonably tractable analysis often dictates performing the work

---

[16] We may, however, choose to consider as costs all future expenditures committed by the end of the period by the induction of men then in the service. This was done in the INS study.

[17] This is not guaranteed *a priori*, however. If costs are likely to rise at five percent a year in programs considered, discounting at five percent or less will never make later costs negligible. This can happen if the effectiveness constraints tend to involve large growth in the military establishment. Such required growth for an indefinite period, however, is very unlikely. Note that the problem does not arise because of inflation. Proper calculation of costs is in terms of resources and thus in constant dollars.

[18] The subject of uncertainty in cost-benefit analysis of defence manpower planning is not treated in this paper. One can, of course, make some allowance for it by considering the expected values of different effects of programs and by using a higher rate of discount when risk is involved than when it isn't, but to say this is hardly even to get into the matter. The discussion in the present paper is relevant whether or not uncertainty is important, however. See the brief summary and references in Prest and Turvey [(1965) p. 699].

at a relatively high level of aggregation. If this is done, the results are likely also to be in broad overall terms: How many men should be inducted? What are efficient incentives for men in general? and so on. On the other hand, keeping the problem at a high level of aggregation may build in unwarranted assumptions as to matters that a more disaggregate analysis would treat more satisfactorily.

Thus, for example, one part of the INS study treated the U.S. Navy as a whole. For this purpose, a man of given length of service was treated as equivalent to any other man of the same experience in the Navy. This is clearly not very satisfactory. Aside from the evident fact that men enter the Navy with different aptitudes and acquired skills, a much more serious problem is raised by the training given in the Navy itself. A man with several years' experience in electronics is a different kind of human capital than a man with the same length of experience as a gunner's mate or a steward. Obviously, such men are not perfect substitutes for one another and it is wrong, in principle, to treat them as though they were perfectly interchangeable without considering the consequences for the results.

On the other hand, the problem treated in the INS study already involved a dynamic programming problem sufficiently large and complicated to strain the capacity even of the most modern computers then available. To have that problem expanded to include explicitly not only inductions and general levels of experience but also assignment and specific training of men would have produced a problem simply not computationally solvable.

Another aspect of the same problem has already been discussed. We saw above that the possibility of substitution among different personnel categories was unlikely to be the same for small units as for the entire military establishment being analyzed. Unless one is willing to specify something about the way in which different small units can substitute for each other, the rate at which men in one personnel category can be substituted for men in another will depend on where these men are assigned and what training they embody. Yet, again, explicitly to keep track of and decide on such assignments in the course of a general analysis can easily lead to an unmanageable problem.

Fortunately, it is possible to get around this difficulty in one or more ways. One such way is to regard the military establishment as made up of its smaller parts, and to neglect substitution possibilities among those parts, if such possibilities exist. This may not be an unreasonable thing to do, if the disaggregation is performed in such a way as to make substitution of men within an analyzed group fairly easy and substitution between groups relatively difficult. Thus, for example, it may be reasonable to say that electronics personnel (once trained) can be separately analyzed. Obviously, substitution between electronics technicians of varying experience is possible to a far greater degree than substitution between electronics personnel and stewards. It may thus be appropriate to analyze costs and benefits in electronics and in stewards separately, whereas, for example, it would be inappropriate to treat electronics personnel on destroyers as separate from and no substitute for electronics personnel on cruisers. (In fact, electronics personnel were separately analyzed in a separate part of the INS study). If the overall problem can be broken up into *separate* subproblems in this way, those separate problems can be separately solved and a realistic level of disaggregation achieved at a manageable computational level.

On the other hand, close attention must be paid to the question of just how disjoint such subproblems really are. We have already pointed out that in breaking up an overall problem into such components, one ignores substitution possibilities that cut across such components. Further, one also ignores the possibility that the costs involved in one subproblem may not be independent of the solution of another. Thus, for example, the cost of providing berths and training facilities for one group may depend in part on whether existing facilities that may be used in common are already being used to capacity for some other group. If this is the case, the two problems cannot be separately analyzed. Nevertheless, the error involved in treating as separate two or more problems related in such a fashion may often be less than that involved in treating them together as a single undifferentiated unit.

Alternatively, analysis on an aggregate level may not be so bad as it at first appears, providing one is willing to make some assumptions about the relations among the units making up the establishment. Furthermore, these assumptions can sometimes be of a relatively general kind. Thus, for example, ignore for the moment difficulties caused by specialized training and consider only the problem raised above as to substitution possibilities for the entire establishment and for small units being different. To take this problem in its purest form, suppose that the mathematical form that such possibilities take is the same for each unit.[19] This means *not* that the trade-offs among different personnel categories are the same in each unit, but merely that such trade-offs would be the same if the number of men in each category assigned to one unit were the same as that assigned to another.

Suppose that we make two further relatively general assumptions. The

---

[19] Thus our discussion may be taken as relevant to the analysis of costs and benefits of men with a particular type of training when these men are assigned to different small units.

first of these is that trade-offs depend only on relative numbers, so that trade-offs would be unchanged if all personnel assignments to a given unit were reduced or increased in the same proportion. Since it is likely to be the composition of the personnel in a unit rather than the absolute size thereof that determines substitution possibilities, this is by no means implausible.

Second, suppose we assume that effectiveness for the establishment as a whole is some increasing function of effectiveness in each unit. That is, we assume that if any unit becomes more effective, and no unit becomes less effective, the establishment as a whole becomes more effective. Were we to specify the form of this relationship, we could be specifying the way in which different units substitute for each other in the establishment as a whole; note, however, that it is not necessary to make such a specification to obtain the results that follow. Thus all that is required here is essentially the statement that such inter-unit substitution is possible; if it is not possible, then (provided that costs can also be broken up) each unit can be analyzed separately anyway and the problem we are now discussing does not arise.

In these circumstances, it can be shown that if the establishment acts in a rational way in its assignment of personnel to different units – that is, if it assigns personnel so as to make overall effectiveness as great as possible, given the available personnel, then whatever the relative importance of the separate units, substitution possibilities for the establishment as a whole take the same form as for the separate units. Analysis can then proceed on an aggregate level with substitution possibilities among personnel categories depending only on the composition of personnel in the establishment as a whole and neglecting the question of the units to which personnel are assigned.[20] The assignment problem can be handled separately, but there may be no need to handle it at all, for cost-benefit analysis at the aggregate level will in fact be appropriate in these circumstances, so far as the problem being considered is concerned.

Naturally, this strong-appearing result rests upon the assumptions made; nevertheless, similar results continue to hold if those assumptions are weakened somewhat. In particular, one can weaken the assumption that substitution possibilities in different units are in precisely the same mathematical form; under some circumstances, one can even weaken the assumption as to optimal assignment.[21]

On the other hand, this result takes care of the problem that substitution possibilities for the entire establishment may be different from

---

[20] A demonstration for a specific case is given in Fisher and Morton (1967b) and in Morton, Fisher, and Nitzberg [(1966), Appendix G].

[21] See Morton, Fisher, and Nitzberg [(1966), Appendix G].

substitution possibilities for individual units on the implicit assumption that men can be shifted between units with no loss of expertise. The problems raised for aggregate analysis by the embodiment of particular training in a particular man are not solved by the theorem under discussion. As already discussed, however, the extreme version of such problems, in which men in one group can at best be substituted for men of another group with great loss of effectiveness, can often be handled by treating the costs and benefits of groups as entirely disjoint.

In general then, the level of aggregation of cost-benefit analysis in defence manpower planning deserves close attention. One wishes to preserve as much realism as possible while still obtaining a solvable problem, for the problem will be solved in practice, even if not by the cost-benefit analyst, through the adoption of a specific policy, optimal or otherwise. It is wrong to suppose that aggregation problems can be glossed over, but equally wrong to suppose that aggregate analyses must be mistaken, for, as the example just given shows, a high level of detail can be irrelevant to at least the broad outlines of the solution.[22,23]

7.   Whose Costs? Whose Benefits?

In this concluding section, I wish briefly to raise an issue of rather a different kind from those so far discussed, although not unrelated to some of them.

What constitutes a cost and what a benefit depends on the point of view from which the question is posed. Indeed, what effects of a policy are to be taken into account at all depends on that point of view. Because cost-benefit analysis is likely to be used to answer relatively specific questions, because the analysis is likely to relate to only a part of the full military establishment, and because even the full military establishment is only a part of governmental operations which in turn are only a part of the life and economy of society as a whole, it is very easy to ignore effects that extend beyond the relatively narrow confines within which the analysis takes place. Such overlooking of wider effects may or may not be justified, but it should always be a matter for conscious decision.

A few examples will make the issues clear. First, once more consider the INS study. That study was concerned with retention of enlisted per-

[22] In this connection, it is interesting to note that the substantive results of the analysis for electronics personnel of the INS study were not qualitatively different from those for the far more aggregative analysis for the Navy as a whole.

[23] The aggregation problems involved in the treatment of human capital are, of course, not unique to that sort of capital. For a discussion of closely related problems raised for aggregation by the existence of different sorts of physical capital, see Fisher (1965) and (1968).

sonnel. Among the incentives offered for such retention was a program of rapid advancement to officer status. Since the study focussed on enlisted personnel, however, men advancing to officer status were treated as equivalent to men leaving the Navy; from the time of their promotion, costs and benefits later attributable to them were counted as zero.

Now, this procedure clearly requires some justification. It is perfectly true that, from the relatively parochial view of the enlisted Navy, such men cease both to incur costs and to perform useful services once they are promoted; from the point of view of the entire Navy, however, this is not the case. If we agree that it ought to be the Navy and not just the enlisted Navy whose costs and effectiveness are analyzed, then at the very least, some analytic support must be given to such treatment of these men.

In fact, it is possible to justify that treatment, providing one is willing to accept one of two alternative (although perhaps not very plausible) assumptions. The first of these is that the training received by such men as enlistees does not improve their efficiency as officers beyond the level ordinarily possessed by men accepted from outside the Navy into officer's training. If the Navy can already easily acquire men from outside whose outside education and experience makes them just as fit for officer status as the men promoted under the incentive program considered, then such promotion does nothing to change the benefits and costs of naval officers. If, on the other hand, training as an enlisted man makes a man better qualified to be an officer than other men educated and trained outside the Navy,[24] or if there is a shortage of suitable officer material, then the benefits and costs of naval officers are affected by the rapid promotion program and this ought not to be ignored.

Alternatively, even if naval officers are in short supply, note that such officers not only contribute benefits but also incur costs. Thus, ignoring such promotions can be justified if the benefits and the costs are thought to just balance. This involves the assumption that such officers are just paid their marginal products, that they are just worth what they cost. This is an assumption that could be defended if the Navy were a profit-maximizing competitive firm, but I should not know how to begin rigorously to justify it in the actual situation, short of ceasing to ignore such benefits and costs and analyzing them as part of an overall cost-benefit analysis for the entire Navy, officers as well as enlisted men.

---

[24] It is important to realize that what is involved is not whether the enlisted experience makes a particular man better suited to be an officer than he was before but rather whether that experience makes him better officer material than can be obtained from other sources.

Just as the viewpoint of the enlisted Navy may be overly narrow when considered from that of the Navy as a whole, however, so may the viewpoint of the Navy as a whole be overly narrow if we consider program effects on the rest of society. Indeed, the example just given has a close parallel in the wider context.

A man taken into the Navy as an untrained man and given specialized training often leaves the Navy a more valuable piece of human capital than he went into it. From the Navy's point of view, indeed, if such a man leaves relatively soon after training, such an increase in value represents an investment by the Navy that is not recouped in the form of services rendered. From society's point of view, however, the case is otherwise, at least in part. The fact that a trained electronics technician, for example, receives a higher civilian wage than does an untrained man reflects the fact that he is performing more valuable services to the economy. This is the case whether or not he is performing them in the place where he was trained. I recognize, of course, that the military establishment is not and perhaps ought not to be in the business of deliberately providing training for men who will then perform their services to society outside that establishment; nevertheless, is it really appropriate to count such men as deadweight losses after they leave the service, as scrapped human capital? From society's point of view, we would not count them as lost had they received their training in a private firm, even if the firm itself properly so counted them. The military establishment is, of course, in a different position, but the question still seems worth raising. It is the same question to which the answer seemed clear when a man was trained in the enlisted Navy and performed his services as a naval officer. Ought the answer to be different here?[25]

This example is one in which benefits from society's point of view are not the same as benefits from the point of view of all or part of the military establishment. Other examples in which costs to society and costs to the military establishment differ are also easy to find. Does a program greatly affect the economy and life of a particular locality or region, and are those effects adequately represented in the prices paid for resources by the military? Does a program require a significant amount of foreign exchange? This may not increase costs from a purely military point of view, but it certainly does so from the point of view of the economy as a whole. In practice, large spillover effects of these sorts are recognized and, sometimes, adjustments are made for them. In performing a rela-

---

[25] Note, incidentally, that this problem could not arise if the military establishment were a competitive private firm paying a market wage. In that case the marginal man would just be worth his cost and his leaving after training would have no effect on profits.

tively abstract cost-benefit analysis, however, such problems are easy to overlook.

One might carry a list of such examples further. At a very different level, annual budgetary allotments are considered absolute constraints by those not responsible for budget making. Such constraints are hardly appropriate, however, as a basis for long-range or overall planning. In such a wider context, as already discussed, such constraints should be replaced by a consideration of the discounted cost of resources.

In all such circumstances – and they are very general – it is important that both analyst and decision-maker recognize that defence manpower planning is a large-scale affair, that planning for part of the establishment is but a part of planning for all of it, and that the wider economic and social effects of defence programs must at least be considered, where these are not entirely reflected in the costs and benefits of the military establishment. Here, as in the specification of trade-offs and measurement of effectiveness and as in other aspects of cost-benefit analysis in defence manpower planning, frequent communication between policy maker and analyst is called for. Such analysis is too technical to be left to the policy maker and too important in its implications to be left to the technicians. Neither can afford a parochial viewpoint.

REFERENCES

Dorfman, R. (1965), "Econometric Analysis for Assessing the Efficacy of Public Investment," *Proceedings of the Study Week (October 1963) on "Le Rôle de l'Analyse Econométrique dans la Formulation de Plans de Developpement*," Pontifical Academy of Sciences, Vatican City, pp. 187–205.

Fisher, F. M. (1965), "Embodied Technical Change and the Existence of an Aggregate Capital Stock," *Review of Economic Studies*, Vol. XXXII, pp. 263–288. Reprinted as Chapter 2 in Fisher (1992–93).

Fisher, F. M. (1968), "Embodied Technology and the Existence of Labour and Output Aggregates," *Review of Economic Studies*, Vol. 35, pp. 391–412. Reprinted as Chapter 3 in Fisher (1992–93).

Fisher, F. M. (1992–93), *Aggregation: Aggregate Production Functions and Related Topics*, Harvester-Wheatsheaf, London, and MIT Press, Cambridge, Mass.

Fisher, F. M. and A. S. Morton (May 1967a), "Reenlistments in the U. S. Navy: A Cost-Effectiveness Study," *American Economic Review*, Vol. LVII, pp. 32–38.

Fisher, F. M. and A. S. Morton (May–June 1967b), "The Costs and Effectiveness of Reenlistment Incentives in the Navy," *Operations Research*, Vol. 15, pp. 373–381.

Hitch, C. J. and R. N. McKean (1960), *The Economics of Defense in the Nuclear Age*, Harvard University Press, Cambridge, Mass.

Morton, A. S., F. M. Fisher, and D. M. Nitzberg (Jan.–Feb. 1966), "Cost/Effectiveness of Reenlistment Incentives," *Navy Manpower Considerations 1970–1980 (U)*, Study 13, Institute of Naval Studies of the Center for Naval Analyses, FOR OFFICIAL USE ONLY.

Prest, A. R. and R. Turvey (Dec. 1965), "Cost-Benefit Analysis: A Survey," *Economic Journal*, Vol. LXXV, pp. 683–735.

PART IV

Industrial Organization, Economics, and the Law

Organizing Industrial Organization: Reflections on the *Handbook of Industrial Organization* (1991)

> Turning and turning in the widening gyre
> The falcon cannot hear the falconer;
> Things fall apart; the centre cannot hold;
> Mere anarchy is loosed upon the world.
>
> W. B. Yeats, "The Second Coming"

> Bliss was it in that dawn to be alive,
> But to be young was very heaven!
>
> William Wordsworth, "French Revolution"

Parts 2 and 3 of the *Handbook of Industrial Organization* are respectively entitled "Analysis of Market Behavior" and "Empirical Methods and Results."[1] The first section is almost exclusively theoretical, whereas the second, as its title makes clear, is empirically oriented. Both sections deal with the analysis of markets, particularly with oligopolistic ones.[2]

Reflection on the *Handbook* has two aspects. First, is the *Handbook* a good book – that is, does it succeed in its stated aims? The second suggests a broader and more important set of questions. Reading the *Handbook* provides the opportunity for thinking about the state of the art, about the field of industrial organization. What does it include? What are the organizing principles? In what direction is the field growing? Is that the correct destination?

This latter set of questions is the subject of most of this paper. But the first question also deserves attention, and the two are not unrelated.

This paper is dedicated to Carl Kaysen on the occasion of his seventieth birthday.

[1] All references to the *Handbook* are to Schmalensee and Willig (1989). In general, these references are to Parts 2 and 3.

[2] A review of the remaining sections of the *Handbook* – "Determinants of Firm and Market Organization" (Part 1), "International Issues and Comparisons" (Part 4), and "Government Intervention in the Marketplace" (Part 5) – is in the paper by Klevorick (1991).

The *Handbook* as a Book

In considering the *Handbook* as a book (and in later assessing the state of the art) I necessarily paint with broad strokes. The *Handbook* is immense, and a detailed review of its chapters would be tedious, if not impossible. As a result, there are exceptions to many of my general comments, and especially to my criticisms, and I hope authors of particular chapters will forgive me for not pointing them out.

This said, my first reaction is enthusiastic praise. The *Handbook* is a very good book. Every chapter is well written and a mine of information. Most of them are far more than surveys of the state of the art in a particular area. They are coherent essays that themselves add to the art. But I do not suggest that one should sit down to read the *Handbook* straight through. It is not intended for cover-to-cover reading (except by exhausted reviewers). I can do no better in this regard than to quote advice given in the introduction to a recent collection of political jokes:

> One final word of advice to any prospective reader of this volume: *Do not read it*! If you try to follow the King's instructions to the White Rabbit in *Alice in Wonderland* – "Begin at the beginning, and go on till you come to the end: then stop," – you will very soon become sated and overcome first with a numbed indifference and then with nausea (as with a box of chocolates – some sweet, some bitter, some hard- and some soft-centered). We advise, rather, judicious sampling.[3]

Rather, the work is intended to be exactly what it says it is: a handbook, a reference whose purpose, as stated by its editors, is "to provide reasonably comprehensive and up-to-date surveys of recent developments and the state of knowledge in the major areas of research . . . as of the latter part of the 1980s, written at a level suitable for use by nonspecialist economists and students in advanced graduate courses."[4]

Is the *Handbook* successful in achieving this goal? I think only partially so. In the first place, particularly in the theoretical chapters of Part 2, the nonspecialist will often find the going heavy, even though the necessary tools have been provided. (Part 2 begins sensibly with Chapter 5, Drew Fudenberg and Jean Tirole's overview of the methods and results of noncooperative game theory.) The authors of chapters in Part 2 sometimes succumb to the temptation to deal with their own most recent, sometimes unpublished work (and perhaps that of their students and friends). This is not necessarily a bad thing – after all, the authors were

---

[3] Lukes and Galnoor (1987, p. xiii).
[4] Schmalensee and Willig (1989, vol. 1, p. xi).

chosen because of their work in their respective subject areas. But the urge to describe all the latest wrinkles occasionally tells the reader more than he or she may want to know, and one comes away from such discussions without a clear sense that the literature has been systematically surveyed.

That is less so in the empirical chapters of Part 3, but here a different problem arises. It is difficult to write a survey of a large set of empirical studies. For one thing, the material is typically less easy to organize than is the case with a theoretical theme. For another, empirical studies vary vastly in quality. It is not easy to describe both what is known and the degree of certainty with which we know it. Here, Richard Schmalensee (Chapter 16) and Wesley Cohen and Richard Levin (Chapter 18) have the daunting task of dealing with cross-industry studies. They do a good job of organizing their respective topics but are less successful in providing a detailed, critical guide to the relevant literature. Because, as we shall see, the studies surveyed are open to considerable theoretical objection, it is of particular importance to single out which studies and which conclusions are solidly based. Although both chapters (especially Schmalensee's) do address the underlying problems, they fail in the perhaps impossible task of carefully separating good, soundly based studies from more questionable ones. Instead the reader gets the author's own (and doubtless often correct) impressions about what the literature shows.

It is also often (but not always) the case that the authors of the theoretical chapters in Part 2 have only a general idea about the results of the empirical work presented in Part 3. This, however, reflects a deeper problem in the field itself, and I shall discuss it later.

In this connection, Dennis Carlton's essay (Chapter 15) on the theory and facts of market clearing stands in sharp contrast to most of the chapters of Part 2.[5] Carlton considers the actual facts on such things as price changes and delivery lags and shows that simple theories cannot explain them. His chapter is a welcome blend of theory and fact. In level and tone, it comes far closer than most of the other chapters of Part 2 to meeting the purpose cited by the editors.

The other theoretical chapters of Part 2, as indicated, spend little time on systematic examination of empirical results. Either they pay little attention to empirical work, or they resort to casual observation. Only occasionally, as in Janusz Ordover and Garth Saloner's excellent piece on predation, monopolization, and antitrust (Chapter 9), does one find

---

[5] The contrast is sharp enough to be jarring. One wonders why Carlton's chapter appears in Part 2 at all.

a real attempt to apply theory to the detailed facts of particular industries.

This brings me to the subject of work in the field that is not well surveyed in the *Handbook*. For a very long time now, a good deal of effort has been spent on detailed industry studies. Such studies – of varying quality and analytic content, to be sure – can provide the basic information from which theory can generalize. I do not know to what extent such work is still common (although I certainly know that it still goes on). More important, I cannot tell much, if anything, about it from the *Handbook*, and this is a gap in coverage.

I realize, of course, that such work is troublesome to survey in a systematic way. Each industry study tends to be idiosyncratic, with organizing principles linking such studies difficult to find. (As we shall see, I do not believe that this is an accident.) But the *Handbook* fails to make the attempt, although some individual studies are mentioned in passing. It is symptomatic of the *Handbook* (and of the profession) that the closest one comes to a survey of work on particular industries is Timothy Bresnahan's essay on empirical studies of industries with market power (Chapter 17). That chapter, excellent and interesting in itself, is focused on work that uses a particular set of techniques; it does not pretend to survey the wider field.

The second area that is not systematically surveyed is related to the first: public policy. Issues of antitrust policy are discussed in several of the chapters – for example, the essay by Ordover and Saloner, already mentioned; that by Hal Varian on price discrimination (Chapter 10); and the one by Michael Katz on vertical contractual relations (Chapter 11). But the *Handbook* makes no separate, concerted attempt to tie together economic and legal thinking about public policy on market power and the related issues. Because much of the practical use of industrial organization comes in antitrust cases, which also supply the occasion for substantial work on particular industries, this is an unfortunate omission.

These two omissions, industry studies and antitrust-related matters, are also troublesome because of the opportunity that a systematic survey (were one possible) might allow one to see theory in action. The authors of the theoretical chapters of Part 2 obviously believe that theory provides a rich set of tools for application when studying particular industries. Thus, Carl Shapiro states, after an extensive discussion of theories of oligopolistic behavior,

Let me close with a sort of user's guide to the many oligopoly models I have discussed. By "user," I mean one who is attempting to use these models to better understand a given industry (not someone out to build yet another model). Here is where the "bag of tools" analogy applies. After learning the basic facts about an industry, the analyst with a working understanding of oligopoly theory should be able to use these tools to identify the main strategic aspects present in that industry.[6]

Had the *Handbook* successfully surveyed industry studies and analyses of particular antitrust cases, it might have been instructive to see how those tools have been used or *might* have been used. As we shall see, however, I suspect that such an exploration would have revealed that views such as Shapiro's cited above are far too sanguine about the usefulness of theory in its present state. There is a serious (and unhappy) gap between theory as revealed in the *Handbook* and the actual analysis of real industries and real antitrust cases. The existence of that gap is by no means the exclusive fault of the theorists. Facts analyzed by means of poorly understood theory are just as big a problem as theory misapplied to poorly understood facts. A survey of the use of industrial organization in antitrust actions could have revealed the problems involved on both sides and might have better indicated which theoretical developments seem promising in practice.

No such survey is provided, however, and the *Handbook* may leave the erroneous impression that economists' expertise is not often called on in antitrust cases. Of course this is far from the truth. Economic expertise is called on all the time. But the tools used in such cases are in general not those of the type of theory that dominates the *Handbook*. I shall return to these matters below.

Before leaving my discussion of the *Handbook* as a book and moving on to the broader question of what it reveals about the state of the art, I must mention a minor matter. The proofreading and copyediting of the *Handbook* are a disgrace. Names are misspelled; sentences are often ungrammatical; cross-references to other chapters are incorrect, and, although meaning is seldom totally obscured, one occasionally has to think about what the author must have meant to say.

Three examples will suffice here. Bresnahan refers to a "higher or at least higherfaulting theoretical language." He also states that he will "mention a consistent notation throughout, rather than adopting the notation of individual papers." But the greatest of all such quotes comes from Stiglitz, who says of the Walrasian auctioneer that "no one probably took the tantamount process seriously."[7] I single out these two

---

[6] Schmalensee and Willig (1989, vol. 1, p. 409).
[7] Schmalensee and Willig (1989, vol. 2, pp. 1020; 1015n; vol. 1, p. 773n).

authors only because the slips are amusing. The level of care here is consistently low, and I suspect that the authors were not given the opportunity to proofread their own papers.

Having made these criticisms, however, I want again to emphasize that my principal reaction is quite favorable. I found every chapter educational (which is not to say that I had no substantive disagreements with the authors). This is a book of which authors and editors should be proud.

Organizing Principles of Industrial Organization

I turn now to the more difficult, but rather more important, task of considering the state of the art as exemplified in Parts 2 and 3 of the *Handbook*. This is not easy to do, for the writing of a systematic essay requires that one find organizing themes. In this regard, the very explosion of material reflected in the *Handbook* is daunting.

After considerable thought, I have decided to proceed in the manner of some authors of the *Handbook*'s chapters. Schmalensee (Chapter 16), for example, organizes his summary in terms of a series of "stylized facts." Similarly, Eaton and Lipsey begin their essay on product differentiation with a list of seven "awkward facts that are available to constrain theorizing."[8] Because this review is empirical to the extent that it reports and summarizes the field as seen through the *Handbook*, I shall proceed in similar fashion with a series of "organizing principles."[9]

Organizing Principle 1:   *Industrial organization has no organizing principles (except for those that are subcases of this one).*

This is no joke. As we shall see, I believe that there are deep reasons for such a lack, and it manifests itself in several different ways. I shall begin with pure theory.

Organizing Principle 2:   *The principal result of theory is to show that nearly anything can happen.*

The principal mode of theorizing in industrial organization is the creation of interesting examples in which problems are stripped of all but their most essential features. The result is, in effect, a formalized anec-

---

[8] Schmalensee and Willig (1989, vol. 1, p. 725).
[9] I trust that I will be forgiven for emulating some of the authors of the *Handbook* in a different way and for referring to my own work a bit too frequently. That, too, as I have mentioned, is characteristic of the field. The views expressed here are consonant with those in Fisher (1989) – an article whose publication certainly contributed to my being asked to write this review.

dote in which the theorist demonstrates that certain outcomes can actually occur – sometimes contrary to what one might have thought.

This sort of theory is what I have elsewhere called "exemplifying theory."[10] It is a powerful method for producing counterexamples to general propositions. Further, it *may* lead to insights about phenomena that can also be found in more general and complex situations. But the result does not appear to be leading to any "generalizing theory" or, indeed, to a theory with much real content in the sense of being suited to empirical verification or rejection.[11] Rather, the method has produced a taxonomy – a laundry list of a vast number of possibilities that rules out little.

This fact has not escaped the attention of some authors of the *Handbook*. Jacquemin and Slade state in their essay on cartels, collusion, and horizontal merger that

Economic thought concerning collusive practices and mergers has changed profoundly, mainly in the light of game-theoretic analysis. Unfortunately, this change has not led to more general and robust conclusions. On the contrary, it is the source of a more fragmented view. The diversity of models and results, which are very sensitive to the assumption selected, suggests a "case-by-case" approach where insight into the ways in which firms acquire and maintain positions of market power becomes essential. It is nevertheless important to bring to light a *typology* of situations and practices for which recent developments in economic analysis offer sounder theoretical characterizations than in the past.[12]

They later say, "The multiplicity of equilibria is one of the problems associated with the repeated-game approach. Instead of providing us with a theory of oligopoly, it can explain all possible behaviors."[13]

Gilbert states in his essay on mobility barriers and the value of incumbency that the "scope for oligopolistic interactions is so wide that a predictive model of how firms behave may be no easier to construct than a model of the weather based on the formation of water droplets." He refers to a "taxonomy of behavior in response to entry."[14]

This situation is not the fault of the theorists. The theoretical facts are as they have recited them, and the possible outcomes are extremely numerous and assumption-dependent. Further, the Folk theorem for repeated games assures us that, with low enough discount rates, this phenomenon is endemic in any situation of serious interest.[15] One must

[10] Fisher (1989).
[11] Fisher (1989).
[12] Schmalensee and Willig (1989, vol. 1, p. 416, emphasis added).
[13] Schmalensee and Willig (1989, vol. 1, p. 441).
[14] Schmalensee and Willig (1989, vol. 1, pp. 478, 509).
[15] An outcome of a game is called "individually rational" if it gives each player at least as much as the minimum amount the player could secure for himself or herself. The Folk

not blame the messenger for the bad news (although one can be skeptical about how surprising the news really is). Yet one can reasonably question whether theorists are working on a useful research agenda. We now know that no general results will emerge that map the route by which simple facts about market structure become performance outcomes.

Organizing Principle 3: *Stripped-down models of theory often fail to provide helpful guides for the analysis of real situations.*

The problem is that real firms operate in a far more complex world than is captured by theory in its present exemplifying state. Real firms do not set only quantity or price. They set a complex variety of strategic variables and frequently offer multiple products in multiple locations. Contrary to the optimistic view expressed in Shapiro's "bag of tools," the analyst working on a particular industry will often not be able to decide what tools apply (if any do).[16]

Quotations from the *Handbook* are illuminating here. Fudenberg and Tirole state that "Firms typically do not only choose a time to enter a market, but also decide on the scale of entry, the type of product to produce, etc. This *detail* can prove unmanageable, which is why industrial organization economists have frequently abstracted it away."[17] Jacquemin and Slade state that

In all of these models, price wars are equilibrium strategies of supergames; no one ever cheats. This is perhaps [!] a shortcoming of the models from a practical if not from a game-theoretic point of view. Our intuitive feeling is that firms do intentionally cheat on collusive agreements (recall the electrical-equipment conspiracy) and that there are many reasons why price wars occur in addition to demand shocks. Nevertheless, economists have devised few theories to explain cheating in collusive agreements.[18]

Reinganum states in her essay on the timing of innovation that

One important goal of future research should be to develop testable models of industry equilibrium behavior. The papers summarized here have used stark models in order to identify the significant characteristics of firms, markets and innovations which are likely to affect incentives to invest and/or adopt [innovations]. But since it is largely restricted to . . . special cases . . . , this work has not yet had a significant impact on the applied literature in industrial organization; its usefulness for policy purposes should also be considered limited. For these

---

theorem states that if discount rates are low enough, then any outcome in an infinitely repeated game that is individually rational is supportable as a Nash equilibrium. See Fudenberg and Tirole's discussion in Chapter 5 of the *Handbook* (pp. 279–81).

[16] Schmalensee and Willig (1989, vol. 1, p. 409).

[17] Schmalensee and Willig (1989, vol. 1, p. 292, emphasis added).

[18] Schmalensee and Willig (1989, vol. 1, p. 447).

purposes, one needs a predictive model which encompasses the full range of firm, industry and innovation characteristics.[19]

Cohen and Levin, writing on empirical studies of innovation and market structure, agree with this, although they are certainly not wholly pessimistic:

One difficulty with testing the implications of recent game-theoretic models of R&D [research and development] rivalry is that they analyze behavior in highly stylized and counterfactual settings. . . . Moreover, many of the results obtained . . . depend on typically unverifiable assumptions concerning the distribution of information, the identity of the decision variables, and the sequence of moves. Nonetheless, empirical effort on the effect and importance of strategic behavior is warranted. Inspiration might be drawn from Lieberman's (1987) empirical examination of the role of strategic entry deterrence in affecting capacity expansion in a sample of chemical and metals industries. He concluded that strategic considerations were not paramount in most industries, but he identified several specific instances in which strategic considerations *may* have been important.[20]

In something of the same vein, Ordover and Saloner state that

[T]heoretical findings and prescriptions are difficult to translate into workable and enforceable standards that in *actual market settings* would, without fail, promote conduct that enhances social welfare and would discourage conduct that harms welfare. The source of the problem is the strategic setting itself. In the context of strategic interactions, it is difficult to distinguish between those actions, which are intended to harm actual (and potential) rivals[,] that stifle competition, and thereby reduce economic welfare, and those actions which harm present rivals and discourage future entry but which, nevertheless, promote economic welfare. Or, as legal scholars are often fond of saying, actions which are consistent with "competition on the merits."[21]

Stripped-down models can, in fact, be very useful, but, as Eaton and Lipsey observe in their essay on product differentiation "Tractability in deriving incorrect results is no advantage."[22] For "incorrect," read "inapplicable." Industrial organization theory has a long and arduous way to go.

Organizing Principle 4: *Some (by no means all) theorists have a casual attitude toward what constitutes verification.*

With a bewildering variety of possible models to choose from, one can reasonably ask what could constitute the verification or falsification of a

---

[19] Schmalensee and Willig (1989, vol. 1, p. 905).
[20] Schmalensee and Willig (1989, vol. 2, p. 1096, emphasis added).
[21] Schmalensee and Willig (1989, vol. 1, pp. 538–39, emphasis in original).
[22] Schmalensee and Willig (1989, vol. 1, p. 759).

particular model. Here there is sometimes an underlying attitude that a theory has been "successful" or "applicable" if one can use it to tell a logically consistent story of what *might* have happened – a story consistent with the few facts that the theorist happens to know.

The excerpt from Cohen and Levin (Chapter 18) given above is one illustration. Others can be found in the very casual citation of certain antitrust cases by some authors.[23] Thus, to take an example that I know well, *Telex* v. *IBM* is cited by Gilbert as providing an example of contracts and entry prevention. But this case does so only in terms of the plaintiff's allegations. It is cited again for the effects of "locked-in" customers in producing alleged price discrimination.[24] Here the allegation made no economic sense, and the principal so-called "lock-in" part of the case was not the one cited. These points are not hard to find.[25]

To continue with the computer industry, Gilbert writes that

Despite its theoretical limitations, the Gaskins model of dynamic limit pricing (along with its refinements) is an appealing description of pricing behavior for industries that are characterized by dominant firms. The exogenous specification of the entry flow is not theoretically justified, but it *may* capture an important element of dynamic competition. . . . If it *were* possible to model [certain underlying] aspects of the entry process, the result *could* be an entry flow rate that appears similar to the . . . Gaskins model. . . . For these reasons, it is not surprising that the Gaskins model has been used *successfully* in empirical models of dominant firm pricing, such as . . . Brock (1975).[26]

The issue, of course, is what constitutes "success." I suggest that a serious knowledge of the complexities of the computer industry does not lead one to believe that this is the best example, however appealing it may seem for its relative simplicity.

Similarly, the notion that merger policy should be made on the assumption that real firms follow Cournot behavior is naive, if not bizarre.[27] That theorists can produce a simplified model with clean results does not mean that the world works in that way. Further, the idea that the cross-section empirical studies surveyed in Part 3 of the *Handbook* somehow verify simplistic theory is simply wrong. The difficulties with such studies (perhaps especially with the use of accounting profitability)

---

[23] This is definitely *not* to say that all authors of the *Handbook* are casual in this regard. Ordover and Saloner (Chapter 9), for example, have clearly read the literature on the cases they cite.

[24] Schmalensee and Willig (1989, vol. 1, pp. 502n, 507n).

[25] See Fisher, McGowan, and Greenwood (1983, pp. 196–204, 316–17, and 325–28).

[26] Schmalensee and Willig (1989, vol. 1, pp. 514–15, emphasis added).

[27] Farrell and Shapiro (1990).

do not appear to be fully appreciated by the theorists in Part 2.[28] I now turn to such empirical work.

Organizing Principle 5: *Much empirical work, especially cross-industry empirical work, is not informed by (or, sometimes, about) theory.*

The years of drought in industrial organization theory were years in which the cross-section farmers went on planting. Not surprisingly, the harvest was not bountiful, and the recent flood of theory has not irrigated the crops.

Cross-sectional attempts to verify (or disprove?) the structure-conduct-performance paradigm have never been very soundly based in theory. Not only has theory not provided much quantitatively useful guidance about exactly how structure affects performance, even at the level of what variables should be used, but also the empirical practitioners often had only a rudimentary understanding of what theory did say.

An outstanding, but not the only, example of this came in the area of capital theory, where inability to move beyond the simplest one-period model was striking indeed. To be more specific, attempts to use profitability as the basic measure of performance simply misunderstood both the role and the measurement of profitability in economic theory.

In the first place, it is not true that there are no economic profits earned in competition. Profits are the driving force of the competitive process. Only in long-run equilibrium are profits (adjusted for risk) driven to zero. It is a great mistake – and one that consistently runs throughout economics – to behave as though all that matters is long-run equilibrium. Competition is a dynamic process; real firms operate in real time, and the fact that economists find it difficult to deal with such dynamics does not make the dynamics go away.

Put this aside, however, and suppose that comparison of a firm or industry's profitability to some "normal" standard is an appropriate way to test for market power. What profitability measure should be used? To the extent that it is appropriate to speak in terms of profit rates at all (as opposed to present values discounted at some suitable rate of return), economic theory teaches that the risk-adjusted profit rate that is equalized under competition is the internal or economic rate of return – the rate that makes the present value of the stream of returns from investment equal to the direct capital costs.

---

[28] See, for example, pp. 437, 449, and 455 of the *Handbook*; and Shapiro (1989, p. 133).

The profitability rate used in cross-section studies is not of this (admittedly hard to measure) magnitude. Rather, many studies have used the accounting rate of return (profits divided by stockholders' equity or by the value of capital stock). Because capital stock purchased now is done so with an eye to future profits, and because current profits are earned in part because of investments made in the past, it should come as no surprise that such measures do not carry a great deal of information about the economic rate of return. (Indeed, the remarkable fact is that there should exist *any* circumstances under which the two are closely related.) Nevertheless, despite others' having made similar points in the past, this fact did cause a great deal of surprise (not to say outraged protest) when John McGowan and I pointed it out some years ago.[29]

A similar problem infects studies using a different profitability measure, the profits-sales ratio. Even making quite favorable assumptions, it turns out that this quantity does not equal (or possibly even approximate) the Lerner measure of monopoly power (price minus marginal cost, all divided by price) except under *very* special circumstances.[30]

These are not difficult results to derive from the theory of the firm. Yet at least one leading practitioner seems to have been wholly unaware that the economic rate of return was of any importance.[31] Others simply found it difficult to believe that they were measuring the wrong thing.

Schmalensee (Chapter 16), who understands the issues involved, attempts to get round them by surveying the literature as providing stylized facts rather than solid results. Those "stylized facts" often concern accounting profitability, and industrial organization theory *may* need to explain them. But one must not yield to the temptation to suppose that the explanation is that the magnitudes studied in empirical work are necessarily closely allied to those that are the objects of theory.

The field has recently moved on a bit. Focus has shifted from profits to prices as measuring performance.[32] The shift to prices has its own serious measurement problems, but the difficulty in this area is not merely one of measurement.[33] Theory does not provide – perhaps theory

---

[29] Fisher and McGowan (1983); see also Long and Ravenscraft (1984), and Fisher (1984).
[30] Fisher (1987a).
[31] See Fisher, McGowan, and Greenwood (1983, p. 257).
[32] Weiss (1989).
[33] Comparison of the prices charged by different firms requires that the goods being priced be (or be made to be) comparable. Even in apparently simple cases, this may not be easy because goods carry such attributes as service, promptness, ease of dealing, and general reputation of the firm. That these attributes can make a substantial difference has been forcefully pointed out by Newmark (1989).

cannot provide – a clean, detailed model that goes from measurable aspects of structure to performance, whether performance is measured by profits or by prices. The Folk theorem and the wealth of exemplifying theory show that market equilibria depend on a host of underlying, often unobservable factors. Further, equilibria are not all that matter in the constantly changing world in which real firms and real industries operate. In the absence of a suitably informing general theory, I do not believe it useful to go on with empirical studies that crudely apply the relatively rudimentary theory of the past to measures that are not the objects that theory discusses.

Somewhat similar (if less pervasive) problems arise in the empirical literature on innovation and returns to scale. Here Peter Temin and I long ago pointed out that the theory of the firm does not yield an unambiguous prediction about the effects of firm size on R&D in the presence of economies of scale.[34] That result holds for both R&D input and R&D output. Yet the literature keeps on growing.

Cohen and Levin's treatment of this issue in their survey of empirical studies of innovation and market structure (Chapter 18) is perhaps indicative of the impatience that empirical workers feel with such demonstrations. They state that

[Fisher and Temin] demonstrated, *among other things*, that an elasticity of R&D [input] with respect to size in excess of one does not necessarily imply an elasticity of innovative output with respect to size greater than one. Kohn and Scott ... established the conditions under which the existence of the former relationship does imply the latter.[35]

They then go on to what they consider the "more fundamental" problem stemming from the argument that "Schumpeter did not postulate a continuous effect of firm size on innovation."

The point is that the proposition about the relations between the two elasticities is a relatively minor one. Among the "other things" that Temin and I demonstrated was that the literature was not actually testing (and probably was not able to test) *any* of the propositions that it purported to examine. Apparently that finding didn't stop anybody.

As in the case of the use of profits as a performance measure, more theory is needed. That theory should not concentrate on showing that under some circumstances the standard empirical approaches are correct. Rather, it should illuminate what variables must be measured to restore the possibility of getting an answer. Unlike the use of profit rates to measure performance, I think there may be some hope here.

---

[34] See Fisher and Temin (1973, 1979); Rodriguez (1979); and Kohn and Scott (1982).
[35] Schmalensee and Willig (1989, vol. 2, p. 1071, emphasis added).

The picture I have painted of careless disregard for theory by empirical workers is, of course, too general to be totally accurate. In at least one area, moreover, it is certainly not correct. Bresnahan's essay (Chapter 17) reports on econometric studies of particular industries that were undertaken to test whether those industries behave competitively and to measure market power. This literature recognizes that "firms' price-cost margins [cannot be] taken to be observables [because] economic marginal cost . . . cannot be directly or straightforwardly observed." At least as important is that

> Individual industries are taken to have important idiosyncrasies. It is likely that institutional detail at the industry level will affect firms' conduct, and even more likely that it will affect the analyst's measurement strategy. Thus, practitioners in this literature are skeptical of using the comparative statics of variations across industries or markets as revealing anything except when the markets are closely related.[36]

This literature stands out from most of the empirical work surveyed in the *Handbook* in that it certainly does use theory. The theory it uses is not closely related to that of the game-theoretic analyses in Part 2, however, but harks back to the earlier literature on conjectural variations. It is not much of an exaggeration to say that the theory involved is much the same as was used by Iwata in his early, important paper in this area.[37]

Further, although some progress has been made in the detection of market power, Bresnahan states that

> Only a very little has been learned from the new methods about the relationship between market power and industrial structure. . . . We know essentially nothing about the causes, or even the systematic predictors of market power, but have come a long way in working out how to measure them.[38]

Maybe so, but I am more skeptical than Bresnahan about our ability to measure market power (or even to know what the right measure is). The work in this area seems most successful in determining whether an industry is in competitive equilibrium. As Bresnahan suggests, it is less convincing in its attempts to locate the sources of departure from competition.

But knowing whether or not an industry is in competitive equilibrium is not usually a remarkably interesting thing to know. Most industries most of the time are not characterized by perfect competition, let alone by perfectly competitive equilibrium. The issues of interest typically

---

[36] Schmalensee and Willig (1989, vol. 2, p. 1012).
[37] Iwata (1974).
[38] Schmalensee and Willig (1989, vol. 2, pp. 1053, 1055).

involve the question of what, if anything, can be done to make an industry more competitive, with the recognition that perfect competition is an unattainable goal.

On this point, as already suggested, the literature surveyed by Bresnahan does not seem helpful. That literature does not appear usually to estimate structural equations; rather, the typical piece sets forth a structural model and derives some quasi-reduced-form implications. Even the conclusions drawn from the estimation of these, I suspect, tend to be heavily dependent on the functional forms used.

Despite such problems, the work surveyed by Bresnahan is miles ahead of much of the field in its use of theory. As I have already emphasized, there *is* no adequate theory on which to base the cross-section empirical work. That has always been true, but it is important to realize that recent developments have not provided the missing foundation. We still have no theory on which to base a *structural* model of the structure-conduct-performance paradigm. That Schmalensee's survey (Chapter 16) is reduced to listing stylized facts is a reflection of this lack. The listing of thirty such stylized facts, moreover, makes one wonder whether this literature has turned up much that is really systematic.

In short, there can be no doubt that empirical attempts to verify, test, or estimate the parameters of the relations between structure and performance have not succeeded. Even if the general empirical literature is taken on its own grounds and the kinds of analytic defects pointed out above are ignored, most results can be said to be uncertain and ambiguous. Further, the explosion in theory is having no effect. The empirical literature makes essentially no use of the modern methods or results, which is hardly surprising because theory is not providing propositions that are testable in practice (Organizing Principle 3).

A Research Agenda

The failure of the empirical literature is no accident. In one (not helpful) sense, that literature does indeed confirm a principal result of theory in this area: nearly anything can happen (Organizing Principle 2). There *is* no simple mapping from elementary (let alone imperfect) measures of structure, such as concentration or firm size, to performance. Those models (such as the simplest Cournot models) that suggest there is arrive at that result by stripping the problem of features essential to the understanding of real industries (Organizing Principle 3). Hence the empirical finding that such relationships are ambiguous does indeed verify the prediction of theory (although not in a helpful way).

In short, the structure-conduct-performance paradigm is dead, *if* (and this is a big if) one thinks of it as relating simple structural measures to characteristics of conduct and performance. The theoretical counterpart is that the program of investigating how perfectly rational opponents will behave in overly simplified settings has also failed (or, if you wish, has succeeded too far). Despite outward appearances, the field of industrial organization is not in a happy state, at least as regards the analysis of oligopolistic markets and related subjects.

But this conclusion rests on a somewhat limited view of what the appropriate research agenda for industrial organization really is. The failures just described come as little surprise to those who carefully read Fellner's *Competition among the Few* or have worked extensively on industry studies.[39] The simple-structure-measures–rational-behavior model does not lead to very useful results because the context of particular industries in which firms operate strongly affects the outcome they will or can achieve.

I give the simplest example. In an infinitely repeated game (with low enough discounting), the cooperative (joint-profit-maximizing) outcome is typically a Nash equilibrium independent of the number of firms or of industry concentration. Yet no sensible person supposes that such an outcome is just as likely when there are a thousand firms of equal size as it is when there are two. In this sense, current theory provides neither a guide nor a justification for studies that attempt to measure the effect of concentration or numbers on outcomes.

Yet such an attempt is not thereby rendered senseless. We think that the two cases just described differ, not because the Nash equilibria are fundamentally different in the two cases but because the two-firm industry will somehow find it easier to achieve the cooperative outcome than will the thousand-firm one. Further, we can all give at least verbal reasons why that is true. If numbers and concentration were all that mattered to such ability, then empirical studies attempting to relate performance (properly measured) to numbers and concentration would be successful despite the Folk theorem.[40]

The difficulty, of course, is that numbers and concentration are not all that matter. A great many other things are likely also to be important. As Carlton states in his essay on how markets clear,

Much of industrial organization seems fixated on answering how the behavior of markets differs as industry concentration changes. Although this is certainly an interesting question, industry concentration is only one of many ways in which

---

[39] Fellner (1949).
[40] Further, merger policy that relies on such measures would be entirely sensible. On this point, see Fisher (1987b).

markets can differ. Market liquidity, heterogeneity of product, variability in demand and supply, the ability to hold inventories, and the ability to plan are also interesting characteristics, and differences in these characteristics lead to different market behavior. Yet the effect of these other characteristics has received much less attention from industrial organization economists than the effect of differences in industry concentration.[41]

Further, once one leaves the question of market clearing, the list of interesting characteristics gets longer still. But empirical studies pay little attention to this, and theory has managed mostly to verify that the list is long indeed.

I believe that the proper research agenda for industrial organization is the study of how the context of particular industries or market situations determines *which* equilibrium will be reached and what happens on the way. In particular, we need to study how context affects the ability to achieve the joint-profit-maximizing outcome. This is not what most of current theory is doing. Further, as I have elsewhere explained in detail, I do not believe that the theoretical tools now so popular are particularly well suited for that task.[42]

In the absence of strong guidance from theory, we need to know what happens *in fact*. This surely requires the *detailed* study of particular industries. The cross-section literature is too simplistic to be of much assistance here, and the somewhat casual attitude of some theorists toward empirical verification (Organizing Principle 4) is of no help at all. (The econometric literature surveyed by Bresnahan in Chapter 17 of the *Handbook* is at least potentially useful in this regard, but it too suffers from a lack of richly articulated structural variables adequate to describe the underlying context.)

It is always dangerous, of course, to jump into empirical description without any guidance from theory, but it would be wrong to suppose that we do not have any such guidance. We do know in general (but only generally) what can matter. The problem is that we have known that for more than forty years. What we need to know now is what aspects of the contextual setting matter in practice.

This may be where experimental methods come in. Plott, in his review of the applications of experimental methods in industrial organization (Chapter 19), lists several cogent reasons for the use of such methods.[43] He does not explicitly mention the possibility that, by carefully controlling the context in which marketlike games are played, one can gain insight into what aspects of context are likely really to matter in

---

[41] Schmalensee and Willig (1989, vol. 1, p. 911).
[42] Fisher (1989).
[43] Schmalensee and Willig (1989, vol. 2, pp. 1165–69).

nonexperimental situations. But that possibility comes across from his survey.

Relating to Antitrust

Plott ends his survey by contemplating that experimental data might be used in court in antitrust cases.[44] At least for the present, that seems to me to be utter fantasy, but it is instructive to consider the extent to which *any* modern developments – especially game-theoretic developments – illuminate the issues in antitrust cases. As I have already suggested, the answer is "not much," and this is a depressing comment on the state of the field.

Do not misunderstand me. Industrial organization analysis has much to contribute to the analysis of antitrust cases and policy. Indeed, it is an indispensable element. The question I am asking is whether the recent developments described in the *Handbook* have added to this usefulness.

To fix ideas, consider an antitrust case involving an oligopoly – in particular, a case in which defendant firms are charged with anticompetitive behavior and collusion. In such a case (as in most areas of antitrust), analysis typically begins with a consideration of market definition – the question of what are the products and services that must be considered.

I have elsewhere pointed out that the question of the definition of the relevant market is not a truly well-posed one, and that the answer should serve only as a classificatory framework for analysis.[45] It is neither surprising nor unfortunate that most recent developments (and all modern theory) ignore this issue.[46]

The second aspect of the case is likely to involve the measurement of market share or concentration. As I have already observed, the empirical literature relating such measures to performance (and hence to competition or the lack of it) is not reliable. The theoretical work is nonexistent. Of course, this reflects the fact the there *are* no simple relations between structure and performance, but, again, what can be said now could have been said long ago.

An attempt may also be made to use profits as an indicator of market power. As discussed above, this has no analytic foundation. Current theoretical developments are (mercifully) silent here.

---

[44] Schmalensee and Willig (1989, vol. 2, pp. 1170–71).
[45] Fisher (1979, pp. 12–17); and Fisher, McGowan, and Greenwood (1983, pp. 31–33, 43–44).
[46] As with other generalizations, this one is too broad. Jacquemin and Slade (Chapter 7, pp. 454–55) survey some suggestions in this area. None of them relies on any development not available years ago.

The last element of market structure that will typically be examined concerns barriers to entry. Here current analysis has more to say. But even here, what can be said about "natural" barriers to entry could have been said years ago. Current theoretical developments do illuminate the analysis of "artificial" barriers, but this is a special case of their illumination of conduct issues, which I consider below.

These structural aspects of the antitrust case all lead to the question of whether departures from competition are possible or, perhaps, likely. They do not address the question of whether such departures have happened. The literature surveyed by Bresnahan (Chapter 17) clearly provides a way of investigating precisely that point (although, as mentioned, it makes no use of current game-theoretic methods).

Even if one can decide that perfectly competitive equilibrium does not characterize the defendants' behavior, one has not gotten very far. One must now examine conduct and decide whether conduct was anti-competitive.

Here, current theory is likely to have more to say. Particular conduct by the defendants can be analyzed in an attempt to decide whether it contributed to an anticompetitive result and whether it appears to have required agreement. Unfortunately, current theory will typically not provide a definitive answer. Instead, the concentration of theorists on providing examples of what *might* happen will come into play. Using a stripped-down, simplified model, an economist may testify for the plaintiff that certain forms of behavior *could* be anticompetitive. Another economist may very well testify for the defendants, explaining the neutral or pro-competitive aspects of the questioned behavior.

Does this mean that it will be impossible to choose between such explanations? Not at all, but doing so is likely to require examination of the detailed facts of the industry and firms involved – detailed examination of the context of the case. Modern theory, by merely showing that a variety of things *can* happen, is likely to stimulate plaintiffs' imagination. It can certainly be suggestive; it will almost never be definitive (Organizing Principle 3).

Further, focus now specifically on an allegation of collusion. In the case of collusion, one has to decide whether departures from competition can be explained only by collusion or whether the observed results could have occurred through oligopolistic rationality without agreement among the defendants.[47] Here, current theory is of no help whatever. Because the principal result of theory at present is (roughly) that anything can happen when rational players oppose each other (Organizing

---

[47] Of course, this supposes that there is no direct evidence of collusion.

Principle 2), the only guidance that one is likely to get from this literature is that the outcome *could* be an equilibrium in a noncooperative game. That is no help at all.

Such a result is no help because it comes from asking the wrong question. The issue is not whether the outcome could be an equilibrium in a stylized noncooperative game. The issue, rather, is whether it is plausible to believe that the defendants could have achieved that particular equilibrium without explicit communication or some form of agreement. This has to do with the rich context in which the defendants operate. Such factors as the difficulty of detecting cheating or the number of variables that must be coordinated come crucially into play. But, although industrial organization economists can have a good deal to say about such matters, current developments have added little, if anything.

At least one principal aim of industrial organization should be to inform public policy toward, and court decisions about, competition or the lack thereof. In this respect progress – at least as revealed by the *Handbook* – has not been remarkably rapid (nor has it been absent). The field is marked by increasing technical sophistication, but that is not the only or the best way of measuring progress. As I have described in this section and the preceding one, the field appears to me to have lost sight of the basic question of how the context within which oligopolists operate determines which equilibrium will be reached and what happens on the way – in particular, the question of whether or to what extent oligopolists will achieve the joint-profit-maximizing solution without collusion.[48]

Concluding Remarks

Despite my favorable remarks on the *Handbook* itself, this essay no doubt conveys a somewhat negative tone. The reactions of some readers, however, suggest that I should be quite explicit about what my message actually is.

In the first place, I am not "antitheory." Indeed, I take the view that theory can and should play an indispensable part in informing empirical analysis. Some of my criticism of empirical work in industrial organization stems precisely from the failure of that work to have a sound theoretical foundation.

Second, I am not even "anti-exemplifying-theory." The stripped-down models often used can and do provide insights into what can happen.

---

[48] See also Fisher (1989).

Moreover, they provide counterexamples to easy generalizations. Some of my own work has been of this nature.[49]

But appreciating such contributions does not imply satisfaction with the state of the art as regards either theory or empirical work. Theory and empirical work need to illuminate each other. Too often, poorly understood scraps of empirical material are used by theorists to provide a suggestive context. Too often, poorly understood theory (and usually not very current theory) is used by empirical workers to reach a conclusion that is not soundly based.

The promise of great advances in industrial organization analysis is there, but that promise has not yet been realized. In its present state, theory does not provide much opportunity for verification or rejection, and often it is not phrased in terms of observable variables. Theorists need to study real industries in depth, and attention needs to shift away from the analysis of pure strategic interaction and toward the effects of context on behavior. Only then will theory be able to provide a model rich enough to serve as the underpinning for cross-industry studies.

Thus, even if one agrees with my comments on the state of the art, one need not be depressed about industrial organization at this juncture. The field has been undergoing a revolution. Even though that revolution has not produced results as exciting or relevant as some of the revolutionaries would have us believe, the revolution is not yet over.

The two poets quoted in the epigraphs to this paper give different accounts of what it is like to live in revolutionary times. The poem by Yeats describes the anarchy consequent on the destruction of an old order; that by Wordsworth describes the opportunity that such times create, especially for the young.

If attention can now be turned to the sort of agenda I have outlined – to the theory and empirical study of the effects of context on outcomes, to the analysis of models rich enough to capture the facts of real industrial situations – then the promise implied in the quote from Wordsworth can be achieved.

But that promise has not yet been achieved. Those who believe that it has (and who are inclined to dismiss my remarks as just those of an old

---

[49] See, for example, Fisher (1985). It is not really correct, however, to suppose that my work on accounting rates of return (Fisher and McGowan, 1983) is exemplifying theory. That work proves some underlying theorems showing that the generalization in question (accounting rate of return equals economic rate of return) is true only under extremely restrictive circumstances. The examples serve to show that the generalization can easily be very far from the truth.

geezer in training) might do well to reflect on the fact that the full title of Wordsworth's poem is "French Revolution, as It Appeared to Enthusiasts at Its Commencement." As I said earlier, industrial organization has a long way to go.

REFERENCES

Brock, Gerald W. 1975. *The U.S. Computer Industry: A Study of Market Power.* Ballinger.

Farrell, Joseph, and Carl Shapiro. 1990. "Horizontal Mergers: An Equilibrium Analysis." *American Economic Review* 80 (March):107–26.

Fellner, William J. 1949. *Competition among the Few.* Knopf.

Fisher, Franklin M. 1979. "Diagnosing Monopoly." *Quarterly Review of Economics and Business* 19 (Summer):7–33. Reprinted as Chapter 1 in Fisher (1990–91).

——— 1984. "The Misuse of Accounting Rates of Return: Reply." *American Economic Review* 74 (June):509–17. Reprinted as Chapter 5 in Fisher (1990–91).

——— 1985. "Can Exclusive Franchises Be Bad?" In *Antitrust and Regulation: Essays in Memory of John J. McGowan,* edited by Franklin M. Fisher. MIT Press. Reprinted as Chapter 9 in Fisher (1990–91).

——— 1987a. "On the Misuse of the Profits-Sales Ratio to Infer Monopoly Power." *Rand Journal of Economics* 18 (Autumn):384–96. Reprinted as Chapter 6 in Fisher (1990–91).

——— 1987b. "Horizontal Mergers: Triage and Treatment." *Journal of Economic Perspectives* 1 (Fall):23–40. Reprinted as Chapter 2 in Fisher (1990–91).

——— 1989. "Games Economists Play: A Noncooperative View." *Rand Journal of Economics* 20 (Autumn):113–24. Reprinted as Chapter 12 in Fisher (1990–91).

——— 1990–91. *Industrial Organization, Economics and the Law.* Harvester-Wheatsheaf and MIT Press.

Fisher, Franklin M., and John J. McGowan. 1983. "On the Misuse of Accounting Rates of Return to Infer Monopoly Profits." *American Economic Review* 73 (March):82–97. Reprinted as Chapter 4 in Fisher (1990–91).

Fisher, Franklin M., John J. McGowan, and Joen E. Greenwood. 1983. *Folded, Spindled, and Mutilated: Economic Analysis and U.S. v. IBM.* MIT Press.

Fisher, Franklin M., and Peter Temin. 1973. "Returns to Scale in Research and Development: What Does the Schumpeterian Hypothesis Imply?" *Journal of Political Economy* 81 (January–February):56–70. Reprinted as Chapter 10 in Fisher (1990–91).

——— 1979. "The Schumpeterian Hypothesis: Reply." *Journal of Political Economy* 87 (April):386–89. Reprinted as Chapter 11 in Fisher (1990–91).

Iwata, Gyoichi. 1974. "Measurement of Conjectural Variations in Oligopoly." *Econometrica* 42 (September):947–66.

Klevorick, A. K. 1991. "Directions and Trends in Industrial Organization: A

Review Essay on the Handbook of Industrial Organization." *Brookings Papers: Microeconomics*, pp. 241–65.

Kohn, Meir G., and John T. Scott. 1982. "Scale Economies in Research and Development: The Schumpeterian Hypothesis." *Journal of Industrial Economics* 30 (March):239–49.

Lieberman, Marvin B. 1987. "Excess Capacity as a Barrier to Entry: An Empirical Reappraisal." *Journal of Industrial Economics* 35 (June):607–27.

Long, William F., and David J. Ravenscraft. 1984. "The Misuse of Accounting Rates of Return: Comment." *American Economic Review* 74 (June): 494–500.

Lukes, Steven, and Itzak Galnoor, eds. 1987. *No Laughing Matter: A Collection of Political Jokes*. Hammondsworth, U.K.: Penguin.

Newmark, C. 1989. "Do High Prices Indicate Collusion? A Critical Review of Price-Concentration Studies." Unpublished manuscript. North Carolina State University.

Rodriguez, Carlos Alfredo. 1979. "A Comment on Fisher and Temin on the Schumpeterian Hypothesis." *Journal of Political Economy* 87 (April): 383–85.

Schmalensee, Richard, and Robert D. Willig, eds. 1989. *Handbook of Industrial Organization*. 2 vols. Amsterdam and New York: North-Holland.

Shapiro, Carl. 1989. "The Theory of Business Strategy." *Rand Journal of Economics* 20 (Spring):125–37.

Weiss, Leonard, ed. 1989. *Concentration and Price*. MIT Press.

CHAPTER 25

Reflections on
Competition Policy (1993)

1. Introduction: Structure vs. Conduct

In writing on competition policy, I shall draw heavily on a century of American experience. I shall do so, not because that experience has been one of unmixed wisdom and success – far from it – but because that is the experience with which I am most familiar.

American antitrust policy (as American competition policy is called for historical reasons) is largely determined by judicial interpretation. In the American legal system, laws are expounded by judges given the nature of the case before them. This has been true of the antitrust laws (which one chief justice called "as broad as the Constitution"). But I do not plan to give a history of court cases; rather, I shall be asking how economic analysis can or should inform public policy, including legal standards.

The first issue in competition policy is a basic one. Should pro-competitive laws be aimed at preventing certain forms of behavior or at preventing the development of certain kinds of market structures? This issue runs through the entire history of American antitrust policy and must inevitably be faced in any thoughtful policy formation.

The conduct vs. structure question is easy to exemplify. Suppose that a firm grows and acquires all or nearly all of the market, attaining monopoly power. If no single act performed by the firm is itself obviously anti-competitive, then a behavioral standard will allow this to happen. A structural standard, by contrast, proceeds from the view that monopolies are bad even though monopolists may be good people. On a structural standard, a monopoly outcome is to be prevented because of the allocative distortion that monopoly produces, even though the monopoly firm has done no particular wrongful act.

On the other hand, there are plainly cases where a behavioral standard is appropriate. Suppose that there are several firms in a generally competitive setting. Suppose that they agree to fix prices. In such a case, a structural standard would not apply, but it would be unreasonable for competition policy to allow such behavior.

384

These examples, of course, are too simple. Competition policy would be easy were it always easy to identify anticompetitive structures or anticompetitive acts. In fact, as we shall see, it is not always (or perhaps even usually) easy, and competition policy is not easily reduced to a few mechanical rules.

2.   Single-Firm Monopoly

2.1.   The Alcoa Decision

The area in which the structure vs. conduct problem arises most often is that of single-firm monopoly, and I shall begin with that topic. Of necessity, my historical sketch of the judicial history of the problem is a superficial one.

The first thirty years of antitrust policy (from 1890 to 1920) involved several large single-firm monopoly cases (called "Section Two cases" because they are brought under Section Two of the Sherman Antitrust Act). None of these, however, forced the courts to deal directly with the structure vs. conduct issue. In each case, the courts found (rightly or wrongly) both that a monopoly structure was present and that the defendant firm had committed anticompetitive acts.

The Supreme Court first began to face the issue in the *United States Steel* case decided in 1920.[1] U.S. Steel was the largest American steel corporation, having been formed by merger around the turn of the century. By the standards of the day, it was a very large and powerful firm, but the Court did not find that it had engaged in anticompetitive conduct. In view of that, the Court declined to find U.S. Steel in violation of the Sherman Act, observing that "the law does not make mere size an offense."[2]

That dictum can be read in two ways. The first is that the Court was refusing to apply a purely structural standard. The second is that size alone does not produce a monopoly structure. I think the first reading is the correct one. In view of later history the second interpretation presumes too high a degree of economic sophistication on the part of the 1920s Court.

Great single-firm monopoly cases do not arise very often, and here matters more or less stood until the *Aluminum Company of America (Alcoa)* case, brought in the 1930s and decided (on liability) just after World War II.[3] Because the case took so long a time to get through the

---

[1] *United States v. United States Steel Corporation, et al.*, 251 US 417 (1920).
[2] *Ibid.* at 451.
[3] *United States v. Aluminum Company of America, et al.*, 148 F. 2d 416 (1945).

court system (or, at least, what seemed like so long a time back then), a majority of the Supreme Court had served in the Department of Justice while the case was pending. As a result, the Supreme Court could not hear the case itself and referred it for decision to a special panel of the Court of Appeals for the Second Circuit. The opinion, which came to have major importance, was therefore written by Judge Learned Hand, one of America's great jurists who never received a Supreme Court appointment.

Judge Hand attempted to deal with the structure-conduct issue. In essence, he held that a firm could violate the anti-monopoly provision of the law without ever doing any single act that was wrongful in itself. Instead, a firm would be held in violation if two things were true: First, the firm had to have monopoly power; second, the firm had to have achieved or maintained that power by deliberate action – by means other than "superior skill, foresight, and industry."

What does such a standard mean? To answer this, we need to look at what monopoly power really is and at how Judge Hand phrased his opinion. This means first examining the problems with a purely structural test for monopoly.

2.2   Monopoly Structure

Monopoly power is the power to charge prices above competitive levels (or, equivalently, offer products below competitive quality) without having your business taken by competitors. Most real firms have a little such power; monopolists have it to a high or long-lasting degree.

So far, so good. The problem is how to *tell* when a given firm has monopoly power. This is where Judge Hand's phraseology became unfortunate and where economic analysis becomes important for competitive policy.

Every student of elementary economic theory learns that a monopoly occurs when a firm has one hundred percent of a market, there are barriers to entry, and there are no close substitutes. In practice, however, there are always some forms of substitutes, entry is seldom impossible, and the firm in question has a large, but not a one hundred percent share of something (exactly what turns out to be a serious issue).

It is very tempting to look for a simple test and, especially, to look at market share. After all, if a firm with one hundred percent is a perfect monopoly, a firm with a high enough share must be close to being a perfect monopoly – close enough to count.

This temptation must be resisted. Aside from the difficulties associated with defining the "relevant market" in which to measure share (I shall have more to say about this a bit later), market share is only a very crude indicator of monopoly power. That indicator operates as follows. Where a firm's share is small, it is likely not to require much effort for its competitors to take away its business should it attempt to charge supra-competitive prices. Where the firm's share is large, on the other hand, taking away its business may require very large expansion or entry.

Notice, however, that the emphasis is on what happens to share if the firm attempts to charge supra-competitive prices. (This has to do with the elasticity of the demand curve facing the firm). The emphasis is *not* on share itself.

This is as it should be. Consider a firm that is more efficient than its rivals and uses that efficiency to charge lower prices. Such a firm will quickly gain a large market share, but one ought not to penalize it for so doing. A firm that gains and keeps a large market share *solely* by being more efficient in this way has no monopoly power. Monopoly power is the ability to keep a large share *without* lower prices and better products.

Judge Hand was quite aware of this, but he made the mistake of phrasing his decision in a way that lent itself to misunderstanding. Although he observed that monopoly power and market share were not equivalent, he essentially made market share the touchstone test for monopoly power, laying down certain quantitative standards based on the facts of the *Alcoa* case. As we shall see, this led to endless problems in later litigation.

Having made market share the test of monopoly power, Hand then had to deal with the issue of what to do in cases such as that of the efficient low-priced firm. Here, instead of stating that such a firm had no monopoly power, he turned to a behavioral standard. As already remarked, a firm that had attained its market share solely through such things as superior skill or efficiency was not to be held liable under the Sherman Act.

Hand was entirely conscious of what was involved here. He stated that "the successful competitor, having been urged to compete, must not be turned upon when he wins".[4] In saying this, he described a central problem for the formation of sensible competition policy.

Competition policy has an incentive effect. When certain structures or behavior are proscribed by the authorities, the actions of firms are and ought to be affected. It follows that the construction of competitive policy must be careful lest competitive behavior be directly or indirectly discouraged. This is likely to be a particular danger when authorities

---

[4] *Ibid.* at 430.

attempt to lay down a simple set of tests or rules. Such rules may be useful for their clarity but risk doing positive harm if they are overly simple.

It is easy to give an example here. Following the train of thought that makes market share the test of monopoly power, it has sometimes been suggested that one ought to have a rule that no firm can have more than a certain percentage of a market (say fifty percent). Aside from the difficulties involved in determining market share, it is easy to see that such a rule has perverse incentives as efficient firms grow larger. That is why Hand carved out an exception to the market-share-alone-is-enough standard.

So far as I know, no country has ever adopted so simple (and perverse) a rule (although the late U.S. Senator, Philip Hart, repeatedly proposed legislation involving it some years ago). But at least one rule that has the same perverse effects in milder form does exist. I refer to the standard used in the EEC which focuses on abuse by a "dominant firm" and defines "dominant" in terms of market share (as I recall, a share greater than thirty percent). Putting aside the exact meaning of "abuse", such a rule makes it clear that firms with more than a certain market share will be treated differently and examined more closely than smaller firms. Like an absolute prohibition against high shares, but more softly, this provides a disincentive to efficient, competitive behavior.

a. Market Definition and Market Share. The problem is greatly exacerbated by the fact that the clarity of a market share test is quite illusory. In most real cases, the measurement of market share is not easy because it is far from clear just what one should mean by "the market". Following *Alcoa*, this has led to a plethora of often bizarre and fruitless argument.

The difficulty arises because it is almost never true that the products of the alleged monopolist have no substitutes. Rather, different goods can substitute for the alleged monopolist's products to a greater or lesser degree. Are such goods "in" or "out" of the market? This will matter if one is going to rely on market share tests.

I believe that the correct way to think about this problem is as follows. In a monopoly case, we are interested in those products and firms whose presence can constrain an attempt by the alleged monopolist to charge supracompetitive prices. Another way of describing this is to say that we are interested in those products and firms that the monopolist must take into account when setting prices.

One set of products that constrain the alleged monopolist's behavior are those to which customers can turn and use in place of the monopolist's products. This phenomenon is called "demand substitutability". A second set of constraints comes from "supply substitutability" – the ability of other firms not currently making demand-substitutable products to do so in the event of an attempt to earn supra-competitive profits.

An example may help. Suppose that there is only one manufacturer of red paint. Then demand substitutability is limited by the extent to which consumers are willing to use other colors. But, even if there is a large group of customers determined to use red and nothing else, the red-paint manufacturer is not a monopolist if other paint manufacturers can easily produce red paint. To count the market as consisting only of red paint and then to count the red-paint manufacturer's share as one hundred percent is to miss the point of what one is trying to do.

Now, it will not have escaped attention that supply substitutability and ease of entry are very, very closely related. Indeed, the statement that certain firms produce supply-substitutable products and the statement that those firms would find it easy to enter differ only in degree and not in kind. That difference does not matter if one is going to be careful about what follows. The conclusion to be drawn in the paint example is the same whether one counts manufacturers of different color paints as already in the market or counts them as poised on the outside with entry very easy. In either case, there is no monopoly power.

The difficulty comes when the exercise is artificially pointed at the calculation of market share as the test of monopoly. Here one gets quite different conclusions depending on whether one defines the market to exclude paints other than red or includes such paints in the market. This problem arises when the test becomes important for its own sake (as legal tests have a way of doing), and one forgets the analysis that lies behind it.

The fact that the market definition question is often not susceptible of any precise answer shows up again when we consider another problem, the role of relative prices. Here the classic example is that of the *Cellophane* case, decided by the Supreme Court in the mid-1950s.[5] This is the classic case on market definition.

In *Cellophane*, the issue was the extent to which other forms of flexible wrapping paper were substitutes for cellophane, a particular transparent type of paper. The Supreme Court found evidence of such substitution and concluded that other flexible wrapping papers were in

---

[5] *U.S. v. E. I. DuPont de Nemours and Company*, 351 U.S. 377 (1956).

the same market as cellophane. That conclusion was heavily criticized by a number of economists.[6] They pointed out that the facts suggested that DuPont (the maker of cellophane) had raised its price up to the point at which customers began to turn to other wrapping papers. At lower, still profitable prices for cellophane, those other papers would not have been seen as acceptable substitutes. The economic commentators concluded that this meant that flexible wrapping papers were *not* in the same market as cellophane.

I believe both sides in this debate to have been in error – largely because the question asked, that of market definition, is not a well-posed one. The facts are that other wrapping papers did not constrain the price of cellophane below a certain level and that, above that level, they did constrain it. Once one has said that, one has said all there is that bears on the monopoly power question. One can only suppress information by trying to press it on the Procrustean bed of market definition in which the other wrapping papers are either in or out. In effect, the other papers were in the same market as cellophane at high cellophane prices and not at low ones. To simplify further than that is to lose the point.

As I have already suggested, however, concentration on the market definition question in an effort to meet Hand's quantitative standards for market share has become a major piece of any American monopoly case (and, indeed, of other types of cases as well). The debate over market definitions has ranged from the reasonably sensible to the truly bizarre. I mention only two examples drawn from the many cases in which I have been personally involved.

The first would be simply amusing if it were not real. Lady Grace is a chain of stores selling women's intimate apparel and foundation garments. They lost their lease in the South Shore Plaza Shopping Mall, a large shopping center in the Boston area, and promptly sued the mall operator under the anti-trust laws (that being the American way). They claimed that the market consisted only of shops selling ladies' lingerie in the South Shore Plaza Shopping Mall and that the mall operator was conspiring with Victoria's Secret (a rather more upscale purveyor of lingerie) to monopolize that market.

Such a claim was, of course, silly. The notion that the only shops that constrained Victoria's Secret's pricing in the South Shore Shopping Mall were the other specialty shops in the mall ignored the possibility of shopping elsewhere and also the enormous lingerie departments of the non-

---

[6] Stocking and Mueller (1955); Kaysen and Turner (1959), p. 102; Posner (1976), pp. 127–8.

specialty stores located in the mall. But the plaintiff maintained a market definition restricted to the narrow business that its own particular shop defined itself as being in.

That was a private suit, as is permitted under the American antitrust laws. A far more important case was one brought by the Department of Justice (with companion private suits), the antitrust case against IBM brought in 1969 and finally withdrawn in 1982 without a decision by the trial judge.[7] I was IBM's chief economic witness in the case and have written about it very extensively,[8] so I shall not discuss it at length here.

In the IBM case, the government claimed the market to consist of "general-purpose, electronic, digital data-processing equipment optimized for commercial purposes". I shall not linger over this except to point out that the last phrase ("optimized for commercial purposes") was designed to remove from the market those areas (scientific uses) in which IBM had been relatively unsuccessful. In any event, after being faced by testimony from their own witnesses that every modern computer was "general purpose", the government finally defined the term to mean only systems with very specialized capabilities. (Indeed, so specialized was the definition that, in at least one version, IBM itself made no systems that met it). Only Burroughs, Univac, and Honeywell machines were said to be in the market.

Now, eleven years after the end of the case, the same people who promulgated that market definition claim that events in the computer industry prove they were right (see Stewart, 1993). They claim that the fact that IBM has suffered considerably from competition from other companies and other forms of computing (smaller machines and distributed processing) means that it was just a sluggish monopoly, slow to respond.

That claim is absurd. If the government's market definition had been correct, IBM would not have had to worry about such forms of competition; such forms were *outside* the market. In fact, the history of the computer industry since the case shows how wide the market was and how competitive it is in fact.

The lesson here is that monopoly power is not easily measured. Market share tests, in particular, are not so simple as they appear. The attempt to find a simple test will often not succeed in doing simple (or any other kind of) justice.

That lesson extends beyond the market-share–market-definition

---

[7] *United States* v. *International Business Machines Corporation*, Docket Number 69 Civ. (DNE) Southern District of New York.
[8] Fisher, McGowan, and Greenwood (1983).

example. Economic analysis does not provide a simple structural test for monopoly. Worse, it is often easy to misunderstand and misapply what economic analysis does provide.

b. Profits. The other leading example here is that of profits. Here there are two issues. One is simply that of measurement. For reasons that it would take too long to go into, accounting profit rates as ordinarily reported do not in fact measure economic rates of return.[9]

The other reason is more fundamental. It is true that *in long-run competitive equilibrium* there are no economic profits. It is a vulgar error to suppose that this means that all profits – even lasting over time – must signal monopoly. It is simply not true that firms in competitive industries earn no profits. Profits are the carrot (and losses the stick) by which the invisible hand guides the economy. To suppose that because profits are zero in long-run competitive equilibrium they must always be zero in competition is to fail to understand the fundamental driving force of competition.

c. Barriers to Entry. Does the fact that there is no simple structural test for monopoly mean that a structural standard cannot be used? Not at all. It is possible to identify monopoly power, but this requires a serious study of the industry rather than reliance on one or two apparently easy-to-measure items. In particular, it requires a study of barriers to entry – more generally of the ability or inability of actual and potential competitors to expand if the alleged monopolist attempts to charge supra-competitive prices.

The subject of barriers to entry, I might add, is one of the many that are easy to get wrong. Merely because an industry is unattractive to entrants does not mean that there are barriers to entry. Fierce competition is not a barrier. Rather, a barrier to entry exists if there is something that would prevent outside firms from entering *while incumbent firms earn supra-normal profits.*

In this connection, I cannot resist telling the following story, especially appropriate for an American publishing in Spain five hundred years after the voyage of Columbus.

In 1986, two United States airlines, Northwest Airlines and Republic Airlines, proposed a merger. That merger (which ultimately took place) was opposed by the Department of Justice's Antitrust Division. Among the reasons for opposing the merger was the claim that competition with the merged airline would require another airline to have a hub (essen-

---

[9] For an extended discussion, see Fisher (1990–91), Chapters 5 and 6.

tially a large connecting airport facility) in the city of Minneapolis, Minnesota, located in the northern part of the central United States. Putting aside the question of whether that was true (it wasn't), let's look at what the Division said were the barriers to entry into acquiring such a hub. These were explicitly not economies of scale. Rather, the first supposed barrier was that the merged Northwest would operate so many flights that an entering hubbing airline would find it unprofitable to compete. But this is not a barrier. The issue is *not* whether an entrant could come in if the merged airline kept producing the pre-merger output but rather whether entry would be possible if the merged airline cut back production in an attempt to raise prices.

The second reason given as a barrier to entry was that Minneapolis is a poor location in which to have a hub because it is too far north to provide efficient connections between East and West Coast cities. This cannot be a barrier to entry either. It is not a barrier to entry that a business is unprofitable for everyone, and, if Minneapolis would be a poor hub for an entrant it would be so for the merged airline.

In fact, Minneapolis is not a poor place for a hub. Its location appears too far north only if one looks at a Mercator projection – a wall map. If one looks at a globe, one finds that Minneapolis lies very close to the great circle routes between East and West Coast cities. In fact, it is second only to Chicago's crowded airport as a large city near which to have such a hub. This fact came as a surprise to the Antitrust Division, leaving one with the inevitable conclusion: When it comes to the analysis of barriers to entry, the Antitrust Division quite literally believed that the earth is flat.

2.3. Monopoly Behavior: Predatory Pricing

If a structural standard applied to monopoly requires more than a simple test, is the same thing true of a behavioral standard? In other words, are there certain acts that monopolists or would-be monopolists are likely to engage in and that can easily be identified as anticompetitive?

Unfortunately, the answer here is "No", and one meets the same problem in trying to formulate a behavioral standard that we met when discussing a structural one. Competition policy must be careful not to *discourage* efficient competitive behavior. The problem can be best illustrated by considering predatory behavior in general and predatory pricing in particular.

Predatory behavior occurs when a firm deliberately chooses an action that is not profit-maximizing without considering the supra-normal profits to be earned when competitors are driven out. Since firms often make mistakes and end up losing money, it is well to add that, to be predatory, an action must also *be* profit-maximizing when one does consider the long-run supra-normal returns to be made after competition has been damaged.

This seems simple enough – and, in principle, it is – but identifying such cases in practice is not always as simple as it appears. Consider, in particular, predatory pricing. Apparently, to be predatory, a price must be below costs with the action making sense because of the monopoly profits to be earned once competition has been driven out and prices raised to supra-competitive levels.[10] (Note the possibility that monopoly might be achieved in this way if there are other barriers to entry.)

The question that naturally arises is that of what it means for prices to be "below costs". Here it is crucial to note that the costs in question must be those of the alleged predator. Rivals are quick to complain and allege predation when prices are cut below *their* costs, but that, standing alone, is irrelevant. Under competition, inefficient firms will indeed see prices cut below their costs. That forces them to become efficient or die. That is how competition works and it is what a pro-competitive policy should encourage. This means that a policy against predatory pricing must be careful not to chill the competitive process itself.

Moreover, even the comparison of the alleged predator's price to its own costs must be done with care. Since 1975, many courts in the United States have adopted some version of the so-called "Areeda-Turner" test (Areeda and Turner, 1975). In that test, price is compared to average variable cost and prices below that level are presumed predatory. Properly understood, that is a reasonable standard for the first prong of the test for predation (the "below cost" part), but, of course, the key lies in the words "properly understood".

Areeda and Turner proposed average variable cost as a standard because they believed that one would seldom be able to estimate marginal cost. Obviously, marginal cost is the preferred alternative; units of output that are sold below marginal cost are units on which the firm is losing money. Average variable cost makes sense both because it *may* lie close to marginal cost and because the simple theory of the firm tells us that firms will shut down rather than produce at prices below average variable cost.

Problems begin to arise when courts or antitrust authorities (or private plaintiffs) misunderstand the genesis of the test and begin to apply it in

---

[10] Under some circumstances, the recoupment can come in a different but related market, but I shall stay with the central example in the text.

a mechanical manner. This is particularly so when the application involves a firm producing multiple products where it requires considerable sophistication to understand what one means by "average variable cost". For, in such cases, "average variable cost" is undefined unless one defines other outputs as negative inputs and the choice to make the given output as involving opportunity costs.

Two related examples may make this clear. Airlines typically sell seats on the same flight at different prices. To simplify greatly, one set of seats is reserved for passengers who cannot commit to the journey far in advance. I shall refer to such passengers as "business passengers". Another set of seats is sold to "leisure passengers" – passengers with more flexible schedules.[11] Business fares are usually considerably higher than leisure fares.

A few years ago, a tour arranger called "International Travel Arrangers" ("ITA") sued Northwest Airlines. Among its claims was the allegation that Northwest had predatorily priced on certain flights because it had priced its leisure seats at a particularly low price – below average cost said ITA.

Now, there can be no question but that this was true in *some* sense: Had Northwest sold *all* the seats on the flights in question at the low price, the flights would have been unprofitable. Further, one might claim that the costs in question were all variable; after all, had no passengers flown, there would have been no flight.

The problem, of course, is that this is superficial nonsense (and was eventually seen to be so by the courts).[12] Northwest was not producing a single output – leisure travel. Rather the low-priced seats were being sold to fill up the plane on which business travel was already being sold. If one steps back from mechanical calculation of average costs and remembers the purpose of the test, then it is plain that the calculation proposed by ITA was irrelevant. Because the flights were going to operate for business travelers in any case, Northwest's only choices were between pricing the leisure seats low enough to attract passengers and allowing those seats to fly empty. The marginal cost of carrying an additional passenger on a flight that will operate in any event is very, very small. It was profit-increasing, not predatory, for Northwest to sell the seats at prices above those low costs rather than earning no revenue from them whatever.

---

[11] Of course not all passengers with inflexible schedules are flying on business, and some business people fly on leisure fares. The terms are used only for mnemonic convenience.
[12] *International Travel Arrangers* v. *NWA, Inc.*, 1993 U.S. App. LEXIS 7882 (8th Cir. 1993).

Note that it is *possible* to express this in terms of average variable costs. The output involved was low-priced passengers. The costs associated with flying the airplane were *fixed* so far as that output was concerned. The only *variable* costs were those associated with extra passengers (baggage and reservation handling, meals, and so forth). The prices involved were above those costs. The difficulty is not that the test used is wrong; it is that one must be fairly sophisticated to understand how to apply the test.

Now consider a second example. In the Spring of 1992, American Airlines, the largest air carrier in the United States, announced what it called "Value Pricing", but what it referred to internally as "Radical Pricing". This involved a drastic lowering of *business* fares, so drastic that it could not reasonably have been believed that most flights would be profitable. Indeed, in the ensuing months, that action, reinforced by later fare actions, led American and other airlines to lose a great deal of money. Two airlines, Continental Airlines and Northwest Airlines, sued American for predatory pricing, and the case was tried before a jury in the summer of 1993. (The jury found for American.) I appeared as a witness for the plaintiffs.

American's lawyers, of course, made the same argument that I gave in the ITA case. (Indeed, they quoted me.) They pointed out that the marginal cost of flying an additional passenger is far below the lowered fares; hence, they argued, the fares cannot have been predatory.

But, of course, this is wrong. Unlike the ITA case, we are now considering prices that affect all the seats on the plane – in particular, prices that affect the business passengers without whom the plane would not operate because it would be unprofitable. Here the marginal decision is not whether to sell the seat at a low price or have it fly anyway. Rather the decision is whether to operate the plane at a profit – to sell the seats to make money or to fly the entire plane (or operate the entire system of the airline) at a loss. In terms of the average variable cost standard, now the costs that are variable are *all* the costs associated with flying the plane (and the market arrangements are such that even some or all of the capital costs can be so counted).

But it is only confusing to attempt to cast this into the apparently simple mold of the Areeda-Turner test. American made a deliberate decision that it must have known would cost it a great deal of money. It charged fares that could not possibly be sustained in the long run, fares well below those that competition would have enforced. Provided that American's action could reasonably have been expected to pay off because of later supra-normal profits to be recovered after the destruction of competition, this was a predatory act. (I believe this to have been the case.) The danger here is that courts, anxious to fit a case into the mold of a standard test, will misapprehend the point of the test and misapply it.

I must not leave the subject of predatory pricing without discussing the second prong of the true test – the destruction of competition and the consequent profits. I do so because, even though the Supreme Court (as we shall see) has been sensible about this, there is still a tendency to look only at the cost part of the test, which deceptively appears to be easily applied.

The most famous modern case that bears directly on this aspect of predation is the *Matsushita* case decided (on summary judgment) in 1986.[13] In *Matsushita*, the plaintiffs charged that various Japanese electronics firms had conspired to price television sets predatorily low with the object of driving American manufacturers (such as the plaintiff) from the market. Apart from other difficulties with such a theory, the Supreme Court pointed out that the predation phase lasted for so long that rational firms could not expect to recoup their losses. Hence, whatever the cost test would have said, predation made no sense.

A second example comes from the IBM antitrust case referred to above. Here, the government alleged that IBM had (among other things) predatorily priced a set of computers known as the 360/90s. These were the top-of-the-line computers introduced in the mid-1960s. The Antitrust Division argued that the 360/90s were priced predatorily low in order to damage Control Data – then putting out its major second-generation large scientific machine, the 6600.

According to the Antitrust Division, IBM had two internal forecasts as to the number of placements of 360/90s that would be made. The first of these estimated that there would be 15 such machines and that the program would then be unprofitable. The second estimated that there would be 24 machines and the program would then be profitable. The Antitrust Division claimed that the second forecast was a fake, produced to satisfy the legal department, and that IBM's true expectations were revealed by the first forecast of 15 placements.

Without going into the details of IBM's accounting system, it is clear that something is wrong here. Suppose that the Antitrust Division were correct. Then expansion of output from 15 to 24 would turn a loss into a profit. Evidently, it must be the case that the price of the 360/90 exceeded its marginal cost. Moreover, it must be the case that the supposed losses on the smaller output were due to large fixed costs. On the

---

[13] *Matsushita Elec. Indus. Co.* v. *Zenith Radio Corp.*, 475 U.S. 574 (1986). For a more extended discussion, see Fisher (1990–91), Chapter 8.

Division's theory, it would have been even more predatory for IBM to have placed *zero* 360/90s and taken a bigger loss. That would surely have swept Control Data from the field!.[14]

In fact, IBM forecast that only 72 large scientific machines would be placed. It therefore cannot have hoped to drive out Control Data by placing 24 machines, let alone by placing 15. Indeed, Control Data's sales and profits on the 6600 exceeded its own forecasts and goals. It takes no more than a little common sense to realize that predation is not a likely explanation here.

Similar statements are true of other behavioral tests. It is typically not the case that simple-appearing tests are in fact simple. More important, they are seldom adequate. As with a structural standard, what is required is informed and detailed investigation.

3.   Oligopoly

3.1.   A Structural Standard: Mergers

The same issues arise again when we consider policy towards oligopoly. Here, indeed, it is difficult to have a structural standard at all. This is so for more than one reason.

To begin, considerations of fairness will often make a structural standard difficult. Consider the following. A firm behaves normally and competitively. Because of the actions of *other* firms, however, the industry structure becomes one of tight oligopoly making non-competitive results likely. It seems quite unfair to penalize the first firm or, indeed, to require it to change or be broken up.

On the other hand, what about a structural policy that primarily affects those firms whose actions caused the tight oligopoly to develop? This seems fair, but there are still substantial difficulties.

The first of these is the same as one we encountered when discussing monopoly. Growth in firm size through efficient competition is not to be discouraged. Moreover, in industries with economies of scale, it will often be the case that there is no efficient way to restrict firms from growing internally and an oligopoly from naturally developing. (This is likely to be a problem of greater practical importance than in the parallel case of natural monopoly.)

Note, however, that this difficulty applies mainly to internal growth. One might restrict the ability of tight oligopolies to form through

---

[14] There is another issue as to whether it was predatory for IBM ever to undertake the 360/90 program at all, but discussion of this would take too long. See Fisher (1990–91), Chapter 7.

mergers, and, indeed, merger policy is about as close as one can come to a structural standard in the case of oligopoly.[15]

I do not mean to suggest, however, that merger policy is without problems – far from it. For one thing, where economies of scale produce a natural oligopoly, successful firms may very well buy out unsuccessful ones. Preventing this is futile. Hence merger policy must allow for the possibility that the merging firms will gain efficiency or that the acquired firm will disappear in any case.

But the principal problem with a structural merger policy is different and far greater. It is the principal problem with any structural policy towards oligopoly. Any such policy supposes that we can recognize a tight oligopoly structure when we see it – and do so in a fairly simple way. This is not the case.

Economic analysis certainly has something to say on the factors that are likely to make oligopolistic rationality and supra-competitive pricing occur. Fewness of numbers and high concentration, simplicity of the product, the ease of detecting cheating on an explicit or implicit agreement, and so forth, form a familiar list.

But that list does not lead to precise or simple tests. How few is few? How concentrated does an industry have to be in order for oligopolistic cooperation to take over? We simply do not know the answers to these questions, and, indeed, we know that the answers are not simple ones. How concentrated an industry must be for oligopoly results to appear certainly depends on such things as the nature of the product and even the history of relationships among the firms. There is no simple mapping taking structural elements into results.

Indeed, to make matters worse, modern economists are not even working on this problem in useful ways. Modern game-theoretic treatments of oligopoly overwhelmingly tend to be studies of what *can* happen in various simplified contexts – formalized anecdotes, as it were. They do not tell us very much about predicting what *must* happen from an examination of structure and context.[16]

This has not stopped designers of merger policy from attempting to use simple structural tests. Since 1982, United States merger policy has been organized in terms of the Department of Justice's merger guidelines which set forth circumstances under which a merger is likely to be carefully studied.[17]

---

[15] Of course, merger policy can also form part of a structural policy towards monopoly. I ignore this in the ensuing discussion.

[16] See Fisher (1990–91), Chapter 12, for a fuller discussion.

[17] There were earlier guidelines, but 1982 marked the point at which the current policies essentially took shape. For a more extended discussion of merger policy, see Fisher (1990–91), Chapter 2.

Those guidelines run in terms of market concentration, more specifically, in terms of the Hirschman-Herfindahl Index (HHI) defined as the sum of squares of market shares multiplied by 10,000.[18] A merger that raises the HHI by 100 points in a market with the HHI already at 1,800 is likely to be opposed (unless there are extenuating factors), and there are other breakpoints similarly defined.

One problem with such a test we have already encountered. Before the HHI can be computed, the "market" must be defined, and, as we have seen, this is not a truly well-posed issue. Here the guidelines do at least an adequate job, defining the "market" as the minimal collection of firms that, if they colluded, could profitably raise prices by five percent for some period of time. This definition has some problems but at least focuses on the constraints on the proposed merged firms.

The problem to which I want to call attention now, however, is not this one. It is the fact that there is no basis whatever for supposing that a particular level of the HHI (1,800 or anything else) is in fact the breakpoint between competitive and oligopolistic behavior. Indeed, it is obvious that such a breakpoint cannot be the same in all industries. Nevertheless, the fact that the antitrust authorities use such a standard has an immense impact on which mergers get proposed and that get consummated.[19] While some standard must be used as a form of triage – a method of deciding which cases merit further investigation – we simply do not know whether the actual standard used is anywhere near optimal. I consider it to be a signal failure of economic analysis that such problems are not intensively studied.

3.2.   Behavioral Standards

All this makes it natural to concentrate on behavioral standards for oligopoly, and, indeed, with the exception of merger policy, this is what is usually done.

Certain forms of behavior are easy to rule out in principle. I have already given the example of overt price fixing. Yet, even here, there are gray areas. It is surely price fixing if you and I agree as to the prices we will set. What if I announce my price and then you follow? What if I

[18] Some idea of what this means can be obtained by observing that if there are n equal-size firms, then the HHI is equal to 10,000n. (Multiplication by 10,000 presumably occurs because lawyers do not like decimals.)

[19] To point out a particular example, the Federal Reserve Board, which has authority over bank mergers, uses the HHI standard (along with other tests) with the HHI calculated in terms of bank *deposits*, which is not even a measure of relevant output. To its credit, the Board has expressed some doubts about its numerical screens.

announce a tentative price and wait to see if you follow before putting it into effect?

A different type of behavioral standard verges on the structural. Oligopolists will find it difficult to collude, especially implicitly, if the product is complex and cheating hard to identify. They may therefore attempt to simplify matters by adopting "facilitating devices" – methods to ensure that conscious parallelism will work.

An old but excellent example of this comes from what are known as the "basing-point" cases. In the steel industry, there are a very large variety of products, shipped from a variety of plants. The members of the steel industry agreed that there would be certain standardized items, with prices of other items related to the standardized ones according to formulae published in an industry book. Further they agreed that, regardless of the origin of a steel shipment, freight would be charged as though it had come from one or, later, a few particular locations, called "basing points".

The industry claimed that these devices made things much simpler for customers. Maybe so, but they also made oligopolistic parallelism much easier. By adopting such devices, the industry no longer had to coordinate a large variety of prices. Rather they had only to coordinate the prices of the standardized items in the basing-point locations. The rest could be mechanically done. Given the difficulty of coordinating oligopoly action under uncertainty, this made such coordination much easier. It was eventually ruled illegal.

Ruling out facilitating devices may not always be simple, however. Some devices that may serve to facilitate coordination may also serve other more positive purposes. As always, it is difficult to formulate standards that can be applied without any investigation whatever.

This brings me to my final point. It may sometimes be difficult to tell whether a particular set of actions is principally designed to aid oligopolistic coordination, but at least competition policy should not positively promote such activity.

In this connection, I am quite skeptical of certain forms of what is called "industrial policy". While some examples of permitted coordination, such as AirBus, may in fact be successful, I do not believe that authorities are likely to be good at picking winners. What is more, permitting competing firms to cooperate in research must be done with caution. Such cooperation may or may not be socially useful, but its utility may be offset if the venturers end up cooperating on more than research. The mere opportunity to get to know each other may facilitate conscious parallelism, and it may be impossible to prevent explicit conversations about prices, products, output, or customer allocation. Policy makers should think long and hard before encouraging such contacts.

In this connection, I can do no better than to quote Adam Smith (1776, 1937 ed., p. 128). (Everyone knows the beginning of the passage, but the end is surprisingly apt.)

People of the same trade seldom meet together, even for merriment and diversion, but the conversation ends in a conspiracy against the public, or in some contrivance to raise prices. It is impossible indeed to prevent such meetings, by any law which either could be executed, or would be consistent with liberty and justice. But though the law cannot hinder people of the same trade from sometimes assembling together, it ought to do nothing to facilitate such assemblies; much less to render them necessary.

A wise competition policy should bear that firmly in mind.

4.   Concluding Remarks

Let me then briefly summarize the strands of thought that run through this paper.

First, competition policy can have either a structural or a behavioral standard or some combination. In the area of monopoly, a sensibly applied structural standard seems helpful. That is less true when it comes to oligopoly with the possible exception of merger policy.

Second, whatever type of standard is used, appropriate tests are generally not simple. Even the deceptively easy task of defining a "market" and calculating market shares is not trivial. Moreover, especially when it comes to oligopoly, economic analysis just does not provide the simple mapping between easy-to-measure structural elements and outcomes that would make tests easy.

Finally, I believe oligopoly to be a more important and frequent problem than is single-firm monopoly. This is especially true in a world open to trade. Here behavioral standards are appropriate.

In general, a sensibly applied competition policy cannot be carried out with quick and simple methods. The facts of the industry in question must be studied in some detail. Here economists have much to contribute, but not if they assist only in devising simple but misleading tests.

REFERENCES

Areeda, P. and Turner, D. (1975): "Predatory Pricing and Related Practices under Section 2 of the Sherman Act". *Harvard Law Review* 88, pp. 697–733.

Fisher, F. M. (1990–91): *Industrial Organization, Economics, and the Law*. Hemel-Hempstead: Harvester-Wheatsheaf and Cambridge, MA. MIT Press.

Fisher, F. M., McGowan, J. J. and Greenwood, J. E. (1983): *Folded, Spindled, and Mutilated: Economic Analysis and U.S. v. IBM*. Cambridge, MA. MIT Press.

Kaysen, C. and Turner, D. (1959): *Antitrust Policy*. Cambridge, MA. Harvard University Press.

Posner, R. (1976): *Antitrust Law: An Economic Perspective*. Chicago and London. University of Chicago Press.

Smith, A. (1937): *An Inquiry into the Nature and Causes of the Wealth of Nations*. New York: Random House, The Modern Library.

Stewart, J. B. (1993): "Whales and Sharks". *The New Yorker*, February 15, pp. 27–43.

Stocking, G. W. and Mueller, W. F. (1955): "The Cellophane Case and the New Competition". *American Economic Review* 45, pp. 29–63.

CHAPTER 26

The Social Costs of Monopoly and Regulation: Posner Reconsidered (1985)

The traditional analysis of the costs of monopoly concentrates on the deadweight loss involved, monopoly rents being considered merely a transfer to the monopolist from the consumer surplus that would exist under competition. Some years ago, that analysis was challenged by Posner (1975), who presented an ingenious argument that monopoly rents in fact measure the resources lost to society through rent-seeking activities and thus should be counted in the costs of monopoly. That argument has recently been used by staff members of the Federal Trade Commission (Long et al., 1982, Chap. 3, esp. pp. 77, 97, 104; see also Tollison, Higgins, and Shugart, 1983, pp. 23–44) in an attempt to estimate the benefits potentially flowing from the use of the FTC's line-of-business program in antitrust enforcement.

Unfortunately, Posner's argument, while a useful corrective to the traditional proposition that deadweight loss is all that matters, is not correct as a general analysis of the costs of monopoly, and conclusions based on it about the benefits of marginal changes in antitrust activities are likely to be particularly fallacious.

Posner's assumptions and conclusion are as follows:

1 Obtaining a monopoly is itself a competitive activity, so that, at the margin, the cost of obtaining a monopoly is exactly equal to the expected profit of being a monopolist. *An important corollary of this assumption is that there are no intramarginal monopolies – no cases, that is, where the expected profits of monopoly exceed the total supply price of the inputs used to obtain the monopoly. If there were such an excess, competition in the activity of obtaining the monopoly would induce the competing firms (or new entrants) to hire additional inputs in an effort to engross the additional monopoly profits.*

2 The long-run supply of all inputs used in obtaining monopolies

I am indebted to Richard Posner and George Stigler for comments, but I retain responsibility for error.

is perfectly elastic. Hence, the total supply price of these inputs includes no rents.

3 The costs incurred in obtaining a monopoly have no socially valuable by-products.

The first two assumptions assure that all expected monopoly rents are transformed into social costs, and the third that these costs do not generate any social benefits. [Posner 1975, p. 809; emphasis added]

The problem, I believe, lies with the first assumption and the fact that the last statement therein does not follow and is unlikely to be true. To begin to see why this is the case, consider for a moment the standard result of competitive theory that profits are reduced to zero in equilibrium. That result follows even when firms are differentially situated, because such differences are defined as rents. Thus, a manufacturing firm particularly well located ends up earning no equilibrium profits in its manufacturing activity despite its favorable location, because we impute to the location the money that flows from that advantage and treat it as a cost when considering manufacturing. *But rents are what Posner's analysis is all about.* If firms are differentially situated in terms of the ease with which monopoly can be obtained, then they will earn rents that will not represent social costs.

Will firms be differentially situated? Posner plainly means to assume that they are not. His assumptions, even if true, are insufficient to guarantee this, however, not only because constant costs may involve imputed rents but also because (contrary to Posner's assertion, p. 810) the assumption that inputs are available at constant prices does not imply that costs are constant. That conclusion also requires that the production function – here the production of monopolies – exhibit constant returns to scale, and Posner fails to assume this.

As a matter of fact, such an assumption would not be a plausible one in most contexts. Consideration of what is involved requires a closer examination of what is meant by the assumption that "obtaining a monopoly is itself a competitive activity" so that there is ease of entry into that activity and profits are competed away.

There are two possible ways to interpret Posner's "production of monopolies." The "competitive activity" involved is either that of obtaining monopolies generally or that of obtaining a particular monopoly. It is useful to examine both versions.

Suppose first that the activity involved is that of obtaining monopolies generally. Here the assumption that there is easy entry is plainly plausible; one can readily imagine potential monopolists searching for an appropriate area to monopolize. On the other hand, the assumption of constant costs – or of no rents – is not easy to maintain in that context. The supply of potential monopolies does not appear infinite. Some industries – the ones with higher entry barriers – are more readily monopolized than others or will yield higher monopoly rents for a given amount of resources spent in monopolizing them. This means that there are decreasing returns to monopolizing activity and inframarginal monopoly rents to firms that acquire the good monopolies. (I deal below with the fact that higher rents will call forth more effort in the securing of a *particular* monopoly.)

More important, even were there constant costs in the production of monopolies generally, it would not follow that monopoly rents corresponded to social costs. Consider the process through which profits are driven to zero in an ordinary competitive activity. In such an activity, when profits are being earned, new entrants come in and existing firms expand. The consequent expansion of supply bids prices down, reducing revenues, and the associated increase in the demand for factors bids input prices up, increasing costs. This goes on until profits have disappeared.

Any attempt to describe this process when the activity is that of the general production of monopolies runs into immediate trouble. Even ignoring the fact that Posner assumes that input prices will not be bid up, the desired conclusion will not follow. What is the "supply" of monopolies generally, the expansion of which will bring down price? Why should the possessor of a monopoly in one industry have his rents reduced because others are attempting to secure monopolies in other industries? Why should his costs be increased? Plainly, this interpretation cannot lead to Posner's results.

Suppose, then, that we consider not the obtaining of monopolies in general but rather the obtaining of a particular monopoly. In this case – even apart from the difficulty of defining successive units of "output" – constant costs cannot be a general property, nor can the activity be characterized as "competitive." Competition involves free entry, and monopolies are typically characterized by barriers to entry with incumbents enjoying advantages over potential entrants. This means that the firm that is foresighted enough to enter such a monopolizable area early will be able to monopolize it at a cost lower than that which latecomers would have to expend to wrest the monopoly away. This will result in a rent that will not be competed away by other potential monopolists. Not all of that rent need be the competitive return to investment in information as to the availability of monopoly; some or all of it can perfectly well be traditional monopoly rent. Even where an oligopoly is involved so that the rent-to-entry-investment process is more continuous than in the single-firm monopoly case, entry barriers can relieve incumbents of the necessity of spending all their rents in the effort to protect them from potential rivals.

Monopolies can also be obtained through luck rather than foresight. It is true that, as Posner says (1975, p. 812), if n risk-neutral firms each have an equal chance of obtaining a monopoly with a present value of V, each of them will be willing to spend V/n in an effort to secure the monopoly. Nevertheless, it does not follow that a total of V will in fact be spent (even apart from the question of whether risk neutrality is a good assumption). Whether the total is spent depends on the mechanism that produces the monopoly. If the monopoly is achieved before V is spent or if the marginal effect of expenditure on the chance of securing the monopoly falls to zero before V/n is spent, then firms will not in fact spend so much. Only the unsupported assumption of constant returns in the activity of securing a particular monopoly produces a mechanism that leads to Posner's result – and then only if one ignores the dynamics that may lead one firm to shut out others.

Note, however, that the fact that resources are expended on the attainment of monopoly certainly means that there are some cases where what appears as monopoly rent *understates* the resources spent on rent-seeking activities. Predictions about monopoly profits can overestimate as well as underestimate the amount to be gained, and luck can be bad as well as good. In some cases (private subways in New York City seem a likely example), more will be expended on the rent-seeking activity than the actual amount that the rents turn out to be. There is still no mechanism that makes such rents exactly equal the costs and no general presumption that overstatement cases must balance understatement ones across the economy. (Indeed, if monopolies keep on being sought and rent seekers are not risk loving there is a presumption that rents exceed costs.)

The point is that once one starts to think of real examples, Posner's result disappears as a general proposition. The Aluminum Company of America, for example, was well placed to monopolize because of the business it was in, an industry requiring particular mineral resources and cheap energy supply. It was in that business because of the patents it had originally obtained. The fact that it may have been drawn into patent research in aluminum by the possibility of monopoly rents does not alter the fact that once it was in and had monopolized the business, no further entry into monopolization of aluminum was possible at the same cost, and no entry into the monopolization of other businesses – even businesses with equally attractive monopoly rents – could bid away the monopoly rents already being earned in aluminum. The fact that a risk-neutral company would have been willing to spend the expected present value of all future monopoly rents to obtain the patents in the first place does not imply that they had to spend so much or that they or their potential rivals did so. Once the patents were obtained, at whatever cost, the future monopoly rents were achieved and further expenditure by anyone was pointless.

Much of this can be summarized by considering Posner's statement that "at the margin, the cost of obtaining a monopoly is exactly equal to the expected profit of being a monopolist." If the activity involved is that of obtaining monopolies generally, then that statement is unquestionably true but has no bearing on the issue. If, on the other hand, the activity is that of obtaining a particular monopoly, then the statement is not true. In equilibrium the costs of wresting the monopoly from the incumbent must be at least as great as the monopoly rents to be earned by doing so, but they need not be equal. This means that the incumbent can, in fact, be earning monopoly rents above the costs expended to secure them (the fact that he would have been willing to spend more if necessary has no bearing). Successful monopolists enjoy inframarginal rents, and there is no general mechanism that competes those rents away.

I say no general mechanism, because there clearly are cases in which some such mechanism operates. These are the cases Posner appears to have in mind; they have to do with government-induced monopoly and with regulation.

Potential monopolists are somewhat more likely to be on an equal footing where barriers to entry arise simply through government action than when such barriers arise for other reasons. The picture of resources expended on lobbying for a monopoly license until the eventually successful applicant has spent all the rents to be earned is one of some plausibility. The extent of that plausibility, however, is more limited than may at first appear. Before a monopoly license is given, all applicants may be on an equal basis. Once the license has been granted, however, regulatory authorities may be reluctant to transfer it. The Federal Communications Commission, for example, has almost never failed to renew the television license of an existing station. If incumbents have an advantage over potential replacements in the licensing process, it does not follow that their incumbency rents are no greater than the value of the resources expended to retain them, including the resources expended by unsuccessful applicants.[1]

---

[1] Rogerson (1982) presents a formal model of the results of advantage to the incumbent in the rent-seeking process.

Furthermore, those rents may exceed even the value of the resources expended to obtain the original monopoly license. It is hard to imagine, for example, that all or most of the originally successful applicants for broadcast licenses in VHF television correctly recognized in the 1940s the size of the rents eventually to be earned or that, if they did, they had to compete against a large body of unsuccessful applicants who shared that recognition. Moreover, there appears to have been some tendency for successful applicants to have been already involved in radio broadcasting. To the extent that the FCC favored such applicants, they earned a monopoly rent even if all applicants recognized the value of television licenses. While it is true that such rent accrued by virtue of the earlier radio license, to attempt to make it the equivalent of social costs by arguing that radio license applicants all expected and competed for the rents later to be made in television is to strain credulity.

The general point of this example is as follows. Even where government regulation is involved in the production of monopoly, not all potential monopolists will be equally situated. While, in such contexts, Posner is undoubtedly correct that some resources are likely to be expended in getting and retaining the monopoly, and while the resources involved are likely to be greater in such contexts than in those areas that do not involve government support, it is still unlikely that the resources expended will match the rents to be earned.

I add one final point related to a use that others have made of Posner's paper rather than directly to the paper itself.[2] Even were Posner's entire analysis correct and applicable, it would not follow that the benefits of increased or better antitrust enforcement should be taken to include the monopoly rents being earned in those additional industries where the improved enforcement restores competition. The monopoly rents being earned in industries where antitrust cases are brought correspond (in Posner's analysis) to resources already wastefully spent to achieve them. Those costs are investments in monopoly; they are generally sunk costs by the time of antitrust enforcement and cannot be recovered by the removal of the resulting monopoly rents.[3] Only if the improved enforcement mechanisms apply to *attempts* to monopolize or if such attempts are deterred by the improvement can the monopoly rents avoided be said to correspond to social costs that are saved. Whether the deterrent effect of marginal improvements in antitrust enforcement is at all impor-

---

[2] See the works on the line-of-business program cited in the opening paragraph of this chapter.

[3] Ongoing expenditures to *retain* the monopoly would be saved, however. In this respect (which Posner does not consider), Posner's assumption (1975, p. 809, n. 3) "that the monopoly is enjoyed for one period only" does affect the analysis.

tant is, of course, debatable;[4] even if that effect is important, decreasing returns to monopolization activity may mean that one catches large-rent monopolies and deters small-rent ones. In any event, the social costs avoided through such deterrence cannot be measured by using the monopoly rents removed in the cases that provide the additional object lessons.

In sum, Posner's analysis does indeed show that the standard analysis of the costs of monopoly as measured only by deadweight loss can understate those costs.[5] While there are thus some circumstances in which some monopoly rents should be included in the construction of such a measure, it is an open question whether those circumstances are so general as to prompt the inclusion of all or nearly all such rents. Broad general theory will not provide the answer here; that answer must rest on a case-by-case analysis.

REFERENCES

Long, William F.; Lean, David F.; Ravenscraft, David J.; and Wagner, C. L., III. *Benefits and Costs of the Federal Trade Commission's Line of Business Program.* Vol. 2. *Staff Analysis.* Washington: Fed. Trade Comm., Bur. Econ., September 1982.
Posner, Richard A. "The Social Costs of Monopoly and Regulation." *J.P.E.* 83 (August 1975): 807–27.
Rogerson, William P. "The Social Costs of Monopoly and Regulation: A Game-theoretic Analysis." *Bell J. Econ.* 13 (Autumn 1982): 391–401.
Tollison, Robert D.; Higgins, Richard S.; and Shugart, William F., II. *Benefits and Costs of the FTC's Line of Business Program: Recommendations of Robert D. Tollison, Richard S. Higgins, and William F. Shugart II.* Washington: Fed. Trade Comm., Bur. Econ., January 20, 1983.

[4] Posner himself is well aware of the deterrence issue as regards antitrust enforcement in general but naturally does not discuss the effect of improvements in enforcement. Even the magnitude of the overall deterrent effect of antitrust policy is speculative; Posner refers in passing to the literature on deterring crime for the suggestion that the costs of deterrence may be low (Posner 1975, pp. 811, 820).

[5] Posner points out that even the inclusion of monopoly rents may understate the costs of monopoly if rent-seeking behavior is active and antimonopoly enforcement expensive and effective (Posner 1975, pp. 811–12). On the other hand, a referee suggests that since one possible way to defend a monopoly is by price cutting, some of the costs of rent seeking may be private but not social costs.

Due Diligence and the Demand for Electricity: A Cautionary Tale (1992)

*written jointly with Peter S. Fox-Penner,
Joen E. Greenwood, William G. Moss,
and Almarin Phillips*

1.   Introduction

Econometrics has proven useful in demand forecasting largely because of its ability to separate the many factors that influence sales. Econometric techniques greatly improve the ability of businesses to understand and respond to market changes. Econometrics can also improve the ability to cope with uncertainty.

It is a commonplace of elementary economics that the quantity demanded depends on price. Yet, in forecasting demand, business people and policy makers often overlook that principle with results that can be very costly indeed. While the immediate subject of this paper is the price elasticity of demand for electricity, the lessons are of wider application.

Carl Kaysen was among the first to recognize the potential of econometrics in analyzing and forecasting demand (and it goes without saying that he did not overlook the importance of price). Nearly 30 years ago, Kaysen suggested to the Research Laboratory of the General Electric Corporation that it sponsor a study

designed to show what modern econometric methods could contribute to the understanding of the forces shaping the demand for electricity. The Corporation had, of course, regularly made forecasts of the growth in demand, in connection with its analyses of markets. However, these forecasts were generally based on correlations of total electricity output with such aggregates as gross national product or industrial production. . . . The Research Laboratory, to which [Kaysen] was a consultant, expressed an interest in the possibility that a more elaborate analytical technique might yield deeper insights into the probable future course of demand.[1]

The result was Fisher and Kaysen's well-known 1962 study of the demand for electricity, which set in motion several waves of successive research.

For Carl Kaysen on his 70th birthday.

[1] Fisher and Kaysen (1962), p. vii.

Fisher and Kaysen, however, were not good enough forecasters to realize that their research would also be at the heart of a dispute over a very costly example of poor demand forecasting. Almost 15 years after their study, a consortium of electric utilities in the Pacific Northwest, the Washington Public Power Supply System (WPPSS), began construction of five nuclear power plants based on inadequate demand forecasts – forecasts that failed to account for the effect that price increases necessitated by cost increases would have on demand. As cost and schedule overruns were encountered and the predicted demand failed to materialize, the utilities were unable to meet their financial obligations and defaulted on the bonds for two of the plants, WPPSS 4 and 5.

In the inevitable ensuing litigation, the literature and methods stemming from Fisher and Kaysen were used to examine the forecasts for the WPPSS utilities, particularly their treatment of uncertainty. Professors Fisher and Phillips and Charles River Associates were retained in this litigation by the plaintiffs, namely, counsel for the Chemical Bank acting as Trustee for the bondholders and by counsel for the Class of bondholders. The defendants included not only WPPSS and the participating utilities, but also R. W. Beck and Associates, which prepared the aggregate demand forecasts, WPPSS's Construction Engineers (United Engineers and Constructors and EBASCO Services, Inc.) and its Financial Advisor (Blyth Eastman Dillon & Co.). Moody's and Standard and Poor, which gave each of the 14 bond issues an initial rating of A1 and A+, respectively, were also among the defendants. This paper is based on our work therein.

The next section briefly reviews the history of forecasting and financial planning methods in the electric utility industry. Section 3 summarizes the WPPSS nuclear power projects. Sections 4 and 5 give our analysis of the original load forecasting techniques and the proper treatment of forecast uncertainty. Section 6 offers concluding observations.

2.   A Brief History of Electric Utility Demand Forecasting

2.1.   Background

Demand forecasting is especially important in the electric utility industry for several reasons. First, by law most electric utilities must serve all demand at the posted price; they cannot sell their products "while supplies last". Second, electricity cannot be stored economically; it must be produced as it is demanded. The electric power system must be sized to supply all electric power demand when and where it is requested. Third, it takes years to add significant new capacity to the system. Utili-

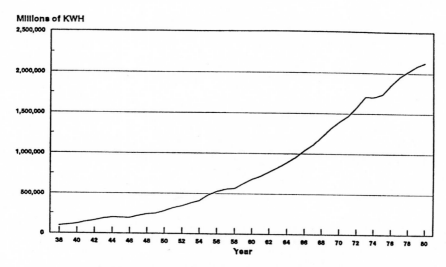

FIGURE 27.1. Energy sales. Total electric utility industry 1938–1980. Source: Edison Electric Institute Historical Statistics of the Electric Utility Through 1970, Statistical Yearbook 1981.

ties must plan well in advance to assure that future supply will meet demand.

These factors combine to necessitate reliable forecasts of electric power demand, making forecasting more prevalent among utilities than in many other industries. A peculiar circumstance initially led most utilities to use deceptively simple forecasting techniques. Figure 27.1 displays the almost perfectly exponential aggregate growth of electric power sales between 1938 and 1980. Figure 27.2 plots the average real price of electricity during this period. Until about 1970, real price declined – dramatically from 1938–1946 and at a modest rate thereafter.

These circumstances led many industry forecasters to use methods that predicted future demand by extrapolating current demand, ignoring any influence of price. A 1969 report to the Federal Power Commission (FPC) found that most utilities estimated future demand by methods such as "compound rates of growth, annual increments, fitting of mathematical growth curves, and use of graphs of treated or untreated historical data".[2] Because exogenous factors did not appear to affect the

---

[2] Federal Power Commission (1969), p. V-1. For a recent survey, see the Edison Electric Institute (1986). Academic demand research is discussed below.

1967 Cents

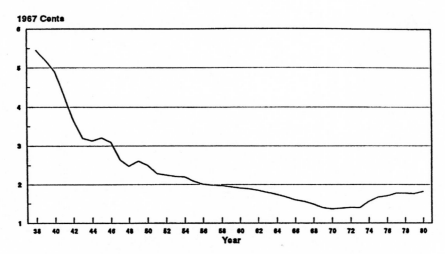

FIGURE 27.2. Average revenue per kWh. Total electric utility industry 1938–1980. Source: Edison Electric Institute Historical Statistics
of the Electric Utility Industry Through 1970, Statistical Yearbook
1981.

rate of growth of demand, forecasters saw no need to understand their
effects.[3] Recognizing this trend, the FPC observed that:

Extrapolation often produces acceptable results because electrical loads exhibit
stable growth patterns over rather long periods. Residential, outdoor lighting and
service loads appear to be largely insulated from the business cycle. However,
forecasters relying predominantly upon this method may fail to recognize underlying changes which eventually will affect future growth.[4]

Academic economists came to be interested in the demand for electricity for somewhat different reasons. During the 1950s, economists such
as Stone, Houthakker, Prais, Brown, Tobin, Wold, and Farrell were interested in the developing empirical estimates of the demand functions for
all consumer goods, individually and in systems that satisfied the con-

---

[3] The report found that virtually all utilities explicitly considered the effects of weather in
their forecasts. For intermediate forecasts (4 to 6 years), 26 out of 30 utilities surveyed
used extrapolation techniques; the remainder considered the effects of economic and
demographic factors (p. V-11). For long-term (greater than 6 years) forecasts, one-fourth
of the sample reported that they did not prepare such forecasts. Half of the rest used
extrapolation methods and half employed "a variety of methods" such as relationships
to land use, marketing information, or population trends (p. V-12).

[4] Federal Power Commission, *supra*, p. V-2.

straints of demand theory.[5] Electric power is one such good. In 1951, Hendrik Houthakker used residential electricity consumption data from 42 English provincial towns to estimate a demand equation for electricity similar to those used in studies of other household goods. It had the form:

$$\log X = \alpha + \beta \log M + \delta \log P + \gamma \log G + \rho \log H + \varepsilon \quad (1)$$

where:

X = average annual electricity consumption per customer;
M = average money income per household;
P = marginal price of electricity on domestic two-part tariffs;
G = marginal price of gas on domestic two-part tariffs;
H = average holding of large domestic electric appliances ("white goods"); and
ε = random error.

The remaining Greek letters represent coefficients to be estimated. With the exception of the term reflecting large appliances, this equation represents the textbook relationship between demand, own-price, income, and the price of substitutes (in this case, natural gas). According to Taylor (1975), Houthakker included stocks of domestic electric appliances because he believed that they and electricity consumption were complementary goods. As a result, Houthakker's analysis treated electricity very much like other commodities in household expenditure systems.

Houthakker examined closely the estimation problems involved in the use of two-part tariffs.[6] His approach to the bias such tariffs introduce was to restrict the sample and use marginal, rather than average price (i.e., the second part of the tariff). To account for the durability of the complementary goods, he estimated Equation (1) and its nonlog counterpart using prices lagged several years. Because Houthakker's data were limited to a single period (1937–1938), and because prices changed little during the surrounding years, he devoted little attention to the temporal structure of demand.

Using this method, Houthakker found a statistically significant price elasticity of demand of approximately −0.9 and an income elasticity of approximately 1.2. His research showed that the demand for electric power, like the demand for most other goods and services, is negatively affected by price.

[5] A survey of this research can be found in Brown and Deaton (1972).
[6] See Taylor (1975) and Taylor, Blattenberger, and Rennhack (1984).

2.2.   *The Fisher/Kaysen Study*

The Fisher and Kaysen study moved beyond Houthakker's analysis in several respects. First, as summarized below, it examined both industrial and residential consumers.[7] Second, Fisher and Kaysen explicitly recognized a difference between short- and long-run demand. For energy forecasting purposes, they defined short run as the period during which the stock of energy-using capital goods is fixed. All responses to price and income changes in the short run affect only the intensity of use of existing appliances. In the long run, consumers can adjust both their stock of appliances and their intensity of use.

Fisher and Kaysen's short-run equation was similar to Houthakker's equation:

$$D_t = \sum_i K_{it} W_{it} \tag{2}$$

where:

$$K_{it} = A_i P_t^{\alpha_i} Y_t^{\beta_i} \tag{3}$$

and:

D_t = demand for electricity in period t;
K_{it} = intensity of use in kilowatt-hours (kWh) in period t for white good i;
W_{it} = the average stock of white good i in period t;
P_t = the price of electricity in period t;
Y_t = income in period t;

and the remaining variables were to be estimated. Note that, in log form, this equation produces an aggregate short-run elasticity of the form:

$$\alpha = \sum_i \alpha_i \tag{4}$$

which is simply the sum of the appliance-specific short-run elasticities.

To allow for changes in the long-run appliance stock, Fisher and Kaysen used a simple form of the then widely accepted stock adjustment model. They defined the equilibrium level of appliance stocks as the level consumers would hold if all exogenous variables remained constant at current values forever. The difference in actual stocks between last year and this year was assumed to be a fraction of the difference between this year's equilibrium stock and last year's actual stock.

Fisher and Kaysen estimated this model using data from a number of

---

[7] For reasons of presentation we concentrate in this section on residential demand.

sources. They noted repeatedly that their effort was greatly hampered by the extremely poor quality of some of the data. Not only did the period of examination in the long-run analysis (1946 to 1957) include the Korean War, but also the data on the stocks of appliances held by consumers and on the intensity of use of each appliance were highly suspect. Data on prices, incomes, and electricity demand were less questionable, but often inconsistent or idiosyncratic.

In view of these limitations it is not surprising that Fisher and Kaysen produced the now-discredited tentative conclusion that, while residential electricity demand was quite sensitive to income, it was generally insensitive to price. Their failure to find a long-run price effect was almost certainly a result of attempting to deal directly with the effect of operating costs on the holdings of electricity-using appliances instead of using a reduced-form, distributed lag structure (as did later researchers). Fisher and Kaysen could find little, if any, evidence of an operating cost effect on appliance holdings (although they did find some suggestion of such an effect for appliances with high electricity operating costs and gas-fired alternatives).[8]

Fisher and Kaysen did find statistically significant short-run price effects, but studies of various periods and regions using the short-run equation led them to conclude that, as the nation grew technologically more mature, short-term price elasticity would diminish and short-term income elasticity would grow.

Research over the 30 years since Fisher and Kaysen has sharply reversed some of these conclusions. The current consensus is that the price elasticity of demand for electricity is significantly different from zero in both the short and the long run for all customer classes. It is also agreed that income (or other appropriate measures of economic activity) is an essential explanatory variable. In some current models, appliance stocks and prices are also important. Table 27.1, reproduced from Bohi (1981), summarizes the pre-1980 empirical literature on residential electricity demand.[9]

While their empirical conclusions may not have survived, Fisher and Kaysen's analytical approach has aged reasonably well. The development of time-series econometrics and more extensive cross-sectional data sets has enabled replacement of the two equations in the Fisher and Kaysen long-run model by a variety of models and estimation methods.[10] In many instances, various forms of a single distributed lag equation are

---

[8] See Fisher and Kaysen (1962), pp. 109–110.

[9] This survey was updated by Bohi and Zimmerman (1984). The more recent results largely confirm the numbers shown in Table 27.1.

[10] Edmonds (1978) and Bohi (1981) provide excellent methodological overviews.

Table 27.1. *Summary of estimated price and income elasticities of residential demand for electricity by type of model and data*

Research study	Sample[1]	Price elasticity[2]		Income elasticity[2]	
		Short-run	Long-run	Short-run	Long-run
I. Reduced-Form Models					
A. Static consumption models					
1. Aggregate level data					
(a) Average prices					
Fisher, Kaysen (1962)	Time-series: states, 1946–57	−0.16 to −0.24		0.07 to 0.33	
Moore (1970)	Cross-section: 407 utilities, 1963		−1.02		n.s.
Wilson (1971)	Cross-section: 77 cities, 1966		−1.33		1.06
Anderson (1973)	Cross-section: states, 1960, 1970		−1.07		0.67
			−1.28		
CRA (1976)	Pooled: states, 1966–72		−1.20		0.48
Halvorsen (1978)	Pooled: states, 1961–69		−1.14		0.52
(b) Marginal prices					
Lacy, Street (1975)	Time-series: Alabama Power Co, 1967–74	−0.45		1.87	
Wills (1977)	Cross-section: Mass. utilities, 1975	−0.08		−0.32	
Halvorsen (1978)	Pooled: states, 1961–69		−1.53		
McFadden, Puig (1975)	Pooled: states, 1961–69		−0.48		
2. Disaggregate level data					
(a) Average prices: none					
(b) Marginal prices					
Acton, Mitchell, Mowill (1976)	Pooled: monthly, Los Angeles County, 1972–74		−0.70		0.40
Hewlett (1977)	Cross-section: household survey, 1973 and 1975	−0.14		0.07	

			1.	Aggregate level data	
B. Dynamic consumption models					
(a) Average prices					
Houthakker, Taylor (1970)	Time series: U.S., 1946–64	−0.13	−1.89	0.13	1.94
Uri (1976)	Time series: monthly, U.S., 1971–75	−0.35		2.00	
Griffin (1974)	Time series: U.S. 1951–71	−0.06	−0.52	0.06	0.88
Mount, Chapman, Tyrrell (1973)	Pooled: states, 1946–70 (3 versions)	−0.14	−1.21	0.03	0.30
		−0.14	−1.20	0.02	0.20
		−0.36	−1.24	0.06	0.21
Gill, Maddala (1976)	Pooled: monthly, TVA area, 1962–67 and 1968–72	−0.49	−0.57	0.10	0.12
		−0.34	−0.62	0.12	0.22
Cohn, Hirst, Jackson (1977)	Pooled: states, 1951–74 and 1969–74	−0.14	−0.16	0.02	0.16
		−0.14	−0.47	0.16	0.56
(b) Marginal prices					
Houthakker, Verleger, Sheehan (1974)	Pooled: states, 1960–71 (3 prices)	−0.09	−1.19	0.13	1.63
		−0.03	−0.44	0.14	2.20
		−0.09	−1.02	0.14	1.64
Taylor, Blattenberger, Verleger (1977)	Pooled: states, 1956–72	−0.08	−0.82	0.10	1.08
2. Disaggregate level data					
(a) Average prices: none					
(b) Marginal prices Hewlett (1977)	Pooled: household survey, 1973 and 1975	−0.16	−0.45	n.s.	n.s.
C. Fuel shares models					
1. Static versions					
Chem (1976)	Pooled: states, 1971–72		−1.34		0.40
2. Dynamic versions					
Baughman, Joskow (1975)	Pooled: states, 1968–72	−0.19	−1.00	n.s.	n.s.
DOE (1978)	Pooled: regions, 1960–75	−0.18 to −0.54	−0.72 to −2.10	n.s.	n.s.

Table 27.1. *(cont.)*

Research study	Sample[1]	Price elasticity[2]		Income elasticity[2]	
		Short-run	Long-run	Short-run	Long-run
II. Structural Models					
A. Aggregate level data					
1. Average prices					
Fisher, Kaysen (1962)	Time-series: states, 1946–57		n.s.		n.s.
Anderson (1973)	Cross-section: states, 1960 and 1970		−1.07		1.06
			−1.28		0.67
2. Marginal prices					
Taylor, Blattenberger, Verleger (1977)	Pooled: states, 1961–72	−0.16	−0.46	0.22	1.00
B. Disaggregate level data					
1. Average prices: none					
2. Marginal prices					
McFadden, Puig, Kirshner (1977)	Cross-section: household survey, 1975	−0.25	−0.66	0.21	0.39

[1] Observation periods are annual except where indicated otherwise.
[2] The estimates given are statistically significant at the 0.05 level. An entry of n.s. indicates not significant. A blank space means no estimate was attempted or reported.
Source: Bohi (1981). Copyright 1981 Resources for the Future, Washington, D.C. The citations for the reported studies can be found in this work.

estimated; other models employ cross-sectional techniques or combined cross-section/time-series methods. The principal improvement of these reduced-form methods over the Fisher and Kaysen approach was in not requiring data on the stocks of appliances held by consumers – data that have continued to be difficult to obtain on a widespread, consistent basis.[11]

2.3. Demand by Industry

Unlike residential users, industrial consumers are extremely heterogeneous. Moreover, individual consumption and price data are often available for large industrial power consumers, making possible separate analyses for various industries. Many researchers, including Fisher and Kaysen, have therefore chosen to measure demand elasticities separately for disparate industries. Table 27.2 summarizes price elasticity estimates by the SIC industry produced by Fisher and Kaysen and others.

2.4. Utility Demand Forecasting in the 1970s

The electric utilities in the United States slowly adopted econometric forecasting techniques and paid increasing attention to price in doing so. This movement first became discernible in the wake of the Arab oil embargo. The embargo-produced shortages and resulting price escalations prompted new research, much of which emanated from the RAND Corporation (e.g., Anderson, 1973; Mooz and Mow, 1973), although some came from elsewhere (Halvorsen, 1975). Mooz and Mow (1973) reported that forecasts by California utilities did not use price and that such models had worked "exceptionally well in the past for short-run projections" (p. 3). Mooz and Mow (1973) computed statistically significant price and income elasticities, however, and concluded that future demand studies should incorporate price effects.

Following Mooz and Mow (1973), RAND researchers continued to analyze the demand for electricity using data from California. In 1976, Acton, Mitchell, and Mowill examined the residential demand for electricity in the Los Angeles area and found significant price and income effects. They also noted a policy concern directly related to capital planning:

---

[11] In recent years, some utilities have begun to accumulate panel data over periods long enough to permit time-series analysis of the relationship between energy use and appliance ownership. (See, for example, Granite State Electric, 1989.) Other utilities have exploited detailed billing data and snapshot appliance saturation surveys using the techniques of conditional demand analysis (Lawrence and Parti, 1983).

Table 27.2. *Demand for electricity: estimates of industrial price elasticities*

SIC code	Name	Halvorsen[1]	Anderson's survey of NERA studies[2]	Chern[3]	Chern & Chang	Fisher & Kaysen	Wilson[4]
20	Food and kindred		−0.483	−1.660	−1.464	−0.780	−1.090
203	Canned, cured and frozen			−0.400	−0.229		
204	Grain mill						
22	Textile mill products		−0.703			−1.620	−1.220
221	Weaving mills, cotton			−0.420	−0.128		
225	Knitting mills			−0.550	−1.002		
23	Apparel	−0.148					
24	Lumber and wood		−0.990				−1.640
25	Furniture and fixtures						−0.970
26	Pulp and paper	−0.203	−1.194				−1.480
262	Papermills, except build paper			−0.290	−0.858	−0.970	
263	Paperboard mills			−3.390	−0.209		
28	Chemicals	−0.684	−0.924			−2.600	−2.230
281	Industrial chemicals			−0.810			
281A	Ind. chem. (see p. 8 in Chern (1975))			−1.380			
282	Plastic materials and synthetics				−0.575		
29	Petroleum and coal products	−1.031	−0.820				
291	Petroleum refining			−0.530	−0.033		
30	Rubber and misc. plastics	−0.124	−0.760				
31	Leather						−0.760

422

Code	Industry						
32	Stone, clay, and glass	−0.312	−1.645			−1.740	−1.080
322	Glass and glassware, pressed or blown			−0.450	−1.069		
324	Cement, hydraulic			−0.120	−0.088		
33	Primary metals	−0.829	−1.035			−1.280	−1.510
331	Blast furnace and basic steel products			−0.082	−0.434		
332	Iron and steel foundries			−0.450	−0.464		
333	Primary nonferrous metal			−0.810	−0.649		
34	Fabricated metal	−1.096	−0.619			+0.550	−1.160
35	Machinery, except elec.	−0.793	−0.522			−1.330	−1.760
36	Electrical machinery	−0.272	−0.560			−1.820	−1.010
37	Transportation equip.		−0.428			+0.690	
371	Motor vehicles and equipment			−1.500	−1.506		
	Weighted average		−0.888				
	All industries			−0.570			
	All remaining industries			−0.720			
	Other				−0.894		

[1] 1971 data.

[2] Long-run static elasticities; electricity only model. Elasticities from Energy Split Models are on average lower.

[3] Short-run elasticities.

[4] Fisher and Kaysen and Wilson estimates are from cross-sectional data and are therefore considered to be long-run estimates.

Source: Halvorsen (1977), pp. 27–28; Anderson (1981) (Appendix Table II); Chern (1975), pp. 15, 32; Fisher and Kaysen (1962); Chern and Chang (1981); Wilson (1969).

423

From a policy perspective, several conclusions are suggested: Because prices have a significant effect on the demand for electricity, estimates of price elasticity should be used in forecasting capital requirements or determining revenue requirements for a utility. (p. vii)

The TVA undertook an extensive investigation of alternative rate structures that would achieve energy conservation (Gill and Maddala, 1976). This study acknowledged the importance of price elasticity but did not find the state of the art sufficiently advanced to allow for the evaluation of different rate structures. That is, although the elasticity of total demand with respect to average price had been studied, the response of demand to changes in separate rate structure elements was unknown.

Starting around 1977, however, econometrics steadily began to creep into utilities' forecasting processes. Much of this work was spearheaded by economic consultants at firms such as Charles River Associates (CRA, 1976), National Economic Research Associates (NERA, 1977), and the Energy Systems Research Group (ESRG). By this time, electricity demand growth had diminished markedly from its pre-oil-embargo pace. As price appeared important in real-world demand changes, the "incorporation of price effects" into load forecasts quickly became topical.

In December 1977, the Electric Power Research Institute (EPRI) held a symposium on load forecasting techniques. Five of the 20 utilities (or other forecasters) participating in the symposium were using an econometric model developed in whole or in part by NERA. Many were using NERA's current "average" long-run price elasticity figure of -0.5. Some were using econometric models as experiments or to compare to their noneconometric forecasts. Although the use of these forecasts in capital planning was not explicitly mentioned in the symposium proceedings, EPRI's summary makes the relationship clear. In arguing that econometric models are more costly to produce than simpler ones, the symposium director wrote (p. xii):

A personal opinion is that it would be prudent for top utility management to use forecasts from both approaches (econometric and non-econometric), when making important capital investment decisions. After all, whereas $300,000 spent on forecasting may seem like a great deal of money, it is only 0.03% of the cost of a billion-dollar power plant.

EPRI itself was then using price effects in its long-range load forecasts for the nation as a whole.

In 1977, EPRI, through Stanford University's Energy Modeling Forum (EMF), convened a task force to survey load forecasting models and methods. The task force examined ten models of electricity demand representing a mixture of techniques, forecasting organizations, applications, and geographic regions. The models were fairly well-known in the industry, each incorporating price effects, even though the models' mathematical structure and degree of responsiveness varied widely. The task force noted that implied average price elasticities varied roughly between -0.2 and -1.0 and that no model went beyond the use of an average price variable.

Around 1979, Booz, Allen, and Hamilton took over management of the Modeling Forum from Stanford. (Its name became the Utility Modeling Forum.) The First Working Group's report from the new organization was issued in September 1980; the Second Working Group's report came out a year later. It covered 16 revenue planning models, cataloging their features and subjecting them to a battery of common tests, including an evaluation of how the models incorporated the effects of price on demand and then on capacity and revenue requirements. Only one of the models incorporated this "price feedback" feature and that model performed very differently from the rest. The Working Group concluded:

Overall, what initially could have been dismissed as an interesting but unsuccessful [model] . . . came to be viewed as a potentially useful and powerful corporate modeling tool. (p. II-13)

The group's fifth formal recommendation read (p. III-34):

Various key elements of the planning environment can best be approached analytically on an iterative basis. For example, the cost of electricity impacts [on] demand, which in turn impacts the capital program, which impacts the cost of electricity, and so on. Whether these effects should always be handled explicitly within the computerized corporate model is debatable. However, when costs are changing rapidly or load is being strongly impacted over a short timeframe the ability to "close the loop" becomes far more important – and can lead to the identification of important analytical findings which would otherwise be obscured.

A model which "closes the loop" is referred to as a dynamic model. It was this dynamic characteristic of Model D – not its strategic nature or limited level of detail – which largely accounted for its unusual patterns of response. Dynamic capability lends itself more readily to strategic models, due to the potentially prohibitive cost and logistical problems involved in operating detailed models in an iterative mode.

Several members of the survey group voiced frustration that their own current corporate modeling system did not do what the old EMF's "Model D" had managed to accomplish.

If "price effect" was a fairly new concept in 1977, by 1980 it had become quite widely discussed. Perhaps the best summary is in a 1985 EPRI report by NERA and the University of Washington that examined the aggregate forecasts of utilities as prepared by a coordinating group, the National Electric Reliability Council (NERC). The report addressed these questions (p. 4-1):

Could NERC, using standard statistical techniques and data available at the time, have made more accurate aggregate forecasts? Were the individual utilities' forecasters too timid in responding to the slowdown in demand for electricity in the mid-1970s?

To answer, the researchers used a simplified aggregate demand model and assumed price elasticities varying between zero and −1.0. The authors found that the −1.0 elasticity model performed best, and that the NERC forecasts made annually between 1971 and 1979 acted as if each year's forecast incorporated a higher value of elasticity, until at last in 1979 the value approximated −1.0. The authors concluded (p. 4-17):

This comparison suggests that, during the past decade, the electric utility industry may have been learning about price elasticity. The mid-1970s may have been a formative experience for electric sales forecasters, one which persuaded them that price effects are stronger than previously thought. The period after 1974 taught everyone two more general lessons: a forecaster cannot count on rapid economic growth nor expect real electricity prices to be flat.

It was in the period after 1974 that the managers of the Washington Public Power Supply System began their ill-fated venture with the last two of five nuclear power plants.

3.   The Background and History of the WPPSS 4 and 5 Projects

The Washington Public Power Supply System was founded in 1957 by 17 public utility districts (PUDs) to acquire, build, and operate generating plants and transmission facilities[12] and to issue tax-exempt bonds. Its first project, a 27.5 megawatt hydroelectric plant, was completed in 1964. Its only other project before it began to build nuclear power plants was an 860 MW generating plant designed to use byproduct steam from an Atomic Energy Commission nuclear reactor at Hanford, Washington. In 1966, this was the largest single plant generating electricity from nuclear

---

[12]   The membership of WPPSS changed over time. At the time of the default, 19 PUDs and four cities – Ellensburg, Richmond, Tacoma, and Seattle – were members. Three members of WPPSS – the City of Seattle, and the Ferry and Kittitas PUDs – did not participate in WPPSS 4 and 5.

  For descriptions of the WPPSS 4 and 5 projects and their development over time, see Mines (1984), Anderson (1985), Chasan (1985), Leigland and Lamb (1986), and Doty (1988).

power. WPPSS sold the plant's output to a number of publicly-owned utilities and some investor-owned companies.

In the late 1960s, demand for electricity in the Pacific Northwest was expected to grow at a rate much faster than new hydroelectric sites could accommodate. A number of organizations that planned and coordinated power supplies already existed in the Northwest, including the Northwest Power Pool, the Pacific Northwest Utilities Conference Committee (PNUCC), the Public Power Planning Council, and the Bonneville Power Administration (BPA). In 1966, BPA and 108 public and private utilities formed the Joint Power Planning Council to produce a 10-year Hydro-Thermal Power Program for the region. Phase 1, announced in 1968, called for completion of five nuclear plants by the early 1980s. Phase 2 added several more.

WPPSS had also participated actively in the attempts to sustain or increase the share of electricity generated by publicly-owned power companies and seemed to be a logical organization to carry out the public part of the Hydro-Thermal Power Program. WPPSS and a number of municipalities, PUDs, and rural electric cooperatives (REAs) made commitments in 1969 to build one of the Phase 1 plants (eventually known as WPPSS 2) and in 1972 to build two more (WPPSS 1 and 3). WPPSS agreed to plan, build, and operate the plants, financing them with tax-exempt revenue bonds.

WPPSS sold the total capability of the plants to "participating" utilities, which provided the revenues to repay the bonds. These utilities signed "take-or-pay" contracts at prices covering all costs, including financing costs, and payments due WPPSS did not depend on plant completion. Moreover, the bondholders of the first three WPPSS nuclear plants had a *de facto* guarantee of revenues from BPA. Through a process known as "net-billing", BPA agreed to buy the plants' output at cost, including the cost of uncompleted plants, to supply the Participants with the power they needed. In this way the costs of the WPPSS plants were to be "regionalized", that is, averaged with the low-cost hydroelectric power and passed on to BPA customers. These financing arrangements provided the framework for planning WPPSS 4 and 5.

In 1973 and 1974, under Phase 2 of the Hydro-Thermal Power Program, WPPSS made a tentative commitment to build two more plants: Number 4 at Hanford (a duplicate of WPPSS 1) and Number 5 at Satsop, Washington (a twin of WPPSS 3). WPPSS agreed to finance, build, and operate the plants, and participating utilities were to purchase the project's total capability in advance. Unlike the first three plants, however, these two could not be financed under BPA net-billing agreements. Other methods of regionalizing the costs were explored, but precluded by a federal district court decision that forced BPA to complete an environmental impact statement before it could participate in Phase 2.[13] This task was expected to take several years. Attempts to pass federal legislation enabling BPA to play an active role failed. Without regionalization, utilities were reluctant to participate. However, after a formal BPA notice of insufficiency of its resources to supply power after July 1, 1983, 88 publicly-owned utilities signed agreements with WPPSS for all the output of WPPSS 4 and 90 percent of the output of WPPSS 5. Pacific Power and Light Company bought the remaining 10 percent of WPPSS 5. Many of the utilities continued to believe they would not ultimately be responsible for the costs of the plants, and attempts to regionalize the costs by federal legislation or other means continued throughout the life of the project.

While holders of WPPSS 4 and 5 bonds did not have BPA's guarantee, two features were intended to improve the bonds' security. The first was the so-called "step-up" provision, which increased the share of non-defaulting utilities by up to 25 percent in the event of default by a utility in its class (municipal or nonmunicipal). The second consisted of WPPSS Assignment Agreements, which enabled WPPSS to purchase surplus output for resale to other Participants, to 14 industrial customers under Short Term Sales Agreements, or "to others".[14] The industrial customers agreed to purchase up to the total capability of the two plants through 1988 and thereafter to purchase shares that declined to 20 percent by 1992. In 1977 WPPSS sold the first of 14 bond issues through which it borrowed $2.25 billion for WPPSS 4 and 5.

3.1.   The Need for Power from WPPSS 4 and 5

WPPSS contracted with R. W. Beck and Associates (Beck), an engineering and consulting firm with an active utility practice in the Pacific Northwest, to provide the information about demand, supply, costs, and revenue requirements of the Participants for prospective bondholders in the Official Statement for this first bond issue.

Late in 1976, WPPSS asked each Participant to provide ". . . its forecasted number of customers and its forecasted power requirements for each customer classification. The forecasts were those currently being used by the utilities for planning purposes".[15] From the utilities and BPA, Beck also obtained forecasts of supplies and the cost of power from other

---

[13] *Port of Astoria v. Hodel*, 5 Envtl. L. Rep. 20657 (D. Or. 1975).
[14] Washington Public Power Supply Service, Official Statement, "Generating Facilities Revenue Bonds, WPPSS 4 and 5", Series 1977A, March 17, 1977, p. 17.
[15] Official Statement, Series 1977A, March 17, 1977, p. A-11.

sources. Beck developed an accounting-type spreadsheet model – called "PORPUS" (Projected Operating Results of Participating Utility Systems) – to extend and aggregate the forecasts. The model used "historical" relationships and trends and "present utility policies" to project other capital and operating costs.[16] These data became the basis for projections of requirements, resources, and operating results for the Participants.[17] Beck's results appeared in the text of the Official Statement and in a letter to the Board of Directors of WPPSS displayed in an Appendix.[18] This information was updated with each bond issue.

The Official Statements reported not only information about the Participants as a group, but also detailed projections for 55 of the 88 Participants. The 55 utilities included 20 PUDs and 10 municipalities in Washington and Oregon and 25 REAs with customers largely in Oregon, Washington, and Idaho, but also in Wyoming, Montana, and Nevada. Their size ranged from large utilities, such as the city of Tacoma and the PUD of Snohomish County, Washington, to small companies with fewer than 3,000 customers and 1976 operating revenues of less than $1 million. Compared to WPPSS 4 and 5, whose initial cost estimate was $3.37 billion, most of the 55 utilities were small: 43 of the 55 had 1976 operating revenues of less than $5,000,000. The remaining 33 utilities were generally among the smaller Participants.

In the first Official Statement, the growth rate for the number of customers was projected to be 3.5 percent per year through 1990. Total sales (kWh) were projected to grow at 6.5 percent annually. Beck's results showed real unit revenue requirements (the price per unit of electricity required to cover the higher costs of WPPSS 4 and 5 and other higher-priced power) increasing by 2.4 percent per year. The average annual increase in the Participants' energy requirements was projected to be 5.5 percent, declining from 11.0 percent in 1977 to under 5.0 percent by 1984. From 1983 through 1988, they would have surplus energy for sale through WPPSS.

In general, as the utilities and Beck revised the forecasts for successive Official Statements, the projected growth rates for energy requirements and sales declined and those for costs and unit revenue requirements increased. The projections of project costs and Participant demand from the Official Statements are summarized in Tables 27.3 and 27.4, respectively.

---

[16] *Ibid.*

[17] In practice, Beck used the model for 55 of the 88 utilities (as well as for projecting aggregate demand), but these 55 accounted for more than 96 percent of the shares of the plants.

[18] This format was consistently used throughout the 14 Official Statements.

Table 27.3. *Chronology of projected costs and completion dates for WPPSS 4 and 5*

			Projected completion date	
Bond issue	Issue date	Projected cost (billions of dollars)	WPPSS 4	WPPSS 5
1977A	3/1/77	3.377	3/83	1/85
1977B	6/1/77	3.434	7/83	3/85
1977C	9/1/77	3.567	6/84	3/85
1978A	2/1/78	3.766	6/84	7/85
1978B	6/1/78	3.766	6/84	7/85
1978C	10/1/78	3.845	6/84	7/85
1979A	2/1/79	4.505	6/85	6/86
1979B	9//1/79	5.075	6/85	6/86
1979C	12/1/79	5.075	6/85	6/86
1980A	5/1/80	5.075	6/86	6/87
1980B	7/1/80	7.231	6/86	6/87
1980C	10/1/80	7.231	6/86	6/87
1980D	12/1/80	7.231	2/87	9/87
1981A	3/1/81	7.824	2/87	9/87

Source: Washington Public Power Supply System, Official Statements, WPPSS 4 and 5, 1977A, pp. 7–8, 11; 1977B, pp. 7–8, 11; 1977C, pp. 7–8, 11; 1978A, pp. 7, 9, 12; 1978B, pp. 7–8, 12; 1978C, pp. 8–9, 13; 1979A, pp. 8–9, 13; 1979B, pp. 21–22, 26; 1979C, pp. 23, 25, 28; 1980A, pp. 25, 27, 30; 1980B, pp. 25–26, 29; 1980C, pp. 23–24, 27; 1980D, pp. 24–25, 28, 1981A, pp. 30–31, 37.

The PNUCC's West Group Area forecasts were published in each Official Statement as confirmation of the WPPSS 4 and 5 forecasts. They showed future deficits in power supplies, but the forecast growth rates for energy requirements were always below those shown by WPPSS for the Participants.

3.2.   Prices and the Demand for Power

WPPSS projected increases in real prices in each Official Statement (see Real Unit Revenue Requirements, Table 27.4).[19] However, it did not explicitly consider how these price changes would affect electricity

---

[19] These increases were due to the costs of WPPSS 4 and 5 and expected increases in BPA rates to cover the "net billing" agreements for WPPSS 1, 2, and 3, and the Trojan Nuclear Project. BPA's announcement of these price increases, scheduled for 1979 and 1981, was made before WPPSS issued its first Official Statement.

Table 27.4. *Forecasts of demand by WPPSS 4 and 5 participants*

Bond issue	Forecast years	Average annual growth rates		Real unit revenue requirements	
		Number of customers	Total sales (MWH)	%	Base year
1977A	1975–1990	3.6%	6.5%	2.4	1975
1977B	1976–1990	3.5	6.1	3.0	1976
1977C	1976–1990	3.5	5.9	3.3	1976
1978A	1976–1990	3.5	5.9	3.3	1976
1978B	1977–1990	3.5	5.7	3.2	1977
1978C	1977–1990	3.5	5.7	3.3	1977
1979A	1977–1990	3.5	5.7	3.7	1977
1979B	1978–1990	5.5	5.5	2.9	1978
1979C	1978–1990	3.9	5.5	2.9	1978
1980A	1978–1990	4.0	5.3	2.3	1978
1980B	1979–1990	3.9	4.8	4.4	1979
1980C	1979–1990	3.9	4.8	4.5	1979
1980D	1979–1990	3.9	4.8	4.5	1979
1981A	1979–1995	3.6	4.2	2.8–3.6	1979

Source: Washington Public Power Supply System, Official Statements (for WPPSS 4 and 5): 1977A, p. A-13; 1977B, p. A-14; 1977C, p. A-15; 1978A, p. A-15; 1978B, p. A-15; 1978C, p. A-15; 1979A, p. A-15; 1979B, p. A-15; 1979C, p. A-16; 1980A, p. A-17; 1980B, p. A-17; 1980C, p. A-16; 1980D, p. A-15; 1981A, p. A-14.

demand.[20] Beck's "spreadsheet" model was not designed to allow for customers' responses to these increases.[21] WPPSS provided Participants with the results of Beck's models for review, but there was apparently no coordinated effort to ascertain whether the utilities thought the price changes would affect demand in their areas, and if so, by how much. In

[20] In late 1980, the Washington State Senate Energy and Utilities Committee held hearings on the WPPSS projects and concluded: "WPPSS has not published any analysis of the degree to which rising real prices, real income levels, the real price of substitute fuels, temporary shortages or other factors might affect its assumption that *per-capita* electricity demand will grow steadily throughout the decade." See Washington State Senate Energy & Utilities Committee (1981), p. 58.

[21] Beck was aware of the shortcomings of an approach that merely aggregated forecasts of the individual utilities and suggested to WPPSS a detailed review of the forecasts of the 20 largest Participants. The review was never undertaken. See *In re* WPPSS Securities Litigation MDL No. 551, *Plaintiffs' Motion in Opposition to Motion for Summary Judgment on Section 10(b) Claims*, March 1, 1988, p. 23.

fact, many utilities could not have supplied reliable information because they relied on trend forecasting techniques.

The Official Statements did not ignore these price increases, but the discussion of prices focused on two points:[22]

1   Prices in real terms would increase at fairly low rates (2 to 4 percent per year);
2   Prices in the Pacific Northwest would continue to be significantly lower than in other regions.

These conclusions, however, like the forecast price increases themselves, depended on price elasticities and on the costs of WPPSS 4 and 5. WPPSS implicitly assumed the former to be zero and grossly underestimated the latter.

3.3.   The Default

In WPPSS's last Official Statement (for Bond Issue 1981A, March 1, 1981), WPPSS 4 and 5 were estimated to be 16 percent and 11 percent complete, respectively. In May, WPPSS revised the estimated cost for the two plants to $11.8 billion and recommended a construction moratorium. The WPPSS 4 and 5 projects were terminated on January 22, 1982. In litigation by Participants, the Chemical Bank as Trustee for the bondholders, and other parties, the Washington Supreme Court concluded on June 15, 1983 that 9 municipal utilities and 20 PUDs in Washington did

---

[22] WPPSS discussed prices at some length in the Official Statements. In the early versions, it noted:

> Until the early 1980's essentially all of the Participants' power supply will be generated at low cost by hydroelectric resources. The higher cost of thermal energy required to meet the Participants' load growth in the 1980's will soon have a significant impact on their power supply costs.... However, for some time into the future, the low-cost hydroelectric resources, when melded with the higher-cost thermal plants, are expected to result in electric power rates to the ultimate power consumer in the Participants' service areas that are significantly lower than comparable costs in areas that must rely on a much larger portion of their power supply to be generated by thermal resources. (OS 1977A, pp. 19 and A-8.)

Similar qualifications appear in later Official Statements, including the expectation that the regional power legislation might affect costs and that upward revisions of BPA rates would be necessary to cover the costs of the "net billed" plants. (OS, 1980D/E, pp. 14 and 17.) In addition, every Official Statement contained projected rates of increase for unit revenue requirements for 55 individual utilities in real and nominal dollars. Beginning with Series 1978C of October 1, 1979, the Official Statements contain a table comparing total costs and mills/kWh for six regions and two or three levels of kWh usage. A chart showing DOE electricity cost forecasts by region through 1990 appeared in later issues.

not have the authority to sign the WPPSS 4 and 5 Participants' Agreements. On August 18, WPPSS defaulted on the bonds.

4. Using the Model: "Substantial Uncertainty"

4.1. Introduction

Chemical Bank and other plaintiffs in the *In re Washington Public Power Supply System Litigation*[23] charged that the WPPSS bonds had been unlawfully issued under the Securities Act of 1933. They alleged that the bonds had been fraudulently issued because the defendants should reasonably have known and disclosed that there was "substantial uncertainty" about their ability to meet the financial obligations that the bonds created. We were asked to develop a model to analyze whether, given plausible values for demand elasticities and recognized probabilities of events that would increase costs and delay construction, the utilities and other defendants should reasonably have recognized and disclosed such "substantial uncertainty".

Our investigation employed a model that combined the main regulatory, accounting, and technological features of utility supply with a contemporary representation of electricity demand. This meant taking Beck's spreadsheet model, explicitly adding a demand equation, and analyzing the consequences of a variety of alternative scenarios.[24]

The 55 utilities for which data were available shared a number of characteristics that simplified the modeling effort. First, each of these utilities was the exclusive supplier of electricity at retail in its service area. Second, these utilities were either REAs, municipals, or PUDs. These entities are all tax-exempt and owned by customers or other public bodies. All three set rates by class so that total annual revenues approximately equal total annual costs.

Our model framework treated each utility as an independent entity for purposes of demand analysis and rate setting. Each utility was assumed to have five customer classes: residential (R), commercial (C), industrial (I), agricultural (largely irrigation, A), and other (O), which included customers such as street lighting, governments, and the utility itself. Each customer class was assumed to face a flat rate tariff. The ratios

---

[23] MDL No. 551 (U.S.D.C., W.D. Washington, 1987).

[24] An initial form of the model was developed by Richard Carlson and his colleagues at Q.E.D. Economics. It is also similar to the model described in Ford and Youngblood (1983), Carlson and Thomas (1986), and Fox-Penner (1988). For a critical assessment of this kind of model, see Hemphill and Costello (1987).

among class tariffs were assumed to remain unchanged from their relationships in 1975.

A separate, structurally identical demand equation was calibrated for each class of each utility. It took the following form:

$$q_t = A^\theta P_t^{\theta\mu} Y_t^{\theta\varepsilon} W_t^{\theta\tau} q_{t-1}^{(1-\theta)},$$

q_t = actual consumption of electricity in year t in mWh;

P_t = the price of electricity in mills per kWh in year t (this is equivalent to dollars per mWh);

Y_t = the customer's income (or output) level in year t; and

W_t = the price of natural gas in year t.

where A, μ, ε, τ, and θ are parameters of the demand equation. Their interpretation is thus:

μ = the long-run price elasticity of demand for electricity;

ε = the long-run income or output elasticity of demand for electricity;

τ = the long-run cross-price elasticity of demand for electricity with respect to the price of natural gas; and

θ = an adjustment or lag factor, $0 < \theta \le 1$.

θ is the portion of the long-run adjustment to price and income/output changes that occurs after one year, and $\theta\mu$, $\theta\varepsilon$, and $\theta\tau$ are the short-run elasticities of demand corresponding to the respective long-run elasticities.

Figure 27.3 helps explain the model's logic. Starting with the first year of the forecast,[25] the model attempts to find an average price that balances revenues and costs.[26] The process begins[27] by assuming (for purposes of starting the calculation) that this year's real price equals the equilibrium real price computed by the model for the prior year. The

[25] The base year of the model was 1976. All of the data for 1976 were actual, and the model performed no calculations for this year.

[26] Referring to the income statement of the utility, the actual criterion used by the model was that year-end cash balances did not change by more than $1,000 from one year to the next. In other words, rates were to be set such that the utility covered costs (including debt service and capital additions), but accumulated neither cash nor additional debt.

[27] The actual computational algorithm guessed that next year's equilibrium price equaled this year's equilibrium price and compared revenues and costs at this guess. If revenues exceeded (were lower than) costs, the model adjusted the price guess downward (upward) by a fraction related to the difference. The process of converging on an equilibrium price for one year often required thousands of iterations. We are indebted to Jack Stuart, a programmer at CRA, who devised an ingenious way of reducing convergence time by an order of magnitude.

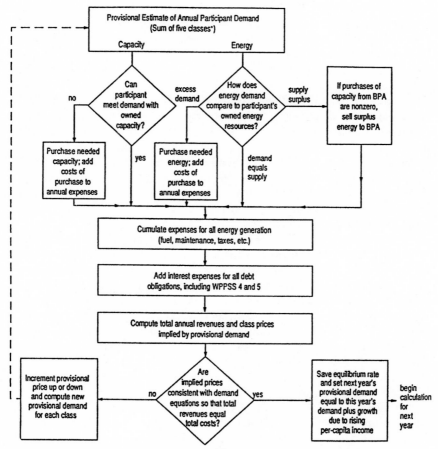

FIGURE 27.3. Schematic of one year of model used to examine effects of demand uncertainty on a WPPSS participant.

demand section combines this "first guess" with forecasts of income growth and gas prices to estimate provisional demand.[28]

Each utility begins the forecast period with a group of generating facilities whose output is fairly certain over that period.[29] If provisional

---

[28] We refer to demand here as if it has a single dimension, quantity. Demand in most electric power systems has two dimensions, energy and capacity (see Fox-Penner, 1990).

[29] Many of the generating facilities are hydroelectric and therefore have output amounts

demand exceeds the utility's supplies, the utility is assumed to purchase energy from BPA according to an assumed schedule of purchase prices.[30] Conversely, if a utility has surplus energy, the model assumes that the utility sells the surplus back to BPA at the same price as it can purchase energy, subject to its maintenance of sufficient capacity reserve margins.[31]

The model accumulates the capacity and energy costs (net of sellback revenue) and adds to them these nonpower expenses: transmission fees, administrative and general costs, customer accounts expenses, taxes, payments in lieu of taxes, debt service, capital additions, and other additions to and deductions from income.[32] The algebraic sum of these items constitutes the total cost of serving customers at the provisional level of demand. In order for the utility to break even, the average price it charges must equal the computed total cost divided by the provisional level of demand.

In the second phase of the model's equilibration loop, calculated average price is disaggregated into the equivalent average price for each customer class. If these equivalent prices equal the model's assumed provisional prices (i.e., last year's equilibrium class prices), equilibrium is achieved. More commonly, however, because of changes in demand conditions and exogenous expenses (such as customer account expenses) between the present year and the last year, last year's real price is not at equilibrium. Thus, the model ends its first complete iteration and concludes that the provisional price was incorrect. The model then uses the revenue overage or shortfall to select a price closer to equilibrium.

A model of this form is ideally suited to analyzing the sensitivity of equilibrium future rates to variables such as the growth rate of real income, the costs of new power supplies, or elasticities of demand. Alternative scenarios merely involve substituting an alternative value for an exogenous assumption and allowing the model to find the new equilibrium price path. This allowed us to explore the effects of uncertainty on the financial condition of the WPPSS Participants.

---

that vary with annual rainfall. Although this introduces additional uncertainty, utilities in the Pacific Northwest usually rate their capacity in a conservative fashion to account for low water years.

[30] The rates for purchase from BPA were equal to BPA's actual 1974–79 nonfirm power rate (3.25 mills/kWh, 1975 dollars).

[31] The model assumes that surplus capacity cannot be sold. The energy generated by the capacity can be sold at BPA nonfirm prices, but these rates typically are sufficient only to cover the variable costs of generating power.

[32] These public utilities operate on a cash basis with 100 percent debt financing, so depreciation usually is not an item on their income statements.

4.2. Use of the Model to Investigate Uncertainty

The model's predictions about ability to pay depend on the choice of parameters (price elasticities, in particular) and on assumed likely contingencies (cost overruns, for example). The question then becomes: How easy is it to find plausible or probable scenarios in which the utilities would be in financial trouble?

There are three broad possibilities. First, suppose that for any reasonable choice of parameters and contingent events the scenarios generated by the model show the utility to be in trouble. In that case, the utility was certainly reckless in undertaking its share of the obligations.

Second, suppose on the contrary that reasonable parameters and contingent events create scenarios that show no difficulty; moreover, that it proves difficult to find scenarios that do show the utility to be in trouble. One has to depart quite far from a "reasonable" case in order to generate financial disaster. While a disaster would still have been possible, one can reasonably say that its likelihood was small – that there was no substantial uncertainty about the utility's ability to meet its obligations.

The third case lies between these extremes. While some possible parameter values and contingent events produce scenarios that permit the utility to meet its obligations, it proves easy to vary the assumptions and generate examples in which financial disaster strikes. In such circumstances there are two possibilities. First, one may have to believe in relatively extreme optimistic parameter values and a rosy set of contingent events to conclude that there is no problem. Second, even if the single best forecast indicates smooth sailing, reasonable deviations from that forecast lead to severe problems. In either of these subcases, there is still substantial uncertainty about the utility's ability to pay.

To take a leading case, if a utility can meet its obligations if the long-run price elasticity of residential electricity demand is some average figure from the literature, but cannot meet its obligations with residential demand only slightly more price-elastic, then there surely is substantial uncertainty for that utility. Price elasticities are hard to estimate; they are hardly known with sufficient certainty to permit the issuing of bonds where repayment relies on a particular elasticity value rather than a slightly different value.

Similarly, if a utility cannot tolerate any sizable cost overrun without disaster, then substantial uncertainty exists even if obligations could be met if costs were on target. By the time of WPPSS 4 and 5, it was already quite clear that large cost overruns for nuclear power plants were the rule rather than the exception.[33]

Perhaps not surprisingly, our results show that, while a few of the participating utilities fall into one of the extreme cases, most of them belong to the intermediate case. For the bulk of the utilities, one can say that there were some outcomes in which they survived, but that those outcomes were hardly certain. Indeed, for most utilities, one would have to believe in relatively extreme favorable assumptions as to parameter values and ultimate costs to conclude that there would be no problem.

Our procedure was to explore, as it were, the relevant portion of some appropriate parameter space. We varied some of the model's parameters and assumptions about the obligations the utilities would be called on to assume. The model parameters that we found to be interesting are first (not surprisingly), own-price elasticities and second, the constant terms in the demand equations for the five customer classes.[34]

The own-price elasticities were chosen as follows. As discussed in the Appendix, the demand function for the residential, commercial, and industrial sectors was assumed to be of the form

[33] The risks and uncertainties associated with cost and time overruns were viewed as of the time the decisions were made to go ahead with the WPPSS project, late 1976. The 25 nuclear power plants in operation by December 31, 1976, had inflation-adjusted construction costs at the dates of their first commercial operation that averaged 219 percent of the amounts estimated at their construction start dates. This figure ranged from a low of 130 percent (Zion I) to a high of 320 percent (Calvert Cliffs I). The actual times between construction start dates and dates of first commercial operation for these plants averaged 259 percent of the times initially estimated, with a low of 195 percent (Brunswick 2) and a high of 340 percent (Indian Point 3).

Many plants that had been started years before remained incomplete, with mounting costs and frequent extensions of estimated completion dates. For example, Brown's Ferry 3 was started in 1966 and was not yet in commercial operation. Inflation-adjusted costs (1982 dollars) had risen from an initial estimate of $170.5 million to an estimate of $462.6 million when the plant was 90 percent complete in September 1975. No plant begun after February 1970 was in operation by the end of 1976. Thirteen plants begun between January 1968 and November 1971 were less than 75 percent complete. All plants over 50 percent complete had experienced cost overruns; no plant had escaped time delays.

The first Official Statement of WPPSS (for bonds issued March 1, 1977) estimated commercial operation dates of March 1, 1983 and January 1985, for Projects 4 and 5, respectively. It was noted that "Any significant delay in obtaining limited work authorization for Project 5 may increase the financing requirements". The financing requirements included $455.4 million for "Escalation" and "Contingency" out of a total of $3,377.0 million.

[34] The values used for the cross-elasticity with respect to gas price were 0.1, 0.3, and 0.2 for the residential, commercial, and industrial sectors, respectively. The respective values for income elasticity for the three sectors (actually "output" elasticity for nonresidential demand) were 0.5, 0.6, and 0.7. As Tables 27.1 and 27.2 demonstrate, these values were consonant with the literature and, in any case, the results are not sensitive to them.

$$\log q_t = \alpha + \beta \log P_t + X_t \gamma + \lambda \log q_{t-1}, \tag{5}$$

where q_t denotes electricity demand in year t, P_t denotes electricity price, X_t denotes a vector of other variables, and Greek symbols denote parameters.

With demand in this form, short-run own-price elasticity is given by β, and long-run own-price elasticity (μ) by $\beta/(1 - \lambda)$. The lag parameters, λ, were set at 0.79, 0.67, and 0.72 for the residential, commercial, and industrial sectors, respectively. This is quite consistent with the literature, and we could then equivalently vary either the short- or the long-run own-price elasticities.

We proceeded by varying long-run own-price elasticities, beginning with the residential, commercial, and industrial long-run own-price elasticities set at -1.2, -1.3, and -1.4, respectively.[35] These values are well within the range in the literature, if a bit elastic (compare Table 27.2).

The precise choice of initial elasticities does not matter so long as the chosen values lie within some reasonable range. What matters is not whether the utilities could meet their obligations at the mean of the price elasticities found in the literature, but whether they could be *sure* they could do so. If choices within a reasonable range really imply disaster, then the utilities' ability to pay was substantially uncertain.

The variations on these elasticity choices are all within the range found in the literature. Starting with the values just described, we increased them (in absolute value) by 0.1, and decreased them (in absolute value) by 0.1 and 0.2.

The remaining demand sector, irrigation, was treated differently. The basic long-run own-price elasticity here was derived (for each utility) from technical studies of irrigation methods.[36] A lag parameter of 0.67 was used. Unlike the case for the three sectors already discussed, however, the long-run own-price elasticities for irrigation varied considerably across utilities. Thus, we thought it too extreme to vary them all by the same additive amount. Instead, we varied them by multiplying. Our rule was simple: when the other elasticities were increased (absolutely) by 0.1, irrigation own-price elasticities were increased (absolutely) by 10 percent. When the other elasticities were decreased (absolutely) by 0.2, irrigation own-price elasticities were decreased (absolutely) by 20 percent, and so on. The variations on elasticities shown in the results below include this treatment.

---

[35] Price elasticity for "other" was set at -1.2.

[36] College of Agricultural Research, Washington State University (1981), also known as *The Whittlesley Report.*

We also varied the value of the constant term α in Equation (5). This requires a bit of explanation. In choosing values for the parameters in the demand equations, we did not perform an econometric study for each utility (nor do we claim that the utilities should have done so). That was not feasible. Instead, parameters we chose for the demand equation reflect the range found in the literature.

The constant terms in the demand equations cannot be set in this way. The constant term reflects the scale of operations of the particular utility. In effect, it must be set to calibrate the demand function to the facts for that utility. In practice, there is not much choice as to how this should be done. For a few utilities, there are data for two successive years, and we could calculate α directly from Equation (5) and the assumed values of the remaining parameters. For the most part, however, such data were unavailable. Thus, the procedure for all utilities was to set q_{t-1} and q_t to the same value, that for 1976, and calculate "1976" αs.[37]

This procedure would be correct if Equation (5) were exact and if *per-capita* demand in 1976 and 1975 were the same. Where *per-capita* demand was growing for reasons not exactly accounted for in the model, our procedure results in too high a value (relative to using actual data for both years); where demand was falling, our procedure results in too low a value.

This inaccuracy does not matter, however, because we varied the resulting estimates anyway. (Indeed, we would have done so even if we had obtained the estimates from actual data for both years, since Equation (5) cannot be expected to fit perfectly.) We varied them by a multiplicative factor. In Table 27.5 the factor is given as a percentage deviation from the original estimates. The five variations, in order of decreasing αs, are: increase by 1 percent, no change, decrease by 1 percent, decrease by 2 percent, and decrease by 5 percent. Since increasing α increases estimated demand for a given level of prices and income, higher values are more favorable to the utilities' financial status than lower ones.

There are also two scenario-type items to vary. They pertain to the obligations that a utility might have to meet if things went badly.[38] The first, the possibility of a cost overrun, was mentioned above. We analyzed cases in which construction costs were on target and cases in

---

[37] Data were available to compare "actual" alphas, that is, alphas derived assuming the equation was correct, to "1976" alphas. This produced a change in the value of alpha on the order of five percent. As described in the text, we experimented with changes of this magnitude and found that our conclusions were not affected by this assumption.

[38] The utilities promised to pay the bondholders even if no electricity was ever produced by the plants (none ever was). All the results reported below are based on such a "dry hole" scenario.

Table 27.5. *Number of utilities with projected rates greater than 17 cents (55 participants)*

No step-up, no cost overrun					Step-up				
	Δ Price elasticity[2]					Δ Price elasticity[2]			
Δalpha[1]	-0.2	-0.1	0	$+0.1$	Δalpha[1]	-0.2	-0.1	0	$+0.1$
$+0.01$	7	14	24	37	$+0.01$	11	19	33	40
0	9	16	28	39	0	15	24	36	44
-0.01	13	21	33	40	-0.01	17	28	39	48
-0.02	15	26	39	45	-0.02	20	34	40	48
-0.05	26	39	45	51	-0.05	33	42	48	52

Step-up and 1.5 cost overrun					Step-up and 2.0 cost overrun				
	ΔPrice elasticity[2]					ΔPrice elasticity[2]			
Δalpha[1]	-0.2	-0.1	0	$+0.1$	Δalpha[1]	-0.2	-0.1	0	$+0.1$
$+0.01$	26	36	43	50	$+0.01$	35	43	49	53
0	30	36	45	50	0	39	46	50	53
-0.01	33	40	49	51	-0.01	41	48	51	53
-0.02	35	43	50	52	-0.02	43	50	52	53
-0.05	43	50	51	53	-0.05	50	51	53	53

Step-up and 3.0 cost overrun				
	ΔPrice elasticity[2]			
Δalpha[1]	-0.2	-0.1	0	$+0.1$
$+0.01$	47	51	53	53
0	49	51	53	53
-0.01	49	52	53	54
-0.02	51	53	53	54
-0.05	52	53	54	55

[1] Deviations from baseline level.
[2] Deviations from baseline level for each of the customer classes.

which they exceeded their target by 50, 100, and 200 percent – all well within the realm of experience for nuclear plant construction by the early 1980s.

The second case concerns the "step-up" feature of the bonds under which each utility undertook up to an increase of 25 percent of its own obligations. Thus, in effect, each utility assured the bondholders that it could pay not merely its own share, but would "step up", if necessary, to pay 25 percent more. We used the model to examine whether such promises were sound.

Since having to step up is analytically equivalent to a 25 percent cost overrun (assuming the step-up occurs at the outset of repayment), it is not necessary to examine all combinations of cost overrun and step-up cases. For each utility, we therefore examined five cost scenarios: (1) no step-up, no cost overrun; (2) step-up, no cost overrun; (3) step-up, costs multiplied by 1.5; (4) step-up, costs multiplied by 2; (5) step-up, costs multiplied by 3.

5.   Results

For each of the five scenarios described above, we examined 20 parameter combinations: 4 sets of price elasticities and 5 choices for alpha. In Table 27.5, the four choices of elasticities are indicated as deviations from the original choice, and are laid out in order of (absolutely) increasing price elasticity as −0.2, −0.1, 0, and +0.1. The criterion used for financial difficulty is as follows. As the model moves forward in time, it seeks the lowest rates that will enable the utility to pay off its obligations in each year.[39] A utility runs into difficulty if the cost-induced price increase reduces demand so far that prices must be raised still further as price elasticity effects take hold in later years. We took as our criterion residential rates[40] reaching a level above \$0.17 per kilowatt-hour in 1987 dollars. This was well above any rate charged in the United States in 1987, and many times the rates being charged in the Pacific Northwest. (Moreover, when the model generates rates over 17 cents per kilowatt-hour, it often generates far higher ones.) The results are presented here by scenario-parameter combination.

In Table 27.5, each of the five step-up-cost combinations corresponds to a single grid. Within each grid, the axes are organized so that relatively optimistic parameter values occur higher up and to the left, and relatively pessimistic ones lower down and to the right. For each combination, the frequency distribution of the maximum residential rate required is given with each utility counting as a single observation.

The results are unambiguous. There was substantial uncertainty about

---

[39] There is no evidence that the utilities thought of establishing a sinking fund with higher rates in the near future to help with later obligations. Nor did they ever seriously contemplate using price discrimination to get around possible problems. Rather, they assured bondholders of their ability to pay without investigating such questions; thus, we too ignore them.

[40] Recall that the model ties together rates for different classes, so we can use a criterion based on any one of them.

the ability of the participating utilities to pay their obligations. That uncertainty involved most of the utilities. When the bonds were issued, WPPSS was a disaster waiting to happen. Financial failure, without extreme good luck, was only a matter of time.

6. Conclusion

The individual defendants settled with Chemical Bank and other plaintiffs prior to and in the first few weeks of trial. The WPPSS bondholders regained only a fraction of their original investments. Our role was small, but, we think, not inconsequential. We were able to demonstrate that, given what was reasonably known to the defendants about demand elasticities and the likelihood of cost-increasing events at the time the bonds were issued, there was indeed "substantial uncertainty" that they would be able to meet their obligations.

The econometric studies on which we relied provided bounds against which to test the sensitivity of the WPPSS utilities to a variety of alternative scenarios. Our data on cost and time overruns came from published studies of the federal regulator. It was so widely recognized that changes in regulations were themselves a primary cause of cost increases and time delays that the failure of the defendants to look more closely at these effects is hard to explain.

Even if it had been possible, it would not have been necessary for the WPPSS defendants to undertake econometric tests or develop complicated feedback models in connection with their proposals. Once it was recognized that there *might* be cost increases beyond those in the Official Statements, the remaining analysis was not complicated: cost increases necessitate price increases in the world in which these utilities operate; price increases necessarily mean that less will be demanded, occasioning further price increases. The question becomes inescapable of how far the process goes before the firms become incapable of meeting their obligations. In fact, there were admissions of a possible "death spiral" in the defendants' own records.

Disclosure would have meant that the bonds would not have been issued and that WPPSS 4 and 5 would not have been started when they were. They should not have been. The uncertain state of public policy about nuclear energy in general and nuclear plant construction in particular desperately needed to be worked out before engaging in an undertaking of that magnitude. Our use of basic economics, econometrics, and historical facts was useful in litigation *after* the damage had been done. Such use in advance would have prevented some very costly mistakes.

ACKNOWLEDGEMENTS

This paper is based on work done for the Chemical Bank as Trustee for the bondholders and for the bondholders as a Class in Multi-District Litigation (MDL) Docket 551. We are grateful to Thomas D. Barr, Robert Baron, Alan Schulman, and Michael Kipling. The work we describe herein owes much to the efforts of Duane Chapman, Richard Carlson, and Q.E.D./Spectrum Economics; we thank these parties as well. We also thank Alan Huntley, the Professional Development Group, Lisa Yeransian, Mark Horton, Michael Ozog, Deanne Samuels, Darris Hess, Jack Stuart, and many others at Charles River Associates. Special thanks are due to Rowan Wilson and Thomas Rafferty. For help in preparing this paper, we thank Stuart Jackson, Tim Hughes, Jo Schlegel, Margaret Bellotti, and Sally Betts.

APPENDIX. THE DEMAND EQUATIONS

Introduction

This appendix describes the demand equations used in the simulation model. Demand equations are used for customers in five separate customer classes: residential, commercial, industrial, irrigation, and other. For each customer class, a demand equation is used to calculate electricity consumption per customer in megawatt-hours. The models are essentially flow adjustment models using a Koyck lag, and the structure of the models is the same for all customer classes. However, a slight variation is required for the residential sector because customers are households, but most studies for which demand parameters are available are of *per-capita* demand.

The Demand Equations

In the demand equations used in the simulation model, electricity consumption per customer is explained by the price of electricity, the price of substitutes represented by the price of natural gas, and a variable representing the level of economic activity conducted by the customer. For residential customers, the variable for economic activity is *per-capita* income, and for other customer classes it is a proxy for the customer's level of output. To derive the demand equations, let

q_t^* = the desired consumption of electricity in year t in mWh;
q_t = actual consumption of electricity in year t in mWh;

P_t = the price of electricity in mills per kWh in year t (this is equivalent to dollars per mWh);

Y_t = the customer's income or output level in year t; and

W_t = the price of natural gas in year t.

The General Form of the Demand Equations

The demand equation derived in this section is used for the commercial, industrial, irrigation, and other sectors. As we mentioned above, a variation is required for the residential equation.

The "desired" consumption of electricity in year t is

$$q_t^* = AP_t^\mu Y_t^\varepsilon W_t^\tau.$$

The "actual" consumption in year t represents a partial adjustment of consumption toward desired consumption from the level of consumption in the previous year:

$$q_t / q_{t-1} = (q_t^* / q_{t-1})^\theta = (AP_t^\mu Y_t^\varepsilon W_t^\tau / q_{t-1})^\theta.$$

Therefore,

$$q_t = A^\theta P_t^{\theta\mu} Y_t^{\theta\varepsilon} W_t^{\theta\tau} q_{t-1}^{(1-\theta)},$$

where A, μ, ε, τ, and θ are parameters of the demand equation. Their interpretation is as follows:

μ = the long-run price elasticity of demand for electricity;

ε = the long-run income or output elasticity of demand for electricity;

τ = the long-run cross-price elasticity of demand for electricity with respect to the price of natural gas; and

θ = an adjustment or lag factor, $0 < \theta \leqslant 1$.

θ is the proportion of the long-run adjustment to price and income/output changes that occurs after one year, and $\theta\mu$, $\theta\varepsilon$, and $\theta\tau$ are the short-run elasticities of demand corresponding to the respective long-run elasticities.

The model does not require absolute levels of natural gas prices and income/economic activity, because projections of demand in future years use constant annual growth rates for these variables. Therefore, the levels of income or output and natural gas prices in any year t are

$$Y_t = Y_0(1 + g_y)^t, \quad \text{and} \quad W_t = W_0(1 + g_w)^t,$$

where g_y and g_w are annual growth rates for income/output and gas prices, respectively, and the subscript "0" indicates the value of the variable in the base year. In addition, the price of electricity in any year t is stated as a price relative to the price in the base year. Let this relative price be p_t, where

$$p_t = (P_t/P_0).$$

Consequently, the demand equation can be written

$$q_t = A' p_t^{\theta\mu} (1 + g_1)^t q_{t-1}^{(1-\theta)}, \qquad\qquad \text{(A-1)}$$

where

$$A' = \left[A^\theta P_0^{\theta\mu} Y_0^{\theta\varepsilon} W_0^{\theta\tau} \right],$$

and

$$(1 + g_1) = \left[(1 + g_y)^{\theta\varepsilon} (1 + g_w)^{\theta\tau} \right].$$

The Demand Equation for Residential Customers

A complication arises for the demand equation for residential customers, because most studies estimating parameters of the demand equation (μ, ε, τ, and θ) for residential customers do so for *per-capita* demand. However, data for the utilities that were Participants of WPPSS were for residential customers. The difference between residential customer demand and residential *per-capita* demand is due to the size of the average household.

This is dealt with by assuming that household consumption of electricity is proportional to household size. Consequently, household demand for electricity, or the demand per residential customer, is

$$q_t^h = A' p_t^{\theta\mu} (1 + g_1)^t q_{t-1}^{(1-\theta)} H_t,$$

where

$$H_t = \text{average household size in year } t.$$

Household size is assumed to grow at a constant rate per year. Therefore,

$$H_t = H_0 (1 + g_h)^t,$$

where g_h is the annual growth rate in household size.

Note that in the residential demand equation above, the left-hand variable is household demand, whereas the lagged variable for demand is *per-capita* demand. With some manipulation, the household demand equation can be written with household demand for both the current and lagged demand variables:

$$q_t^h = B p_t^{\theta \mu} (1 + g_2)^t \left(q_{t-1}^h \right)^{(1-\theta)}, \tag{A-2}$$

where

$$B = \left[A' H_0^\theta (1 + g_h)^{(1-\theta)} \right]$$

and

$$(1 + g_2) = \left[(1 + g_1)(1 + g_h)^\theta \right].$$

REFERENCES

Acton, J. P., Mitchell, B. M., and Mowill, R. S. (1976) *Residential Demand for Electricity in Los Angeles: An Econometric Study of Disaggregated Data*, Santa Monica, CA: Rand Corp., Report R-1899-NSF.

Anderson, D. V. (1985) *Illusions of Power: A History of the Washington Public Power Supply System (WPPSS)*, New York: Praeger.

Anderson, Kent P. (1971) *Toward Econometric Estimation of Industrial Energy Demand: An Experimental Application to the Primary Metals Industry*, Santa Monica, CA: Rand Corp., Report R-719-NSF.

Anderson, Kent P. (1973) *Residential Energy Use: An Econometric Analysis*, Santa Monica, CA: Rand Corp., Report R-1296-NSF.

Anderson, Kent P. (1974) *The Price Elasticity of Residential Energy Use*, Santa Monica, CA: Rand Corp., Report P-5180.

Anderson, Kent P. (September 1981) *A Review of Studies of the Demand for Electricity*, National Economic Research Associates.

Bohi, D. (1981) *Analyzing Demand Behavior – A Study of Energy Elasticities*, Baltimore, MD: Johns Hopkins University Press.

Bohi, D. and Zimmerman, M. D. (1984) "Econometric Studies of Energy Demand Behavior", *Annual Review of Energy* 9, 105–154.

Box, G. E. P. and Jenkins, G. M. (1976) *Time Series Analysis: Forecasting and Control*, San Francisco: Holden-Day.

Brown, J. A. C. and Deaton, A. S. (1972) "Models of Consumer Behavior: A Survey", *Economic Journal*, 82, 1145–1236.

Carlson, R. and Thomas, T. (1986) "The Death Spiral: Implications for Regulations", Q.E.D. Research, Palo Alto, CA. Mimeo.

Charles River Associates Inc. (CRA) (1976) *Long-Range Forecasting Properties of State-of-the-Art Models of Demand for Electric Energy*, Palo Alto, CA: Electric Power Research Institute, Report EA-221.

Charles River Associates Inc. (CRA) (1976) *Long-Range Forecasting Properties of State-of-the-Art Models of Demand for Electric Energy*, CRA-230. Palo Alto, CA: Electric Power Research Institute.

Chasan, D. J. (1985) *The Fall of the House of WPPSS*, Seattle, WA: Sasquatch Publishing.

Chern, W. (November 1975) *Electricity Demand by Manufacturing Industries in the U.S.*, Oak Ridge National Laboratories.

Chern, W. and Chang, C. (1981) "Specification, Estimation of the Demand for Electricity", *Energy Systems and Policy* **228**.

College of Agricultural Research Center, Washington State University (1981) *Demand Response to Increasing Electricity Prices by Pacific Northwest Irrigated Agriculture*, Bulletin 0897.

Doty, R. W. (1988) *Life After WPPSS: Issuer Disclosure in the State and Local Government Securities Market*, Philadelphia, PA: Packard Press.

Edison Electric Institute (1986) *A Guide to Electricity Forecasting Methodology*, Washington, D.C.: Edison Electric Institute, Report 04-86-01.

Edmonds, J. A. (1978) *A Guide to Price Elasticities of Demand for Energy: Studies and Methodologies*, Oak Ridge, TN: Institute for Energy Analysis, Oak Ridge Associated Universities Report ORAU/IEA-78-15(R).

Federal Power Commission (October 1969) *The Methodology of Load Forecasting*, Technical Advisory Committee on Load Forecasting Methodology for the National Power Survey. (On file with the authors.)

Fisher, F. M. and Kaysen, C. (1962) *Demand for Electricity in the United States*, Amsterdam: North Holland.

Ford, A. and Youngblood, A. (1983) "Simulating the Spiral of Impossibility in the Electric Utility Industry", *Energy Policy* **11**(1).

Fox-Penner, P. (1988) "Allowing for Regulation in Forecasting Load and Financial Performance", *Public Utilities Fortnightly*, January 7, 1988.

Fox-Penner, P. (1990) *Electric Power Transmission and Wheeling: A Technical Primer*, Washington, D.C.: Edison Electric Institute.

Gill, G. S. and Maddala, G. S. (1976) "Residential Demand for Electricity in the TVA Area: An Analysis of Structural Change", in *1976 Proceedings of the Business and Economic Statistics Section*, pp. 315–19, American Statistical Association.

Granite State Electric Company (1989) *Integrated Least Cost Resource Plan for the Fifteen Year Period 1989–2003*, Submitted to the New Hampshire Public Utilities Commission, May 1, 1989.

Halvorsen, R. (1977) *Industrial Demand for Electricity*, Cambridge: National Bureau of Economic Research.

Hemphill, R. and Costello, K. (1987) *The Death Spiral: An Assessment of Its Likelihood in Electric Utilities*, Presented at the 51st Annual Meeting of the Midwest Economics Association, St. Louis, MO, March 1987. (On file with the authors.)

Houthakker, H. S. (1951) "Some Calculations of Electricity Consumption in Great Britain", *Journal of the Royal Statistical Society (A)* 114, Part III: 359–71.

Joskow, P. L. (1989) *Regulatory Failure, Regulatory Reform, and Structural Change in the Electrical Power Industry*, Washington, D.C.: Brookings Papers on Economic Activity.

Lawrence, A. and Parti, M. (1983) *Survey of Conditional Energy Demand Models for Estimating Residential Unit Energy Consumption Coefficients*, Palo Alto, CA: Electric Power Research Institute RP576-3.

Leigland, J. and Lamb, R. (1986) *WPP$$: Who is to Blame for the WPPSS Disaster?* Cambridge, MA: Ballinger.

Mines, M. (1984) "Background and Survey of Current Litigation Arising Out of the Washington Public Power Supply System Termination of Nuclear Projects 4 and 5", in D. L. Goelzer and R. S. Simmons (eds.), *Municipal and Agency Securities After WPPSS*, New York, NY: Law & Business, Inc./ Harcourt Brace Jovanovich.

Mooz, W. E. and Mow, C. C. (1973) *A Methodology for Projecting the Electrical Energy Demand of the Manufacturing Sector in California*, Santa Monica, CA: Rand. Corp., Report R-991-NSF/CSRA.

National Economic Research Associates, Inc. (NERA) (1977) *Consideration of the Price Elasticity of Demand for Electricity: Topic 2*, New York, NY: NERA.

Office of Environmental Affairs, Seattle Department of Lighting (1976) *Energy 90 Study*, 7 vols. [Consultants Team headed by Northwest Environmental Technology Laboratories.] Seattle, WA.

Port of Astoria v. Hodel (1975) *Environmental Law Reporter*, 5:20657. District of Oregon.

Prais, S. J. and Houthakker, H. S. (1955) *The Analysis of Family Budgets*, Cambridge (England): Cambridge University Press.

Taylor, L. D. (1975) "The Demand for Electricity: A Survey", *Bell Journal of Economics* 6, 74–110.

Taylor, L. D., Blattenberger, G., and Rennhack, R. (1984) "Residential Energy Demand in the U.S.: Results for Electricity", *Advances in the Economics of Energy and Resources* 5, 103–112.

Washington Public Power Supply Service (1977–1981) Official Statement. "Generating Facilities Revenue Bonds, WPPSS 4 and 5", Series 1977A–1981A.

Washington State Senate Energy and Utilities Committee (1981) "Causes of Cost Overruns and Schedule Delays on the Five WPPSS Nuclear Power Plants", *WPPSS Inquiry*. Vol. 1. January 12, 1981.

Wilson, J. (1969) "Residential and Industrial Demand for Electricity: An Empirical Analysis", Ph.D. diss., Cornell University.

In re WPPSS Securities Litigation MDL No. 551. U.S. District Court for the Western District of Washington (1988) *Plaintiff's Motion in Opposition to Motion for Summary Judgment on Section 10(b) Claims*, March 1, 1988.

CHAPTER 28

Estimating the Effects of Display Bias
in Computer Reservation Systems (1990)

written jointly with Kevin Neels

1.   Introduction

Today, the majority of airline reservations are made and tickets are sold through computer reservation systems (CRSs). The history of these systems, however, has been one of continuous controversy, involving both regulatory and antitrust proceedings.[1] This paper is drawn from our work in one of those proceedings, the antitrust suit brought by Continental Airlines (and its associated corporate family) against American Airlines and United Airlines.[2] Our work focused on the so-called bias period – before the Civil Aeronautics Board (CAB) issued its CRS Rules in 1984 (see C.F.R., 1984). The history and issues involved are recounted briefly below.

Computer reservation systems grew out of the internal reservation systems of the airlines. In the mid-1970s, there was discussion of extending the advancing reservation and information technology to travel agencies. This discussion resulted in the formation of an industry committee, a joint development that soon came to naught, however, when United

This paper is based on work done for Continental Airlines by Fisher and Charles River Associates (by whom Neels was then employed) in *Continental Airlines, Inc. and Texas Int'l Airlines, Inc. v. American Airlines, Inc. and United Airlines, Inc.*, No. CV 0696 ER (Mcx) (C.D.Cal.) and *New York Airlines, Inc. v. American Airlines, Inc. and United Airlines, Inc.*, No. CV 86-0697 (C.D.Cal.), and on Fisher's testimony therein. We are grateful to Benjamin Hirst, David Boies, Dominic Surprenant, Alan Vickery, Peter Barbur, R. Craig Romaine, Glenn Ellison, Chris Maxwell, Jeff Wooldridge, and especially Brian Palmer, but retain responsibility for errors and for the views expressed here.

[1] A number of papers have discussed that history, and we shall not attempt a full discussion here. See, for example, U.S. Department of Transportation, 1988, or DOT, 1990.

[2] American and United were also sued separately by a different group of airlines. That case was tried to a jury in Los Angeles in late 1989, and the jury found for the defendants. (*USAir, Inc. et al. v. American Airlines, Inc. and United Airlines, Inc.*, No. 84-8918 ER (Mcx) (C.D.Cal.), see also *In Re Air Passenger Computer Reservations Systems Antitrust Litigation*, 694 F. Supp. 1443 (C.D.Cal. 1988), *affd sub nom, Alaska Airlines, Inc. v. United Airlines, Inc.* 948 F.2d 536 (9th Cir. 1991), *Cert. denied*, 112 S.Ct. 1603 (1992)) American and Continental settled before the trial of the Continental case, and that trial went forward against United only. The trial took place in early 1990, but no verdict was reached, as the parties settled after closing statements but before the jury had produced a decision.

Airlines and American Airlines pulled out of the committee and each announced it would develop its own system. With the withdrawal of the two largest domestic airlines and (and – not coincidentally – the two with the best-developed internal reservations systems), cooperative development effectively stopped.

Deregulation of the airline industry created powerful incentives for United and American to develop their own proprietary systems. As new carriers began operations and established carriers entered new routes, the number of different flights and itineraries that might suit a particular customer's request could become very large. A traveler wishing to go from point A to B on a particular day could travel at different times, on different carriers and through different connecting points. The number of available fares also grew dramatically.

In this environment, a travel agent who queried a CRS as to travel options from A to B would be presented with a large variety of choices – often more than would fit on a single computer screen. As a result, CRSs had to employ algorithms to decide the order of presentation. Such algorithms involved tradeoffs between such things as closeness to desired departure time, number of stops, whether a change of carrier was involved, and so forth.

In their proprietary systems, American and United inserted preference for their own flights into their respective display algorithms. For example, the SABRE system, American's CRS, used an algorithm that ranked options by elapsed time after adding in penalty minutes to reflect undesirable characteristics. A flight leaving an hour after the desired departure time would receive a 60-minute penalty; an itinerary involving a change of planes would receive a penalty of some number of minutes measuring (in some sense) equivalent inconvenience to the traveler and so on. But American also assigned additional penalty minutes to the flights of its competitors, independent of their quality of service or fit with passengers' desired itineraries. APOLLO, United's CRS, accomplished the same end only in more complicated ways.[3]

Such algorithms increased the bookings of the CRS owners at the expense of other subscribers. It is easy to see how this occurred. A large number of transactions begin with a phone call by the customer to the travel agent. There is a natural tendency for the travel agent to offer the flights in the order in which they are presented on the screen and to

---

[3] The algorithms became very complicated indeed. Carriers other than the host (the airline owning the CRS) were permitted to buy in and become "co-hosts." The algorithms would then give them an advantage relative to non-co-host carriers, but would still leave them at a disadvantage relative to the host. It is worth noting that neither American nor United became co-hosts in the other's system.

stop when the customer finds one that is acceptable. To investigate all flights would require a substantial amount of time. So, although many travel agents were aware of the bias introduced into the display by CRS vendors, most choices were nonetheless made from the first line presented, and an even greater fraction were made from the first screen.[4]

United and American's own internal estimates of the magnitude of the diversion of traffic from other carriers to themselves indicated that the associated profit was enormous. These profits were attributable not just to the size of the diversion, but also to the fact that airline profitability is naturally very sensitive to changes in the fraction of the available seats filled by paying passengers.[5]

Eventually, of course, the existence of display bias became known to other carriers and, in 1984, the CAB issued rules that, *inter alia*, forbade the use of carrier identity in CRS display algorithms. This ruling greatly reduced (although it did not end) the use of biased displays. Immediately following the issuance of these Rules there was a short episode in which United and American took advantage of a loophole in the Rules, bribing travel agencies to lock in a biased secondary screen as the first one that the agent would see. After that, manipulation of the display algorithms became more subtle.[6]

Not surprisingly, American's and United's behavior gave rise to litigation by other airlines and to debates over regulatory policy for CRSs. A major issue was the magnitude of the damage suffered by other airlines as a result of display bias. This paper reports our study of that question as it pertains to Continental Airlines.

2.   Did Display Bias Actually Result in Revenue Diversion?

Despite the existence of numerous internal documents describing the gains to American and United from display bias, the defendants maintained in pleadings and expert testimony that, in fact, this bias had very little effect on market shares. Disagreements over this question have per-

---

[4] The 1988 DOT report cites on page 1 the widely held belief within the industry that screen placement does affect choice of carrier. Empirical studies conducted by CRS owners confirm this belief.

[5] Estimates by the U.S. Department of Transportation of internal rates of return earned by American through the SABRE system in 1986 ranged from 22.8 percent through 129.5 percent, depending what assumptions are made regarding the profit earned on revenues diverted to American through the effects of bias. Internal documents of American cited in the DOT report support the higher figure. See DOT, 1988.

[6] For some examples of such subtle use, see Fisher, 1987.

sisted to this day.[7] Thus, our first task is to determine whether Continental was in fact injured as a result of display bias.

One obvious approach is to compare Continental's CRS bookings in the periods before and after the CRS Rules were issued.[8] Although the results of such a study may be suggestive, they cannot provide definitive evidence. While the Rules presumably brought about changes, they were not the only factor influencing Continental's bookings in the early and mid-1980s. Consider some obvious examples of other factors: Continental experienced a pilots' strike followed by its first bankruptcy in 1983; thereafter, its route structure and level of service changed dramatically. The pilots at United – a major Continental competitor – struck in 1985. More generally, the amount of air travel in the United States as a whole changed over this period. Clearly, a raw before-and-after comparison cannot provide a defensible estimate of the effects of the Rule.

Many of these factors could be expected to have similar proportional effects on both the overall number of passengers on Continental and bookings through a CRS. Removal of display bias, however, would have a disproportionate effect on CRS bookings.[9] Based upon this observation, we compared the ratio of Continental CRS bookings to Continental enplanements before and after the elimination of display bias.[10] We took into account bookings through the three CRSs that were said to have been heavily biased in the pre-Rule period.[11] Calculating their ratio to Continental enplanements and regressing the resulting measure on the display bias dummy variable generated the results shown in Table 28.1. Also included in the model is an indicator variable identifying the period of the 1985 pilots' strike against United Airlines.[12] Since casual inspection of the booking data suggested strongly that this strike had a

[7] There is widespread agreement that host carriers tended to enjoy disproportionate shares of sales through their own systems. Opinions have varied, however, over the explanation for this advantage. It has been variously attributed to goodwill from ongoing business relationships; the tendency of travel agents to choose the CRS of the carrier they tend to book on anyway; the effects of special incentive or "override" agreements; and various other non-display-bias-related factors.

[8] This is in fact how the study began. We were asked to review an internal study that had been prepared by Continental staff based upon a before-and-after comparison.

[9] Total enplanements would also be affected, although to a lesser extent, because the additional CRS bookings gained by Continental would be made by passengers who would eventually fly and be counted as enplanements.

[10] We are indebted to a reviewer of an earlier draft of this paper for this suggestion.

[11] These included SABRE, APOLLO, and PARS, which at the time was owned by TWA. The latter carrier was not a defendant in the case.

[12] This variable is defined more fully elsewhere in this paper.

Table 28.1. *Effect of the removal of display bias on the ratio of biased CRS bookings to total enplanements*

Summary Statistics

Observations:	36		
Degrees of Freedom:	33		
R Squared:	0.361		

Variable	Coefficient	Standard error	Ratio
Intercept	0.694	0.005	153.287
United strike	0.104	0.034	3.078
Primary bias period	−0.021	0.008	−2.502

major effect on Continental's APOLLO bookings, we did not want to mistakenly attribute this jump to the absence of display bias. Results shown in Table 28.1 confirm that the ratio of CRS bookings on allegedly biased systems to enplanements was significantly lower in the pre-Rule period than in the post-Rule period, confirming our hypothesis.

This ratio model provides a simple way of addressing a concern expressed by many over the reliability of efforts to measure the effects of display bias that relied either directly or indirectly on before-and-after comparisons. Many comments elicited both by the original testimony at trial and by early drafts of this paper expressed a suspicion that SABRE and APOLLO bookings were trending upward over time, probably as a result of growth in these systems, and that our bias coefficient was simply picking up the effects of this trend.[13] In the context of the ratio model it is a simple matter to include both a time trend and a display bias dummy variable, and to determine whether the presence of the former eliminates the statistical significance of the latter. Results of this test are shown in Table 28.2. Contrary to the expectations of virtually all of our reviewers, the coefficient of the time trend variable is negative (i.e., the ratio of SABRE, APOLLO, and PARS bookings to enplanements for Continental was *declining* over time), and the presence of this variable both increases the estimated magnitude of the bias effect and strengthens its statistical significance.

Further evidence that CRS display bias did result in diversion of passenger revenue arrived at time of trial from a different source. Testify-

---

[13] One reviewer even characterized our failure to consider this possibility as "inexcusable."

Table 28.2. *Effect of the removal of display bias
on the ratio of biased CRS bookings to total
enplanements, controlling for time trends*

Summary Statistics
Observations:	36
Degrees of Freedom:	32
R Squared:	0.394

Variable	Coefficient	Standard error	Ratio
Intercept	0.714	0.015	46.744
Time trend	−0.0008	0.0006	−1.324
United strike	0.093	0.035	2.677
Primary bias period	−0.036	0.014	−2.548

ing for United, Jerry Hausman presented a study of his own in which he
looked at travel agents in several hundred locations (i.e., cities or sections of cities). He compared shares of total bookings made on United
by agents in 1984 and 1986, to see whether there was a systematic tendency for United bookings made by APOLLO agents to decrease as
compared with agents automated with SABRE or one of the three
smaller systems. By comparing agents in the same location, he controlled
for factors affecting travel from a particular location. Hausman's results
cannot be interpreted directly as measuring the effect of bias in
APOLLO. However, if correct, they measure the total effect on United
of the removal of bias both in APOLLO and in the system with which
it is compared. Thus, they can be taken as a test for the presence or
absence of a display bias effect.

Testing for display bias on a location-by-location basis, Hausman
found that in a majority of cases he was unable to reject the null hypothesis of no change over the period in United's market share in APOLLO
relative to its share in other CRSs. He concluded and testified on the
basis of this evidence that the removal of display bias had no effect on
booking patterns.

While Hausman failed to find many significant coefficients, the number
of significant ones he did find and, indeed, the sign pattern of coefficients,
shows that something significant happened between 1984 and 1986.[14]

---

[14] Of 542 estimated coefficients, Hausman found 319 with a sign indicating display bias.
This is significant at the 0.01 percent level on a one-tailed test.

While the individual coefficients often failed the usual statistical tests, they tended in most cases to take signs suggesting that the removal of display bias harmed United in APOLLO and helped it in other CRSs. It was possible to reject the hypothesis that the pattern of positive and negative coefficients arose by chance with a high degree of confidence. Hausman's results thus suggested that between those two years, United's bookings with APOLLO agents decreased relative to its bookings with agents using other systems. It is not possible to determine from this analysis alone whether revenue diversion occurred in APOLLO, in the other systems, or in both.

3.   How Much Revenue Was Diverted from Continental in SABRE and APOLLO?

A very important issue at trial, clearly, was the magnitude of the revenue diversion from Continental. How much business did Continental lose as a result of display bias? By how much was it injured as a result? It was also important to know how much of the diversion occurred in SABRE and how much in APOLLO. In addition to these private concerns, it is also important from a policy perspective to know the magnitude of the display bias effect. Drastic solutions have sometimes been proposed to the problem of CRS bias.[15] In order to assess the merits of such proposals, accurate knowledge of the magnitude and severity of the problems they purport to correct is essential.

The analyses whose results are summarized above provide only limited information on the magnitude of the display bias effect and shed very little light on differences across systems. Providing answers to these more specific questions required a different approach.

3.1.   Effects of Display Bias in SABRE

One obvious approach in attempting to measure the effects of display bias in SABRE is to compare Continental's SABRE bookings in the periods before and after the CRS Rules were issued. As noted above, however, while the results of such a study may be suggestive, they cannot provide definitive evidence. A variety of different influences affected the level of passenger demand and hence also the level of CRS bookings during the period surrounding the prohibition of display bias.

---

[15] These have included divestiture and prohibition of "hosting," the phenomenon in which the airline owner of the CRS uses that system as its internal reservation system.

To account properly for these effects and to isolate the influence of display bias we developed an econometric model of Continental's bookings on SABRE. The dependent variable is the natural log of the number of segments booked in the SABRE system on Continental as of the time of flight departure.[16] The independent variables are summarized in Table 28.3. Parameters of this model were estimated using monthly observations for the period January 1983 through December 1986. This period is approximately centered on the issuance of the Rules in November 1984 and represents a time of relative stability for Continental's organization and route structure. In October 1982, shortly before the start of the period, Continental merged with Texas International. In early 1987, shortly after the end of the period, Continental merged with People Express and New York Air.[17] The rationale for inclusion of most of the variables shown in Table 28.3 is fairly obvious. They measure the extent and quality of Continental's service, the quality of service provided by Continental's competitors, the overall level of air travel demand and relative prices.[18]

The industry event variables require somewhat more explanation. The

[16] This definition is the basis for the booking fees charged to Continental by American. Note that it implies that passengers who do not show up at departure time are still recorded as bookings. The dependent variable thus overstates the number of passenger trips booked in SABRE and actually flown. A more precise discussion of date and data sources is given in the Appendix.

[17] Extending the period either backward – to include the period prior to the Texas International merger – or forward – to the period after the People Express/New York Air merger – gave us similar estimates of the magnitude of the CRS display bias effect.

[18] A suggestion made by a reviewer of an earlier draft involved replacement of total U.S. enplanements as a measure of overall demand levels with total bookings made through SABRE. Such a substitution, this reviewer argued, would have resulted in a model that better reflected the growth in the SABRE system that took place during the period. This suggestion has merit, although as a practical matter our inability to obtain monthly data on total SABRE bookings made its implementation impossible.

Although we accept the general validity of this suggestion, we note that growth in the total number of SABRE bookings could arise from a number of different sources, not all of which would be expected to influence the number of bookings made on Continental. Clearly, a change in total SABRE bookings resulting from a relocation by American of the line separating its internal reservation system from the SABRE system would have little effect on Continental bookings. The same could be said of an increase resulting from a decision by a new carrier to become a SABRE participant. On the other hand, growth in bookings resulting from the conversion of travel agencies from other CRSs, from the automation by SABRE of previously non-automated agencies, or from increases in the number of individual agents using the system could all be expected to influence Continental's booking levels on the system. Data were available measuring the growth of the SABRE system in terms both of the number of locations automated and the number of travel agent CRTs connected to the system. When entered into the model, these variables invariably had insignificant coefficients and had no effect on the other estimated parameters.

Table 28.3. *SABRE model specification*

	Minimum	Maximum	Mean	Standard deviation	Source
Continental Service					
Log of mainland cities served	3.22	4.41	3.88	0.30	Monthly Continental schedule analyses
Log of domestic departures per city	5.04	5.91	5.64	0.24	U.S. Department of Transportation
Log of continental complaint rate	−11.39	−7.75	−10.02	0.63	U.S. Department of Transportation
Competitor Service					
Log of Competitor domestic departures	12.67	13.09	12.91	0.09	U.S. Department of Transportation
Demand for Travel					
Log of domestic enplanements	16.88	17.45	17.14	0.14	U.S. Department of Transportation
Price Levels					
Log of Continental yield over air fare CPI	−8.74	−8.11	−8.49	0.16	Monthly Continental revenue reports and monthly CPI detail reports
Industry Events					
Continental pilot strike	0.00	0.87	0.03	0.15	Trade press accounts
Continental bankruptcy	0.00	0.75	0.03	0.13	Trade press accounts
United pilot strike	0.00	0.48	0.02	0.10	Trade press accounts
Display Bias					
Primary display bias	0.00	1.00	0.47	0.50	CAB regulations
Secondary display bias	0.00	1.00	0.09	0.29	Trade press accounts

first is an indicator variable for the direct effects of the Continental pilots' strike in August and September 1983. The variable is zero except for those two months. For August, the variable is equal to the fraction of the month that Continental pilots were on strike. For September, the variable equals the fraction of the month from September 1st to the day on which Continental declared bankruptcy and abrogated its labor contracts. Note that, since the pilots' strike lasted only a short time before the bankruptcy, we should not be surprised if we fail to find that the strike had a significant effect that can be separated from that of the bankruptcy.

The second event variable relates to the bankruptcy itself. Part of the effect of the bankruptcy (and of the pilots' strike) was to cause a dramatic reduction in the number of cities served and in departures per city. These effects are captured in the Continental service variables. However, even controlling for the level of Continental's service, the bankruptcy probably had other effects, causing passengers and travel agents to avoid Continental when making travel arrangements. This latter effect was doubtless greatest at the time of the bankruptcy and diminished as the situation stabilized.

To represent this effect, we use an indicator variable in the following form. The variable is zero before September 1983. For September 1983, the variable is equal to the fraction of the month during which Continental was in bankruptcy. In essence, this makes the variable zero for all days before the declaration of bankruptcy and unity for all days (in September) following it. For the following months, the variable declines linearly from unity until it reaches zero in January 1984. The latter date is not arbitrary but is estimated by varying the month in which the variable declined to zero and choosing the particular month that provided the best fit.[19]

Continental was not the only carrier experiencing difficulties during the estimation period. As already noted, United experienced a pilots' strike in May and June of 1985. We capture the effects of that strike with an indicator variable equal to zero except for the two strike months. In each of those months this variable is equal to the fraction of the month during which the strike was in effect.

The last two variables measure the effects of display bias. The first is an indicator variable equal to unity before November 1984 and zero for all months thereafter. For November itself, the variable equals the fraction of the month before the Rules were issued. We refer to this variable as an indicator variable for the "primary bias period" – the period before issuance of the rules.

As mentioned earlier, there was also a "secondary" bias period from the middle of November 1984 through March 1985. Immediately after the promulgation of the CRS Rules, American and United encouraged a number of travel agencies to lock in so-called secondary screens with

---

[19] The standard errors presented in this paper do not take into account that the duration of the post-bankruptcy effect is an estimated coefficient. An approximate and asymptotic test confirms that our estimate of the CRS display effect remains significant when this is corrected.

Table 28.4. *OLS results for the SABRE model*

Summary Statistics
Observations:	48	
Degrees of Freedom:	36	
Adjusted R Squared:	0.986	

Variable	Coefficient	Standard error	t-statistic
Intercept	0.920	2.352	0.391
Log cities served	0.524	0.055	9.502
Log departures per city	0.859	0.159	5.385
Log complaint rate	−0.050	0.028	−1.816
Log competitor departures	−1.129	0.302	−3.736
Log total enplanements	1.076	0.139	7.765
Log relative fares	−0.077	0.135	−0.572
Bankruptcy	−0.380	0.143	−2.652
Continental strike	−0.056	0.076	−0.744
United strike	0.035	0.098	0.357
Primary bias period	−0.135	0.041	−3.253
Secondary bias period	−0.004	0.035	−0.127

the old biased display as the screen agents would see first upon signing on to the system. That practice was "voluntarily" ended on March 31, 1985, following a storm of protests by other carriers and a Congressional hearing. Our indicator variable for the secondary bias period is zero, except for the months from November 1984 to March 1985. It is unity for December 1983, and for January to March 1985. For November 1984, the variable equals the fraction of the month after the promulgation of the CRS Rules.

The results obtained by estimating this model using ordinary least squares are given in Table 28.4. They are very satisfactory. Every coefficient has the expected sign, and most are highly significant. The four variables that relate to Continental and competitor service and to total air traffic have coefficients that sum to a bit more than unity (1.33). This result is roughly of the correct order of magnitude, since it suggests that a 1 percent increase in all airline activity, other things equal, would increase Continental's bookings on SABRE by roughly 1 percent.

The non-bias variables that fail to be significant even on a one-tailed test are the relative-fare variable and the two strike-indicator variables. The relative-fare variable is only a rough measure of relative prices.

Unlike the service variables that are fixed by Continental two months in advance, fares vary up to the day of departure. Thus, while the service variable can be regarded as predetermined, fares should perhaps be regarded as endogenous. Moreover, because fare levels and availability change continuously over the period leading up to departure, passengers making reservations at different points in time very likely faced different relative prices. Our average fare variable can at best only approximate this sequence of relative prices. Hence it is not too surprising to find the coefficient of the fare variable to be of the correct sign but insignificant.

The Continental strike indicator marks a very short period (less than two months). Moreover, the second of the two months for which it is non-zero is the month in which the Continental bankruptcy variable first becomes non-zero. It is not surprising that we fail to find a separate significant effect here.

We also fail to find a significant effect for the United strike variable. That variable also takes on non-zero values only for a short time. More important, we should expect the effects of the United strike on *Continental* to be most pronounced for bookings made in cities with a great deal of United service. Those cities generally have a large number of APOLLO agents. SABRE agents, by contrast, tend to predominate in cities with a great deal of American service. As we shall see below, we do find a significant effect of the United strike when we examine APOLLO bookings.

The effect of display bias, however, is unmistakably significant as regards the primary bias period (the period before the Rules). The implication is that display bias during that period reduced Continental's bookings in SABRE by approximately 12.6 percent.[20] We discuss the order of magnitude of this effect later.

The secondary-screen episode, however, for all the controversy it generated, apparently had little or no effect. Not only does the coefficient of the relevant variable not differ significantly from zero, but that coefficient itself is also very close to zero. The estimated coefficient for this variable remained very close to zero in all variants of the model we examined while testing the robustness of our findings. These facts suggest that American was unsuccessful in persuading travel agencies to lock in the secondary screen.[21]

---

[20] This effect is calculated as $1 - \exp(-0.135) = 0.1263$.

[21] Interestingly, anecdotal evidence from the trade press suggests that in recent years, as both travel agents and their corporate customers have become more oriented toward relationships with preferred carriers, the demand for deliberately biased displays has increased.

Table 28.5. *OLS results for the APOLLO model,*
with raw bookings data

Summary Statistics

Observations:	48
Degrees of Freedom:	36
Adjusted R Squared:	0.833

Variable	Coefficient	Standard error	t-statistic
Intercept	0.230	8.890	0.026
Log cities served	0.650	0.209	3.117
Log departures per city	0.658	0.603	1.092
Log complaint rate	0.019	0.104	0.179
Log competitor departures	0.566	1.142	0.496
Log total enplanements	−0.265	0.524	−0.506
Log relative fares	−0.419	0.509	−0.823
Bankruptcy	−1.033	0.541	−1.908
Continental strike	−0.429	0.286	−1.498
United strike	0.807	0.369	2.186
Primary bias period	−0.095	0.156	−0.610
Secondary bias period	−0.109	0.132	−0.831

3.2.   *Effects of Display Bias on APOLLO Bookings by Time of Booking*

The same logic that led to the analysis of SABRE bookings described above suggests that a similar approach should lead to a valid estimate of the effect that display bias in the APOLLO system had on Continental's bookings. Although effects of bias could well differ between the two systems, we would expect variables describing broad industry trends to have comparable effects. If we are on the right track, the APOLLO results should at least resemble those presented in Table 28.4.

Direct estimation of the same specification using data on APOLLO bookings quickly shows that something is very wrong. The results of this estimation are displayed in Table 28.5. While most coefficients have the correct sign, many do not. In particular, the effect of total air travel demand on APOLLO bookings appears perverse. Significance levels are generally quite low. This is true not only for the estimated effects of bias, but also for the variables relating to Continental and competitor departures. Further striking differences arose when we tested these results for robustness. While the SABRE results are quite stable with respect to small changes in specification, the results in Table 28.5 are extremely sensitive to such changes.

The source of the problem is easy to find. The two systems maintain their bookings records in very different ways. SABRE bookings recorded for a given month are the bookings made through SABRE and still resident therein on the date when the relevant flights depart. APOLLO bookings, on the other hand, are recorded *as of the date when the reservations are made*. Thus, for example, SABRE bookings data for December 1983 indicate how many passengers made reservations through the system for travel in that month, regardless of whether the agent was contacted in December or in some earlier month. The APOLLO data for the same month indicate how many passengers initially contacted travel agents in December, regardless of whether they intended to travel in that month or in some later month. Since many of the independent variables in the model describe conditions as of the time of flight, it is hardly surprising that they do a better job of predicting movements in SABRE bookings than in bookings on APOLLO.

While easily diagnosed, this timing problem is not so easily solved. The time lag between the date on which a reservation is made and the actual date of travel varies from passenger to passenger and systematically from month to month. Some reservations are made shortly before the travel date; others are made months in advance. Further, the time pattern of such advance bookings is not constant over the course of the year. Bookings for such heavy leisure-travel times as Thanksgiving or Christmas are likely to be made well in advance. As a result, use of a traditional fixed-lag structure cannot correct the timing problem.

4. Estimating the Propensity to Book Ahead

In order to proceed, therefore, we needed to express Continental's APOLLO bookings on a time-of-flight basis. To do this, we needed to measure variations in passengers' propensity to book ahead over the course of the year. We accomplished this by developing a model that related the number of segments actually flown on Continental to the number of reservations made through the different CRS systems over a three-month period leading up to the time of flight.

Passengers who flew on Continental could obtain tickets from a number of different sources. They could, of course, purchase them from an automated travel agent. These passengers appear in the counts of bookings through SABRE, APOLLO, or one of the smaller CRSs.[22] They could also obtain tickets from non-automated travel agents or directly from Continental itself.[23]

If comprehensive data had been available on the number of passengers who obtained tickets on Continental in these various ways, it would have been a relatively simple matter to relate these data to counts of the number of segments actually flown. We would have related enplaned passengers for a month to the number of bookings reported for SABRE and the secondary systems in that month. We would have related enplanements in a month to the number of APOLLO bookings reported in that month and previous months.

Data limitations hampered this analysis. We were able to obtain complete data on SABRE and APOLLO bookings, but data for the minor CRS systems were limited, covering only a portion of the period. Data on direct bookings or bookings through non-automated travel agencies were completely unavailable. Fortunately, however, these limitations were not insuperable. Bookings on SABRE and APOLLO during this period accounted for a large fraction of total Continental travel.[24] Further, it did not seem unreasonable to assume that no-shows, direct bookings and bookings through the minor reservations systems were closely related to bookings through SABRE and APOLLO.

Considering that relationship to be linear enabled us to construct this formula:

$$C_t = a_A A_t + a_S S_t + e_t \tag{1}$$

Here C_t denotes the number of passengers actually flying on Continental in month t; S_t is the number of bookings made through SABRE for travel in month t; A_t is the number of bookings made through APOLLO for travel in month t; and e_t is a random disturbance term.

Now, A_t – the number of bookings made through APOLLO for travel in month t – is made up both of bookings made in month t and bookings made in previous months. Thus:

$$A_t = \lambda_0 A_t^* + \lambda_1 A_{t-1}^* + \lambda_2 A_{t-2}^* \tag{2}$$

---

[22] During the relevant period, those systems were PARS (owned initially by TWA and later also by Northwest), System One (owned initially by Eastern and later by Texas Air Corporation), and DATAS II (owned by Delta).

[23] Bookings are also made through non-CRS-owning airlines so passengers do show up at the gate without a reservation but with a valid ticket.

[24] In 1985, for example, Continental's domestic enplanements totaled 14,598,461. Its total bookings through the SABRE and APOLLO systems were 9,307,790.

where A_t^* denotes bookings made during month t.[25] However, the seasonal nature of airline traffic and booking patterns means that the λ_i are likely to vary from month to month. To capture this effect we modify equation (2):

$$A_t = \lambda_{0m(t)}A_t^* + \lambda_{1m(t)}A_{t-1}^* + \lambda_{2m(t)}A_{t-2}^* \tag{3}$$

where m(t) is the month number (i.e., 1 for January, 2 for February, etc.) associated with time period t. Estimation of the $\lambda_{im(t)}$ permits us to convert data by time of booking to data by time of flight.

Development of an estimable form required two steps. First, we substituted (3) into (1), reparameterizing the model slightly and deriving two coefficients for each of the 12 months. Second, we added a number of independent variables to the model to capture changes in the relationship between our bookings data series and the series on the number of enplaned passengers.

To illustrate the nature of the reparameterization, consider the month of January. The first of the two coefficients for January (JAN1) gives the fraction of bookings made in January that pertain to travel in January (λ_{01}). The second coefficient (JAN2) gives the fraction of the *remaining* bookings made in January that pertain to travel in February. Thus, λ_{11} equals $(1 - JAN1)(JAN2)$. The fraction of bookings made in January that pertain to travel in March (λ_{21}) equals $(1 - JAN2)(1 - JAN1)$, since we have assumed that no bookings are made more than two months in advance.

This reparameterization allowed us to impose three plausible constraints on these coefficients. The first two are obvious. The coefficients cannot be negative and cannot exceed 100 percent. The third constraint requires the fraction of bookings made in a particular month for travel in the following month to be at least as great as the fraction for travel two months later. (In the example above, this constraint is imposed by requiring JAN2 to be greater than or equal to 0.500.) This constraint guarantees that the fraction of bookings made for a future point in time declines as the interval between the time of booking and the time of flight increases.

A number of different factors changed the relationship between enplanements and bookings over the period. We capture their effects through the addition of a number of independent variables to the timing model. We first assume that the contributions of SABRE and APOLLO,

---

[25] Expanding equation (2) to capture bookings made more than two months in advance adds trivially to the explanatory power of the model and yields essentially identical estimates of the effects of CRS display bias on Continental's APOLLO bookings.

respectively, grew over time with the expansion of the two systems. Thus:

$$a_S = a_{S0} + (a_{S1}/L_{St}) \tag{4}$$

where a_{S0} and a_{S1} are constants, and L_{St} denotes the number of SABRE-automated travel agency locations in month t.[26] The corresponding expression for APOLLO contained an additional term to account for the effects of the United strike on the importance of APOLLO in Continental bookings:[27]

$$a_A = a_{A0} + (a_{A1}/L_{At}) + a_{A2}U_t \tag{5}$$

where U_t is the indicator variable for the United strike, previously defined. We then added two additional variables. The first is the indicator variable for the period prior to the Rule. Its presence in the model was implied by the premise of our investigation. If removal of display bias increased the number of bookings on Continental, we would expect SABRE and APOLLO to account for relatively greater fractions of Continental enplanements in the post-Rule period. The second variable added was an indicator variable equal to unity for the period before the merger of Continental and Texas International. It captures the effects of the changes in network structure and in the geographical distribution of bookings that occurred as a result of the merger.[28]

The timing equation finally estimated was thus:

$$\begin{aligned}
C_t = &\{a_{S0} + (a_{S1}/L_{St}) + a_M M_t + a_B B_t\} S_t \\
&+ \{a_{A0} + (a_{A1}/L_{At}) + a_{A2}U_t + a_M M_t + a_B B_t\} \\
&\{\lambda_{0m(t)}A_t^* + \lambda_{1m(t)}A_{t-1}^* + \lambda_{2m(t)}A_{t-2}^*\} + e_t
\end{aligned} \tag{6}$$

where M_t is an indicator variable identifying the time period prior to the Continental–Texas International merger and B_t is an indicator variable identifying the primary bias period.

Table 28.6 presents the results derived from estimation of equation (6)

---

[26] Data on the number of SABRE and APOLLO installations were available only on an annualized basis. Monthly values were calculated through interpolation. We experimented with a number of functional forms for the installations variables and found that the reciprocal gave the best fit.

[27] The temporary surge in Continental's APOLLO bookings as a result of the strike, discussed above, implies a temporary increase in APOLLO's contribution to Continental enplanements.

[28] The merger is likely to have affected the relations between the various industry and airline variables and the *level* of Continental bookings on APOLLO (or SABRE) in complex ways. It is far less likely to have so affected the *timing* of Continental bookings on APOLLO. Hence we use a longer time period (and an indicator variable) for the timing equation than for the bookings equation.

Table 28.6. *Timing model results*

Summary Statistics

Observations:	71
Degrees of Freedom:	40
R squared:	0.9867

Variable	Coefficient	Standard error	t-statistic
JAN1	0.554	0.418	1.324
FEB1	0.528	0.259	2.038
MAR1	0.545	0.533	1.023
APR1	0.371	0.300	1.236
MAY1	0.191	0.245	0.778
JUN1	0.539	0.308	1.747
JUL1	0.615	0.228	2.697
AUG1	0.594	0.496	1.197
SEP1	0.615	0.247	2.484
OCT1	0.395	0.117	3.367
NOV1	0.651	0.186	3.490
DEC1	0.812	0.491	1.655
JAN2	0.634	0.512	1.238
FEB2	0.500		
MAR2	0.680	0.823	0.826
APR2	1.000		
MAY2	0.641	0.271	2.362
JUN2	0.500		
JUL2	1.000		
AUG2	0.711	0.517	1.374
SEP2	1.000		
OCT2	0.500		
NOV2	0.500		
DEC2	1.000		
APOLLO constant	1.770	0.794	2.227
1/APOLLO locns.	0.000		
SABRE constant	1.029	0.441	2.331
1/SABRE locns.	−5,016.890	1,644.460	−3.051
Pre-TI merger	−0.353	0.055	−6.393
Primary bias	−0.094	0.048	−1.942
United strike	−0.996	0.395	−2.521

Note: Equation was estimated using nonlinear least squares.

using data for the period February 1980 through December 1986. A binding boundary constraint appears as a coefficient of zero or unity without a reported standard error; a binding inequality constraint appears as a coefficient of 0.500 without a reported standard error. We are most interested in the estimated timing parameters. Although the individual coefficients are not always estimated precisely, as a group they are highly significant.[29] The individual parameter values are intuitively plausible. Note, in particular, that in the months preceding the heavy travel times – Thanksgiving, Christmas, and the end of the academic year – bookings are shown to be made farther in advance than at other times. The coefficient for the installations variable is significant for SABRE, but the corresponding coefficient for APOLLO was not significant and had the wrong sign. As a result, that coefficient was constrained to zero. The pre-Texas International merger variable, the primary bias variable, and the United strike variable all had coefficients that were significantly different from zero.

5.   Effects of Display Bias on APOLLO Bookings by Time of Departure

A second and, from the point of view of this analysis, more important test of the validity of these results is the quality of results we obtain when we use the timing model coefficients to calculate the number of APOLLO bookings by time of departure. The coefficients shown in Table 28.6 tell us what fractions of the bookings made in each month are for travel in succeeding months. Using these estimates, we can construct a new dependent variable that reflects the number of bookings made for travel in a month, regardless of when they were made. With this dependent variable in hand, reestimation of the model shown in Table 28.5 is straightforward.[30] The results appear in Table 28.7. Note that the

---

[29] The fact that many of the parameter boundary constraints bind appears to be attributable to the imprecision of the individual coefficient estimates. The point estimates for many imprecisely estimated coefficients happened to fall on the wrong side of a constraint.

[30] The fact that bookings are often made for travel some weeks or months in the future raises questions about our representation of some of the other factors included in the model. Does an event like the United strike affect bookings that are made while the strike is ongoing? Or do travelers anticipate the strike and avoid the affected airline for trips scheduled for the period of the strike, even if bookings are made in advance? Our analysis of United data, discussed in a later footnote, supports the former view. The effect of the strike on United appears to have been restricted to bookings made during the months of May and June 1985, while the strike was taking place.

These two points of view lead to two different ways of constructing the indicator vari-

Table 28.7. *APOLLO bookings model: bookings by time of departure*

Summary Statistics
Observations: 48
Degrees of Freedom: 24

Variable	Coefficient	Standard error	Ratio
Intercept	−2.925	8.618	−0.339
Log Cities Served	0.608	0.104	5.866
Log Departures per City	0.219	0.273	0.804
Log Complaint Rate	−0.054	0.055	−0.981
Log Competitor Depart.	−0.994	1.019	−0.976
Log Total Enplanements	1.144	0.472	2.425
United Strike	0.360	0.282	1.276
Continental Strike	−0.440	0.163	−2.696
Bankruptcy	−0.711	0.480	−1.481
Primary Bias Period	−0.213	0.069	−3.112
Secondary Bias Period	−0.002	0.039	−0.063
Log Relative Fares	−0.548	0.455	−1.203
February	−0.143	0.129	−1.119
March	−0.124	0.133	−0.933
April	−0.102	0.108	−0.945
May	−0.047	0.109	−0.432
June	0.092	0.136	0.681
July	0.185	0.139	1.330
August	0.169	0.149	1.334
September	0.082	0.102	0.808
October	0.109	0.131	0.835
November	0.029	0.103	0.282
December	0.014	0.101	0.139

ables that capture the effects of factors such as the United strike or the Continental strike. One approach relates the indicator variables directly to the adjusted APOLLO bookings. It assumes, in effect, that passengers accurately anticipate events such as the United strike and avoid the affected airline only if they plan to travel during the period of the strike. The results presented in the text use this approach. The second approach uses the timing coefficients from Table 28.4 to adjust the indicator variables in such a way as to relate the effects of the strike to bookings made during the period of the strike, regardless of when the travel was to take place. The results using this approach generally differ from those presented only in detail. (A similar statement is true of reestimation of the SABRE model along these lines.) Since the effects of bias must occur as of the time of booking, the results in the text do adjust the bias variables for timing.

asymptotic standard errors in Table 28.7 account for the fact that the dependent variable has been constructed using the estimates in Table 28.6, which themselves are subject to error.[31]

The reestimation shows a dramatic change. The muddled results of Table 28.5 have disappeared, and the new results look satisfyingly like those of Table 28.4 (although there is no reason to expect them to be precisely identical with the results in that table). The coefficients of the variables representing Continental and competitor activity and total air traffic are all of the correct sign; three are of roughly the same magnitude as in Table 28.4. Further, as with the results for SABRE, the sum of the coefficients for those variables is roughly unity – a sensible order of magnitude. The relative fare variable again has a negative coefficient.

As in Table 28.4, the Continental bankruptcy is seen to have a negative effect on bookings on Continental – an effect, however, that is rather larger for APOLLO than it was for SABRE. We also find here a "significant" negative effect of the Continental pilot strike. The complaint variable takes a negative sign. Further, we find a more strongly positive effect of the United strike of 1985, although this coefficient fails to achieve statistical "significance." Since this last finding is more likely for APOLLO than for SABRE, the fact that we find it here provides some confirmation of our results.[32]

The fact that the variables for the Continental strike and bankruptcy and the United strike had bigger effects in the case of APOLLO than they did for SABRE may reflect the fact that Continental overlapped with United more than it did with American. If competition between Continental and United tends to be sharper than competition between Continental and American, then such effects should be larger on APOLLO bookings than they are on SABRE.

This is consistent with our next finding. As shown in Table 28.1, our estimate of the effects of bias in APOLLO on Continental is that it

---

[31] This is not a trivial matter. For details, see Neels et al., unpublished. Because only asymptotic distributional results can be obtained, references to "significance" should be taken as asymptotic only.

[32] Unlike our treatment of the Continental bankruptcy variable, we did not directly estimate the duration of the United strike variable. (This was the subject of criticism by Jerry Hausman, testifying for United.) However, examination of the residuals from the model estimated without including such a variable shows effects mainly for the time of the strike. Further, a similar monthly model for total enplanements on United itself shows the effects of the strike to have been restricted to May and June 1985 with the effect for May about half that for June. This corresponds to our indicator variable in the model for Continental. Obviously, the United strike can only have helped Continental in the months in which it hurt United.

depressed bookings by about 19 percent, as opposed to 12.6 percent for SABRE.[33]

Note, however, that, as with SABRE, we estimate the effect of the secondary screen episode to be essentially zero. This is one of the differences between Table 28.5 and Table 28.7 that lend credence to our timing adjustments.

There is one obvious difference between the results given in Table 28.7 and Table 28.4. Our results for APOLLO contain monthly dummy variables that capture seasonal effects in APOLLO bookings on Continental not already captured by seasonal movements in the other included variables. No such variables appear in the SABRE model results of Table 28.4 because their inclusion does not materially alter the other results. Further, their coefficients are not significant and do not follow the pattern of those in Table 28.7. That pattern is striking. The coefficients in question describe shifts in the relationship each month relative to January (arbitrarily set equal to zero). It is obvious that this is not random noise but a true seasonal pattern. These monthly indicator variables clearly belong in the relationship being estimated.

Why do we find such effects for the APOLLO model but not for the SABRE model? There may be more than one reason. First, the destinations being flown to by travelers in cities with a high proportion of APOLLO agents may differ from those in cities with a high proportion of SABRE agents. It is therefore possible that seasonal effects in SABRE bookings on Continental are all closely related to the seasonal effects in the other included variables (e.g., total air travel), whereas some seasonal effects in APOLLO bookings on Continental are not.

Beyond this possibility, there is another reason. Our construction of the dependent variable in the APOLLO model relied upon estimated coefficients from our timing model. To the extent that such construction is only approximately correct, there may still remain a seasonal effect not otherwise accounted for in the relations between bookings by month of booking and bookings by month of flight. That would produce a seasonal effect in the ultimate APOLLO model, but could have nothing to do with the SABRE model, where no such transformation of data was required.[34]

---

[33] This effect is calculated as $1 - \exp(-0.213) = 0.19$ (approximately). This is one place where the two approaches to the timing of indicator variables do produce different results. If such variables are all assumed to influence behavior at the time of booking, the estimated effect of bias falls to about 15 percent. This is, of course, a material difference but one that does not affect the discussion below.

[34] The same cause is likely to have produced another difference between the results for the

6.   Consistency with Other Results

One is naturally led to wonder whether the bias effects shown in Tables 28.4 and 28.7 are consistent with the results produced by the simple ratio models presented in Tables 28.1 and 28.2. Because those simple models fail to distinguish between the different systems, precise comparisons between the two sets of results are impossible. Nonetheless, if one assumes that bias effects are uniform across the three biased systems and account carefully for differences in the mathematical structure of the two models, it is possible to place them on a comparable basis.[35] After appropriate adjustments, the bias parameter shown in Table 28.1 implies a bias percentage of 17.1, a value comfortably between our estimates for SABRE and APOLLO.

One can also use Hausman's results to estimate the full effect of the removal of bias on United bookings. If one does this, the result described above is statistically significant, but it is also small, amounting to 3.43 percent of United's 1984 bookings through automated travel agents. When one recalls that this is the *total* effect of the removal of bias in all CRS systems, so that the effect on United of the removal of bias in APOLLO must have been even smaller, the result seems quite at variance with our result for Continental, 19 percent (see Table 28.7).

Is this really the case? Examination of this question requires several steps. First, the Hausman result just quoted is expressed as a percentage of United's bookings by all automated travel agents. Expressing the same

two models. We find the residuals in the APOLLO model to be significantly serially correlated – something not true in the SABRE model – and the results in Table 28.5 are estimated accounting for this. The serial correlation turns out to be negative. This is unusual for econometric models. This is not surprising in this case, however. Our timing regressions depicted in Table 28.6 assumed that the distributions of bookings over present and future months were the same each year for the same month. This is unlikely to be exactly true, however. For example, in some years, Thanksgiving comes later in the month than in other years. If travelers book the same number of days in advance each year, then a higher fraction of September and October bookings will be for November when Thanksgiving is early than when it is late. But since we assign all bookings to some future month, a negative error in assigning September bookings to November will lead to a positive error in assigning them to October (and possibly September). A similar statement is true of the date of Easter. Such effects will produce negative serial correlation when the constructed data are used as the dependent variable in our final regressions.

[35] Specifically, the value implied by the ratio model results for the bias parameter shown in Tables 28.4, 28.5, and 28.7 is given by the following formula:

$$\gamma = \ln((CE - C^2(1-\lambda) - \delta E^2 - \delta EC(1-\lambda))/(EC + \delta EC(1-\lambda) - C^2(1-\lambda)))$$

where E is total enplanements on Continental; C is total bookings through the biased CRSs; λ is the "no-show" rate, or the fraction of bookings that don't eventually generate enplaned passengers; and δ is the estimated bias coefficient from the ratio model. To carry out this calculation we assumed a no-show rate of 15 percent and used enplanement and booking data for October 1985.

lost bookings as a percent of United's bookings by *APOLLO-automated* travel agents yields a larger figure. Expressing them as a percent of *Continental's bookings by APOLLO-automated agents* – our basis – yields a larger percentage still. Furthermore, some additional adjustments are required. 1984 was the last year before the Rules took effect (and 1986 was the first year after the Rules took effect that was not affected by the United strike). But the Rules came into effect not at the end of 1984 but in mid-November. Hence bookings made at the end of 1984 were made during the post-Rule period but counted as if made in the pre-Rule period. This tends to bias the Hausman number downwards.[36]

Beyond this, there are reasons for believing that the Hausman procedure does not fully control for all the changes between 1984 and 1986. This is because comparing travel agents in the same location does not control for phenomena that systematically affect travel agents automated with one system rather than another. One possibility along these lines is as follows. Travel agents automated with the system of a particular carrier are often likely to be those booking heavily on that carrier even in the absence of pure display bias. An agent booking heavily on United, for example, is likely to want the best possible interface with the United computer and therefore will want to use APOLLO. An agent booking heavily on Delta will tend to be automated with Delta's CRS. In this situation, any change between 1984 and 1986 affecting traffic on United but not on Delta may not be reflected equally when bookings on United are compared for the two agents. For example, suppose that a Delta-automated agent in Chicago tends to serve a relatively high proportion of customers traveling south, while a United-automated agent tends to serve customers traveling east and west. Comparing these two agents may not control adequately for changes differentially affecting Chicago-originating travelers going to different destinations.[37]

---

[36] Moreover, even though the Hausman number measures the total effect on United of the removal of bias in APOLLO and in the other systems, the phenomenon just discussed does not apply equally to both parts of that effect. As we have seen, APOLLO records bookings by month of booking whereas SABRE records them by month of flight. To the extent that bookings made after the Rules took effect were for flights in 1985 rather than in 1984, SABRE bookings on United would not count them in 1984, whereas APOLLO bookings on United would. Hence APOLLO bookings for 1984 include a bigger piece of post-Rule activity than do SABRE bookings. This means that, were the true effect on United of the removal of bias in SABRE the same as that of the removal of bias in APOLLO, so that the "true" Hausman number was twice the latter effect, the *estimated* Hausman number must be interpreted as involving a larger effect from the removal of bias in APOLLO than from the removal of bias in SABRE.

[37] One such change in the industry certainly took place. United's acquisition of Pan American's Pacific Division greatly expanded its trans-Pacific traffic between 1984 and 1986.

Finally, there is one phenomenon that certainly does affect the Hausman number but not our estimate. When the CRS Rules went into effect, the various host airlines sought to compensate by offering increased commission overrides to travel agents. While carriers were not permitted to differentiate in their override structure so as to favor agents automated with their particular CRS, such agents were far more likely than others to be able to respond to the override incentives. This is because agents who book heavily with a particular airline tend to use the CRS of that carrier. Since overrides pay off if the agent concentrates bookings on a particular carrier, it was easier for an agent automated with SABRE, say, and already booking heavily on American to respond to American's override incentives than it was for an agent in the same location whose primary business was with Delta.

Now, to the extent that the change in overrides following the Rules operated to offset the effects of bias removal, Hausman's method will tend to underestimate the latter effect. The matter is a bit more complicated than that, however, because part of the same phenomenon will lead our own estimate to understate the effect of bias removal. This is because we (using regression to control for other factors) also use a before-and-after comparison and the effect of United's increased overrides will dampen that comparison.

This does not apply, however, to the effect of increased overrides by other host carriers. Such increases will not affect our estimates of the effect of APOLLO display bias on Continental, but, as observed, they will affect (and reduce) the Hausman estimates, which necessarily count any offset to the removal of bias in any system as a lower effect of bias.

All these facts taken together offer some explanation for the difference in the two sets of results.[38] Whether they fully resolve it, we cannot say.

7.   Magnitude of the Revenue Diversion

The results shown in Tables 28.4 and 28.7 indicate that during the pre-Rule period Continental's bookings through SABRE and APOLLO

In turn, this made United a more desirable airline for feeder flights serving trans-Pacific travelers than had previously been the case. Agents already booking travelers to destinations served by United were more likely to be affected by this than agents largely booking travelers to destinations primarily served by a different carrier. This may have masked the effect of the removal of bias in APOLLO. On the other hand, the same phenomenon may have affected our own estimate of the effects of APOLLO bias. The fact that we use more than two years and control for non-Continental departures probably mitigates this effect. Of course, this phenomenon tends to make our estimate of the effect of APOLLO bias conservative.

[38] It should also be mentioned that the Hausman estimate becomes somewhat larger if his model is estimated using ratios rather than differences.

were 12.6 percent and 19.0 percent lower respectively than they would have been absent display bias. These surprisingly large estimates indicate that the magnitude of the revenue diversion resulting from display bias was substantial. Assuming that 85 percent of passengers booking reservations on Continental through SABRE and APOLLO eventually purchase and use tickets and that they pay the same fares on average as other passengers, our estimates of the bias effects suggest that in 1984 alone the revenue diversion on the two systems amounted to almost $58 million. To place this amount in perspective, we note that in that same year Continental's total domestic passenger revenues amounted to $844 million. Clearly the effects of CRS display bias on Continental were very substantial.

8.   Subsequent Events and Policy Implications

Following issuance of the Rules prohibiting display bias and the resolution of related litigation, the focus of the CRS debate shifted to "architectural bias," or differences in CRS features and functionality in favor of the airline owner, which, it was argued, created unfair incentives of travel agents to steer passengers toward the owner and that continued to divert revenue away from non-owners.[39] Architectural bias was generally thought to arise from the owner's status as "host" on its system. The tight integration between CRS and the internal reservation system that this arrangement created had the inevitable effect, it was argued, of creating a situation where the CRS worked better and faster and more reliably for the host than for other carriers. Architectural bias was a major focus of the debate preceding the issuance of updated CRS regulations by the US Department of Transportation in 1992. During the course of that debate a number of bold solutions to the problem of architectural bias were proposed. These included divestiture by the owner airlines to eliminate incentives for the creation of bias, and prohibition of host status. The 1992 rules dictated that features and enhancements had to be offered to all participants on a non-discriminatory basis but otherwise refrained from adoption of structural solutions to the bias problem.

---

[39] Some observers believe that the effects of CRS display bias persisted even after the publication of the 1984 Rules. Stories circulated within the industry of major research efforts on the part both of American and United to identify the "carrier-neutral" display algorithms that gave them the best screen placements. If true, they suggest that these carriers continued to benefit from display bias even after the Rules. Our analysis, however, shows that even if this were the case, the magnitude of the benefit decreased as a result of the Rules. And most observers recognize that the Rules prohibiting display bias represent as good a solution as one is likely to achieve in the absence of divestiture.

Recognition of the advantages an airline could gain from a CRS led to major changes in the ownership structure of the major CRSs. In 1986 Northwest Airlines bought a half interest in TWA's PARS system and through a major effort became hosted there. Texas Air, the corporate parent of Continental, purchased Eastern Airlines. As a result, Continental eventually became the owner of System One, the CRS developed by Eastern. Ownership of the APOLLO system was eventually transferred by United to a subsidiary whose ownership broadened to include a number of different carriers, among them USAir. USAir, however, refrained from converting to host status. After a proposed merger with SABRE was called off under pressure from federal regulatory authorities, Delta's CRS merged with PARS to form the present WORLDSPAN system.

What is perhaps most surprising about our results is the magnitude of the revenue diversion resulting from display bias. They indicate that at least in the pre-Rule period, relatively simple manipulations of the information presented to travel agents and passengers were capable of altering the carrier choices of a great many travelers. The potential for such diversion can be attributed to two factors: the absence of strong brand preference in the face of relatively undifferentiated airline "products"; and the relatively limited ability of passengers and travel agents to make informed evaluations of the quality of the advice offered by CRSs.[40] In the aftermath of airline deregulation, the number of routing, scheduling, and pricing options available to travelers exploded. Many new carriers entered the market, many existing carriers expanded rapidly, entry and exit occurred frequently at the city-pair level, and the development of hub and spoke systems dramatically increased the availability of one-stop routings. The growth of CRSs was fueled in large part by the need of travel agents and passengers for assistance in sorting through this plentitude of options. It is perhaps, then, not surprising that the presentation by the CRSs of distorted information would go undetected for so long or have such a large effect on market shares.

It is also not surprising that the years since the prohibition of display bias have seen strenuous efforts on the part of airlines to inject more brand preference into the booking process. These represent an inevitable effort by the airlines to capture the rents that display bias revealed were available and have taken a number of forms. Frequent flier programs reward travelers for concentrating their purchases on particular carriers.

---

[40] One might also cite as a contributing factor the relatively large number of travelers whose travel expenses are paid by their employers. Such travelers are likely to be relatively less price sensitive, which reduces the effectiveness of price as a differentiating factor among carriers.

Travel agent override commissions reward agents for concentrating their sales on particular carriers. Corporate discounts reward businesses for directing their employees toward particular travel suppliers. All of these practices have become more common and more highly developed in the years since the prohibition of display bias.

The welfare implications of these practices have been hotly debated. It has often been charged that frequent business travelers select higher-cost and more circuitous travel options at their employer's expense in order to maximize their frequent flyer payouts. However, to our knowledge, no good information exists on the real extent or cost of such practices. It has also been argued that override commissions exploit principal-agent problems in the passenger/travel agent relationship and prompt agents to offer distorted recommendations to passengers in a way not unlike that of display bias. Others have argued, however, that the benefits of override agreements are routinely passed on to business customers.[41]

The net effect of all of these efforts is that the parties involved in the booking decision are much more likely now than in the past to come to the transaction with a well-formed brand preference. This means that much less revenue is being sold "off the display" and, hence, bias in all of its forms – display or architectural – is less of an issue now than it once was.

The more recent CRS debate has tended to focus less on the issue of bias and more on the issue of cost. CRS booking fees have risen to the point where they have become a major cost item for the airline industry, and many of the carriers with a "negative balance of trade" in CRS bookings[42] have complained about their inability to take action to reduce their costs. Such statements are understandable, given the structure of the CRS market.

The provision of CRS services is characterized by economies of scale because of the high fixed cost involved in the hardware, software, and personnel required to operate the central system. Indeed, as the recent history of consolidations of CRS systems makes clear, it is not viable to have more than a handful of competing systems. Competition for agents – even if severe – necessarily ends up with at most a few large systems.

A direct result of this is that every large CRS vendor has monopoly

---

[41] Robert Moss, "Override Review", *Business Travel News*, January 20, 1992.

[42] Such carriers lose more revenue through the fees they pay on other systems than they gain through payments by other carriers for bookings on their systems. In the United States carriers with such negative balances probably include everyone except American and United.

power over airlines. That monopoly power arises as follows. Since the economies of scale involved in the provision of CRS services imply a natural oligopoly vis-à-vis agents, every successful CRS will contract with a large group of agents. Accordingly, the question of whether and how an airline is presented on a particular CRS is the question of whether and how that airline is presented to a large group of agents.

This is a vital matter to airlines. Airline economics are such that no national airline can afford to be materially disadvantaged in reaching a large group of agents.

As a result, each CRS has monopoly power over all national airlines. The different CRSs are not substitutes for one another. Northwest, for example, cannot evade a high booking fee on SABRE by increasing its listing on APOLLO. One can describe this by saying that each major CRS has monopolized a different market – the market consisting of access to its group of travel agents.

It is important to realize that competition among CRSs for agents will not reduce the monopoly power involved. At best, such competition will transfer some monopoly rents to agents from CRS vendors. The monopoly power that generates such rents will remain, however. That power stems inevitably from the economics of CRS operation.

In an unregulated environment, this situation inevitably leads to distortions affecting the market for air transportation. This is particularly true because of the ownership of CRSs by air carriers. Such distortions are of two types: direct and indirect effects. Direct effects occur when a CRS is used directly to favor one or more carriers over others. Indirect effects occur when monopoly booking fees affect the costs of non-host carriers.

The most obvious example of direct effects was the situation that existed before the 1984 CAB Rules took effect, when carrier identity played a major role in the algorithms used by SABRE and APOLLO to order the display seen by agents. We have seen that those effects were large ones.

There are also indirect effects of CRS monopoly power through the charging of monopoly levels of booking fees. When a host airline charges its rivals a high booking fee, it raises their marginal costs (as it also does when distorting the CRS display and functions). It costs a rival carrier more than it does the host to book a passenger. With marginal cost higher, price must also be higher or quantity cut back. Hence, the host airline gets the benefit of a situation in which its rivals have higher costs and it does not. This means supranormal profits in air transportation.

Note that it makes no difference to this conclusion that there are several CRSs and that they are owned by different airlines. Of course United, for example, would be better off if it were not disadvantaged by having to pay high booking fees for bookings made through SABRE. But all the CRS owners as a group have an advantage relative to non-CRS owners, and the price of airline tickets is raised by the high booking fees, to the disadvantage of the traveling public.

Neither the direct nor the indirect distortions caused by CRSs in the market for air transportation will be cured in the absence of some form of regulation. Is there a self-enforcing mechanism that will solve the difficulties described? Such a mechanism does exist, but to adopt it would involve so drastic a change in the way CRSs and travel agents operate as probably to make it politically impractical. Nevertheless, a discussion of the ideal case provides a useful benchmark.

The self-enforcing mechanism consists of two rules, which have already been (separately) proposed in some form to the Department of Transportation. They are:

- *Divestiture: No air carrier shall have any direct or indirect ownership interest in a CRS.*
- *Zero Fee: No CRS vendor shall receive any direct or indirect payment from an air carrier.*

We now consider how these rules would operate in an unregulated environment. Under divestiture, the incentive for air carriers to use CRSs to distort the choices made by passengers would appear to be removed. In fact, however, divestiture alone would not solve such problems, for it would not prevent a CRS vendor from contracting with an airline to provide display or architectural bias. Hence, divestiture alone would not eliminate the need for further regulation.

The addition of the zero fee rule, however, changes this. Since no CRS vendor could receive any money from an air carrier, such a sale of bias could not take place. Hence no CRS vendor would have an incentive to bias its display. Further, because of divestiture, no air carrier would have an incentive to cooperate more closely with one CRS than with another. Competition among CRSs for travel agents would then take place on the basis of service and price.

Adoption of the zero fee rule would correct a problem of incentives that now exists and has been thought by some to contribute to growth in CRS costs. Travel agents currently make many of the important decisions regarding CRS use. They select the system they will use, and they are in a position to strongly influence the "booking intensity" of the booking process.[43] Most of the costs of the system, however, are borne by airlines in the form of booking fees. Travel agents have no incentive to select a system with lower booking fees, so there is little price competition in the CRS market.[44] Travel agents do have an incentive to select a system on the basis of features and functionality, which has forced the systems to compete on that basis, tending to drive up costs.

Would any supranormal returns remain? It is possible that they would because, as already explained, CRSs are a natural oligopoly vis-à-vis travel agents. On the other hand, divestiture would mean that existing CRSs have no special advantages over new entrants. That would certainly make entry easier than it is today when air carrier owners have an incentive to make their own CRS offer better service with regard to their airline than do other CRSs. The increased possibility of entry would certainly act to reduce the possibility of supranormal profits vis-à-vis travel agents and might eliminate it altogether. In any case, the remaining oligopoly structure and profits remaining would present no problem different from those of any other oligopoly market. In particular, the effects would be limited to the market in which they occur and would not distort the market for air transportation.

Obviously, in such a system, CRSs would be supported by fees coming from travel agents in the first instance. That does not mean that travel agents would end up paying for CRSs. Agents will use CRSs only if it is profitable for them to do so. That means that the costs of CRSs would in fact be passed to the public. Indeed, in equilibrium, CRSs would be paid for as they are now – by airlines and eventually by air travelers. The difference would be that there would be no payment for monopoly power.

But, of course, the transition to such a system would be a wrenching one. In the course of making the necessary readjustments, travel agents in particular would experience great dislocation. Hence adoption of the rules just discussed is quite unlikely. While some movement in the right direction is possible by requiring CRS-owning airlines to divorce their CRSs from their internal computer systems and provide the same functionality to other airlines that they provide themselves, this will not lead

---

[43] Most CRSs charge fees to airlines on a per-transaction basis. Travel agents influence the booking process by deciding whether to make a reservation for a traveler whose plans are uncertain, how frequently to search for lower fares, whether to double book, etc.

[44] Many travel agent contracts contain productivity pricing clauses whereby the charges they pay for a CRS decline as the volume of booking revenues they generate increases. Some have charged that this creates an incentive for travel agents to create spurious bookings, driving up CRS costs to airlines and inhibiting their ability to manage their inventory effectively.

to a self-regulating mechanism. Not only would compliance with such rules require continuing oversight, but the problem of monopoly power in booking fees would surely remain.

Indeed, without the zero-fee rule, CRS vendors can still exercise monopoly power over carriers in the form of monopoly booking fees. This raises rivals' costs and distorts competition in air transportation.

More can be said in favor of a zero-fee rule than this, however. The use of CRS bias is but one example of how airlines can and do use their relations with travel agents to distort competition in air transportation. The outstanding other example is that of commission overrides, where an agent that books sufficiently on a single carrier receives a bonus commission payment. This gives agents an incentive to concentrate bookings (as it is intended to do). Moreover, since agents in a hub or other city principally served by a particular airline will find it easiest to earn their overrides by booking on that airline, there will be a distortion of agents' incentives even if all carriers offer the same overrides. And that distortion will carry over into a distortion of the information and advice presented to the traveling public.

It is important to note that such distortions could not easily be avoided even if customers were to shop travel agents much more actively than they now do. Most agents in a particular hub city are likely to offer the same distorted service, making shopping ineffective.

Evidently, the problem arises here (as, in part, it does in regard to CRSs) because travel agents are paid by airlines and not by travelers. An extension of the zero-fee rule proposed above would cure this. If no travel agent could receive any money from an airline (directly or indirectly), then such opportunities for distortion would disappear. In such a system, travelers using an agency would have to be charged directly for that agency's services. Price competition would be promoted, and travel agencies would be forced fully to become what they already purport to be – agents of the traveler rather than of the airline. The history of the effects of display bias in CRS does not suggest that less drastic remedies or reliance on competition among travel agencies will suffice.

APPENDIX

Data Sources

Data on domestic enplaned passengers, revenue passenger miles, and departures were obtained from the Form 41 reports filed monthly by airlines to the Civil Aeronautics Board and its successor, the Federal Aviation Administration (FAA). Total U.S. enplanements and departures were defined as the sum of these variables for all major and national domestic carriers as defined by the FAA. Continental domestic enplanements were defined as the sum of enplanements reported by Continental and Texas International prior to their merger.[45]

Data on Continental bookings through SABRE and APOLLO were obtained from Continental Airlines. These data were taken from the monthly statements received by Continental from these two systems. Continental Airlines also supplied monthly data on its domestic passenger revenues[46] derived from its revenue accounting system and counts of the number of mainland cities served taken from its monthly schedule analysis reports.

Monthly figures on Continental revenue per passenger mile were deflated using the consumer price index for airline fares. These data were obtained from monthly issues of the *CPI Detail Report* published by the U.S. Bureau of Labor Statistics.

Data on passenger complaints were obtained from monthly reports published by the U.S. Department of Transportation summarizing the calls and letters that organization has received about airline service.

Data on number of travel agency locations automated by SABRE and APOLLO were provided by reports filed by the two systems in response to information requests made by the U.S. Department of Transportation as part of the investigation of Airline Computer Reservation Systems summarized in its May 1988 report.

REFERENCES

"Carrier-Owned Computer Reservation Systems." 49 C.F.R. 255 (August 15, 1984). Washington, DC: U.S. Government Printing Office.

Fisher, F. M. "Pan American to United: The Pacific Division Transfer Case," *Rand Journal of Economics*, Vol. 18 (1987), pp. 492–508. Reprinted as Chapter 4 in Fisher (1990–91).

Fisher, F. M. *Industrial Organization, Economics, and the Law*. London: Harvester-Wheatsheaf and Cambridge, MA: MIT Press, 1990–91.

Neels, K., Palmer, B. L., and Woolbridge, J. M. "Estimation and Inference with Adjusted Data." Unpublished.

U.S. Department of Transportation. *Study of Airline Computer Reservation*

---

[45] Enplanements for Continental and Texas International were summed to make this series consistent with the CRS bookings data, which combined the bookings for the two airlines. Note that the inclusion of the Texas International enplanements affected only the timing model. By the start of the estimation period for the bookings model Texas International had ceased to exist as a distinct operating airline.

[46] Publicly available Form 41 data report revenues by quarter and were judged to be too coarse for use in this analysis.

Systems. Office of the Secretary of Transportation. Washington, DC: U.S. Government Printing Office, May 1988.

U.S. Department of Transportation. *Secretary's Task Force on Competition in the Domestic Airline Industry: Airline Marketing Practices.* Office of the Secretary of Transportation. Washington, DC: U.S. Government Printing Office, February 1990.

PART V

Public Policy Applications

CHAPTER 29

Standing Up to Be Counted: The Decision not to Adjust the 1990 Census (1994)

written jointly with Brian Palmer

1.   Introduction

It has long been well known that the decennial census of population systematically undercounts certain groups not only absolutely but in relation to the population as a whole. Those groups tend to be black or Hispanic and/or poor. The reasons for this are not hard to find: (1) Some members of such groups tend to distrust government and tend not to want to be found; (2) illiteracy rates are higher in such groups and addresses uncertain, making mail-back techniques unreliable; and (3) the neighborhoods in which those groups live often do not seem inviting or safe to census takers, leading to less accurate follow-ups. In any event, the fact of differential undercount has long been documented.[1] The effects are important in a democratic society. First, the distribution of seats in the House of Representatives depends on the Census. This means that states with a high proportion of the undercounted groups may receive less representation in Congress than that to which they are entitled. Second, the distribution of federal funds to the states is affected. Third, if the census figures are relied on within states for apportionment purposes, rural and suburban areas will receive more representation in state legislatures than that to which they are really entitled, and urban areas – particularly inner-city areas – will receive less.

It should not (and typically does not) escape attention that these

This paper is based on Fisher's testimony for the plaintiffs (a large number of cities and states) in the suit brought to compel adjustment of the 1990 census (cited below), and on the materials prepared therefor. We are grateful to James Burrows, Stephen Carter, Sandra Goldstein, Daniel Levy, Christopher Maxwell, Bradley Miller, Robert Rifkind, Robert Stoddard, David Stone, Jack Stuart, John Tukey, Rowan Wilson, and especially Bruce Spencer for assistance and discussion, but retain responsibility for error.

[1] See, for example, the discussion in Feinberg (1993) pp. 68–9. Thomas Jefferson recognized an absolute undercount in the very first census, and the existence of a differential undercount for blacks was observed at least as early as 1890. Letter from Thomas Jefferson to David Humphreys, in Cullen (1986); and Walker (1890).

matters have partisan consequences. As a general matter, urban areas tend to vote Democratic. Further, state legislatures apportion districts for Congressional elections. Hence, not only does the differential under-count disenfranchise minorities and the poor, it also aids the Republican party. The first effect is unconstitutional and unethical if it is unnecessary. The second is merely unfair.

Suggestions as to how to improve this situation have been made for a long time. They involve the use of statistical methods to correct the undercount, typically by making use of a post-enumeration survey (PES).[2] By the 1980 census, such methods were sufficiently advanced to be considered practical and desirable by some. The Bureau of the Census disagreed, however, believing that the PES was not sufficiently accurate. A number of states and cities brought suit to compel adjustment;[3] those suits failed.

Despite its belief that retroactive adjustment would not be desirable for the 1980 census, the Bureau of the Census began, in the 1980s, to make plans for adjustment of the 1990 census. The problem was studied well in advance (in part with the assistance of a National Academy of Sciences Panel[4]), and plans for adjustment began to be made.

Those plans were interrupted in 1987 when the announcement was made (apparently without serious consultation with the Bureau) that no adjustment would take place. A series of (eventually consolidated) law-suits parallel to the earlier ones were then brought.[5] With the trial date nearing, the suit was (temporarily, as it turned out) settled by an agreement. That agreement provided that a special eight-person advisory panel would be appointed (four members by each side); that plans for adjustment would go forward; that the Secretary (by then Robert Mosbacher) would set forth explicit guidelines for the decision as to whether to adjust; and that the decision itself (to be made in July 1991) would be made with an open mind.

In the event, the Bureau of the Census recommended adjustment, the eight-member special panel split along expected lines, and Secretary

---

[2] See the references in the November 1994 issue of *Statistical Science*, which contains a symposium on census adjustment. (9 *Statistical Science* 458).

[3] These include *Cuomo* v. *Baldridge*, 674 F. Supp. 1089 (S.D.N.Y. 1980) and *Carey* v. *Klutznick*, 508 F. Supp. 404 (S.D.N.Y. 1980).

[4] See Cirto and Cohen (1985).

[5] The consolidated suits were *The City of New York, et al.*, v. *United States Department of Commerce, et al.*, 88 Civ. 3474, *City of Atlanta, et al.* v. *Ronald H. Brown, as Secretary of United States Department of Commerce, et al.*, 92 Civ. 1566, and *Florida House of Representatives, et al.* v. *Ronald H. Brown, as Secretary of the United States Department of Commerce, et al.* 92 Civ. 2037. (By the time of the judge's opinion, the Administration had changed and with it the name of the Secretary of Commerce and the exact titles of the cases. The names given above are as of the time of the District Court's opinion.)

Mosbacher decided not to adjust. The court case then resumed and reached trial in the Spring of 1992.

In the Spring of 1993, Judge Joseph M. McLaughlin decided for the defendants. He stated that he would have ordered adjustment if deciding the issue *de novo* but that he had no power so to decide, being only able to review the decision under the Administrative Practices Act. He found that Secretary Mosbacher's decision was not "so beyond the pale of reason as to be arbitrary or capricious."[6]

The plaintiffs then appealed, arguing that the Constitution entitled them to a complete review. The Court of Appeals for the Second Circuit heard argument in January 1994 and issued its opinion the following August, vacating the judgment of the District Court and remanding the case for further proceedings. In her opinion, Judge Amalia Kearse held that:[7]

[The] plaintiffs amply showed that the Secretary did not make the required effort to achieve numerical accuracy as nearly as practicable, and that the burden thus shifted to the Secretary to justify his decision not to adjust the census in a way that the court found would for most purposes be more accurate and would lessen the disproportionate [under]counting of minorities. The Secretary's decision not to make that adjustment is subject to scrutiny not under an arbitrary-and-capricious standard of review but rather under the more traditional standard applicable to an equal protection claim that a fundamental right has been denied on the basis of race or ethnicity. While precise equality is a goal that at the national level may be illusory, there must be a good-faith effort to approach that goal as nearly as is practicable, and the substantive question becomes what choice should be made among imperfect alternatives. When the official answer is that it is preferable to undercount minorities, that answer must be supported by an official showing that the result (a) furthers a governmental objective that is legitimate, and (b) is essential for the achievement of that objective.

This holding was reversed by the Supreme Court.

This paper is concerned with some of the issues involved in Secretary Mosbacher's opinion, in particular, with the criteria he used and the way in which he applied them. Statistical issues involved in the adjustment mechanism itself will not be discussed except as necessary; those issues have been the subject of a number of other articles.[8]

One word before proceeding: Technical, statistical issues are not the only ones involved in deciding whether to adjust the census. Secretary Mosbacher could have made his decision on other grounds. To a very

---

[6] Slip opinion at 47. See also pp. 48–50. Judge McLaughlin added (p. 47n) that "in light of recent improvement in statistical tools and the practical benefits that the 1990 PES has provided, the use of adjustment in the next census is probably inevitable."

[7] Docket No. 93-6183, slip opinion at 44. Cited hereafter as "Appeals Court Decision."

[8] For references, see the symposium in *Statistical Science, supra.*

large extent, however, he did not do this, choosing instead to rest his decision on technical matters. Having made that choice, the Secretary surely had an obligation to get those matters right. As we shall see, he failed to live up to that obligation.

2.   Measuring Accuracy: the Use of Statistical Methods

The first "Guideline" adopted by the Secretary was as follows:[9]

The Census shall be considered the most accurate count of the population of the United States, at the national, state, and local level, unless an adjusted count is shown to be more accurate. The criteria for accuracy shall follow accepted statistical practice and shall require the highest level of professional judgment from the Bureau of the Census. No statistical or inferential procedure may be used as a substitute for the Census. Such procedures may only be used as supplements to the Census.

In effect, this calls for non-adjustment unless adjustment can be shown to give a more accurate result. The question then naturally arises as to what this criterion means.

Obviously, one can never literally show that adjusting the Census gives a more accurate result than not adjusting it. To do this would require that we know the true population (possibly by state, locality, or even census tract). If we had that information, however, there would be nothing left to adjust.

The only sensible way to compare the accuracy of the adjusted and the unadjusted enumeration must therefore be to ask which of them is *expected* to give a more accurate result, where "expected" has a technical meaning. In order to understand that meaning and to follow some of the ensuing discussion, a small digression is necessary for non-statisticians.

Suppose, for simplicity, that we are interested only in measuring the population of one geographic area (a census district, a state, the nation as a whole, etc.).[10] Because the proposed adjustment to be made employs statistical methods, the result of that adjustment is subject to some random error. We do not know what that error is (otherwise, we would correct for it), but statistical theory permits us to analyze its distribution. In other words, we can attach probabilities to different possible outcomes. (This is made possible because we know the mathematics of the

---

[9] Mosbacher (1991). Cited hereafter as "Decision." The decision was issued on July 15, 1991. The Guidelines had earlier been published in the *Federal Register* for March 15, 1990.

[10] In fact, in deciding whether to adjust, we will need to decide how to combine error measures across different geographic areas. This is taken up at length below.

adjustment process.) Having done this, we can ask whether, if we envisage all the different possible values of the random errors involved in the process, the error in the adjusted count will be greater or less than the error in the unadjusted one *on average*. This is the meaning of "expected" as used above.

In practice, we will be interested in two properties of the adjusted count. These are called its *bias* and its *variance*.

It is important not to confuse the technical use of the term "bias" with its everyday usage to mean "discrimination" or "prejudgment." The bias of an "estimator" (a procedure used to measure some true number) has to do with the question of whether *on average* the estimator will give the true number to be measured. If so, then the estimator is said to be "unbiased." This can be put slightly differently. Where there are random errors, estimation procedures lead to estimates that are themselves subject to such errors. Those estimates have a probability distribution.[11] An unbiased estimator generates an estimate whose probability distribution is centered on the true value that one is trying to measure. Biased procedures have a *systematic* (i.e., a non-random) tendency to over- or underestimate the true values sought. In this sense, the unadjusted enumeration is known to be biased in the statistical sense, as well as in terms of ordinary parlance. The purpose of adjustment is to correct bias (in both senses).

Unbiasedness, however, is not the only desirable property of an estimator. Suppose, for example, that the true value of the number to be estimated is 5. We might very well prefer an estimator that is always 5.1 to a second estimator which would be 5 on average but which has a 50% probability of being 10 and a 50% probability of being 0. The first estimator is definitely biased. The second is not, but has a much greater dispersion. The measure of that dispersion is called "variance".[12]

A non-census example may assist here and will illustrate other points as well. Suppose that we were interested in knowing the average height of attorneys in New York City. Imagine two ways of obtaining such an estimate.

The first way is non-statistical. We actually go out and measure the height of every *male* attorney in the city. We calculate the average and report it. This estimator has only negligible variance – there may be random errors of measurement, but they are likely to cancel out and not affect the average. On the other hand, since female and male heights tend

---

[11] Even where there are no random errors, any procedure can be said to generate a probability distribution with all the probability (unity) at a single value.

[12] Technically, variance is the expected (average) value of the sum of squared deviations of a random variable from its own average.

to be systematically different, the estimator is surely biased – it has a systematic error.

The second method is statistical. Suppose that we choose a random sample of attorneys (male and female) and take the average height in the sample as our estimate of the average height of the attorney population. It is easy to see that this procedure is unbiased; on average, were we to repeat the procedure many times, we would neither overestimate nor underestimate the average height of the attorney population. On the other hand, the procedure is surely subject to random error and hence to variance; unless we take an extremely large random sample, we would have to be very lucky to hit the true result on the nose.

Which procedure is more accurate? Since we do not know the true value we seek, that question can only be answered in terms of which procedure is expected to be more accurate. Perhaps surprisingly, it is possible to answer that question without knowing the true average height of attorneys in New York.

To see how this can be done, consider again the second, statistical, procedure. That procedure generates an estimate of its own uncertainty, of its own variance, in the following way. Suppose that the spread of heights in the sample we obtain is very small (in practice, this would be measured by the variance of the sample heights). Assuming a reasonably large sample, this would indicate that the spread of heights in the attorney population is also likely to be small. That, in turn, would suggest that taking a different sample would be unlikely to yield a very different result for average height.

On the other hand, suppose (as is more likely to be the case in fact) that the variance of heights in our sample was fairly large. That, in turn, would suggest that taking a different sample might very well yield a somewhat different result for average height.

The point is that we can use the variance of heights in the sample to estimate in turn the variance in heights of the population. Given that estimate, we can make a statement about how far our sample average is likely to be from the true population average. *Statistical methods generate measures of their own expected inaccuracy* – and that without knowing the true values they are trying to measure.

This property can also be used to compare the expected accuracy of the two estimators in the example. Because it is unbiased, the second, statistical, estimator generates an estimate of the bias of the first one (the enumeration of male heights). That estimate is simply the difference between the results of the two methods. Moreover, the statistical method also generates a measure of how reliable its estimate of first-method-bias is. Using this, one can calculate whether, on average, the variance of the statistical measure is or is not likely to introduce greater error than the systematic bias of the male enumeration. Again, this does not require knowing the true average height of all attorneys in New York, the magnitude whose measurement is sought.

This example is similar to that involved in adjusting the census (although it is, of course, fantastically more simple). In essence, the unadjusted enumeration is known to be biased, but has very little variance.[13] The use of statistical adjustment removes some bias but introduces more variance. By use of statistical methods, we can determine which method is expected to be more accurate, which method will have lower error on average.

Of course, the matter is not as simple as this. For one thing, we may care about the trade-off between bias and variance; as we shall see, it is not necessarily true that all errors are created equal. For another, we are not estimating the population of just one geographic area but are doing it for many. We thus need to decide how we would combine error measures for different geographic areas into a single measure, in effect, the way in which we would trade off greater error in one area for less error in another.

These are matters of vital importance, and we shall discuss them at length below. For the present, however, we assume that they have been resolved and that accuracy is to be measured in terms of the expected value of some overall measure of error. In that context, we need to consider what the presumption in favor of retaining the original enumeration means when the measure of accuracy becomes a measure of *expected* accuracy.

This is not hard to do. Suppose that we look at the difference in expected accuracy between the adjusted census and the original enumeration, so that a positive number suggests that adjustment is more accurate. The question of dealing with the presumption in favor of the original enumeration can then be put in terms of the classical statistical theory of null hypothesis testing.[14]

The way in which null hypothesis testing works can best be illustrated by an example. Suppose that we suspect that a particular coin is weighted towards heads. An obvious thing to do is to toss it some number of times and then ask how probable it is that a fair coin would come up heads at

[13] This is because there is no reason to think that the *random* errors involved in the unadjusted count are particularly important. There may be a great many such errors, but, by a statistical property known as the "Law of Large Numbers," they will tend to cancel out. (This is definitely not true of the systematic errors known to be in the unadjusted count.)

[14] For a more detailed description of null hypothesis testing in a legal framework, see Fisher (1980).

least as many times as the actual coin does. If that probability is low enough (traditionally below five or one percent), then the null hypothesis that the coin is fair is rejected. Otherwise, the null hypothesis that the coin is fair is not rejected.[15]

Note that this procedure does not lead to acceptance of the null hypothesis (that the coin is unweighted). It merely asks whether, *if* the coin is unweighted, we would be likely to obtain the results that we do in the experiment performed. Because the null hypothesis is not rejected unless that probability is quite small, the procedure is one that favors the retention of the null hypothesis unless the evidence is convincing that the observed results are likely to be inconsistent with it.

The application of this to the case of the census is immediate. We seek to know the probability that an observed positive value for the random variable measuring the difference in expected accuracy would occur if in fact the true difference in accuracy was non-positive. In other words, we must test the null hypothesis that the adjusted census is no more accurate than the original enumeration. This is a statistical problem with which we can deal.[16]

3.   Loss Functions and Their Meaning

Before we can perform such a statistical test, however, we must decide what criterion of accuracy is to be used. This is not a trivial matter, and there are at least three issues to consider.

The first of these concerns the geographic unit to be considered. Are we to be concerned with measuring the population of the United States as a whole, the populations of the several states, the populations of particular cities, or even of census tracts?

Obviously, the answer here largely depends on the use to which the final Census figures are to be put. The Constitution requires the apportionment of representatives "among the several States . . . according to their respective numbers, counting the whole number of persons in each State . . . ,"[17] so that both the total population and the population of the

---

[15] In this example, the question is whether the coin is weighted towards heads as opposed to being not so weighted. The test described is called a "one-tail test." If the issue was whether the coin was weighted at all – i.e., in either direction – then the test would be slightly different – a "two-tail test." In the case of the census, a one-tail test is appropriate, since we are interested in whether adjustment improves expected accuracy (coin weighted towards heads) and not simply in whether adjusting *changes* expected accuracy (coin weighted either towards heads or towards tails as opposed to being unweighted).

[16] It also answers the call by Under Secretary Michael Darby (Appendix 6 of Secretary Mosbacher's Decision) for the application of tests of statistical significance.

[17] Fourteenth Amendment, Section 2.

several states are involved. On the other hand, the Census is used for a number of purposes, at least some of which (legislative apportionment, for example) involve measuring the population of units within states. It is difficult to imagine any independent reason for being interested in the population of census tracts, however – any reason, that is, other than the fact that census tract estimates can be used to build up estimates for larger units.

The second issue is also closely related to the uses to which the results are to be put. Although the Constitution speaks in terms of the absolute number of people, both Congressional apportionment and the allocation of federal funds depends not (or not merely) on absolute numbers but on the *relative* populations of the several states. (Similarly, legislative apportionment involves the relative populations of different areas within a state.) Indeed, what is objectionable about the differential undercount of minorities is not that it is an undercount but that it is differential. If all states were undercounted by five percent, then Congressional apportionment would be unaffected. This suggests that we care not about (or not only about) accuracy measured in terms of numbers of people but about accuracy measured in terms of percent of the true population that ends up being measured.

Moreover (speaking in terms of "states" for ease of exposition), if what one cares about is *relative* accuracy, then one cares about measuring the relative size of any two states. One ought to choose a measure that reflects this.[18] An outcome that under- (or over-) estimates every state's population by five percent is to be preferred to one that has an average error over states of five percent but varies around that figure.

This is related to the third issue. Having decided how to measure accuracy for a single state (percent of the true population, for example),[19] one needs to combine such measures for all states together. This means deciding how to trade off greater accuracy for one state for lesser accuracy for another.

An example will make this clear. Suppose that, with one method, the population of one state is underestimated by thirty percent, while that of every other state is correctly estimated. Suppose that we have an alternative method that will produce a one percent underestimate in each of thirty states while measuring the population of the remaining twenty

---

[18] On the appropriate choice of such a measure, see John W. Tukey, Affidavit in *Cuomo* v. *Baldridge*, Civil Action 80-45550, U.S. District Court, Southern District of New York (1983).

[19] The discussion just given suggests that there is no satisfactory measure of accuracy for a state taken alone, since all that matters is measurement of the population of that state relative to that of others or to that of the United States as a whole.

states correctly. Which method should be preferred? In other words, is one large error better or worse than several small ones (controlling the total in some sense.)

This sort of question is not exactly a novel one in statistics, and two measures immediately come to mind. The first of these is as follows: Express the error for each state as an error in the percentage of the country's population to be found in that state. Then take the sum of squared errors. The second measure does the same thing but sums the absolute errors. In fact, the Bureau of the Census did both of these things.

There is something to be said in favor of each of these measures. The use of the sum of squares (an obviously familiar choice) counts large errors in single states as more important than several small ones. The use of the sum of absolute errors makes no such distinction.

Either of these measures constitutes a "loss function," that is, it produces a function that summarizes in a single value the loss (more precisely, the expected loss) that comes from the inaccuracies involved in the use of a particular method. By comparing the expected values of such loss functions for the original enumeration and the adjusted count, one can see which method is expected to be the more accurate – given that one has now decided how accuracy should be measured.

The two loss functions used by the Bureau are not the only possible ones. But one must beware. The choice of a loss function is the choice of how one is willing to trade off accuracy in measurement of one state's population for accuracy in measurement of another's. *Having chosen a loss function, it is inappropriate to abandon it and look at the contribution to its value made by the expected errors in each of the individual states.* To do so and make some count of the states in which one method or another appears superior is to lose sight of the purpose for which one chose a loss function in the first place. Alternatively, it is to substitute for a carefully chosen loss function one with quite undesirable properties – a loss function that implies that any error in one state is equivalent to any error in another, no matter how large the first error or how small the second. We shall have more to say on this below.

Of course, it is completely inappropriate to change one's loss function because one does not like the results given by the loss function previously chosen.

Note that it is impossible to avoid specifying a loss function at least implicitly if one is to make a rational decision. Such a specification amounts to choosing the criterion on which the decision will be made. In the present context, this amounts to describing the standard by which one will judge accuracy. This necessarily involves specifying the trade-offs that will balance greater accuracy in one geographic area against lesser accuracy in another.

One other matter requires discussion before we proceed. Our discussion of loss functions in terms of expected loss paid no attention to one important fact. When we substitute a statistically adjusted estimate for the original count, we risk purchasing reduced bias at the expense of increased variance. In effect, we reduce systematic error but increase random error. In most contexts, it would be natural to treat both types of error equally. After all, error is error, and we wish to minimize it whatever its source.

In the context of census adjustment, however, there is a powerful argument in favor of the proposition that bias and random error should *not* be treated on an equal footing – that some kinds of error are worse than others.

That argument is as follows. Suppose that the adjusted count and the original enumeration ranked the same according to our chosen way of measuring accuracy (sum-of-squared errors or sum of absolute errors, or any other measure). Then substituting the adjusted estimate for the original count would substitute random error for bias with the amount of expected total error (as measured by our chosen criterion) remaining the same.

Such a substitution would not necessarily be ethically or constitutionally neutral, however. The unadjusted enumeration is known to discriminate against certain specific groups – minorities, in particular. The adjusted count would substitute for this a set of estimates with the same expected inaccuracy but with the error randomly distributed. In effect, the same number of people would be disadvantaged in terms of Congressional representation (and other things),[20] but, as opposed to the unadjusted count, the errors would not affect known, specific groups.

Such an arrangement seems fairer than retaining the unadjusted count. In effect, each person would have the same chance of being undercounted as any other. In terms of Congressional representation, the expected number of voters per congressional seat would be the same. Adapting the language in the line of cases following *Baker* v. *Carr*,[21] the landmark Supreme Court decision on apportionment, "one person, one expected vote" seems fairer than a system with the same overall inaccuracy but one in which we know that blacks and Hispanics are partially disenfranchised relative to other groups.

Two remarks about this argument seem appropriate. First, despite the danger of confusion of language, the force of the argument comes from the fact that, in the present context, "bias" is not merely "bias" in the statistical sense. It is also "bias" in the sense of "discrimination."

---

[20] This would be literally true if all states had equal true populations or if the loss function were appropriately weighted to reflect population sizes.

[21] 369 U.S. 186 (1962). See Appeals Court Decision, slip opinion at 30.

Second, and more important, this argument is quite in accord with the opinion of Appeals Judge Kearse quoted above.[22] The view that the government had better have a legitimate purpose in adopting a method that is known to discriminate against minorities is a view that exchanging non-random bias for random error is desirable even if the size of the resulting expected inaccuracy due to random error is a bit greater than the size of the inaccuracy that would have been due to bias.

In fact, as we shall see, there is no need to appeal to this argument, however convincing. The results of the tests performed turn out to be overwhelmingly in favor of adjustment even when random error and bias are treated equally.

4.   The Bureau's Loss Functions

The Census Bureau proceeded along the lines indicated in the preceding section. They used two mathematical forms with which to measure inaccuracy – the sum of squared errors and the sum of absolute values of errors,[23] both sums being taken over geographic areas, and both with errors expressed as fractions of the nation's population.

In mathematical symbols, the two loss functions were, respectively:

$$L_1 = \sum_{i=1}^{n}(X_i - \theta_i)^2 \tag{1}$$

and

$$L_2 = \sum_{i=1}^{n}|X_i - \theta_i|, \tag{2}$$

where i denotes a geographic area (a state or a census tract, for example), X_i is the estimate of that area's fraction of the nation's population, and θ_i can (for purposes of this article) be taken as the true value of that fraction. In fact, since the true values are unknown, these loss functions cannot be computed directly; however, for each of the two loss functions, it is possible to obtain a measure of the expected *difference* between the value of the function for the unadjusted count and the similar value for the adjusted count. This enables one to say whether adjustment is expected to increase or decrease accuracy.[24]

---

[22] *Supra*, p. 5.
[23] Mulry and Spencer comment that, in using these particular forms, the Census Bureau was in keeping with government tradition. (See Mulry and Spencer (1993), p. 1083.) Of course, these forms (particularly the sum-of-squares) are also the forms most often used in the general statistical and other technical literature.
[24] See, for example, Mulry and Spencer (1993) and three internal memoranda of the Bureau of Census: Bateman (1991); Thompson (1991); and Woltman (1991).

While one can (and the Bureau did) perform the analysis for several different choices of geographic area, the results are not particularly sensitive to this choice. We present the results for the most interesting case, that of states (plus the District of Columbia).[25]

Table 29.1 gives the results.[26] For reasons of later discussion, we give not only the results when the errors are summed to obtain the difference in the expected values of the loss function arising from adjusting and not adjusting, but also the contribution to that difference made by the error in each state. For the present, however, we are interested only in the overall result.

That result is plainly in favor of adjustment. Using the convention that a positive sign favors adjustment (that is, we measure the expected difference in the loss function subtracting the value of the loss function for the adjusted count from the value of the loss function for the unadjusted count), the value that is obtained for the absolute-value loss function is approximately $+ 6.9 \times 10^{-3}$, while that obtained for the sum-of-squares loss function is $+ 7.1 \times 10^{-6}$.[27]

Because these results are both positive, the analysis favors adjustment. But that by itself is not dispositive. Are the loss differences obtained large or small? More important, could they just be due to chance?

---

[25] We also omit variations stemming from the choice of which of two alternative methods were used to allocate certain types of error in census tracts to "poststrata" – collections of people defined by such things as race, gender, and so forth. The results are quite insensitive to the choice of such procedures. The results presented here are for the so-called PRODSE method. That appears to be the method the results of which were relied on by Secretary Mosbacher.

One more issue of this type requires explanation. The Bureau of the Census revised its estimates quite late in the process (but prior to the Secretary's decision). Those revisions first produced what was called the "Updated" version of the results for the sum-of-squares loss function and then (a second change) what was called the "Final" version. Secretary Mosbacher's decision appears to have been based on the earlier, "Updated" version. We present both sets of results in Table 29.1, but, save where necessary for discussion of the Secretary's decision, most of our analysis of the results for the sum-of-squares loss function uses the "Final" version. While that version is marginally more favorable to adjustment than the (earlier) "Updated" version, the differences are relatively small and make no difference to our qualitative discussion. (There is no "Updated" version of the results for the absolute-value loss function.) It is worth noting that Robert Fay, a Senior Mathematical Statistician at the Bureau of the Census, appears to have been referring to the "Updated" version of the results for the sum-of-squares loss function when he told Secretary Mosbacher on July 8, 1991 – a week before the decision – that the results "might overstate the amount of error due to adjustment." Notes of Secretary's Meeting on Census Adjustment – Technical Issues.

[26] The values reported in the tables and calculations in the present paper are based on Census Bureau methodology and data. Since some of the values are based on averages over 1000 simulations, our computed values may differ slightly (but trivially) from those reported in various Census Bureau memoranda.

[27] For those not used to mathematical notation, 6.9×10^{-3} is the same as 6.9 divided by 10 three times, or 0.0069. Similarly, 7.1×10^{-6} is 7.1 divided by 10 six times, or 0.0000071.

Table 29.1. *Table of loss function comparisons (states)* *(Target = PRODSE)*

State	Census counts	Target counts	Adjusted counts	"Final" absolute value loss difference ($\times 10^5$)	"Final" sum of squares loss difference ($\times 10^{10}$)	"Updated" sum of squares loss difference ($\times 10^{10}$)
Alabama	4,040,587	4,127,180	4,143,089	2.8	−7.0	−26.6
Alaska	550,043	558,412	560,411	−0.7	−1.3	−1.6
Arizona	3,665,228	3,802,649	3,787,981	18.8	696.9	678.2
Arkansas	2,350,725	2,397,651	2,401,160	−0.9	−19.3	−26.9
California	29,760,021	30,847,229	30,868,287	191.8	50,160.7	48,144.4
Colorado	3,294,394	3,367,111	3,373,860	2.1	−15.8	−33.9
Connecticut	3,287,116	3,280,826	3,303,717	18.3	477.1	463.7
Delaware	666,168	683,780	686,200	1.8	4.2	3.3
District of Columbia	606,900	631,293	638,452	3.9	24.5	24.6
Florida	12,937,926	13,223,867	13,270,202	13.9	168.8	−49.0
Georgia	6,478,216	6,609,796	6,628,385	1.5	−59.1	−112.0
Hawaii	1,108,229	1,134,208	1,135,677	1.2	0.8	−3.0
Idaho	1,006,749	1,026,224	1,034,693	−1.9	−10.2	−11.1
Illinois	11,430,602	11,560,500	11,587,121	15.3	275.9	60.1
Indiana	5,544,159	5,557,324	5,583,879	27.2	932.3	857.4
Iowa	2,776,755	2,793,650	2,805,532	8.5	96.6	86.3
Kansas	2,477,574	2,493,970	2,504,939	8.0	81.9	73.6
Kentucky	3,685,296	3,758,091	3,765,150	−2.1	−56.1	−71.0
Louisiana	4,219,973	4,310,312	4,329,168	3.6	7.1	−18.7
Maine	1,227,928	1,228,810	1,239,624	5.1	41.7	37.2
Maryland	4,781,468	4,861,476	4,866,135	−13.9	−150.3	−177.1
Massachusetts	6,016,425	5,994,518	6,035,830	38.0	2,002.7	1,954.1
Michigan	9,295,297	9,368,205	9,400,121	26.3	877.2	708.2

Minnesota	4,375,099	4,394,618	4,416,274	17.6	392.3	370.8
Mississippi	2,573,216	2,662,141	2,630,532	-2.1	-26.7	-33.0
Missouri	5,117,073	5,160,995	5,181,094	12.6	201.3	170.0
Montana	799,065	815,480	821,587	-0.9	-5.3	-5.6
Nebraska	1,578,385	1,587,060	1,593,953	5.6	41.1	37.9
Nevada	1,201,833	1,228,181	1,230,801	0.7	-2.5	-4.6
New Hampshire	1,109,252	1,106,649	1,115,438	6.4	59.8	56.7
New Jersey	7,730,188	7,768,024	7,831,271	22.6	899.1	740.7
New Mexico	1,515,069	1,583,435	1,585,585	14.5	268.4	265.3
New York	17,990,455	18,221,027	18,296,408	12.1	-121.3	-986.1
North Carolina	6,628,637	6,784,983	6,810,200	12.4	196.3	132.9
North Dakota	638,800	644,707	647,427	1.1	1.3	0.5
Ohio	10,847,115	10,879,438	10,928,781	51.4	3,261.2	3,014.3
Oklahoma	3,145,585	3,207,953	3,211,538	-1.0	-28.0	-42.5
Oregon	2,842,321	2,885,840	2,895,965	-2.9	-23.6	-41.4
Pennsylvania	11,881,643	11,865,918	11,948,470	68.7	6,425.8	6,149.1
Rhode Island	1,003,464	998,733	1,005,555	6.7	62.4	60.6
South Carolina	3,486,703	3,571,995	3,587,334	7.0	60.7	44.0
South Dakota	696,004	703,688	706,500	0.5	-0.7	-1.1
Tennessee	4,877,185	4,987,206	5,008,564	6.2	36.3	3.8
Texas	16,986,510	17,425,437	17,537,982	43.2	2,746.4	2,142.6
Utah	1,722,850	1,744,934	1,756,133	-1.2	-19.0	-23.3
Vermont	562,758	565,005	570,486	1.3	2.1	1.0
Virginia	6,187,358	6,328,787	6,348,646	9.9	123.3	69.0
Washington	4,866,692	4,963,880	4,983,136	0.9	-34.6	-87.7
West Virginia	1,793,477	1,838,483	1,840,998	3.5	15.8	11.6
Wisconsin	4,891,769	4,899,379	4,921,956	25.7	816.0	759.0
Wyoming	453,588	462,500	465,793	-0.6	-1.5	-1.8
Totals	248,709,873	252,863,558	253,828,020	690.5	70,875.6	65,362.7

Note: Loss Difference = Expected Census Loss – Expected Adjusted Loss.

The magnitudes of the numbers just quoted appear very small, but that is because of the way in which errors have been measured. We begin with the absolute-value loss function.

Recall that the error for any given state is measured in terms of the fraction of the nation's population residing in that state. This is equivalent to measuring each error as a fraction of the national population. Hence, 6.9×10^{-3} corresponds to approximately 0.7% of the population or roughly 1,750,000 people.

The result for the sum-of-squares loss function appears much smaller, but this is because squaring a number less than one makes that number smaller. Hence one obtains a result involving 10^{-6} rather than 10^{-3}.

But the more important question is whether we are really observing a difference in accuracy here or whether the apparent difference is likely to arise by chance. To deal with that issue requires testing the null hypothesis that the unadjusted count is more accurate.

5.   Testing the Null Hypothesis

The results just presented suggest that (using either loss function) the adjusted count is to be preferred to the original enumeration. But, without further analysis, that suggestion remains just that – a suggestion. Like any good point estimate in statistics,[28] the estimated value of the expected difference in the loss function results may be the best single estimate of the true value of that expected difference, but that does not tell us how confident we are that the true value is close to the estimate. Put differently, merely obtaining the results already presented does not overcome the presumption of the guidelines that the original enumeration is to be preferred unless adjustment is proven to be superior.

As already discussed, that presumption can be put into workable form,[29] through the use of null hypothesis testing. Null hypothesis testing gives the benefit of the doubt to the retention of the null hypothesis (here, the hypothesis that the unadjusted count is more accurate). That hypothesis is retained unless, in order to do so, one would have to believe that a very improbable event has occurred. Traditionally, the level of probability required for rejection is 5% or 1%. When the null hypothesis is rejected with such standards, the results obtained are said to be "significant at the 5% (or 1%) level."

---

[28] A point estimate is a single number giving an estimate of the value of some parameter. Statistical theory typically provides intervals around such point estimates ("confidence intervals") measuring how accurate the point estimate is likely to be.

[29] Unless, of course, one is determined not to do so. See the discussion below.

Null hypothesis testing is thus the natural way in which to enforce the presumption of the Guidelines that the unadjusted count is to be retained unless the adjusted count is shown to be more accurate.[30] To perform such a test requires only that we obtain an estimate of the variance (in effect, a measure of the uncertainty) of the estimated difference in expected losses. This can be done using the simulations performed by the Bureau of the Census.[31]

The results are striking indeed. Recall that the usual criterion is to retain the null hypothesis unless the probability of obtaining results as strong as those observed is less than 5% or 1%.[32] In the case of the absolute-value loss function, calculation of the corresponding probability shows it to be 0.0000000000068%! In the case of the sum-of-squares loss function, the corresponding probability is 0.00000066%!

This is not a joke. The usual standard is to reject the null hypothesis if to retain it requires belief that an event with probability below one in a hundred (or even only one in twenty) has occurred. By contrast, retention of the null hypothesis that the unadjusted count is more accurate requires belief in the occurrence of an event with probability less than one in *one hundred and fifty million*, using the sum-of-squares loss function and less than one in *fourteen trillion* for the absolute-value loss function!

Plainly, if one has agreed to measure accuracy by the use of either loss function, there can be no doubt as to what to do. The presumption of the guideline has been overwhelmingly overcome.

6. Secretary Mosbacher's Decision: The Propriety of Counting the States

When Secretary Mosbacher came to make his decision in July, 1990, he did so in a manner that at best can be described as showing a thorough misunderstanding of the Bureau's work on loss functions. He stated:[33]

---

[30] It also complies with the insistence of Under Secretary Michael Darby that standard statistical tests be used to determine whether the adjusted count is more accurate.

[31] Technical note: In the tests, the results of which are here reported, the bias and variance of the adjusted count were treated as known rather than as estimated. This cannot be a problem for results so overwhelmingly strong as those obtained. Even if the true variances were orders of magnitude larger than those used, the results of the hypothesis tests would lead to the same conclusion.

[32] For example, in testing whether a coin is weighted towards heads, one retains the null hypothesis that it is not unless the number of heads that comes up is so great as to occur with probability less than 5% (alternatively, 1%) for an unweighted coin.

[33] Decision p. 1–4.

Based on the measurements so far completed, the Census Bureau estimated that the proportional share of about 29 states would be made more accurate and about 21 states would be made less accurate by adjustment.

He stated[34] that this conclusion was reached on the basis of "an absolute value loss function." The Secretary went on to remark that if one increased the estimated variance of the adjusted estimates due to smoothing by a factor of 2 (thought reasonable by the Undercount Steering Committee), the proportions were reversed with 28 or 29 states having their proportional shares made worse by adjustment.

These statements represent a cascade of errors. We begin with the least important one. In fact, the finding that 21 states would have their proportional shares made worse by adjustment comes from the sum-of-squares loss function and not from the absolute-value loss function. The corresponding number for the absolute-value loss function is 11, a number far less than that asserted by the Secretary.[35]

More important than this, the use of such a statistic is fundamentally meaningless (and, as we shall see, the Secretary actually *mis*used it as well). To understand why this is so requires discussion.

The first question to ask is whether one ought to use *any* count of states that will in some sense have their proportional shares made less accurate by adjustment as an aid in the adjustment decision. It is very doubtful whether one should. To do so is to decide that a decrease in accuracy in one state, however small, balances an increase in accuracy in another state, however large.

Consider the following example. Suppose that it were known that the original count measured the population of 48 states[36] with no error, but counted the population of New York at zero and the population of Texas as the sum of the true population of that state and the true population of New York. In this situation, the 48 states other than Texas and New York would have their proportional shares exactly right. Now suppose that an adjustment mechanism is proposed that would accurately measure the populations of Texas and New York but would introduce errors of one person in each of the other 48 states, with the errors

---

[34] Decision, p. 2–29.
[35] As already explained, the Secretary appears to have used the "Updated" rather than the "Final" version of the results for the sum-of-squares loss function. There is no record of an "Updated" version for the absolute-value loss function.
[36] In fact, there are 51 relevant political subdivisions at the state level, the District of Columbia also being represented in the House of Representatives. For ease of exposition, however, we shall use 50 as the number when giving illustrative examples.

summing to zero. A count of the states would show that adjustment would make the proportional shares of 48 states less accurate and would increase accuracy for only 2 states, yet no rational person would choose not to adjust. Counting states in this manner is thus not a sensible loss function.

Nevertheless, suppose that one does wish to count states. One might be interested in either of two counts. The first of these is the number of states in which adjustment can be expected to make proportional shares more accurate; the second is the expected number of states where adjustment will make proportional shares more accurate.

These are not the same thing. The first is a count of the states where the probability that adjustment improves distributive accuracy is greater than 0.5. The second consists of the sum over states of the probabilities that adjustment improves distributive accuracy. (That these can be very different is shown in the example in the next paragraph.)[37]

Even if one chooses to use a count of states, it is hard to see why one would want to use the first count (that of states in which adjustment is more likely than not to improve distributive accuracy). Consider the following example. Suppose that there were 10 states in which the probability of improvement was very close to unity. Suppose that in each of the other 40 states that probability was 0.499999. Then a count of states in which adjustment is more likely than not to improve distributive accuracy would show only 10. Yet the expected number of states that would be improved by adjustment is approximately 30 (the 10 states in which improvement is virtually certain plus almost exactly half the remaining 40). To use the count of states in which improvement is more likely than not is to say that any probability of improvement over 1/2, however large, is offset by any probability under 1/2, even if the latter probability is very close to 1/2. (In a way, this repeats with probabilities the failure to consider magnitudes that makes a count of states unreasonable in the first place.)

Although these examples may seem unrealistic, they are illuminating when one considers what actually happened. As Table 29.1 shows, there are a few states in which adjustment would have a large effect

---

[37] Another way to see that the two counts are not the same is by considering the following non-Census example. Suppose that one had a coin that was weighted towards heads in such a way that the probability of its coming up heads was 60%. Suppose that the coin were tossed 100 times. Then the expected number of heads would be 60, but the number of tosses in which the coin is more likely than not to come up heads would be 100.

(California and the District of Columbia being outstanding examples). In many states, however, only small adjustments in proportional shares are called for, because the estimated percentage undercount for that state is approximately the same as that for the nation as a whole. In the latter group of states, it basically does not matter much whether or not adjustment is made,[38] and hence it is not surprising that one is relatively unsure that adjustment will improve things. To use this *de minimis* risk of increasing inaccuracy to offset the clear great improvement that adjustment brings in states such as California is wholly unjustified. We shall examine this phenomenon more closely when we again discuss hypothesis testing below.

For the present, however, it suffices to observe that whether one counts the states with probability of improvement greater than 1/2 or takes the expected number of states that will be improved, the results are much the same.[39] On either standard, the results are overwhelmingly in favor of adjustment. As shown in Table 29.2, the number of states in either count is approximately 40, far above the "about 29" referred to by the Secretary. (A similar count using numerical accuracy rather than distributive accuracy yields 39.)[40] Further, if one increases the estimated variance of the adjustment method by a factor of 2, as did the Secretary, the count decreases only to 36. One would have to multiply that variance by a factor of more than 7 (more than double the high end of the range suggested by the Undercount Steering Committee) to reduce to 25 the expected number of states that would have distributive accuracy improved by adjustment.

Indeed, one can go further than this. While states are an important political subdivision, some interest surely attaches to people. This generally suggests weighting observations on states by population. In the present instance (using the original enumeration), approximately 90 percent of the population lives in states where it is more likely than not that adjustment will improve distributive accuracy. The expected number of people for whom adjustment would improve distributive accuracy is about 85 percent of the population.[41]

---

[38] The decision involved was whether to adjust all states or none. The question of adjusting some but not others does not appear to have been considered.

[39] Mulry and Spencer (1992) shows how the computations are done.

[40] The exact numbers depend on the precise assumptions used in distributing certain biases over the states, but are not sensitive to them.

[41] These are two different calculations. The first sums the population living in the 40 states where the probability of improvement is greater than 1/2. The second multiplies the population of each state by the probability of improvement and sums the result. As with the count of states, the second method takes the magnitude of the probabilities involved into account.

Table 29.2. *Probability that adjustment brings the population shares closer to the truth (Target = PRODSE)*

State	Probability
California	1.000
Indiana	1.000
New Mexico	1.000
Ohio	1.000
Wisconsin	1.000
Pennsylvania	1.000
Minnesota	1.000
Rhode Island	1.000
Massachusetts	0.999
New Hampshire	0.999
Nebraska	0.998
Kansas	0.997
Connecticut	0.997
Arizona	0.991
Michigan	0.990
Missouri	0.986
Iowa	0.984
District of Columbia	0.970
Maine	0.967
Delaware	0.964
New Jersey	0.961
North Carolina	0.946
Texas	0.938
Virginia	0.926
South Carolina	0.925
North Dakota	0.903
West Virginia	0.887
Florida	0.853
Illinois	0.847
Tennessee	0.842
Vermont	0.826
Louisiana	0.789
Hawaii	0.780
Alabama	0.759
South Dakota	0.758
Colorado	0.713
Nevada	0.701
Georgia	0.662
Washington	0.610
New York	0.599
Arkansas	0.496
Oklahoma	0.481
Utah	0.472
Kentucky	0.462
Montana	0.420
Mississippi	0.400
Wyoming	0.363
Oregon	0.289
Alaska	0.275
Idaho	0.273
Maryland	0.005
	39.998*

*Note: The expected number of states with improved accuracy is 40.
The number of states in which the probability of improving accuracy is greater than 0.5, a different measure, is 40.

7.   Secretary Mosbacher's Decision:
     Understanding Mosbacher's Count

Obviously, these results are quite different from those implied by Secretary Mosbacher's statement quoted above. Where then did the figure of 29 states that he mentions come from? The answer lies in a total misuse of loss functions.

The count of "about 29" states to be made more accurate (and "about 21" worse) is a count of states in which the given state's contribution to the sum-of-squares loss function[42] is favorable to adjustment. What this means precisely is as follows. The sum-of-squares loss function compares for each state the expected square of the bias of the original count with the variance (plus remaining expected squared bias) of the adjusted count.[43] The latter is subtracted from the former and the result is summed over states. As can be verified from Table 29.1, there are 33 states in which that subtraction yields a positive result. (For the "Updated" version, apparently used by the Secretary, the corresponding number is 30).

This is a nonsensical way to proceed. It asks how many states there are in which the expected squared bias exceeds *not* the square of the error introduced by adjustment, but the *expected value* of that square. Why does anyone care?

What the Secretary did here was (in part) to seriously misunderstand and misuse loss functions. Recall that we have adopted the convention that a negative number for a state corresponds to an adjustment-produced decrease in distributive accuracy, while a positive number corresponds to an adjustment-produced improvement. The Secretary's method of counting states implies that any negative number, no matter how small, offsets any positive number, no matter how large. The sum-of-squares criterion was chosen precisely as one way to consider trade-offs among large and small errors. To then simply count the signs of the errors is to destroy the purpose for which the loss function was created.

Moreover, it is important to emphasize that the Secretary's count was *not* a count of the states in which adjustment can be expected to improve

---

[42] As already mentioned, the Secretary was in error when he attributed this count to the absolute-value loss function. For ease of exposition, we discuss only the sum-of-squares loss function in the text. A similar analysis applies to the absolute-value loss function.

[43] The original enumeration has bias but essentially no random error. The adjusted count has random error (and hence a positive variance) but has a considerably reduced, but not zero bias. Of course, the reduction in bias relates to the whole purpose of adjustment.

accuracy. Similarly, it was *not* an estimate of the expected number of states in which adjustment would improve accuracy. Those counts are discussed and given in the previous section; the results for both of them are approximately 40 to 11 in favor of adjustment. Rather the Secretary's count was precisely as described: a count of the states in which the expected squared bias of the original count was greater than the expected squared random error due to adjustment.

Not only is that count meaningless in theory, it is also misleading in the way the Secretary applied it. As the Secretary pointed out, when one doubles the variance of the adjustment process, the count of states in which adjustment appears to make matters worse rises to 28 or 29, a majority of the states. The Secretary apparently thought this important, presumably because it is natural to think of 25 1/2 (half of 51) as the break point. That is, since the number of states with accuracy appearing better after adjustment is less than half the total, it looks as though adjustment is the poorer choice.

Surprisingly, this is incorrect. Although half the states is the natural break point for either of the two relatively more sensible counts of states discussed above, it is almost certainly well below the appropriate break point for the Secretary's meaningless count. To understand why this is so requires a bit of technical discussion. That discussion is given in the Appendix and shows that the appropriate break point is not 25 1/2 but approximately 17.

It is also worth pointing out that the fact that the break point is not 25 1/2 but is close to 17 appears to have been known to Secretary Mosbacher. The document from which he appears to have obtained his count deals with the break-point issue.[44] Further, that issue was discussed at a meeting held on July 8, 1991 (a week before the Secretary's decision), a meeting at which the Secretary was present. The point was explained to him by Robert Fay, a Senior Mathematical Statistician at the Bureau of the Census.[45]

It is hard to avoid the view that Secretary Mosbacher was dead set against adjustment and went out of his way to rule against it. He misstated the numerical results, overrode the loss functions used by the Bureau, implicitly adopted a most implausible loss function, did a count for that loss function that made little sense, and then (apparently knowingly) failed to observe that even that count favored adjustment.

---

[44] Addendum to the Report of the Undercount Steering Committee, June 21, 1991.
[45] "Notes of Secretary's Meeting on Census Adjustment – Technical Issues" (Plaintiff's Exhibit 41).

8.   Secretary Mosbacher's Decision: Hypothesis Tests

Similar problems arose when Secretary Mosbacher came to consider issues of hypothesis testing.

As Under Secretary Michael Darby had urged, the Secretary attempted to apply the principles of hypothesis testing to his decision. He found[46] that "[o]nly 18 of the 51 states have an undercount rate that is significantly different from the national average," and then went on to say that this means that "in 33 states *we do not know* if the undercount rate is higher, lower or the same as the national average." He apparently considered this of some importance.

The Secretary here misapplied both loss functions and the theory of null hypothesis tests. We begin with the misapplication of loss functions.

Although he did not make this explicit, the Secretary's remarks only make sense if he took as a criterion for his decision that adjustment would not take place unless hypothesis testing showed at least a majority of states with a percentage undercount significantly different from the national average. (Indeed, perhaps he would have required that all states have such an undercount.) This is not a sensible decision criterion.

To see this, consider the following example. Suppose that it were the case that (continuing to work in terms of 50 states) 48 states had an estimated undercount identical to the national average, one state had a huge undercount statistically significantly greater than the national average, and the last state had an undercount much smaller than that average, with the difference again statistically significant. In that circumstance, adjustment will not change the distributive shares of the first 48 states but will change those of the latter two states, changing them in the obviously desirable direction. To refuse to adjust because only 2 states have an undercount significantly different from the national average makes no sense.

There are two more things to say about this example. First, both in the Secretary's decision and several times during the trial, the point was brought up that the differential undercount statistics were heavily dominated by a few states – principally California. This is hardly a reason to refuse to adjust, however. California was admitted to the Union in 1850, and is, in fact, the state with the largest population.

Second, a glance at the results on which the Secretary apparently relied for the statement quoted shows that the example given above is on point. Figure 29.1 presents those results graphically. In Figure 29.1,

---

[46] Decision, p. 2–34. Emphasis in original.

Undercount Percentage by State
with 95% Confidence Intervals

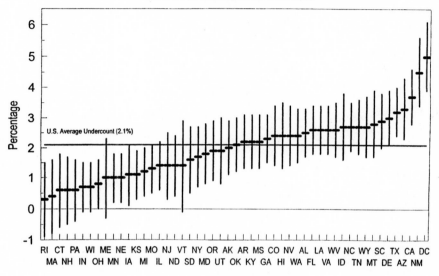

FIGURE 29.1

the states are arrayed in increasing order of percentage undercount, from Rhode Island and Massachusetts to California, New Mexico, and the District of Columbia. For each state, the short horizontal line indicates the estimated percentage undercount and the vertical line shows the 95% confidence interval – the interval that, with 95% probability, covers the true value. The national average percentage undercount is 2.1%, and this is indicated by the long horizontal line. A state's percentage undercount differs significantly from the national average at the 5% significance level[47] if the vertical line for that state does not cross or touch the long horizontal line.

It is evident from Figure 29.1 that the fact that there are many states that do not have percentage undercounts significantly different from the national average merely reflects the fact that many states do not have percentage undercounts that are very different from the national average at all. (That is only to be expected, given the nature of averages.) These

---

[47] Recall that this means that the probability of observing so great a difference from the national average is less than 5% on the null hypothesis that the state's percentage undercount is not different from the national average.

Table 29.3. *Relative undercounts and significance levels*

Undercount Relative to National Average (Percentage Points – Absolute Value)

	Greater than 1	Greater than 0.5 and no more than 1	No more than 0.5	Totals
Definitely significant	15	2	0	17
Possibly significant	0	3	0	3
Not significant	1	10	20	31
Totals	16	15	20	51

are the states in the middle of Figure 29.1. But adjustment will affect the estimated proportional share of the national population in such states hardly at all. The states that will be affected by adjustment are those with estimated percentage undercounts that do differ from the national average by a large amount. These are the states at the right and left sections of the array in Figure 29.1, and these are the states in which the difference from the national average is usually significant.

Table 29.3 shows this numerically. In that table, states are classified in two ways. The first classification (the columns) is in terms of the (absolute) number of percentage points by which their percentage undercount differs from the national average. The second classification (the rows) is in terms of the statistical significance of that difference.[48]

Note the concentration of the numbers in the upper left-hand and lower right-hand corners. The states whose estimated percentage undercounts differ the most from the national average are overwhelmingly the states where that estimated difference is statistically significant. These are the states that would be most affected by adjustment. The states

---

[48] The significance level used is the 5% level. The classification of "Possibly Significant" comes about because in three cases the 95% confidence interval for the state's percentage undercount ends exactly at the national average, given that there was only one significant digit reported in the Census Bureau's document. The Secretary's count of 18 states with statistical significance suggests that he assigned one of these to the "Significant" category and two to the "Not Significant" category (either arbitrarily or on the basis of more detailed information). It does not matter to the conclusions or to the discussion in the text how these cases are treated.

where the estimated difference is not statistically significant tend also to be the states where that estimated difference is small. (Indeed, in 13 cases, such states have percentage undercounts that differ from the national average by no more than 0.3 percentage points.) Hence the states about which we are relatively uncertain as to whether adjustment will improve accuracy tend also to be the states where the effect of adjustment would be small.

It is inevitable that one will be uncertain as to whether correction of very small differences will be a gain or a loss. However, the fact that one is uncertain as to whether some essentially trivial adjustments will make things more or less accurate is no excuse for refusing to adjust when one is quite sure that the large adjustments involved will help matters.

Another way of saying this is to observe that the reason for dealing with loss functions in the first place is to provide trade-offs between greater accuracy in some states and lesser accuracy in others. Having done so, the only null hypothesis of interest is the one considered in Section 4, above, the hypothesis that the expected loss from the original enumeration is not greater than the expected loss from adjustment. To insist on significant evidence of improvement in all states is to impose a criterion that will generally be impossible to meet and one that makes no sense.

Putting this aside, what in fact should one conclude from the finding that 18 states have an undercount significantly different from the national average?[49] The first thing to say is that one must *not* conclude that this means that in 33 states adjustment will not improve distributive accuracy. In null hypothesis testing, the test is loaded, as it were, against the rejection of the null hypothesis. One rejects only if one can explain the results given the truth of the null hypothesis only by believing that an event with a probability as low as 5% (or 1%) occurred. Failure to reject the null hypothesis thus does not mean that it is true. Indeed, the best single estimate available of the undercount for each state is the one given.

Further, one cannot even read the probability that the null (or the alternative) hypothesis is true out of the level at which the results would be significant. That level is the probability of observing results as inconsistent with the null hypothesis as those observed if in fact the null hypothesis is true.

---

[49] We here assign the states in the "Possibly Significant" category in the same way as did the Secretary.

In the present case, the probability of adjustment improving distributive accuracy in each state is given in Table 29.2. We have already discussed the expected number of states that will be improved.

Returning to the Secretary's use of hypothesis testing, we must ask what one would expect to see if in fact the null hypothesis that adjustment does not improve matters were true. In such a case, one would expect to find results significant at the 5% level in 5% of the states – i.e., 2.6 states. In fact, such results are found in 18 states. This is very strong evidence in favor of adjustment. Yet the Secretary took it as evidence against adjustment.

9.   Conclusion

It will not have escaped the reader's attention that we feel fairly strongly about what occurred. We do. A serious injustice was permitted to continue when it could have been cured. While there are arguments against adjustment (some cited by the Secretary), most of the arguments presented at trial played no apparent role in Secretary Mosbacher's decision.

Indeed, the Secretary needed no such arguments. Having shown himself against adjustment from the outset, he misunderstood or deliberately perverted the evidence in favor of it, riding roughshod over the recommendations of the Census Bureau and over his own criteria to do so.

As we said earlier, the Secretary could have chosen other criteria on which to make his decision. Having explicitly chosen technical criteria, however, he had an obligation to use them correctly. This he did not do.

During a break in Fisher's deposition in the case, David Freedman, the government's chief statistical witness, and a man dedicated to opposing adjustment, asked him "What are two guys like us doing here?" His answer was: "Standing up to be counted." It still is.

APPENDIX

The Appropriate Break Point for the Secretary's Count of States

In this Appendix, we show that, even if one accepts Secretary Mosbacher's method of counting the states, the appropriate break point for judging whether adjustment makes things better or worse is not half the states, or 25 1/2, but about 1/3 of the states, or 17.

Figure 29.2 shows a graph of the normal probability distribution

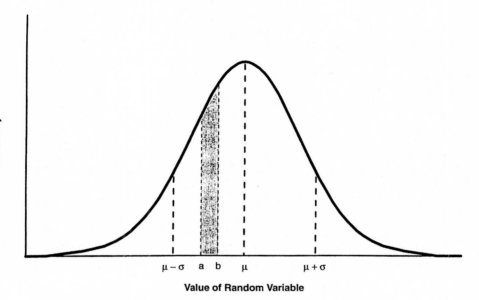

Value of Random Variable

FIGURE 29.2

(popularly or unpopularly called the "bell curve"). This is the standard probability distribution used in statistics, and with good reason. Not only are many things naturally distributed normally, but also various theorems state that in large samples averages tend to be distributed this way even if the original variable being averaged is not.

Now, the height of the curve above any given value on the horizontal axis gives the probability density associated with that point. For purposes of this exposition, one can think of that density as the probability that the corresponding value on the horizontal axis will be observed.[50] More precisely, the probability of observing a value within a given interval (the interval between a and b, for example), is equal to the area under the curve and above that interval (the shaded area in the diagram in the same example). The total area under the curve is 1, of course, since some value will be obtained.

[50] This is technically not correct. Since all points on the horizontal axis can (in principle) occur, and there is a continuum of such points, the probability of observing any particular value (to an infinite number of decimal places) is zero. The technically correct statement is as follows. Choose a very small distance, w. For any point, x, on the horizontal axis, the probability of observing a point between $x - w$ and $x + w$ is proportional to the height of the curve above x.

Now, the distribution in Figure 29.2 has a mean or expected value, denoted by μ. This is the value that will be observed on average.[51] The distribution also has a variance. This (as always) is a measure of dispersion – how scattered are the observations likely to be around the mean. It is the expected (average) value of squared deviations from the mean. Conventionally, the variance is denoted by σ^2, and its square root – called the "standard deviation" – by σ.

In Figure 29.2, the point that falls short of μ by exactly one standard deviation (the point $\mu - \sigma$) and the point that exceeds μ by exactly one standard deviation (the point $\mu + \sigma$) are both depicted.

Now we come to an important fact. The area under the normal curve between the points $\mu - \sigma$ and $\mu + \sigma$ is considerably greater than the area outside that interval. This corresponds to the fact that an observation taken at random is much more likely to fall between $\mu - \sigma$ and $\mu + \sigma$ (i.e., within one standard deviation of the mean) than it is to fall outside that interval. As a matter of fact, the probability that a value taken at random will lie within one standard deviation of the mean is very close to 2/3.

We are now ready to return to the Census. The sum-of-squares criterion that gives rise to the Secretary's count of states is one that compares the (estimated) squared bias of the unadjusted enumeration with the variance of the random error introduced by adjustment.[52] Equivalently, the absolute value of the bias of the unadjusted enumeration is compared to the standard deviation of the random error.[53] In the Secretary's count of states, this is done for each state.

Suppose that the (estimated) biases of the original count are normally distributed over states with mean 0 and variance b^2. Suppose that the random errors introduced by adjustment have mean 0 and variance σ^2 (normality is not required). Then, in terms of an expected sum-of-squares loss function, adjustment is superior if and only if $\sigma^2 < b^2$.[54] Now suppose

---

[51] In the case of the normal distribution (and many others), this is also the value with the greatest probability density (the "mode") and the one with half the probability on one side and half on the other (the "median"), but these properties are irrelevant for our purposes.

[52] This is not quite correct. As earlier observed, the adjusted estimates do not have zero bias but do have bias much smaller than does the original enumeration. For simplicity, the discussion in the text assumes zero bias after adjustment. This makes that discussion illustrative only, but the illustration is clear as to why the break point will not be 25 1/2 states.

[53] Squared bias is used to compare to variance, since variance is expected squared error. In comparing bias to standard deviation, the absolute value of the bias is used, since one does not wish to say that a huge negative bias is less than a small (naturally positive) standard deviation in any helpful sense.

[54] This is because in such a case the expected sum of squared errors over all states would be lower after adjustment ($51\sigma^2$) than before adjustment ($51b^2$).

that $\sigma^2 = b^2$, so that the two methods are tied. What would the Secretary's count show?

Let b_i be the estimated bias for state i. Then the Secretary counts a state in the favorable-to-adjustment category if and only if $b_i^2 > \sigma^2 = b^2$. But with the b_i normally distributed with mean 0, the expected number of them that will lie within σ (i.e., within one standard deviation) of 0 is approximately *two-thirds* of the total. In this case, therefore, the results favor adjustment if the Secretary's count of states with results favorable to adjustment is greater than 17 ($1/3 \times 51$). In fact, that count (29 or 30) is considerably greater than 17. Moreover, the count remains greater than 17 (becoming 22 or 23) even when one doubles the estimated variance due to adjustment. Thus even the Secretary's own count of states favored adjustment.

Against this there are only two arguments, and both are weak at best. The first is to say that the case of $b^2 = \sigma^2$ is a tie only if one works in terms of the sum-of-squares loss function. By going to a count of states, the Secretary abandoned that function.

This is not persuasive. It is true that by going to a count of states the Secretary effectively abandoned the sum-of-squares loss function. But the count done by the Secretary has its origin in that loss function. We have already seen that to make such a count is not a sensible procedure on any basis, but to do so is totally inexplicable if one is not thinking in terms of the sum-of-squares loss function.

The second argument is that the example given depends on normality. With a non-normal distribution, the break point might not occur at 17.[55] That is true. But normality is surely the leading case, and if one cannot conclude that the break point is 17, then one is even less justified in concluding that it is 25 1/2. It is worth pointing out that, in the case of the more sensible counts of states discussed in the text, there is no doubt as to where the break point is.

REFERENCES

Bateman, D., "Final Report for 1990 PES Evaluation Project P16: Total Error Model – Loss Function Evaluation," Memorandum for John H. Thompson, July 11, 1991.

Cirto, C. F., and M. L. Cohen (eds.), *The Bicentennial Census: New Directions for Methodology in 1990*, Panel on Decennial Census Methodology, National Research Council, National Academy Press, Washington, 1985.

---

[55] The presence of some residual bias in the adjusted estimates might also change the exact location of the break point.

Cullen, C. T. (ed.), *The Papers of Thomas Jefferson*, Princeton University Press, Princeton, 1986.

Feinberg, S. E., "The New York City Census Adjustment Trial: Witness for the Plaintiffs," *Jurimetrics* 34, 1993, 65–85.

Fisher, F. M., "Multiple Regression in Legal Proceedings," *Columbia Law Review* 702, 1980. Reprinted as Chapter 23 in Fisher (1990–91).

   Industrial Organization, Economics, and the Law. London: Harvester-Wheatsheaf and Cambridge, MA: MIT Press, 1990–91.

Mosbacher, R. A., "The Decision of the Secretary of Commerce on Whether a Statistical Adjustment of the 1990 Census for Population and Housing Should be Made for Coverage Deficiencies Resulting in an Overcount or Undercount of the Population," *Federal Register* 56 (No. 140), July 22, 1991.

Mulry M. H., and B. D. Spencer, "Loss Functions and the 1990 Census," unpublished mimeo, 1992.

   "Accuracy of the 1990 Census and Undercount Adjustments," *Journal of the American Statistical Association* 88, September 1993, 1080–1091.

Thompson, J. H., "Updated Loss Function Analysis for States and Places," Memorandum for the Undercount Steering Committee, June 27, 1991.

Walker, F. A., "Statistics of the Colored Race in the United States," *Publications of the American Statistical Association* 2, 1890.

Woltman, H. F., "Loss Function Analysis at the Poststratum Level," Memorandum for John H. Thompson, September 24, 1991.

CHAPTER 30

The Economics of Water Dispute Resolution, Project Evaluation and Management: An Application to the Middle East (1995)

Introduction

Water disputes among and within countries are common sources of friction. In particular, one of the conditions for the success of the current peace process in the Middle East is the reaching of an agreement over water rights and water allocations. The waters of the Jordan and Yarmouk rivers and those of the mountain aquifer shared between Israel and the Palestinians are all subject to various claims.

This paper reports on an economics-based approach to such issues that may assist their resolution as well as promoting efficient management of the water resources involved.

Ownership and Usage of Water: The General Approach

Water disputes are usually thought of as disputes over the ownership rights to quantities of water. But economic analysis suggests that, however important such rights may be, the question of water ownership rights and the question of water usage are analytically independent and

This ongoing work involves a large number of people, including: Yehuda Bachmat, Zvi Eckstein, Gideon Fishelson, Yuval Nachtom, and Hillel Shuval in Israel; Jad Isaac, Numar Mizyed, Yousef Nasser, Taher Naser El-Din, Mustafa Nusseibeh, Abdel Rahman Tamimi and Mohammed Al Turshan in connection with the Palestine Consultancy Group (Sari Nusseibeh, Chairperson, and Issa Khater, Director) in the Palestinian territory; Iyad Abu-Moghli, Maher Abu-Taleb and Elias Salameh in Jordan; Atif Kubursi in Canada; and Robert Dorfman, N. Harshadeep and Aviv Nevo in the United States. The contributions made by these participants in the project vary in nature and in magnitude, but space does not here permit a detailed description which must await later and longer publication. We are also very grateful to Shaul Arlosoroff, Jeremy Berkoff, Ellen P. Fisher, Munther Haddadin, Theodore Panayotou, Uri Shamir, Naomi Zikmund-Fisher and many others for advice and assistance. The entire project is under the auspices of the Institute for Social and Economic Policy in the Middle East at the John F. Kennedy School of Harvard University. We are indebted to Leonard Hausman, Anni Karasik and Bishara Bahbah for tireless and enthusiastic support and to Shula Gilad and others for administrative assistance. *Inclusion in this note does not imply agreement with the opinions here expressed.*

should not be confused. Moreover, analysis of water *scarcity rents* – of efficiency prices for water in different locations – can assist in resolving disputes over ownership rights by producing estimates of their monetary value. Such analysis also provides a powerful tool for efficient water management, particularly for the evaluation of various projects such as the construction of pipelines, dams, recycling plants or desalination plants.

The Harvard Middle East Water Project – a joint effort of Israeli, Palestinian, Jordanian, and North American scholars – is performing such an analysis for the water systems of Israel, Jordan and the Palestinian entity. In doing so, we take into account the fact that water has social, as well as private, value as revealed by the policies of the entities involved.

In the long run, this economic approach to regional water management can lead to optimal allocation of the region's scarce water resources and to rational planning of infrastructure projects. More immediately, we hope to help the parties to the Middle East peace negotiations perceive their water problem in a new way. By estimating the true economic value of the quantities of water in dispute, we hope to facilitate negotiations over water rights, for, when this is done, the size of the dispute ceases to be formidable, and it should thus become amenable to resolution.[1] In the short run, our results can be used to generate the amount of compensation for water usage that should be paid after a water settlement is reached.

The approach is based on the following points:

(1)   Water is a scarce resource. Scarce resources have value. In the case of water, however, that value is not merely the price that water would obtain in a free market. Indeed, water often has social value that is not merely private value. For example, the allocation of water can implement national policies towards agriculture that go beyond the promotion of privately profitable farms. Further, water usage can often involve externalities – positive ones such as the provision of green spaces or negative ones where pumping in one location affects costs in another. Issues of social stability can also be bound up in the question of how water should be allocated.

(2)   In particular, the fact that water is necessary for human life is an important element of the value of water. Were water sufficiently scarce, that fact would be reflected in a private or

---

[1] So far as I know, Gideon Fishelson was the first person to suggest that such valuation was possible and (because of the cap on value placed by the possibility of desalination of essentially unlimited amounts of seawater) could not lead to very large numbers.

national willingness to pay large sums for small amounts of water. Where water is somewhat more abundant (although still scarce), the value of water will be lower. But, no matter how scarce water is, every person requires and is entitled to at least the minimal amount of water consistent with human life and dignity.

(3) Countries that own water and use their water themselves do not in fact get the water at no cost. Such countries give up the money that they could make by selling the water to others. They will do this if and only if they value the water more than the money involved. But this is no different than the case of a country that does not own water and must consider whether to purchase it. Such a country will do so if and only if it values the water more than the money involved. Hence water owners (like anyone who uses the water) are buying the water and giving up money. The only difference consists of who gets the money that the water represents.

(4) Therefore, the right of water ownership is a property right entitling the owner to the value of the water. That is true regardless of who *uses* the water.

(5) As a result, the two questions, first, that of property rights – of who *owns* the water – and, second, the question of who *uses* the water, are analytically separate questions. Both questions are important, and both must be answered in any agreement, but one can and should think about them separately.[2]

The following concrete example, taken from our work on the Middle East, may be helpful here. The value of water in the Gaza strip will surely be high. That reflects the urgent fact that there is a large population and relatively little sweet water in Gaza. No matter who owns the water in dispute among the parties in the Middle East and no matter whether the cost is borne privately or publicly, the Palestinian government will find it expensive to supply its Gazan citizens with the water they must have. This is obvious if water has to be purchased from others, but it is also true – and true in the same measure – if the water is Palestinian. In that case, Gaza will be supplied by giving up the money for which the water could otherwise be sold. The expense will have to be incurred, *but it will be incurred regardless of the solution to the ownership question.*[3]

---

[2] This proposition is an application of the well-known Coase Theorem of economics (Coase, 1960).

[3] There may, of course, be options that would reduce the expense, but these too are independent of water ownership.

Discussion and Exemplification: Valuing Disputed Water

Our project has built a model of the connected water economies of Israel, Jordan and the Palestinian entity, and the discussion that follows draws heavily on our experience and results. To facilitate understanding, a map of the region and its principal water resources is given as Figure 30.1.[4] The major water sources that are (or have been) under dispute are: the water of the Jordan River (roughly 600 million cubic meters (MCM)/year); the water of the Yarmouk (roughly 500 MCM/year of which approximately 250 MCM/year flows south of Syria); and the water of the mountain aquifer that extends from the mountains of the West Bank into pre-1967 Israel (roughly 600 MCM/year).[5] The amounts given are annual renewable quantities. Together, the three sources account for roughly 60% of the water consumption of the three entities modelled.

Our model is an annual, steady-state model (i.e. a model for an average year), with data for 1990 and projections for the years 2010 and 2020. The model considers water demand by households, industry and agriculture. Water supply includes both fresh water and recycled water, that is, wastewater treated to a level safe for agricultural use. The model is disaggregated into districts within each country; water supply costs in each district and transportation costs between districts are taken into account and play a significant role. As explained below, the model takes account of the fact that water has a social as well as a private value by examining national policies toward water.[6]

Our work emphasizes the calculation of efficiency prices for both fresh and recycled water in each of the many districts that make up the region. Those prices equate demand and supply in each district, but, by a central and deep theorem of microeconomics, they play a basic role in guiding decisions as to water allocation. That role and the calculation of the prices are discussed at length below.

Such prices also permit us to value the water in dispute among the parties. We find that such valuation does not result in very high figures, with the water in dispute being worth no more than US $110 million per year at present and no more than $500 million per year by 2020 (figures in 1990 dollars). These are small numbers relative to the economies involved.

---

[4] The map is adapted from that in Wolf (1994), p. 27.
[5] Properly, there is not one mountain aquifer but several, and not all drain as described. I use the term as shorthand.
[6] The pioneering version of such a model (and one to which our project owes a great deal) was constructed by a team headed by Zvi Eckstein. See Eckstein et al. (1994).

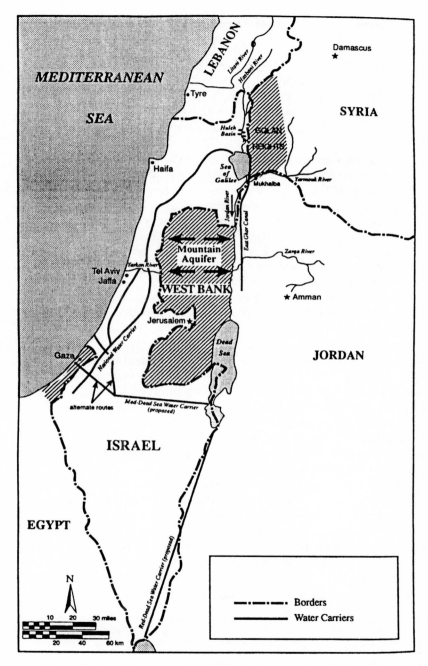

FIGURE 30.1. Map of study region with principal water sources.

These results are not so surprising as they may first appear. To take an outer limit, no matter how important fresh water is, it cannot be worth more than the cost of replacing it. Hence the possibility of desalination puts an upper bound on the value of water. In fact, that upper bound is lower than the cost of desalination, even when desalination is economically feasible on the coast.[7] This is a consequence of the following, much more general point.

The value of water is different in different locations. To understand this, consider the following example. As already discussed, water is (and will remain) quite valuable in Gaza where the population density is high and naturally occurring sweet water sources relatively low. (Indeed, relieving the Gazan water situation is an urgent matter.) An upper limit to the value of water in Gaza is the cost of desalination there. But whether or not Gaza is supplied by desalination, the high value of water in that city does not produce an equally high value for the water of the mountain aquifer or the Jordan River *in situ*. This is because supplying Gaza from those sources involves considerable pumping and transportation costs. The same water which, delivered in Gaza, would have a relatively high value, thus has a much lower one *in situ* in the West Bank.

An even more compelling case is that of Amman. In our results, we find that if the existing conveyance facilities to take water to Amman are not expanded,[8] there will be a major fresh water crisis there by 2010. That fact is reflected in the very high scarcity prices that we find would obtain in Amman in the absence of such expansion (more than $8/m^3$ in 2010). Those prices would add nothing to the value of the disputed water *in situ*, however, because the scarcity would not lie in the water but in the inability to transport it to Amman.[9]

Our first conclusion can thus be stated as follows: Despite the importance of water in use, and despite the consequent importance of the question of who uses the water, the property rights issue – the question of who owns the water – should not be nearly so difficult to resolve as is generally supposed. In the case of Israel, Jordan and the Palestinian entity, the value of the property rights at issue is small enough that it should prove possible to settle the issue in the context of a general peace agreement. The magnitudes involved are not such as cause war among

---

[7] In fact, we do not find desalination to be a likely efficient outcome on the Mediterranean coast of the entities involved until at least 2020 and perhaps not even then.

[8] We believe that plans for such an expansion are under way.

[9] Related to this is the following. In public discussions of our project, it is sometimes pointed out that if we were lost in the desert the value of water would be very great indeed. So it would be *in the desert*. But that fact would not increase the value of water *at the riverside*.

nations. If the parties will step back from a narrow focus on water quantities and consider the matter from the vantage point of the need to reach a workable and lasting settlement, the problem of water ownership should not stand in the way.

In this connection, the peace treaty between Israel and Jordan appears to settle water issues sensibly within a larger context. The quantity of water that Israel is to give Jordan in the short run is important but not earthshaking; based on our results, its value is less than $10 million per year.[10]

Note that we do not offer a specific solution for the issue of who owns the water in the sense of offering a specific allocation of the property rights involved. Nor do we claim that the question of who owns the water is unimportant. Indeed, that question must be solved as a prerequisite for any further arrangements. We do claim, however, that clarifying the value of the property rights involved can facilitate reaching a general peace agreement.

No matter how the question of who *owns* the water is resolved, however, the question of who *uses* the water will remain a very important one. Here the model we have constructed should be useful in a different way, as we now outline.

The model generates the allocation of water that would be optimal for the peoples of the region, given social as well as private goals. As explained below, a consequence of that optimization is the appearance of prices associated with water in different locations. Those prices can serve as guides to rational water management either by individual entities or jointly.

One way to think about our model is to envisage a water authority jointly operated by (at least) Jordan, Israel and the Palestinian entity. (This can happen only after ownership rights are established.) At the very least, some such joint arrangement will be necessary to monitor compliance with any eventual water agreement. We believe, however, that there would be considerable benefit to be gained from rational joint management of the water resources of the region. Such joint management would involve the transfer of water from one entity to another at prices reflecting the full social value of water as determined by each party.

It is crucial to realize that such prices need not be those that would prevail in a private market for water. The deep social importance of water makes the question of who uses the water one that does not simply

---

[10] And the value is unlikely to exceed $30 million per year by 2020. The exact quantity involved is difficult to determine from the text of the treaty. There are also transfers from Jordan to Israel.

have a private answer. Rather, the answer depends on the values of the political entities involved. That is why we seek to construct demand curves that include national goals as revealed in national water policies. The prices at which water would be traded reflect those goals.

In this regard, it is important to recognize that when a political entity determines for itself how much water it demands at a particular price – including the demand coming from considerations of national policy – then that entity should be willing to sell additional water to a neighbour at that price or any higher one. If it does so, it can use the money obtained for greater social benefit than (according to its own policies) would be obtained from the water itself. In effect, the selling country has already said what additional water is worth to it. At that price, it must be indifferent between using and selling such additional water. If it wishes not to sell, then it has placed too low a value on the water, and the price should be adjusted upwards.

Our project does not suppose a world in which poorer countries necessarily sell their water to richer ones. Nor does it ignore the fact that all humans must receive at least that minimal amount of water required for a decent life. There is no requirement here that there be an internal or international private market for water. Instead, we adapt the market mechanism to reflect national policies and goals.

Further, the transfers envisaged in our work are only temporary ones. We are not talking of a permanent sale of historic rights. Rather, we envisage the sale of permits allowing some party other than the owner to use the water for a limited time. As with all voluntary trades, such permit sales will benefit both buyer and seller. As populations grow and economies develop, the quantity of water traded by such permits and even the direction of the trade may change.

A model such as ours can be used to predict such changes and as a guide in setting the prices involved in cooperative arrangements. Further, the model can forecast now what those prices are likely to be in the future. Perhaps most important for future developments, it can serve as a guide to the wisdom of various proposed projects such as new canals, water treatment and recycling plants, desalination facilities, or water import programmes. To take imports as an example, since the model generates the equilibrium price of water at each location, it tells us the maximum price that the participating entities should be willing to pay for imports from outside (from the Litani River in Lebanon or from Turkey, for example).

Water management along these lines is not a simple matter. Water systems are often complex, making precise modelling difficult. Further, policy makers faced with the demand-curve implications of their national policies may decide that national goals are not correctly reflected and may wish to change those policies. There will probably be a good deal of refinement and interaction between policy makers and technocrats in the process of assuring that the model reflects the national value of water, and that is all to the good.

It is also likely that there will be continuing interplay among the policy makers of the different entities. The issues involved in who uses the water do not go away because one has provided a systematic framework with which to analyse them. In particular, the national policies of one of the entities will affect the water prices and uses of another. A subsidy to water for agriculture in one country, for example, will generally lead to higher water prices in the others. This may seem to require continuing negotiations over what policies are to be adopted.

Our model appears helpful in two ways in this regard. First, it permits a systematic investigation of the effects of the policies of any one party on the water prices, flows, costs and benefits as seen by the others. This permits the focusing of the negotiations involved.

The other point is somewhat surprising. Our results strongly suggest that (at least for the region studied), the effects of one party's water subsidies on the other parties involved are not very large. Further, if the imposition of a subsidy causes the subsidizing entity to import more water from its neighbours, the non-subsidizing countries can actually benefit. The extent to which this occurs depends on the allocation of property rights. (It should be noted, however, that these findings take no account of any effects on competition in agricultural outputs.)

Shadow Prices, Scarcity Rents and Value

Clearly, prices and values play a very large role in our analysis, as they do in economics generally. It is therefore important to give a discussion of that role and to make clear what we mean by the "value of water".

In competitive markets, price comes to reflect both what buyers are just willing to spend for additional units of the good in question (marginal value) and the cost of producing such additional units (marginal cost). A price higher than marginal cost is a signal that the unit is worth producing, for the value placed by buyers on that unit is greater than the cost of production; similarly, a price less than marginal cost is a signal to cut back on production. Prices and the profits and losses they generate thus serve as guides to the efficient allocation of resources.

In the case of water, there are reasons for not relying on a totally private market to serve such functions. A principal reason has to do with the social as opposed to the private value of water. Our model deals with this by augmenting and modifying private demand curves to include social values as reflected by national policies. For example, a subsidy to water users of a given amount per cubic meter shows a national value to water that exceeds the private value by that same amount. More complex cases can also be handled; indeed, any logically consistent policy can be represented as a change in the demand curve for water. Once this is done, the prices generated by equating supply and demand can play the same role as those in a competitive private market.

There is a wholly different way to think about this: Embedded in every optimization problem is a system of prices. Our model operates by allocating water (including recycled water) to maximize the net benefit received from water. That net benefit consists of a measure of the total amount that buyers (consumers or nations) would be willing to pay for the water, less the production and conveyance costs required to provide it.

This maximization process is done subject to a number of constraints, essentially all concerned with water availability. For example, in a particular district, the amount of water consumed cannot exceed the amount produced there plus net imports into that district. There are also constraints on the amount of water that can be taken from each source and on the capacity of the transportation system.

Associated with each of these constraints is a "shadow price" that shows the extent by which the benefits from water would increase if that constraint were loosened just a little. For example, where a pipeline is limited in capacity, the associated shadow price shows the amount by which benefits would increase per unit of pipeline capacity if that capacity were slightly increased. This is the amount that those benefiting would just be willing to pay for more capacity.

The central shadow prices in the model, however, are those of water itself. The shadow price of water at a given location is the amount by which the benefits to water users (in the system as a whole) would increase were there an additional cubic meter per year available free *at that location*. It is also the price that the buyers at that location who value additional water the most would just be willing to pay to obtain an additional cubic meter per year, given the optimal water flows of the model solution.

It is important to note that the shadow price of water in a given location does not generally equal the direct cost of providing it there: Suppose a limited water source whose pumping costs are zero. If demand for water from that source is sufficiently high, the shadow price of that water will not be zero; equivalently, benefits to water users would be increased if the capacity of the source were greater. Equivalently, buyers will be willing to pay a non-zero price for water in short supply, even though its direct costs are zero.

A proper view of costs accommodates this phenomenon. When demand at the source exceeds capacity, it is not costless to provide a particular user with an additional unit of water. That water can be provided only by depriving some *other* user of the benefits of the water; that loss of benefits represents an *opportunity cost*.

Another way of saying this is to observe that scarce resources have positive values and positive prices even if their direct cost of production is zero. This should surprise nobody. Land in the center of Manhattan sells for a considerable price even though (up to the point at which it is fully utilized) it costs nothing to produce. The positive price of that land occurs because demand for it exceeds the available supply; equivalently, could additional land be produced at zero cost, there would be positive benefits from doing so.

In the case of zero direct cost, the shadow price of the resource involved consists entirely of "scarcity rent". More generally, the scarcity rent of water at a particular location equals the shadow price at that location less the direct marginal cost of providing the water there.[11] This is the same as the per-unit profit that a private owner of a water source at that location could obtain by producing an additional unit. Just as in a competitive market, a positive scarcity rent is a signal that more water from that source would be beneficial were it available.

It is important to note that water shadow prices and hence water scarcity rents depend upon the infrastructure assumed to be in place.

When water is efficiently allocated, the relationships listed below must hold. Equivalently, if they do not hold, then water is *not* being efficiently allocated. Since our model allocates water efficiently, these relations hold in the solution of our model (all values are per unit of water):

(1) Shadow price equals direct marginal cost plus scarcity rent.

(2) Water will be produced at a given location only if the shadow price of water at that location exceeds the marginal cost of production. Equivalently, water will be produced only from sources whose scarcity rents are non-negative.

(3) If water can be transported from location a to location b, then the shadow price of water at b can never exceed the shadow price at a by more than the cost of such transportation. Water will actually be transported from a to b only if the shadow price

---

[11] If this calculation gives a negative figure, then scarcity rent is zero, and water is not scarce at the given location.

at b exactly equals the shadow price at a plus the transportation cost. Equivalently, if water is transported from a to b, then the scarcity rent of that water will be the same in the two locations.

(4)   At each location, the shadow price of water is the price at which buyers of water would be just willing to buy and sellers of water just willing to sell an additional cubic meter of water.

(5)   Consider a body of water at a particular location, a (for example, the Sea of Galilee). At all locations to which that water can be transported, buyers of water will not be willing to purchase additional water for more than an amount equal to the shadow price at a plus the transport costs of conveying the water to the location of the buyer. If water is actually transported from a to such a location, then buyers at that location will be just willing to purchase additional water for exactly the described amount.

Thus, the maximum price users of any body of water are just willing to pay for more water is the common scarcity rent associated with that water in all locations plus the transport and lifting costs required to get the water to the buyer. This is also the price at which sellers of water will be just willing to sell.

This immediately implies how the water in question should be valued. Water *in situ* should be valued at its scarcity rent. That value is the price at which buyers value additional water, less the direct costs involved in getting it to them.

One should not be confused by the use of marginal valuation here (the value of an additional unit of water). The fact that people would be willing to pay much larger amounts for the amount of water necessary for human life is important. It is taken into account in our optimizing model by assigning correspondingly large benefits to the first relatively small quantities of water allocated. But the fact that the benefits derived from the first units are greater than the marginal value does not distinguish water from any other economic good. It merely reflects the fact that water would be (even) more valuable if it were scarcer.

It is the scarcity of water and not merely its importance for existence that gives it its value. Where water is not scarce, it is not valuable.

Results of the Project to Date

Water Values

At present our model is an annual, steady-state model. We currently deal with fresh water and recycled water. Work is under way to include: more dimensions of water quality; seasonal variation; and inter-year effects important for water-system management. We are also adding more sophistication in our modelling of joint aquifers in terms of a number of interconnected cells with costs of pumping in any cell affected by pumping rates in the others. Nevertheless, while the model continues to be refined, the major conclusions so far reached seem unlikely to change. I begin with the results bearing on water valuation and negotiations. The first, and most important of these, has already been mentioned.

(1) The value of the water in dispute among the parties is not great. Using a liberal estimate, it is currently a maximum of $110 million per year (all figures in 1990 dollars) and will rise to a maximum of less than $500 million per year by 2020. Such values are small compared with the economies involved or (perhaps more pointedly) compared with the cost of military equipment.

(2) There will be no crisis of water for human consumption in the region or for domestic, industrial or commercial use. What is required there is not more water but better conveyance facilities permitting more efficient use of the existing water. For example, by 2010, if no additional conveyance facilities beyond those existing in 1990 were to be built, there would be a major crisis in the areas of Jordan near Amman (with shadow prices of $8/m^3 or more, compared with $0.50–0.60/m^3 elsewhere in the region). This would not increase the value of Jordan River water to the Kingdom of Jordan, however, because the true scarcity would be that of the limited capacity of the 1990 pipeline system. The model shows that additional capacity makes the crisis disappear with shadow prices falling into line with those of the remainder of the region.

(3) There will, however, be a crisis in unsubsidized agriculture unless further infrastructure facilities are built. That crisis can largely be cured by the construction of wastewater recycling and treatment plants.

(4) As already mentioned, we obtain the following result: National policies that subsidize water for agriculture are expensive for the subsidizing country but do not have a large negative effect on the other parties so far as water itself is concerned. Moreover, if the imposition of a subsidy causes the subsidizing entity to import more water from its neighbours, the non-subsidizing entities can actually benefit. The extent to which this happens depends on the allocation of property rights. (Note, however,

that effects on competition in agricultural *outputs* are not studied.) This is a matter of considerable importance, since it suggests that an initial agreement on joint efficient water use and management need not be followed by continual difficult negotiations over what policies are to be permitted to each entity, as would be the case if a subsidy by one party were very harmful to the others.

Project Evaluation

In addition to facilitating negotiations, models of this type can provide a powerful tool for assessing proposed capital projects. By running the model with and without a proposed project, the net benefits of having such a project in existence can be assessed and compared with the capital costs involved.

Indeed, one can gain considerable insight even before including capital costs explicitly, for the model can be used to tell at what capital costs a particular proposed project would be worth constructing and using. Running the model in this way provides a useful screen for selecting projects as candidates for deeper investigation.

In addition, examination of the shadow prices obtained when the model is run with a particular infrastructure can suggest projects that may be attractive. This is particularly true of conveyance projects. We have performed a number of such screening runs, and the results (while still preliminary) are quite interesting. They are as follows:

(1) In the absence of considerable technological improvement, desalination facilities on the Mediterranean coast will not be needed until at least 2020 if other reasonable recycling and conveyance facilities are put in place. On reasonable assumptions, shadow prices of water on that coast will not rise above roughly $0.70/m^3$ (in 1990 dollars). That is the target which desalination costs will have to meet in order to make desalination an efficient technology in 2020.

(2) Similarly, it is doubtful that the major canal projects now under discussion (such as the Red Sea–Dead Sea canal) will be economically justified so far as water is concerned. Our results do not suggest that the shadow price of water will be high enough to justify such projects simply as methods of desalination.

(3) On the other hand, certain facilities stand out as candidates for construction. These include: (a) pipeline facilities to bring water

to Amman and neighbouring regions of Jordan; (b) storage facilities to capture the excess winter flow of the Yarmouk and lower Jordan Rivers; (c) pipeline facilities to bring Jordan River water to the Nablus region of the West Bank and a West Bank pipeline system generally with possible connections to the Israeli system; (d) increased capacity of the pipeline connecting Gaza to the Israeli National Water Carrier; and (e) wastewater recycling plants in the major cities of the West Bank with conveyance to the Jordan valley. It is interesting to note that construction of the facilities in (a) is already under way (and those facilities are expected to become operational very soon). The facilities described in (b) are being planned. One should also observe that the combination of (c) and (d) could create a situation of mutual interdependence and hence of cooperation for Israel and the Palestinian entity.

Full development of the model for purposes of optimal management will require a good deal more work. In particular, it would be desirable to make the model dynamic so as to study the effect of decisions in a particular year on conditions in later years and to optimize over a long time horizon. In addition, one should study decision making under variable hydrological conditions. All this remains to be done.

Can Water Be Priced?

Of course, all these results depend on being able to think of water as something that has a price, on considering the monetary equivalent of water. That, we know, is an unfamiliar way of thinking about water. To those who believe that water is beyond price, however, we pose the following questions (while the examples are drawn from the Middle East, the lessons are of global applicability).

Why does Jordan not desalinate water at Aqaba and pump it to Amman? Why, no matter how much or how little of the disputed water it receives, is it unlikely to make sense for the Palestinian entity to plan to desalinate water at Gaza and pump it to the cities of the West Bank? Why does Israel not desalinate water at Haifa and Tel Aviv? Why don't all the entities of the region plan on importing water from anyone who will sell it, no matter where located?

The answer in each case is the same. These actions are not or will not be taken because they would be too expensive. But then the value of the water at the places receiving it cannot be greater than the expense of producing or transporting water there. Note that this is so even if (indeed, partly *because*) those places can be more cheaply supplied in other ways. If water were beyond price, this would not matter. The fact that scarcity prices are inevitably associated with efficient allocation of scarce resources is among the central propositions of economic analysis. Water is not an exception.

Conclusion

The Harvard Middle East Water Project has two principal aims. First, it aims to assist negotiations among the parties. It does so by monetizing the value of the property rights in dispute and thus evaluating the rate at which such rights can be traded off for other concessions. There is reason to believe that ownership rights are not, in fact, tremendously valuable, so that a water settlement can form part of a more general agreement.

The project's focus on values and prices, rather than quantities, also assists in achieving a second principal aim. The project provides a powerful tool with which the parties, either separately or together, can decide on water flows and evaluate proposed projects and infrastructure improvements.

That tool, of course, can assist individual entities in managing their own water systems. (That is one reason for them to be interested in our work.) But the project will not have achieved its objectives if it merely becomes an aid to separate management by separate entities. Joint management of joint resources is important for efficiency, and the cooperation required may contribute to a stable peace.

Indeed, the cooperative effort required to build models such as ours can itself contribute to a peaceful settlement of disputes. At the very least, it changes the dialogue from one of repeated statements of irreconcilable historical claims to a dispassionate discussion of facts and assumptions. The fact that the optimizing nature of the model leads to efficient water use and provides the parties with a useful policy tool can also lead to a concentration on joint benefits, removing the belief that a zero-sum game is being played.

The project has aroused considerable (if often carefully unofficial) interest among the parties in the region, as well as among analysts and policy makers outside it. We have been given substantial reason to believe that it has already indirectly facilitated the peace negotiations. At present, there is great interest among Israelis, Jordanians and Palestinians in further developing the model so as to make it an even better tool for water policy planning.

One final word: The region whose water systems we have modelled does not exist in isolation. The water resources of Israel, Jordan and the Palestinian territory are connected to those of Syria and Lebanon, and the water systems of those countries are in turn connected to those of Turkey and Iraq. Extension of the model is an obvious possibility.

It has also not escaped our attention that the methods used by the project are applicable to other water systems and other water disputes.

REFERENCES

Coase, R. (1960) "The problem of social cost", *Journal of Law and Economics*, 1, pp. 1–44.
Eckstein, Z., Zackay, D., Nachtom, Y. and Fishelson, G. (1994) The Allocation of Water Resources between Israel, the West Bank and Gaza: An Economic Viewpoint (Tel Aviv, The Armand Hammer Fund for Economic Cooperation, Tel Aviv University, unpublished).
Wolf, A. (1994) "A hydropolitical history of the Nile, Jordan and Euphrates river basins", in: A. K. Biswas (Ed.) *International Waters of the Middle East from Euphrates–Tigris to Nile* (Oxford, Oxford University Press), Ch. 2.

Epilogue

My Career in Economics: A Hindcast (1997)

1. How I Wandered into Economics and Then to MIT

Most children do not grow up dreaming of becoming an economist, and I was no exception. I wandered into the subject.

I was born in New York City in 1934, the oldest of three children. My father, Mitchell S. Fisher, was a rabbi who became a prominent attorney specializing in divorce work. My mother, Esther Oshiver Fisher, had a law degree but never practiced. Eventually, she became a marriage counselor.

Despite a strong high-school training and interest in mathematics, I decided not to continue in that subject when I entered Harvard College in September 1952. One of my best friends was a mathematics genius and, although I was good, I plainly could not compare with him.

I began by majoring in philosophy but was quickly turned off by exposure to quite a bad teacher in that subject. By contrast, I had an excellent teaching assistant, Gavin Langmuir (later a professor of history at Stanford) for my instructor in a history-oriented social science course. History had always interested me, and I decided to become a history major.

One of the requirements for that major was a course in either political science or economics. At the beginning of my sophomore year, I consulted Langmuir and was strongly advised to take economics, political science being deemed "too easy". I duly registered for Harvard's Principles of Economics course – Ec 1, as it was then called.

The course (which used the second edition of Paul Samuelson's text, Samuelson 1951) was a revelation to me in more than one respect. First, it was fun. Second, it combined both mathematics (a mild amount in those days) and real-world issues – just right for me. Third, I found that the roles of my mathematically-minded friend and I were now reversed. He was good, but I had found a subject that came naturally.

It was when the course got to microeconomics, however (in the second term), that I began to think seriously about majoring in and perhaps making a career in economics. At the time, I had no idea what econo-

539

mists actually did. (I sometimes think that I am but little better informed now.) I consulted a distant cousin, Philip Glaessner, who worked for the New York Federal Reserve Bank, and he was encouraging. Nevertheless, I remained mystified. It truly never occurred to me that one could be paid for going on and studying the subject; I had never thought of an academic career.

In the Spring of 1954, the course turned briefly to the subject of oligopoly, emphasizing what was then known as the "oligopoly problem" – the fact that oligopolists are mutually interdependent, so that one cannot predict the actions of one without knowing the reactions of the others which, in turn, requires knowing the thing that is to be predicted. I was literally sophomoric and assumed that anything called a "problem" was there to be solved.[1] I therefore wrote a paper on the issue, the contents of which I (mercifully) have long forgotten.

There now occurred an event of major importance for my career. It was an occasion on which the Harvard educational system (about which I shall be critical below) actually functioned extremely well.

I first gave the paper to my section instructor, a teaching assistant named Ted Boyden. Boyden found he could not understand it (possibly nobody could have done so), and turned it over to the head teaching assistant for the course, Merton J. Peck. Joe Peck in turn referred it to his dissertation advisor, Assistant Professor Carl Kaysen. Kaysen read the paper and spotted enough raw ability to call me in to see him. He offered to be my tutor in the following academic year, suggesting strongly that I should switch my major to economics instead of waiting for graduate school.

I had no real idea of what I was getting into. (Least of all did I think that I was beginning a life-long friendship.) It simply did not occur to me that Junior-year tutorials tended to involve several students and that I was being singled out for very special attention. Nor did I realize what Carl had in mind for me for the next year. But I did have enough sense to know that I was being complimented, and I agreed.

Carl took the view that smart undergraduates ought not to take Harvard's undergraduate economics courses. Moreover, he regarded Harvard's first-year graduate theory course (taught by Edward Chamberlin) as not very good. He therefore tutored me himself in economic theory and, at the same time, placed me in John Chipman's course in mathematical economics. (Having taken some elementary calculus in prior years or in summer school, I also went directly into a rather badly

---

[1] I had achieved some success in my history course the year before with a paper on the "Schleswig-Holstein problem", a topic I chose for the same reason.

taught intermediate calculus course). It was planned that I would take Wassily Leontief's second-year graduate theory course in the following year. Finally, Carl had me take the graduate course in industrial organization, taught by himself and Edward S. Mason.

To put it mildly, this was an ambitious program. John Chipman's course, in particular, scared me to death. I was (barely) acquiring the necessary mathematics at the same time, and I never worked so hard in my life, believing that I had to understand every line in every derivation. I ended the first term by finding all the typographical errors in the main textbook – Samuelson's *Foundations of Economic Analysis* (Samuelson 1947) – and (as I later discovered) frightening all the graduate students in the course who were not working with the same timorous tenacity as was I.

It is interesting to note how much times have changed. In those days (1954–55), Harvard required no mathematics of its graduate students (let alone its undergraduates).[2] Chipman's course – typically taken only by a minority of advanced graduate students – was in style and content fairly close to what is now regularly taught in first-year graduate or even advanced undergraduate theory courses. The ordinary graduate student received little exposure to the advances in economic theory (in general equilibrium, for example) that were then taking place.

Fortunately, my education was a special one. While Chipman's course helped, Kaysen's tutorial sessions were what really taught me microeconomic theory. Focusing on the relations between the functioning of the price system and the welfare of consumers, Carl managed a style that combined serious insight with just the necessary level of technique. He did not lack rigor, but he never allowed me to become so involved with the mathematics as to lose sight of the economic insights involved. This was a teaching style that is altogether too rare in the profession and that I have ever since tried to emulate (perhaps not always successfully).

In the course of this tutorial, I wrote what became my first published paper (Fisher, 1956). While parts of it showed the incomplete nature of my education,[3] I was (and still am) amazed that students could so quickly explore matters on – or even near – the frontier of the subject. I am not certain that this speaks well for the serious connection of economic

---

[2] Although one could satisfy part of the foreign language requirement for the Ph.D. by passing what would now be thought of as a fairly elementary mathematics examination!

[3] I implicitly assumed that since indifference curves could not cross, indifference maps had to be homothetic (a property to which I had not been exposed as special). As a result, a later note was necessary to correct the minor errors flowing from this (Fisher and Kenen, 1957).

theory with empirical fact, however exciting it is for the students involved.

As already mentioned, Kaysen placed me in the graduate course in industrial organization. This was not industrial organization as the field is usually taught today. Industrial organization theory was in the doldrums, and the brighter students usually did not go into the field. The course was largely empirical, with the second part (taught by Mason) heavily oriented towards public policy, especially antitrust.

This was my first exposure to antitrust, a field in which I was much later to work intensively. At the time, it aroused my interest considerably, enough so that in the following year and for several thereafter, I participated in the antitrust seminar run jointly by the Harvard Economics Department and the Harvard Law School.[4] The seminar covered a different topic each year and was largely taught in the Socratic style of the Law School. This was my first systematic exposure to lawyers.

In 1955–56, my senior year, Carl went on sabbatical, bequeathing me to James Duesenberry as a tutee. At Carl's suggestion, I attempted to formalize Schumpeter's model of innovation and imitation (Schumpeter, 1951). I failed and returned to the subject many years later (Fisher, 1983). In any event, my interests began to move away from economic theory and towards econometrics.

Here too my education was peculiar, and here too what Harvard offered was inadequate by modern standards. Every graduate student was required to take a statistics course, then taught by Guy Orcutt. This was a very good course, but it went no farther than ordinary least squares regression (and did not use linear algebra or anything else that might frighten the student). There was a graduate econometrics course (taught at the time first by John Chipman and later by Stefan Valavanis), but it was not required. More than that, it was not a course that most people even thought of taking. That was also true of me, even though I was fast studying the subject.

Instead, my further education in econometrics began when I went to work as a research assistant for John R. Meyer in the Spring of 1956. The project involved various studies for the Canadian Pacific Railroad, and John was smart enough to turn me loose on a study of the demand for aluminum which made use of the monopolized character of that

[4] In 1956, the faculty were Kaysen and Mason for the Economics Department and Donald F. Turner and Kingman Brewster for the Law School. Turner, with whom Kaysen was writing a to-be-well-known book on antitrust policy (Kaysen and Turner, 1959), later became Assistant Attorney General for Antitrust in the Kennedy administration. Brewster went on to become President of Yale. It was a good course.

industry in the interwar period. This study later became a chapter in my doctoral dissertation (of which John was the director) and was the first piece of empirical econometrics I ever did. My only other formal training in the subject came in a reading course in 1956–57 with Robert Solow – not himself an econometrician – on simultaneous equation methods.[5] Apart from that, I was self taught (as I was also in linear algebra).

This idiosyncratic training (or the lack of it) was both to benefit and hamper my work in the subject, as I shall later discuss.

In the Fall of 1956, I became a graduate student at Harvard, receiving a teaching fellowship and tutorship in Winthrop House in my first year, which was unusual. I was elected to Harvard's Society of Fellows for a three-year term starting in the Fall of 1957. I did not complete that term, but, in 1959 joined the faculty of the University of Chicago as an Assistant Professor for one year, intending to return to Harvard, where I had the promise of a similar job.

The University of Chicago in those days was at a low point as regards economics. The Cowles Commission had left for Yale a couple of years before, and there was nothing to replace it in the technical areas. Moreover, in the great Chicago tradition, the Economics Department was very ideologically oriented. Finally, with the exception of Zvi Griliches, who was on leave that year, there was no one in the department within ten years of my age. Hence, although the department was extremely kind to me, I felt no temptation to change my mind and stay on.

In the meantime, however, my view that Harvard was the natural, indeed the only, place at which to work changed dramatically. For one thing, I discovered that (in a story not worth relating) I had been the victim of the ongoing fight over the usefulness of technical economics. That was a fight that had been going on at Harvard since Paul Samuelson's day, and was not to be satisfactorily resolved for another ten years. I found that agreements would not necessarily be kept. As a result, I was only mildly tempted by later Harvard offers in the early 1960s.

Having become aware that there were other places besides Harvard, my wife, Ellen, and I considered the question of where we would like to be. We quickly decided that MIT was at the top of our list. When we visited Cambridge in December of 1959, I hinted as much to Bob Solow.

---

[5] Looking back, this seems even more peculiar than it did at the time. Bob Solow (to whom Carl Kaysen had sent my first paper in 1955 and whom I had met at that time) can teach anybody anything. But consider how odd it was for one of Harvard's best students to go to MIT for a reading course in econometrics with someone not really an expert in that subject.

(For some reason I felt it improper to ask him directly whether MIT would like to hire me.) Some days later, he took the hint.

That was in 1960. I have been at MIT ever since – usually happily.

2.   Themes in My Work and Changes in My Interests

Several times in my professional career I have been fortunate enough to find research in a vein similar to mine. By that I mean that I have come upon a line of research in which a succession of topics suggests itself.[6]

a.   Econometric Theory: Identification and Block Recursive Systems

The first of these lines was in econometrics and was, in part, a result of my relatively inadequate education in the subject. The specific set of topics involved centered around the identification problem in simultaneous equations, and my work in the area ultimately led to my book on that subject (Fisher, 1966, 1976).

Because I had not received much statistical training, I tended not to think of econometrics as a branch of mathematical statistics but rather as economic modeling with statistical methods a necessary appendage. This caused me to think of identification at first not as a plateau in the likelihood function but rather in terms of the uniqueness of solution of the normal equations of ordinary least squares. This led naturally to the view that, in large part, identification was not a statistical problem at all: the stochastic problems involved could be made to disappear in large enough samples, but the identification problem would nevertheless remain.

This approach (largely, but not always quite correct) led naturally to a series of papers in which I investigated identification as the uniqueness-of-solution problem when the information at hand differed in various ways.[7] These included non-linear constraints, constraints on

---

[6] For a different and somewhat more extended discussion of some of my work, see the introductions to the three volumes of my collected articles published earlier (Fisher 1990–91, 1991–92, 1992–93), and the introduction to this volume.

[7] Even here, I was somewhat hampered by inadequate training, since I knew rather less about uniqueness issues than I thought. A conversation with Paul Samuelson kept me from asserting that the Implicit Function Theorem was a global one but led me to other false assertions based on an error that Paul himself had made in a different context. (See Fisher, 1959, p. 438, n. 9, and 1965b, p. 205, n. 19). It was not until my identification book that I finally got these matters really right.

the variance of the disturbance terms, constraints on their covariances, non-linearities in the variables, and so forth.

Some of this work was closely related to a more fundamental investigation I had undertaken in 1959–60. T. C. Liu had raised a set of questions that seemed to challenge the entire possibility of structural estimation. (See, for example, Liu 1960.) He pointed out the following: (1) Identifying restrictions typically take the form of excluding variables from equations. But econometric models are approximations, so "excluded" variables may really appear with small coefficients. (2) Identification is usually achieved by using as instruments exogenous variables that do not appear in the equation of interest. But (again because of the approximative nature of econometric models), such variables are not "really" exogenous at all; they are themselves endogenous in a wider system of equations. Under these circumstances, how can any equation ever be identified, and how can consistent structural estimates ever be achieved?[8]

I was able to deal with these issues because of the way I thought about identification. If identification involved the solution of equations when certain parameters were zero, then it was natural to notice that solutions would also exist when those parameters were small and (most importantly) that the solutions would be continuous in the parameter values. This meant that the extent of inconsistency in parameter estimates brought about by assuming coefficients to be zero would be satisfactorily small if the true coefficients were sufficiently close to zero. Moreover, I showed that the exogeneity problem could be reduced to the same case.

I published these findings in 1961 in a paper that I still regard as my most important contribution to econometrics (Fisher, 1961). That contribution lay only partly in the continuity results as to approximations. More important, I think, was the analysis of exogeneity (and nearexogeneity) that occurred on the way. This was the discovery of what I termed "block-recursive" systems.

Block-recursive systems were the answer to Liu's observation that, since every variable is connected to every other in the total system of equations describing the world, no variable can be exogenous. I showed that this is not true, provided that the matrix of coefficients of current endogenous variables is block triangular and the covariance matrix of the disturbance terms block diagonal. Given the approximation theorem,

---

[8] Liu thought that the moral was that one should work only with unrestricted least squares estimates of the reduced form. He failed to notice that, were his objections to exogeneity well taken, one could not even obtain consistent estimates of reduced form equations.

it is good enough if such conditions hold approximately. If they do, then variables from low-numbered "blocks" can be taken as exogenous when dealing with higher-numbered blocks.

I regard this analysis as having established the foundations of structural estimation. As it turns out, the conditions involved are intimately related to conditions for identification, and the subject was expanded in my book on that subject (Fisher, 1966, 1976).

The exploration of block-recursive systems and approximations also led me into a non-econometric area. This was the exploration of dynamic systems with only very small feedbacks from higher- to lower-numbered sectors. A series of papers resulted, several with Albert Ando, the principal theorem being a generalization of one that Ando and Herbert Simon had proved on systems with only very small feedbacks connecting *any* two sectors. The papers were then collected and published as Ando, Fisher, and Simon (1963). Interestingly, they included Simon's well known paper on the structure of identification.

At the end of the 1960s, I again ventured into the area of the underpinning of structural estimation. This time the issue was that of the consequences of supposing that the simultaneous equations of econometrics were in fact approximations to equations with very small time lags (Fisher, 1970). While I thought the results obtained quite interesting, the rest of the profession paid them almost no attention.

By that time, my interests had moved on. Indeed, the identification book was the high point of my foray into theoretical econometrics. In 1970, as discussed below, I made a deliberate decision to leave that subject.

b.   *The Existence of Aggregate Production Functions*

Meanwhile, I had come across another vein of research involving economic theory rather than econometrics.

It was and is common in macroeconomics to deal with large aggregates. In particular, such concepts as Gross Domestic Product, Capital, Investment, and Labor are treated as meaningful constructs. Further, the production side of the economy is treated as though aggregate output were related to aggregate capital and aggregate labor by a production function such as is typically thought to represent the technology of micro-units. Such a production function is treated as though it had the standard properties. For example, wages are supposed to be related to marginal products. Such treatments are common in theory, in econometric modeling, and in statements about policy.

But is there any sound justification for such treatment? It is far from obvious that the diverse technology of a modern economy can be so represented. If not, then not only are analyses explicitly based on aggregate production functions likely to prove misleading, but the usefulness of the aggregates used in national accounts can be called into question.

In the late 1950s and early 1960s, these matters had been forcibly brought to the attention of the profession by Joan Robinson (e.g., Robinson 1953–4) and were the subject of the so-called "Cambridge v. Cambridge" debate, with Robert Solow figuring most prominently on the side of the American Cambridge (e.g., Solow 1955–6). Mrs. Robinson, however, took a zealot's view of the subject. For her, the existence of aggregate production functions was bound up with the validity of neoclassical *micro*-economics – a subject to which it is orthogonal – and, indeed, with capitalism versus socialism.

I inadvertently wandered into the debate around 1964. My first paper on the subject (Fisher, 1965a) considered the question of the conditions under which technical changes embodied in capital equipment could be captured in a capital aggregate. It was not until the paper was in press that I realized that the problem was isomorphic to the more interesting one of aggregating capital over firms.

Perhaps because of the way I entered the subject I did not become caught up in the (at least on one side) emotional debate. Instead, I approached the aggregation problem as a purely technical one with a purely technical answer. In that first paper, I was able to prove that, under constant returns, perfect aggregation was possible if and only if all technical differences were capital-augmenting – that is, if and only if a different kind of capital had all the properties of more of the same kind. (Sufficiency had been proven by Solow.) I then went on to a number of generalizations.

That first paper was followed by a number of others considering aggregation problems when capital was specific to firms. Some of these papers dealt with aggregation of variable factors. Another dealt with the question of approximate aggregation if the Leontief conditions for exact aggregation (which lay behind the exact aggregation results) did not even hold approximately. I and others also performed simulation experiments to see what happened if one estimated aggregate production functions in circumstances when they were known not to exist. I used the occasion of the Fisher-Schultz Lecture at the European meetings of the Econometric Society in 1968 to summarize the results.[9]

---

[9] All of the papers referred to in this and the next paragraph can be found in Fisher (1992–3).

In general, my findings were that exact aggregation conditions were very unlikely to be satisfied, although there were some very interesting exceptions. But the reasons had very little to do with the possibility that capital and labor might have to be used in fixed proportions, as Mrs. Robinson had claimed. Indeed, years later I returned to the problem and showed that, in all but the simplest cases, aggregation still remained difficult if all factors were mobile. In that sense, the specificity of capital had little to do with the matter.

I would have thought it a fair claim that this work settled the Cambridge v. Cambridge debate. Indeed, I made that claim in the preface to the volume of my collected works that deals with this subject (Fisher, 1992–3). But some things never die, and one should be wary of such claims. In the Spring of 1994, I had a chance conversation with a (non-MIT) graduate student who had studied at Cambridge. He asked me whether the existence of aggregate capital was regarded on my side of the Atlantic as so important a subject as on the other. The discussion revealed that he had recently had a course in the subject at the English Cambridge, that the subject was still taught there with great fervor, and that he had no idea that I had ever written on it. So much for pride.

c.   *The Economic Theory of Price Indices*

Somewhat related to my work on aggregation was my work with Karl Shell on the economic theory of price indices. In the mid-1960s, I served briefly on an advisory panel set up by the Federal Reserve Board to consider research on price indices. We were each asked for suggestions. This was a time in which the modeling of various forms of technical change in terms of factor augmentation was much discussed, and, of course, I had recently written my first paper on aggregate production functions which contained the capital-augmentation theorem. Struggling to come up with a topic at the meeting of the panel, I suggested that one might examine taste changes and the cost-of-living index by modeling taste changes in consumption in the way that technical changes in production were treated.

Having generated this idea, I returned to MIT from the meeting and enlisted Karl Shell (who had the office next to mine) to make it real. We worked and argued and eventually produced our paper on "Taste and Quality Change in the Pure Theory of the True Cost of Living Index." After publication elsewhere, this became the first of two essays in our book, *The Economic Theory of Price Indices* (Fisher and Shell, 1972).

To understand the rest of that book, one must consider the nature of the subject. Historically and currently, price index theory has received a great deal of attention. Most of the work in the area, however, has concentrated on highly useful but relatively non-economic properties of indices. The desirable properties of a price index are axiomatized, and the existence (or non-existence) and construction of an index satisfying those axioms is then considered. Other work concerns the approximation properties of various constructible indices.

Shell and I approached the subject in a different way. We returned to the foundations of price indices in economic theory and asked what such indices were supposed to do, what questions they were supposed to answer in terms of the underlying theory. In our first paper, we found that the supposed inability of the cost-of-living index to handle taste change resulted from a sloppy statement of the question that the index was designed to answer. That question, concerning whether the consumer was better off in the base or current period, turns out not to be answerable whether or not tastes change. A rigorous restatement of the question led to the incorporation of taste changes into the theory. Pursuing such lines also led to results on quality change and on new goods.

Further, it occurred to Shell and me that a similar investigation of the production sector might prove fruitful. In particular, we set about analyzing output price indices such as the GNP deflator from the point of view of production theory. Nobody had ever asked what questions such indices were supposed to answer in terms of the underlying economics of production. We created a theory isomorphic in many respects to that of the cost-of-living index, and obtained many results. Together with our cost-of-living paper, these were published in Fisher and Shell 1972.[10]

With few exceptions, this line was not pursued by others laboring in the index number field. This is, perhaps, not surprising. As indicated above, most of those writing on index numbers were and are interested in other things – axiomatic properties and approximations. In effect, they work on a different subject.

An important exception to that rule was John Muellbauer. He

---

[10] A comment on the methods used seems in order. These were the days when duality theory was beginning to dominate the theory of the theory of the individual agent in the form of the expenditure function and the restricted profits function. In our cost-of-living paper, Shell and I made no use of such methods, but did things the old fashioned way. By the time we wrote on production, the new methods had pressed themselves on us and (in the form of the Envelope Theorem) we used them. One has only to compare the two studies in Fisher and Shell 1972 to see the gains in elegance and ease produced by the new ways.

observed that our theory of output deflation could be used to construct an isomorphic theory of input deflation (Muellbauer, 1972), something that had simply not occurred to us. Unfortunately, that isomorphic theory involves supposing that the firm (or, more generally, the production sector being considered) is committed to producing a fixed vector of outputs. This is not an interesting case for a multi-product firm or sector.

Shell and I began considering this issue in the late 1970s. We quickly realized that the appropriate case was that of constant revenue received by the firm. But that led us to realize that our theory of output deflation had also been too narrow. Once one leaves the case of a closed economy and deals either with an open one or with individual firms, industries, or sectors, the isomorphic device of assuming a fixed vector of inputs no longer made sense. We thus set out to generalize the theory of both input and output deflation.

Unfortunately, this turned out to be one of those enterprises that hangs fire. We substantially completed the work by 1980, but then, with a first draft of the book more-or-less done, first one and then the other of us lost interest. We finally returned to the job in 1993, and the finished product (Fisher and Shell, 1998) finally appeared.

d.   *I Decide to Leave Econometric Theory*

One of the reasons for the slow rewriting of the second Fisher-Shell book was that 1970 brought two important changes in my interests. The first of these – my decision to leave econometric theory and to study stability theory – was deliberate. The second – my reentry into industrial organization and involvement with antitrust – was largely accidental. I discuss the deliberate change now and the accidental one at length below.

As already discussed, I was poorly trained in the statistical aspects of econometric theory. Nevertheless, I was able to make considerable progress by dealing with the subject in terms of the underlying economic models involved and in terms of linear algebra. I was not the only one to do this. In the late 1950s and the 1960s, many (not all) advances in econometrics were made by people who had good intuitive ideas and were then able to work out the statistical formalities. The invention of two-stage least squares and three-stage least squares stand out in this regard. While the inventors were much better trained in mathematical statistics than was I, the style of invention was, I think, largely the same as mine.

By about 1970, it was clear that this period was ending. The future of econometric theory lay in systematic application of the methods of mathematical statistics rather than in the kind of thing I had been doing. To participate in that future would have required retraining. I did not want to do that, especially because I had only limited interest in the kind of developments I foresaw. Moreover, there were other things I wanted to do. I therefore made a deliberate decision to leave the field.

That decision did not mean that I left econometrics altogether, for I had been doing empirical work from the time of my study of the demand for aluminum ingot begun in 1956 and included in my first book (Fisher, 1962). But econometric theory was no longer a serious interest of mine.

e.   *Disequilibrium Foundations of Equilibrium Economics*

The area I decided to pursue was that of stability theory, more generally, of micro-economic disequilibrium. I believed then and believe now that the issues involved are the greatest unanswered questions of economics.

Economic theory is preeminently an equilibrium subject. The theory of value and the associated welfare theorems form the centerpiece of microeconomics and the principal propositions that economists have to say to the outside world. It is no exaggeration to say that these are the fundamental precepts of Western capitalism and free-market economics. The theories involved are elegant and powerful treatments of the behavior of optimizing agents and the properties of situations in which the plans of those agents mesh.

So powerful are these theories that it is easy to overlook the fact that they are silent on what happens when plans do not mesh – on what happens out of equilibrium. We have an elegant theory of what the world looks like after the Invisible Hand has finished its work. Yet that is not a substitute for a full theory of how (or whether) the Invisible Hand brings such a situation about. This is a major lacuna and not merely a formal one. For example, the question of whether a formerly communist economy will be better off with free markets cannot be answered by reference to the efficiency properties of free-market equilibrium alone. Whether such an economy gets to equilibrium, how long it takes, and what happens on the way, are all likely to matter a great deal.

Yet these questions are largely ignored by modern theorists, and what is known about them is pretty unsatisfactory. There is a general presumption that an economy of rational agents will be driven to equilibrium, but no proper theory of how or whether this happens. In particular, we lack a theory of how individual agents set prices. In a world in which all agents take prices as given, how do prices ever change? (Koopmans, 1957).

I began an investigation of such issues around 1970, publishing a series of articles that culminated in my book, *Disequilibrium Foundations of Equilibrium Economics* (Fisher, 1983). I began with the existing literature on the stability of general equilibrium and attempted to answer the question of whether an economy of rational agents, perceiving the arbitrage opportunities thrown up by disequilibrium, will drive the economy to equilibrium and, if so, to what sort of equilibrium. For it is far from evident that the equilibria that will be approached in such a process (if any are) will be Walrasian. Rather, such equilibria may resemble Keynes' liquidity trap with agents prevented from buying because they believe (possibly correctly) that they cannot sell and so obtain money.

Probably the least interesting result in the book was the stability result itself. I was able to show that convergence would take place if no new and unforeseen opportunities arose in the course of the adjustment process. That condition is very strong, but, if one thinks about it, one cannot hope for much more than this.

More interesting were the results I obtained as to the behavior of agents in disequilibrium and the properties of equilibrium itself. I showed how agents act on arbitrage opportunities. More important, equilibrium in my model is not the exhaustion of trading opportunities but the carrying out of previously made plans under foreseen conditions and at foreseen prices. As such, the role of money does not vanish in equilibrium. Perhaps most important of all, the question of Walrasian versus non-Walrasian equilibrium turns out to involve the question of how agents' own perceptions of their monopoly (or monopsony) power change over time.

I gather that this last problem has now become a central issue in macroeconomics (as are some of the others). So far as I know, however, most macroeconomists writing on it have not been aware of my work which approached the problem from a microeconomic perspective, that of general equilibrium and the theory of value. Of course, since I do not pretend to know much about macroeconomics, the style of my book was not conducive to such consultation. Indeed, in my discovery that I was writing on macroeconomic issues, I was much like Molière's *bourgeois gentilhomme*, who was surprised to learn that he was speaking prose.

3. I Reenter Industrial Organization and Cease Being a Pure Academic

a.   The IBM Case

The other change in my interests that occurred in 1970 was not inten-
tional. It radically changed my career.

I had engaged in consulting activities in at least a minor way for quite
some time. Apart from the writing of a chapter of my thesis in connection with John Meyer's project for the Canadian Pacific Railroad, the
first such venture occurred in 1959. In association with Carl Kaysen, I
studied the demand for electricity in the United States for a research laboratory of General Electric. This became a fairly well-known book
(Fisher and Kaysen, 1962). Continuing on from there, for the next decade
I engaged in consulting projects, usually econometric oriented ones. As
with the electricity project, these often led to publication, and, indeed, a
great deal of my empirical work in econometrics has grown out of such
ventures.

In 1967, I became heavily involved with a private firm, Charles River
Associates (CRA), that specialized in microeconomic consulting. This
provided skilled colleagues and assistants as well as systematic management. The type of consulting I did continued as before, generally econometric investigations rather than litigation. I considered it an interesting
sidelight to my main activities.

Then, in May 1970, the telephone call came from Armonk.

The call came from Nicholas DeB. Katzenbach, then General Counsel
of IBM. He had been referred to me by Carl Kaysen, whom he had
known in the Kennedy administration.[11] He wanted to know whether I
and CRA would be interested in assisting IBM, which was being sued
by the government under Section Two of the Sherman Act (the principal anti-monopoly provision of the antitrust laws). There were private
suits as well.

This proposition seemed interesting to me for a number of reasons.
First, consulting was something that I did in my spare time. Second, CRA
could certainly use the work. Third, and most important, I thought, great
single-firm monopoly cases come along perhaps once in a generation and
change the law. Here was a chance to put good economics into judicial

[11] I did not (and do not) often get calls from persons so distinguished as Katzenbach, who
had been Attorney General and Acting Secretary of State of the United States before
going to IBM. As a result, when I got home that night, I opened the door and called out
"Guess who called me today!" My wife promptly called back "Nicholas Katzenbach!".
I have yet to forgive her.

interpretations of the Sherman Act. Not realizing what was involved, I accepted Katzenbach's invitation, thus beginning a project that was to last for thirteen years and change my professional life.[12]

How large the case was quickly became clear. Because my younger daughter, Naomi, was born on May 11, 1970,[13] I could not attend the first meeting. The CRA people who did told me that there appeared to be a whole floor of people working on the case. After the second meeting, they reported that it might be a whole building.

In fact, the IBM case (and its associated private and foreign suits) was one of the largest antitrust cases ever pursued and was certainly the greatest antitrust fiasco in the history of the United States. I have written extensively about the misuse of economics in the case (Fisher, McGowan, and Greenwood, 1983) and shall not discuss that issue at any length here.

What is worth discussing is the more general phenomenon of which the misuse of economic analysis in the IBM case was a symptom. That phenomenon has to do with the relatively shallow understanding of economics that often pervades its practical use in antitrust cases, with the desire for simple answers to complicated questions, and with the general state of the industrial organization field in the 1970s and today.

When I began work on the IBM case in 1970, I had been away from the applied industrial organization area for several years. What struck me upon reentry was how little the field had changed during that period. And the field was not in good shape. Perhaps because of the difficulty of making advances in the theory of oligopoly, industrial organization was not then what it is today, a hot topic for the best young analytically-oriented economists. There had been little progress in industrial organization theory for the past quarter century.

In antitrust, in particular, the field was weak. The natural tendency of attorneys and judges to look for "bright-line" tests (simple quantitative rules) had led to over-concentration on the measurement of market share and hence on the badly posed problem of market definition. Since the question of what is *the* market is not susceptible of any precise answer and since market share is at best only a very rough indicator of market power, such concentration tends to lead to very superficial answers at the expense of the thoughtful, serious analysis of industry

---

[12] I used to be asked whether I regretted having done so. Certainly, with my pre-IBM tastes in economics, I would not have accepted had I fully realized what was involved. On the other hand, participating in the IBM case changed my tastes in economics. Given my post-IBM tastes, I am glad that I did it. (The analysis of Fisher and Shell 1972 shows that the question of whether accepting made me better off is without meaning.)

[13] The case lasted long enough that she assisted in proofreading my book on it (Fisher, McGowan, and Greenwood, 1983).

facts that is really required.[14] In the IBM case, the Antitrust Division and its economists used market definitions and ways of measuring market share that were bereft of any semblance of rationality or any sense of what such measures are supposed to accomplish.

Market definition and market share remain the shibboleths of many antitrust cases today (although somewhat more sanely than in the IBM case), but the wish for a simple answer to an inherently complex question is not limited to those subjects. In particular, there is (or was) a large literature purporting to use profit rates as a measure of market power.

This is an enterprise that is wholly misguided, and the principal reason for such endeavors is a manifestation of the fact that economists tend to concentrate on equilibrium. As discussed above, that was the other area that was receiving my attention in the 1970s and early 1980s.

The proposition on which the use of profits as a measure of market power is based is the true result that, *in long-run equilibrium*, profits (*properly measured*) are zero in competitive markets. For the moment, concentrate on the first italicized phrase. When the Invisible Hand is done working, it is indeed true that profits will be zero. But it is a gross misunderstanding of the competitive process to suppose that this means that profits do not occur in competitive markets. On the contrary. The carrot of profits and the stick of losses are precisely the tools that the Invisible Hand uses to bring about its desirable results. Profits, in particular, are the reward of the foresighted and efficient. They may disappear in long-run equilibrium, but they are very much a part of the competitive process. Particularly in industries characterized by repeated innovation (as was the computer industry), the identification of profits with market power is a major mistake.

Less fundamental but still important is the second italicized phrase above. To guide analysis in any way, profit rates must be properly measured. This involves such things as the treatment of intangibles, the opportunity cost of capital, and the problem of unimputed rents. But it also involves the serious treatment of the fact that real firms do not live in the one-period world of elementary textbooks. Merely looking at accounting rates of return – profits divided by equity or by the book value of the capital stock – does not come close to dealing with the issue. Capital stock is acquired to bring future profits; current profits depend on past investments; and only a really careful treatment of depreciation will lead to correct results.

---

[14] My Harvard training in the field can be found in such statements. Edward S. Mason, from whom I had my first course in antitrust, was the father of the industry study.

Part of my work on the IBM case involved the analysis of such issues. Besides our book, John McGowan and I published an article on them in the *American Economic Review* in early 1983.[15] This aroused a storm of controversy. As I later remarked (Fisher, 1984), one would think we had defaced the national monument. Particularly since we were not the first to point out the problem, it was surprising how much feeling was aroused. While the issue appears now to be reasonably settled in our favor, I still continue to receive related papers.

One other aspect of the IBM case deserves mention. This was a case in which the actions complained of all involved either better products or lower prices. The inability of the Antitrust Division to distinguish such actions (leading to greater market share) from the acts of a monopolist bespeaks a wider difficulty. Competition in real industries is a more complex animal than in elementary textbooks or standard theory. If one fails to understand how competition really works, then a superficial comprehension of competitive theory will lead to policy conclusions that are positively harmful.

b.   Economics and Antitrust

The IBM case ended in 1982, when the government withdrew its complaint, stipulating that the case had been "without merit." By that time, I had been involved in other antitrust cases as well. A primary theme in my work in such cases (and in other forms of economic litigation) has been the insistence that economic analysis, *properly understood*, has a great deal to contribute.

In this regard, the revolution that has swept industrial organization in the last fifteen years has not proved of much help. (I have elsewhere given my views on this (Fisher, 1989 and 1991), and shall only summarize them here.) It is my position that modern game-theoretic treatments of oligopoly are not, in fact, advancing the subject along very useful lines. Many papers are little more than stylized anecdotes – stories of what *can* happen. They do not help much in the analysis of real industries and real firms where one wants to know what *has* happened or what *will* happen. The embarrassing multiplicity of Nash equilibria corresponds to the fact that oligopoly behavior depends on context, a fact we knew long ago. The crucial question of when that context is likely to lead to co-ordinated rather than to rivalrous behavior is very little studied. Yet it is that question that is the important one in practice and certainly in antitrust cases.

[15] Fisher and McGowan, 1983; see also Fisher, 1984, 1987.

Antitrust cases continue to be fought without much help from modern theory. Unfortunately, they are often also fought without much understanding of old-fashioned theory on the part of at least one side. Often, this comes about because the economists on one side are not strong, and the economic basis for the case very superficial. That does not guarantee that the good guys win, since judges and juries may be more impressed with simplistic arguments than with deeper analyses. The matter is not helped when skilled economists who do (or ought to) know better take the attitude that theirs is a partisan task and feel free to say in court what they would never say in seminars.[16]

As this suggests, I have tried (I hope successfully) to maintain a standard of intellectual honesty in the cases in which I have been involved. I have found such involvement to be quite rewarding. While the work can be tiresome, at its best, as in the IBM case, one gets a major opportunity to study an industry in depth and to acquire a real understanding of how things actually work. Often (certainly not always) this leads to insights that deserve publication.[17] Despite the substantial strains put on my relations with the MIT Economics Department which has (or had) a general presumption that one should not engage heavily in such activities, I have not regretted having done so. Much of my research for the last two decades has stemmed from such involvement, and I believe that I am a better applied economist for it.

There have been other rewards as well. I mentioned above that one reason for my entering the IBM case was that I thought it would provide an opportunity to put good economics into judicial interpretations of the antitrust laws. It has been a continuing satisfaction to feel that I am assisting in the proper use and proper understanding of the tools and results of my profession. Since, as remarked above, it often happens that much of the economics being done by one side or the other is over-simplified or, as in the IBM case, positively distorted, I get that satisfaction with some regularity.

c. The Census Case

The upholding of proper economic analysis, however, is not the only socially desirable activity that my consulting practice has involved. On a few occasions, I have felt that my professional abilities and intellectual capital plus the communication skills I have learned from being an expert witness have permitted me to make a real contribution towards

---

[16] Some discussion of these matters can be found in Fisher, 1986.
[17] In addition to Fisher, McGowan, and Greenwood, 1983, see Fisher, McKie, and Mancke, 1983 and various chapters in Fisher, 1990–1 and 1991–2.

justice or even peace. I shall briefly discuss the two most important of these.

It has long been recognized that the United States decennial census tends to undercount minorities and does so relative to the general population. The reasons are not hard to understand. Minorities tend to live in relatively high-crime neighborhoods where census takers are nervous. Minorities have a higher illiteracy rate. Some members of minorities distrust the government and do not want to be found. As a result, states with a relatively high minority population tend to be underrepresented in Congress. A similar statement is true of cities versus rural regions as regards the apportionment of state legislatures (which in turn design Congressional districts). The distribution of federal funds across (and even within states) is also affected.

For many years it has been known that this situation might be improved and the population count made relatively and absolutely more accurate by the use of statistical methods. Indeed, following the 1980 census, a large number of states and cities sued the Department of Commerce (within which the Bureau of the Census is located) to compel the use of such methods.

That suit came to trial in 1984, and I testified in it on behalf of the plaintiffs. My role was that of an expositor. I was not myself responsible for the invention or application of the statistical methods involved; rather, it fell to me to explain to the judge how generally one ought to think about the use of statistical methods.

The suit was opposed by the government, with the Bureau of the Census contending that the data gathered and studies done just after the 1980 census were not of sufficient quality to warrant using them for adjustment. After a considerable delay, the judge (who did not appear to have made a great effort to understand what was involved) refused to order adjustment. That may have been the right result.

Having argued that the 1980 census could not reasonably be retroactively adjusted, the Bureau of the Census quite reasonably began to plan for the use of statistical adjustment methods in connection with the 1990 census. That effort was brought to a halt in 1987 when the Secretary of Commerce (not, of course, an expert) decreed that there would be no adjustment.

This prompted a second suit by the same sorts of plaintiffs as before. That suit was temporarily settled when the Secretary, Robert Mosbacher, agreed to allow the Bureau to plan for adjustment and to consider the matter with an open mind and explicit criteria.

In the event, no adjustment was made. In 1991, Secretary Mosbacher overrode the recommendations of the Census Bureau and ruled against adjustment. He then went on to become the chairman of George Bush's reelection campaign. I do not believe it to be coincidental that cities with large minority populations tend to vote Democratic.

Indeed, I believe that a great injustice was perpetrated here. As I testified at the trial of the resumed lawsuit, Secretary Mosbacher's opinion was a "cascade of errors." To reach the result he wanted, the Secretary had to misunderstand or deliberately misinterpret result after result of the analyses done by the Census Bureau. He managed a result in which two-thirds of the people of the United States were partially disenfranchised. As the Court of Appeals for the Second Circuit wrote in remanding the case for a new trial, if the government is going to do that, there had better be an "overriding governmental purpose."

I was glad to be able to testify in these cases, especially the second one, and to use the testimonial skills I had developed to assist in attempting to right what I consider a great wrong.[18] During a break in my deposition in the case, a statistician on the other side asked me what two fellows like him and me were doing in this case. I was glad to be able to say "Standing up to be counted."

d. The Harvard Middle East Water Project

The other endeavor that I have found fulfilling in this way does not involve litigation, but it has certainly called on the communications skills I have developed in testifying before non-economists.

Water disputes occur all over the world and are a potentially explosive issue in the current Middle East peace negotiations.

Although it is hard for non-economists to recognize, economics has a lot to say about this problem. Water is a scarce resource; scarce resources have prices. Moreover, since a country that owns water and uses that water itself pays an opportunity cost equal to the money for which the water could have been sold, ownership of water is really only an entitlement to the money value that the water represents. This is true even when that value includes a social component. To put it differently, the question of who owns the water and the question of who uses the water are both very important, but they are analytically separate questions.

I am the Chairman of a project of the Institute for Social and Economic Policy in the Middle East (located at Harvard's Kennedy School), which deals with such matters. With a team of Israeli, Jordanian, and

---

[18] Chapter 29 of the present volume is drawn up from an unpublished paper with Brian Palmer in which I have set out my arguments.

Palestinian scholars, we are building a model of the region's water economy. We seek both to assist in sensible water management and also to ask what the value of the water in dispute actually is.

Apparently, very few, if any, people have considered water in this way. Moreover, our estimates suggest that the value of the water involved is quite low (perhaps $100–$300 million per year depending on scenarios and future dates). This is not the sort of sum over which nations go to war.

The project has attracted a good deal of interest among the governments involved and is playing a very unofficial role in the peace negotiations. It has provided me with two challenges: first, the project itself is intellectually very interesting; second, it is an exercise not only in political economy but also in economic politics. The skills and intellectual capital acquired over my professional lifetime are all being called upon. This is perhaps the most exciting and important thing I have ever done.[19]

Incidentally, I mean the term "professional lifetime" quite literally. Some of the expository material I use goes back to the very first lecture I gave – a lecture in Carl Kaysen's undergraduate course in industrial organization more than forty years ago.

REFERENCES

Ando, A., F. M. Fisher, and H. A. Simon (1963). *Essays on the Structure of Social Science Models*. Cambridge, MA: MIT Press.
Fisher, F. M. (1956). "Income Distribution, Value Judgments, and Welfare". *Quarterly Journal of Economics* **70**. Reprinted as Chapter 12 in this volume.
    (1959). "Generalization of the Rank and Order Conditions for Identifiability." *Econometrica*, **27**.
    (1961). "On the Cost of Approximate Specification in Simultaneous Equations Estimation". *Econometrica*, **29**. Reprinted in Fisher (1991–2).
    (1962). *A Priori Information and Time Series Analysis: Essays in Economic Theory and Measurement*. Amsterdam: North-Holland.
    (1965a). "Embodied Technical Change and the Existence of an Aggregate Capital Stock". *Review of Economic Studies*, **XXXII**. Reprinted in Fisher (1992–3).
    (1965b). "Identifiability Criteria in Nonlinear Systems: A Further Note". *Econometrica*, **33**.
    (1966, 1976). *The Identification Problem in Econometrics*. New York: McGraw-Hill (1966) and Huntington, NY: Robert E. Krieger (1976).
    (1970). "A Correspondence Principle for Simultaneous Equation Models". *Econometrica*, **38**. Reprinted in Fisher (1991–2).

[19] Chapter 30 of the present volume is the first article published out of this ongoing work.

(1983). *Disequilibrium Foundations of Equilibrium Economics*. Cambridge, UK: Cambridge University Press.

(1984). "On the Misuse of Accounting Rates of Return: Reply". *American Economic Review*, **74**. Reprinted in Fisher (1990–1).

(1986). "Statisticians, Econometricians and Adversary Proceedings". *Journal of the American Statistical Association (Applications)*, **81**. Reprinted in Fisher (1990–1).

(1987). "On the Misuse of the Profits-Sales Ratio to Infer Monopoly Power". *RAND Journal of Economics*, **18**. Reprinted in Fisher (1990–1).

(1989). "Games Economists Play." *RAND Journal of Economics*, **20**. Reprinted in Fisher (1990–1).

(1991). "Organizing Industrial Organization: Reflections on *The Handbook of Industrial Organization*". In *Brookings Papers on Economic Activity: Microeconomics* (M. N. Baily and C. Winston, eds.). Washington: The Brookings Institution. Reprinted as Chapter 24 in this volume.

(1990–1). *Industrial Organization, Economics, and the Law*. Hemel Hempstead: Harvester-Wheatsheaf and Cambridge, MA: MIT Press.

(1991–2). *Econometrics: Essays in Theory and Applications*. Hemel Hempstead: Harvester-Wheatsheaf and Cambridge, MA: MIT Press.

(1992–3). *Aggregation: Aggregate Production Functions and Related Topics*. Hemel Hempstead: Harvester-Wheatsheaf and Cambridge, MA: MIT Press.

Fisher, F. M., in association with C. Kaysen (1962). *A Study in Econometrics: The Demand for Electricity in the United States*. Amsterdam: North-Holland.

Fisher, F. M. and P. Kenen (1957). "Income Distribution, Value Judgments, and Welfare: A Correction". *Quarterly Journal of Economics*, **71**. Reprinted as Chapter 13 in this volume.

Fisher, F. M. and J. J. McGowan (1983). "On the Misuse of Accounting Rates of Return to Infer Monopoly Profits". *American Economic Review*, **74**. Reprinted in Fisher (1990–91).

Fisher, F. M., J. J. McGowan, and J. E. Greenwood (1983). *Folded, Spindled, and Mutilated: Economic Analysis and U.S. v. IBM*. Cambridge, MA: MIT Press.

Fisher, F. M., J. McKie, and R. Mancke (1983). *IBM and the U.S. Data Processing Industry: An Economic History*. New York: Praeger.

Fisher, F. M. and K. Shell (1972). *The Economic Theory of Price Indices*. New York: Academic Press.

(1998). *The Economic Theory of Production Price Indexes*. Cambridge, UK: Cambridge University Press.

Kaysen, C. and D. Turner (1959). *Antitrust Policy*. Cambridge: Harvard University Press.

Koopmans, T. C. (1957). *Three Essays on the State of Economic Science*. New York: McGraw-Hill.

Liu, T. C. (1960). "Underidentification, Structural Estimation, and Forecasting". *Econometrica*, **28**.

Muellbauer, J. (1972). "The Theory of True Input Price Indices". Revision of University of Warwick Economic Research Paper 17, University of Warwick, Coventry, UK.

Robinson, J. (1953–4). "The Production Function and the Theory of Capital". *Review of Economic Studies*, **XXI**.

Samuelson, P. A. (1947). *Foundations of Economic Analysis*. Cambridge, MA: Harvard University Press.

   (1951). *Economics, an Introductory Analysis*. New York: McGraw-Hill (second edition).

Schumpeter, J. (1951). *The Theory of Economic Development*. Cambridge, MA: Harvard University Press (fourth printing).

Solow, R. M. (1955–6). "The Production Function and the Theory of Capital". *Review of Economic Studies*, **XXIII**.

Indexes

Author Index

565

Subject Index

accuracy of census: criterion used, 494–8; loss function related to, 496; using statistical methods to measure, 490–4

agriculture sector: of countries importing food surpluses, 296, 307–8

airline industry *See also* computer reservation systems (CRSs): competition and predation in, 395–7; computer reservation systems within, 450–1; deregulation, 451; proving injury related to reservation systems' display bias, 453–6

Alcoa case. *See United States* v. *Aluminum Company of America* (1945)

antitrust policy: in *Handbook of Industrial Organization*, 378–80; related to oligopoly behavior, 398–402; related to single-firm monopolies, 385–98

arbitrage: with disequilibrium, 35; effect on prices, 43–4; opportunities for, 26; in stability analysis, 46–7

Arrow-Debreu model of general equilibrium, 33, 41, 42

Arrow-Hahn price-adjustment model, 88, 90, 93, 95n11, 104, 105–7, 111

auctioneer: in price-adjustment model without, 88–91; price adjustment without, 87–108; role in markets of, 29, 87

Baker v. *Carr* (1962), 497

barriers to entry: arising through government action, 408–9; conditions for existence of, 392–3

benefits: discounting of, 348; point of view related to, 354–7; use of measures for, 346–7

boundedness of prices: in Hahn process models, 119–20; in price adjustment without auctioneer, 99–101

buyers (consumers): in price-adjustment model, 52–60

Cellophane case. *See U. S.* v. *E. I. DuPont de Nemours and Company* (1956)

census adjustment: Bureau of the Census recommendation for, 488; counting the states, 503–17; decision of Secretary of Commerce against, 488–9, 503–7; loss functions related to, 494–502; measurement of accuracy, 490–4; testing null hypothesis of, 502–3; understanding decision of Secretary of Commerce, 508–14

coalitions: of agents in Edgeworth process assumption, 143–4

Coase theorem, 521n2

Cobb-Douglas utility function: weak gross substitute property, 178

competition: among airline computer reservation systems, 478; convergence to competitive equilibrium, 80–6; models of competitive equilibrium, 87

competition policy. *See* antitrust policy

computer reservation systems (CRSs): airlines' individual proprietary systems, 451–2; architectural bias in, 475; change in ownership structure (1986), 476; of combined airline industry, 450–1; effect of display bias in SABRE system, 456–61; effects of display bias on APOLLO bookings, 462–3; effects of display bias on APOLLO bookings by time of departure, 468–71; estimation of propensity to book in advance, 463–8; proposed self-enforcing mechanism for, 479–81; regulation related to display bias in, 452, 475, 478–9; revenue diversion from display bias, 474; SABRE, APOLLO, and PARS display algorithms, 451, 454–79

constraints: in cost-benefit analysis, 332–42; disequilibrium with quantity, 110–11; in making public policy, 332–4, 340–2; related to water availability, 528; shadow price of cost constraint, 328–9; shadow price of water consumption, 525–6, 528; in substitution between men and capital, 335

568

(Houthakker), 415; predatory pricing of monopolist, 393–8; price setting by firms in price-adjustment model, 52–60; quasi- and competitive equilibria, 91–3; in water allocation model, 528

property rights: related to ownership of water, 521, 524–5; value related to water, 525

public policy *See also* antitrust policy: choosing criteria for cost-benefit analysis, 328–32; constraints in making, 332–4; effectiveness constraint in, 340–2; effects of, 354–7; environment for decision making, 332; using cost-benefit analysis to find efficient, 333

quantity constraints: incorporated into Hahn process, 12
quantity-rationing, 132
queue-rationing, 132

rationing: queue-, coupon-, and quantity-rationing in trading mechanisms, 132–3
rents: scarcity rents for water, 529–30
research agenda: in *Handbook of Industrial Organization*, 375–8

sellers (firms): in price-adjustment model, 52–60
shadow prices: of constraints, 328–9, 333–4; of constraints on water consumption, 528; of water, 528–30; in water allocation model, 525–6, 528
shocks, exogenous, 46
Simple Simon, 38–9
social cost, 521n2
social welfare function: Fisher's model of, 255; Goodman's and Markowitz's model of, 252–3; Harsanyi's model of, 253–5; Hildreth's model, 251–2; Strotz's model of, 230–51
Solow's Theorem, 6, 161–2
spillovers: disequilibrium with, 110–11; incorporated into Hahn process, 112
stability: of adjustment process, 119–25; Hicksian perfect, 30; pure exchange with quasi-stability, 113–19; related to tâtonnment, 31–2
stability analysis: dynamic model in, 28; introduction of money in, 39; No Favorable Surprise assumption in, 47; purpose of, 46; under quantity constraints, 110–27; question of equilibrium in, 27; tâtonnement analysis in, 29

Strotz's income distribution paradox: Certainty Equivalence Postulate, 242–7, 250–1, 254; Convexity Postulate, 232, 235–6, 242–7, 250–1, 254; Isomorphism Postulate, 231, 235–6, 238–40, 242, 254; postulates of, 231–3; statement of, 230; Strong Independence Postulate, 232, 250; using value judgments to judge, 233–5

substitution: at aggregate level of units in the military, 353–4; among different types of labor and personnel types, 335–7; among personnel in small units, 351–2; gross substitute process, 174–9; between men and capital, 334–5; substitutability of demand and supply, 388–9; trade-offs related to personnel with, 338–40

target utilities: in Hahn process, 37, 101–4; Lyapounov function from sum of, 104–5, 124

tâtonnement *See also* auctioneer; non-tâtonnement; price adjustment: agents' acceptance of prices under, 130; defects and failure of, 29–33; in Lyapounov function, 33–4; in stability analysis, 29; treatment of agents' behavior in models of, 28–9

time: costs and benefits over, 342–50

trade-offs: in substitutions among personnel, 338–40

trades: analysis of compound, 155–9; analysis of simple, 150–3; in deterministic disequilibrium awareness model, 131–40; in Edgeworth process, 34–5; in endowments, 32–4; number of participants in Edgeworth-process, 143–59; out of equilibrium, 32–6; Pareto-improving, 34–5, 144–5; in price-adjustment model without auctioneer, 96–9; simple and compound Edgeworth process, 144–59

trading processes *See also* non-tâtonnement; tâtonnement: agents' demands based on understanding of, 131; disequilibrium in, 131; Edgeworth Process, 3–5, 33–6; Hahn Process, 3–4, 36–42; No Swindling assumption, 33–4, 118; price-adjustment equation in, 33; quantity constraints in, 110–11; queue-, coupon-, and quantity-rationing in, 132

U.S. v. E. I. DuPont de Nemours and Company (1956), 389–90

Printed in the United States
39272LVS00007BB/94-96

9 780521 023290